THE **SOURCEBOOK** OF

LOCAL COURT AND COUNTY RECORD RETRIEVERS

THE NATIONAL GUIDE OF INFORMATION RETRIEVERS
WHO PULL FILES AND DOCUMENTS FROM US, STATE, AND LOCAL COURTS AND FROM COUNTY AGENCIES.

The Public Record Research Library®
from
BRB PUBLICATIONS, INC.

The Sourcebook of Local Court and County Record Retrievers

ISBN: 1-879792-09-5
Copyright @ 1993 by BRB Publications, Inc.

BRB Publications, Inc.
4653 South Lakeshore, Suite 3 • Tempe, Arizona • 85282
FAX: (602) 838-8324

Cover Design by Robin Fox & Associates
Cover Photos by Lynn B. Sankey

ACKNOWLEDGEMENTS

There are two distinct groups of people whom we wish to thank...

The Companies and Individuals Profiled in this Book - Your assistance and cooperation was superb and it was a pleasure working with you all. Our sincere thanks to all of you for having the interest and taking the time to help us put this book together!

The Research and Production Staff and BRB - A great amount of extra effort was contributed by some key people to develop and produce this Sourcebook. We wish to personally thank and acknowledge the efforts of Nancy White, Annette Talley, Mary Beth Reith, and Audrey Akhavan!

Carl Ernst, Editor & Research Director
Michael Sankey, Publisher
BRB Publications, Inc.
March 20, 1993

Other Books in **THE PUBLIC RECORD RESEARCH LIBRARY®**
Published by BRB Publications

- **THE SOURCEBOOK OF COUNTY COURT RECORDS**

  A directory of over 5,300 local and state courts detailing where and hoe you can obtain information on civil and criminal cases as well as probate, lien, real estate, tax, and vital statistic records.

- **THE SOURCEBOOK OF FEDERAL COURTS—US DISTRICT AND BANKRUPTCY**

  The only complete guide to searching the more than 500 US courts and 12 Federal Records Centers for information on civil, criminal, and bankruptcy cases.

- **THE SOURCEBOOK OF PUBLIC RECORD PROVIDERS**

  A compendium profiling 400 companies specializing in various information products, including UCC and court record retrieval, on-line public record and proprietary databases, tenant screening, and other sources of individual and business information.

- **THE SOURCEBOOK OF ASSET/LIEN SEARCHING**

  A national directory of names, addresses, and telephone numbers for all 4,283 US filing offices where real property, lien, and corporate records are located.

- **LOCUS—THE ULTIMATE LOCATOR**

  The only directory that accurately matches ZIP codes to place names and counties, including these indexes:
  - 90,000+ Places—Real Geographic ZIP Codes—Counties
  - 10,000+ ZIP Codes That Cross County Borders
  - All 99,999 Possible ZIP Codes—Places—Counties
  - 3,140 Counties—ZIP Codes

- **THE MVR BOOK**

  The definitive (and only) national reference detailing and summarizing—in practical terms—the descriptions, access, automation, regulations, and privacy restrictions of driver and vehicle records for all 50 states and the District of Columbia.

- **THE MVR DECODER DIGEST**

  A companion volume to *The MVR Book*, translating the codes and abbreviations of violations, classes, restrictions, endorsements, etc., that appear on motor vehicle-related records.

- **THE SOURCEBOOK OF INSURANCE SERVICES VENDORS**

  A unique directory for property and casualty insurers, profiling firms that providing premium audits, property inspections, motor vehicle record reporting, and more.

For More Information, Call 800-929-3764
or See the Order Form on the Back Page

CONTENTS

Editor's Notes

All the listings in this Sourcebook are based upon responses to surveys conducted by our staff. The geographic coverage and profile information listed for each retriever is based upon their own responses to our survey. We have tried to reflect these responses accordingly, but we are not responsible for the accuracy of the answers.

The retriever entries in Section One—County Index are solely based on regular, physical, hands-on retrieval of court records within the county:

- The individual listed; or

- People working exclusively for the retriever as employees (not independent contractors or correspondents).

We recognize the importance of independent contractors and correspondents (see pages vii and viii). Many of the retrievers listed in this book employ such people and are duly noted in Section Two—Retriever Profiles.

Finally, any company or individual wishing to appear in future editions of *The Sourcebook of Local Court and County Record Retrievers* may reach the BRB Publications Research Center at:

4653 South Lakeshore, Suite 3

Tempe AZ, 85282

(602) 838-8909

Introduction

The Sourcebook of Local Court and County Record Retrievers is divided into two sections:

SECTION ONE—COUNTY INDEX

Each of the 3140 counties, parishes, independent cities and equivalent jurisdictions in the United States is listed here by state. Each heading indicates the types of records available in that jurisdictions. Chart I—Summary of Codes, on page xi, explains the meaning of each heading abbreviation.

Federal Courts

Federal courts are designated only for those jurisdictions where courts that keep records are located. The number of locations is

- 241 US District Courts (DT), and
- 169 US Bankruptcy Courts (BK)

For more complete searching information about the Federal court system, see our publication, *The Sourcebook of Federal Courts.*

Retriever Line

Each retriever who accesses government offices in a jurisdiction is listed under that jurisdiction heading. The bullets beside each retriever indicate the specific types of information accessed. The one to four digit number that appears to the right of each retriever name is the key to the location of a profile about that retriever in Section Two.

Exceptions

Many states also include a special heading—"ALL COUNTIES"—that includes retrievers who have indicated their own people access the bulleted record types in every jurisdiction within that state.

In a few remote counties, no retriever other than possible a state wide retriever was located. These counties read "See **All Counties**" or "See adjoining counties."

SECTION TWO—RETRIEVER PROFILES

Information about the 2127 Retrievers included in this Sourcebook is include here. Each profile contains

- Address
- Telephone #, including 800 # if available
- Fax #
- Local retrieval area—a list of counties served
- Billing and payment terms
- Project turn around times
- Other geographic areas serviced through correspondents
- Special expertise

Retrievers are listed in numerical order by the key number that appears in Section One. Names are primarily in alphabetical order. Individual names are alphabetized last name first unless they appear as part of a company name.

You vs. Retriever vs. Provider

Do It Yourself

There are two ways to obtain a piece of information—whether the information is pubic record or not:

1. Look it up yourself, or
2. Have someone else look it up for you.

In the world of public records, you may be able to look it up (or "do the search") yourself under two circumstances:

1. The information is available on-line so you can dial it up, or
2. The information is available in your geographic area in searchable form (paper, microfilm, etc.).

In addition, you need to be comfortable with the online search logic and/or with the type of information you seek before trying to obtain it yourself.

If you are not able to look it up yourself, to whom do you go?

Two Categories of Public Record Professionals

We distinguish public record Retrievers from public record Providers as follows:

*   Providers—Companies which furnish search and retrieval services through a network of sources, including their own employees, correspondents and on-line databases.
*   Retrievers—Companies and individuals which directly access sources (repositories) of information.

In other words, a Retriever's personnel (or the Retriever himself), just like you might have done yourself, goes directly to the agency to look up the information. (Of course, in some agencies, the jurisdiction personnel do the looking for them.)

Another Difference Between Retrievers and Providers

A practical distinction of importance to our readers is that a Retriever may be relied upon for local knowledge whereas a Provider has a breadth of knowledge and experience in a wider geographic area.

Many Do Both

Remember that many companies act as both Retrievers and Providers. They retrieve records in the areas surrounding their offices and use correspondents for other areas. Also many Providers, like many Retrievers, are specialists in a specific type of public` record, such as court records or UCC records.

Which to Use?

Chart II—Seven Questions to Ask Yourself, on page xii, outlines a way to answer this question. Basically, before you use a Retriever, you should be comfortable that you know exactly what you want and where it is located. Otherwise you may look for the wrong information in the wrong place, and interpret the results wrong as well.

How to Choose a Competent Retriever

The two most significant attributes of the kind of Retriever you want on your side are:

1. In depth local experience and expertise
   - Knows exactly where to go to obtain the information you need
   - Knows personally the people who work at the government agency
   - Knows exactly what the records look like and what the contents mean

2. Reliability
   - Knows just how long the project will take
   - Knows whether it is possible to expedite the project
   - Completes the project as promised
   - Knows and explains the possible pitfalls involved in obtaining the information you need

When You Call

Chart III—Eleven Questions to Ask a Retriever, on page xiii, illustrates the kinds of questions you want answered before committing your project to a Retriever. Retrievers who are experienced and who do the searches themselves, as is frequently the case in real estate searching, are often more complete and accurate than the jurisdiction itself would be.

Survey of Retrievers

You may have the impression that quality of service is a given in the search business if you are used to using Providers, but your impression may be inaccurate. Although the editors of this *Sourcebook* have no intention of grading firms, a survey was conducted to determine generally the kind of responsiveness our readers may expect from these firms. We called 130 firms at random with a general request for information about whether they could do a particular kind of document retrieval and what the project would cost. Here are the results):

- Didn't get through on initial call (27%)
  - Telephone not answered.. 3%
  - Telephone busy 3%
  - Got an answering machine 20%
  - Put on hold too long 1%

- Answered the telephone immediately (73%)
  - Said they would call back , but didn't.......................... 8%
  - Were either unhelpful or did not know
    if requested documents was available................. 27%
  - Answered our call promptly
    and our questions competently............................ 38%

Of those in the last category, 10 not only showed competence, but also offered helpful advice about the documents. Some of these ten were the only firms that asked for our name and address.

CHART I—SUMMARY OF CODES

COURT RECORDS

CODE*	GOVERNMENT AGENCY	TYPE OF INFORMATION
DT	US District Court	Federal civil and criminal cases
BK	Bankruptcy Court	United States bankruptcy cases
CV	Civil Court	Municipal, county and state level civil cases
CR	Criminal Court	Municipal, county and state level criminal cases
PR	Probate Court	Wills and estate cases

COUNTY RECORDS

CODE*	GOVERNMENT AGENCY	TYPE OF INFORMATION
UC	UCC Filing Office	Uniform Commercial Code and other personal property liens
RE	Recorder of Deeds	Real property transactions and liens
TX	Tax Assessor	Real property tax information
VR	Vital Records Office	Birth, death, marriage, divorce, etc.

*The "CODE" designates the agency and type of information obtainable in each county.

CHART II—SEVEN QUESTIONS TO ASK YOURSELF

Here is a handy chart to help you decide whether to use a Retriever or a Provider to perform your public record search project:

	Date: _____ Project: _____			
1.	What is my level of expertise in the type of information I need?	HIGH	MODERATE	LOW
2.	Do I know where the information is located?	YES	NOT SURE	NO
3.	Do I know how to search for the information?	YES	NOT SURE	NO
4.	Can I obtain the information directly?	YES	DON'T KNOW	NO
5.	What is the age of the information that is accessible?	KNOW	DON'T KNOW	
6.	Does the information in its final form need interpretation?	YES	DON'T KNOW	NO
7.	What is my budget to obtain the information?	LOW	MEDIUM	HIGH

⬇ ⬇ ⬇

If you circled a preponderance of answers in one column, you should

Call a Retriever	Consider a Provider	Call a Provider

If you decide a Provider is right for your project, our companion publication, *The Sourcebook of Public Record Providers*, may be helpful.

Chart III—ELEVEN QUESTIONS TO ASK A RETRIEVER

Once you know if you want to use a Retriever, use these questions, addressed to the Retriever, to determine if the Retriever you call is right for your project. The questions are also generally applicable to choosing a Provider.

Date: _____
Project: _____
Retriver: _____
Telephone: _____
Conatact Name:

1a.	What is your expertise in the type of informatin I need?	HIGH	MEDIUM	LOW
1b.	What is your expertise in dealing with the agency where the information is stored?	HIGH	MEDIUM	LOW
2a.	How frequently do you access the agency where the information I need is stored?	DAILY	WEEKLY	OTHER
2b.	How frequently do you access the specific information I need?	DAILY	WEEKLY	OTHER
3.	Are the original documents stored at this agency?	YES	NO	DON'T KNOW
4.	Do you access the information yourself or through a third party?	SELF		THIRD PARTY
5.	Who does the actual search for the information?	WE DO	AGENCY	
6.	How long before some results are known?	1-2 DAYS	LESS THAN A WEEK	OTHER
7.	In what form will I receive the information?	AS YOU WISH	VERBAL	DOCS ONLY
8.	Will you interpret the information for me?	YES	NO	
9.	Will my search be legal and remain confidential?	YES		DON'T KNOW
10.	What are all the costs I will (may) incur to obtain the information?	EXPLAINED	NOT FULLY EXPLAINED	DON'T KNOW
11.	Do you serve other clients who have needs like mine and may I talk to a few of them?	YES		NO
		⬇	⬇	⬇

If you circled a preponderance of answers in one column, you should

Consider This Retriever	Consider Other Retrievers	Do Not Use This Retriever

Section One

County Index

SUMMARY OF CODES

COURT RECORDS

CODE*	Government Agency	Type of Information
DT	US DISTRICT COURT	Federal civil and criminal cases
BK	BANKRUPTCY COURT	Unites States bankruptcy cases
CV	CIVIL COURT	Municipal, county, and state-level civil cases
CR	CRIMINAL COURT	Municipal, county and state-level criminal cases
PR	PROBATE COURT	Wills and estate cases

COUNTY RECORDS

CODE*	Government Agency	Type of Information
UC	UCC FILING OFFICE	Uniform Commercial Code and other personal property liens
RE	RECORDER OF DEEDS	Real property transactions and liens
TX	TAX ASSESSOR	Real property tax information
VR	VITAL RECORDS OFFICE	Birth, death, marriage, divorce, etc.

*The "CODE" designates the agency and type of information obtainable in each county.

Alabama

AUTAUGA

CV	CR	PR	Provider	Page	UC	RE	TX	VR
●	●	●	Advantage Title Co	90	●	●	●	
		●	Autauga Abstract	220	●	●	●	
●	●	●	Mid-State Attorney Service Inc	1343		●	●	●

BALDWIN

CV	CR	PR	Provider	Page	UC	RE	TX	VR
●	●	●	Brabston Legal Investigations Inc	335	●	●	●	
●	●	●	Hollingsworth Court Reporting Inc	983	●	●	●	●
●		●	Klyce, Thomas W	1132	●	●	●	

BARBOUR

CV	CR	PR	Provider	Page	UC	RE	TX	VR
●	●	●	Hollingsworth Court Reporting Inc	983	●	●	●	●
●	●	●	McNeal Investigations	1318	●	●	●	●

BIBB

CV	CR	PR	Provider	Page	UC	RE	TX	VR
		●	Capstone Title Services	405	●	●	●	
●	●	●	Mid-South Investigations Inc	1342	●	●	●	●

BLOUNT

CV	CR	PR	Provider	Page	UC	RE	TX	VR
●	●	●	Charles F Edgar & Associates	438	●	●	●	
●	●	●	Facts Title Service	732	●	●	●	●
●	●	●	Mid-South Investigations Inc	1342	●	●	●	●

BULLOCK

CV	CR	PR	Provider	Page	UC	RE	TX	VR
●	●	●	Advantage Title Co	90	●	●	●	
●	●	●	McNeal Investigations	1318	●	●	●	●

BUTLER

CV	CR	PR	Provider	Page	UC	RE	TX	VR
●	●	●	Advantage Title Co	90	●	●	●	
●	●	●	McNeal Investigations	1318	●	●	●	●
●	●	●	Mid-State Attorney Service Inc	1343		●	●	●

CALHOUN

BK	CV	CR	PR	Provider	Page	UC	RE	TX	VR
●	●	●	●	Charles F Edgar & Associates	438	●	●	●	●
	●	●	●	Facts Title Service	732	●	●	●	●
			●	H & M Research Co	903	●	●	●	
●	●	●	●	Mid-South Investigations Inc	1342	●	●	●	●

CHAMBERS

CV	CR	PR	Provider	Page	UC	RE	TX	VR
●	●	●	Wright III, Wyatt	2118	●	●	●	●

CHEROKEE

CV	CR	PR	Provider	Page	UC	RE	TX	VR
●	●	●	Charles F Edgar & Associates	438	●	●	●	●
●		●	Facts Title Service	732	●	●	●	●
		●	H & M Research Co	903	●	●	●	
●		●	Stimpson, Frances	1869	●	●	●	
		●	Title Guaranty and Trust of Chattanooga	1953	●	●	●	

CHILTON

CV	CR	PR	Provider	Page	UC	RE	TX	VR
●	●	●	Advantage Title Co	90	●	●	●	
●	●	●	Mid-South Investigations Inc	1342	●	●	●	●
●	●	●	Mid-State Attorney Service Inc	1343		●	●	●

CHOCTAW

CV	CR	PR	Provider	Page	UC	RE	TX	VR
●			Chambless, Linda	435	●	●	●	
●	●	●	McNeal Investigations	1318	●	●	●	●

CLARKE

CV	CR	PR	Provider	Page	UC	RE	TX	VR
●	●	●	Brabston Legal Investigations Inc	335	●	●	●	
		●	Chambless, Linda	435	●	●	●	
●	●	●	Hollingsworth Court Reporting Inc	983	●	●	●	●
●	●	●	McNeal Investigations	1318	●	●	●	●

CV	CR	PR	CLAY		UC	RE	TX	VR
●	●	●	Hollingsworth Court Reporting Inc...................................983		●	●	●	●
●	●	●	Wright III, Wyatt...2118		●	●	●	●

CV	CR	PR	CLEBURNE		UC	RE	TX	VR
●	●	●	Hollingsworth Court Reporting Inc...................................983		●	●	●	●
●	●	●	Wright III, Wyatt...2118		●	●	●	●

CV	CR	PR	COFFEE		UC	RE	TX	VR
●	●	●	Hollingsworth Court Reporting Inc...................................983		●	●	●	●
●	●	●	McNeal Investigations..1318		●	●	●	●
●	●	●	Willingham, Jeanette..2098		●	●	●	

CV	CR	PR	COLBERT		UC	RE	TX	VR
●	●	●	Charles F Edgar & Associates...438		●	●	●	●
●	●	●	Facts Title Service...732		●	●	●	●
		●	H & M Research Co..903		●	●	●	
●	●	●	Legal Research Services Inc..1208		●	●	●	

CV	CR	PR	CONECUH		UC	RE	TX	VR
●	●	●	Hollingsworth Court Reporting Inc...................................983		●	●	●	●
●	●	●	McNeal Investigations..1318		●	●	●	●

CV	CR	PR	COOSA		UC	RE	TX	VR
●	●	●	Hollingsworth Court Reporting Inc...................................983		●	●	●	●

CV	CR	PR	COVINGTON		UC	RE	TX	VR
●	●	●	Hollingsworth Court Reporting Inc...................................983		●	●	●	●
●	●	●	McNeal Investigations..1318		●	●	●	●
●	●	●	Willingham, Jeanette..2098		●	●	●	

CV	CR	PR	CRENSHAW		UC	RE	TX	VR
●	●	●	Advantage Title Co...90		●	●	●	
●	●	●	McNeal Investigations..1318		●	●	●	●

CV	CR	PR	CULLMAN		UC	RE	TX	VR
●	●	●	Charles F Edgar & Associates...438		●	●	●	●
●	●	●	Facts Title Service...732		●	●	●	●
●	●	●	Mid-South Investigations Inc..1342		●	●	●	●

CV	CR	PR	DALE		UC	RE	TX	VR
●	●	●	Hollingsworth Court Reporting Inc...................................983		●	●	●	●
●	●	●	McNeal Investigations..1318		●	●	●	●
●	●	●	Willingham, Jeanette..2098		●	●	●	

CV	CR	PR	DALLAS		UC	RE	TX	VR
		●	Capstone Title Services..405		●	●	●	
●	●	●	McNeal Investigations..1318		●	●	●	●
●	●	●	Mid-State Attorney Service Inc..1343			●	●	●

CV	CR	PR	DE KALB		UC	RE	TX	VR
●	●	●	B & B Reporting...226		●	●	●	●
●	●	●	Charles F Edgar & Associates...438		●	●	●	●
●	●	●	Facts Title Service...732		●	●	●	●
		●	Title Guaranty and Trust of Chattanooga.........................1953		●	●	●	

CV	CR	PR	ELMORE		UC	RE	TX	VR
●	●	●	Advantage Title Co...90		●	●	●	
		●	Autauga Abstract...220		●	●	●	
●	●	●	Mid-State Attorney Service Inc..1343			●	●	●

CV	CR	PR	ESCAMBIA		UC	RE	TX	VR
●	●	●	Hollingsworth Court Reporting Inc...................................983		●	●	●	●

DT	BK	CV	CR	PR	Provider	Ref	UC	RE	TX	VR
		●	●	●	McNeal Investigations	1318	●	●	●	●
		CV	**CR**	**PR**	**ETOWAH**		**UC**	**RE**	**TX**	**VR**
		●	●	●	Charles F Edgar & Associates	438	●	●	●	●
		●	●	●	Facts Title Service	732	●	●	●	●
				●	H & M Research Co	903	●	●	●	
		●	●	●	Hollingsworth Court Reporting Inc	983	●	●		●
		●	●	●	Mid-South Investigations Inc	1342	●	●	●	●
		CV	**CR**	**PR**	**FAYETTE**		**UC**	**RE**	**TX**	**VR**
				●	Capstone Title Services	405	●	●	●	
		●	●	●	Facts Title Service	732	●	●	●	●
		CV	**CR**	**PR**	**FRANKLIN**		**UC**	**RE**	**TX**	**VR**
		●	●	●	Charles F Edgar & Associates	438	●	●	●	●
		●	●	●	Facts Title Service	732	●	●	●	●
		●	●	●	Legal Research Services Inc	1208	●	●	●	
		CV	**CR**	**PR**	**GENEVA**		**UC**	**RE**	**TX**	**VR**
		●	●	●	Hollingsworth Court Reporting Inc	983	●	●	●	●
		●	●	●	McNeal Investigations	1318	●	●	●	●
		●	●	●	Willingham, Jeanette	2098	●	●	●	●
		CV	**CR**	**PR**	**GREENE**		**UC**	**RE**	**TX**	**VR**
		●	●	●	Burdett, Russell	365	●	●	●	
				●	Capstone Title Services	405	●	●	●	
		CV	**CR**	**PR**	**HALE**		**UC**	**RE**	**TX**	**VR**
				●	Capstone Title Services	405	●	●	●	
		CV	**CR**	**PR**	**HENRY**		**UC**	**RE**	**TX**	**VR**
		●	●	●	Hollingsworth Court Reporting Inc	983	●	●	●	●
		●	●	●	McNeal Investigations	1318	●	●	●	
		●	●	●	Willingham, Jeanette	2098	●	●	●	
		CV	**CR**	**PR**	**HOUSTON**		**UC**	**RE**	**TX**	**VR**
		●	●	●	Hollingsworth Court Reporting Inc	983	●	●	●	●
			●	●	McNeal Investigations	1318	●	●	●	
				●	Title Guaranty and Trust of Chattanooga	1953	●	●	●	
		●	●	●	Willingham, Jeanette	2098	●	●	●	
		CV	**CR**	**PR**	**JACKSON**		**UC**	**RE**	**TX**	**VR**
		●	●	●	B & B Reporting	226	●	●	●	●
		●	●	●	Charles F Edgar & Associates	438	●	●	●	●
		●	●	●	Facts Title Service	732	●	●	●	●
				●	H & M Research Co	903	●	●	●	
DT	**BK**	**CV**	**CR**	**PR**	**JEFFERSON**		**UC**	**RE**	**TX**	**VR**
				●	Blankney, Betty	310	●	●	●	
●	●	●	●	●	Fidelity Legal Investigation INc	759	●	●		●
	●	●	●	●	Hollingsworth Court Reporting Inc	983	●	●		●
●		●	●	●	Mid-South Investigations Inc	1342	●	●	●	
		CV	**CR**	**PR**	**LAMAR**		**UC**	**RE**	**TX**	**VR**
		●	●	●	Facts Title Service	732	●	●	●	●
DT		**CV**	**CR**	**PR**	**LAUDERDALE**		**UC**	**RE**	**TX**	**VR**
●		●	●	●	Charles F Edgar & Associates	438	●	●	●	●
●		●	●	●	Facts Title Service	732	●	●	●	●
			●	●	H & M Research Co	903	●	●	●	
●		●	●	●	Legal Research Services Inc	1208	●	●	●	
		CV	**CR**	**PR**	**LAWRENCE**		**UC**	**RE**	**TX**	**VR**
		●	●	●	Charles F Edgar & Associates	438	●	●	●	●

DT	BK	CV	CR	PR	Company	Page	UC	RE	TX	VR
				•	H & M Research Co	903	•	•	•	
		•	•	•	Legal Research Services Inc	1208	•	•	•	

LEE

DT	BK	CV	CR	PR	Company	Page	UC	RE	TX	VR
		•	•	•	Mid-State Attorney Service Inc	1343		•	•	•
		•	•	•	Samford Denson Horsley et al	1731	•	•	•	

LIMESTONE

DT	BK	CV	CR	PR	Company	Page	UC	RE	TX	VR
		•		•	Blackwell, Bob & Karen	306	•	•	•	
		•	•	•	Charles F Edgar & Associates	438	•	•	•	•
		•	•	•	Facts Title Service	732	•	•	•	•
				•	H & M Research Co	903	•	•		
		•	•	•	Legal Research Services Inc	1208	•	•	•	

LOWNDES

DT	BK	CV	CR	PR	Company	Page	UC	RE	TX	VR
		•	•	•	Advantage Title Co	90	•	•	•	
		•	•	•	Grant, Louise	865	•	•	•	•
		•	•	•	McNeal Investigations	1318	•	•	•	•
		•		•	Rittenour, Frances	1700	•	•	•	•

MACON

DT	BK	CV	CR	PR	Company	Page	UC	RE	TX	VR
		•	•	•	Advantage Title Co	90	•	•	•	

MADISON

DT	BK	CV	CR	PR	Company	Page	UC	RE	TX	VR
		•	•	•	B & B Reporting	226	•	•	•	•
		•		•	Blackwell, Bob & Karen	306	•	•		
•		•	•	•	Charles F Edgar & Associates	438	•	•	•	•
•		•	•	•	Facts Title Service	732	•	•	•	•
				•	H & M Research Co	903	•	•		
•		•	•	•	Legal Research Services Inc	1208	•	•	•	
•		•	•	•	Mid-South Investigations Inc	1342	•	•	•	•

MARENGO

DT	BK	CV	CR	PR	Company	Page	UC	RE	TX	VR
		•	•	•	Burdett, Russell	365	•	•	•	
		•		•	Chambless, Linda	435	•	•	•	
		•	•	•	McNeal Investigations	1318	•	•	•	•

MARION

DT	BK	CV	CR	PR	Company	Page	UC	RE	TX	VR
		•	•	•	Charles F Edgar & Associates	438	•	•	•	•

MARSHALL

DT	BK	CV	CR	PR	Company	Page	UC	RE	TX	VR
		•	•	•	B & B Reporting	226	•	•	•	•
		•	•	•	Charles F Edgar & Associates	438	•	•	•	•
		•		•	Facts Title Service	732	•	•	•	•
				•	H & M Research Co	903	•	•		

MOBILE

DT	BK	CV	CR	PR	Company	Page	UC	RE	TX	VR
•	•	•	•	•	Brabston Legal Investigations Inc	335	•	•	•	
	•	•	•	•	Hollingsworth Court Reporting Inc	983	•	•	•	•
•	•	•	•	•	McNeal Investigations	1318	•	•	•	•

MONROE

DT	BK	CV	CR	PR	Company	Page	UC	RE	TX	VR
		•	•	•	Hollingsworth Court Reporting Inc	983	•	•	•	•
		•	•	•	McNeal Investigations	1318	•	•	•	

MONTGOMERY

DT	BK	CV	CR	PR	Company	Page	UC	RE	TX	VR
		•	•	•	Advantage Title Co	90	•	•	•	
•	•	•	•	•	McNeal Investigations	1318	•	•	•	•
•	•	•	•	•	Mid-South Investigations Inc	1342	•	•	•	•
•	•	•	•	•	Mid-State Attorney Service Inc	1343		•	•	•

MORGAN

BK	CV	CR	PR	Company	Page	UC	RE	TX	VR
	•		•	Blackwell, Bob & Karen	306	•	•	•	

BK	CV	CR	PR			UC	RE	TX	VR
•	•	•	•	Charles F Edgar & Associates	438	•	•	•	•
			•	H & M Research Co	903	•	•	•	

PERRY

	CV	CR	PR			UC	RE	TX	VR
	•	•	•	Barnes Jr, James M	245	•	•	•	•

PICKENS

	CV	CR	PR			UC	RE	TX	VR
			•	Capstone Title Services	405	•	•	•	
	•	•	•	Magnolia Title Co	1266	•	•	•	•

PIKE

	CV	CR	PR			UC	RE	TX	VR
	•	•	•	Advantage Title Co	90	•	•	•	
	•	•	•	McNeal Investigations	1318	•	•	•	•
	•	•	•	Mid-State Attorney Service Inc	1343		•	•	•

RANDOLPH

	CV	CR	PR			UC	RE	TX	VR
	•	•	•	Wright III, Wyatt	2118	•	•	•	•

RUSSELL

	CV	CR	PR			UC	RE	TX	VR
	•	•	•	Columbus Land Title Co	499	•	•	•	•

ST. CLAIR

	CV	CR	PR			UC	RE	TX	VR
	•	•	•	Charles F Edgar & Associates	438	•	•	•	•
	•	•	•	Facts Title Service	732	•	•	•	•
	•	•	•	Fidelity Legal Investigation INc	759	•	•	•	•
	•	•	•	Hollingsworth Court Reporting Inc	983	•	•	•	•
	•	•	•	Mid-South Investigations Inc	1342	•	•	•	•

SHELBY

	CV	CR	PR			UC	RE	TX	VR
	•	•	•	Fidelity Legal Investigation INc	759	•	•	•	•
	•	•	•	Mid-South Investigations Inc	1342	•	•	•	•

SUMTER

	CV	CR	PR			UC	RE	TX	VR
	•	•	•	Burdett, Russell	365	•	•	•	

TALLADEGA

	CV	CR	PR			UC	RE	TX	VR
	•	•	•	Facts Title Service	732	•	•	•	•
	•	•	•	Hollingsworth Court Reporting Inc	983	•	•	•	•
	•	•	•	Mid-South Investigations Inc	1342	•	•	•	•

TALLAPOOSA

	CV	CR	PR			UC	RE	TX	VR
	•	•	•	Wright III, Wyatt	2118	•	•	•	•

TUSCALOOSA

BK	CV	CR	PR			UC	RE	TX	VR
•			•	Capstone Title Services	405	•	•	•	
•	•	•	•	Mid-South Investigations Inc	1342	•	•		•
	•	•	•	Montz, Mary Ann	1377	•			•

WALKER

	CV	CR	PR			UC	RE	TX	VR
			•	Capstone Title Services	405	•	•	•	
	•	•	•	Mid-South Investigations Inc	1342	•	•	•	•

WASHINGTON

	CV	CR	PR			UC	RE	TX	VR
	•		•	Chambless, Linda	435	•	•	•	
	•	•	•	Hollingsworth Court Reporting Inc	983	•	•		
	•	•	•	McNeal Investigations	1318	•	•	•	

WILCOX

	CV	CR	PR			UC	RE	TX	VR
	•	•	•	McNeal Investigations	1318	•	•	•	•

WINSTON

	CV	CR	PR			UC	RE	TX	VR
	•	•	•	Charles F Edgar & Associates	438	•	•	•	•
	•	•	•	Hunt, Bill	1002	•	•	•	

Alaska

		CV	CR	PR	**ALEUTIAN ISLANDS, EAST**	UC	RE	TX	VR
					See adjoining counties..				

		CV	CR	PR	**ALEUTIAN ISLANDS, WEST**	UC	RE	TX	VR
					See adjoining counties..				

DT	BK	CV	CR	PR	**ANCHORAGE BOROUGH**	UC	RE	TX	VR
●	●	●	●	●	Anchorage and Matsu Process Service............................144	●	●	●	●
●	●	●	●	●	Freelance Legal Secretary 813	●	●	●	●
●	●	●	●	●	Informa Alaska Inc..1027	●	●	●	
●	●	●	●	●	Information Services of Anchorage.........................1030	●	●		●
●	●	●	●	●	Kennedy's Private Eye..1118	●	●	●	●
●	●	●	●	●	Legal Search..1209	●	●	●	●
●	●	●	●	●	McCord Company...1307	●	●	●	●
●	●	●	●	●	Paladin Legal Services 1502	●	●	●	●

		CV	CR	PR	**BETHEL**	UC	RE	TX	VR
		●	●	●	Fairbanks Courier Service....................................733	●	●	●	●

		CV	CR	PR	**BRISTOL BAY BOROUGH**	UC	RE	TX	VR
					See adjoining counties..				

DT		CV	CR	PR	**FAIRBANKS NORTH STAR BOROUGH**	UC	RE	TX	VR
●		●	●	●	Fairbanks Courier Service....................................733	●	●	●	●
●		●	●	●	Fairbanks Process Service....................................734	●	●	●	●
●		●	●	●	Fort Enterprises Process Srv & Inv 796		●	●	●
●		●	●	●	Lawyer Support Services......................................1181	●	●	●	●

		CV	CR	PR	**HAINES BOROUGH**	UC	RE	TX	VR
					See adjoining counties..				

DT		CV	CR	PR	**JUNEAU BOROUGH**	UC	RE	TX	VR
●		●	●		Alaska Process 98		●	●	●
●		●	●	●	Complete Corporate Services of Alaska................509	●	●	●	●

		CV	CR	PR	**KENAI PENINSULA BOROUGH**	UC	RE	TX	VR
					See adjoining counties..				

		CV	CR	PR	**KETCHIKAN GATEWAY BOROUGH**	UC	RE	TX	VR
					See adjoining counties..				

		CV	CR	PR	**KODIAK ISLAND BOROUGH**	UC	RE	TX	VR
					See adjoining counties..				

		CV	CR	PR	**MATANUSKA-SUSITNA BOROUGH**	UC	RE	TX	VR
		●	●	●	Legal Search..1209	●	●	●	●
		●	●	●	Paladin Legal Services 1502	●	●	●	●

DT		CV	CR	PR	**NOME**	UC	RE	TX	VR
					See adjoining counties..				

		CV	CR	PR	**NORTH SLOPE BOROUGH**	UC	RE	TX	VR
					See adjoining counties..				

		CV	CR	PR	**NORTHWEST ARCTIC BOROUGH**	UC	RE	TX	VR
					See adjoining counties..				

		CV	CR	PR	**PRINCE OF WALES-OUTER KETCHIKAN**	UC	RE	TX	VR
					See adjoining counties..				

		CV	CR	PR	**SKAGWAY-YAKUTAT-ANGOON**	UC	RE	TX	VR
					See adjoining counties..				

CV	CR	PR	**SOUTHEAST FAIRBANKS**	UC	RE	TX	VR
			See adjoining counties...				

CV	CR	PR	**VALDEZ-CORDOVA**	UC	RE	TX	VR
			See adjoining counties...				

CV	CR	PR	**WADE HAMPTON**	UC	RE	TX	VR
			See adjoining counties...				

CV	CR	PR	**WRANGELL-PETERSBURG**	UC	RE	TX	VR
			See adjoining counties...				

CV	CR	PR	**YUKON-KOYUKUK**	UC	RE	TX	VR
			See adjoining counties...				

CV	CR	PR	**SITKA BOROUGH**	UC	RE	TX	VR
			See adjoining counties...				

CV	CR	PR	**BARROW DISTRICT**	UC	RE	TX	VR
●		●	Fairbanks Title Agency 735	●	●	●	

CV	CR	PR	**CAPE NOME DISTRICT**	UC	RE	TX	VR
●		●	Fairbanks Title Agency 735	●	●	●	

CV	CR	PR	**FAIRBANKS DISTRICT**	UC	RE	TX	VR
●	●	●	Allied/Northland Investigations 117	●	●		●
●	●	●	Fairbanks Courier Service....................................733	●	●	●	●
●		●	Fairbanks Title Agency 735	●	●	●	
●	●	●	Lawyer Support Services......................................1181	●	●	●	●

CV	CR	PR	**FORT GIBBON DISTRICT**	UC	RE	TX	VR
●		●	Fairbanks Title Agency 735	●	●	●	

CV	CR	PR	**HOMER DISTRICT**	UC	RE	TX	VR
●	●	●	Freelance Legal Secretary 813	●	●	●	●

CV	CR	PR	**KENAI DISTRICT**	UC	RE	TX	VR
●	●	●	Freelance Legal Secretary 813	●	●	●	●

CV	CR	PR	**KODIAK DISTRICT**	UC	RE	TX	VR
●	●	●	Freelance Legal Secretary 813	●	●	●	●

CV	CR	PR	**KOTZEBUE DISTRICT**	UC	RE	TX	VR
●		●	Fairbanks Title Agency 735	●	●	●	

CV	CR	PR	**MANLEY HOT SPRINGS DISTRICT**	UC	RE	TX	VR
●		●	Fairbanks Title Agency 735	●	●	●	

CV	CR	PR	**MOUNT MCKINLEY DISTRICT**	UC	RE	TX	VR
●		●	Fairbanks Title Agency 735	●	●	●	

CV	CR	PR	**NENANA DISTRICT**	UC	RE	TX	VR
●		●	Fairbanks Title Agency 735	●	●	●	

CV	CR	PR	**NULATO DISTRICT**	UC	RE	TX	VR
●		●	Fairbanks Title Agency 735	●	●	●	

CV	CR	PR	**PALMER DISTRICT**	UC	RE	TX	VR
●	●	●	Anchorage and Matsu Process Service...............144	●	●	●	●
●	●	●	Freelance Legal Secretary 813	●	●	●	●

CV	CR	PR	**RAMPART DISTRICT**	UC	RE	TX	VR
●		●	Fairbanks Title Agency 735	●	●	●	

CV	CR	PR	**VALDEZ DISTRICT**	UC	RE	TX	VR
●	●	●	Freelance Legal Secretary 813	●	●	●	●

Arizona

DT	BK	CV	CR	CR	ALL COUNTIES		UC	RE	TX	VR
	●	●	●	●	Hollingsworth Court Reporting Inc....................983		●	●	●	●

		CV	CR	CR	APACHE		UC	RE	TX	VR
					See ALL COUNTIES............................					

		CV	CR	CR	COCHISE		UC	RE	TX	VR
					See ALL COUNTIES............................					

		CV	CR	CR	COCONINO		UC	RE	TX	VR
		●	●	●	David Granger Investigations....................600		●	●		
		●	●	●	Fleming Attorney Service....................783		●	●	●	●
		●	●	●	Northern Arizona Investigations 1444		●	●	●	●

		CV	CR	CR	GILA		UC	RE	TX	VR
					See ALL COUNTIES............................					

		CV	CR	CR	GRAHAM		UC	RE	TX	VR
					See ALL COUNTIES............................					

		CV	CR	CR	GREENLEE		UC	RE	TX	VR
					See ALL COUNTIES............................					

		CV	CR	CR	LA PAZ		UC	RE	TX	VR
		●	●	●	Desert Investigations....................625		●	●	●	●
		●	●	●	Riviera Research 1701		●	●	●	●

DT	BK	CV	CR	CR	MARICOPA		UC	RE	TX	VR
●	●	●	●	●	AccuSearch Business Service....................63		●	●	●	
●	●	●	●	●	Beacom Attorney Services....................267		●	●	●	●
●	●	●	●	●	Capitol Document Services Inc....................393		●	●	●	●
●	●	●	●	●	David Granger Investigations....................600		●	●		
●	●	●	●	●	Educated Legals Inc....................693		●	●		●
●	●	●	●	●	Fleming Attorney Service....................783		●	●	●	●
●	●	●	●	●	Hawkins and Campbell Inc 939		●	●	●	●
●	●	●	●	●	National Document Retrieval Inc....................1407		●	●	●	
●	●	●	●	●	Phelps & Phelps Investigations....................1546		●	●	●	●
●	●	●	●	●	Track Down Inc....................1975		●	●	●	●

		CV	CR	CR	MOHAVE		UC	RE	TX	VR
		●	●	●	MHR and Associates....................1260		●	●	●	●
		●	●	●	Riviera Research 1701		●	●	●	●

		CV	CR	CR	NAVAJO		UC	RE	TX	VR
		●	●	●	Northern Arizona Investigations 1444		●	●	●	●

DT	BK	CV	CR	CR	PIMA		UC	RE	TX	VR
●	●	●	●	●	AccuSearch Business Service....................63		●	●	●	
●	●	●	●	●	E-Z Messenger Attorney Service Inc 669		●	●	●	
●	●	●	●	●	Educated Legals Inc 693		●	●		●
●	●	●	●	●	Fleming Attorney Service....................783		●	●		●
●	●	●	●	●	Kroes Detective Agency....................1135					
●	●	●	●	●	National Document Retrieval Inc....................1407		●	●	●	
●	●	●	●	●	Trace Unlimited....................1973			●	●	●

		CV	CR	CR	PINAL		UC	RE	TX	VR
		●	●	●	David Granger Investigations....................600		●	●		
		●	●	●	Educated Legals Inc 693		●	●		●
		●	●	●	Fleming Attorney Service....................783		●	●		●
		●	●	●	National Document Retrieval Inc....................1407		●	●	●	

	CV	CR	CR	SANTA CRUZ	UC	RE	TX	VR
				See ALL COUNTIES..				

	CV	CR	CR	YAVAPAI	UC	RE	TX	VR
	●	●	●	Fleming Attorney Service.......................................783	●	●	●	●
	●	●	●	Palmer Investigative Services..............................1506	●	●	●	

BK	CV	CR	CR	YUMA	UC	RE	TX	VR
		●	●	AWS Investigations Inc...37			●	●
●	●	●	●	Desert Investigations...625	●	●	●	●
●	●	●		Wallace Investigations 2048	●	●	●	●

SUMMARY OF CODES

COURT RECORDS

CODE*	GOVERNMENT AGENCY	TYPE OF INFORMATION
DT	US District Court	Federal civil and criminal cases
BK	Bankruptcy Court	United States bankruptcy cases
CV	Civil Court	Municipal, county and state level civil cases
CR	Criminal Court	Municipal, county and state level criminal cases
PR	Probate Court	Wills and estate cases

COUNTY RECORDS

CODE*	GOVERNMENT AGENCY	TYPE OF INFORMATION
UC	UCC Filing Office	Uniform Commercial Code and other personal property liens
RE	Recorder of Deeds	Real property transactions and liens
TX	Tax Assessor	Real property tax information
VR	Vital Records Office	Birth, death, marriage, divorce, etc.

*The "CODE" designates the agency and type of information obtainable in each county.

Arkansas

CV	CR	CR	ALL COUNTIES		UC	RE	TX	VR
•	•	•	Quest Research Inc...........1635		•	•	•	
•		•	Wilson & Associates 2100		•	•	•	

CV	CR	CR	ARKANSAS		UC	RE	TX	VR
			Arkansas County Title Co Inc...........159		•	•	•	

CV	CR	CR	ASHLEY		UC	RE	TX	VR
			See ALLCOUNTIES...........					

CV	CR	CR	BAXTER		UC	RE	TX	VR
•		•	Baxter County Abstract Co 259		•	•	•	
•	•	•	Carroll, D Garvin 411		•	•	•	•

CV	CR	CR	BENTON		UC	RE	TX	VR
•	•	•	Bronson Title Services 349		•	•	•	
•	•	•	North Winds Investigations Inc...........1440		•	•	•	•
•		•	Tucker Abstract Co 1987		•	•	•	

CV	CR	CR	BOONE		UC	RE	TX	VR
•	•	•	Carroll, D Garvin 411		•	•	•	
•		•	Ozark Title & Guaranty Co...........1487		•	•	•	

CV	CR	CR	BRADLEY		UC	RE	TX	VR
•	•	•	Martin Abstract Co...........1289		•	•	•	•

CV	CR	CR	CALHOUN		UC	RE	TX	VR
•	•	•	Lyon Abstract Company...........1251		•	•	•	•
•	•	•	Rollins and Ives PA...........1710		•	•	•	

CV	CR	CR	CARROLL		UC	RE	TX	VR
•	•		Berryville Abstract and Title Co 290			•	•	•
•	•	•	Jackson Abstract Inc...........1073		•	•	•	
•	•	•	North Winds Investigations Inc...........1440		•	•	•	
•		•	Ozark Title & Guaranty Co 1487		•	•	•	

CV	CR	CR	CHICOT		UC	RE	TX	VR
•	•	•	Chicot County Abstract...........452		•	•	•	
•	•	•	David F Gillison Jr PA...........599		•	•	•	

CV	CR	CR	CLARK		UC	RE	TX	VR
•	•	•	Clark County Abstract Co...........465		•	•	•	

CV	CR	CR	CLAY		UC	RE	TX	VR
•	•	•	Hollingsworth Court Reporting Inc...........983		•	•	•	•

CV	CR	CR	CLEBURNE		UC	RE	TX	VR
•	•	•	Professional Title & Abstract Co 1619		•	•	•	•

CV	CR	CR	CLEVELAND		UC	RE	TX	VR
•	•	•	Martin Abstract Co...........1289		•	•	•	
•	•	•	Tinnon Beshear Abstract Co 1949		•	•	•	•

CV	CR	CR	COLUMBIA		UC	RE	TX	VR
•	•		Dauzat, Sondra...........597		•	•	•	
•		•	DeSoto Abstract 609		•	•	•	
•	•	•	Lyon Abstract Company...........1251		•	•	•	•
•	•	•	Rollins and Ives PA...........1710		•	•	•	
•	•	•	Security Abstract Co 1762		•	•	•	

CONWAY

CV	CR	CR	Company	UC	RE	TX	VR
•	•	•	Mercantile Data Resources..................1327	•	•	•	•
•		•	Morrilton Abstract Co.........................1387	•	•	•	

CRAIGHEAD

DT	CV	CR	CR	Company	UC	RE	TX	VR
	•	•	•	Abstracts Inc..................................54		•	•	
	•	•	•	Craighead County Abstract.................548	•	•	•	
•	•	•	•	Easy Way.......................................687		•	•	•
	•	•	•	Hollingsworth Court Reporting Inc.........983	•	•	•	•

CRAWFORD

CV	CR	CR	Company	UC	RE	TX	VR
•	•	•	Crawford County Abstract Co................553	•	•	•	
•	•	•	Deister Ward & Witcher of AR...............615	•	•	•	•
•		•	Hebert Land Services.........................947	•	•	•	•
•		•	Mac Abstract & Title Insurance Co........1262	•	•	•	
•		•	Mercantile Data Resources..................1327	•	•	•	
		•	Mosley Abstract Co..........................1391	•	•	•	
•	•	•	North Winds Investigations Inc............1440	•	•	•	•

CRITTENDEN

CV	CR	CR	Company	UC	RE	TX	VR
•	•	•	Hollingsworth Court Reporting Inc.........983	•	•	•	•
•	•	•	Investigative Services for Attorneys......1049	•	•	•	•
•	•	•	RecordServe/John Kelley Enterprises......1664	•	•	•	•
•	•	•	Schaeffer Papers.............................1743		•		

CROSS

CV	CR	CR	Company	UC	RE	TX	VR
•	•	•	East Arkansas Abstract Co..................677	•	•	•	
•	•	•	Hollingsworth Court Reporting Inc.........983	•	•	•	•

DALLAS

CV	CR	CR	Company	UC	RE	TX	VR
•	•	•	Lyon Abstract Company......................1251	•	•	•	•
•	•	•	Rollins and Ives PA.........................1710	•	•	•	

DESHA

CV	CR	CR	Company	UC	RE	TX	VR
•		•	Smith Abstract Co Inc.......................1812		•	•	

DREW

CV	CR	CR	Company	UC	RE	TX	VR
•	•	•	Drew County Abstract & Title Co...........662	•	•	•	

FAULKNER

CV	CR	CR	Company	UC	RE	TX	VR
•	•	•	Mercantile Data Resources..................1327	•	•	•	•
•	•	•	Pro Facto Inc................................1606	•	•	•	•

FRANKLIN

CV	CR	CR	Company	UC	RE	TX	VR
•	•	•	Deister Ward & Witcher of AR...............615	•	•	•	•
•		•	Hebert Land Services.........................947	•	•	•	
•		•	Mercantile Data Resources..................1327	•	•	•	
		•	Mosley Abstract Co..........................1391	•	•	•	

FULTON

CV	CR	CR	Company	UC	RE	TX	VR
•	•	•	Carroll, D Garvin............................411	•	•	•	•
•	•	•	Fulton Title Company........................819	•	•	•	
•	•	•	Reavis, Dorotha.............................1661	•	•	•	•

GARLAND

DT	CV	CR	CR	Company	UC	RE	TX	VR
	•		•	Guaranty Title Co...........................892	•	•	•	
	•	•	•	Hot Spring County Title Services Inc......994	•	•	•	•

GRANT

CV	CR	CR	Company	UC	RE	TX	VR
•	•	•	Hot Spring County Title Services Inc......994	•	•	•	•

	CV	CR	CR	GREENE	UC	RE	TX	VR
	●	●	●	Easy Way................................687		●	●	●
	●	●	●	Hollingsworth Court Reporting Inc................983	●	●	●	●

	CV	CR	CR	HEMPSTEAD	UC	RE	TX	VR
	●	●	●	Hempstead County Abstract and Title................951	●	●	●	

	CV	CR	CR	HOT SPRING	UC	RE	TX	VR
	●	●	●	Hot Spring County Title Services Inc 994	●	●	●	●

	CV	CR	CR	HOWARD	UC	RE	TX	VR
	●			Credit Bureau of Sevier County.................560	●	●	●	●
	●	●		Dauzat, Sondra.................597	●	●	●	

	CV	CR	CR	INDEPENDENCE	UC	RE	TX	VR
	●	●	●	Independence County Abstract Co...............1020	●	●	●	

	CV	CR	CR	IZARD	UC	RE	TX	VR
	●	●	●	Carroll, D Garvin 411	●	●	●	●
	●	●	●	Izard County Abstract Co................1061	●	●	●	

	CV	CR	CR	JACKSON	UC	RE	TX	VR
	●		●	Miller Newell Abstract...............1353	●	●	●	

DT	CV	CR	CR	JEFFERSON	UC	RE	TX	VR
●	●	●	●	Pro Facto Inc 1606	●	●	●	●

	CV	CR	CR	JOHNSON	UC	RE	TX	VR
	●	●	●	Deister Ward & Witcher of AR...............615	●	●	●	●
	●	●	●	Mercantile Data Resources.................1327	●	●	●	●

	CV	CR	CR	LAFAYETTE	UC	RE	TX	VR
	●	●		Dauzat, Sondra................597	●	●	●	
	●		●	DeSoto Abstract 609	●	●	●	
	●	●	●	Lyon Abstract Company.................1251	●	●	●	●
	●	●	●	Patton Abstract and Title Inc................1525	●	●	●	●

	CV	CR	CR	LAWRENCE	UC	RE	TX	VR
	●	●	●	Mullen Abstract Co.................1396	●	●	●	

	CV	CR	CR	LEE	UC	RE	TX	VR
	●	●	●	Daggett Abstract Co................583	●	●	●	
	●	●	●	Hollingsworth Court Reporting Inc................983	●	●	●	●

	CV	CR	CR	LINCOLN	UC	RE	TX	VR
	●	●	●	Lincoln Abstract Co.................1226	●	●	●	

	CV	CR	CR	LITTLE RIVER	UC	RE	TX	VR
	●	●		Dauzat, Sondra.................597	●	●	●	
	●	●	●	McIver Abstract & Insurance Co 1312	●	●	●	

	CV	CR	CR	LOGAN	UC	RE	TX	VR
	●	●	●	Deister Ward & Witcher of AR...............615	●	●	●	●
	●		●	Hebert Land Services 947	●	●	●	●

	CV	CR	CR	LONOKE	UC	RE	TX	VR
	●	●	●	First State Abstract................778	●	●	●	

	CV	CR	CR	MADISON	UC	RE	TX	VR
	●	●	●	Mercantile Data Resources.................1327	●	●	●	
	●	●	●	Town & Country Abstract Co 1969	●	●	●	

	CV	CR	CR	MARION	UC	RE	TX	VR
	●	●	●	Carroll, D Garvin 411	●	●	●	●

DT		CV	CR	CR	MILLER		UC	RE	TX	VR
		●	●		Dauzat, Sondra 597		●	●	●	
		●	●	●	Marion County Abstract Co 1278		●	●	●	
●		●		●	Miller County Abstract Co 1352		●	●	●	

		CV	CR	CR	MISSISSIPPI		UC	RE	TX	VR
		●	●	●	Hollingsworth Court Reporting Inc 983		●	●	●	●
		●		●	Prewitt-Rogers Abstract Co 1601		●	●	●	

		CV	CR	CR	MONROE		UC	RE	TX	VR
		●	●	●	Menard Title & Abstract Co Inc 1325		●	●	●	

		CV	CR	CR	MONTGOMERY		UC	RE	TX	VR
		●	●	●	Deister Ward & Witcher of AR 615		●	●	●	●

		CV	CR	CR	NEVADA		UC	RE	TX	VR
		●	●	●	Rollins and Ives PA 1710		●	●	●	

		CV	CR	CR	NEWTON		UC	RE	TX	VR
		●	●	●	Mercantile Data Resources 1327		●	●	●	●
		●		●	Ozark Title & Guaranty Co 1487		●	●	●	

		CV	CR	CR	OUACHITA		UC	RE	TX	VR
		●		●	DeSoto Abstract 609		●	●	●	
		●	●	●	Lyon Abstract Company 1251		●	●	●	●
		●	●	●	Rollins and Ives PA 1710		●	●	●	

		CV	CR	CR	PERRY		UC	RE	TX	VR
		●	●	●	Deister Ward & Witcher of AR 615		●	●	●	●

		CV	CR	CR	PHILLIPS		UC	RE	TX	VR
		●	●	●	Hollingsworth Court Reporting Inc 983		●	●	●	●
		●		●	Hornor-Morris Abstract Co 992		●	●	●	
		●		●	Tappan Abstract 1902		●	●	●	

		CV	CR	CR	PIKE		UC	RE	TX	VR
		●	●	●	Deister Ward & Witcher of AR 615		●	●	●	●

		CV	CR	CR	POINSETT		UC	RE	TX	VR
		●	●	●	Hollingsworth Court Reporting Inc 983		●	●	●	●
		●	●	●	Poinsett County Abstract Co 1564		●	●	●	

		CV	CR	CR	POLK		UC	RE	TX	VR
		●	●	●	Deister Ward & Witcher of AR 615		●	●	●	●
		●	●	●	Martin Abstract Co 1288		●	●	●	

		CV	CR	CR	POPE		UC	RE	TX	VR
		●		●	Hebert Land Services 947		●	●	●	●
		●	●	●	Mercantile Data Resources 1327		●	●	●	●

		CV	CR	CR	PRAIRIE		UC	RE	TX	VR
		●	●	●	Moody Abstract Co 1378		●	●	●	●

DT	BK	CV	CR	CR	PULASKI		UC	RE	TX	VR
●	●	●	●	●	North Winds Investigations Inc 1440		●	●	●	●
●	●	●	●	●	Pro Facto Inc 1606		●	●	●	●

		CV	CR	CR	RANDOLPH		UC	RE	TX	VR
		●	●	●	Service Abstract Company 1784		●	●	●	

		CV	CR	CR	ST. FRANCIS		UC	RE	TX	VR
		●	●	●	Hollingsworth Court Reporting Inc 983		●	●	●	●

	CV	CR	CR	SALINE		UC	RE	TX	VR
	●	●	●	Pro Facto Inc 1606		●	●	●	●
	●	●	●	Saline County Abstract.....................1729		●	●	●	●

	CV	CR	CR	SCOTT		UC	RE	TX	VR
	●	●	●	Deister Ward & Witcher of AR.....................615		●	●	●	●
	●		●	Hebert Land Services 947		●	●	●	●
			●	Mosley Abstract Co......................1391		●	●	●	

	CV	CR	CR	SEARCY		UC	RE	TX	VR
	●	●	●	Carroll, D Garvin 411		●	●	●	●
	●	●	●	Mercantile Data Resources.....................1327		●	●	●	●

		CV	CR	CR	SEBASTIAN		UC	RE	TX	VR
DT		●	●	●	Deister Ward & Witcher of AR.....................615		●	●	●	●
		●		●	Hebert Land Services 947		●	●	●	●
●		●	●	●	Mac Abstract & Title Insurance Co.....................1262		●	●	●	
●		●		●	Mosley Abstract Co......................1391		●	●	●	
●		●	●	●	North Winds Investigations Inc.....................1440		●	●	●	●

	CV	CR	CR	SEVIER		UC	RE	TX	VR
	●			Credit Bureau of Sevier County 560		●	●	●	●
	●	●		Dauzat, Sondra.....................597		●	●	●	
	●		●	DeQueen Abstract Co.....................608		●	●	●	

	CV	CR	CR	SHARP		UC	RE	TX	VR
	●	●	●	Sharp County Abstract Co Inc.....................1789		●	●	●	

	CV	CR	CR	STONE		UC	RE	TX	VR
	●	●	●	Mercantile Data Resources.....................1327		●	●	●	●
	●	●	●	Mountain View Abstract Co 1392		●	●	●	

		CV	CR	CR	UNION		UC	RE	TX	VR
DT		●		●	DeSoto Abstract 609		●	●	●	
●		●	●	●	Lyon Abstract Company.....................1251		●	●	●	●
		●	●	●	Rollins and Ives PA.....................1710		●	●	●	
		●		●	Union Abstract Co.....................2004		●	●	●	

	CV	CR	CR	VAN BUREN		UC	RE	TX	VR
	●	●	●	Mercantile Data Resources.....................1327		●	●	●	●

		CV	CR	CR	WASHINGTON		UC	RE	TX	VR
DT		●	●	●	Bronson Abstract Co.....................348		●	●	●	
●		●	●	●	Mercantile Data Resources.....................1327		●	●	●	●
●		●	●	●	North Winds Investigations Inc.....................1440		●	●	●	●

	CV	CR	CR	WHITE		UC	RE	TX	VR
	●	●	●	Citizen's Abstract Co.....................459		●	●	●	
	●		●	Strother-Wilbourn Land Title Co.....................1875		●	●	●	

	CV	CR	CR	WOODRUFF		UC	RE	TX	VR
	●	●	●	Eldridge III, John D 697		●	●	●	

	CV	CR	CR	YELL		UC	RE	TX	VR
	●	●	●	Deister Ward & Witcher of AR.....................615		●	●	●	●
	●		●	Hebert Land Services 947		●	●	●	●
	●	●	●	Mercantile Data Resources.....................1327		●	●	●	●

California

DT	BK	CV	CR	PR	ALL COUNTIES	UC	RE	TX	VR
		•	•		Accelerated Legal Services (ALS) 57				
	•				Bankruptcy Bulletin Weekly Inc 240				
•	•	•	•	•	Global Projects Ltd 851	•	•	•	•

BK	CV	CR	PR	ALAMEDA	UC	RE	TX	VR
				A Fast Copy Inc 5		•		
•	•	•	•	ACE Legal Assistance 19		•		•
•	•	•	•	AD Services 23		•	•	•
•	•	•	•	Adila-Gray Process Servers 83	•	•	•	•
•	•	•	•	Attorney's Diversified Services 200	•	•	•	•
•	•	•	•	Attorney's Messenger Service 205		•	•	•
•	•	•	•	Attorneys' Service Limited 212		•	•	•
•	•	•	•	Bay Area Courthouse Services 261	•	•	•	•
•	•	•	•	Berkeley Base Ltd 286		•	•	
•	•	•	•	Court Record Consultants 544	•	•	•	•
•	•	•	•	Direct Legal Support Services 634		•	•	•
•	•	•	•	Fax & File Legal Services Inc 745	•	•	•	•
•	•	•	•	Lone Star Legal 1236		•	•	•
•	•	•	•	Marco & Company 1276	•	•	•	•
•	•	•	•	McCord Company 1307	•	•	•	•
•	•	•	•	Metro Legal Services Inc 1335		•	•	•
	•	•	•	PFC Information Services 1490	•	•	•	
	•	•	•	Patten Investigations 1523	•	•	•	•
•	•	•	•	Rafael Jorge Investigations 1644	•	•	•	•
•	•	•	•	Ramey Investigative Services 1647	•	•	•	•
	•	•	•	Researchers 1690	•			
	•	•	•	Ross Legal Services 1716				
	•	•	•	Specialized Investigations 1841	•	•	•	•
	•	•	•	St Ives 1846	•	•	•	•
	•	•	•	Systems Resource 1897	•	•	•	•
	•	•	•	Wakeman Microfilm Service 2043		•	•	•
	•	•	•	Western Attorney Services 2081	•	•	•	•

CV	CR	PR	ALPINE	UC	RE	TX	VR
•	•	•	Amador/Calaveras County Attorneys Svc 124	•	•	•	•

CV	CR	PR	AMADOR	UC	RE	TX	VR
•	•	•	Amador/Calaveras County Attorneys Svc 124	•	•	•	•
•	•	•	Attorney's Document Production 202	•	•	•	•
•	•	•	Rafael Jorge Investigations 1644	•	•	•	•
		•	Valley Copy Service Inc 2019				
•	•	•	Vigil Enterprises 2029	•	•	•	•

CV	CR	PR	BUTTE	UC	RE	TX	VR
•	•	•	Attorney's Document Production 202	•	•	•	•
•	•	•	North State Process 1438	•	•	•	•
•	•	•	St Ives 1846	•	•	•	•
•	•	•	The Legal Source 1936			•	

CV	CR	PR	CALAVERAS	UC	RE	TX	VR
•	•	•	Amador/Calaveras County Attorneys Svc 124	•	•	•	•
•	•	•	Attorney's Document Production 202	•	•	•	•
•	•	•	Rafael Jorge Investigations 1644	•	•	•	•
•	•	•	Ray Feller Investigatons 1652	•	•	•	•

CV	CR	PR	COLUSA	UC	RE	TX	VR
•	•	•	Capitol Legal Service Inc 396				
•	•	•	Dave Kern Attorney Service Inc 598		•	•	•
•	•	•	St Ives 1846	•	•	•	•

					UC	RE	TX	VR
●	●	●	The Legal Source ...1936			●		

CONTRA COSTA

CV	CR	PR		UC	RE	TX	VR
			A Fast Copy Inc ...5		●		
●	●	●	ACE Legal Assistance ...19		●		●
●	●	●	AD Services ...23		●	●	●
●	●		Accelerated Legal Services (ALS) ...57				
●	●	●	Adila-Gray Process Servers ...83	●	●	●	●
●	●	●	Attorney's Messenger Service ...205		●		●
●	●	●	Bay Area Courthouse Services ...261	●	●	●	●
●	●	●	Berkeley Base Ltd ...286		●	●	
●	●	●	Court Record Consultants ...544	●	●	●	●
●	●	●	Direct Legal Support Services ...634		●	●	●
●	●	●	Fax & File Legal Services Inc ...745	●	●	●	●
●	●	●	Lone Star Legal ...1236		●	●	●
●	●	●	McCord Company ...1307	●	●	●	●
●	●	●	Metro Legal Services Inc ...1335		●	●	●
●	●	●	Patten Investigations ...1523	●	●	●	●
●	●	●	Rafael Jorge Investigations ...1644	●	●	●	●
●	●	●	Researchers ...1690	●			
●	●	●	Ross Legal Services ...1716				
●	●	●	St Ives ...1846	●	●	●	●
●	●	●	Wakeman Microfilm Service ...2043		●	●	●
●	●	●	Western Attorney Services ...2081	●	●	●	●

DEL NORTE

CV	CR	PR		UC	RE	TX	VR
●	●		Crescent Legal Service ...564	●			
●	●	●	Research and Investigative Associates ...1688	●	●	●	●

EL DORADO

CV	CR	PR		UC	RE	TX	VR
●	●	●	Attorney's Document Production ...202	●	●	●	●
●	●	●	Attorney's Service Centers ...208	●	●	●	●
●	●	●	Baker Attorney Service ...236	●	●	●	●
●	●	●	Bay Area Courthouse Services ...261	●	●		
●	●	●	Capitol Legal Service Inc ...396				
●	●	●	El Dorado Co Attorney Service ...695				
●	●	●	Koogler and Associates Inc ...1133	●	●	●	●
●	●	●	Legalese ...1218	●	●	●	●
●	●	●	Rafael Jorge Investigations ...1644	●	●	●	●
●	●	●	Researchers ...1690	●			
●	●	●	Sierra Legal Services ...1801		●	●	
●	●	●	St Ives ...1846	●	●	●	●
●	●	●	UCC Network Inc ...1996	●	●	●	●
●	●	●	Vigil Enterprises ...2029	●	●	●	●
	●	●	William Olmsted Investigations ...2092	●	●	●	●

FRESNO

DT	BK	CV	CR	PR		UC	RE	TX	VR
	●	●	●	●	Accessible Legal Service ...60		●		●
●	●	●	●	●	Action Process ...72				
●	●	●	●	●	Attorney Service of Merced ...185	●	●	●	●
●	●	●	●	●	Attorney's Diversified Services ...195	●	●	●	●
●	●	●	●	●	Court Record Consultants ...544	●	●	●	●
●	●	●	●	●	Drum, Dora ...664	●	●	●	●
●	●	●	●	●	Loss Protection & Investigations Inc ...1244				
●	●	●	●	●	McCord Company ...1307	●	●	●	●
●	●	●	●	●	Rafael Jorge Investigations ...1644	●	●	●	●
●	●	●	●	●	St Ives ...1846	●	●	●	●
		●		●	Valley Copy Service Inc ...2019				
●	●	●	●		Wilson Enterprises ...2103				

CV	CR	PR	GLENN		UC	RE	TX	VR
•	•	•	Attorney's Document Production	202	•	•	•	•
•	•	•	St Ives	1846	•	•	•	
•	•	•	The Legal Source	1936			•	

CV	CR	PR	HUMBOLDT		UC	RE	TX	VR
•	•	•	Research and Investigative Associates	1688	•	•	•	•
•	•	•	St Ives	1846	•	•	•	•

CV	CR	PR	IMPERIAL		UC	RE	TX	VR
•	•	•	American Messenger Service	137		•	•	•
•	•	•	Britton, Frank	346		•		•
•	•	•	Desert Investigations	625	•	•		•
•	•	•	Rafael Jorge Investigations	1644	•	•		•
•	•	•	St Ives	1846	•	•		•

CV	CR	PR	INYO		UC	RE	TX	VR
•	•	•	Andrews, Sharron	153	•	•	•	•
•	•	•	Rafael Jorge Investigations	1644	•	•	•	•
•	•	•	Sierra Attorney Service	1800	•	•	•	•

CV	CR	PR	KERN		UC	RE	TX	VR
•	•	•	Accessible Legal Service	60		•		•
•	•	•	Attorney's Diverisfied Services	192	•	•	•	•
•	•	•	Bay Area Courthouse Services	261	•	•	•	•
•	•	•	Court Record Consultants	544	•	•	•	•
•	•	•	Rafael Jorge Investigations	1644	•	•	•	•
•		•	The Daily Report	1929	•	•	•	•

CV	CR	PR	KINGS		UC	RE	TX	VR
•	•	•	Accessible Legal Service	60		•		•
•	•	•	Arval Legal Service	164	•		•	•
•	•		Mike Moore Private Investigations	1349				•
•	•	•	Rafael Jorge Investigations	1644	•	•	•	•
•	•	•	St Ives	1846	•	•	•	•

CV	CR	PR	LAKE		UC	RE	TX	VR
•	•	•	Mendo-Lake Paralegals	1326	•	•	•	
•	•	•	North Coast Attorney Service	1433				
•	•	•	St Ives	1846	•			•

CV	CR	PR	LASSEN		UC	RE	TX	VR
•	•	•	The Legal Source	1936			•	

DT	BK	CV	CR	PR	LOS ANGELES		UC	RE	TX	VR
•	•	•	•	•	A & M Attorney Services Inc	3		•		•
•	•	•	•	•	A California Process and Attorney Svc	4	•	•	•	•
•	•	•	•	•	ABI Attorney Service	16		•		
•	•	•	•	•	Abbas Attorney Service	39	•	•	•	
•	•	•	•	•	American Attorney Service	129		•		
•	•	•	•	•	American Messenger Service	137		•		
•	•	•	•	•	Arrow Attorney Assistance	163		•		
		•	•	•	Attorney Services--Antelope Valley	188		•		
•	•	•	•	•	Barristers Attorney Service	250	•	•	•	
•	•	•	•	•	Bay Area Courthouse Services	261	•	•	•	
•	•	•	•	•	Bollinger Attorney Service	317		•		
•	•	•	•	•	Cal Info	380	•	•	•	
•	•	•	•	•	Copy Central	519		•		
•	•	•	•	•	Court Record Consultants	544	•	•	•	
•	•	•	•	•	Dante's Attorney Service	590		•		
•	•	•	•	•	Dave Kern Attorney Service Inc	598		•	•	
•	•	•	•	•	Executive Attorney Service Inc	722	•	•	•	•

CV	CR	PR				Service	Page	UC	RE	TX	VR
●	●	●	●	●		Express Network	727	●	●	●	●
		●	●	●		Five C's	780			●	●
●	●	●	●	●		General Services	838				
			●	●		Green, Richard J	873			●	
●	●	●	●	●		Investigative and Attorney Services	1050	●	●	●	●
●	●	●	●	●		LegalNet Inc	1217	●	●	●	●
●	●	●	●	●		Los Angeles Legal Service	1243	●	●	●	●
●	●	●	●	●		McCord Company	1307	●	●	●	●
●	●	●	●	●		Parasec	1519	●	●	●	●
●	●	●	●	●		Prentice Hall Legal & Financial Services	1583	●	●	●	●
●	●	●	●	●		Rafael Jorge Investigations	1644	●	●	●	●
●	●	●	●	●		Research and Retrieval	1689	●	●	●	●
●	●	●	●	●		S & J Attorney Service	1721	●	●	●	●
●	●	●	●	●		Specialized Investigations	1841	●	●	●	●
●	●	●	●	●		Valley Legal Support Services Inc	2021		●		●

CV	CR	PR	MADERA	Page	UC	RE	TX	VR
●	●	●	Accessible Legal Service	60		●		●
●	●	●	Attorney Service of Merced	185	●	●	●	●
●	●	●	Loss Protection & Investigations Inc	1244				
●	●	●	Rafael Jorge Investigations	1644	●	●	●	●
●	●	●	St Ives	1846	●	●	●	●

CV	CR	PR	MARIN	Page	UC	RE	TX	VR
●	●	●	ACE Legal Assistance	19		●		●
●	●	●	Bay Area Courthouse Services	261	●	●		●
●	●	●	Capitol City Network	392	●	●		●
●	●	●	Direct Legal Support Services	634		●		●
●	●	●	Fax & File Legal Services Inc	745	●	●		●
●	●	●	Lone Star Legal	1236		●		●
●	●	●	Marco & Company	1276		●		●
●	●	●	McCord Company	1307	●	●		●
●	●	●	Metro Legal Services Inc	1335		●	●	●
●	●	●	Rafael Jorge Investigations	1644	●	●	●	●
●	●	●	Ramey Investigative Services	1647	●	●	●	●
●	●	●	Randall, Jean	1648	●	●		●
●	●	●	Researchers	1690	●			
●	●	●	Ross Legal Services	1716		●		●
●	●	●	St Ives	1846	●	●	●	●
●	●	●	Wakeman Microfilm Service	2043		●	●	●
●	●	●	Western Attorney Services	2081	●	●	●	●

CV	CR	PR	MARIPOSA	Page	UC	RE	TX	VR
●	●	●	Attorney Service of Merced	185	●	●	●	●
●	●	●	Rafael Jorge Investigations	1644	●	●	●	●

CV	CR	PR	MENDOCINO	Page	UC	RE	TX	VR
●	●	●	North Coast Attorney Service	1433				
●	●	●	Research and Investigative Associates	1688	●	●	●	●

CV	CR	PR	MERCED	Page	UC	RE	TX	VR
●	●	●	Attorney Service of Merced	185	●	●	●	●
●	●	●	Rafael Jorge Investigations	1644	●	●	●	●
●	●	●	Ray Feller Investigatons	1652	●	●	●	●
●	●	●	St Ives	1846	●	●	●	●
		●	Valley Copy Service Inc	2019				

CV	CR	PR	MODOC		UC	RE	TX	VR
			See ALLCOUNTIES					

MONO

CV	CR	PR		UC	RE	TX	VR
●	●	●	Hill's Records Research ... 971	●	●	●	●
●	●	●	Rafael Jorge Investigations ... 1644	●	●	●	●

MONTEREY

CV	CR	PR		UC	RE	TX	VR
●	●	●	Attorney Service of California ... 184	●	●	●	●
●	●	●	Bay Area Courthouse Services ... 261	●	●	●	●
●	●	●	Monterey County Attorneys Service ... 1371	●	●	●	●
●	●	●	Rafael Jorge Investigations ... 1644	●	●	●	●
●	●	●	Researchers ... 1690	●			
●	●	●	St Ives ... 1846	●	●	●	●
●	●	●	SuperBureau Inc ... 1885	●	●	●	●
●	●	●	Tri County Process Service ... 1978		●	●	

NAPA

CV	CR	PR		UC	RE	TX	VR
●	●	●	Bay Area Courthouse Services ... 261	●	●	●	●
●	●	●	Lone Star Legal ... 1236		●	●	●
●	●	●	Metro Legal Services Inc ... 1335		●	●	●
●	●	●	Patten Investigations ... 1523	●	●	●	●
●	●	●	Rafael Jorge Investigations ... 1644	●	●	●	●
●	●	●	St Ives ... 1846	●	●	●	●

NEVADA

CV	CR	PR		UC	RE	TX	VR
●	●	●	Capitol Legal Service Inc ... 396				
●	●	●	Researchers ... 1690	●			
●	●	●	Sierra Legal Services ... 1801		●	●	
●	●	●	St Ives ... 1846	●	●	●	●
●	●	●	The Legal Source ... 1936			●	
●	●	●	Vigil Enterprises ... 2029	●	●	●	●

ORANGE

BK	CV	CR	PR		UC	RE	TX	VR
●	●	●	●	A & M Attorney Services Inc ... 3		●		●
●	●	●	●	A California Process and Attorney Svc ... 4	●	●		●
●	●	●	●	ABI Attorney Service ... 16		●		●
●	●	●	●	Abbas Attorney Service ... 39	●	●		●
●	●	●	●	All Counties Attorney Service ... 105		●		●
●	●	●	●	American Attorney Service ... 129		●		●
●	●	●	●	American Messenger Service ... 137		●		●
●	●	●	●	Arrow Attorney Assistance ... 163		●		●
●	●	●	●	Barristers Attorney Service ... 250	●	●		●
●	●	●	●	Bay Area Courthouse Services ... 261	●	●		●
●	●	●	●	Bollinger Attorney Service ... 317		●		●
●	●	●	●	Bosic and Bosic ... 328		●		●
●	●	●	●	Cal Info ... 380	●	●		●
●	●	●	●	Court Record Consultants ... 544	●	●		●
●	●	●	●	Dante's Attorney Service ... 590		●		●
●	●	●	●	Dave Kern Attorney Service Inc ... 598		●		●
●	●	●	●	Executive Attorney Service Inc ... 722	●	●		●
●	●	●	●	Express Network ... 727	●	●		●
●	●	●	●	General Services ... 838		●		●
●	●	●	●	Investigative and Attorney Services ... 1050	●	●	●	●
●	●	●	●	LegalNet Inc ... 1217	●	●	●	●
●	●	●	●	McCord Company ... 1307	●	●	●	●
●				One Hour Court Services ... 1470				
●	●	●	●	Prentice Hall Legal & Financial Services ... 1583	●	●		●
●	●	●	●	Rafael Jorge Investigations ... 1644	●	●	●	●
●	●	●	●	S & J Attorney Service ... 1721	●	●	●	●

PLACER

CV	CR	PR		UC	RE	TX	VR
●	●	●	Attorney's Document Production ... 202	●	●	●	●
●	●	●	Attorney's Service Centers ... 208	●	●	●	●

CV	CR	PR			UC	RE	TX	VR
•	•	•	Baker Attorney Service	236	•	•	•	•
•	•	•	Bay Area Courthouse Services	261	•	•	•	•
•	•	•	Capitol City Network	392	•	•	•	•
•	•	•	Capitol Legal Service Inc	396				
•	•	•	El Dorado Co Attorney Service	695				
•	•	•	Fax & File Legal Services Inc	745	•	•	•	•
•	•	•	Fred Waters Inv	809		•	•	•
•	•	•	Koogler and Associates Inc	1133	•	•	•	•
•	•	•	Legalese	1218	•	•	•	•
•	•	•	Rafael Jorge Investigations	1644	•	•	•	
•	•	•	Researchers	1690	•			
•	•	•	Sierra Legal Services	1801		•	•	
•	•	•	St Ives	1846	•	•	•	•
•	•	•	UCC Network Inc	1996	•	•	•	•
•	•	•	United Attorneys' Services	2008	•	•	•	•
•	•	•	Vigil Enterprises	2029	•	•	•	•
•	•	•	William Olmsted Investigations	2092	•	•	•	•

CV	CR	PR	PLUMAS		UC	RE	TX	VR
•	•	•	The Legal Source	1936			•	

CV	CR	PR	RIVERSIDE		UC	RE	TX	VR
•	•	•	A California Process and Attorney Svc	4	•	•	•	•
		•	A Professional Attorney Service Inc	7	•		•	
•	•	•	Abbas Attorney Service	39	•	•	•	•
•	•	•	American Legal Services	135				
•	•	•	Arrow Attorney Assistance	163		•	•	•
•	•	•	Bay Area Courthouse Services	261	•	•	•	•
•	•	•	Bollinger Attorney Service	317		•	•	•
•	•	•	Bosic and Bosic	328		•		•
•	•	•	Court Record Consultants	544	•	•	•	•
		•	Crystal Clear Copy Service	571			•	•
•	•	•	Dante's Attorney Service	590		•	•	•
•	•	•	Dave Kern Attorney Service Inc	598		•	•	•
•	•	•	Executive Attorney Service Inc	722	•	•	•	•
•	•	•	Green, Richard J	873			•	
•	•	•	McCord Company	1307	•	•	•	•
		•	RASCAL	1640		•	•	
•	•	•	Rafael Jorge Investigations	1644	•	•	•	•

DT	BK	CV	CR	PR	SACRAMENTO		UC	RE	TX	VR
•	•	•	•	•	Attorney's Aid Inc of Sacramento	190	•			
•	•	•	•	•	Attorney's Diversified Services	201	•	•	•	•
•	•	•	•	•	Attorney's Document Production	202	•	•	•	•
•	•	•	•	•	Attorney's Service Centers	208	•	•	•	•
•	•	•	•	•	Baker Attorney Service	236	•	•	•	•
•	•	•	•	•	Bay Area Courthouse Services	261	•	•	•	•
•	•	•	•	•	Capitol City Network	392	•	•	•	•
•	•	•	•	•	Capitol Legal Service Inc	396				
					Capitol Services	399	•			
		•	•	•	Court Record Consultants	544	•	•	•	•
		•	•	•	El Dorado Co Attorney Service	695				
•	•	•	•	•	Fax & File Legal Services Inc	745	•	•	•	•
•	•	•	•	•	Fred Waters Inv	809		•	•	•
•	•	•	•	•	Koogler and Associates Inc	1133	•	•	•	•
•	•	•	•	•	Legalese	1218	•	•	•	•
•	•	•	•	•	McCord Company	1307	•	•	•	•
•	•	•	•	•	Parasec	1519	•	•	•	•
•	•	•	•	•	Prentice Hall Legal & FInancial Services	1582	•	•	•	•
•	•	•	•	•	Rafael Jorge Investigations	1644	•	•	•	•

DT	BK	CV	CR	PR			UC	RE	TX	VR
		●	●	●	Researchers	1690	●			
	●	●	●	●	Sierra Legal Services	1801		●	●	
	●	●	●	●	St Ives	1846	●	●	●	●
	●	●	●	●	UCC Network Inc	1996	●	●	●	●
	●	●	●	●	United Attorneys' Services	2008	●	●	●	●
		●		●	Valley Copy Service Inc	2019				
	●	●	●	●	Vigil Enterprises	2029	●	●	●	●
	●	●	●	●	William Olmsted Investigations	2092	●	●	●	●

	CV	CR	PR	SAN BENITO		UC	RE	TX	VR
	●	●	●	Attorney Service of California	184	●	●	●	●
	●	●	●	Monterey County Attorneys Service	1371	●	●	●	●
	●	●	●	Rafael Jorge Investigations	1644	●	●	●	●
	●	●	●	St Ives	1846	●	●	●	●
	●	●	●	Systems Resource	1897	●		●	●
	●	●	●	Tri County Process Service	1978		●	●	

BK	CV	CR	PR	SAN BERNARDINO		UC	RE	TX	VR
●	●	●	●	A California Process and Attorney Svc	4	●	●	●	●
	●		●	A Professional Attorney Service Inc	7	●			●
●	●	●	●	ABI Attorney Service	16		●		●
●	●	●	●	Abbas Attorney Service	39	●	●	●	●
●	●	●	●	American Attorney Service	129		●	●	●
●	●	●	●	American Legal Services	135				
●	●	●	●	American Messenger Service	137		●	●	●
●	●	●	●	Bay Area Courthouse Services	261	●	●	●	●
●	●	●	●	Bollinger Attorney Service	317		●	●	●
●	●	●	●	Bosic and Bosic	328		●		●
●	●	●	●	Court Record Consultants	544	●	●	●	●
	●			Crystal Clear Copy Service	571				●
●	●	●	●	Dante's Attorney Service	590		●	●	●
●	●	●	●	Executive Attorney Service Inc	722	●	●	●	●
●	●	●	●	McCord Company	1307	●	●	●	●
●	●	●	●	Rafael Jorge Investigations	1644	●	●	●	●

DT	BK	CV	CR	PR	SAN DIEGO		UC	RE	TX	VR
●	●	●	●	●	Abbas Attorney Service	39	●	●	●	●
●	●	●	●	●	Accu-Tech Professional Services	62	●	●	●	●
●	●	●	●	●	Adjuster's Photo Copy	84	●	●	●	●
●	●	●	●	●	Alpha Attorney Service	121	●	●	●	●
●	●	●	●	●	American Attorney Service	129		●	●	●
●	●	●	●	●	American Messenger Service	137		●	●	●
●	●	●	●	●	Arrow Attorney Assistance	163		●	●	●
●	●	●	●	●	Bay Area Courthouse Services	261	●	●	●	●
●	●	●	●	●	Campanella Attorney Services Inc	386	●	●	●	●
●	●	●	●	●	Court Record Consultants	544	●	●	●	●
●	●	●	●	●	DataFile	595	●	●	●	●
●	●	●	●	●	Dave Kern Attorney Service Inc	598		●	●	●
●	●	●	●	●	Krotzer Legal Service	1136	●	●		●
●	●	●	●	●	McCord Company	1307	●	●	●	●
●	●	●	●	●	Owens & Associates Investigations	1485	●	●	●	●
●	●	●	●	●	Parasec	1519	●	●	●	●
		●		●	RASCAL	1640		●	●	
●	●	●	●	●	Rafael Jorge Investigations	1644	●	●	●	●
●	●	●	●	●	San Diego Attorney Service Inc	1732				
●	●	●	●	●	Specialized Investigations	1841	●	●	●	●
●	●	●	●	●	WE Investigate Inc	2039	●	●	●	●

BK	CV	CR	PR	SAN FRANCISCO		UC	RE	TX	VR
●	●	●	●	A & A Legal Services	2	●	●	●	●

BK	CV	CR	PR	SANTA BARBARA	UC	RE	TX	VR
●	●	●	●	Associated Attorney Services 170	●	●	●	●
	●	●	●	Commercial Process Service 505		●	●	●
●	●	●	●	Court Record Consultants 544	●	●	●	●
●	●	●	●	Express Network 727	●	●	●	●
	●	●	●	Five C's 780				
●	●	●	●	Rafael Jorge Investigations 1644	●	●	●	●
●	●	●	●	Services for Attorneys 1785	●	●	●	●
●	●	●	●	Specialized Investigations 1841	●	●	●	●

DT	BK	CV	CR	PR	SANTA CLARA	UC	RE	TX	VR
●	●	●	●	●	ACE Legal Assistance 19		●		●
	●	●	●	●	AD Services 23		●		●
●	●	●	●	●	Addie's Attorneys Services 82				●
●	●	●	●	●	Attorney's Document Production 202	●	●	●	●
●	●	●	●	●	Attorneys' Service Limited 212		●	●	●
●	●	●	●	●	Bay Area Courthouse Services 261	●	●	●	●
●	●	●	●	●	Court Record Consultants 544	●	●	●	●
●	●	●	●	●	Direct Legal Support Services 634		●	●	●
●	●	●	●	●	Fax & File Legal Services Inc 745	●	●	●	●
●	●	●	●	●	Lone Star Legal 1236		●	●	●
●	●	●	●	●	McCord Company 1307	●	●	●	●
●	●	●	●	●	Metro Legal Services Inc 1335		●	●	●
●	●	●	●	●	Rafael Jorge Investigations 1644	●	●	●	●
			●	●	Researchers 1690	●			
	●	●	●	●	St Ives 1846	●	●	●	●
	●	●	●	●	Systems Resource 1897	●	●	●	
			●	●	Wakeman Microfilm Service 2043		●	●	●
	●	●	●	●	Western Attorney Services 2081	●	●	●	●

CV	CR	PR	SANTA CRUZ	UC	RE	TX	VR
●	●	●	Attorney Service of California 184	●	●	●	●
●	●	●	Monterey County Attorneys Service 1371	●	●	●	●
●	●	●	Rafael Jorge Investigations 1644	●	●	●	●
●	●	●	Researchers 1690	●			
●	●	●	St Ives 1846	●	●	●	●
●	●	●	Systems Resource 1897	●	●	●	
●	●	●	Tri County Process Service 1978		●	●	

CV	CR	PR	SHASTA	UC	RE	TX	VR
●	●	●	Attorney's Diversified Services 198	●	●	●	●
●	●	●	Capitol City Network 392	●	●	●	●
●	●	●	North State Process 1438	●	●	●	●
●	●	●	St Ives 1846	●	●	●	●
●	●	●	The Legal Source 1936			●	

CV	CR	PR	SIERRA	UC	RE	TX	VR
●	●	●	The Legal Source 1936			●	

CV	CR	PR	SISKIYOU	UC	RE	TX	VR
●	●	●	North State Process 1438	●	●	●	●

CV	CR	PR	SOLANO	UC	RE	TX	VR
●	●	●	Attorney's Document Production 202	●	●	●	●
●	●	●	Bay Area Courthouse Services 261	●	●		
●	●	●	Capitol Legal Service Inc 396				
●	●	●	Metro Legal Services Inc 1335		●	●	●
●	●	●	Patten Investigations 1523	●	●	●	●
●	●	●	Rafael Jorge Investigations 1644	●	●	●	●
●	●	●	Researchers 1690	●			
●	●	●	St Ives 1846	●	●	●	●

BK	CV	CR	PR		Page	UC	RE	TX	VR
	•	•	•	Wakeman Microfilm Service	2043		•	•	•

SONOMA

BK	CV	CR	PR		Page	UC	RE	TX	VR
•	•	•	•	Attorney's Diversified Services	199	•	•	•	•
•	•	•	•	Bay Area Courthouse Services	261	•	•	•	•
•	•	•	•	Capitol City Network	392	•	•	•	•
•	•	•	•	Lone Star Legal	1236		•	•	•
•	•	•	•	McCord Company	1307	•	•	•	•
•	•	•	•	Metro Legal Services Inc	1335		•	•	•
•	•	•	•	Rafael Jorge Investigations	1644	•	•	•	•
	•	•	•	Researchers	1690	•			
•	•	•	•	Ross Legal Services	1716				
•	•	•	•	St Ives	1846	•	•	•	•

STANISLAUS

BK	CV	CR	PR		Page	UC	RE	TX	VR
•	•	•	•	Attorney Service of Merced	185	•	•	•	•
	•	•	•	Attorney's Aid Inc of Modesto	189	•			
•	•	•	•	Attorney's Diversified Services	196	•	•	•	•
•	•	•	•	Bay Area Courthouse Services	261	•	•	•	•
•	•	•	•	Capitol City Network	392	•	•	•	•
•	•	•	•	Rafael Jorge Investigations	1644	•	•	•	•
	•	•	•	Ray Feller Investigatons	1652	•	•	•	•
	•	•	•	Researchers	1690	•			
•	•	•	•	St Ives	1846	•			•
•			•	Valley Copy Service Inc	2019	•			

SUTTER

BK	CV	CR	PR		Page	UC	RE	TX	VR
	•	•	•	Attorney's Document Production	202	•	•	•	•
	•	•	•	Capitol Legal Service Inc	396				
	•	•	•	Fred Waters Inv	809		•	•	•
	•	•	•	Koogler and Associates Inc	1133	•	•	•	•
	•	•	•	Legalese	1218	•	•	•	•
	•	•	•	Rafael Jorge Investigations	1644	•	•	•	•
	•	•	•	Researchers	1690	•			
	•	•	•	St Ives	1846	•	•	•	•
	•	•	•	The Legal Source	1936		•		
	•	•	•	William Olmsted Investigations	2092	•	•	•	•

TEHAMA

BK	CV	CR	PR		Page	UC	RE	TX	VR
	•	•	•	Attorney's Document Production	202	•	•	•	•
	•	•	•	North State Process	1438	•	•	•	•
	•	•	•	St Ives	1846	•	•	•	•
	•	•		The Legal Source	1936			•	
			•	Valley Copy Service Inc	2019				

TRINITY

BK	CV	CR	PR		Page	UC	RE	TX	VR
	•	•	•	Research and Investigative Associates	1688	•	•	•	•

TULARE

BK	CV	CR	PR		Page	UC	RE	TX	VR
	•	•	•	Accessible Legal Service	60		•		•
	•	•	•	Arval Legal Service	164	•		•	•
	•	•		Loss Protection & Investigations Inc	1244				
	•	•		Mike Moore Private Investigations	1349				•
	•	•	•	Rafael Jorge Investigations	1644	•	•	•	•
	•	•	•	St Ives	1846	•	•	•	•
			•	Valley Copy Service Inc	2019				

TUOLUMNE

BK	CV	CR	PR		Page	UC	RE	TX	VR
	•	•	•	Rafael Jorge Investigations	1644	•	•	•	•
	•	•	•	Ray Feller Investigatons	1652	•	•	•	•

VENTURA

CV	CR	PR			UC	RE	TX	VR
●	●	●	Bollinger Attorney Service	317		●	●	●
●	●	●	Commercial Process Service	505		●	●	●
●	●	●	Court Record Consultants	544	●	●	●	●
●	●	●	Dante's Attorney Service	590		●	●	●
●	●	●	Executive Attorney Service Inc	722	●	●	●	●
●	●	●	Express Network	727	●	●	●	●
●	●	●	Green, Richard J	873			●	
●	●	●	Investigative and Attorney Services	1050	●	●	●	●
●	●	●	Rafael Jorge Investigations	1644	●	●	●	●
●	●	●	S & J Attorney Service	1721	●	●	●	●

YOLO

CV	CR	PR			UC	RE	TX	VR
●	●	●	Attorney's Document Production	202	●	●	●	●
●	●	●	Attorney's Service Centers	208	●	●	●	●
●	●	●	Baker Attorney Service	236	●	●	●	●
●	●	●	Capitol City Network	392	●	●	●	●
●	●	●	Capitol Legal Service Inc	396				
●	●	●	Fred Waters Inv	809		●	●	●
●	●	●	Koogler and Associates Inc	1133	●	●	●	●
●	●	●	Legalese	1218	●	●	●	●
●	●	●	Researchers	1690	●			
●	●	●	St Ives	1846	●	●	●	●
●	●	●	United Attorneys' Services	2008	●	●	●	●
●	●	●	Vigil Enterprises	2029	●	●	●	●
●	●	●	William Olmsted Investigations	2092	●		●	●

YUBA

CV	CR	PR			UC	RE	TX	VR
●	●	●	Attorney's Document Production	202	●	●	●	●
●	●	●	Fred Waters Inv	809		●	●	●
●	●	●	Koogler and Associates Inc	1133	●	●	●	●
●	●	●	Legalese	1218	●	●	●	●
●	●	●	Rafael Jorge Investigations	1644	●	●	●	●
●	●	●	Researchers	1690	●			
●	●	●	Sierra Legal Services	1801		●	●	
●	●	●	St Ives	1846	●	●	●	●
●	●	●	The Legal Source	1936			●	
●	●	●	William Olmsted Investigations	2092	●	●	●	●

Colorado

DT	BK	CV	CR	PR	ALL COUNTIES		UC	RE	TX	VR
	●	●	●	●	Hollingsworth Court Reporting Inc.....................983		●	●	●	●

		CV	CR	PR	ADAMS		UC	RE	TX	VR
		●	●	●	AAA Process Servers Inc.....................13		●	●		
		●	●	●	BGB Enterprises/Investigations.....................232		●	●	●	●
		●	●	●	Baxter Investigations.....................260		●	●	●	●
		●	●	●	Blue Moon Investigations.....................313		●	●	●	
		●	●	●	Burley, Wade.....................367		●	●	●	
		●	●	●	Centennial Coverages Inc.....................422		●	●	●	
		●	●	●	Colorado Records Search Inc.....................495		●	●	●	●
		●	●	●	DJM Enterprises.....................582		●	●	●	●
		●	●	●	Deister Ward & Witcher Inc.....................614		●	●	●	●
		●	●	●	Interwest Investigations.....................1042		●	●	●	●
		●	●	●	Larry Nasi LTD.....................1173		●	●	●	●
		●	●		Peregrine Investigation & Research.....................1537		●	●		●
		●	●	●	Prentice Hall Legal & Financial Services.....................1584		●	●	●	●
		●	●	●	R A Heales & Associates Ltd.....................1639		●	●	●	●
		●	●		Research & Revisions Etc.....................1682		●	●	●	●
		●	●	●	SPS Investigations & Process Serving.....................1725		●	●	●	
		●	●	●	Search Company International.....................1754		●	●	●	●

		CV	CR	PR	ALAMOSA		UC	RE	TX	VR
		●	●	●	Alamosa Abstract Co.....................96		●	●	●	●

		CV	CR	PR	ARAPAHOE		UC	RE	TX	VR
		●	●	●	AAA Process Servers Inc.....................13		●	●		
		●	●	●	Access Information.....................58		●	●	●	●
		●	●	●	BGB Enterprises/Investigations.....................232		●	●	●	●
		●	●	●	Baxter Investigations.....................260		●	●	●	●
		●	●	●	Blue Moon Investigations.....................313		●	●	●	
		●	●	●	Burley, Wade.....................367		●	●	●	
		●	●	●	Centennial Coverages Inc.....................422		●	●	●	
		●	●	●	Colorado Records Search Inc.....................495		●	●	●	●
		●	●	●	DJM Enterprises.....................582		●	●	●	●
		●	●	●	Deister Ward & Witcher Inc.....................614		●	●	●	●
		●	●	●	Interwest Investigations.....................1042		●	●	●	●
		●	●	●	Larry Nasi LTD.....................1173		●	●	●	●
		●	●		Peregrine Investigation & Research.....................1537		●	●		
		●	●	●	Prentice Hall Legal & Financial Services.....................1584		●	●	●	●
		●	●	●	R A Heales & Associates Ltd.....................1639		●	●	●	●
		●	●	●	SPS Investigations & Process Serving.....................1725		●	●	●	
		●	●	●	Search Company International.....................1754		●	●	●	●

		CV	CR	PR	ARCHULETA		UC	RE	TX	VR
					Colorado Land Title.....................494		●	●	●	
		●	●	●	Pagosa Springs Title Co.....................1500		●	●	●	

		CV	CR	PR	BACA		UC	RE	TX	VR
					See ALL COUNTIES.....................					

		CV	CR	PR	BENT		UC	RE	TX	VR
		●	●	●	Bent County Abstract Co.....................279		●	●	●	●

		CV	CR	PR	BOULDER		UC	RE	TX	VR
		●	●	●	AAA Process Servers Inc.....................13		●	●		
		●	●	●	Access Information.....................58		●	●	●	●
		●	●	●	BGB Enterprises/Investigations.....................232		●	●	●	●
		●	●	●	Baxter Investigations.....................260		●	●	●	●
		●	●	●	Burley, Wade.....................367		●	●	●	●

CV	CR	PR		UC	RE	TX	VR
•	•	•	Colorado Records Search Inc 495	•	•	•	•
•	•	•	Interwest Investigations 1042	•	•	•	•
•	•	•	Larry Nasi LTD 1173	•	•	•	•
•	•		Peregrine Investigation & Research 1537	•	•	•	
•	•	•	Prentice Hall Legal & Financial Services 1584	•	•	•	•
•	•	•	SPS Investigations & Process Serving 1725	•	•	•	•
•	•	•	Search Company International 1754	•	•	•	•

CV	CR	PR	CHAFFEE	UC	RE	TX	VR
			Chaffee Title-Abstract Co 432	•	•	•	

CV	CR	PR	CHEYENNE	UC	RE	TX	VR
		•	Cheyenne County Abstract Co 451	•	•	•	
•	•	•	Deister Ward & Witcher Inc 614	•	•	•	•

CV	CR	PR	CLEAR CREEK	UC	RE	TX	VR
•	•	•	Baxter Investigations 260	•	•	•	•
•	•	•	Clear Creek-Gelpin Abstract & Title Corp 472	•	•	•	

CV	CR	PR	CONEJOS	UC	RE	TX	VR
•	•	•	Alamosa Abstract Co 96	•	•	•	•

CV	CR	PR	COSTILLA	UC	RE	TX	VR
•	•	•	Alamosa Abstract Co 96	•	•	•	•

CV	CR	PR	CROWLEY	UC	RE	TX	VR
			Crowley County Insurance & Title 569	•	•	•	
•	•	•	Deister Ward & Witcher Inc 614	•	•	•	•

CV	CR	PR	CUSTER	UC	RE	TX	VR
•		•	Fremont/Custer County Abstract Co 814	•	•	•	

CV	CR	PR	DELTA	UC	RE	TX	VR
			Western Title Insurance Agency Inc 2082	•	•	•	

DT	BK	CV	CR	PR	DENVER	UC	RE	TX	VR
•	•	•	•	•	AAA Process Servers Inc 13	•	•		
•	•	•	•	•	Access Information 58	•	•	•	•
•	•	•	•	•	BGB Enterprises/Investigations 232	•	•	•	•
•	•	•	•	•	Baxter Investigations 260	•	•	•	•
•	•	•	•	•	Blue Moon Investigations 313	•	•	•	
•	•	•	•	•	Burley, Wade 367	•	•	•	•
•	•	•	•	•	Centennial Coverages Inc 422	•	•	•	•
•	•	•	•	•	Colorado Records Search Inc 495	•	•	•	•
•	•	•	•	•	DJM Enterprises 582	•	•	•	•
•	•	•	•	•	Interwest Investigations 1042	•	•	•	•
•	•	•	•	•	Larry Nasi LTD 1173	•	•	•	•
•	•	•	•	•	Peregrine Investigation & Research 1537	•	•		
•	•	•	•	•	R A Heales & Associates Ltd 1639	•	•	•	•
•	•	•	•	•	SPS Investigations & Process Serving 1725	•	•	•	
•	•	•	•	•	Search Company International 1754	•	•	•	•

CV	CR	PR	DOLORES	UC	RE	TX	VR
			Montezuma-Dolores Title Co 1372	•	•	•	

CV	CR	PR	DOUGLAS	UC	RE	TX	VR
•	•	•	AAA Process Servers Inc 13	•	•		•
•	•	•	BGB Enterprises/Investigations 232	•	•	•	•
•	•	•	Baxter Investigations 260	•	•	•	•
•	•	•	Blue Moon Investigations 313	•	•	•	
•	•	•	Colorado Records Search Inc 495	•	•	•	
•	•	•	DJM Enterprises 582	•	•	•	•
•	•	•	Deister Ward & Witcher Inc 614	•	•	•	•

●	●		Peregrine Investigation & Research 1537	●	●		●
●	●	●	R A Heales & Associates Ltd.............................1639	●	●	●	●
●	●	●	SPS Investigations & Process Serving 1725	●	●	●	
●	●	●	Search Company International 1754	●	●	●	●

CV	CR	PR	EAGLE	UC	RE	TX	VR
●	●	●	JMAC Enterprises 1071	●	●	●	●

CV	CR	PR	ELBERT	UC	RE	TX	VR
●	●	●	Baxter Investigations..260	●	●	●	●
●	●	●	Deister Ward & Witcher Inc................................614	●	●	●	●

CV	CR	PR	EL PASO	UC	RE	TX	VR
●	●	●	BGB Enterprises/Investigations 232	●	●	●	●
●	●	●	Baxter Investigations..260	●	●	●	●
●	●	●	Colorado Records Search Inc................................495	●	●	●	●
●	●	●	Legal Express 1202	●	●	●	

CV	CR	PR	FREMONT	UC	RE	TX	VR
●		●	Fremont/Custer County Abstract Co....................814	●	●	●	●

CV	CR	PR	GARFIELD	UC	RE	TX	VR
●	●	●	Deister Ward & Witcher Inc................................614	●	●	●	●

CV	CR	PR	GILPIN	UC	RE	TX	VR
●	●	●	Baxter Investigations..260	●	●	●	●
●	●	●	Clear Creek-Gelpin Abstract & Title Corp...........472	●	●	●	
●	●	●	Colorado Records Search Inc................................495	●	●	●	●

CV	CR	PR	GRAND	UC	RE	TX	VR
●	●	●	JMAC Enterprises 1071	●	●	●	●

CV	CR	PR	GUNNISON	UC	RE	TX	VR
●	●	●	Deister Ward & Witcher Inc................................614	●	●	●	●

CV	CR	PR	HINSDALE	UC	RE	TX	VR
●	●	●	Hinsdale County Title Co....................................977	●	●	●	●

CV	CR	PR	HUERFANO	UC	RE	TX	VR
			Dotter Abstract & Associates 648	●	●	●	●

CV	CR	PR	JACKSON	UC	RE	TX	VR
●	●	●	JMAC Enterprises 1071	●	●	●	●

CV	CR	PR	JEFFERSON	UC	RE	TX	VR
●	●	●	AAA Process Servers Inc 13	●	●		
●	●	●	Access Information...58	●	●	●	●
●	●	●	BGB Enterprises/Investigations 232	●	●	●	●
●	●	●	Baxter Investigations..260	●	●	●	●
●	●	●	Blue Moon Investigations 313	●	●	●	
●	●	●	Burley, Wade..367	●	●	●	
●	●	●	Centennial Coverages Inc....................................422	●	●	●	
●	●	●	Colorado Records Search Inc................................495	●	●	●	●
●	●	●	DJM Enterprises...582	●	●	●	
●	●	●	Interwest Investigations......................................1042	●	●	●	
●	●	●	Larry Nasi LTD...1173	●	●	●	●
●	●	●	Peregrine Investigation & Research 1537	●	●	●	●
●	●	●	Prentice Hall Legal & Financial Services.............1584	●	●	●	●
●	●	●	R A Heales & Associates Ltd.............................1639	●	●	●	●
●	●	●	SPS Investigations & Process Serving 1725	●	●	●	
●	●	●	Search Company International 1754	●	●	●	●

CV	CR	PR	KIOWA	UC	RE	TX	VR
●	●	●	Deister Ward & Witcher Inc................................614	●	●	●	●

			Kiowa County Abstract Co 1127	●	●	●	

CV	CR	PR	**KIT CARSON**	UC	RE	TX	VR
●	●	●	Deister Ward & Witcher Inc................................614	●	●	●	●

CV	CR	PR	**LAKE**	UC	RE	TX	VR
●	●	●	Lake County Abstract Co....................................1156	●	●	●	●

CV	CR	PR	**LA PLATA**	UC	RE	TX	VR
●	●	●	La Plata Abstract Co 1145	●	●	●	

CV	CR	PR	**LARIMER**	UC	RE	TX	VR
●	●	●	Colorado Records Search Inc.................................495	●	●	●	●
●	●	●	Interwest Investigations....................................1042	●	●	●	●
●	●	●	Larry Nasi LTD..1173	●	●	●	●
●	●		Research & Revisions Etc....................................1682	●	●	●	●
●	●	●	Search Company International 1754	●	●	●	●

CV	CR	PR	**LAS ANIMAS**	UC	RE	TX	VR
●		●	Southern Colorado Title Co................................1828	●	●	●	●

CV	CR	PR	**LINCOLN**	UC	RE	TX	VR
●	●	●	Deister Ward & Witcher Inc................................614	●	●	●	●

CV	CR	PR	**LOGAN**	UC	RE	TX	VR
●	●	●	Deister Ward & Witcher Inc................................614	●	●	●	●
●	●		Research & Revisions Etc....................................1682	●	●	●	●

CV	CR	PR	**MESA**	UC	RE	TX	VR
			Abstract & Title Co of Mesa County Inc...................44		●	●	●
●	●	●	Deister Ward & Witcher Inc................................614	●	●	●	●

CV	CR	PR	**MINERAL**	UC	RE	TX	VR
●	●	●	Alamosa Abstract Co..96	●	●	●	●

CV	CR	PR	**MOFFAT**	UC	RE	TX	VR
●	●	●	JMAC Enterprises 1071	●	●	●	●

CV	CR	PR	**MONTEZUMA**	UC	RE	TX	VR
			Montezuma-Dolores Title Co...............................1372	●	●	●	

CV	CR	PR	**MONTROSE**	UC	RE	TX	VR
●	●	●	Deister Ward & Witcher Inc................................614	●	●	●	●
			Western Title Insurance Agency Inc 2083	●	●	●	

CV	CR	PR	**MORGAN**	UC	RE	TX	VR
●	●		Research & Revisions Etc....................................1682	●	●	●	●

CV	CR	PR	**OTERO**	UC	RE	TX	VR
●	●	●	Deister Ward & Witcher Inc................................614	●	●	●	●

CV	CR	PR	**OURAY**	UC	RE	TX	VR
●	●	●	Attorneys' Title Agency Inc..................................213	●	●	●	

CV	CR	PR	**PARK**	UC	RE	TX	VR
●	●	●	Baxter Investigations...260	●	●	●	●
●	●	●	Deister Ward & Witcher Inc................................614	●	●	●	●

CV	CR	PR	**PHILLIPS**	UC	RE	TX	VR
●	●	●	Deister Ward & Witcher Inc................................614	●	●	●	●
●	●		Research & Revisions Etc....................................1682	●	●	●	●

CV	CR	PR	**PITKIN**	UC	RE	TX	VR
●	●	●	Deister Ward & Witcher Inc................................614	●	●	●	●

CV	CR	PR	PROWERS	UC	RE	TX	VR
●	●	●	Guaranty Abstract Co............887	●	●	●	

CV	CR	PR	PUEBLO	UC	RE	TX	VR
●	●	●	Colorado Records Search Inc............495	●	●	●	●

CV	CR	PR	RIO BLANCO	UC	RE	TX	VR
●	●	●	Deister Ward & Witcher Inc............614	●	●	●	●

CV	CR	PR	RIO GRANDE	UC	RE	TX	VR
●	●	●	Alamosa Abstract Co............96	●	●	●	●

CV	CR	PR	ROUTT	UC	RE	TX	VR
●	●	●	JMAC Enterprises............1071	●	●	●	●

CV	CR	PR	SAGUACHE	UC	RE	TX	VR
●	●	●	Alamosa Abstract Co............96	●	●	●	●

CV	CR	PR	SAN JUAN	UC	RE	TX	VR
●	●	●	Attorneys' Title Agency Inc............213	●	●	●	

CV	CR	PR	SAN MIGUEL	UC	RE	TX	VR
●	●	●	Attorneys' Title Agency Inc............213	●	●	●	

CV	CR	PR	SEDGWICK	UC	RE	TX	VR
●	●	●	Deister Ward & Witcher Inc............614	●	●	●	●
●	●		Research & Revisions Etc............1682	●	●	●	●

CV	CR	PR	SUMMIT	UC	RE	TX	VR
●	●	●	Deister Ward & Witcher Inc............614	●	●	●	●

CV	CR	PR	TELLER	UC	RE	TX	VR
●	●	●	Baxter Investigations............260	●	●	●	●
●	●	●	Legal Express............1202	●	●	●	

CV	CR	PR	WASHINGTON	UC	RE	TX	VR
●	●		Research & Revisions Etc............1682	●	●	●	●
			Washington County Title Company............2058	●	●	●	

CV	CR	PR	WELD	UC	RE	TX	VR
●	●	●	Burley, Wade............367	●	●	●	●
●	●	●	Colorado Records Search Inc............495	●	●	●	●
●	●	●	Deister Ward & Witcher Inc............614	●	●	●	●
●	●	●	Interwest Investigations............1042	●	●	●	●
●	●	●	Larry Nasi LTD............1173	●	●	●	●
●	●		Research & Revisions Etc............1682	●	●	●	●

CV	CR	PR	YUMA	UC	RE	TX	VR
●	●		Research & Revisions Etc............1682	●	●	●	●

Connecticut

DT	BK	CV	CR	PR	ALL COUNTIES	UC	RE	TX	VR
•	•		•	•	Data Reporting Corp 593	•	•	•	
•	•	•			Nationwide Information Services....................1411	•	•	•	•

DT	BK	CV	CR	PR	FAIRFIELD	UC	RE	TX	VR
•	•	•	•	•	LegalEase Inc 1215	•	•	•	•
•	•	•	•	•	Mandelbaum-Edgerton Grooup......................1274	•	•	•	•
•	•	•	•	•	North East Court Services Inc 1434	•	•	•	
			•		Pro Search Inc 1607	•	•	•	•

DT	BK	CV	CR	PR	HARTFORD	UC	RE	TX	VR
•	•	•	•	•	Applied Investigative Group.......................156	•	•	•	•
•	•	•	•	•	First Security Service Corp 777	•	•	•	•
•	•	•	•	•	Ricard Assocates Inc 1692	•	•	•	•

		CV	CR	PR	LITCHFIELD	UC	RE	TX	VR
					See ALL COUNTIES..				

		CV	CR	PR	MIDDLESEX	UC	RE	TX	VR
		•	•	•	Ricard Assocates Inc 1692	•	•	•	•
		•		•	Shickel, Valerie...............................1798	•	•		•

DT		CV	CR	PR	NEW HAVEN	UC	RE	TX	VR
		•		•	Shickel, Valerie...............................1798	•	•	•	•
				•	Sullivan, Joan................................1881	•	•	•	

		CV	CR	PR	NEW LONDON	UC	RE	TX	VR
				•	Arnold, Platt................................161	•	•	•	
					Kittrell, Katherine G............................1131	•	•	•	•
		•	•	•	Ricard Assocates Inc 1692	•	•	•	•
		•		•	Shickel, Valerie...............................1798	•	•	•	•

		CV	CR	PR	TOLLAND	UC	RE	TX	VR
		•	•	•	Applied Investigative Group.......................156	•	•	•	•
		•	•	•	Ricard Assocates Inc 1692	•	•	•	•

		CV	CR	PR	WINDHAM	UC	RE	TX	VR
		•	•	•	Ricard Assocates Inc 1692	•	•	•	•

Delaware

DT	BK	CV	CR	PR	ALL COUNTIES	UC	RE	TX	VR
●	●	●	●	●	CorpAmerica Inc 523	●	●	●	
●	●	●	●		Golt Adjustment Service 853	●	●	●	
●	●	●	●		Incorporating Services Ltd 1019		●	●	●
●	●	●	●	●	Interstate Abstract Inc 1040	●	●	●	●
●	●	●	●		National Legal Process 1409	●	●	●	●

		CV	CR	PR	KENT	UC	RE	TX	VR
		●	●	●	Corporation Service Co - Delaware 529	●	●	●	●
		●	●		Delaware Attorney Services 617	●	●	●	●

DT	BK	CV	CR	PR	NEW CASTLE	UC	RE	TX	VR
●	●	●	●	●	Corporation Service Co - Delaware 529	●	●	●	●
●	●	●	●		Delaware Attorney Services 617	●	●	●	●
●	●	●	●	●	Legal Beagles Inc 1193	●	●	●	●

		CV	CR	PR	SUSSEX	UC	RE	TX	VR
		●	●	●	Corporation Service Co - Delaware 529	●	●	●	●
		●	●		Delaware Attorney Services 617	●	●	●	●
		●	●	●	Researchers Ltd 1691	●	●	●	

District of Columbia

DT	BK	CV	CR	PR	DISTRICT OF COLUMBIA	UC	RE	TX	VR
•	•	•	•	•	ABIS Inc ...17	•	•	•	
		•		•	Accurate Legal Service Co ...66	•	•		•
		•	•	•	CorpAssist ...524	•	•	•	•
•	•	•			Court House Retrieval Inc ...543	•		•	•
		•	•	•	Davis Detective Agency Inc ...602	•	•	•	•
		•			Douglas Investigations Ltd ...655				
		•	•	•	Federal Information Service ...749	•	•	•	•
		•	•	•	Instant Information Systems ...1032	•	•	•	•
		•	•	•	M & M Search Service Inc ...1254	•	•	•	•
•	•	•		•	Pascal & Carter Process Service Inc ...1522	•			
		•	•	•	Security Intelligence Bureau ...1774	•	•	•	•
•	•	•	•	•	University Process Service ...2012				
		•	•	•	W A Haag & Associates Inc ...2036	•	•	•	•

SUMMARY OF CODES

COURT RECORDS

CODE*	GOVERNMENT AGENCY	TYPE OF INFORMATION
DT	US District Court	Federal civil and criminal cases
BK	Bankruptcy Court	United States bankruptcy cases
CV	Civil Court	Municipal, county and state level civil cases
CR	Criminal Court	Municipal, county and state level criminal cases
PR	Probate Court	Wills and estate cases

COUNTY RECORDS

CODE*	GOVERNMENT AGENCY	TYPE OF INFORMATION
UC	UCC Filing Office	Uniform Commercial Code and other personal property liens
RE	Recorder of Deeds	Real property transactions and liens
TX	Tax Assessor	Real property tax information
VR	Vital Records Office	Birth, death, marriage, divorce, etc.

*The "CODE" designates the agency and type of information obtainable in each county.

Florida

DT	BK	CV	CR	PR	ALL COUNTIES	UC	RE	TX	VR
•	•	•	•	•	Global Projects Ltd 851	•	•	•	•

		CV	CR	PR	ALACHUA	UC	RE	TX	VR
		•	•	•	SIC Inc 1724	•	•	•	•

		CV	CR	PR	BAKER	UC	RE	TX	VR
		•		•	Tri-County Title Services 1982	•	•	•	

		CV	CR	PR	BAY	UC	RE	TX	VR
		•		•	Bay County Land and Abstract Co Inc 264	•	•	•	•

		CV	CR	PR	BRADFORD	UC	RE	TX	VR
		•	•	•	Crummy Investigations Inc 570	•	•	•	•

		CV	CR	PR	BREVARD	UC	RE	TX	VR
		•	•	•	Andrews Agency Inc 152	•	•	•	
		•	•	•	Fidelity Title and Guaranty Company 760	•	•	•	•
		•	•	•	Hollingsworth Court Reporting Inc 983	•	•	•	•
		•			Independent Research 1024	•	•	•	
		•	•		J Mike Kelley Investigative Services 1066	•	•	•	•
		•	•	•	Pacific Photocopy & Research - Orlando 2127	•	•	•	•
		•	•	•	Paladin Investigations Inc 1501	•	•	•	•
		•	•	•	World Class Investigations 2114		•	•	

DT		CV	CR	PR	BROWARD	UC	RE	TX	VR
•		•	•	•	Bill Greenberg Special Services Inc 302	•	•		•
•		•	•	•	Civil Process Plus Inc 461	•	•	•	•
•		•	•	•	Compass Investigations 508		•		
•		•	•	•	EJB Service Corp 670		•	•	•
•		•	•	•	FLA Search Company 729	•	•	•	•
•		•	•	•	Pacific Photocopy & Research 1493	•	•	•	•
•		•	•	•	Paralegal Field Research Service 1512	•	•	•	•
•		•	•	•	SIC Inc 1724	•	•	•	•
•		•	•	•	The Records Reviewer Inc 1941	•	•	•	•

		CV	CR	PR	CALHOUN	UC	RE	TX	VR
		•	•	•	Calhoun-Liberty Abstract Co 381	•	•	•	
		•		•	Corporation Information Services 528	•	•	•	•
		•	•	•	Pacific Photocopy & Research 1494	•	•	•	•
		•			Sunstate Research Associates Inc 1884	•			

		CV	CR	PR	CHARLOTTE	UC	RE	TX	VR
		•	•	•	Accurate Legal Services 67	•	•	•	
		•	•	•	Hollingsworth Court Reporting Inc 983	•	•	•	•
		•	•	•	Youngblood Process Service 2122	•	•	•	•

		CV	CR	PR	CITRUS	UC	RE	TX	VR
		•	•		J Mike Kelley Investigative Services 1066	•	•	•	•
		•	•	•	On-Line Investigation & Recovery Inc 1469		•	•	•

		CV	CR	PR	CLAY	UC	RE	TX	VR
		•	•	•	First Coast Investigations Inc 772	•	•	•	•
		•	•	•	Pacific Photocopy & Research 1494	•	•	•	•

		CV	CR	PR	COLLIER	UC	RE	TX	VR
		•	•	•	Hollingsworth Court Reporting Inc 983	•	•	•	•
		•	•	•	Lawyers' Abstract Service Inc 1188	•	•	•	•
		•	•	•	Midwest Title Guarantee Company of Fl 1347	•	•	•	
		•	•	•	Pacific Photocopy & Research 1493	•	•	•	•
		•	•	•	SIC Inc 1724	•	•	•	•

COLUMBIA

DT	BK	CV	CR	PR	Name	#	UC	RE	TX	VR
		•		•	Tri-County Title Services	1982	•	•	•	

DADE

DT	BK	CV	CR	PR	Name	#	UC	RE	TX	VR
•	•	•	•	•	Bill Greenberg Special Services Inc	302	•	•		•
•	•	•	•	•	Civil Process Plus Inc	461	•	•	•	•
•	•	•	•	•	Compass Investigations	508		•		
•	•	•	•	•	FLA Search Company	729	•	•	•	•
•	•	•	•	•	Julien Process Service	1106	•	•	•	•
•	•	•	•	•	Pacific Photocopy & Research - Miami	1495	•	•	•	•
•	•	•	•	•	Paralegal Field Research Service	1512	•	•	•	•
•	•	•	•	•	SIC Inc	1724	•	•	•	•
•	•	•	•	•	The Records Reviewer Inc	1941	•	•	•	•
•	•	•	•	•	Vollrath, Robert	2034	•	•	•	•

DE SOTO

CV	CR	PR	Name	#	UC	RE	TX	VR
•	•	•	Accurate Legal Services	67	•	•	•	
•	•	•	Chambers Investigations	434	•	•	•	•
•	•	•	DeSoto Abstract Co	610	•	•	•	•
•	•	•	Hollingsworth Court Reporting Inc	983	•	•	•	•

DIXIE

CV	CR	PR	Name	#	UC	RE	TX	VR
•	•	•	Gilchrist Title Services Inc	842	•	•	•	•
•		•	Suwanne Title and Abstract Inc	1895	•	•	•	

DUVAL

DT	BK	CV	CR	PR	Name	#	UC	RE	TX	VR
		•	•	•	Collins Title & Abstract Co Inc	490	•	•	•	•
•	•	•	•	•	Fidelity Title and Guaranty Company	760	•	•	•	•
•	•	•	•	•	First Coast Investigations Inc	772	•	•	•	•
•	•	•	•	•	SIC Inc	1724	•	•	•	•

ESCAMBIA

DT	BK	CV	CR	PR	Name	#	UC	RE	TX	VR
•	•	•	•	•	Aalpha Omega Investigations Inc	38	•	•	•	•
		•	•	•	Carol Ann Bailey CLA Inc	408		•		•
		•	•	•	Hollingsworth Court Reporting Inc	983	•	•	•	•
•	•	•	•	•	Marshall Services Inc	1287	•	•	•	

FLAGLER

CV	CR	PR	Name	#	UC	RE	TX	VR
•	•	•	Collins Title & Abstract Co Inc	490	•	•	•	•
		•	East Florida Title Services Inc	678	•	•	•	
•		•	Fidelity Title and Guaranty Company	760	•	•	•	
		•	Flagher County Abstract Co	781	•	•		
•		•	Hollingsworth Court Reporting Inc	983	•	•	•	•

FRANKLIN

CV	CR	PR	Name	#	UC	RE	TX	VR
•	•	•	Acumen Investigations	75	•	•	•	•
•	•	•	Advanced Investigations Inc	88	•	•	•	•
•	•	•	Corporation Information Services	528	•	•	•	•

GADSDEN

CV	CR	PR	Name	#	UC	RE	TX	VR
•	•	•	Acumen Investigations	75	•	•	•	•
•	•	•	Advanced Investigations Inc	88	•	•	•	•
			Capitol Services	400				
•		•	Corporation Information Services	528	•	•	•	•
•		•	Gadsden Abstract Co	826	•	•	•	
•	•	•	State Information Bureau	1854	•	•	•	•
•			Sunstate Research Associates Inc	1884	•			

GILCHRIST

CV	CR	PR	Name	#	UC	RE	TX	VR
•	•	•	Gilchrist Title Services Inc	842	•	•	•	•
•		•	Suwanne Title and Abstract Inc	1895	•	•	•	
•		•	Tri-County Title Services	1982	•	•	•	

GLADES

CV	CR	PR		UC	RE	TX	VR
●	●	●	Okeechobee Abstract and Title Ins Inc............1461	●	●	●	

GULF

CV	CR	PR		UC	RE	TX	VR
●		●	Bay County Land and Abstract Co Inc..............264	●	●	●	●

HAMILTON

CV	CR	PR		UC	RE	TX	VR
●		●	Tri-County Title Services............1982	●	●	●	

HARDEE

CV	CR	PR		UC	RE	TX	VR
●	●	●	Accurate Legal Services............67	●	●	●	
●	●	●	Hollingsworth Court Reporting Inc............983	●	●	●	●

HENDRY

CV	CR	PR		UC	RE	TX	VR
●	●	●	Pacific Photocopy & Research............1493	●	●	●	●
●	●	●	Palm Title Inc............1504	●	●	●	●

HERNANDO

CV	CR	PR		UC	RE	TX	VR
●	●	●	Hollingsworth Court Reporting Inc............983	●	●	●	●
●	●		J Mike Kelley Investigative Services............1066	●	●	●	●

HIGHLANDS

CV	CR	PR		UC	RE	TX	VR
●		●	Highlands Abstract and Title Co............969	●	●	●	
●	●	●	Hollingsworth Court Reporting Inc............983	●	●	●	●
●	●	●	South Ridge Abstract and Title Co............1823	●	●	●	●
●	●	●	Sunshine State Abstract & Title............1883	●	●	●	●

HILLSBOROUGH

DT	BK	CV	CR	PR		UC	RE	TX	VR
●	●	●	●	●	Bay Area Search Inc............262	●	●	●	
●	●	●	●	●	EX-CEL Investigations............672	●	●	●	●
●	●	●	●	●	Gietren & Associates Inc............841		●	●	
		●	●	●	Hollingsworth Court Reporting Inc............983	●	●	●	●
●	●	●	●	●	Intelligence Network Inc............1034	●	●	●	●
●	●	●	●	●	Pacific Photocopy & Research Services............1496	●	●	●	●

HOLMES

CV	CR	PR		UC	RE	TX	VR
●			Sunstate Research Associates Inc............1884	●			

INDIAN RIVER

CV	CR	PR		UC	RE	TX	VR
●	●	●	Crummy Investigations Inc............570	●	●	●	●
●	●	●	Hollingsworth Court Reporting Inc............983	●	●	●	●
●	●	●	Paralegal Field Research Service............1512	●	●	●	●
		●	Treasure Coast Abstract & Title Ins Co............1977	●	●	●	
●	●	●	World Class Investigations............2114		●	●	

JACKSON

CV	CR	PR		UC	RE	TX	VR
●	●	●	Corporation Information Services............528	●	●	●	●
●			Sunstate Research Associates Inc............1884	●			

JEFFERSON

CV	CR	PR		UC	RE	TX	VR
●	●	●	Acumen Investigations............75	●	●	●	●
●	●	●	Advanced Investigations Inc............88	●	●	●	●
●	●	●	Corporation Information Services............528	●	●	●	●
●	●	●	North Florida Abstract............1435	●	●	●	●
●	●	●	State Information Bureau............1854	●	●	●	●
●			Sunstate Research Associates Inc............1884	●			

LAFAYETTE

CV	CR	PR		UC	RE	TX	VR
●		●	Tri-County Title Services............1982	●	●	●	

LAKE

CV	CR	PR		UC	RE	TX	VR
●	●	●	Andrews Agency Inc............152	●	●	●	
●	●	●	Fidelity Title and Guaranty Company............760	●	●	●	●

CV	CR	PR		UC	RE	TX	VR
•	•	•	Hollingsworth Court Reporting Inc 983	•	•	•	•
•	•		J Mike Kelley Investigative Services 1066	•	•	•	•
•		•	Lake Research Inc 1159	•	•	•	
•	•	•	Pacific Photocopy & Research - Orlando 2127	•	•	•	•
•	•	•	Paladin Investigations Inc 1501	•	•	•	•

DT		CV	CR	PR	LEE	UC	RE	TX	VR
		•	•	•	Hollingsworth Court Reporting Inc 983	•	•	•	•
		•	•	•	Midwest Title Guarantee Company of Fl 1347	•	•	•	•

DT	BK	CV	CR	PR	LEON	UC	RE	TX	VR
•	•	•	•	•	Acumen Investigations 75	•	•	•	•
•	•	•	•	•	Advanced Investigations Inc 88	•	•	•	•
•	•				Capitol Services 400				
•	•	•	•	•	Corporation Information Services 528	•	•		•
•	•	•	•	•	Florida Information Associates 788	•	•	•	
•	•	•	•	•	International Research Bureau Inc (IRB) 1039	•	•	•	
•	•	•	•	•	Prentice Hall Legal & Financial Services 1585	•	•	•	•
•	•	•	•	•	State Information Bureau 1854	•	•	•	•
•	•	•			Sunstate Research Associates Inc 1884	•			

CV	CR	PR	LEVY	UC	RE	TX	VR
•	•	•	Gilchrist Title Services Inc 842	•	•	•	•
•		•	Suwanne Title and Abstract Inc 1895	•	•	•	

CV	CR	PR	LIBERTY	UC	RE	TX	VR
•	•	•	Acumen Investigations 75	•	•	•	•
•	•	•	Advanced Investigations Inc 88	•	•	•	•
•	•	•	Calhoun-Liberty Abstract Co 381	•	•	•	
•	•	•	Corporation Information Services 528	•	•		•
•			Sunstate Research Associates Inc 1884	•			

CV	CR	PR	MADISON	UC	RE	TX	VR
•	•	•	Corporation Information Services 528	•	•	•	•
•			Sunstate Research Associates Inc 1884	•			

CV	CR	PR	MANATEE	UC	RE	TX	VR
•	•	•	Accurate Legal Services 67	•	•	•	
•	•	•	Bay Area Search Inc 262	•	•	•	
•	•	•	Chambers Investigations 434	•	•	•	•
•	•	•	Hollingsworth Court Reporting Inc 983	•	•	•	•
•	•	•	Pacific Photocopy & Research Services 1496	•	•	•	•

CV	CR	PR	MARION	UC	RE	TX	VR
		•	Fidelity Title and Guaranty Company 760	•	•	•	•
•	•		J Mike Kelley Investigative Services 1066	•	•	•	
	•		Lake Research Inc 1159	•	•	•	
•		•	On-Line Investigation & Recovery Inc 1469		•	•	•
•		•	Paladin Investigations Inc 1501	•			

CV	CR	PR	MARTIN	UC	RE	TX	VR
•	•	•	FLA Search Company 729	•	•	•	•
•	•	•	Okeechobee Abstract and Title Ins Inc 1461	•	•	•	
•	•	•	Paralegal Field Research Service 1512	•	•	•	•
		•	Treasure Coast Abstract & Title Ins Co 1977	•	•	•	

DT		CV	CR	PR	MONROE	UC	RE	TX	VR
•		•	•	•	Civil Process Plus Inc 461	•	•	•	•
		•	•	•	Independent Abstract & Title 1021	•	•	•	•
•		•	•	•	SIC Inc 1724	•	•	•	•

CV	CR	PR	NASSAU	UC	RE	TX	VR
•	•	•	First Coast Investigations Inc 772	•	•	•	•

CV	CR	PR			UC	RE	TX	VR
•	•	•	Pacific Photocopy & Research ...1494		•	•	•	•

OKALOOSA

CV	CR	PR			UC	RE	TX	VR
•	•	•	Aalpha Omega Investigations Inc...38		•	•	•	•
•	•	•	Marshall Services Inc...1287		•	•	•	

OKEECHOBEE

CV	CR	PR			UC	RE	TX	VR
•	•	•	Okeechobee Abstract and Title Ins Inc...1461		•	•	•	
•	•	•	Paralegal Field Research Service ...1512		•	•	•	•
		•	Treasure Coast Abstract & Title Ins Co ...1977		•	•	•	

ORANGE

DT	BK	CV	CR	PR			UC	RE	TX	VR
•	•	•	•	•	Andrews Agency Inc...152		•	•	•	•
•	•	•	•	•	Fidelity Title and Guaranty Company...760		•	•	•	•
		•	•	•	Hollingsworth Court Reporting Inc...983		•	•	•	•
•	•	•			Independent Research ...1024		•	•	•	
•	•	•	•	•	Investigative Legal Services...1047		•	•	•	•
•	•	•	•		J Mike Kelley Investigative Services...1066		•	•	•	•
•	•	•	•	•	Pacific Photocopy & Research - Orlando...2127		•	•	•	•
•	•	•	•	•	Paladin Investigations Inc ...1501		•	•	•	•
•	•	•	•	•	SIC Inc ...1724		•	•	•	•

OSCEOLA

CV	CR	PR			UC	RE	TX	VR
•	•	•	Andrews Agency Inc...152		•	•	•	
•	•	•	Fidelity Title and Guaranty Company...760		•	•	•	•
•	•	•	Hollingsworth Court Reporting Inc...983		•	•	•	•
•			Independent Research ...1024		•	•	•	
•	•	•	Investigative Legal Services...1047		•	•	•	•
•	•		J Mike Kelley Investigative Services...1066		•	•	•	•
•	•	•	Pacific Photocopy & Research - Orlando...2127		•	•	•	•
•	•	•	Paladin Investigations Inc ...1501		•	•	•	•

PALM BEACH

DT	CV	CR	PR			UC	RE	TX	VR
•	•	•	•	Attorney's Professional Process Srvc ...207		•	•	•	•
•	•	•	•	Bill Greenberg Special Services Inc...302		•	•		
•	•	•	•	Civil Process Plus Inc ...461		•	•	•	•
•	•	•	•	Compass Investigations...508			•		
•	•	•	•	FLA Search Company...729		•	•	•	
•	•	•	•	Mulberry, David...1395		•	•	•	
•	•	•	•	Pacific Photocopy & Research...1493		•	•	•	
•	•	•	•	Paralegal Field Research Service ...1512		•	•	•	
•	•	•	•	SIC Inc ...1724		•	•	•	
•	•	•	•	Scholtes Investigation & Attorney Svcs...1746			•	•	

PASCO

CV	CR	PR			UC	RE	TX	VR
•	•	•	Bay Area Search Inc...262		•	•	•	
•	•	•	Gietren & Associates Inc...841			•	•	
•	•	•	Hollingsworth Court Reporting Inc...983		•	•	•	•
•	•	•	Pacific Photocopy & Research Services...1496		•	•	•	•

PINELLAS

CV	CR	PR			UC	RE	TX	VR
•	•	•	Bay Area Search Inc...262		•	•	•	
•	•	•	EX-CEL Investigations ...672		•	•	•	•
•	•	•	Gietren & Associates Inc...841			•	•	
•	•	•	Hollingsworth Court Reporting Inc...983		•	•	•	•
•	•	•	Intelligence Network Inc ...1034		•	•	•	•
•	•	•	SIC Inc ...1724		•	•	•	•

POLK

CV	CR	PR			UC	RE	TX	VR
•	•	•	Bay Area Search Inc...262		•	•	•	
•	•	•	Fidelity Title and Guaranty Company...760		•	•	•	•
•	•	•	Gietren & Associates Inc...841			•	•	

CV	CR	PR		UC	RE	TX	VR
●	●	●	Hollingsworth Court Reporting Inc ...983	●	●	●	●
●	●	●	Pacific Photocopy & Research Services ...1496	●	●	●	●
●	●	●	Paladin Investigations Inc ...1501	●	●	●	●

CV	CR	PR	PUTNAM	UC	RE	TX	VR
●	●	●	Collins Title & Abstract Co Inc ...490	●	●	●	●

CV	CR	PR	ST. JOHNS	UC	RE	TX	VR
●	●	●	Collins Title & Abstract Co Inc ...490	●	●	●	●
●	●	●	Pacific Photocopy & Research ...1494	●	●	●	●

CV	CR	PR	ST. LUCIE	UC	RE	TX	VR
●	●	●	FLA Search Company ...729	●	●	●	●
●	●	●	Paralegal Field Research Service ...1512	●	●	●	
		●	Treasure Coast Abstract & Title Ins Co ...1977	●	●	●	

CV	CR	PR	SANTA ROSA	UC	RE	TX	VR
●	●	●	Aalpha Omega Investigations Inc ...38	●	●	●	●
●	●	●	Carol Ann Bailey CLA Inc ...408		●		
●	●	●	Hollingsworth Court Reporting Inc ...983	●	●	●	●
●	●	●	Marshall Services Inc ...1287	●	●	●	

CV	CR	PR	SARASOTA	UC	RE	TX	VR
●	●	●	Accurate Legal Services ...67	●	●	●	
●	●	●	Bay Area Search Inc ...262	●	●	●	
●	●	●	Chambers Investigations ...434	●	●	●	●
●	●	●	Hollingsworth Court Reporting Inc ...983	●	●	●	●

CV	CR	PR	SEMINOLE	UC	RE	TX	VR
●	●	●	Andrews Agency Inc ...152	●	●	●	
●	●	●	Fidelity Title and Guaranty Company ...760	●	●	●	●
●	●	●	Hollingsworth Court Reporting Inc ...983	●	●	●	●
●			Independent Research ...1024	●	●	●	
●	●	●	Investigative Legal Services ...1047	●	●	●	●
●	●		J Mike Kelley Investigative Services ...1066	●	●	●	●
●	●	●	Paladin Investigations Inc ...1501	●	●	●	●
●			Title Searchers Inc ...1955			●	●

CV	CR	PR	SUMTER	UC	RE	TX	VR
●	●	●	Hollingsworth Court Reporting Inc ...983	●	●	●	●
●	●		J Mike Kelley Investigative Services ...1066	●	●	●	●
		●	Lake Research Inc ...1159	●	●	●	
●	●	●	Paladin Investigations Inc ...1501	●	●	●	●

CV	CR	PR	SUWANNEE	UC	RE	TX	VR
●		●	Tri-County Title Services ...1982	●	●	●	

CV	CR	PR	TAYLOR	UC	RE	TX	VR
			Capitol Services ...400				
●	●	●	Corporation Information Services ...528	●	●	●	●

CV	CR	PR	UNION	UC	RE	TX	VR
●		●	Tri-County Title Services ...1982	●	●	●	

CV	CR	PR	VOLUSIA	UC	RE	TX	VR
		●	East Florida Title Services Inc ...678	●	●	●	
●	●	●	Fidelity Title and Guaranty Company ...760	●	●	●	●
●	●	●	Hollingsworth Court Reporting Inc ...983	●	●	●	●
●			Independent Research ...1024	●	●	●	
●	●	●	Pacific Photocopy & Research - Orlando ...2127	●	●	●	●
●	●	●	Paladin Investigations Inc ...1501	●	●	●	●
	●	●	Professional Title of Edgewater Inc ...1623	●	●	●	●
●	●	●	SIC Inc ...1724	●	●	●	●

CV	CR	PR		UC	RE	TX	VR
●	●	●	Volusia Legal Services 2035				
●	●	●	Ziegler and Associates Inc 2126	●	●	●	●

CV	CR	PR	WAKULLA	UC	RE	TX	VR
●	●	●	Acumen Investigations...75	●	●	●	●
●	●	●	Advanced Investigations Inc 88	●	●	●	●
			Capitol Services 400				
●	●	●	Corporation Information Services.....................................528	●	●	●	●
●	●	●	State Information Bureau 1854	●	●	●	●
●			Sunstate Research Associates Inc....................................1884	●			

CV	CR	PR	WALTON	UC	RE	TX	VR
●	●	●	Marshall Services Inc 1287	●	●	●	

CV	CR	PR	WASHINGTON	UC	RE	TX	VR
●	●	●	Corporation Information Services.....................................528	●	●	●	●
●			Sunstate Research Associates Inc....................................1884	●			

Georgia

DT	BK	CV	CR	PR	ALL COUNTIES		UC	RE	TX	VR
•	•	•	•	•	Ed Knight Information Service	689	•	•	•	
•	•	•	•	•	Liberty Corporate Services Inc	1224	•	•	•	•
•	•	•	•	•	MLQ Attorney Services	1261	•	•	•	•

		CV	CR	PR	APPLING		UC	RE	TX	VR
		•	•	•	Betty M Rowell CLA	295	•	•	•	•
		•	•		Wilson, Cindy	2104	•	•	•	•

		CV	CR	PR	ATKINSON		UC	RE	TX	VR
		•	•	•	Betty M Rowell CLA	295	•	•	•	•
		•	•	•	John E Jones Jr Land Title Services	1091	•	•	•	•
		•	•	•	Roberts Abstracting Inc	1705	•	•	•	

		CV	CR	PR	BACON		UC	RE	TX	VR
		•	•	•	Betty M Rowell CLA	295	•	•	•	•

		CV	CR	PR	BAKER		UC	RE	TX	VR
		•		•	Dougherty Abstract & Title Service Inc	650		•	•	
		•	•		Thurman Investigative Services Inc	1948				

		CV	CR	PR	BALDWIN		UC	RE	TX	VR
		•	•	•	Bigler & Associates Inc	300	•	•	•	•
		•	•	•	John E Jones Jr Land Title Services	1091	•	•	•	•
		•	•	•	Preferred Research Inc	1581	•	•	•	

		CV	CR	PR	BANKS		UC	RE	TX	VR
		•	•	•	EL-Ru Inc	671	•		•	
		•	•	•	Hollingsworth Court Reporting Inc	983	•	•	•	•
		•	•	•	Wilmot, Sally	2099	•	•	•	•

		CV	CR	PR	BARROW		UC	RE	TX	VR
		•	•	•	EL-Ru Inc	671	•		•	
		•	•	•	Gladden, Roger	847	•	•	•	
		•	•	•	Hollingsworth Court Reporting Inc	983	•	•	•	•
		•		•	S D Moody Co	1722	•	•	•	
		•	•	•	Wilmot, Sally	2099	•	•	•	•

		CV	CR	PR	BARTOW		UC	RE	TX	VR
		•	•	•	Hollingsworth Court Reporting Inc	983	•	•	•	•
		•	•	•	Perry Field Services	1541	•	•	•	
					Robinson Real Estate Services	1707	•	•	•	
				•	S D Moody Co	1722	•	•	•	

		CV	CR	PR	BEN HILL		UC	RE	TX	VR
		•	•	•	John E Jones Jr Land Title Services	1091	•	•	•	•

		CV	CR	PR	BERRIEN		UC	RE	TX	VR
		•	•	•	Roberts Abstracting Inc	1705	•	•	•	

DT	BK	CV	CR	PR	BIBB		UC	RE	TX	VR
•	•	•	•	•	Bigler & Associates Inc	300	•	•	•	•
•	•	•	•	•	John E Jones Jr Land Title Services	1091	•	•	•	•
•	•	•	•	•	Preferred Research Inc	1581	•	•	•	

		CV	CR	PR	BLECKLEY		UC	RE	TX	VR
		•	•	•	Cartwright Abstracting	412	•	•	•	
		•	•	•	John E Jones Jr Land Title Services	1091	•	•	•	•
		•	•	•	Preferred Research Inc	1581	•	•	•	

		CV	CR	PR	BRANTLEY		UC	RE	TX	VR
		•	•	•	Betty M Rowell CLA	295	•	•	•	•

		DT	BK	CV	CR	PR		UC	RE	TX	VR
				●	●	●	John E Jones Jr Land Title Services..............1091	●	●	●	●

			CV	CR	PR	**BROOKS**	UC	RE	TX	VR
			●	●	●	John E Jones Jr Land Title Services..............1091	●	●	●	●
			●			Sunstate Research Associates Inc..............1884	●			

			CV	CR	PR	**BRYAN**	UC	RE	TX	VR
			●	●	●	John E Jones Jr Land Title Services..............1091	●	●	●	●
			●	●	●	Josey, Cheryl S..............1105	●	●	●	●

			CV	CR	PR	**BULLOCH**	UC	RE	TX	VR
			●	●	●	John E Jones Jr Land Title Services..............1091	●	●	●	●
			●	●	●	Josey, Cheryl S..............1105	●	●	●	●
			●	●	●	Kirkland Jr, R Carrol..............1130	●	●	●	●

			CV	CR	PR	**BURKE**	UC	RE	TX	VR
			●	●	●	John E Jones Jr Land Title Services..............1091	●	●	●	●

			CV	CR	PR	**BUTTS**	UC	RE	TX	VR
			●	●	●	Gladden, Roger..............847	●	●	●	
			●	●	●	Hollingsworth Court Reporting Inc..............983	●	●	●	●
			●	●	●	Preferred Research Inc..............1581	●	●	●	

			CV	CR	PR	**CALHOUN**	UC	RE	TX	VR
			●		●	Dougherty Abstract & Title Service Inc..............650	●	●		
			●	●		Thurman Investigative Services Inc..............1948				

			CV	CR	PR	**CAMDEN**	UC	RE	TX	VR
			●	●	●	John E Jones Jr Land Title Services..............1091	●	●	●	●

			CV	CR	PR	**CANDLER**	UC	RE	TX	VR
			●	●	●	John E Jones Jr Land Title Services..............1091	●	●	●	●

			CV	CR	PR	**CARROLL**	UC	RE	TX	VR
			●		●	S D Moody Co..............1722	●	●	●	
			●	●	●	Wright III, Wyatt..............2118	●	●	●	●

			CV	CR	PR	**CATOOSA**	UC	RE	TX	VR
						Bele, Jan..............278	●	●	●	
			●	●	●	Hollingsworth Court Reporting Inc..............983	●	●	●	●
			●		●	Hurst, Pam..............1009	●	●	●	●
			●		●	Title Guaranty and Trust of Chattanooga..............1953	●	●	●	

			CV	CR	PR	**CHARLTON**	UC	RE	TX	VR
			●	●	●	Betty M Rowell CLA..............295	●	●	●	●
			●	●	●	Frederick, June..............810	●	●	●	●
			●	●	●	John E Jones Jr Land Title Services..............1091	●	●	●	●

	DT	BK	CV	CR	PR	**CHATHAM**	UC	RE	TX	VR
	●	●	●	●	●	John E Jones Jr Land Title Services..............1091	●	●	●	●
			●	●	●	Josey, Cheryl S..............1105	●	●		●

			CV	CR	PR	**CHATTAHOOCHEE**	UC	RE	TX	VR
			●	●	●	Columbus Land Title Co..............499	●	●	●	●

			CV	CR	PR	**CHATTOOGA**	UC	RE	TX	VR
			●		●	Title Guaranty and Trust of Chattanooga..............1953	●	●	●	

			CV	CR	PR	**CHEROKEE**	UC	RE	TX	VR
			●	●	●	Attorneys' Personal Services..............211	●	●	●	●
			●	●	●	Hollingsworth Court Reporting Inc..............983	●	●	●	●
			●	●	●	Perry Field Services..............1541	●	●	●	
			●		●	S D Moody Co..............1722	●	●	●	

CV	CR	PR	CLARKE		UC	RE	TX	VR
•	•	•	Attorneys' Personal Services........................211		•	•	•	•
•	•	•	EL-Ru Inc..................................671		•		•	
•	•	•	Gladden, Roger 847		•	•	•	
•	•	•	Wilmot, Sally 2099		•	•	•	•

CV	CR	PR	CLAY		UC	RE	TX	VR
•		•	Dougherty Abstract & Title Service Inc...........650		•	•		
•	•		Thurman Investigative Services Inc..............1948					

CV	CR	PR	CLAYTON		UC	RE	TX	VR
•	•	•	ASAP Inc 34		•	•	•	•
•	•	•	Atlanta Courthouse Services 178		•	•	•	•
•	•	•	Attorneys' Personal Services....................211		•	•	•	•
•	•	•	EL-Ru Inc..................................671		•		•	
•	•	•	FACFIND Network Inc..........................728		•	•	•	•
•	•	•	Gladden, Roger 847		•	•	•	
•	•	•	Hollingsworth Court Reporting Inc...............983		•	•	•	•
•	•	•	Perry Field Services 1541		•	•	•	
•		•	S D Moody Co 1722		•	•	•	

CV	CR	PR	CLINCH		UC	RE	TX	VR
•	•	•	Betty M Rowell CLA 295		•	•	•	•
•	•	•	John E Jones Jr Land Title Services...............1091		•	•	•	•

CV	CR	PR	COBB		UC	RE	TX	VR
•	•	•	ASAP Inc 34		•	•	•	•
•	•		ASAP Legal Documents.........................35			•	•	•
•	•	•	Atlanta Courthouse Services 178		•	•	•	•
•	•	•	Attorneys' Personal Services....................211		•		•	
•	•	•	EL-Ru Inc..................................671		•			•
•	•	•	FACFIND Network Inc..........................728		•	•	•	•
•	•	•	Gladden, Roger 847		•	•	•	
•	•	•	Hollingsworth Court Reporting Inc...............983		•	•	•	•
•	•	•	Perry Field Services 1541		•	•	•	
•	•	•	Phoenix Investigations 1549		•	•	•	•
•		•	S D Moody Co 1722		•	•	•	

CV	CR	PR	COFFEE		UC	RE	TX	VR
•	•	•	APS Attorney Service 33		•	•	•	•
•	•	•	Betty M Rowell CLA 295		•	•	•	•

CV	CR	PR	COLQUITT		UC	RE	TX	VR
•	•	•	John E Jones Jr Land Title Services...............1091		•	•	•	•
•			Sunstate Research Associates Inc.................1884		•			

CV	CR	PR	COLUMBIA		UC	RE	TX	VR
•	•	•	Freeflight Inc.................................812		•	•	•	•
•	•	•	John E Jones Jr Land Title Services...............1091		•	•	•	•
•	•	•	Weber, Attorney David V 2070		•	•	•	•

CV	CR	PR	COOK		UC	RE	TX	VR
•	•	•	John E Jones Jr Land Title Services...............1091		•	•	•	•
•	•	•	Roberts Abstracting Inc.........................1705		•	•	•	
•			Sunstate Research Associates Inc.................1884		•			

DT	BK	CV	CR	PR	COWETA		UC	RE	TX	VR
•	•	•	•	•	Atlanta Courthouse Services 178		•	•	•	•
	•	•	•	•	Hollingsworth Court Reporting Inc...............983		•	•	•	•
		•	•	•	Perry Field Services 1541		•	•	•	

CRAWFORD

CV	CR	PR	Company	#	UC	RE	TX	VR
●	●	●	Bigler & Associates Inc	300	●	●	●	●
●	●	●	Preferred Research Inc	1581	●	●	●	

CRISP

CV	CR	PR	Company	#	UC	RE	TX	VR
●	●	●	John E Jones Jr Land Title Services	1091	●	●	●	●
●	●	●	South Georgia Title	1821	●	●	●	
●	●		Thurman Investigative Services Inc	1948				

DADE

CV	CR	PR	Company	#	UC	RE	TX	VR
●	●	●	Hollingsworth Court Reporting Inc	983	●	●	●	●
●		●	Title Guaranty and Trust of Chattanooga	1953	●	●	●	

DAWSON

CV	CR	PR	Company	#	UC	RE	TX	VR
●	●	●	EL-Ru Inc	671	●		●	
●		●	S D Moody Co	1722	●	●	●	

DECATUR

CV	CR	PR	Company	#	UC	RE	TX	VR
●			Sunstate Research Associates Inc	1884	●			

DE KALB

CV	CR	PR	Company	#	UC	RE	TX	VR
●	●	●	APS Attorney Service	33	●	●	●	●
●	●	●	ASAP Inc	34	●	●	●	●
●	●		ASAP Legal Documents	35		●	●	●
●	●	●	Atlanta Courthouse Services	178	●	●	●	
●	●	●	Attorneys' Personal Services	211	●	●	●	●
●	●		EL-Ru Inc	671	●			
●	●	●	FACFIND Network Inc	728	●	●	●	●
●	●	●	Gladden, Roger	847	●	●	●	
●	●	●	Hollingsworth Court Reporting Inc	983	●	●	●	●
●	●	●	John Reberson Investigations	1093	●	●	●	●
●	●	●	Perry Field Services	1541	●	●	●	●
●	●	●	Phoenix Investigations	1549	●	●	●	●
●		●	S D Moody Co	1722	●	●	●	

DODGE

CV	CR	PR	Company	#	UC	RE	TX	VR
●	●	●	Cartwright Abstracting	412	●	●	●	
●	●	●	John E Jones Jr Land Title Services	1091	●	●	●	●
●	●	●	Preferred Research Inc	1581	●	●	●	
●	●	●	South Georgia Title	1821	●	●	●	

DOOLY

CV	CR	PR	Company	#	UC	RE	TX	VR
●	●	●	John E Jones Jr Land Title Services	1091	●	●	●	●
●	●	●	Preferred Research Inc	1581	●	●	●	
●	●	●	South Georgia Title	1821	●	●	●	

DOUGHERTY

DT	CV	CR	PR	Company	#	UC	RE	TX	VR
	●		●	Dougherty Abstract & Title Service Inc	650		●	●	
●	●	●	●	John E Jones Jr Land Title Services	1091	●	●	●	●
	●	●	●	South Georgia Title	1821	●	●	●	
	●	●		Thurman Investigative Services Inc	1948				

DOUGLAS

CV	CR	PR	Company	#	UC	RE	TX	VR
●	●	●	ASAP Inc	34	●	●	●	●
●	●	●	Attorneys' Personal Services	211	●	●	●	●
●	●	●	FACFIND Network Inc	728	●	●	●	●
●	●	●	Hollingsworth Court Reporting Inc	983	●	●	●	●
●	●	●	Perry Field Services	1541	●	●	●	
●		●	S D Moody Co	1722	●	●	●	

EARLY

CV	CR	PR	Company	#	UC	RE	TX	VR
●	●		Thurman Investigative Services Inc	1948				

		CV	CR	PR	ECHOLS	UC	RE	TX	VR
		●	●	●	John E Jones Jr Land Title Services................................1091	●	●	●	●

		CV	CR	PR	EFFINGHAM	UC	RE	TX	VR
		●	●	●	John E Jones Jr Land Title Services................................1091	●	●	●	●

		CV	CR	PR	ELBERT	UC	RE	TX	VR
		●	●	●	Wilmot, Sally 2099	●	●	●	●

		CV	CR	PR	EMANUEL	UC	RE	TX	VR
		●	●	●	John E Jones Jr Land Title Services................................1091	●	●	●	●

		CV	CR	PR	EVANS	UC	RE	TX	VR
		●	●	●	John E Jones Jr Land Title Services................................1091	●	●	●	●
		●	●	●	Josey, Cheryl S..1105	●	●	●	●

		CV	CR	PR	FANNIN	UC	RE	TX	VR
		●	●	●	Hollingsworth Court Reporting Inc....................................983	●	●	●	●
		●		●	Title Guaranty and Trust of Chattanooga.......................1953	●	●	●	

		CV	CR	PR	FAYETTE	UC	RE	TX	VR
		●	●	●	ASAP Inc 34	●	●	●	●
		●	●	●	Attorneys' Personal Services...211	●	●	●	●
		●	●	●	Perry Field Services 1541	●	●	●	
		●		●	S D Moody Co 1722	●	●	●	

DT	BK	CV	CR	PR	FLOYD	UC	RE	TX	VR
●	●	●	●	●	Attorneys' Personal Services...211	●	●	●	●
					Robinson Real Estate Services.......................................1707	●	●	●	

		CV	CR	PR	FORSYTH	UC	RE	TX	VR
		●	●	●	Attorneys' Personal Services...211	●	●	●	●
		●	●	●	EL-Ru Inc...671	●			
		●	●	●	Hollingsworth Court Reporting Inc....................................983	●	●	●	
		●	●	●	Perry Field Services 1541	●	●	●	
		●		●	S D Moody Co 1722	●	●	●	

		CV	CR	PR	FRANKLIN	UC	RE	TX	VR
		●	●	●	Accurate Investigative Services...65	●	●	●	●

DT	BK	CV	CR	PR	FULTON	UC	RE	TX	VR
●	●	●	●	●	APS Attorney Service 33	●	●	●	●
●	●	●	●	●	ASAP Inc 34	●	●	●	●
●	●	●	●	●	Atlanta Courthouse Services...178	●	●	●	●
●	●	●	●	●	Attorneys' Personal Services...211	●	●	●	●
●	●	●	●	●	EL-Ru Inc...671	●	●	●	●
●	●	●	●	●	FACFIND Network Inc...728	●		●	
●	●	●	●	●	Gladden, Roger 847	●		●	
		●	●	●	Hollingsworth Court Reporting Inc....................................983	●		●	
●	●	●	●	●	John Reberson Investigations...1093	●	●	●	●
		●	●	●	Perry Field Services 1541	●		●	
●	●	●	●	●	Phoenix Investigations 1549	●	●	●	
		●		●	S D Moody Co 1722	●	●	●	

		CV	CR	PR	GILMER	UC	RE	TX	VR
					Bele, Jan..278	●	●	●	
		●	●	●	Hollingsworth Court Reporting Inc....................................983	●	●	●	●
		●		●	Title Guaranty and Trust of Chattanooga.......................1953	●	●	●	

		CV	CR	PR	GLASCOCK	UC	RE	TX	VR
		●	●	●	John E Jones Jr Land Title Services................................1091	●	●	●	●

GLYNN

DT	CV	CR	PR		UC	RE	TX	VR
•	•	•	•	John E Jones Jr Land Title Services 1091	•	•	•	•
	•	•	•	Josey, Cheryl S 1105	•	•	•	•

GORDON

CV	CR	PR		UC	RE	TX	VR
			Robinson Real Estate Services 1707	•	•	•	
•		•	Title Guaranty and Trust of Chattanooga 1953	•	•	•	

GRADY

CV	CR	PR		UC	RE	TX	VR
•			Sunstate Research Associates Inc 1884	•			

GREENE

CV	CR	PR		UC	RE	TX	VR
•	•	•	Merritt Jr, Charles W 1331	•	•	•	•

GWINNETT

CV	CR	PR		UC	RE	TX	VR
•	•	•	APS Attorney Service 33	•	•	•	•
•	•	•	ASAP Inc 34	•	•	•	•
•	•		ASAP Legal Documents 35		•		
•	•	•	Atlanta Courthouse Services 178	•	•	•	
•	•	•	Attorneys' Personal Services 211	•	•	•	
•	•	•	EL-Ru Inc 671	•		•	
•	•	•	FACFIND Network Inc 728	•	•	•	•
•	•	•	Gladden, Roger 847	•	•	•	
•	•	•	Hollingsworth Court Reporting Inc 983	•	•	•	•
•	•	•	Perry Field Services 1541	•	•	•	
•	•	•	Phoenix Investigations 1549	•	•	•	•
•		•	S D Moody Co 1722	•	•	•	
•	•	•	Wilmot, Sally 2099	•	•	•	•

HABERSHAM

CV	CR	PR		UC	RE	TX	VR
•	•	•	Hollingsworth Court Reporting Inc 983	•	•	•	•

HALL

DT	BK	CV	CR	PR		UC	RE	TX	VR
•	•	•	•	•	Attorneys' Personal Services 211	•	•	•	•
•	•	•	•	•	EL-Ru Inc 671	•			
		•	•	•	Perry Field Services 1541	•	•	•	
		•	•	•	Wilmot, Sally 2099	•	•		•

HANCOCK

CV	CR	PR		UC	RE	TX	VR
•	•	•	John E Jones Jr Land Title Services 1091	•	•	•	•
•	•	•	Preferred Research Inc 1581	•	•	•	

HARALSON

CV	CR	PR		UC	RE	TX	VR
•	•	•	FACFIND Network Inc 728	•	•	•	•
•	•	•	Hollingsworth Court Reporting Inc 983	•	•	•	•
•	•	•	Robinson Real Estate Services 1707	•	•	•	

HARRIS

CV	CR	PR		UC	RE	TX	VR
•	•	•	Columbus Land Title Co 499	•	•	•	•

HART

CV	CR	PR		UC	RE	TX	VR
•	•	•	Accurate Investigative Services 65	•	•	•	•

HEARD

CV	CR	PR		UC	RE	TX	VR
•	•	•	Wright III, Wyatt 2118	•	•	•	•

HENRY

CV	CR	PR		UC	RE	TX	VR
•	•	•	EL-Ru Inc 671	•		•	
•	•	•	Gladden, Roger 847	•	•	•	
•	•	•	Hollingsworth Court Reporting Inc 983	•	•	•	•
•	•	•	Perry Field Services 1541	•	•	•	

CV	CR	PR	HOUSTON		UC	RE	TX	VR
•	•	•	Bigler & Associates Inc............................300		•	•	•	•
•	•	•	John E Jones Jr Land Title Services.............1091		•	•	•	•
•	•	•	South Georgia Title............................1821		•	•	•	

CV	CR	PR	IRWIN		UC	RE	TX	VR
•	•	•	John E Jones Jr Land Title Services.............1091		•	•	•	•

CV	CR	PR	JACKSON		UC	RE	TX	VR
•	•	•	EL-Ru Inc......................................671		•		•	
•	•	•	FACFIND Network Inc.............................728		•	•	•	•
•	•	•	Gladden, Roger..................................847		•	•	•	
•	•	•	Hollingsworth Court Reporting Inc...............983		•	•	•	•
•	•	•	Wilmot, Sally...................................2099		•	•	•	•

CV	CR	PR	JASPER		UC	RE	TX	VR
•	•	•	Gladden, Roger..................................847		•	•	•	
•	•	•	Hollingsworth Court Reporting Inc...............983		•	•	•	•
•	•	•	Merritt Jr, Charles W...........................1331		•	•	•	
•	•	•	Preferred Research Inc..........................1581		•	•	•	

CV	CR	PR	JEFF DAVIS		UC	RE	TX	VR
•	•	•	Betty M Rowell CLA..............................295		•	•	•	•

CV	CR	PR	JEFFERSON		UC	RE	TX	VR
•	•	•	John E Jones Jr Land Title Services.............1091		•	•	•	•

CV	CR	PR	JENKINS		UC	RE	TX	VR
•	•	•	John E Jones Jr Land Title Services.............1091		•	•	•	•

CV	CR	PR	JOHNSON		UC	RE	TX	VR
•	•	•	John E Jones Jr Land Title Services.............1091		•	•	•	•
•	•	•	Preferred Research Inc..........................1581		•	•	•	

CV	CR	PR	JONES		UC	RE	TX	VR
•	•	•	Bigler & Associates Inc............................300		•	•	•	•
•	•	•	John E Jones Jr Land Title Services.............1091		•	•	•	•
•	•	•	Preferred Research Inc..........................1581		•	•	•	

CV	CR	PR	LAMAR		UC	RE	TX	VR
•	•	•	Hollingsworth Court Reporting Inc...............983		•	•	•	•
•	•	•	Preferred Research Inc..........................1581		•	•	•	

CV	CR	PR	LANIER		UC	RE	TX	VR
•	•	•	John E Jones Jr Land Title Services.............1091		•	•	•	•
•	•	•	Roberts Abstracting Inc.........................1705		•	•	•	

CV	CR	PR	LAURENS		UC	RE	TX	VR
•	•	•	John E Jones Jr Land Title Services.............1091		•	•	•	•
•	•	•	Preferred Research Inc..........................1581		•	•	•	

CV	CR	PR	LEE		UC	RE	TX	VR
•		•	Dougherty Abstract & Title Service Inc..........650			•	•	
•	•	•	South Georgia Title............................1821		•	•	•	
•	•		Thurman Investigative Services Inc..............1948					

CV	CR	PR	LIBERTY		UC	RE	TX	VR
•	•	•	John E Jones Jr Land Title Services.............1091		•	•	•	•
•	•	•	Josey, Cheryl S.................................1105		•	•	•	•

CV	CR	PR	LINCOLN		UC	RE	TX	VR
•	•	•	John E Jones Jr Land Title Services.............1091		•	•	•	•

DT	BK	CV	CR	PR		UC	RE	TX	VR
					LONG				
		•	•	•	John E Jones Jr Land Title Services 1091	•	•	•	•
		•	•	•	Josey, Cheryl S 1105	•	•	•	•
					LOWNDES				
•		•	•	•	John E Jones Jr Land Title Services 1091	•	•	•	•
		•	•	•	Roberts Abstracting Inc 1705	•	•	•	
•		•			Sunstate Research Associates Inc 1884	•			
					LUMPKIN				
		•	•	•	EL-Ru Inc 671	•		•	
					McDUFFIE				
		•	•	•	Freeflight Inc 812	•	•	•	•
		•	•	•	John E Jones Jr Land Title Services 1091	•	•	•	•
					McINTOSH				
		•	•	•	John E Jones Jr Land Title Services 1091	•	•	•	•
					MACON				
		•	•	•	John E Jones Jr Land Title Services 1091	•	•	•	
		•	•	•	Preferred Research Inc 1581	•	•	•	
					MADISON				
		•	•	•	Wilmot, Sally 2099	•	•	•	•
					MARION				
		•	•	•	Columbus Land Title Co 499	•	•	•	•
		•		•	Dougherty Abstract & Title Service Inc 650		•	•	
					MERIWETHER				
		•	•	•	Columbus Land Title Co 499	•	•	•	•
					MILLER				
		•		•	Dougherty Abstract & Title Service Inc 650		•	•	
		•			Sunstate Research Associates Inc 1884	•			
					MITCHELL				
		•		•	Dougherty Abstract & Title Service Inc 650		•	•	
		•			Sunstate Research Associates Inc 1884	•			
		•	•		Thurman Investigative Services Inc 1948				
					MONROE				
		•	•	•	Bigler & Associates Inc 300	•	•	•	•
		•	•	•	Preferred Research Inc 1581	•	•	•	
					MONTGOMERY				
		•	•	•	John E Jones Jr Land Title Services 1091	•	•	•	•
					MORGAN				
		•	•	•	Gladden, Roger 847	•	•	•	
		•	•	•	Hollingsworth Court Reporting Inc 983	•	•	•	•
		•	•	•	Merritt Jr, Charles W 1331	•	•	•	•
					MURRAY				
					Bele, Jan 278	•	•	•	
		•	•	•	Hollingsworth Court Reporting Inc 983	•	•	•	•
		•		•	Title Guaranty and Trust of Chattanooga 1953	•	•	•	
					MUSCOGEE				
	•	•	•	•	Columbus Land Title Co 499	•	•	•	•
					NEWTON				
		•	•	•	EL-Ru Inc 671	•		•	

●	●	●	Gladden, Roger 847	●	●	●	
●	●	●	Hollingsworth Court Reporting Inc...............983	●	●	●	●

CV	CR	PR	OCONEE	UC	RE	TX	VR
●	●	●	EL-Ru Inc...............671	●		●	
●	●	●	Gladden, Roger 847	●	●	●	
●	●	●	Merritt Jr, Charles W...............1331	●	●	●	●
●	●	●	Wilmot, Sally 2099	●	●	●	●

CV	CR	PR	OGLETHORPE	UC	RE	TX	VR
●	●	●	EL-Ru Inc...............671	●		●	
●	●	●	Wilmot, Sally 2099	●	●	●	●

CV	CR	PR	PAULDING	UC	RE	TX	VR
●	●	●	Hollingsworth Court Reporting Inc...............983	●	●	●	●
			Robinson Real Estate Services...............1707	●	●	●	
●		●	S D Moody Co 1722	●	●	●	

CV	CR	PR	PEACH	UC	RE	TX	VR
●	●	●	John E Jones Jr Land Title Services...............1091	●	●	●	●
●	●	●	Preferred Research Inc 1581	●	●	●	

CV	CR	PR	PICKENS	UC	RE	TX	VR
●	●	●	FACFIND Network Inc...............728	●	●	●	
●	●	●	Hollingsworth Court Reporting Inc...............983	●	●	●	●

CV	CR	PR	PIERCE	UC	RE	TX	VR
●	●	●	Betty M Rowell CLA 295	●	●	●	●

CV	CR	PR	PIKE	UC	RE	TX	VR
●	●	●	Hollingsworth Court Reporting Inc...............983	●	●	●	●
●	●	●	Preferred Research Inc 1581	●	●	●	

CV	CR	PR	POLK	UC	RE	TX	VR
			Robinson Real Estate Services...............1707	●	●	●	

CV	CR	PR	PULASKI	UC	RE	TX	VR
●	●	●	Cartwright Abstracting...............412	●	●	●	
●	●	●	John E Jones Jr Land Title Services...............1091	●	●	●	●
●	●	●	Preferred Research Inc 1581	●	●	●	
●	●	●	South Georgia Title...............1821	●	●	●	

CV	CR	PR	PUTNAM	UC	RE	TX	VR
●	●	●	Gladden, Roger 847	●	●	●	
●	●	●	Hollingsworth Court Reporting Inc...............983	●	●	●	●
●	●	●	Merritt Jr, Charles W...............1331	●	●	●	●
●	●	●	Preferred Research Inc 1581	●	●	●	

CV	CR	PR	QUITMAN	UC	RE	TX	VR
●	●	●	Columbus Land Title Co...............499	●	●	●	
●		●	Dougherty Abstract & Title Service Inc...............650		●	●	

CV	CR	PR	RABUN	UC	RE	TX	VR
●	●	●	Hollingsworth Court Reporting Inc...............983	●	●	●	

CV	CR	PR	RANDOLPH	UC	RE	TX	VR
●	●	●	Columbus Land Title Co...............499	●	●	●	●
●		●	Dougherty Abstract & Title Service Inc...............650		●	●	

DT	BK	CV	CR	PR	RICHMOND	UC	RE	TX	VR
●	●	●	●	●	Freeflight Inc...............812	●	●	●	
●	●	●	●	●	Weber, Attorney David V 2070	●	●	●	●

CV	CR	PR	ROCKDALE		UC	RE	TX	VR
●	●	●	Atlanta Courthouse Services 178		●	●	●	●
●	●	●	Attorneys' Personal Services 211		●	●	●	●
●	●	●	EL-Ru Inc..671		●			
●	●	●	FACFIND Network Inc...............................728		●	●	●	●
●	●	●	Gladden, Roger 847		●	●	●	●
●	●	●	Hollingsworth Court Reporting Inc..............983		●	●	●	●
●	●	●	Perry Field Services 1541		●	●	●	

CV	CR	PR	SCHLEY		UC	RE	TX	VR
●	●	●	Columbus Land Title Co.............................499		●	●	●	●
●		●	Dougherty Abstract & Title Service Inc........650					

CV	CR	PR	SCREVEN		UC	RE	TX	VR
●	●	●	John E Jones Jr Land Title Services...........1091		●	●	●	●

CV	CR	PR	SEMINOLE		UC	RE	TX	VR
●		●	Dougherty Abstract & Title Service Inc........650			●	●	
●			Sunstate Research Associates Inc..............1884		●			

CV	CR	PR	SPALDING		UC	RE	TX	VR
●	●	●	FACFIND Network Inc...............................728		●	●	●	●
●	●	●	Hollingsworth Court Reporting Inc..............983		●	●	●	●

CV	CR	PR	STEPHENS		UC	RE	TX	VR
●	●	●	Hollingsworth Court Reporting Inc..............983		●	●	●	●

CV	CR	PR	STEWART		UC	RE	TX	VR
●	●	●	Columbus Land Title Co.............................499		●	●	●	●
●		●	Dougherty Abstract & Title Service Inc........650			●	●	

CV	CR	PR	SUMTER		UC	RE	TX	VR
●		●	Dougherty Abstract & Title Service Inc........650			●	●	
●	●	●	South Georgia Title 1821		●	●	●	

CV	CR	PR	TALBOT		UC	RE	TX	VR
●	●	●	Columbus Land Title Co.............................499		●	●	●	●

CV	CR	PR	TALIAFERRO		UC	RE	TX	VR
●	●	●	John E Jones Jr Land Title Services...........1091		●	●	●	●

CV	CR	PR	TATTNALL		UC	RE	TX	VR
●	●	●	John E Jones Jr Land Title Services...........1091		●	●	●	●
●	●	●	Josey, Cheryl S.......................................1105		●	●	●	●

CV	CR	PR	TAYLOR		UC	RE	TX	VR
●	●	●	Preferred Research Inc 1581		●	●	●	

CV	CR	PR	TELFAIR		UC	RE	TX	VR
●	●	●	Cartwright Abstracting..............................412		●	●	●	
●	●	●	John E Jones Jr Land Title Services...........1091		●	●		●
●	●	●	Preferred Research Inc 1581		●	●	●	

CV	CR	PR	TERRELL		UC	RE	TX	VR
●	●	●	Columbus Land Title Co.............................499		●	●	●	●
●		●	Dougherty Abstract & Title Service Inc........650			●	●	

CV	CR	PR	THOMAS		UC	RE	TX	VR
●		●	Dougherty Abstract & Title Service Inc........650			●	●	
●	●	●	South Georgia Title 1821		●	●	●	
●			Sunstate Research Associates Inc..............1884		●			
●	●		Thurman Investigative Services Inc............1948					

	CV	CR	PR	TIFT	UC	RE	TX	VR
	●		●	Dougherty Abstract & Title Service Inc..........................650		●	●	
	●	●	●	Roberts Abstracting Inc...1705	●	●	●	

	CV	CR	PR	TOOMBS	UC	RE	TX	VR
	●	●	●	John E Jones Jr Land Title Services...............................1091	●	●	●	●

	CV	CR	PR	TOWNS	UC	RE	TX	VR
	●	●	●	Accurate Investigative Services...65	●	●	●	●

	CV	CR	PR	TREUTLEN	UC	RE	TX	VR
	●	●	●	John E Jones Jr Land Title Services...............................1091	●	●	●	●
	●	●	●	Preferred Research Inc 1581	●	●	●	

	CV	CR	PR	TROUP	UC	RE	TX	VR
	●	●	●	Columbus Land Title Co...499	●	●	●	●
	●	●	●	Wright III, Wyatt...2118	●	●	●	●

	CV	CR	PR	TURNER	UC	RE	TX	VR
	●		●	Dougherty Abstract & Title Service Inc..........................650		●	●	
	●	●	●	John E Jones Jr Land Title Services...............................1091	●	●	●	●
	●	●	●	South Georgia Title...1821	●	●	●	

	CV	CR	PR	TWIGGS	UC	RE	TX	VR
	●	●	●	John E Jones Jr Land Title Services...............................1091	●	●	●	●
	●	●	●	Preferred Research Inc 1581	●	●	●	

	CV	CR	PR	UNION	UC	RE	TX	VR
	●	●	●	Accurate Investigative Services...65	●	●	●	●

	CV	CR	PR	UPSON	UC	RE	TX	VR
	●	●	●	Preferred Research Inc 1581	●	●	●	

	CV	CR	PR	WALKER	UC	RE	TX	VR
	●	●	●	Hollingsworth Court Reporting Inc.................................983	●	●	●	●
	●		●	Title Guaranty and Trust of Chattanooga.......................1953	●	●	●	

	CV	CR	PR	WALTON	UC	RE	TX	VR
	●	●	●	Atlanta Courthouse Services...178	●	●	●	●
	●	●	●	EL-Ru Inc...671	●			
	●	●	●	Gladden, Roger 847	●			
	●	●	●	Hollingsworth Court Reporting Inc.................................983	●	●	●	●
	●		●	S D Moody Co 1722	●	●	●	
	●	●	●	Wilmot, Sally 2099	●	●	●	●

	CV	CR	PR	WARE	UC	RE	TX	VR
	●	●	●	Betty M Rowell CLA...295	●	●	●	●

	CV	CR	PR	WARREN	UC	RE	TX	VR
	●	●	●	John E Jones Jr Land Title Services...............................1091	●	●	●	●

	CV	CR	PR	WASHINGTON	UC	RE	TX	VR
	●	●	●	John E Jones Jr Land Title Services...............................1091	●	●	●	●
	●	●	●	Preferred Research Inc 1581	●	●	●	

	CV	CR	PR	WAYNE	UC	RE	TX	VR
	●	●	●	Betty M Rowell CLA...295	●	●	●	●

	CV	CR	PR	WEBSTER	UC	RE	TX	VR
	●	●	●	Columbus Land Title Co...499	●	●	●	●
	●		●	Dougherty Abstract & Title Service Inc..........................650		●	●	

	CV	CR	PR	WHEELER	UC	RE	TX	VR
	●	●	●	Cartwright Abstracting..412	●	●	●	

CV	CR	PR			UC	RE	TX	VR
●	●	●	John E Jones Jr Land Title Services 1091		●	●	●	●
●	●	●	Preferred Research Inc 1581		●	●	●	

CV	CR	PR	WHITE		UC	RE	TX	VR
●	●	●	EL-Ru Inc...671		●		●	

CV	CR	PR	WHITFIELD		UC	RE	TX	VR
			Bele, Jan..278		●	●	●	
●	●	●	Hollingsworth Court Reporting Inc....................................983		●	●	●	●
●		●	Title Guaranty and Trust of Chattanooga........................1953		●	●	●	

CV	CR	PR	WILCOX		UC	RE	TX	VR
●	●	●	Cartwright Abstracting..412		●	●	●	
●	●	●	John E Jones Jr Land Title Services...................................1091		●	●	●	●

CV	CR	PR	WILKES		UC	RE	TX	VR
●	●	●	John E Jones Jr Land Title Services...................................1091		●	●	●	●
●	●	●	South Georgia Title..1821		●	●	●	

CV	CR	PR	WILKINSON		UC	RE	TX	VR
●	●	●	John E Jones Jr Land Title Services...................................1091		●	●	●	●
●	●	●	Preferred Research Inc 1581		●	●	●	

CV	CR	PR	WORTH		UC	RE	TX	VR
●		●	Dougherty Abstract & Title Service Inc...........................650			●	●	
●	●	●	John E Jones Jr Land Title Services...................................1091		●	●	●	●
●	●	●	South Georgia Title..1821		●	●	●	

Hawaii

DT	BK	CV	CR	PR	ALL COUNTIES	UC	RE	TX	VR
●	●	●	●	●	Global Projects Ltd 851	●	●	●	●

		CV	CR	PR	HAWAII	UC	RE	TX	VR
		●	●	●	Doc-U-Search Hawaii 640	●		●	
		●	●	●	Honolulu Information Service...........................988	●	●	●	●

DT	BK	CV	CR	PR	HONOLULU	UC	RE	TX	VR
●	●	●	●	●	Honolulu Information Service...........................988	●	●	●	●
●	●	●	●	●	Roadrunner Messenger Service.......................1702	●	●	●	●
●	●	●	●	●	The Niles Agency...1938	●	●	●	●

		CV	CR	PR	KALAWAO	UC	RE	TX	VR
		●	●	●	Doc-U-Search Hawaii 640	●		●	

		CV	CR	PR	KAUAI	UC	RE	TX	VR
		●	●	●	Honolulu Information Service...........................988	●	●	●	●

		CV	CR	PR	MAUI	UC	RE	TX	VR
		●	●	●	Doc-U-Search Hawaii 640	●		●	
		●	●	●	Honolulu Information Service...........................988	●	●	●	●

Idaho

DT	BK	CV	CR	PR	ALL COUNTIES		UC	RE	TX	VR
●	●	●	●	●	Detective Referral Service	626	●	●	●	
●	●	●	●	●	Record Search and Information Services	1662	●	●	●	●

DT	BK	CV	CR	PR	ADA		UC	RE	TX	VR
●	●	●	●	●	Burr Investigation	370	●	●	●	●
●	●	●	●	●	Drake Detective Agency	659	●	●	●	●
		●	●	●	Hickox, Carol	964	●	●	●	●
●	●	●	●	●	Lord and Associates	1242	●	●	●	
●	●	●	●	●	McCord Company	1307	●	●		●
●	●	●	●	●	Tri-County Process Serving	1981	●	●	●	●

		CV	CR	PR	ADAMS		UC	RE	TX	VR
		●	●	●	Burr Investigation	370	●	●	●	●
		●	●		Hickox, Carol	964	●	●	●	●

		CV	CR	PR	BANNOCK		UC	RE	TX	VR
		●	●	●	C.I. & S.	374	●	●	●	●
		●	●	●	Eagle Rock Investigations & Surveillance	675	●	●		●
		●	●	●	M R Daniel & Associates	1255		●	●	●

		CV	CR	PR	BEAR LAKE		UC	RE	TX	VR
		●	●	●	Niemier, Leslie	1426		●		●

		CV	CR	PR	BENEWAH		UC	RE	TX	VR
		●	●	●	Action Agency	71	●	●	●	●
		●	●	●	Gem State Investigations	837	●	●	●	●

		CV	CR	PR	BINGHAM		UC	RE	TX	VR
		●	●	●	C.I. & S.	374	●	●	●	●
		●	●	●	Eagle Rock Investigations & Surveillance	675	●	●	●	●

		CV	CR	PR	BLAINE		UC	RE	TX	VR
		●	●	●	American Eagle Invest & Pers Security	130	●	●	●	●
		●	●	●	Burr Investigation	370	●	●	●	●

		CV	CR	PR	BOISE		UC	RE	TX	VR
		●	●	●	Burr Investigation	370	●	●	●	●
		●	●	●	Drake Detective Agency	659	●	●	●	●
		●	●		Hickox, Carol	964	●	●	●	●
		●	●	●	Lord and Associates	1242	●	●	●	
		●	●	●	Tri-County Process Serving	1981	●	●	●	●

		CV	CR	PR	BONNER		UC	RE	TX	VR
		●	●	●	Action Agency	71	●	●	●	●
		●	●	●	Best Investigations	292	●	●	●	●

		CV	CR	PR	BONNEVILLE		UC	RE	TX	VR
		●	●	●	Eagle Rock Investigations & Surveillance	675	●	●	●	●
		●	●	●	M R Daniel & Associates	1255		●	●	●

		CV	CR	PR	BOUNDARY		UC	RE	TX	VR
		●	●	●	Action Agency	71	●	●	●	●

		CV	CR	PR	BUTTE		UC	RE	TX	VR
		●	●	●	M R Daniel & Associates	1255		●	●	●

		CV	CR	PR	CAMAS		UC	RE	TX	VR
		●	●	●	American Eagle Invest & Pers Security	130	●	●	●	●

		CV	CR	PR	CANYON		UC	RE	TX	VR
		●	●	●	Burr Investigation	370	●	●	●	●

CV	CR	PR		Page	UC	RE	TX	VR
●	●	●	Drake Detective Agency	659	●	●	●	●
●	●		Hickox, Carol	964	●	●	●	
●	●	●	Lord and Associates	1242	●	●	●	
●	●	●	Tri-County Process Serving	1981	●	●	●	●

CARIBOU

CV	CR	PR		Page	UC	RE	TX	VR
●	●	●	C.I. & S.	374	●	●		
●	●	●	M R Daniel & Associates	1255		●	●	●
●	●	●	Niemier, Leslie	1426		●		●

CASSIA

CV	CR	PR		Page	UC	RE	TX	VR
●	●	●	Burr Investigation	370	●	●	●	●
		●	Cassia County Abstract Co	417	●	●	●	

CLARK

See ALL COUNTIES...

CLEARWATER

CV	CR	PR		Page	UC	RE	TX	VR
●	●	●	Gem State Investigations	837	●	●	●	●

CUSTER

CV	CR	PR		Page	UC	RE	TX	VR
●	●	●	C.I. & S.	374	●	●	●	●

ELMORE

CV	CR	PR		Page	UC	RE	TX	VR
●	●	●	Burr Investigation	370	●	●	●	●
●	●		Hickox, Carol	964	●	●	●	
●	●	●	Lord and Associates	1242	●	●	●	
●	●	●	Tri-County Process Serving	1981	●	●	●	●

FRANKLIN

CV	CR	PR		Page	UC	RE	TX	VR
●	●	●	Preston Land Title Co	1600	●	●	●	●

FREMONT

See ALL COUNTIES...

GEM

CV	CR	PR		Page	UC	RE	TX	VR
●	●	●	Burr Investigation	370	●	●	●	●
●	●		Hickox, Carol	964	●	●	●	
●	●	●	Lord and Associates	1242	●	●	●	
●	●	●	Tri-County Process Serving	1981	●	●	●	●

GOODING

CV	CR	PR		Page	UC	RE	TX	VR
●	●	●	American Eagle Invest & Pers Security	130	●	●	●	●
●	●	●	Burr Investigation	370	●	●	●	●

IDAHO

CV	CR	PR		Page	UC	RE	TX	VR
●			Anderson, Edith L	149	●	●	●	
●	●	●	Gem State Investigations	837	●	●	●	●

JEFFERSON

CV	CR	PR		Page	UC	RE	TX	VR
●	●	●	Eagle Rock Investigations & Surveillance	675	●	●	●	●
●	●	●	M R Daniel & Associates	1255		●	●	●

JEROME

CV	CR	PR		Page	UC	RE	TX	VR
●	●	●	American Eagle Invest & Pers Security	130	●	●	●	●

KOOTENAI

CV	CR	PR		Page	UC	RE	TX	VR
●	●	●	Action Agency	71	●	●	●	●
●	●	●	Best Investigations	292	●	●	●	●

LATAH

CV	CR	PR		Page	UC	RE	TX	VR
●	●	●	Action Agency	71	●	●	●	●
●	●	●	Gem State Investigations	837	●	●		
●	●	●	Pullman Process Service	1630				

CV	CR	PR	LEMHI		UC	RE	TX	VR
•	•	•	Lemhi Title Co 1219		•	•	•	•

CV	CR	PR	LEWIS		UC	RE	TX	VR
•	•	•	Gem State Investigations 837		•	•	•	•
•	•	•	Lewis County Abstract 1221			•	•	

CV	CR	PR	LINCOLN		UC	RE	TX	VR
•	•	•	American Eagle Invest & Pers Security 130		•	•	•	•

CV	CR	PR	MADISON		UC	RE	TX	VR
•	•	•	Eagle Rock Investigations & Surveillance 675		•	•	•	•
•	•	•	M R Daniel & Associates 1255			•	•	•

CV	CR	PR	MINIDOKA		UC	RE	TX	VR
•	•	•	Burr Investigation 370		•	•	•	•

CV	CR	PR	NEZ PERCE		UC	RE	TX	VR
•	•	•	Action Agency 71		•	•	•	•
•	•	•	Gem State Investigations 837		•	•	•	•

CV	CR	PR	ONEIDA		UC	RE	TX	VR
•	•	•	C.I. & S. 374		•	•	•	•

CV	CR	PR	OWYHEE		UC	RE	TX	VR
•	•	•	Burr Investigation 370		•	•	•	•
•	•		Hickox, Carol 964		•	•	•	•
•	•	•	Lord and Associates 1242		•	•	•	

CV	CR	PR	PAYETTE		UC	RE	TX	VR
•	•		Hickox, Carol 964		•	•	•	•
•	•	•	Lord and Associates 1242		•	•	•	
•	•	•	Tri-County Process Serving 1981		•	•	•	•

CV	CR	PR	POWER		UC	RE	TX	VR
•	•	•	C.I. & S. 374		•	•	•	•

CV	CR	PR	SHOSHONE		UC	RE	TX	VR
•	•	•	Action Agency 71		•	•	•	•
•	•	•	Best Investigations 292		•	•	•	•

CV	CR	PR	TETON		UC	RE	TX	VR
•	•	•	M R Daniel & Associates 1255			•	•	•

CV	CR	PR	TWIN FALLS		UC	RE	TX	VR
•	•	•	American Eagle Invest & Pers Security 130		•	•	•	•
•	•	•	Burr Investigation 370		•	•	•	

CV	CR	PR	VALLEY		UC	RE	TX	VR
•	•	•	Burr Investigation 370		•	•	•	•
•	•	•	Drake Detective Agency 659		•	•	•	•
•	•		Hickox, Carol 964		•	•	•	•
•	•	•	Lord and Associates 1242		•	•	•	
•	•	•	Tri-County Process Serving 1981		•	•	•	•

CV	CR	PR	WASHINGTON		UC	RE	TX	VR
•	•		Hickox, Carol 964		•	•	•	•
•	•	•	Lord and Associates 1242		•	•	•	

Illinois

DT	BK	CV	CR	PR	ALL COUNTIES		UC	RE	TX	VR
●	●	●	●	●	Accurate Research Inc.................................68		●		●	●
●	●	●	●	●	Legal Services...1210		●	●	●	●

		CV	CR	PR	ADAMS		UC	RE	TX	VR
		●	●	●	Falcon Investigations 739		●	●	●	●
		●		●	Marion County Abstract Co.......................1280		●	●	●	●

		CV	CR	PR	ALEXANDER		UC	RE	TX	VR
		●	●	●	Terry Sharp Law Office..............................1911		●	●	●	●

		CV	CR	PR	BOND		UC	RE	TX	VR
		●	●	●	Terry Sharp Law Office..............................1911		●	●	●	●

		CV	CR	PR	BOONE		UC	RE	TX	VR
		●	●	●	McCabe and Hubly Adj Co.........................1300				●	
		●		●	Northwestern Illinois Title........................1448		●	●	●	

		CV	CR	PR	BROWN		UC	RE	TX	VR
		●	●		Chattel Mortgage Reporters Inc 442		●	●	●	●

		CV	CR	PR	BUREAU		UC	RE	TX	VR
		●	●	●	Associated Title Co.....................................174		●	●	●	●
		●		●	Northwestern Illinois Title........................1448		●	●	●	

		CV	CR	PR	CALHOUN		UC	RE	TX	VR
		●	●	●	Moses, Ralph J 1390		●	●	●	●

		CV	CR	PR	CARROLL		UC	RE	TX	VR
		●		●	Northwestern Illinois Title........................1448		●	●	●	
		●	●	●	Steward and Associates Inc.......................1868		●	●	●	●

		CV	CR	PR	CASS		UC	RE	TX	VR
		●	●	●	Hylind Info Quest......................................1012		●	●	●	●

		CV	CR	PR	CHAMPAIGN		UC	RE	TX	VR
		●	●	●	CPD Inc..377		●	●	●	●
		●	●		Chattel Mortgage Reporters Inc 442		●	●	●	●
		●	●	●	Hurst Security Service Inc.........................1008					

		CV	CR	PR	CHRISTIAN		UC	RE	TX	VR
		●	●	●	Hylind Info Quest......................................1012		●	●	●	●

		CV	CR	PR	CLARK		UC	RE	TX	VR
		●		●	Everhart and Everhart Abstractors 721		●	●	●	●

		CV	CR	PR	CLAY		UC	RE	TX	VR
					Chattel Mortgage Reporters Inc 442		●			
		●	●	●	Terry Sharp Law Office..............................1911		●	●	●	●

		CV	CR	PR	CLINTON		UC	RE	TX	VR
		●	●	●	D & L Invesgiations...................................577		●	●	●	●
		●	●	●	Heil Investigations Agency Inc...................948		●	●	●	●
		●	●	●	St Vrain Resources....................................1848		●	●	●	
		●	●	●	Terry Sharp Law Office..............................1911		●	●	●	●

		CV	CR	PR	COLES		UC	RE	TX	VR
		●	●	●	CPD Inc..377		●	●	●	●

DT	BK	CV	CR	PR	COOK				UC	RE	TX	VR
●	●	●	●	●	AM Legal Service Inc 29				●	●	●	●
●	●	●	●	●	All Investigations 107				●			●
●	●	●	●	●	Centennial Coverages Inc............... 422				●	●	●	●
●	●	●	●	●	Chattel Mortgage Reporters Inc 442				●	●	●	●
●	●	●	●	●	LaSalle Process Servers............... 1151							
●	●	●	●	●	Legal Data Resources............... 1198				●	●	●	●
●	●	●	●	●	Research Information Services............... 1683				●	●	●	●
●	●	●	●	●	VTS............... 2018				●	●	●	●

		CV	CR	PR	CRAWFORD				UC	RE	TX	VR
		●	●	●	Lawrence County Title............... 1180				●	●	●	●
		●	●	●	Terry Sharp Law Office............... 1911				●	●	●	●

		CV	CR	PR	CUMBERLAND				UC	RE	TX	VR
		●		●	Everhart and Everhart Abstractors 721				●	●	●	●

		CV	CR	PR	DE KALB				UC	RE	TX	VR
		●	●		Chattel Mortgage Reporters Inc 442					●	●	●
		●		●	Northwestern Illinois Title 1448				●	●	●	●
		●	●	●	VTS............... 2018				●	●	●	●

		CV	CR	PR	DE WITT				UC	RE	TX	VR
		●	●	●	CPD Inc............... 377				●	●	●	●
		●	●		Conover Detective Agency............... 513				●	●	●	●

		CV	CR	PR	DOUGLAS				UC	RE	TX	VR
		●	●	●	Douglas County Abstract Co Inc............... 653				●	●	●	●

		CV	CR	PR	DU PAGE				UC	RE	TX	VR
		●	●	●	All Investigations 107				●			●
		●	●		Chattel Mortgage Reporters Inc 442				●	●	●	●
		●	●	●	Legal Data Resources............... 1198				●	●	●	●
		●	●	●	Research Information Services............... 1683				●	●	●	●
		●	●	●	VTS............... 2018				●	●	●	●

		CV	CR	PR	EDGAR				UC	RE	TX	VR
		●	●	●	Edgar County Title Co 692				●	●	●	●

		CV	CR	PR	EDWARDS				UC	RE	TX	VR
		●	●	●	Terry Sharp Law Office............... 1911				●	●	●	●

		CV	CR	PR	EFFINGHAM				UC	RE	TX	VR
		●	●	●	Terry Sharp Law Office............... 1911				●	●	●	●

		CV	CR	PR	FAYETTE				UC	RE	TX	VR
		●	●	●	Terry Sharp Law Office............... 1911				●	●	●	●

		CV	CR	PR	FORD				UC	RE	TX	VR
		●	●	●	CPD Inc............... 377				●	●	●	●

	BK	CV	CR	PR	FRANKLIN				UC	RE	TX	VR
		●		●	Kotner, Jeff............... 1134				●	●	●	
		●	●	●	Palmer and Murrie Abstract Co............... 1507				●	●	●	●
		●		●	Real Estate Data Inc 1655				●	●	●	
	●	●	●	●	Terry Sharp Law Office............... 1911				●	●	●	●

		CV	CR	PR	FULTON				UC	RE	TX	VR
		●	●		Conover Detective Agency............... 513				●	●	●	●
		●	●	●	Turnquist & Associates 1991				●	●	●	●
		●	●	●	Wilson Abstract Co 2101				●	●	●	●

		CV	CR	PR	GALLATIN				UC	RE	TX	VR
		●		●	Kotner, Jeff............... 1134				●	●	●	

Court Records				County Records			
●	●	●	Terry Sharp Law Office.......1911	●	●	●	●
CV	**CR**	**PR**	**GREENE**	**UC**	**RE**	**TX**	**VR**
●	●	●	Falcon Investigations 739	●	●	●	●
●		●	O H Vivell Title Co.......1449		●	●	
CV	**CR**	**PR**	**GRUNDY**	**UC**	**RE**	**TX**	**VR**
●	●		Chattel Mortgage Reporters Inc.......442	●	●	●	●
●	●	●	Hurst Security Service Inc.......1008				
CV	**CR**	**PR**	**HAMILTON**	**UC**	**RE**	**TX**	**VR**
●		●	Kotner, Jeff.......1134	●	●	●	
●	●	●	Terry Sharp Law Office.......1911	●	●	●	●
CV	**CR**	**PR**	**HANCOCK**	**UC**	**RE**	**TX**	**VR**
●		●	Marion County Abstract Co.......1280	●	●	●	●
●	●	●	Wilson Abstract Co.......2101	●	●	●	●
CV	**CR**	**PR**	**HARDIN**	**UC**	**RE**	**TX**	**VR**
●	●	●	Hardin County Abstract Company.......923	●	●	●	●
●		●	Kotner, Jeff.......1134	●	●	●	
●	●	●	Neuf & Associates.......1418	●	●	●	●
●	●	●	Terry Sharp Law Office.......1911	●	●	●	
CV	**CR**	**PR**	**HENDERSON**	**UC**	**RE**	**TX**	**VR**
●	●	●	Wilson Abstract Co.......2101	●	●	●	●
CV	**CR**	**PR**	**HENRY**	**UC**	**RE**	**TX**	**VR**
●	●	●	J M White Investigations.......1065	●	●	●	●
●		●	Northwestern Illinois Title.......1448	●	●	●	
●	●	●	Turnquist & Associates.......1991	●	●	●	
CV	**CR**	**PR**	**IROQUOIS**	**UC**	**RE**	**TX**	**VR**
●	●		Chattel Mortgage Reporters Inc.......442	●	●	●	●
CV	**CR**	**PR**	**JACKSON**	**UC**	**RE**	**TX**	**VR**
●		●	Kotner, Jeff.......1134	●	●	●	
●		●	Real Estate Data Inc.......1655	●	●	●	
●	●	●	Terry Sharp Law Office.......1911	●	●	●	●
CV	**CR**	**PR**	**JASPER**	**UC**	**RE**	**TX**	**VR**
●	●	●	Eaton Abstract Company.......688	●	●	●	
●	●	●	Terry Sharp Law Office.......1911	●	●	●	●
CV	**CR**	**PR**	**JEFFERSON**	**UC**	**RE**	**TX**	**VR**
●	●	●	Terry Sharp Law Office.......1911	●	●	●	●
CV	**CR**	**PR**	**JERSEY**	**UC**	**RE**	**TX**	**VR**
●	●	●	Hayes & Associates.......942	●	●	●	
●	●	●	St Vrain Resources.......1848	●	●	●	
CV	**CR**	**PR**	**JO DAVIESS**	**UC**	**RE**	**TX**	**VR**
●		●	Northwestern Illinois Title.......1448	●	●	●	
●	●	●	Steward and Associates Inc.......1868	●	●	●	●
CV	**CR**	**PR**	**JOHNSON**	**UC**	**RE**	**TX**	**VR**
●		●	Johnson County Abstract.......1094	●	●	●	
●		●	Kotner, Jeff.......1134	●	●	●	
●	●	●	Neuf & Associates.......1418	●	●	●	
●	●	●	Palmer and Murrie Abstract Co.......1507	●	●	●	●
●		●	Real Estate Data Inc.......1655	●	●	●	
●	●	●	Terry Sharp Law Office.......1911	●	●	●	●

CV	CR	PR	KANE	UC	RE	TX	VR
●	●		Chattel Mortgage Reporters Inc 442	●	●	●	●
●	●	●	VTS...2018	●	●	●	●

CV	CR	PR	KANKAKEE	UC	RE	TX	VR
●	●		Chattel Mortgage Reporters Inc 442	●	●	●	●
●	●	●	Hurst Security Service Inc.............................1008				

CV	CR	PR	KENDALL	UC	RE	TX	VR
●	●		Chattel Mortgage Reporters Inc 442	●	●	●	●
●	●	●	VTS...2018	●	●	●	●

CV	CR	PR	KNOX	UC	RE	TX	VR
●	●	●	Turnquist & Associates 1991	●	●	●	●

CV	CR	PR	LAKE	UC	RE	TX	VR
●	●		Chattel Mortgage Reporters Inc 442	●	●	●	●
●	●	●	Legal Data Resources......................................1198	●	●	●	●
●	●	●	VTS...2018	●	●	●	●

CV	CR	PR	LA SALLE	UC	RE	TX	VR
●	●		Chattel Mortgage Reporters Inc 442	●	●	●	●
●		●	Northwestern Illinois Title 1448	●	●	●	

CV	CR	PR	LAWRENCE	UC	RE	TX	VR
●	●	●	Lawrence County Title......................................1180	●	●	●	
●	●	●	Terry Sharp Law Office.....................................1911	●	●	●	●

CV	CR	PR	LEE	UC	RE	TX	VR
●	●		Chattel Mortgage Reporters Inc 442	●	●	●	●
●		●	Northwestern Illinois Title 1448	●	●	●	
●	●	●	Steward and Associates Inc 1868	●	●	●	●

CV	CR	PR	LIVINGSTON	UC	RE	TX	VR
●	●		Chattel Mortgage Reporters Inc 442	●	●	●	●

CV	CR	PR	LOGAN	UC	RE	TX	VR
●	●	●	CPD Inc...377	●	●	●	●
●	●		Conover Detective Agency...................................513	●	●	●	●
●	●	●	Hylind Info Quest...1012	●	●	●	●

CV	CR	PR	MCDONOUGH	UC	RE	TX	VR
●	●	●	Turnquist & Associates 1991	●	●	●	●
●	●	●	Wilson Abstract Co 2101	●	●	●	●

CV	CR	PR	MCHENRY	UC	RE	TX	VR
●	●		Chattel Mortgage Reporters Inc 442	●	●	●	●
●		●	Northwestern Illinois Title 1448	●	●	●	
●	●	●	VTS...2018	●	●	●	●

CV	CR	PR	MCLEAN	UC	RE	TX	VR
●	●	●	CPD Inc...377	●	●	●	●
●	●		Conover Detective Agency...................................513	●	●	●	●

CV	CR	PR	MACON	UC	RE	TX	VR
●	●	●	CPD Inc...377	●	●	●	●
			Chattel Mortgage Reporters Inc 442	●			
●	●	●	Falcon Investigations 739	●	●	●	●
●	●	●	Hurst Security Service Inc.............................1008	●	●	●	●
●	●	●	Hylind Info Quest...1012	●	●	●	●

CV	CR	PR	MACOUPIN	UC	RE	TX	VR
●	●	●	CPD Inc...377	●	●	●	●

		CV	CR	PR	MADISON		UC	RE	TX	VR
		•	•	•	D & L Invesgiations....................577		•	•	•	•
		•	•	•	Hayes & Associates....................942		•	•	•	•
		•	•	•	Heil Investigations Agency Inc....................948		•	•	•	•
		•	•	•	Legal System Services....................1213		•	•	•	•
		•	•	•	St Vrain Resources....................1848		•	•	•	•
		•	•	•	Terry Sharp Law Office....................1911		•	•	•	•

		CV	CR	PR	MARION		UC	RE	TX	VR
		•	•		Chattel Mortgage Reporters Inc....................442		•	•	•	•
		•	•	•	Monroe County Title Co....................1365		•	•	•	•
		•	•	•	Terry Sharp Law Office....................1911		•	•	•	•

		CV	CR	PR	MARSHALL		UC	RE	TX	VR
		•	•		Conover Detective Agency....................513		•	•	•	•
		•		•	Northwestern Illinois Title....................1448		•	•	•	

		CV	CR	PR	MASON		UC	RE	TX	VR
		•	•		Conover Detective Agency....................513		•	•	•	•

		CV	CR	PR	MASSAC		UC	RE	TX	VR
		•	•	•	Neuf & Associates....................1418		•	•	•	
		•	•	•	Terry Sharp Law Office....................1911		•	•	•	•

		CV	CR	PR	MENARD		UC	RE	TX	VR
		•	•		Conover Detective Agency....................513		•	•	•	•
		•	•	•	Hylind Info Quest....................1012		•	•	•	•

		CV	CR	PR	MERCER		UC	RE	TX	VR
		•	•	•	J M White Investigations....................1065		•	•	•	•

		CV	CR	PR	MONROE		UC	RE	TX	VR
		•	•	•	D & L Invesgiations....................577		•	•	•	•
		•	•	•	Heil Investigations Agency Inc....................948		•	•	•	•
		•	•	•	Legal System Services....................1213		•	•	•	•
		•	•	•	St Vrain Resources....................1848		•	•	•	•
		•	•	•	Terry Sharp Law Office....................1911		•	•	•	•

		CV	CR	PR	MONTGOMERY		UC	RE	TX	VR
		•	•	•	CPD Inc....................377		•	•	•	•

		CV	CR	PR	MORGAN		UC	RE	TX	VR
		•	•	•	Falcon Investigations....................739		•	•	•	•
		•	•	•	Hylind Info Quest....................1012		•	•	•	•

		CV	CR	PR	MOULTRIE		UC	RE	TX	VR
		•	•	•	CPD Inc....................377		•	•	•	•
		•		•	Citzen Abstract Co....................460		•	•	•	•

		CV	CR	PR	OGLE		UC	RE	TX	VR
		•		•	Northwestern Illinois Title....................1448		•	•		
		•	•	•	Steward and Associates Inc....................1868		•	•		

DT	BK	CV	CR	PR	PEORIA		UC	RE	TX	VR
•	•	•	•		Conover Detective Agency....................513		•	•	•	•
•	•	•	•	•	J M White Investigations....................1065		•	•	•	•
•		•	•	•	Turnquist & Associates....................1991		•	•	•	•

		CV	CR	PR	PERRY		UC	RE	TX	VR
		•	•	•	Terry Sharp Law Office....................1911		•	•	•	•
		•	•	•	Uhe, Lois....................2003		•	•	•	•

		CV	CR	PR	PIATT		UC	RE	TX	VR
		•	•	•	CPD Inc....................377		•	•	•	•

	•	•	•	Hurst Security Service Inc........................1008						

		CV	**CR**	**PR**	**PIKE**		**UC**	**RE**	**TX**	**VR**
		•	•	•	Falcon Investigations 739		•	•	•	•
		•		•	Marion County Abstract Co......................1280		•	•	•	•

		CV	**CR**	**PR**	**POPE**		**UC**	**RE**	**TX**	**VR**
		•		•	Kotner, Jeff.......................................1134		•	•	•	
		•	•	•	Terry Sharp Law Office..........................1911		•	•	•	•

		CV	**CR**	**PR**	**PULASKI**		**UC**	**RE**	**TX**	**VR**
		•		•	Pulaski County Abstract Company...............1629		•	•	•	•
		•	•	•	Terry Sharp Law Office..........................1911		•	•	•	•

		CV	**CR**	**PR**	**PUTNAM**		**UC**	**RE**	**TX**	**VR**
		•	•	•	Associated Title Co..............................174		•	•	•	•
		•		•	Northwestern Illinois Title.....................1448		•	•	•	

		CV	**CR**	**PR**	**RANDOLPH**		**UC**	**RE**	**TX**	**VR**
		•	•	•	St Vrain Resources..............................1848		•	•	•	
		•	•	•	Terry Sharp Law Office..........................1911		•	•	•	•

		CV	**CR**	**PR**	**RICHLAND**		**UC**	**RE**	**TX**	**VR**
		•	•	•	Lawrence County Title..........................1180		•	•	•	
		•	•	•	Terry Sharp Law Office..........................1911		•	•	•	•

DT		**CV**	**CR**	**PR**	**ROCK ISLAND**		**UC**	**RE**	**TX**	**VR**
•		•	•	•	J M White Investigations........................1065		•	•	•	•
•		•		•	Northwestern Illinois Title.....................1448		•	•	•	

DT	**BK**	**CV**	**CR**	**PR**	**ST. CLAIR**		**UC**	**RE**	**TX**	**VR**
•	•	•	•	•	D & L Invesgiations.............................577		•	•	•	•
•	•	•	•	•	Hayes & Associates..............................942		•	•	•	•
•	•	•	•	•	Heil Investigations Agency Inc..................948		•	•	•	•
•	•	•	•	•	Legal System Services..........................1213		•	•	•	
•	•	•	•	•	St Vrain Resources..............................1848		•	•	•	
•	•	•	•	•	Terry Sharp Law Office..........................1911		•	•	•	•

		CV	**CR**	**PR**	**SALINE**		**UC**	**RE**	**TX**	**VR**
		•		•	Kotner, Jeff.......................................1134		•	•	•	
		•	•	•	Palmer and Murrie Abstract Co..................1507		•	•	•	•
		•		•	Real Estate Data Inc...........................1655		•	•	•	
		•	•	•	Terry Sharp Law Office..........................1911		•	•	•	•

DT	**BK**	**CV**	**CR**	**PR**	**SANGAMON**		**UC**	**RE**	**TX**	**VR**
•	•	•	•	•	CPD Inc..377		•	•	•	•
•	•	•	•	•	Corporation Associates of Illinois...............527		•	•	•	•
•	•	•	•	•	Hylind Info Quest..............................1012		•	•	•	•
•	•	•	•	•	Prentice Hall Legal & Financial Services.........1586		•	•	•	•

		CV	**CR**	**PR**	**SCHUYLER**		**UC**	**RE**	**TX**	**VR**
		•	•	•	Falcon Investigations 739		•	•	•	•
		•	•	•	Wilson Abstract Co.............................2101		•	•	•	•

		CV	**CR**	**PR**	**SCOTT**		**UC**	**RE**	**TX**	**VR**
		•	•	•	Falcon Investigations 739		•	•	•	•

		CV	**CR**	**PR**	**SHELBY**		**UC**	**RE**	**TX**	**VR**
		•	•	•	Shelby County Land Title Corp..................1794		•	•	•	•

		CV	**CR**	**PR**	**STARK**		**UC**	**RE**	**TX**	**VR**
		•	•	•	J M White Investigations........................1065		•	•	•	•

DT	BK	CV	CR	PR	STEPHENSON		UC	RE	TX	VR
		•	•	•	McCabe and Hubly Adj Co	1300			•	
				•	Northwestern Illinois Title	1448	•	•	•	
		•	•	•	Steward and Associates Inc	1868	•	•	•	•

DT	BK	CV	CR	PR	TAZEWELL		UC	RE	TX	VR
		•	•		Conover Detective Agency	513	•	•	•	•
		•	•	•	J M White Investigations	1065	•	•	•	•

DT	BK	CV	CR	PR	UNION		UC	RE	TX	VR
		•		•	Real Estate Data Inc	1655	•	•	•	
		•	•	•	Terry Sharp Law Office	1911	•	•	•	•

DT	BK	CV	CR	PR	VERMILION		UC	RE	TX	VR
•		•	•	•	Hurst Security Service Inc	1008	•	•	•	•

DT	BK	CV	CR	PR	WABASH		UC	RE	TX	VR
		•	•	•	Lawrence County Title	1180	•	•	•	
		•	•	•	Terry Sharp Law Office	1911	•	•	•	•

DT	BK	CV	CR	PR	WARREN		UC	RE	TX	VR
		•	•	•	Turnquist & Associates	1991	•	•	•	•
		•	•	•	Wilson Abstract Co	2101	•	•	•	•

DT	BK	CV	CR	PR	WASHINGTON		UC	RE	TX	VR
		•	•	•	Heil Investigations Agency Inc	948	•	•	•	•
		•	•	•	Terry Sharp Law Office	1911	•	•	•	•

DT	BK	CV	CR	PR	WAYNE		UC	RE	TX	VR
		•	•	•	Terry Sharp Law Office	1911	•	•	•	•

DT	BK	CV	CR	PR	WHITE		UC	RE	TX	VR
		•		•	Kotner, Jeff	1134	•	•	•	
		•	•	•	Terry Sharp Law Office	1911	•	•	•	•

DT	BK	CV	CR	PR	WHITESIDE		UC	RE	TX	VR
		•	•		Chattel Mortgage Reporters Inc	442	•	•	•	•
		•		•	Northwestern Illinois Title	1448	•	•	•	
		•	•	•	Steward and Associates Inc	1868	•	•	•	•

DT	BK	CV	CR	PR	WILL		UC	RE	TX	VR
		•	•		Chattel Mortgage Reporters Inc	442	•	•	•	•
		•	•	•	Legal Data Resources	1198	•	•	•	•
		•	•	•	VTS	2018	•	•	•	•

DT	BK	CV	CR	PR	WILLIAMSON		UC	RE	TX	VR
		•		•	Kotner, Jeff	1134	•	•	•	
		•	•	•	Palmer and Murrie Abstract Co	1507	•	•	•	•
		•		•	Real Estate Data Inc	1655	•	•	•	
		•	•	•	Terry Sharp Law Office	1911	•	•	•	•

DT	BK	CV	CR	PR	WINNEBAGO		UC	RE	TX	VR
•	•	•	•		Chattel Mortgage Reporters Inc	442	•	•	•	
•	•	•	•	•	Gregg Investigations Inc of Madison	879	•	•	•	•
•	•	•	•	•	McCabe and Hubly Adj Co	1300			•	
•	•			•	Northwestern Illinois Title	1448	•	•	•	
•	•	•	•	•	Steward and Associates Inc	1868	•	•	•	•

DT	BK	CV	CR	PR	WOODFORD		UC	RE	TX	VR
		•	•		Conover Detective Agency	513	•	•	•	•

Indiana

DT	BK	CV	CR	PR	ALL COUNTIES		UC	RE	TX	VR
●	●	●	●	●	National Service Information Inc 1410		●		●	●

		CV	CR	PR	ADAMS		UC	RE	TX	VR
		●	●	●	Tri-County Land Title.......................1980		●	●	●	●

DT	BK	CV	CR	PR	ALLEN		UC	RE	TX	VR
					See ALL COUNTIES....................................					

		CV	CR	PR	BARTHOLOMEW		UC	RE	TX	VR
		●			Boone County Abstract Co 324		●	●	●	●
		●	●	●	Indiana Title Co 1025		●	●	●	●
		●	●	●	Trace Investigations 1972		●	●	●	●

		CV	CR	PR	BENTON		UC	RE	TX	VR
		●		●	Benton County Abstract & Title......................282		●	●	●	
		●	●	●	Tippecanoe Title Services Inc 1950		●	●	●	

		CV	CR	PR	BLACKFORD		UC	RE	TX	VR
		●		●	King's Title & Abstract Co......................1124		●	●	●	●

		CV	CR	PR	BOONE		UC	RE	TX	VR
		●	●	●	Abstract and Title Services......................52		●	●	●	
		●			Boone County Abstract Co 324		●	●	●	●
		●	●	●	Central Indiana Paralegal Service Inc 424		●		●	
		●	●	●	International Investigators Inc......................1038		●	●	●	●

		CV	CR	PR	BROWN		UC	RE	TX	VR
		●	●	●	Indiana Title Co 1025		●	●	●	●
		●	●	●	Trace Investigations 1972		●	●	●	●

		CV	CR	PR	CARROLL		UC	RE	TX	VR
		●	●	●	Tippecanoe Title Services Inc......................1950		●	●	●	

		CV	CR	PR	CASS		UC	RE	TX	VR
		●	●	●	Gundrum Realty Inc......................901		●	●	●	●
		●	●	●	Tippecanoe Title Services Inc......................1950		●	●	●	

		CV	CR	PR	CLARK		UC	RE	TX	VR
		●	●	●	Eagle Investigations Inc 673		●	●	●	●
		●	●	●	Indiana Title Co 1025		●	●	●	●
		●	●	●	Sam Steele Investigations......................1730		●	●	●	●
		●		●	Shanks Abstract and Title Co......................1786		●	●	●	●
		●		●	Southern Indiana Abstract & Title Co......................1829		●	●	●	●

		CV	CR	PR	CLAY		UC	RE	TX	VR
		●		●	Hendrich Abstract Co Inc......................952		●	●	●	●
		●	●	●	Indiana Title Co 1025		●	●	●	●
		●	●	●	Moomaw Abstract Corp......................1380		●	●	●	

		CV	CR	PR	CLINTON		UC	RE	TX	VR
		●	●	●	Tippecanoe Title Services Inc......................1950		●	●	●	

		CV	CR	PR	CRAWFORD		UC	RE	TX	VR
		●	●	●	Indiana Title Co 1025		●	●	●	●
		●		●	Shanks Abstract and Title Co......................1786		●	●	●	●

		CV	CR	PR	DAVIESS		UC	RE	TX	VR
		●	●	●	Indiana Title Co 1025		●	●	●	●
		●		●	James F Havill Attorney at Law PC......................1076		●	●	●	●
		●	●	●	Moomaw Abstract Corp......................1380		●	●	●	

		CV	CR	PR	**DEARBORN**	UC	RE	TX	VR
		●	●	●	Indiana Title Co 1025	●	●	●	●

		CV	CR	PR	**DECATUR**	UC	RE	TX	VR
		●	●	●	Indiana Title Co 1025	●	●	●	●
		●		●	King's Title & Abstract Co....................................1124	●	●	●	●

		CV	CR	PR	**DeKALB**	UC	RE	TX	VR
		●	●	●	TWT Title..1899	●	●	●	

		CV	CR	PR	**DELAWARE**	UC	RE	TX	VR
		●		●	King's Title & Abstract Co....................................1124	●	●	●	●

		CV	CR	PR	**DUBOIS**	UC	RE	TX	VR
		●	●	●	Indiana Title Co 1025	●	●	●	●

		CV	CR	PR	**ELKHART**	UC	RE	TX	VR
		●	●	●	Elkhart County Abstract Co 700	●	●	●	●
		●	●	●	Holley, Mickey..982	●	●	●	●
		●	●	●	J-C Investigations..1069	●	●	●	●
		●	●	●	Main Street Title Corp 1270	●	●	●	●
		●	●	●	Security Consulting Svc of South Bend....................1771	●	●	●	●

		CV	CR	PR	**FAYETTE**	UC	RE	TX	VR
		●	●	●	Carl Watson & Associates..406	●	●	●	●
		●	●	●	Indiana Title Co 1025	●	●	●	●
		●		●	King's Title & Abstract Co....................................1124	●	●	●	●

DT	BK	CV	CR	PR	**FLOYD**	UC	RE	TX	VR
●	●	●	●	●	Eagle Investigations Inc 673	●	●	●	●
		●	●	●	Indiana Title Co 1025	●	●	●	●
●	●	●	●	●	Sam Steele Investigations......................................1730	●	●	●	●
		●		●	Shanks Abstract and Title Co..................................1786	●	●	●	●
	●	●		●	Southern Indiana Abstract & Title Co.....................1829	●	●	●	●

		CV	CR	PR	**FOUNTAIN**	UC	RE	TX	VR
		●		●	Massey Abstract and Real Estate.............................1294	●	●	●	
		●	●	●	Tippecanoe Title Services Inc 1950	●	●	●	

		CV	CR	PR	**FRANKLIN**	UC	RE	TX	VR
		●	●	●	Indiana Title Co 1025	●	●	●	●
		●		●	King's Title & Abstract Co....................................1124	●	●		●

		CV	CR	PR	**FULTON**	UC	RE	TX	VR
		●	●	●	Deamer & Deamer..612	●	●	●	●
		●	●	●	Gundrum Realty Inc...901	●	●	●	●
		●	●	●	Holley, Mickey..982	●	●	●	●

		CV	CR	PR	**GIBSON**	UC	RE	TX	VR
		●	●	●	Druley, Ray M...663	●	●	●	●
		●	●	●	Indiana Title Co 1025	●	●	●	●

		CV	CR	PR	**GRANT**	UC	RE	TX	VR
		●	●	●	Corant County Abstract Co......................................520	●	●	●	

		CV	CR	PR	**GREENE**	UC	RE	TX	VR
		●	●	●	Indiana Title Co 1025	●	●	●	●
		●	●	●	Moomaw Abstract Corp 1380	●	●	●	
		●	●	●	Trace Investigations 1972	●	●	●	●

		CV	CR	PR	**HAMILTON**	UC	RE	TX	VR
		●	●	●	Central Indiana Paralegal Service Inc 424	●		●	
		●	●	●	International Investigators Inc...............................1038	●	●	●	●

CV	CR	PR	HANCOCK		UC	RE	TX	VR
•	•	•	Hancock County Abstract Co Inc 914		•	•	•	•
•	•	•	Indiana Title Co 1025		•	•	•	•
•	•	•	International Investigators Inc 1038		•	•	•	•

CV	CR	PR	HARRISON		UC	RE	TX	VR
•	•	•	Indiana Title Co 1025		•	•	•	•
•		•	Shanks Abstract and Title Co 1786		•	•	•	•
•		•	Southern Indiana Abstract & Title Co 1829		•	•	•	•

CV	CR	PR	HENDRICKS		UC	RE	TX	VR
•			Boone County Abstract Co 324		•	•	•	•
•	•	•	Central Indiana Paralegal Service Inc 424		•			
•	•	•	Indiana Title Co 1025		•	•	•	•
•	•	•	International Investigators Inc 1038		•	•	•	•

CV	CR	PR	HENRY		UC	RE	TX	VR
•		•	Henry County Abstract Co 954		•	•	•	
•	•	•	Indiana Title Co 1025		•	•	•	•
•		•	King's Title & Abstract Co 1124		•	•	•	•

CV	CR	PR	HOWARD		UC	RE	TX	VR
•		•	Anderson Land Title Co 148		•	•	•	•

CV	CR	PR	HUNTINGTON		UC	RE	TX	VR
•	•	•	Jones Abstract & Title Co Inc 1100		•	•	•	
•		•	Three Rivers Title Co 1947		•	•	•	•

CV	CR	PR	JACKSON		UC	RE	TX	VR
•	•	•	Indiana Title Co 1025		•	•	•	•
•	•	•	Nierman & Nierman Law Office 1427		•			
•		•	Shanks Abstract and Title Co 1786		•	•	•	•

CV	CR	PR	JASPER		UC	RE	TX	VR
•	•	•	Holley, Mickey 982		•	•	•	•
•	•	•	Jasper County Abstract Company 1079		•	•	•	
•	•	•	Tippecanoe Title Services Inc 1950		•	•	•	

CV	CR	PR	JAY		UC	RE	TX	VR
•		•	Jay County Abstract Company Inc 1080		•	•	•	•
•		•	Jay Portland Abstract Inc Co 1081		•	•	•	•
•		•	King's Title & Abstract Co 1124		•	•	•	•
•	•	•	Tri-County Land Title 1980		•	•	•	•

CV	CR	PR	JEFFERSON		UC	RE	TX	VR
•	•	•	Indiana Title Co 1025		•	•	•	•

CV	CR	PR	JENNINGS		UC	RE	TX	VR
•	•	•	Indiana Title Co 1025		•	•	•	•
•		•	North Vernon Abstract Co Inc 1439		•	•	•	

CV	CR	PR	JOHNSON		UC	RE	TX	VR
•	•	•	Central Indiana Paralegal Service Inc 424		•		•	
•	•	•	Indiana Title Co 1025		•	•	•	•
•	•	•	International Investigators Inc 1038		•	•	•	•
•	•	•	Trace Investigations 1972		•	•		•

CV	CR	PR	KNOX		UC	RE	TX	VR
•	•	•	Indiana Title Co 1025		•	•	•	•
•	•	•	L Fay Hedden Abstract Office Inc 1141		•	•	•	•

CV	CR	PR	KOSCIUSKO		UC	RE	TX	VR
•	•	•	Bodkin Abstract Company Inc 314		•	•	•	•

DT	BK	CV	CR	PR		UC	RE	TX	VR
		•	•	•	Holley, Mickey 982	•	•	•	•
		CV	**CR**	**PR**	**LAGRANGE**	**UC**	**RE**	**TX**	**VR**
		•	•	•	Holley, Mickey 982	•	•	•	•
		•	•	•	J-C Investigations 1069	•	•	•	•
		•	•	•	LaGrange Title Company 1147	•	•	•	
		•	•	•	TWT Title 1899	•	•		
DT	**BK**	**CV**	**CR**	**PR**	**LAKE**	**UC**	**RE**	**TX**	**VR**
		•	•	•	Elkhart County Abstract Co 700	•	•	•	•
		CV	**CR**	**PR**	**LA PORTE**	**UC**	**RE**	**TX**	**VR**
		•	•	•	Holley, Mickey 982	•	•	•	•
		•	•	•	J-C Investigations 1069	•	•	•	•
		CV	**CR**	**PR**	**LAWRENCE**	**UC**	**RE**	**TX**	**VR**
		•	•	•	Indiana Title Co 1025	•	•	•	•
		•		•	Shanks Abstract and Title Co 1786	•	•	•	•
		•	•	•	Trace Investigations 1972	•	•	•	•
		CV	**CR**	**PR**	**MADISON**	**UC**	**RE**	**TX**	**VR**
				•	King's Title & Abstract Co 1124	•	•	•	•
DT	**BK**	**CV**	**CR**	**PR**	**MARION**	**UC**	**RE**	**TX**	**VR**
•	•	•	•	•	Central Indiana Paralegal Service Inc 424	•		•	
•	•	•	•	•	International Investigators Inc 1038	•	•	•	•
•	•	•	•	•	Trace Investigations 1972	•	•	•	•
		CV	**CR**	**PR**	**MARSHALL**	**UC**	**RE**	**TX**	**VR**
		•	•	•	Gundrum Realty Inc 901	•	•	•	•
		•	•	•	Holley, Mickey 982	•	•	•	•
		•			McKesson Title Corp 1315	•	•	•	•
		•	•	•	Oressner & Company Inc 1478	•	•		
			•		Terry Investigations Inc 1910				
		CV	**CR**	**PR**	**MARTIN**	**UC**	**RE**	**TX**	**VR**
		•	•	•	Indiana Title Co 1025	•	•	•	•
		CV	**CR**	**PR**	**MIAMI**	**UC**	**RE**	**TX**	**VR**
		•	•	•	Gundrum Realty Inc 901	•	•	•	•
		•			Wabash Valley Abstract Co Inc 2040	•	•	•	
		CV	**CR**	**PR**	**MONROE**	**UC**	**RE**	**TX**	**VR**
		•	•	•	Bloomington Abstract Co 312	•	•	•	•
		•	•	•	Indiana Title Co 1025	•	•	•	•
		•	•	•	Trace Investigations 1972	•	•	•	•
		CV	**CR**	**PR**	**MONTGOMERY**	**UC**	**RE**	**TX**	**VR**
		•			Boone County Abstract Co 324	•	•	•	•
		•	•	•	Tippecanoe Title Services Inc 1950	•	•	•	
		CV	**CR**	**PR**	**MORGAN**	**UC**	**RE**	**TX**	**VR**
		•			Boone County Abstract Co 324	•	•	•	•
		•	•	•	Central Indiana Paralegal Service Inc 424	•		•	
		•	•	•	Indiana Title Co 1025	•	•	•	
		•	•	•	Trace Investigations 1972	•	•	•	•
		CV	**CR**	**PR**	**NEWTON**	**UC**	**RE**	**TX**	**VR**
		•	•	•	Holley, Mickey 982	•	•	•	•
		CV	**CR**	**PR**	**NOBLE**	**UC**	**RE**	**TX**	**VR**
		•	•	•	Bodkin Abstract Company Inc 314	•	•	•	•
		•	•	•	TWT Title 1899	•	•	•	•
		•		•	Three Rivers Title Co 1947	•	•	•	•

DT	BK	CV	CR	PR	**OHIO**		UC	RE	TX	VR
		•	•	•	Indiana Title Co 1025		•	•	•	•

DT	BK	CV	CR	PR	**ORANGE**		UC	RE	TX	VR
		•	•	•	Indiana Title Co 1025		•	•	•	•
		•		•	Orange County Abstract and Title Co Inc 1475		•	•	•	•
		•		•	Shanks Abstract and Title Co 1786		•	•	•	•

DT	BK	CV	CR	PR	**OWEN**		UC	RE	TX	VR
		•			Boone County Abstract Co 324		•	•	•	•
		•	•	•	Indiana Title Co 1025		•	•	•	•
		•	•	•	Trace Investigations 1972		•	•	•	•

DT	BK	CV	CR	PR	**PARKE**		UC	RE	TX	VR
					See ALL COUNTIES...............					

DT	BK	CV	CR	PR	**PERRY**		UC	RE	TX	VR
		•	•	•	Indiana Title Co 1025		•	•	•	•

DT	BK	CV	CR	PR	**PIKE**		UC	RE	TX	VR
		•	•	•	Indiana Title Co 1025		•	•	•	•

DT	BK	CV	CR	PR	**PORTER**		UC	RE	TX	VR
		•	•	•	Holley, Mickey 982		•	•	•	•

DT	BK	CV	CR	PR	**POSEY**		UC	RE	TX	VR
		•	•	•	Indiana Title Co 1025		•	•	•	•

DT	BK	CV	CR	PR	**PULASKI**		UC	RE	TX	VR
		•	•	•	Holley, Mickey 982		•	•	•	•
		•	•	•	Shurn, Michael A 1799		•	•	•	•

DT	BK	CV	CR	PR	**PUTNAM**		UC	RE	TX	VR
		•			Boone County Abstract Co 324		•	•	•	•
		•	•	•	Indiana Title Co 1025		•	•	•	•

DT	BK	CV	CR	PR	**RANDOLPH**		UC	RE	TX	VR
		•		•	King's Title & Abstract Co 1124		•	•	•	•

DT	BK	CV	CR	PR	**RIPLEY**		UC	RE	TX	VR
		•	•	•	Indiana Title Co 1025		•	•	•	•

DT	BK	CV	CR	PR	**RUSH**		UC	RE	TX	VR
		•	•	•	Indiana Title Co 1025		•	•	•	•
		•		•	King's Title & Abstract Co 1124		•	•	•	•

DT	BK	CV	CR	PR	**ST. JOSEPH**		UC	RE	TX	VR
		•	•	•	Holley, Mickey 982		•	•	•	•
•	•	•	•	•	J-C Investigations 1069			•	•	•
•	•	•	•	•	Security Consulting Svc of South Bend 1771			•	•	•
•	•	•		•	Terry Investigations Inc 1910			•	•	•

DT	BK	CV	CR	PR	**SCOTT**		UC	RE	TX	VR
		•	•	•	Indiana Title Co 1025		•	•	•	•
		•		•	Shanks Abstract and Title Co 1786		•	•	•	•

DT	BK	CV	CR	PR	**SHELBY**		UC	RE	TX	VR
		•	•	•	Carl Watson & Associates 406		•	•	•	
		•	•	•	Central Indiana Paralegal Service Inc 424		•		•	
		•	•	•	Indiana Title Co 1025		•	•	•	•
		•	•	•	International Investigators Inc 1038		•	•	•	
		•		•	King's Title & Abstract Co 1124		•	•	•	•

Court Records					County Records			
	CV	CR	PR	SPENCER	UC	RE	TX	VR
	•	•	•	Indiana Title Co 1025	•	•	•	•
	•	•	•	Wetherill, Richard 2084	•	•	•	•
	CV	CR	PR	STARKE	UC	RE	TX	VR
	•	•	•	Holley, Mickey 982	•	•	•	•
	•	•	•	Starke County Abstract Title & Guaranty 1852	•	•	•	•
	CV	CR	PR	STEUBEN	UC	RE	TX	VR
	•	•	•	Holley, Mickey 982	•	•	•	•
	•	•	•	Indiana Title Co 1025	•	•	•	•
	•	•	•	TWT Title 1899	•	•	•	
	•	•	•	Tippecanoe Title Services Inc 1950	•	•	•	
	CV	CR	PR	SULLIVAN	UC	RE	TX	VR
	•	•	•	Moomaw Abstract Corp 1380	•	•	•	
	•	•	•	Sullivan County Abstract Inc 1880	•	•	•	
	CV	CR	PR	SWITZERLAND	UC	RE	TX	VR
	•	•	•	Indiana Title Co 1025	•	•	•	•
DT	CV	CR	PR	TIPPECANOE	UC	RE	TX	VR
				See ALL COUNTIES				
	CV	CR	PR	TIPTON	UC	RE	TX	VR
	•	•	•	Carl Watson & Associates 406	•	•	•	•
	CV	CR	PR	UNION	UC	RE	TX	VR
	•	•	•	Indiana Title Co 1025	•	•	•	•
DT BK	CV	CR	PR	VANDERBURGH	UC	RE	TX	VR
	•	•	•	Indiana Title Co 1025	•	•	•	•
	CV	CR	PR	VERMILLION	UC	RE	TX	VR
	•		•	Massey Abstract and Real Estate 1294	•	•	•	
	•	•	•	Swayze Abstract 1896	•	•	•	
DT BK	CV	CR	PR	VIGO	UC	RE	TX	VR
	•		•	Hendrich Abstract Co Inc 952	•	•	•	•
	•	•	•	Indiana Title Co 1025	•	•	•	•
	CV	CR	PR	WABASH	UC	RE	TX	VR
	•		•	Three Rivers Title Co 1947	•	•	•	•
	CV	CR	PR	WARREN	UC	RE	TX	VR
	•	•	•	Held Abstract Co Inc 949	•	•	•	
	•		•	Massey Abstract and Real Estate 1294	•	•	•	
	•	•	•	Tippecanoe Title Services Inc 1950	•	•	•	
	CV	CR	PR	WARRICK	UC	RE	TX	VR
	•	•	•	Indiana Title Co 1025	•	•	•	•
	CV	CR	PR	WASHINGTON	UC	RE	TX	VR
	•	•	•	Indiana Title Co 1025	•	•	•	•
	•		•	Shanks Abstract and Title Co 1786	•	•	•	•
	CV	CR	PR	WAYNE	UC	RE	TX	VR
	•	•	•	Indiana Title Co 1025	•	•	•	•
	•		•	King's Title & Abstract Co 1124	•	•	•	•
	CV	CR	PR	WELLS	UC	RE	TX	VR
	•		•	Three Rivers Title Co 1947	•	•	•	•
	•	•	•	Tri-County Land Title 1980	•	•	•	•

CV	CR	PR	WHITE		UC	RE	TX	VR
●	●	●	Tippecanoe Title Services Inc 1950		●	●	●	

CV	CR	PR	WHITLEY		UC	RE	TX	VR
●	●	●	Gates Land Title Corp......................836		●	●	●	●
●		●	Three Rivers Title Co......................1947		●	●	●	●

SUMMARY OF CODES

COURT RECORDS

CODE*	GOVERNMENT AGENCY	TYPE OF INFORMATION
DT	US District Court	Federal civil and criminal cases
BK	Bankruptcy Court	United States bankruptcy cases
CV	Civil Court	Municipal, county and state level civil cases
CR	Criminal Court	Municipal, county and state level criminal cases
PR	Probate Court	Wills and estate cases

COUNTY RECORDS

CODE*	GOVERNMENT AGENCY	TYPE OF INFORMATION
UC	UCC Filing Office	Uniform Commercial Code and other personal property liens
RE	Recorder of Deeds	Real property transactions and liens
TX	Tax Assessor	Real property tax information
VR	Vital Records Office	Birth, death, marriage, divorce, etc.

*The "CODE" designates the agency and type of information obtainable in each county.

Iowa

DT	BK	CV	CR	PR	ALL COUNTIES		UC	RE	TX	VR
●	●	●	●	●	Search Network 1758		●	●	●	●

		CV	CR	PR	ADAIR		UC	RE	TX	VR
		●	●	●	Adair County Abstract.................................76		●	●	●	
		●	●	●	Thomas, Donna 1944				●	●
		●	●	●	Williamson Abstract Co 2096		●	●	●	

		CV	CR	PR	ADAMS		UC	RE	TX	VR
		●	●	●	Thomas, Donna 1944				●	●

		CV	CR	PR	ALLAMAKEE		UC	RE	TX	VR
		●	●	●	Palmer Abstract Inc 1505		●	●	●	●

		CV	CR	PR	APPANOOSE		UC	RE	TX	VR
		●	●	●	Drake, Wilson and Jay.................................661		●	●	●	●

		CV	CR	PR	AUDUBON		UC	RE	TX	VR
		●	●	●	Thomas, Donna 1944				●	●

		CV	CR	PR	BENTON		UC	RE	TX	VR
		●	●	●	Benton County Title Co 284		●	●	●	●
		●	●	●	Starr Investigations & Security 1853		●	●	●	●

		CV	CR	PR	BLACK HAWK		UC	RE	TX	VR
		●	●	●	Black Hawk Abstract Co..............................305		●	●	●	●
		●	●	●	Prins, Bob...1602		●	●	●	●
		●	●	●	Starr Investigations & Security 1853		●	●	●	●

		CV	CR	PR	BOONE		UC	RE	TX	VR
		●	●	●	Boone County Abstract Co 323		●	●	●	●

		CV	CR	PR	BREMER		UC	RE	TX	VR
		●	●	●	Bremer County Abstract Co.........................341		●	●	●	●

		CV	CR	PR	BUCHANAN		UC	RE	TX	VR
		●	●	●	Gary Pratt Investigations............................835		●	●	●	●

		CV	CR	PR	BUENA VISTA		UC	RE	TX	VR
		●	●	●	Fritcher Abstract Co 817		●	●	●	●

		CV	CR	PR	BUTLER		UC	RE	TX	VR
		●	●	●	Gary Pratt Investigations............................835		●	●	●	●

		CV	CR	PR	CALHOUN		UC	RE	TX	VR
					See ALL COUNTIES.......................................					

		CV	CR	PR	CARROLL		UC	RE	TX	VR
		●	●	●	Thomas, Donna 1944				●	●

		CV	CR	PR	CASS		UC	RE	TX	VR
		●	●	●	Cass County Abstract Co 413		●	●	●	●
		●	●	●	Thomas, Donna 1944				●	●

		CV	CR	PR	CEDAR		UC	RE	TX	VR
		●	●	●	Land Title Corp..1164		●	●	●	●
					Miller, Joan 1356		●	●	●	●
		●	●	●	Starr Investigations & Security 1853		●	●	●	●

		CV	CR	PR	CERRO GORDO		UC	RE	TX	VR
		●	●	●	Cerro Gordo Abstract Co 431		●	●	●	●

CV	CR	PR	CHEROKEE	UC	RE	TX	VR
●	●	●	First Abstract and Loan Co 766	●	●	●	
●	●	●	Intra-Lex Investigations Inc 1043	●	●	●	●

CV	CR	PR	CHICKASAW	UC	RE	TX	VR
●	●	●	G T Murphy Abstractor........................824	●	●	●	●
●	●	●	Gary Pratt Investigations 835	●	●	●	●

CV	CR	PR	CLARKE	UC	RE	TX	VR
●	●	●	Banta Abstract Co 242	●	●	●	●

CV	CR	PR	CLAY	UC	RE	TX	VR
●	●		Fransen, Barbara 806				
●	●	●	Security Land Title Co 1776	●	●	●	

CV	CR	PR	CLAYTON	UC	RE	TX	VR
●	●	●	Clayton County Abstract Co 470	●	●	●	●

CV	CR	PR	CLINTON	UC	RE	TX	VR
●		●	Abstract & Title Guaranty Co 45	●	●	●	●
			Miller, Joan 1356	●	●	●	●

CV	CR	PR	CRAWFORD	UC	RE	TX	VR
●		●	Crawford County Abstract Co........................554		●	●	●
●	●	●	Thomas, Donna 1944			●	●

CV	CR	PR	DALLAS	UC	RE	TX	VR
●	●	●	J R Investigations.....................................1067	●	●	●	●

CV	CR	PR	DAVIS	UC	RE	TX	VR
●	●	●	Ball Abstracting 238		●	●	●

CV	CR	PR	DECATUR	UC	RE	TX	VR
●	●	●	Elson & Fulton Abstractors..............................710	●	●	●	●

CV	CR	PR	DELAWARE	UC	RE	TX	VR
●	●	●	Delaware County Abstract Co..........................618	●	●	●	●

CV	CR	PR	DES MOINES	UC	RE	TX	VR
●	●	●	American Investigation Agency 133	●	●	●	●
●	●	●	Pohlpeter, Marilyn 1563	●	●	●	●

CV	CR	PR	DICKINSON	UC	RE	TX	VR
●	●	●	Cornell Abstract Co..522	●	●	●	●
●	●	●	Intra-Lex Investigations Inc 1043	●	●	●	●

CV	CR	PR	DUBUQUE	UC	RE	TX	VR
●		●	Abelin Abstract Co..40	●	●	●	●

CV	CR	PR	EMMET	UC	RE	TX	VR
●	●	●	Estherville Abstract Co 716	●	●	●	●

CV	CR	PR	FAYETTE	UC	RE	TX	VR
●	●	●	Gary Pratt Investigations.....................................835	●	●	●	●

CV	CR	PR	FLOYD	UC	RE	TX	VR
●	●	●	Iowa Title & Realty Co 1054	●	●	●	●

CV	CR	PR	FRANKLIN	UC	RE	TX	VR
●	●	●	Franklin County Abstract Co 804	●	●	●	●

CV	CR	PR	FREMONT	UC	RE	TX	VR
●	●	●	Thomas, Donna..1944			●	●

CV	CR	PR	GREENE		UC	RE	TX	VR
●	●	●	Greene County Abstract Company Inc............874		●	●	●	●

CV	CR	PR	GRUNDY		UC	RE	TX	VR
●	●	●	Community Title Co............507		●	●	●	●

CV	CR	PR	GUTHRIE		UC	RE	TX	VR
●	●	●	Guthrie County Abstract............902		●	●	●	●

CV	CR	PR	HAMILTON		UC	RE	TX	VR
●	●	●	Dingman, Nadine............633		●	●	●	●
●	●	●	Neuroth, Tim............1419		●	●	●	●

CV	CR	PR	HANCOCK		UC	RE	TX	VR
●	●	●	Hancock County Abstract Co............913		●	●	●	

CV	CR	PR	HARDIN		UC	RE	TX	VR
●	●	●	Harding County Abstract and Title............925		●	●	●	●
●	●	●	Munsigner, Maxine............1398		●	●	●	●

CV	CR	PR	HARRISON		UC	RE	TX	VR
		●	Harrison County Title and Guaranty............931		●		●	
●	●	●	Thomas, Donna............1944					●

CV	CR	PR	HENRY		UC	RE	TX	VR
●	●	●	Henry County Abstract Co............953		●	●	●	●

CV	CR	PR	HOWARD		UC	RE	TX	VR
●	●	●	Howard County Abstract & Title Co............998		●	●	●	●

CV	CR	PR	HUMBOLDT		UC	RE	TX	VR
●	●	●	Snyder, Ed............1816		●	●	●	●

CV	CR	PR	IDA		UC	RE	TX	VR
●	●	●	Ida County Abstract Co............1018		●	●	●	●

CV	CR	PR	IOWA		UC	RE	TX	VR
●	●	●	Greene County Abstract Company Inc............874		●	●	●	●
●	●	●	Iowa County Abstract Company............1052		●	●	●	
●	●	●	Starr Investigations & Security............1853		●	●		●
●	●	●	Thomas, Donna............1944					●

CV	CR	PR	JACKSON		UC	RE	TX	VR
●	●	●	Iowa Title & Guaranty Co............1053		●	●	●	●

CV	CR	PR	JASPER		UC	RE	TX	VR
●	●	●	J R Investigations............1067		●	●	●	●

CV	CR	PR	JEFFERSON		UC	RE	TX	VR
●	●	●	Jefferson County Abstract & Land Titles............1085		●	●	●	

CV	CR	PR	JOHNSON		UC	RE	TX	VR
			Miller, Joan............1356		●	●	●	●
●	●	●	Reliance Title Services............1677		●	●	●	●
●	●	●	Starr Investigations & Security............1853		●	●	●	●

CV	CR	PR	JONES		UC	RE	TX	VR
●	●	●	McCarn Abstract Co............1301		●	●	●	●
●	●	●	Starr Investigations & Security............1853		●	●	●	●

CV	CR	PR	KEOKUK		UC	RE	TX	VR
●	●	●	Daniels, Mabel............589		●	●	●	●
●	●	●	J R Investigations............1067		●	●	●	●

		CV	CR	PR	KOSSUTH	UC	RE	TX	VR
		●	●	●	Buchanan Abstract Co............................361		●	●	

		CV	CR	PR	LEE	UC	RE	TX	VR
		●		●	American Abstract and Title Gty Corp............128	●	●	●	●
		●	●	●	Johnson, Edith F.............................1095	●	●	●	●

DT	BK	CV	CR	PR	LINN	UC	RE	TX	VR
●	●	●	●	●	Starr Investigations & Security 1853	●	●	●	●
		●	●	●	United Title Services Inc......................2010	●	●	●	●

		CV	CR	PR	LOUISA	UC	RE	TX	VR
		●	●	●	Street, Kieth 1874		●		●

		CV	CR	PR	LUCAS	UC	RE	TX	VR
		●	●	●	Chariton Abstract Co...........................437	●	●	●	●

		CV	CR	PR	LYON	UC	RE	TX	VR
		●	●	●	Dirks, Lewis..................................635	●	●	●	●
		●	●	●	Lynn County Title............................1250	●	●	●	●

		CV	CR	PR	MADISON	UC	RE	TX	VR
		●	●	●	Security Abstract and Title Inc................1769	●	●	●	●

		CV	CR	PR	MAHASKA	UC	RE	TX	VR
		●	●	●	Daniels, Mabel 589	●	●	●	●
		●	●	●	J R Investigations............................1067	●	●	●	●
		●	●	●	Mahaska Title - Johnson Abstract Co 1267	●	●	●	●

		CV	CR	PR	MARION	UC	RE	TX	VR
		●	●	●	Marion County Abstract Co......................1279	●	●	●	

		CV	CR	PR	MARSHALL	UC	RE	TX	VR
		●	●	●	Bair, Bob.....................................235	●	●	●	●
		●	●	●	Marshall County Abstract Company...............1285	●	●	●	●

		CV	CR	PR	MILLS	UC	RE	TX	VR
		●	●	●	Thomas, Donna.................................1944			●	●

		CV	CR	PR	MITCHELL	UC	RE	TX	VR
		●	●	●	Mitchell County Abstract Co 1361	●	●	●	●

		CV	CR	PR	MONONA	UC	RE	TX	VR
		●	●	●	Cutler, Sue...................................575	●	●	●	●
		●		●	Harder, Mary K 922		●		●
		●	●	●	Intra-Lex Investigations Inc 1043	●	●	●	●
		●	●	●	Johnson, Janice I 1096			●	●
		●	●	●	Thomas, Donna.................................1944			●	●

		CV	CR	PR	MONROE	UC	RE	TX	VR
		●	●	●	Graham Abstract Co............................857	●	●	●	●

		CV	CR	PR	MONTGOMERY	UC	RE	TX	VR
		●	●	●	Thomas, Donna.................................1944			●	●

		CV	CR	PR	MUSCATINE	UC	RE	TX	VR
		●	●	●	Legal Abstract Co.............................1192	●	●	●	●
					Miller, Joan 1356	●	●	●	●

		CV	CR	PR	O'BRIEN	UC	RE	TX	VR
					See ALL COUNTIES..............................				

		CV	CR	PR	OSCEOLA	UC	RE	TX	VR
		●	●	●	Dirks, Lewis..................................635	●	●	●	●
		●	●	●	The Title Co Inc..............................1943	●	●	●	●

DT	BK	CV	CR	PR		UC	RE	TX	VR
					PAGE				
		•	•	•	Page County Abstract and Title Company 1499	•	•	•	
		•	•	•	Thomas, Donna 1944			•	•
					PALO ALTO				
		•	•	•	Palo Alto County Abstract Co 1509	•	•	•	•
					PLYMOUTH				
		•	•	•	Intra-Lex Investigations Inc 1043	•	•	•	•
				•	Plymouth County Abstract 1561	•	•	•	
					POCAHONTAS				
		•	•	•	Peduska, Paul 1528	•	•	•	•
					POLK				
•	•	•	•	•	J R Investigations 1067	•	•	•	•
•	•	•	•	•	Process Associates 1609	•	•	•	•
					POTTAWATTAMIE				
•		•	•	•	Thomas, Donna 1944			•	•
					POWESHIEK				
			•		Pittman, Julie 1557		•	•	
					RINGGOLD				
		•	•	•	Ringgold County Abstract Co 1699	•	•	•	•
					SAC				
		•	•	•	Sac County Abstract Co 1727	•	•	•	•
					SCOTT				
		•	•	•	Bettendorf Abstract Co 294		•	•	•
•		•	•	•	J M White Investigations 1065	•	•	•	•
		•	•	•	Miller, Joan 1356	•	•	•	•
					SHELBY				
		•	•	•	Ouren Title Inc 1483	•	•	•	
		•	•	•	Thomas, Donna 1944			•	•
					SIOUX				
		•	•	•	Dirks, Lewis 635	•	•	•	•
		•	•	•	Intra-Lex Investigations Inc 1043	•	•	•	•
					STORY				
		•	•	•	Batman-Sayers Abstract & Title Co 258	•	•	•	•
		•	•	•	J R Investigations 1067	•	•	•	•
					TAMA				
		•	•	•	Tama County Abstract 1901	•	•	•	•
					TAYLOR				
		•	•	•	Parks, June 1521	•	•	•	•
		•	•	•	Thomas, Donna 1944			•	•
					UNION				
		•	•	•	Thomas, Donna 1944			•	•
					VAN BUREN				
		•	•	•	Van Buren Abstract Co 2022	•	•	•	•
					WAPELLO				
		•	•	•	Box & Box 334	•	•	•	•
					WARREN				
		•	•	•	J R Investigations 1067	•	•	•	•

DT	CV	CR	PR		UC	RE	TX	VR
	•	•	•	Warren County Abstract Company 2054	•	•	•	•
	CV	**CR**	**PR**	**WASHINGTON**	**UC**	**RE**	**TX**	**VR**
	•	•	•	Day Abstract Co 607	•	•	•	•
	CV	**CR**	**PR**	**WAYNE**	**UC**	**RE**	**TX**	**VR**
	•	•	•	John H Rider Abstract & Real Estate 1092	•	•	•	
	CV	**CR**	**PR**	**WEBSTER**	**UC**	**RE**	**TX**	**VR**
			•	Webster County Records..2071	•	•		•
	•	•	•	Webster County-Butler & Rhodes Abstract....................2072	•	•	•	•
	CV	**CR**	**PR**	**WINNEBAGO**	**UC**	**RE**	**TX**	**VR**
	•	•	•	Winnebago County Abstract..2107	•	•	•	
	CV	**CR**	**PR**	**WINNESHIEK**	**UC**	**RE**	**TX**	**VR**
	•	•	•	Gary Pratt Investigations...835	•	•	•	•
DT	**CV**	**CR**	**PR**	**WOODBURY**	**UC**	**RE**	**TX**	**VR**
	•		•	Harder, Mary K 922		•		•
	•	•	•	Intra-Lex Investigations Inc 1043	•	•	•	•
	CV	**CR**	**PR**	**WORTH**	**UC**	**RE**	**TX**	**VR**
	•	•	•	Worth County Abstract Co Inc..2115		•	•	•
	CV	**CR**	**PR**	**WRIGHT**	**UC**	**RE**	**TX**	**VR**
	•	•	•	Wright County Land Title Co 2117	•	•	•	•

Kansas

DT	BK	CV	CR	PR	ALL COUNTIES	UC	RE	TX	VR
●	●	●	●	●	Search Network................................1758	●	●	●	●

		CV	CR	PR	ALLEN	UC	RE	TX	VR
					See ALL COUNTIES........................				

		CV	CR	PR	ANDERSON	UC	RE	TX	VR
		●	●		Anderson County Abstract Co 146	●	●	●	

		CV	CR	PR	ATCHISON	UC	RE	TX	VR
		●	●	●	Fred McDaniel and Associates.........................807	●	●	●	●
		●	●	●	Wilson Associates 2102	●	●	●	●

		CV	CR	PR	BARBER	UC	RE	TX	VR
		●		●	Slamal & Swayden Inc.................................1811	●	●	●	●

		CV	CR	PR	BARTON	UC	RE	TX	VR
		●		●	Barton County Abstract and Title Co..................255	●	●	●	
		●	●	●	Kansas Investigative Services Inc 1111	●	●	●	●

		CV	CR	PR	BOURBON	UC	RE	TX	VR
		●	●	●	Linn County Abstract Co 1230	●	●	●	

		CV	CR	PR	BROWN	UC	RE	TX	VR
		●	●	●	Brown County Title Co 352	●		●	

		CV	CR	PR	BUTLER	UC	RE	TX	VR
		●	●	●	Allen Abstract Co...112	●	●	●	●
		●	●	●	Kansas Investigative Services Inc 1111	●	●	●	●

		CV	CR	PR	CHASE	UC	RE	TX	VR
		●	●	●	Moon Abstract Co 1381	●	●	●	●

		CV	CR	PR	CHAUTAUQUA	UC	RE	TX	VR
		●	●	●	Chautauqua County Abstract Co 443	●	●	●	●

		CV	CR	PR	CHEROKEE	UC	RE	TX	VR
		●	●	●	Kunkel, Joan..1138	●	●	●	●
		●		●	Olson Abstract and Title Co..........................1466	●	●	●	●

		CV	CR	PR	CHEYENNE	UC	RE	TX	VR
		●	●	●	The R M Jaqua Abstract Co 1940	●	●	●	

		CV	CR	PR	CLARK	UC	RE	TX	VR
		●		●	Ashland Abstract & Title Co............................166	●	●	●	●
		●	●	●	Credit Bureau Services Inc.............................556	●	●	●	●

		CV	CR	PR	CLAY	UC	RE	TX	VR
		●	●	●	Attorney's Title Co 209	●	●	●	●
		●	●	●	Eric H Swenson Co Abstracters 713	●	●	●	●

		CV	CR	PR	CLOUD	UC	RE	TX	VR
		●	●	●	Attorney's Title Co 209	●	●	●	●

		CV	CR	PR	COFFEY	UC	RE	TX	VR
		●	●	●	Moon Abstract Co 1381	●	●	●	●
		●	●	●	Street Abstract Co 1873	●	●	●	●

		CV	CR	PR	COMANCHE	UC	RE	TX	VR
		●		●	Comanche Abstract and Title Co 501	●	●	●	

		CV	CR	PR	COWLEY	UC	RE	TX	VR
		●	●	●	Barbour Title Co 244	●	●	●	●

			Kansas Investigative Services Inc 1111				
•	•	•		•	•	•	•

CV	CR	PR	**CRAWFORD**	UC	RE	TX	VR
•	•	•	Kunkel, Joan...1138	•	•	•	•

CV	CR	PR	**DECATUR**	UC	RE	TX	VR
•	•	•	Farmers Loan and Abstract Co.............................742	•	•	•	
•	•	•	First Insurance Agency of Hoxie Inc....................773	•	•	•	

CV	CR	PR	**DICKINSON**	UC	RE	TX	VR
•		•	Wyatt Land Title Services Inc..............................2119	•	•	•	

CV	CR	PR	**DONIPHAN**	UC	RE	TX	VR
•	•	•	Guier Abstract & Title Co....................................899	•	•	•	•
•	•	•	Wilson Associates..2102	•	•	•	•

CV	CR	PR	**DOUGLAS**	UC	RE	TX	VR
•	•	•	Fred McDaniel and Associates.............................807	•	•	•	•
•	•	•	Mercury Messengers Inc 1329	•	•	•	•

CV	CR	PR	**EDWARDS**	UC	RE	TX	VR
•		•	Richardson Abstract Co Inc 1694	•	•	•	
			See ALL COUNTIES..				

CV	CR	PR	**ELK**	UC	RE	TX	VR
•	•	•	Elk County Abstract & Title Co............................699	•	•	•	•

CV	CR	PR	**ELLIS**	UC	RE	TX	VR
•	•	•	Ellis County Abstract & Title Co..........................708	•	•	•	•
•	•	•	Kansas Investigative Services Inc 1111	•	•	•	•

CV	CR	PR	**ELLSWORTH**	UC	RE	TX	VR
•	•	•	G & H Abstract 822	•	•	•	•
•	•	•	Kansas Investigative Services Inc 1111	•	•	•	•

CV	CR	PR	**FINNEY**	UC	RE	TX	VR
•		•	Campbell Abstract Inc..388	•	•	•	
•	•	•	Credit Bureau Services Inc...................................556	•	•	•	•

CV	CR	PR	**FORD**	UC	RE	TX	VR
•	•	•	Credit Bureau Services Inc...................................556	•	•	•	•
•	•	•	Gray County Abstract Co Inc................................867	•	•	•	
•	•	•	Kansas Investigative Services Inc 1111	•	•	•	•

CV	CR	PR	**FRANKLIN**	UC	RE	TX	VR
•	•	•	Haley Abstract & Title Co....................................907	•	•	•	•

CV	CR	PR	**GEARY**	UC	RE	TX	VR
			See ALL COUNTIES..				

CV	CR	PR	**GOVE**	UC	RE	TX	VR
•	•	•	First Insurance Agency of Hoxie Inc....................773	•	•	•	

CV	CR	PR	**GRAHAM**	UC	RE	TX	VR
•	•	•	First Insurance Agency of Hoxie Inc....................773	•	•	•	

CV	CR	PR	**GRANT**	UC	RE	TX	VR
•	•	•	American Title & Abstract Specialists 140	•	•	•	•
•	•	•	PC Fraze Abstract Co 1489	•	•	•	•

CV	CR	PR	**GRAY**	UC	RE	TX	VR
•	•	•	Credit Bureau Services Inc...................................556	•	•	•	•
•	•	•	Gray County Abstract Co Inc................................867	•	•	•	

CV	CR	PR		Page	UC	RE	TX	VR
			GREELEY					
•		•	Scott County Abstract and Title Co Inc	1751	•	•	•	
			GREENWOOD					
•	•	•	Moon Abstract Co	1381	•	•	•	•
			HAMILTON					
•	•	•	PC Fraze Abstract Co	1489	•	•	•	•
			HARPER					
•	•	•	Couch Abstract and Title Co	536	•	•	•	
			HARVEY					
•		•	Columbian National Title Ins of Wichita	498		•	•	•
•	•		Hutchinson Title Co	1010	•	•	•	•
•	•	•	Kansas Investigative Services Inc	1111	•	•	•	•
•		•	Regier Agency Inc	1672	•	•	•	•
			HASKELL					
•	•	•	Haskell County Abstract and Title	936	•	•	•	
			HODGEMAN					
•	•	•	Hodgeman County Abstract & Title	978	•	•	•	
			JACKSON					
•	•	•	Title Abstract Co	1951	•	•	•	
			JEFFERSON					
•	•	•	Finley Abstract & Title Co	764	•	•	•	•
			JEWELL					
•	•	•	Miller, Gail L	1355	•	•	•	
•		•	Weltmer Law Office	2077	•	•		•
			JOHNSON					
•	•	•	Executive Investigative Services	723		•	•	
•	•	•	Fred McDaniel and Associates	807	•	•	•	•
•	•	•	RSI	1643				
•	•	•	Silk Attorney Service	1804	•	•	•	•
			KEARNY					
•	•	•	PC Fraze Abstract Co	1489	•	•	•	•
			KINGMAN					
•		•	Kingman Abstract and Title Co Inc	1125	•	•	•	
			KIOWA					
•	•	•	Church & Grau	458	•	•	•	
			LABETTE					
•	•	•	Kunkel, Joan	1138	•	•	•	•
			LANE					
•	•	•	Credit Bureau Services Inc	556	•	•	•	•
•	•	•	Lane County Abstract Co Inc	1171	•	•	•	
•		•	Scott County Abstract and Title Co Inc	1751	•	•	•	
			LEAVENWORTH					
•	•	•	Fred McDaniel and Associates	807	•	•	•	•
•	•	•	G & H Abstract	822	•	•	•	•
•	•	•	Silk Attorney Service	1804	•	•	•	•
•	•	•	Wilson Associates	2102	•	•	•	•
			LINCOLN					
•	•	•	Crawford Abstract & Real Estate Co	551		•	•	

CV	CR	PR	LINN	UC	RE	TX	VR
•	•	•	Linn County Abstract Co 1230	•	•	•	

CV	CR	PR	LOGAN	UC	RE	TX	VR
•		•	Scott County Abstract and Title Co Inc 1751	•	•	•	
•	•	•	The Gordon Company of Colby............................1932	•	•	•	

CV	CR	PR	LYON	UC	RE	TX	VR
•	•	•	Greenwood Abstract Co 876	•	•	•	•

CV	CR	PR	McPHERSON	UC	RE	TX	VR
•	•		Hutchinson Title Co...1010	•	•	•	•
•		•	McPherson County Abstract 1319	•	•	•	

CV	CR	PR	MARION	UC	RE	TX	VR
•	•	•	Hannaford Abstract & Title Co 918	•	•	•	•

CV	CR	PR	MARSHALL	UC	RE	TX	VR
			See ALL COUNTIES..				

CV	CR	PR	MEADE	UC	RE	TX	VR
•	•	•	KOBS Abstracting..1110	•	•	•	•

CV	CR	PR	MIAMI	UC	RE	TX	VR
•	•	•	Fred McDaniel and Associates................................807	•	•	•	•
•	•	•	Winkler, Wendell D 2106	•	•	•	

CV	CR	PR	MITCHELL	UC	RE	TX	VR
			See ALL COUNTIES..				

CV	CR	PR	MONTGOMERY	UC	RE	TX	VR
			Montgomery County Abstract Co 1373	•	•	•	

CV	CR	PR	MORRIS	UC	RE	TX	VR
•	•	•	Moon Abstract Co 1381	•	•	•	•

CV	CR	PR	MORTON	UC	RE	TX	VR
•	•	•	Farmers & Lawyers Title Co.....................................741	•	•	•	•

CV	CR	PR	NEMAHA	UC	RE	TX	VR
•	•	•	Nemaha County Abstract Co...................................1417	•	•	•	•

CV	CR	PR	NEOSHO	UC	RE	TX	VR
•		•	Locke-Neosho Abstracts Inc 1234	•	•	•	

CV	CR	PR	NESS	UC	RE	TX	VR
•	•	•	Credit Bureau Services Inc.......................................556	•	•	•	•
•	•	•	Floyd & Floyd...789	•	•	•	•

CV	CR	PR	NORTON	UC	RE	TX	VR
•	•	•	Security Abstract Company.....................................1768	•	•	•	•

CV	CR	PR	OSAGE	UC	RE	TX	VR
•	•	•	Mercury Messengers Inc 1329	•	•	•	•
•	•	•	Moon Abstract Co 1381	•	•	•	•

CV	CR	PR	OSBORNE	UC	RE	TX	VR
•	•	•	Gregory Abstract and Title Co Inc............................880	•	•	•	•

CV	CR	PR	OTTAWA	UC	RE	TX	VR
•	•	•	Scheibeler's..1744	•	•	•	•

CV	CR	PR	PAWNEE	UC	RE	TX	VR
•		•	Taylor Abstract Co 1903	•	•	•	

		CV	CR	PR	PHILLIPS	UC	RE	TX	VR
		●	●	●	Keesee Abstracting Co 1116	●	●	●	●

		CV	CR	PR	POTTAWATOMIE	UC	RE	TX	VR
		●		●	Pottawatomie County Abstract Co 1574	●	●	●	●

		CV	CR	PR	PRATT	UC	RE	TX	VR
		●		●	Centennial Abstract of Pratt Inc 421		●	●	

		CV	CR	PR	RAWLINS	UC	RE	TX	VR
		●	●	●	Rawlings County Abstract and Title Co 1651	●	●	●	●

		CV	CR	PR	RENO	UC	RE	TX	VR
		●	●		Hutchinson Title Co 1010	●	●	●	●
		●	●	●	Kansas Investigative Services Inc 1111	●	●	●	●

		CV	CR	PR	REPUBLIC	UC	RE	TX	VR
		●	●	●	Attorney's Title Co 209	●	●	●	●

		CV	CR	PR	RICE	UC	RE	TX	VR
					See ALL COUNTIES......				

		CV	CR	PR	RILEY	UC	RE	TX	VR
		●		●	Charlson & Wilson Bonded Abstracters Inc 440	●	●	●	

		CV	CR	PR	ROOKS	UC	RE	TX	VR
		●	●	●	Ellis County Abstract & Title Co 708	●	●	●	●

		CV	CR	PR	RUSH	UC	RE	TX	VR
		●	●	●	American Title & Abstract Specialists 138	●	●	●	●

		CV	CR	PR	RUSSELL	UC	RE	TX	VR
		●	●	●	G & H Abstract 822	●	●	●	●
		●	●	●	Kansas Investigative Services Inc 1111	●	●	●	●

		CV	CR	PR	SALINE	UC	RE	TX	VR
		●		●	C W Lynn Abstract Co Inc 373				

		CV	CR	PR	SCOTT	UC	RE	TX	VR
		●	●	●	Credit Bureau Services Inc 556	●	●	●	●
		●		●	Scott County Abstract and Title Co Inc 1751	●	●	●	

DT	BK	CV	CR	PR	SEDGWICK	UC	RE	TX	VR
		●	●		Hutchinson Title Co 1010	●	●	●	●
●	●	●	●	●	Kansas Investigative Services Inc 1111	●	●	●	●

		CV	CR	PR	SEWARD	UC	RE	TX	VR
		●	●	●	American Title & Abstract Specialists 139	●	●	●	●
		●	●	●	Kansas Investigative Services Inc 1111	●	●	●	●

DT	BK	CV	CR	PR	SHAWNEE	UC	RE	TX	VR
		●	●	●	Comstock Search Reporting 511	●	●	●	
●	●	●	●	●	Fred McDaniel and Associates 807	●	●	●	
●	●	●	●	●	Mercury Messengers Inc 1329	●	●	●	
●	●	●	●	●	Search Network Ltd 1759	●	●	●	

		CV	CR	PR	SHERIDAN	UC	RE	TX	VR
		●	●	●	First Insurance Agency of Hoxie Inc 773	●	●	●	
		●	●	●	The Gordon Company of Colby 1932	●	●	●	

		CV	CR	PR	SHERMAN	UC	RE	TX	VR
		●		●	Teeters Abstract and Title Co 1908	●	●	●	
		●	●	●	The Gordon Company of Colby 1932	●	●	●	

CV	CR	PR	SMITH	UC	RE	TX	VR
•		•	Collier Abstracts Inc.............489	•	•	•	

CV	CR	PR	STAFFORD	UC	RE	TX	VR
•		•	Stafford County Abstract & Title Co Inc..........1849	•	•	•	•

CV	CR	PR	STANTON	UC	RE	TX	VR
•	•	•	Farmers & Lawyers Title Co.............741	•	•	•	•
•	•	•	PC Fraze Abstract Co.............1489	•	•	•	•
•	•	•	Tomson Abstract Co.............1966		•	•	•

CV	CR	PR	STEVENS	UC	RE	TX	VR
•	•	•	Farmers & Lawyers Title Co.............741	•	•	•	•
•	•	•	McQueen Abstract Company.............1321		•	•	

CV	CR	PR	SUMNER	UC	RE	TX	VR
•	•	•	Kansas Investigative Services Inc.............1111	•	•	•	•
•		•	Kansas Title Service.............1112	•	•	•	•

CV	CR	PR	THOMAS	UC	RE	TX	VR
•	•	•	First Insurance Agency of Hoxie Inc.............773	•	•	•	
•	•	•	The Gordon Company of Colby.............1932	•	•	•	

CV	CR	PR	TREGO	UC	RE	TX	VR
•		•	Fowler Abstract Co.............801	•	•	•	

CV	CR	PR	WABAUNSEE	UC	RE	TX	VR
•	•	•	Moon Abstract Co.............1381	•	•	•	•

CV	CR	PR	WALLACE	UC	RE	TX	VR
•		•	Teeters Abstract and Title Co.............1908	•	•	•	

CV	CR	PR	WASHINGTON	UC	RE	TX	VR
•	•	•	Attorney's Title Co.............209	•	•	•	•
•	•	•	Hyland Abstract Co.............1011	•	•	•	•

CV	CR	PR	WICHITA	UC	RE	TX	VR
•	•	•	Credit Bureau Services Inc.............556	•	•	•	•
•		•	Scott County Abstract and Title Co Inc.............1751	•	•	•	

CV	CR	PR	WILSON	UC	RE	TX	VR
•		•	Fink Abstract Co.............763	•	•	•	•

CV	CR	PR	WOODSON	UC	RE	TX	VR
•	•	•	Street Abstract Co.............1873	•	•	•	•

DT	BK	CV	CR	PR	WYANDOTTE	UC	RE	TX	VR
•	•	•	•	•	Executive Investigative Services.............723		•	•	
•	•	•	•	•	Fred McDaniel and Associates.............807	•	•	•	•
•	•	•	•	•	RSI.............1643				
•	•	•	•	•	Silk Attorney Service.............1804	•	•	•	•

Kentucky

DT	BK	CV	CR	PR	ALL COUNTIES	UC	RE	TX	VR
●	●	●	●	●	Equisearch Company...........712	●	●	●	●
	●	●	●	●	National Service Information Inc...........1410	●		●	●

		CV	CR	PR	ADAIR	UC	RE	TX	VR
		●	●	●	Harvey, Gayle...........934				●

		CV	CR	PR	ALLEN	UC	RE	TX	VR
		●	●	●	Hollingsworth Court Reporting Inc...........983	●	●	●	●

		CV	CR	PR	ANDERSON	UC	RE	TX	VR
					Holman, Beverly Gail...........984		●		

		CV	CR	PR	BALLARD	UC	RE	TX	VR
		●	●	●	Kelley Law Offices...........1117	●	●	●	●

		CV	CR	PR	BARREN	UC	RE	TX	VR
		●	●	●	Goodman & Nichols...........855	●	●	●	●
		●	●	●	Hollingsworth Court Reporting Inc...........983	●	●	●	●
		●	●	●	Moore Jr, Attorney Reed...........1382	●	●	●	

		CV	CR	PR	BATH	UC	RE	TX	VR
					See ALL COUNTIES...........				

		CV	CR	PR	BELL	UC	RE	TX	VR
		●	●	●	Daniel Agency...........588	●	●	●	●
		●	●	●	Footprints...........790	●	●	●	●
		●	●	●	Weatherly Law Office...........2068	●	●	●	●

		CV	CR	PR	BOONE	UC	RE	TX	VR
		●		●	Independent Abstract Inc...........1022	●	●	●	

		CV	CR	PR	BOURBON	UC	RE	TX	VR
					See ALL COUNTIES...........				

DT		CV	CR	PR	BOYD	UC	RE	TX	VR
●		●	●	●	Daniel Agency...........588	●	●	●	●
●		●	●	●	Davis Investigatons Inc...........603	●	●	●	●
●		●	●	●	McBrayer McDennis Leslie & Kirkland...........1299	●	●	●	●

		CV	CR	PR	BOYLE	UC	RE	TX	VR
					Holman, Beverly Gail...........984		●		
		●	●	●	Layton, Attorney David K...........1189	●	●	●	●

		CV	CR	PR	BRACKEN	UC	RE	TX	VR
		●		●	Clarke, Attorney J Kirk...........466		●	●	

		CV	CR	PR	BREATHITT	UC	RE	TX	VR
		●	●	●	Daniel Agency...........588	●	●	●	●
		●	●	●	Friend, Irene...........816	●	●	●	●
		●	●	●	Long, Gordon B...........1238	●	●	●	

		CV	CR	PR	BRECKINRIDGE	UC	RE	TX	VR
		●		●	Eagle Investigations Inc...........673	●	●	●	●
		●	●	●	McCarty, Attorney John...........1303	●	●	●	
		●	●	●	Mitchener, Kent D...........1363	●	●	●	●

		CV	CR	PR	BULLITT	UC	RE	TX	VR
		●	●	●	County Process Inc...........538	●	●	●	●
		●	●	●	Eagle Investigations Inc...........673	●	●	●	●

		CV	CR	PR	BUTLER	UC	RE	TX	VR
		●	●	●	Hollingsworth Court Reporting Inc...........983	●	●	●	●

	CV	CR	PR	CALDWELL	UC	RE	TX	VR
	•	•	•	Hollingsworth Court Reporting Inc................983	•	•	•	•
	•	•	•	Stout, Attorney Alan 1870	•	•	•	•

	CV	CR	PR	CALLOWAY	UC	RE	TX	VR
	•	•	•	Kelley Law Offices..............................1117	•	•	•	•
	•	•		Lattus, Helen 1178	•	•	•	

	CV	CR	PR	CAMPBELL	UC	RE	TX	VR
	•		•	Independent Abstract Inc 1022	•	•	•	

	CV	CR	PR	CARLISLE	UC	RE	TX	VR
	•	•	•	Kelley Law Offices..............................1117	•	•	•	•

	CV	CR	PR	CARROLL	UC	RE	TX	VR
				Berry & Floyd 288	•	•	•	

	CV	CR	PR	CARTER	UC	RE	TX	VR
				Albright, Gary 102	•	•	•	
	•	•	•	Daniel Agency...................................588	•	•	•	•
	•	•	•	McBrayer McDennis Leslie & Kirkland 1299	•	•	•	•

	CV	CR	PR	CASEY	UC	RE	TX	VR
				Holman, Beverly Gail............................984		•		

	CV	CR	PR	CHRISTIAN	UC	RE	TX	VR
	•	•	•	Hollingsworth Court Reporting Inc................983	•	•	•	•

	CV	CR	PR	CLARK	UC	RE	TX	VR
	•	•	•	AD Investigations..................................22	•	•	•	•

	CV	CR	PR	CLAY	UC	RE	TX	VR
	•	•	•	Daniel Agency...................................588	•	•	•	•
	•	•		Feltner, Angela...................................752	•	•		
	•	•	•	Weatherly Law Office 2068	•	•	•	•

	CV	CR	PR	CLINTON	UC	RE	TX	VR
				See ALL COUNTIES...............................				

	CV	CR	PR	CRITTENDEN	UC	RE	TX	VR
	•	•	•	Stout, Attorney Alan 1870	•	•	•	•

	CV	CR	PR	CUMBERLAND	UC	RE	TX	VR
	•	•	•	Harvey, Gayle....................................934				•

DT	CV	CR	PR	DAVIESS	UC	RE	TX	VR
	•		•	Hicks III, Attorney John O.......................965	•	•	•	
	•	•	•	McCarty, Attorney John 1303	•	•	•	
	•	•		Stephen's Research 1862				

	CV	CR	PR	EDMONSON	UC	RE	TX	VR
	•	•	•	Hollingsworth Court Reporting Inc................983	•	•	•	•

	CV	CR	PR	ELLIOTT	UC	RE	TX	VR
	•	•	•	Daniel Agency...................................588	•	•	•	•
	•	•	•	Ison, Reeda.....................................1059	•	•	•	

	CV	CR	PR	ESTILL	UC	RE	TX	VR
	•	•	•	Daniel Agency...................................588	•	•	•	•
	•	•	•	Friend, Irene....................................816	•	•	•	•
	•	•	•	Marcum, Hannah................................1277	•	•	•	

DT	BK	CV	CR	PR	FAYETTE	UC	RE	TX	VR
•	•	•	•	•	AD Investigations..................................22	•	•	•	•
•	•	•	•	•	County Process Inc...............................538	•	•	•	•

●	●	●	●	●	McBrayer McDennis Leslie & Kirkland 1299	●	●	●	●

	CV	CR	PR	FLEMING	UC	RE	TX	VR
	●		●	Clarke, Attorney J Kirk 466		●	●	
	●	●	●	Daniel Agency............588	●	●	●	●
	●	●	●	Suit McCartney Price 1878	●	●	●	●

	CV	CR	PR	FLOYD	UC	RE	TX	VR
	●	●	●	Combs and Combs PSC 503	●	●		
	●	●	●	Daniel Agency............588	●	●	●	●

DT	CV	CR	PR	FRANKLIN	UC	RE	TX	VR
●	●	●	●	McBrayer McDennis Leslie & Kirkland 1299	●	●	●	●

	CV	CR	PR	FULTON	UC	RE	TX	VR
	●	●	●	Kelley Law Offices............1117	●	●	●	●
	●	●		Lattus, Helen 1178	●	●	●	

	CV	CR	PR	GALLATIN	UC	RE	TX	VR
	●	●	●	Huddleston, Stephen P 1001	●	●	●	

	CV	CR	PR	GARRARD	UC	RE	TX	VR
				Holman, Beverly Gail............984		●		
	●	●	●	Layton, Attorney David K............1189	●	●	●	●

	CV	CR	PR	GRANT	UC	RE	TX	VR
				See ALL COUNTIES............				

	CV	CR	PR	GRAVES	UC	RE	TX	VR
	●	●	●	Kelley Law Offices............1117	●	●	●	●
	●	●		Lattus, Helen 1178	●	●	●	

	CV	CR	PR	GRAYSON	UC	RE	TX	VR
	●	●	●	Guffy, Jerry 898	●	●	●	●

	CV	CR	PR	GREEN	UC	RE	TX	VR
	●	●	●	Harvey, Gayle............934				●

	CV	CR	PR	GREENUP	UC	RE	TX	VR
	●	●	●	Daniel Agency............588	●	●	●	●
	●	●	●	McBrayer McDennis Leslie & Kirkland 1299	●	●	●	●

	CV	CR	PR	HANCOCK	UC	RE	TX	VR
	●	●	●	McCarty, Attorney John............1303	●	●	●	

	CV	CR	PR	HARDIN	UC	RE	TX	VR
	●	●	●	Eagle Investigations Inc 673	●	●	●	●
	●		●	Lincoln Trail Title Services Inc............1228	●	●	●	

	CV	CR	PR	HARLAN	UC	RE	TX	VR
	●	●	●	Daniel Agency............588	●	●	●	●
	●	●	●	Footprints............790	●		●	

	CV	CR	PR	HARRISON	UC	RE	TX	VR
	●	●	●	Hood & Whaler 989	●	●	●	●

	CV	CR	PR	HART	UC	RE	TX	VR
	●	●	●	Goodman & Nichols............855	●	●	●	●

	CV	CR	PR	HENDERSON	UC	RE	TX	VR
				See ALL COUNTIES............				

	CV	CR	PR	HENRY	UC	RE	TX	VR
				Berry & Floyd 288	●	●	●	
	●	●	●	Eagle Investigations Inc 673	●	●	●	●

DT	BK	CV	CR	PR		UC	RE	TX	VR
		●	●	●	Jeffries, Keith A 1086	●	●	●	

		CV	CR	PR	**HICKMAN**	UC	RE	TX	VR
		●	●	●	Kelley Law Offices.........................1117	●	●	●	●

		CV	CR	PR	**HOPKINS**	UC	RE	TX	VR
		●	●	●	Hollingsworth Court Reporting Inc...................983	●	●	●	●

		CV	CR	PR	**JACKSON**	UC	RE	TX	VR
		●	●	●	Daniel Agency.........................588	●	●	●	●

DT	BK	CV	CR	PR	**JEFFERSON**	UC	RE	TX	VR
●	●	●	●	●	County Process Inc........................538	●	●	●	●
●	●	●	●	●	Eagle Investigations Inc 673	●	●	●	●
●	●	●	●	●	Sam Steele Investigations.................1730	●	●	●	●

		CV	CR	PR	**JESSAMINE**	UC	RE	TX	VR
		●	●	●	AD Investigations.......................22	●	●	●	●
					Holman, Beverly Gail.....................984		●		
		●	●	●	Layton, Attorney David K...................1189	●	●	●	●

		CV	CR	PR	**JOHNSON**	UC	RE	TX	VR
		●	●	●	Daniel Agency.........................588	●	●	●	●
		●	●	●	Long, Gordon B 1238	●	●	●	
		●		●	McCay Marcum & Triplett...................1304	●	●	●	

DT		CV	CR	PR	**KENTON**	UC	RE	TX	VR
		●		●	Independent Abstract Inc 1022	●	●	●	

		CV	CR	PR	**KNOTT**	UC	RE	TX	VR
		●	●	●	Daniel Agency.........................588	●	●	●	●
		●	●		Feltner, Angela........................752	●	●	●	
		●	●	●	Long, Gordon B 1238	●	●	●	

		CV	CR	PR	**KNOX**	UC	RE	TX	VR
		●	●	●	Daniel Agency.........................588	●	●	●	●
		●	●	●	Weatherly Law Office.....................2068	●	●	●	●

		CV	CR	PR	**LARUE**	UC	RE	TX	VR
		●	●	●	Goodman & Nichols.....................855	●	●	●	●

DT		CV	CR	PR	**LAUREL**	UC	RE	TX	VR
●		●	●	●	Daniel Agency.........................588	●	●	●	●
		●	●	●	Weatherly Law Office.....................2068	●	●	●	●

		CV	CR	PR	**LAWRENCE**	UC	RE	TX	VR
		●	●	●	Daniel Agency.........................588	●	●	●	●
		●		●	McCay Marcum & Triplett...................1304	●	●	●	

		CV	CR	PR	**LEE**	UC	RE	TX	VR
		●	●	●	Friend, Irene........................816	●	●	●	●

		CV	CR	PR	**LESLIE**	UC	RE	TX	VR
		●	●	●	Brashear, Attorney Leonard.....................339	●	●	●	
		●	●	●	Daniel Agency.........................588	●	●	●	●
		●	●		Feltner, Angela........................752	●	●	●	

		CV	CR	PR	**LETCHER**	UC	RE	TX	VR
		●	●	●	Daniel Agency.........................588	●	●	●	●
		●	●		Feltner, Angela........................752	●	●	●	

		CV	CR	PR	**LEWIS**	UC	RE	TX	VR
		●	●	●	Daniel Agency.........................588	●	●	●	●
		●	●	●	McBrayer McDennis Leslie & Kirkland 1299	●	●	●	●

LINCOLN

DT	CV	CR	PR	Name	Page	UC	RE	TX	VR
				Holman, Beverly Gail	984		●		
	●	●	●	Layton, Attorney David K	1189	●	●	●	●

LIVINGSTON

DT	CV	CR	PR	Name	Page	UC	RE	TX	VR
	●	●	●	Neuf & Associates	1418	●	●	●	
	●	●	●	Stout, Attorney Alan	1870	●	●	●	●

LOGAN

DT	CV	CR	PR	Name	Page	UC	RE	TX	VR
	●	●	●	Hollingsworth Court Reporting Inc	983	●	●	●	●

LYON

DT	CV	CR	PR	Name	Page	UC	RE	TX	VR
	●	●	●	Stout, Attorney Alan	1870	●	●	●	●

MCCRACKEN

DT	CV	CR	PR	Name	Page	UC	RE	TX	VR
	●	●	●	Kelley Law Offices	1117	●	●	●	●
	●	●		Lattus, Helen	1178	●	●	●	
●	●	●	●	Neuf & Associates	1418	●	●	●	

MCCREARY

DT	CV	CR	PR	Name	Page	UC	RE	TX	VR
	●	●	●	King & King	1123	●	●	●	

MCLEAN

DT	CV	CR	PR	Name	Page	UC	RE	TX	VR
	●		●	Hicks III, Attorney John O	965	●	●	●	

MADISON

DT	CV	CR	PR	Name	Page	UC	RE	TX	VR
	●	●	●	Daniel Agency	588	●	●	●	●
	●	●	●	Layton, Attorney David K	1189	●	●	●	●

MAGOFFIN

DT	CV	CR	PR	Name	Page	UC	RE	TX	VR
	●	●	●	Long, Gordon B	1238	●	●	●	

MARION

DT	CV	CR	PR	Name	Page	UC	RE	TX	VR
	●	●	●	Avritt & Avritt	221	●	●	●	●
				Holman, Beverly Gail	984		●		

MARSHALL

DT	CV	CR	PR	Name	Page	UC	RE	TX	VR
	●	●	●	Kelley Law Offices	1117	●	●	●	●
	●	●	●	Neuf & Associates	1418	●	●	●	

MARTIN

DT	CV	CR	PR	Name	Page	UC	RE	TX	VR
	●	●	●	Daniel Agency	588	●	●	●	●
	●		●	McCay Marcum & Triplett	1304	●	●	●	

MASON

DT	CV	CR	PR	Name	Page	UC	RE	TX	VR
	●		●	Clarke, Attorney J Kirk	466		●	●	

MEADE

DT	CV	CR	PR	Name	Page	UC	RE	TX	VR
	●	●	●	Eagle Investigations Inc	673	●	●	●	●
	●	●	●	Mitchener, Kent D	1363	●	●	●	●

MENIFEE

DT	CV	CR	PR	Name	Page	UC	RE	TX	VR
	●	●	●	Daniel Agency	588	●	●		●

MERCER

DT	CV	CR	PR	Name	Page	UC	RE	TX	VR
				Holman, Beverly Gail	984		●		

METCALFE

DT	CV	CR	PR	Name	Page	UC	RE	TX	VR
	●	●	●	Harvey, Gayle	934				●

MONROE

DT	CV	CR	PR	Name	Page	UC	RE	TX	VR
	●	●	●	Moore Jr, Attorney Reed	1382	●	●	●	

MONTGOMERY

DT	CV	CR	PR	Name	Page	UC	RE	TX	VR
	●	●	●	Daniel Agency	588	●	●	●	●

	CV	CR	PR	MORGAN	UC	RE	TX	VR
	•	•	•	Daniel Agency..588	•	•	•	•

	CV	CR	PR	MUHLENBERG	UC	RE	TX	VR
	•		•	Hicks III, Attorney John O................................965	•	•	•	
	•	•	•	Hollingsworth Court Reporting Inc....................983	•	•	•	•

	CV	CR	PR	NELSON	UC	RE	TX	VR
	•	•	•	Eagle Investigations Inc...................................673	•	•	•	•

	CV	CR	PR	NICHOLAS	UC	RE	TX	VR
				See ALL COUNTIES....................................				

	CV	CR	PR	OHIO	UC	RE	TX	VR
	•	•	•	McCarty, Attorney John...................................1303	•	•	•	

	CV	CR	PR	OLDHAM	UC	RE	TX	VR
				Berry & Floyd..288	•	•	•	
	•	•	•	County Process Inc..538	•	•	•	•
	•	•	•	Eagle Investigations Inc...................................673	•	•	•	•
	•	•	•	Sam Steele Investigations................................1730	•	•	•	•

	CV	CR	PR	OWEN	UC	RE	TX	VR
				See ALL COUNTIES....................................				

	CV	CR	PR	OWSLEY	UC	RE	TX	VR
	•	•	•	Daniel Agency..588	•	•	•	•
	•	•	•	Friend, Irene..816	•	•	•	•

	CV	CR	PR	PENDLETON	UC	RE	TX	VR
				See ALL COUNTIES....................................				

	CV	CR	PR	PERRY	UC	RE	TX	VR
	•	•	•	Daniel Agency..588	•	•	•	•
	•	•		Feltner, Angela...752	•	•	•	
	•	•	•	Friend, Irene..816	•	•	•	•

DT	CV	CR	PR	PIKE	UC	RE	TX	VR
•		•	•	Combs and Combs PSC.....................................503	•	•		
•	•	•	•	Daniel Agency..588	•	•	•	•
	•	•	•	Long, Gordon B..1238	•	•	•	

	CV	CR	PR	POWELL	UC	RE	TX	VR
	•	•	•	Daniel Agency..588	•	•	•	•
	•	•	•	Friend, Irene..816	•	•	•	•

	CV	CR	PR	PULASKI	UC	RE	TX	VR
	•	•	•	King & King...1123	•	•	•	
	•	•	•	Weatherly Law Office......................................2068	•	•	•	•

	CV	CR	PR	ROBERTSON	UC	RE	TX	VR
				See ALL COUNTIES....................................				

	CV	CR	PR	ROCKCASTLE	UC	RE	TX	VR
	•	•	•	Weatherly Law Office......................................2068	•	•	•	•

	CV	CR	PR	ROWAN	UC	RE	TX	VR
	•	•	•	Daniel Agency..588	•	•	•	•

	CV	CR	PR	RUSSELL	UC	RE	TX	VR
				See ALL COUNTIES....................................				

	CV	CR	PR	SCOTT	UC	RE	TX	VR
				See ALL COUNTIES....................................				

SHELBY

CV	CR	PR			UC	RE	TX	VR
•	•	•	County Process Inc	538	•	•	•	•
•	•	•	Eagle Investigations Inc	673	•	•	•	•
•	•	•	Sam Steele Investigations	1730	•	•	•	•

SIMPSON

CV	CR	PR			UC	RE	TX	VR
•	•	•	Hollingsworth Court Reporting Inc	983	•	•	•	•

SPENCER

CV	CR	PR			UC	RE	TX	VR
•	•	•	Eagle Investigations Inc	673	•	•	•	•

TAYLOR

CV	CR	PR			UC	RE	TX	VR
•	•	•	Harvey, Gayle	934				•
•	•	•	Kunkel, Joan	1138	•	•	•	•

TODD

CV	CR	PR			UC	RE	TX	VR
•	•	•	Hollingsworth Court Reporting Inc	983	•	•	•	•

TRIGG

CV	CR	PR			UC	RE	TX	VR
•	•	•	Hollingsworth Court Reporting Inc	983	•	•	•	•

TRIMBLE

CV	CR	PR			UC	RE	TX	VR
			Berry & Floyd	288	•	•	•	
•	•	•	Jeffries, Keith A	1086	•	•	•	

UNION

CV	CR	PR			UC	RE	TX	VR
•	•	•	Stout, Attorney Alan	1870	•	•	•	•

WARREN

DT	CV	CR	PR			UC	RE	TX	VR
DT	•	•	•	Hollingsworth Court Reporting Inc	983	•	•	•	•
	•	•		Spidel, R Scott	1843	•	•	•	

WASHINGTON

CV	CR	PR			UC	RE	TX	VR
			Holman, Beverly Gail	984		•		

WAYNE

CV	CR	PR			UC	RE	TX	VR
•	•	•	King & King	1123	•	•	•	

WEBSTER

CV	CR	PR			UC	RE	TX	VR
•	•	•	Stout, Attorney Alan	1870	•	•	•	•

WHITLEY

CV	CR	PR			UC	RE	TX	VR
•	•	•	Daniel Agency	588	•	•	•	•
•	•	•	King & King	1123	•	•	•	
•	•	•	Weatherly Law Office	2068	•	•	•	•

WOLFE

CV	CR	PR			UC	RE	TX	VR
•	•	•	Daniel Agency	588	•	•	•	•
•	•	•	Friend, Irene	816	•	•	•	•
•	•	•	Long, Gordon B	1238	•	•		

WOODFORD

CV	CR	PR			UC	RE	TX	VR
•	•	•	AD Investigations	22	•	•	•	•

Louisiana

DT	BK	CV	CR	PR	ALL PARISHES	UC	RE	TX	VR
●	●	●	●	●	Access Louisiana Inc 59	●	●	●	●
	●	●	●	●	Hollingsworth Court Reporting Inc 983	●	●	●	●
●	●	●	●	●	J L & A 1063	●	●	●	●

CV	CR	PR	ACADIA PARISH	UC	RE	TX	VR
●	●	●	ABC Investigators Inc 14	●	●	●	●
●	●		Bayou Investigations Inc 266	●	●	●	●
●		●	Bordelon, Leroy 325		●	●	
●	●	●	Forest & Forest 794	●	●		●
●		●	Pelican Land and Abstract Co Inc 1529	●	●		
●	●	●	Professional Services Bureau 1562	●	●		●

CV	CR	PR	ALLEN PARISH	UC	RE	TX	VR
●	●	●	Abstracting and Legal Research Inc 53	●	●	●	●
●		●	Bordelon, Leroy 325		●	●	

CV	CR	PR	ASCENSION PARISH	UC	RE	TX	VR
●	●	●	Abstracts by Godail 56	●	●	●	
●	●	●	Ascension Title Services Inc 165	●	●	●	
●	●	●	Bombet & Associates 319	●	●	●	●

CV	CR	PR	ASSUMPTION PARISH	UC	RE	TX	VR
●	●	●	Abstracts by Godail 56	●	●	●	
●	●	●	Braud, Jerry M 340	●	●	●	

CV	CR	PR	AVOYELLES PARISH	UC	RE	TX	VR
●	●	●	Abstracting and Legal Research Inc 53	●	●	●	●

CV	CR	PR	BEAUREGARD PARISH	UC	RE	TX	VR
●		●	Pelican Land and Abstract Co Inc 1529	●	●	●	

CV	CR	PR	BIENVILLE PARISH	UC	RE	TX	VR
●		●	DeSoto Abstract 609	●	●	●	
●	●	●	North Louisiana Title Co Inc 1436	●	●	●	

CV	CR	PR	BOSSIER PARISH	UC	RE	TX	VR
●		●	DeSoto Abstract 609	●	●	●	
●	●	●	North Louisiana Title Co Inc 1436	●	●	●	
●	●	●	Southern Research Company 1831	●	●	●	●
●		●	Taylor Title Inc 1904	●	●	●	

DT	BK	CV	CR	PR	CADDO PARISH	UC	RE	TX	VR
●	●	●	●	●	Aymond Investigations Inc 224	●	●	●	●
		●		●	DeSoto Abstract 609	●	●	●	
●	●	●	●	●	North Louisiana Title Co Inc 1436	●	●	●	
●	●	●	●	●	Southern Research Company 1831	●	●	●	●
		●		●	Taylor Title Inc 1904	●	●	●	

DT		CV	CR	PR	CALCASIEU PARISH	UC	RE	TX	VR
		●	●	●	Herbert Abstract Co Inc 958	●	●	●	
		●		●	Pelican Land and Abstract Co Inc 1529	●	●	●	

CV	CR	PR	CALDWELL PARISH	UC	RE	TX	VR
●	●	●	Colvin, Melanie 500	●	●	●	●
●	●	●	North Louisiana Title Co Inc 1436	●	●	●	

CV	CR	PR	CAMERON PARISH	UC	RE	TX	VR
●	●	●	Herbert Abstract Co Inc 958	●	●	●	
●		●	Pelican Land and Abstract Co Inc 1529	●	●	●	

CATAHOULA PARISH

CV	CR	PR	Name	Page	UC	RE	TX	VR
●	●	●	North Louisiana Title Co Inc	1436	●	●	●	

CLAIBORNE PARISH

CV	CR	PR	Name	Page	UC	RE	TX	VR
●		●	DeSoto Abstract	609	●	●	●	
●	●	●	North Louisiana Title Co Inc	1436	●	●	●	

CONCORDIA PARISH

CV	CR	PR	Name	Page	UC	RE	TX	VR
●	●	●	North Louisiana Title Co Inc	1436	●	●	●	

DE SOTO PARISH

CV	CR	PR	Name	Page	UC	RE	TX	VR
●		●	DeSoto Abstract	609	●	●	●	

EAST BATON ROUGE PARISH

DT	BK	CV	CR	PR	Name	Page	UC	RE	TX	VR
		●	●	●	Abstracts by Godail	56	●	●	●	
●	●	●	●	●	Bombet & Associates	319	●	●		●
●	●	●			Information Research	1028		●		
				●	Pelican Land and Abstract Co Inc	1529	●	●	●	
●	●	●	●	●	Professional Services Bureau	1562	●	●		●
●	●	●			Statewide Abstract and Title Co Inc	1856	●			
				●	Universal Research	2011		●		●

EAST CARROLL PARISH

CV	CR	PR	Name	Page	UC	RE	TX	VR
●	●	●	North Louisiana Title Co Inc	1436	●	●	●	

EAST FELICIANA PARISH

CV	CR	PR	Name	Page	UC	RE	TX	VR
●		●	Universal Research	2011		●		●

EVANGELINE PARISH

CV	CR	PR	Name	Page	UC	RE	TX	VR
●	●	●	Abstracting and Legal Research Inc	53	●	●	●	●
●	●		Bayou Investigations Inc	266	●	●	●	●
●		●	Bordelon, Leroy	325		●	●	
●	●	●	Professional Services Bureau	1562	●	●	●	●

FRANKLIN PARISH

CV	CR	PR	Name	Page	UC	RE	TX	VR
●	●	●	Colvin, Melanie	500	●	●	●	●
●	●	●	North Louisiana Title Co Inc	1436	●	●	●	

GRAND PARISH

CV	CR	PR	Name	Page	UC	RE	TX	VR
●	●	●	Abstracting and Legal Research Inc	53	●	●	●	●
●	●	●	North Louisiana Title Co Inc	1436	●	●	●	

IBERIA PARISH

CV	CR	PR	Name	Page	UC	RE	TX	VR
●	●		Bayou Investigations Inc	266	●	●	●	●
●	●	●	Professional Services Bureau	1562	●	●	●	
●		●	RND Realty Corp	1642	●	●	●	

IBERVILLE PARISH

CV	CR	PR	Name	Page	UC	RE	TX	VR
●	●	●	Ascension Title Services Inc	165	●	●	●	
●	●	●	Bombet & Associates	319	●	●	●	●

JACKSON PARISH

CV	CR	PR	Name	Page	UC	RE	TX	VR
●	●	●	Colvin, Melanie	500	●	●	●	●
●	●	●	North Louisiana Title Co Inc	1436	●	●	●	

JEFFERSON PARISH

CV	CR	PR	Name	Page	UC	RE	TX	VR
●	●	●	Braud, Jerry M	340	●	●	●	●
●	●	●	Caliva, Kevin H	382			●	●
●	●	●	Vinson Detective Agency	2031	●	●	●	●

JEFFERSON DAVIS PARISH

CV	CR	PR	Name	Page	UC	RE	TX	VR
●	●	●	ABC Investigators Inc	14	●	●	●	●
●	●		Bayou Investigations Inc	266	●	●	●	●
●		●	Bordelon, Leroy	325		●	●	

DT	BK	CV	CR	PR		UC	RE	TX	VR
•				•	Pelican Land and Abstract Co Inc 1529	•	•	•	
•		•		•	Professional Services Bureau 1562	•	•	•	•

LAFAYETTE PARISH

DT	CV	CR	PR		UC	RE	TX	VR
•	•	•	•	ABC Investigators Inc 14	•	•	•	•
•	•	•		Bayou Investigations Inc 266	•	•	•	•
•	•		•	Forest & Forest 794	•	•	•	•
•	•		•	Professional Services Bureau 1562	•	•	•	•
		•	•	RND Realty Corp 1642	•	•	•	

LAFOURCHE PARISH

CV	CR	PR		UC	RE	TX	VR
•	•	•	Braud, Jerry M 340	•	•	•	

LA SALLE PARISH

CV	CR	PR		UC	RE	TX	VR
•	•	•	Caliva, Kevin H 382	•	•	•	
•	•	•	North Louisiana Title Co Inc 1436	•	•	•	

LINCOLN PARISH

CV	CR	PR		UC	RE	TX	VR
•	•	•	Colvin, Melanie 500	•	•	•	•
		•	DeSoto Abstract 609	•	•	•	
•	•	•	North Louisiana Title Co Inc 1436	•	•	•	

LIVINGSTON PARISH

CV	CR	PR		UC	RE	TX	VR
•	•	•	Abstracts by Godail 56	•	•	•	
•			Information Research 1028		•		
•	•	•	Speed, Toni 1842	•	•	•	•
		•	Universal Research 2011		•		•

MADISON PARISH

CV	CR	PR		UC	RE	TX	VR
•	•	•	North Louisiana Title Co Inc 1436	•	•	•	

MOREHOUSE PARISH

CV	CR	PR		UC	RE	TX	VR
•	•	•	Colvin, Melanie 500	•	•	•	•
•	•	•	North Louisiana Title Co Inc 1436	•	•	•	

NATCHITOCHES PARISH

CV	CR	PR		UC	RE	TX	VR
•	•	•	Abstracting and Legal Research Inc 53	•	•	•	•

ORLEANS PARISH

DT	BK	CV	CR	PR		UC	RE	TX	VR
•	•	•	•	•	Caliva, Kevin H 382	•	•	•	
•	•	•	•	•	Vinson Detective Agency 2031		•		•

OUACHITA PARISH

DT	CV	CR	PR		UC	RE	TX	VR
	•	•	•	Colvin, Melanie 500	•	•	•	•
•	•	•	•	North Louisiana Title Co Inc 1436	•	•	•	

PLAQUEMINES PARISH

CV	CR	PR		UC	RE	TX	VR
•	•	•	Caliva, Kevin H 382	•	•	•	•
•	•	•	Fleming, Glenn A 784	•	•	•	•

POINTE COUPEE PARISH

CV	CR	PR		UC	RE	TX	VR
•	•	•	Abstracts by Godail 56	•	•	•	

RAPIDES PARISH

DT	BK	CV	CR	PR		UC	RE	TX	VR
•	•	•	•	•	Abstracting and Legal Research Inc 53	•	•	•	•
•	•	•	•	•	North Louisiana Title Co Inc 1436	•	•	•	
•	•	•	•	•	Professional Services Bureau 1562	•	•	•	•

RED RIVER PARISH

CV	CR	PR		UC	RE	TX	VR
•	•	•	Red River Title Research 1667	•	•	•	•

RICHLAND PARISH

CV	CR	PR		UC	RE	TX	VR
•	•	•	Colvin, Melanie 500	•	•	•	•
•	•	•	North Louisiana Title Co Inc 1436	•	•	•	

		CV	CR	PR	SABINE PARISH	UC	RE	TX	VR
		•	•	•	Abstracting and Legal Research Inc..................53	•	•	•	•

		CV	CR	PR	ST. BERNARD PARISH	UC	RE	TX	VR
		•	•	•	Caliva, Kevin H..................382	•	•	•	•
		•	•	•	Vinson Detective Agency..................2031		•		•

		CV	CR	PR	ST. CHARLES PARISH	UC	RE	TX	VR
		•	•	•	Braud, Jerry M..................340	•	•	•	
		•	•	•	Breuille, Billie..................343	•	•	•	•

		CV	CR	PR	ST. HELENA PARISH	UC	RE	TX	VR
		•	•	•	Speed, Toni..................1842	•	•	•	•
		•		•	Universal Research..................2011		•		•

		CV	CR	PR	ST. JAMES PARISH	UC	RE	TX	VR
		•	•	•	Ascension Title Services Inc..................165	•	•	•	

		CV	CR	PR	ST. JOHN THE BAPTIST PARISH	UC	RE	TX	VR
		•	•	•	Breuille, Billie..................343	•	•	•	•

BK		CV	CR	PR	ST. LANDRY PARISH	UC	RE	TX	VR
•		•	•	•	ABC Investigators Inc..................14	•	•	•	•
•		•	•	•	Abstracting and Legal Research Inc..................53	•	•	•	•
•		•	•	•	Bayou Investigations Inc..................266	•	•	•	•
•		•		•	Bordelon, Leroy..................325		•	•	•
•		•	•	•	Professional Services Bureau..................1562	•	•	•	•

		CV	CR	PR	ST. MARTIN PARISH	UC	RE	TX	VR
		•	•		Bayou Investigations Inc..................266	•	•	•	•
		•	•	•	Forest & Forest..................794	•	•	•	•
		•	•	•	Professional Services Bureau..................1562	•	•	•	•
		•		•	RND Realty Corp..................1642	•	•	•	

		CV	CR	PR	ST. MARY PARISH	UC	RE	TX	VR
		•	•		Bayou Investigations Inc..................266	•	•	•	•
		•	•	•	Professional Services Bureau..................1562	•	•	•	•

		CV	CR	PR	ST. TAMMANY PARISH	UC	RE	TX	VR
		•	•	•	Legal Data Services..................1199	•	•	•	•
		•	•	•	Speed, Toni..................1842	•	•	•	•

		CV	CR	PR	TANGIPAHOA PARISH	UC	RE	TX	VR
		•	•	•	Speed, Toni..................1842	•	•	•	•

		CV	CR	PR	TENSAS PARISH	UC	RE	TX	VR
		•	•	•	Colvin, Melanie..................500	•	•	•	•
		•	•	•	North Louisiana Title Co Inc..................1436	•	•	•	

		CV	CR	PR	TERREBONNE PARISH	UC	RE	TX	VR
		•	•	•	Braud, Jerry M..................340	•	•	•	
		•	•	•	Caliva, Kevin H..................382	•	•	•	•

		CV	CR	PR	UNION PARISH	UC	RE	TX	VR
		•	•	•	Colvin, Melanie..................500	•	•	•	•
		•	•	•	North Louisiana Title Co Inc..................1436	•	•	•	

		CV	CR	PR	VERMILION PARISH	UC	RE	TX	VR
		•	•	•	ABC Investigators Inc..................14	•	•	•	•
		•	•		Bayou Investigations Inc..................266	•	•	•	
		•	•	•	Forest & Forest..................794	•	•	•	•
		•	•	•	Professional Services Bureau..................1562	•	•	•	•
		•		•	RND Realty Corp..................1642	•	•	•	

CV	CR	PR	VERNON PARISH		UC	RE	TX	VR
●	●	●	Abstracting and Legal Research Inc......53		●	●	●	●

CV	CR	PR	WASHINGTON PARISH		UC	RE	TX	VR
●	●	●	Legal Data Services......1199		●	●	●	●
●	●	●	Speed, Toni......1842		●	●	●	●

CV	CR	PR	WEBSTER PARISH		UC	RE	TX	VR
●		●	DeSoto Abstract......609		●	●	●	
●	●	●	North Louisiana Title Co Inc......1436		●	●	●	

CV	CR	PR	WEST BATON ROUGE PARISH		UC	RE	TX	VR
●	●	●	Abstracts by Godail......56		●	●	●	
●	●	●	Bombet & Associates......319		●	●	●	●
●			Information Research......1028			●		
●	●	●	Professional Services Bureau......1562		●	●	●	●
●			Statewide Abstract and Title Co Inc......1856		●			

CV	CR	PR	WEST CARROLL PARISH		UC	RE	TX	VR
●	●	●	North Louisiana Title Co Inc......1436		●	●	●	

CV	CR	PR	WEST FELICIANA PARISH		UC	RE	TX	VR
●		●	Universal Research......2011			●		●

CV	CR	PR	WINN PARISH		UC	RE	TX	VR
●	●	●	Colvin, Melanie......500		●	●	●	●
●	●	●	North Louisiana Title Co Inc......1436		●	●	●	

Maine

		CV	CR	PR	ANDROSCOGGIN	UC	RE	TX	VR
		●	●	●	Public Information Resource..............1626	●	●	●	●

		CV	CR	PR	AROOSTOOK	UC	RE	TX	VR
		●	●	●	Private Eyes Investigations 1605	●	●	●	●

DT	BK	CV	CR	PR	CUMBERLAND	UC	RE	TX	VR
●	●	●	●	●	Public Information Resource..............1626	●	●	●	●

		CV	CR	PR	FRANKLIN	UC	RE	TX	VR
		●	●	●	Public Information Resource..............1626	●	●	●	●

		CV	CR	PR	HANCOCK	UC	RE	TX	VR
		●	●	●	Private Eyes Investigations 1605	●	●	●	●

		CV	CR	PR	KENNEBEC	UC	RE	TX	VR
		●	●	●	Facts Investigative Services 731	●	●	●	●
		●	●	●	Public Information Resource..............1626	●	●	●	●
		●	●	●	Sentry Security..............1783	●	●	●	●

		CV	CR	PR	KNOX	UC	RE	TX	VR
					See adjoining counties				

		CV	CR	PR	LINCOLN	UC	RE	TX	VR
					See adjoining counties..............				

		CV	CR	PR	OXFORD	UC	RE	TX	VR
		●	●	●	Public Information Resource..............1626	●	●	●	●

DT	BK	CV	CR	PR	PENOBSCOT	UC	RE	TX	VR
		●	●	●	Private Eyes Investigations 1605	●	●	●	●

		CV	CR	PR	PISCATAQUIS	UC	RE	TX	VR
					See adjoining counties..............				

		CV	CR	PR	SAGADAHOC	UC	RE	TX	VR
		●	●	●	Public Information Resource..............1626	●	●	●	●

		CV	CR	PR	SOMERSET	UC	RE	TX	VR
		●	●	●	Facts Investigative Services 731	●	●	●	●
		●	●	●	Sentry Security..............1783	●	●	●	●

		CV	CR	PR	WALDO	UC	RE	TX	VR
					See adjoining counties..............				

		CV	CR	PR	WASHINGTON	UC	RE	TX	VR
					See adjoining counties..............				

		CV	CR	PR	YORK	UC	RE	TX	VR
		●	●	●	Public Information Resource..............1626	●	●	●	●

Maryland

DT	BK	CV	CR	PR	ALL COUNTIES		UC	RE	TX	VR
●	●	●	●	●	CorpAssist...524		●	●	●	●
●	●		●		Court House Retrieval Inc..........................543		●		●	●
●	●	●	●	●	Mid-Point Services....................................1341		●	●		
●	●	●	●	●	Security Intelligence Bureau......................1774		●	●	●	●

		CV	CR	PR	ALLEGANY		UC	RE	TX	VR
					See ALL COUNTIES....................................					

		CV	CR	PR	ANNE ARUNDEL		UC	RE	TX	VR
		●	●	●	A P Legal Support Services.............................6		●	●	●	●
		●	●	●	Chesapeake Services 448					
		●	●	●	Davis Detective Agency Inc.........................602		●	●	●	●
		●			Douglas Investigations Ltd...........................655					
		●	●	●	Federal Information Service..........................749		●	●	●	●
		●	●	●	Federal Research Corporation......................751		●	●	●	●
		●		●	Harbor City Research Inc............................921		●	●	●	
		●	●	●	IH Publishing 1016			●	●	●
		●	●	●	University Process Service...........................2012					

DT		CV	CR	PR	BALTIMORE		UC	RE	TX	VR
●		●	●	●	A P Legal Support Services.............................6		●	●	●	●
●		●	●	●	ABIS Inc 17		●	●	●	●
		●	●	●	Crystal Systems Legal Services Division...........572		●	●	●	●
●		●	●	●	Federal Information Service..........................749		●	●	●	●
●		●	●	●	Federal Research Corporation......................751		●	●	●	●
●		●		●	Harbor City Research Inc............................921		●	●	●	
●		●	●	●	IH Publishing 1016			●	●	●
●		●		●	Maryland Research and Abstract Co...............1291		●	●	●	
		●			Prentice Hall Legal & Financial Services.........1588		●			
●		●	●	●	Process Service Unlimited Inc 1610		●	●	●	●
●		●	●	●	University Process Service...........................2012					

	BK	CV	CR	PR	CITY OF BALTIMORE		UC	RE	TX	VR
	●	●	●	●	A P Legal Support Services.............................6		●	●	●	●
	●	●	●	●	ABIS Inc 17		●	●	●	
	●	●	●	●	Federal Information Service..........................749		●	●	●	●
	●	●	●	●	Federal Research Corporation......................751		●	●	●	●
	●	●		●	Harbor City Research Inc............................921		●	●	●	
	●	●	●	●	IH Publishing 1016			●	●	●
		●		●	Prentice Hall Legal & Financial Services.........1588		●			
	●	●	●	●	University Process Service...........................2012					

		CV	CR	PR	CALVERT		UC	RE	TX	VR
		●	●	●	Davis Detective Agency Inc.........................602		●	●	●	●

		CV	CR	PR	CAROLINE		UC	RE	TX	VR
		●	●	●	Accurate Abstracts Inc 64		●	●	●	●
		●			Paralegal Services 1514		●	●	●	●
		●	●	●	Vinson, Lynda P..2032		●	●	●	●

		CV	CR	PR	CARROLL		UC	RE	TX	VR
		●	●	●	A P Legal Support Services.............................6		●	●	●	●
		●	●	●	IH Publishing 1016			●	●	●
		●	●	●	Process Service Unlimited Inc 1610		●	●	●	●
		●	●	●	University Process Service...........................2012					

		CV	CR	PR	CECIL		UC	RE	TX	VR
		●	●	●	IH Publishing 1016			●	●	●

CHARLES

CV	CR	PR	Name	Page	UC	RE	TX	VR
•	•	•	Associated Investigative Services Inc	171	•	•	•	•
•			Davis Detective Agency Inc	602				

DORCHESTER

CV	CR	PR	Name	Page	UC	RE	TX	VR
•	•	•	Accurate Abstracts Inc	64	•	•	•	•
•		•	Paralegal Services	1514	•	•	•	•
•	•	•	Vinson, Lynda P	2032	•	•	•	•

FREDERICK

CV	CR	PR	Name	Page	UC	RE	TX	VR
•	•	•	Process Service Unlimited Inc	1610	•	•	•	
•	•	•	Quality Abstractors Inc	1633	•	•	•	
•	•	•	University Process Service	2012				

GARRETT

CV	CR	PR	Name	Page	UC	RE	TX	VR
•		•	Acton, Frances	74	•	•	•	
			Search In USA	1756	•			

HARFORD

CV	CR	PR	Name	Page	UC	RE	TX	VR
•	•	•	A P Legal Support Services	6	•	•	•	
•	•	•	Federal Research Corporation	751	•	•	•	
•		•	Harbor City Research Inc	921	•			
•	•	•	IH Publishing	1016				•
•		•	Maryland Research and Abstract Co	1291	•	•	•	

HOWARD

CV	CR	PR	Name	Page	UC	RE	TX	VR
•	•	•	A P Legal Support Services	6	•	•	•	•
•	•	•	Davis Detective Agency Inc	602	•	•	•	•
•	•	•	Federal Research Corporation	751	•	•	•	•
•		•	Harbor City Research Inc	921	•	•	•	
•	•	•	IH Publishing	1016		•	•	•
•	•	•	Process Service Unlimited Inc	1610	•	•	•	•
•	•	•	University Process Service	2012				

KENT

CV	CR	PR	Name	Page	UC	RE	TX	VR
•		•	Paralegal Services	1514	•	•	•	•
•	•	•	Van Dyke, Leona	2024	•	•	•	•

MONTGOMERY

BK	CV	CR	PR	Name	Page	UC	RE	TX	VR
•	•		•	Accurate Legal Service Co	66	•	•		•
•	•	•	•	Associated Investigative Services Inc	171	•			
•	•			Douglas Investigations Ltd	655		•		
			•	Elder Abstracts	696		•		
•	•	•	•	Federal Information Service	748				
•	•	•	•	Federal Information Service	749	•	•	•	•
•	•		•	Harbor City Research Inc	921	•	•	•	
•	•	•	•	IH Publishing	1016		•	•	•
•	•	•	•	Instant Information Systems	1032	•	•	•	•
•	•	•		Montgomery Investigative Services	1375				
•	•		•	Pascal & Carter Process Service Inc	1522		•		
•	•	•	•	Process Service Unlimited Inc	1610	•	•	•	•
•	•	•	•	University Process Service	2012				

PRINCE GEORGE'S

CV	CR	PR	Name	Page	UC	RE	TX	VR
•	•	•	A P Legal Support Services	6	•	•	•	•
•		•	Accurate Legal Service Co	66	•	•		•
•	•	•	Associated Investigative Services Inc	171	•	•	•	•
•	•	•	Davis Detective Agency Inc	602	•	•	•	•
•			Douglas Investigations Ltd	655		•		
		•	Elder Abstracts	696		•		
•	•	•	Federal Information Service	748				
•		•	Harbor City Research Inc	921	•	•	•	

CV	CR	PR			UC	RE	TX	VR
•	•	•	University Process Service	2012				

CV	CR	PR	QUEEN ANNE'S		UC	RE	TX	VR
•	•	•	Accurate Abstracts Inc	64	•	•	•	•
•	•	•	Chesapeake Services	448				
•		•	Paralegal Services	1514	•	•	•	•
•	•	•	Van Dyke, Leona	2024	•	•	•	•

CV	CR	PR	ST. MARY'S		UC	RE	TX	VR
•	•	•	Davis Detective Agency Inc	602	•	•	•	•

CV	CR	PR	SOMERSET		UC	RE	TX	VR
			See ALL COUNTIES					

CV	CR	PR	TALBOT		UC	RE	TX	VR
•	•	•	Accurate Abstracts Inc	64	•	•	•	•
•		•	Paralegal Services	1514	•	•	•	•
•	•	•	Vinson, Lynda P	2032	•	•	•	•

CV	CR	PR	WASHINGTON		UC	RE	TX	VR
			See ALL COUNTIES					

CV	CR	PR	WICOMICO		UC	RE	TX	VR
•	•	•	Vinson, Lynda P	2032	•	•	•	•

CV	CR	PR	WORCESTER		UC	RE	TX	VR
•	•	•	Ayres, Judith	225	•	•	•	•

Massachusetts

DT	BK	CV	CR	PR	ALL COUNTIES	UC	RE	TX	VR
●	●	●	●	●	Barry Shuster Co 253	●	●	●	●

		CV	CR	PR	BARNSTABLE	UC	RE	TX	VR
		●	●	●	Michael B Fixman & Associates 1338	●	●	●	●
		●	●	●	Simmons Agency 1807	●	●	●	●

		CV	CR	PR	BERKSHIRE	UC	RE	TX	VR
					Registry Research 1674	●	●		

		CV	CR	PR	BRISTOL	UC	RE	TX	VR
		●	●	●	Michael B Fixman & Associates 1338	●	●	●	●
		●	●	●	Simmons Agency 1807	●	●	●	●

		CV	CR	PR	DUKES	UC	RE	TX	VR
					See ALL COUNTIES............................				

		CV	CR	PR	ESSEX	UC	RE	TX	VR
		●	●	●	A Scott Broadhurst and Associates 8	●	●	●	
		●	●	●	DiNatale Detective Agency 630	●	●	●	
		●	●	●	First Security Service Corp 777	●	●	●	
		●	●	●	Kaufman & Harlow Inc of Cambridge 1114	●	●	●	
		●	●	●	Simmons Agency 1807	●	●	●	

		CV	CR	PR	FRANKLIN	UC	RE	TX	VR
		●	●		Harmon Personnel Services Inc 928				
		●	●	●	Simmons Agency 1807	●	●	●	●

DT		CV	CR	PR	HAMPDEN	UC	RE	TX	VR
●		●	●	●	Simmons Agency 1807	●	●	●	●

		CV	CR	PR	HAMPSHIRE	UC	RE	TX	VR
		●	●		Harmon Personnel Services Inc 928				
		●	●	●	Simmons Agency 1807	●	●	●	●

		CV	CR	PR	MIDDLESEX	UC	RE	TX	VR
		●	●	●	A Scott Broadhurst and Associates 8	●	●	●	
		●	●	●	DiNatale Detective Agency 630	●	●	●	●
		●	●	●	First Security Service Corp 777	●	●	●	●
		●	●	●	Kaufman & Harlow Inc of Cambridge 1114	●	●	●	●
		●	●	●	Quirk Associates 1637	●	●	●	●
		●	●	●	Simmons Agency 1807	●	●	●	●
		●	●	●	Suburban Record Research 1877	●		●	

		CV	CR	PR	NANTUCKET	UC	RE	TX	VR
					See ALL COUNTIES............................				

		CV	CR	PR	NORFOLK	UC	RE	TX	VR
		●	●	●	A Scott Broadhurst and Associates 8	●	●	●	
		●	●	●	DiNatale Detective Agency 630	●	●		●
		●	●	●	First Security Service Corp 777	●	●		●
		●	●	●	Kaufman & Harlow Inc of Cambridge 1114	●	●	●	
		●	●	●	Quirk Associates 1637	●	●	●	
		●	●	●	Simmons Agency 1807	●	●	●	
		●	●	●	Suburban Record Research 1877	●		●	

		CV	CR	PR	PLYMOUTH	UC	RE	TX	VR
		●	●	●	A Scott Broadhurst and Associates 8	●	●	●	
		●	●	●	DiNatale Detective Agency 630	●	●	●	●
		●	●	●	Michael B Fixman & Associates 1338	●	●	●	●
		●	●	●	Simmons Agency 1807	●	●	●	●

DT	BK	CV	CR	PR	SUFFOLK	UC	RE	TX	VR
●	●	●	●	●	A Scott Broadhurst and Associates 8	●	●	●	
●	●	●	●		Capitol Services Inc 401	●			
●	●	●	●	●	DiNatale Detective Agency 630	●	●	●	●
●	●	●	●	●	First Security Service Corp 777	●	●	●	●
●	●	●	●	●	Kaufman & Harlow Inc of Cambridge 1114	●	●	●	●
●	●	●	●	●	Paralegal Resource Center Inc 1513	●	●	●	●
					Prentice Hall Legal & Financial Services 1587		●		
		●	●	●	Quirk Associates 1637	●	●		●
		●			Simmons Agency 1807				

DT	BK	CV	CR	PR	WORCESTER	UC	RE	TX	VR
●	●	●	●	●	A Scott Broadhurst and Associates 8	●	●	●	
●	●	●	●	●	Kaufman & Harlow Inc of Cambridge 1114	●	●	●	●
●	●	●	●	●	Simmons Agency 1807	●	●	●	●

Court
Records

MICHIGAN
101

County
Records

Michigan

DT	BK	CV	CR	PR	ALL COUNTIES		UC	RE	TX	VR
•	•	•	•	•	Advanced Information Consultants......87		•	•	•	•
	•	•	•	•	Hollingsworth Court Reporting Inc......983		•	•	•	•
•	•	•	•	•	Legal Services......1210		•	•	•	•

		CV	CR	PR	ALCONA		UC	RE	TX	VR
		•	•	•	Landmark Title Corp......1168		•	•	•	•
		•	•	•	Research North Inc of Alpena......1684		•	•	•	•

		CV	CR	PR	ALGER		UC	RE	TX	VR
				•	Upper Penninsula Title and Abstract......2013		•	•	•	

		CV	CR	PR	ALLEGAN		UC	RE	TX	VR
		•	•	•	I & S Consulting......1014			•	•	
		•		•	Special Private Investigations Inc......1840		•	•	•	•

		CV	CR	PR	ALPENA		UC	RE	TX	VR
		•	•	•	Huron Shares Abstract & Title......1005		•	•	•	
		•	•	•	Research North Inc of Alpena......1684		•	•	•	•

		CV	CR	PR	ANTRIM		UC	RE	TX	VR
		•	•	•	Research North Inc of Traverse City......1686		•	•	•	•

		CV	CR	PR	ARENAC		UC	RE	TX	VR
		•	•	•	Arenae Abstract & Title Co......158		•	•	•	•
		•		•	Bay County Abstract Co......263		•	•	•	•

		CV	CR	PR	BARAGA		UC	RE	TX	VR
		•	•	•	Copper Range Abstract & Title Co......518		•	•	•	•

		CV	CR	PR	BARRY		UC	RE	TX	VR
		•		•	Metropolitan Title Co......1336		•	•	•	•
		•		•	Special Private Investigations Inc......1840		•	•	•	•

DT	BK	CV	CR	PR	BAY		UC	RE	TX	VR
•	•	•		•	Bay County Abstract Co......263		•	•	•	•

		CV	CR	PR	BENZIE		UC	RE	TX	VR
		•	•		Behind the Scene Investigations......276		•	•	•	
					Benzie County Abstract & Title Co......285		•	•	•	
		•	•	•	Research North Inc of Traverse City......1686		•	•	•	•

		CV	CR	PR	BERRIEN		UC	RE	TX	VR
		•	•	•	Security Consulting Svc of Cassopolis......1770		•	•	•	•

		CV	CR	PR	BRANCH		UC	RE	TX	VR
		•		•	Branch County Abstract & Title Inc......338		•	•	•	•

		CV	CR	PR	CALHOUN		UC	RE	TX	VR
		•	•	•	The Fatman Intl Private Detective Svc......1931		•	•	•	•

		CV	CR	PR	CASS		UC	RE	TX	VR
		•	•	•	Security Consulting Svc of Cassopolis......1770		•	•	•	•
		•	•	•	St Joseph County Abstract Office Inc......1847		•	•	•	•

		CV	CR	PR	CHARLEVOIX		UC	RE	TX	VR
		•	•	•	Research North Inc of Petoskey......1685		•	•	•	•

		CV	CR	PR	CHEBOYGAN		UC	RE	TX	VR
		•	•	•	Cheboygan Straits Area Title......445		•	•	•	•
		•	•	•	Research North Inc of Petoskey......1685		•	•	•	•

	CV	CR	PR	CHIPPEWA		UC	RE	TX	VR
	●	●	●	Askwith, Elizabeth 168		●	●	●	
			●	Chippewa Abstract and Title Co 455			●	●	
	●	●		Eastern Upper Pennensula Title Co 685		●	●	●	●
			●	Mackinac Abstract and Title Co 1263		●	●	●	

	CV	CR	PR	CLARE		UC	RE	TX	VR
			●	Great Lakes Title of Cadillac 868		●	●	●	
			●	Houghton Lake Title & Escrow Co 996		●	●	●	●
	●		●	Land Title & Abstract Inc 1162		●	●	●	●
	●		●	Mt Pleasant Abstract and Title Co 1394		●	●	●	

	CV	CR	PR	CLINTON		UC	RE	TX	VR
	●	●	●	Ingham County Sheriff's Dept-Civil Div 1031		●	●	●	
	●			Lawyers Title Insurance Corp 1186		●	●	●	

	CV	CR	PR	CRAWFORD		UC	RE	TX	VR
			●	Alpine Title Co 122			●	●	
	●		●	AuSable Valley Abstract and Title Co 214		●	●	●	
	●	●	●	Crawford County Abstract & Title Co 552		●	●	●	●
			●	Houghton Lake Title & Escrow Co 996		●	●	●	●
			●	Main Abstract & Title Co 1269		●	●	●	●

	CV	CR	PR	DELTA		UC	RE	TX	VR
			●	Upper Penninsula Title and Abstract 2013		●	●	●	

	CV	CR	PR	DICKINSON		UC	RE	TX	VR
	●	●	●	Penninsula Title and Abstract Corp 1534		●	●	●	
	●		●	Superior Title and Abstract 1888			●	●	

	CV	CR	PR	EATON		UC	RE	TX	VR
	●	●	●	Ingham County Sheriff's Dept-Civil Div 1031		●	●	●	
	●			Lawyers Title Insurance Corp 1186		●	●	●	
	●	●	●	The Eaton County Sheriff's Civil Div 1930					

	CV	CR	PR	EMMET		UC	RE	TX	VR
	●	●	●	Research North Inc of Petoskey 1685		●	●	●	●

DT	BK	CV	CR	PR	GENESEE	UC	RE	TX	VR
				●	Centennial Title & Abstract Co 423	●	●	●	
●	●	●	●	●	Fidelity Abstract & Title Co 756	●	●	●	●
		●	●	●	Homestead Title 987	●	●	●	●
●	●	●	●	●	Mallard Investigations 1273	●	●	●	●
●	●	●	●	●	Sargents Abstract & Title Co 1740	●	●	●	●

	CV	CR	PR	GLADWIN		UC	RE	TX	VR
				Gladwin County Abstract Company 848			●	●	
			●	Gladwin Title Co 849		●	●	●	●
			●	Houghton Lake Title & Escrow Co 996		●	●	●	●
	●		●	Land Title & Abstract Inc 1162		●	●	●	●

	CV	CR	PR	GOGEBIC		UC	RE	TX	VR
	●		●	Iron Title & Abstract Co 1056		●	●	●	●

	CV	CR	PR	GRAND TRAVERSE		UC	RE	TX	VR
	●	●		Behind the Scene Investigations 276		●	●	●	
				Benzie County Abstract & Title Co 285		●	●	●	
			●	Grand Traverse Title Co 860		●	●	●	
	●	●	●	Research North Inc of Traverse City 1686		●	●	●	●

	CV	CR	PR	GRATIOT		UC	RE	TX	VR
			●	Alma Abstract and Title Co 119		●	●	●	●

			CV	CR	PR	**HILLSDALE**	UC	RE	TX	VR
					•	Hillsdale Title Company 975		•	•	•

			CV	CR	PR	**HOUGHTON**	UC	RE	TX	VR
			•	•	•	Copper Range Abstract & Title Co 518	•	•	•	•

			CV	CR	PR	**HURON**	UC	RE	TX	VR
						See ALL COUNTIES..........................				

DT			CV	CR	PR	**INGHAM**	UC	RE	TX	VR
			•	•	•	Ingham County Sheriff's Dept-Civil Div.................1031	•	•	•	
•			•			Lawyers Title Insurance Corp.....................1186	•	•	•	

			CV	CR	PR	**IONIA**	UC	RE	TX	VR
			•		•	Special Private Investigations Inc 1840	•	•	•	•

			CV	CR	PR	**IOSCO**	UC	RE	TX	VR
			•		•	Iosco County Abstract Office Ltd 1051	•	•	•	•
			•	•	•	Landmark Title Corp....................1168	•	•	•	•

			CV	CR	PR	**IRON**	UC	RE	TX	VR
			•	•	•	Penninsula Title and Abstract Corp.................1534	•	•	•	

			CV	CR	PR	**ISABELLA**	UC	RE	TX	VR
					•	Isabella County Abstract.....................1058		•	•	
			•		•	Midland Title Co.....................1344	•	•	•	•
			•		•	Mt Pleasant Abstract and Title Co 1394	•	•	•	

			CV	CR	PR	**JACKSON**	UC	RE	TX	VR
						See ALL COUNTIES..........................				

DT			CV	CR	PR	**KALAMAZOO**	UC	RE	TX	VR
			•	•	•	Magic P I & Security Inc.....................1265	•	•	•	•

			CV	CR	PR	**KALKASKA**	UC	RE	TX	VR
			•	•		Behind the Scene Investigations.....................276	•	•	•	
			•	•	•	Research North Inc of Traverse City....................1686	•	•	•	

DT	BK		CV	CR	PR	**KENT**	UC	RE	TX	VR
•	•	•	•	•	•	I & S Consulting 1014		•	•	
•	•	•	•	•	•	Professional Courier Service.....................1616	•	•	•	•
•	•	•	•	•	•	Special Private Investigations Inc 1840	•	•	•	•
•	•	•	•	•	•	The Fatman Intl Private Detective Svc....................1931	•	•	•	

			CV	CR	PR	**KEWEENAW**	UC	RE	TX	VR
			•	•	•	Copper Range Abstract & Title Co 518	•	•	•	•

			CV	CR	PR	**LAKE**	UC	RE	TX	VR
						Great Lakes Title of Cadillac.....................868	•	•	•	
			•	•	•	Lake County Abstract Co Inc.....................1157	•	•	•	
						Suveyors Title Co Inc.....................1894	•	•	•	

			CV	CR	PR	**LAPEER**	UC	RE	TX	VR
			•	•	•	Homestead Title 987	•	•	•	•
			•	•	•	LaPeer County Abstract & Title Co Inc..................1149	•	•	•	•
			•	•	•	Mallard Investigations.....................1273	•	•	•	•

			CV	CR	PR	**LEELANAU**	UC	RE	TX	VR
			•	•		Behind the Scene Investigations.....................276	•	•	•	
					•	Leelanau Title Co.....................1191	•	•	•	

			CV	CR	PR	**LENAWEE**	UC	RE	TX	VR
			•	•	•	American Title Company of Lenawee....................141	•	•	•	•
			•	•	•	Central Investigation 425	•	•	•	•

●	●	●	Research North Inc of Traverse City 1686	●	●	● ●

CV	**CR**	**PR**	**LIVINGSTON**	**UC**	**RE**	**TX**	**VR**
●	●	●	Homestead Title 987	●	●	●	●
●		●	Landmark Title Service 1169	●	●	●	●

CV	**CR**	**PR**	**LUCE**	**UC**	**RE**	**TX**	**VR**
		●	Mackinac Abstract and Title Co 1263	●	●	●	

CV	**CR**	**PR**	**MACKINAC**	**UC**	**RE**	**TX**	**VR**
●	●		Eastern Upper Pennensula Title Co 685	●	●	●	●
		●	Mackinac Abstract and Title Co 1263	●	●	●	
●	●	●	Research North Inc of Petoskey 1685	●	●	●	●
		●	Whiteside Abstract and Title Insurance.............2087	●	●	●	

CV	**CR**	**PR**	**MACOMB**	**UC**	**RE**	**TX**	**VR**
●	●	●	Ameripro Attorney Service Bureau Inc...............142	●	●	●	●
		●	Finders Inc 762	●	●	●	
●	●	●	MGI..1259	●	●	●	●
●	●	●	Mallard Investigations.......................................1273	●	●	●	●
●	●	●	Mason and Associates 1293	●	●	●	●
●	●	●	VISTA Inc..2017	●	●	●	●

CV	**CR**	**PR**	**MANISTEE**	**UC**	**RE**	**TX**	**VR**
			Great Lakes Title of Manistee 869	●	●	●	
●	●	●	Manistee Abstract & Title Co 1275	●	●	●	●
●	●	●	Research North Inc of Traverse City 1686	●	●	●	●

DT	**BK**	**CV**	**CR**	**PR**	**MARQUETTE**	**UC**	**RE**	**TX**	**VR**
				●	Great Northern Title & Abstract Inc...................870	●	●	●	
				●	Upper Penninsula Title and Abstract.................2013	●	●	●	

CV	**CR**	**PR**	**MASON**	**UC**	**RE**	**TX**	**VR**
			Great Lakes Title of Manistee 869	●	●	●	
			Mason County Abstract......................................1292	●	●	●	

CV	**CR**	**PR**	**MECOSTA**	**UC**	**RE**	**TX**	**VR**
			Great Lakes Title of Cadillac............................868	●	●	●	
			Suveyors Title Co Inc..1894	●	●	●	●

CV	**CR**	**PR**	**MENOMINEE**	**UC**	**RE**	**TX**	**VR**
●	●	●	Associated Peninsula Title Co............................172	●	●	●	●
		●	Upper Penninsula Title and Abstract.................2013	●	●	●	

CV	**CR**	**PR**	**MIDLAND**	**UC**	**RE**	**TX**	**VR**
●		●	Midland Title Co 1344	●	●	●	●

CV	**CR**	**PR**	**MISSAUKEE**	**UC**	**RE**	**TX**	**VR**
		●	Houghton Lake Title & Escrow Co.....................996	●	●	●	●
●	●	●	Missaukee Realty Co..1359	●	●	●	●
●	●	●	Research North Inc of Traverse City 1686	●	●	●	●

CV	**CR**	**PR**	**MONROE**	**UC**	**RE**	**TX**	**VR**
		●	Centennial Title & Abstract Co 423	●	●	●	
●	●	●	Central Investigation 425	●	●	●	●
●	●	●	VISTA Inc..2017	●	●	●	●

CV	**CR**	**PR**	**MONTCALM**	**UC**	**RE**	**TX**	**VR**
			See ALL COUNTIES..				

CV	**CR**	**PR**	**MONTMORENCY**	**UC**	**RE**	**TX**	**VR**
●		●	Montmorency County Abstract...........................1376	●	●	●	●
●	●	●	Research North Inc of Alpena............................1684	●	●	●	●

	CV	CR	PR	MUSKEGON		UC	RE	TX	VR
	●	●	●	Duran, James C 668			●	●	●
	●	●	●	I & S Consulting 1014			●	●	
	●	●	●	Professional Courier Service......................1616		●	●	●	●
	●		●	Special Private Investigations Inc 1840		●	●	●	●

	CV	CR	PR	NEWAYGO		UC	RE	TX	VR
	●	●	●	Newaygo County Abstract and Title Co...........1424		●	●	●	●

	CV	CR	PR	OAKLAND		UC	RE	TX	VR
	●	●	●	Ameripro Attorney Service Bureau Inc................142		●	●	●	●
			●	Finders Inc 762		●	●	●	
	●		●	Homestead Title.................................987		●	●	●	
	●		●	Landmark Title Service........................1169		●	●	●	
	●	●	●	MGI.......................................1259		●	●	●	
	●	●	●	Mallard Investigations..........................1273		●	●	●	
	●	●	●	Mason and Associates 1293		●	●	●	
	●	●	●	Midwest Search Ltd 1346		●	●	●	
	●	●	●	VISTA Inc...................................2017		●	●	●	

	CV	CR	PR	OCEANA		UC	RE	TX	VR
	●	●	●	Duran, James C 668			●	●	●
	●	●	●	I & S Consulting 1014			●	●	
	●	●	●	Oceana Land Title Co 1455		●	●	●	●

	CV	CR	PR	OGEMAW		UC	RE	TX	VR
	●		●	AuSable Valley Abstract and Title Co 214		●	●	●	
			●	Houghton Lake Title & Escrow Co...................996		●	●	●	●
	●	●	●	Landmark Title Corp............................1168		●	●	●	●
	●	●	●	Ogeman Title Co...............................1457		●	●	●	●
			●	Ogemaw County Abstract Co......................1458		●	●	●	

	CV	CR	PR	ONTONAGON		UC	RE	TX	VR
	●	●	●	Copper Range Abstract & Title Co 518		●	●	●	●

	CV	CR	PR	OSCEOLA		UC	RE	TX	VR
				Great Lakes Title of Cadillac......................868		●	●	●	
	●	●	●	Lake County Abstract Co Inc.....................1157		●	●	●	●
				Suveyors Title Co Inc...........................1894		●	●	●	

	CV	CR	PR	OSCODA		UC	RE	TX	VR
	●		●	AuSable Valley Abstract and Title Co 214		●	●	●	
	●		●	Oscoda County Abstract Inc......................1480		●	●	●	
	●	●	●	Research North Inc of Alpena.....................1684		●	●	●	●

	CV	CR	PR	OTSEGO		UC	RE	TX	VR
			●	Alpine Title Co.................................122			●	●	
	●	●	●	Otsego County Abstract Co.......................1482		●	●	●	●
	●	●	●	Research North Inc of Petoskey 1685		●	●	●	●

	CV	CR	PR	OTTAWA		UC	RE	TX	VR
	●	●	●	I & S Consulting 1014			●	●	
	●	●	●	Professional Courier Service......................1616		●	●	●	●
	●		●	Special Private Investigations Inc 1840		●	●	●	●

	CV	CR	PR	PRESQUE ISLE		UC	RE	TX	VR
	●	●	●	Huron Shares Abstract & Title....................1005		●	●	●	
	●		●	Presque Isle County Abstract.....................1599		●	●	●	
	●	●	●	Research North Inc of Alpena.....................1684		●	●	●	●

	CV	CR	PR	ROSCOMMON		UC	RE	TX	VR
			●	Houghton Lake Title & Escrow Co...................996		●	●	●	●
			●	Main Abstract & Title Co.........................1269		●	●	●	●

DT	BK	CV	CR	PR		UC	RE	TX	VR
					SAGINAW				
		•		•	Bay County Abstract Co 263	•	•	•	•
					ST. CLAIR				
		•		•	Huron Title Co 1006	•	•	•	
					ST. JOSEPH				
		•	•	•	St Joseph County Abstract Office Inc 1847	•	•	•	•
					SANILAC				
				•	Mid Michigan Title & Abstract Co Inc 1339	•	•	•	•
					SCHOOLCRAFT				
				•	Upper Penninsula Title and Abstract 2013	•	•	•	
					SHIAWASSEE				
		•	•	•	Homestead Title 987	•	•	•	•
		•			Lawyers Title Insurance Corp 1186	•	•	•	
					TUSCOLA				
		•		•	Bay County Abstract Co 263	•	•	•	•
					VAN BUREN				
				•	Lake Michigan Title Co 1158	•	•	•	
		•	•	•	VanBuren County Abstract Office 2025	•	•	•	•
					WASHTENAW				
•				•	Finders Inc 762	•	•	•	
		•	•	•	Homestead Title 987	•	•	•	•
		•		•	Landmark Title Service 1169	•	•	•	•
•		•	•	•	Mason and Associates 1293	•	•	•	•
•		•	•	•	VISTA Inc 2017	•	•	•	•
					WAYNE				
•	•	•	•	•	Ameripro Attorney Service Bureau Inc 142	•	•	•	•
•	•			•	Finders Inc 762	•	•	•	
•	•	•	•	•	MGI 1259	•	•	•	•
•	•	•	•	•	Mallard Investigations 1273	•	•	•	•
•	•	•	•	•	Mason and Associates 1293	•	•	•	•
•	•	•	•	•	Midwest Search Ltd 1346	•	•	•	•
•	•	•	•	•	VISTA Inc 2017	•	•	•	•
					WEXFORD				
		•	•		Behind the Scene Investigations 276	•	•	•	
					Great Lakes Title of Cadillac 868	•	•	•	
		•	•	•	Research North Inc of Traverse City 1686	•	•	•	•
					Suveyors Title Co Inc 1894	•	•	•	•

Minnesota

DT	BK	CV	CR	PR	ALL COUNTIES	UC	RE	TX	VR
●	●	●	●	●	Capitol Lien Records and Research Inc 397	●	●	●	

		CV	CR	PR	AITKIN	UC	RE	TX	VR
		●			Aitkin County Abstract Co.......................92		●	●	
		●	●	●	Port-o-Wild's Security Services...................1572	●	●	●	●
		●	●		Reid, Ann C.......................1675	●	●	●	●

		CV	CR	PR	ANOKA	UC	RE	TX	VR
		●	●	●	Accountable Process Servers...................61	●	●	●	●
		●	●	●	Acorn 3 Inc.......................70	●	●	●	●
		●	●	●	Associated Abstracting Services of MN...........169	●	●	●	●
		●	●	●	Dovolos & Associates...................657	●	●	●	●
		●	●	●	Heartland Information Services Inc...............944	●	●	●	●
		●		●	Independent Abstracting Service Inc..........1023	●	●	●	●
				●	Land Title Inc.......................1165		●	●	●
		●	●	●	Legal Courier Service...................1195	●	●	●	●
		●	●	●	Metro Legal Services...................1334	●	●	●	●
		●	●	●	Professional Research Services Inc...............1617	●	●	●	●
		●		●	Twin City Abstract Corp...................1993	●	●	●	
		●	●	●	Verified Credentials...................2028	●	●	●	●

		CV	CR	PR	BECKER	UC	RE	TX	VR
		●	●	●	Consolidated Abstract Co of Becker..............515	●	●	●	●
		●	●	●	P.I. Services...................1488	●	●	●	●
		●	●	●	Port-o-Wild's Security Services...................1572	●	●	●	●

		CV	CR	PR	BELTRAMI	UC	RE	TX	VR
		●	●	●	ACME Research...................20	●	●	●	●
		●	●	●	Port-o-Wild's Security Services...................1572	●	●	●	●
		●	●		Reid, Ann C.......................1675	●	●	●	
					Sathre Abstractors Inc 1741	●			

		CV	CR	PR	BENTON	UC	RE	TX	VR
		●	●	●	Associated Abstracting Services of MN...........169	●	●	●	●
		●		●	Benton County Abstract Company...............283	●	●	●	●
		●		●	Heartland Title and Abstract Co.................945	●	●	●	●
		●	●		Reid, Ann C.......................1675	●	●	●	●
		●		●	Tri-County Abstract and Title Guaranty..........1979	●	●	●	
		●	●		Walker, Marilyn...................2046	●	●	●	●

		CV	CR	PR	BIG STONE	UC	RE	TX	VR
		●	●		Walker, Marilyn...................2046	●	●	●	●

		CV	CR	PR	BLUE EARTH	UC	RE	TX	VR
		●	●	●	Associated Abstracting Services of MN...........169	●	●	●	●
		●	●	●	Olson Detective Agency...................1467	●	●	●	●

		CV	CR	PR	BROWN	UC	RE	TX	VR
		●	●	●	Associated Abstracting Services of MN...........169	●	●	●	●
		●	●	●	Olson Detective Agency...................1467	●	●	●	●

		CV	CR	PR	CARLTON	UC	RE	TX	VR
		●		●	Carlton County Abstract and Title Co............407	●	●	●	●
		●	●		Reid, Ann C.......................1675	●	●	●	●
		●	●		Seehus, Penny 1781		●	●	

		CV	CR	PR	CARVER	UC	RE	TX	VR
		●	●	●	Acorn 3 Inc.......................70	●	●	●	●
		●	●	●	Associated Abstracting Services of MN...........169	●	●	●	●
		●		●	Independent Abstracting Service Inc..........1023	●	●	●	●

CV	CR	PR			UC	RE	TX	VR
●	●	●	Legal Courier Service	1195	●	●	●	●
●	●	●	Metro Legal Services	1334	●	●	●	●
●	●	●	Professional Research Services Inc	1617	●	●	●	●
●		●	Twin City Abstract Corp	1993	●	●	●	
●	●	●	Verified Credentials	2028	●	●	●	●

CV	CR	PR	CASS		UC	RE	TX	VR
●	●	●	ACME Research	20	●	●	●	●
●			Complete Title Service of Walker Inc	510		●	●	
	●	●	Cygneture Title Inc	576	●	●	●	●
●	●	●	Port-o-Wild's Security Services	1572	●	●	●	●
●	●		Reid, Ann C	1675	●	●	●	●
●	●		Walker, Marilyn	2046	●	●	●	●

CV	CR	PR	CHIPPEWA		UC	RE	TX	VR
●	●	●	Libby Law Office	1223		●	●	●
●	●		Walker, Marilyn	2046	●	●	●	

CV	CR	PR	CHISAGO		UC	RE	TX	VR
●	●	●	Associated Abstracting Services of MN	169	●	●	●	●
●		●	Independent Abstracting Service Inc	1023	●	●	●	
●		●	Land Title Inc	1165		●	●	●
●	●	●	Peterson Abstract Co	1543	●	●	●	●

CV	CR	PR	CLAY		UC	RE	TX	VR
●		●	Clay County Abstract Co	469	●	●	●	
●	●	●	P.I. Services	1488	●	●	●	●

CV	CR	PR	CLEARWATER		UC	RE	TX	VR
●	●	●	Port-o-Wild's Security Services	1572	●	●	●	●

CV	CR	PR	COOK		UC	RE	TX	VR
●	●		Reid, Ann C	1675	●	●	●	●
●	●		Seehus, Penny	1781		●	●	

CV	CR	PR	COTTONWOOD		UC	RE	TX	VR
●		●	Cottonwood County Abstract Company	535		●	●	

CV	CR	PR	CROW WING		UC	RE	TX	VR
●		●	Crow Wing County Abstract Co	567	●	●	●	
	●	●	Cygneture Title Inc	576	●	●	●	●
●	●	●	Port-o-Wild's Security Services	1572	●	●	●	●
●	●		Reid, Ann C	1675	●	●	●	●

CV	CR	PR	DAKOTA		UC	RE	TX	VR
●	●	●	Acorn 3 Inc	70	●	●	●	●
●	●	●	Associated Abstracting Services of MN	169	●	●	●	●
●		●	Dakota County Abstract Co	585	●	●	●	
●	●	●	Dovolos & Associates	657	●	●	●	●
●	●	●	Heartland Information Services Inc	944	●	●	●	●
●		●	Independent Abstracting Service Inc	1023	●	●	●	
●		●	Land Title Inc	1165		●	●	●
●	●	●	Legal Courier Service	1195	●	●	●	●
●	●	●	Metro Legal Services	1334	●	●	●	●
●	●	●	Professional Research Services Inc	1617	●	●	●	●
●		●	Twin City Abstract Corp	1993	●	●	●	
●	●	●	Verified Credentials	2028	●	●	●	●

CV	CR	PR	DODGE		UC	RE	TX	VR
			See ALL COUNTIES					

CV	CR	PR	DOUGLAS		UC	RE	TX	VR
●		●	Douglas County Abstract Co	652	●	●	●	

DT	BK	CV	CR	PR		UC	RE	TX	VR
		•	•		Walker, Marilyn..2046	•	•	•	•
		CV	**CR**	**PR**	**FARIBAULT**	**UC**	**RE**	**TX**	**VR**
		•		•	Sharon K Hannaman Abstracter........................1788	•	•	•	
		CV	**CR**	**PR**	**FILLMORE**	**UC**	**RE**	**TX**	**VR**
					See ALL COUNTIES..				
		CV	**CR**	**PR**	**FREEBORN**	**UC**	**RE**	**TX**	**VR**
		•	•	•	Albert Lea Abstract Co...100	•	•	•	•
		•	•	•	Associated Abstracting Services of MN..............169	•	•	•	•
		CV	**CR**	**PR**	**GOODHUE**	**UC**	**RE**	**TX**	**VR**
		•	•	•	Born, Shirley..327	•	•	•	•
		CV	**CR**	**PR**	**GRANT**	**UC**	**RE**	**TX**	**VR**
		•	•		Walker, Marilyn..2046	•	•	•	•
DT	**BK**	**CV**	**CR**	**PR**	**HENNEPIN**	**UC**	**RE**	**TX**	**VR**
•	•	•	•	•	Accountable Process Servers.................................61	•	•	•	•
•	•	•	•	•	Acorn 3 Inc..70	•	•	•	•
•	•	•	•	•	Associated Abstracting Services of MN..............169	•	•	•	•
•	•	•	•	•	Dovolos & Associates...657	•	•	•	•
•	•	•	•	•	Heartland Information Services Inc.....................944	•	•	•	•
		•	•	•	Independent Abstracting Service Inc..................1023	•			
		•	•	•	Land Title Inc..1165		•	•	•
		•	•	•	Legal Courier Service..1195	•	•	•	•
•	•	•	•	•	Metro Legal Services...1334	•	•	•	•
•	•	•	•	•	Professional Research Services Inc....................1617	•	•	•	•
•	•	•	•	•	Twin City Abstract Corp....................................1993	•	•	•	
•	•	•	•	•	Verified Credentials...2028	•	•	•	•
		CV	**CR**	**PR**	**HOUSTON**	**UC**	**RE**	**TX**	**VR**
		•		•	Search Associates...1753	•	•	•	•
		CV	**CR**	**PR**	**HUBBARD**	**UC**	**RE**	**TX**	**VR**
		•	•	•	ACME Research...20	•	•	•	•
		•			Complete Title Service of Walker Inc.................510		•	•	
		•		•	Hubbard County Abstract Co Inc........................999		•	•	
		•	•	•	Port-o-Wild's Security Services.........................1572	•	•	•	•
		•	•		Reid, Ann C..1675	•	•	•	•
		CV	**CR**	**PR**	**ISANTI**	**UC**	**RE**	**TX**	**VR**
		•		•	Associated Abstracting Services of MN..............169	•	•	•	•
		•		•	Independent Abstracting Service Inc..................1023	•	•	•	•
		CV	**CR**	**PR**	**ITASCA**	**UC**	**RE**	**TX**	**VR**
			•	•	Itasca County Abstract Co.................................1060	•	•	•	•
		•	•	•	Port-o-Wild's Security Services.........................1572	•	•	•	•
		•	•		Reid, Ann C..1675	•	•	•	•
		•	•		Seehus, Penny..1781		•	•	
		CV	**CR**	**PR**	**JACKSON**	**UC**	**RE**	**TX**	**VR**
					See ALL COUNTIES..				
		CV	**CR**	**PR**	**KANABEC**	**UC**	**RE**	**TX**	**VR**
		•	•		Reid, Ann C..1675	•	•	•	•
		CV	**CR**	**PR**	**KANDIYOHI**	**UC**	**RE**	**TX**	**VR**
		•	•		Walker, Marilyn..2046	•	•	•	•
		CV	**CR**	**PR**	**KITTSON**	**UC**	**RE**	**TX**	**VR**
		•	•	•	Port-o-Wild's Security Services.........................1572	•	•	•	•
		•	•	•	Welch & Ekman PC..2073	•	•	•	•

CV	CR	PR	KOOCHICHING	UC	RE	TX	VR
●	●	●	Port-o-Wild's Security Services....................1572	●	●	●	●
●	●		Reid, Ann C....................1675	●	●	●	●

CV	CR	PR	LAC QUI PARLE	UC	RE	TX	VR
●	●	●	Libby Law Office....................1223		●	●	●

CV	CR	PR	LAKE	UC	RE	TX	VR
●	●		Reid, Ann C....................1675	●	●	●	●
●	●		Seehus, Penny....................1781		●	●	

CV	CR	PR	LAKE OF THE WOODS	UC	RE	TX	VR
●	●	●	Lake of the Woods County Title Company....................1160	●	●	●	●
●	●	●	Port-o-Wild's Security Services....................1572	●	●	●	●

CV	CR	PR	LE SUEUR	UC	RE	TX	VR
●	●	●	Associated Abstracting Services of MN....................169	●	●	●	●

CV	CR	PR	LINCOLN	UC	RE	TX	VR
●	●	●	Dirks, Lewis....................635	●	●	●	●

CV	CR	PR	LYON	UC	RE	TX	VR
			See ALL COUNTIES....................				

CV	CR	PR	MCLEOD	UC	RE	TX	VR
●	●	●	Associated Abstracting Services of MN....................169	●	●	●	●
●	●	●	Public Records Recovery Services....................1628	●	●	●	●
●	●		Reid, Ann C....................1675	●	●	●	●

CV	CR	PR	MAHNOMEN	UC	RE	TX	VR
●		●	Mahnomen County Abstract Company....................1268	●	●	●	
●	●	●	Port-o-Wild's Security Services....................1572	●	●	●	●

CV	CR	PR	MARSHALL	UC	RE	TX	VR
●	●	●	Port-o-Wild's Security Services....................1572	●	●	●	●
●	●	●	Welch & Ekman PC....................2073	●	●	●	●

CV	CR	PR	MARTIN	UC	RE	TX	VR
			See ALL COUNTIES....................				

CV	CR	PR	MEEKER	UC	RE	TX	VR
●		●	Heartland Title and Abstract Co....................945	●	●	●	●
●	●		Reid, Ann C....................1675	●	●	●	●

CV	CR	PR	MILLE LACS	UC	RE	TX	VR
●	●	●	Associated Abstracting Services of MN....................169	●	●	●	●

CV	CR	PR	MORRISON	UC	RE	TX	VR
	●	●	Larson Abstract Co....................1175	●	●	●	●
●	●		Reid, Ann C....................1675	●	●	●	●
●		●	Tri-County Abstract and Title Guaranty....................1979	●	●	●	

CV	CR	PR	MOWER	UC	RE	TX	VR
●	●	●	Associated Abstracting Services of MN....................169	●	●	●	●
●		●	Attorney Services....................186				●

CV	CR	PR	MURRAY	UC	RE	TX	VR
●	●	●	Dirks, Lewis....................635	●	●	●	●

CV	CR	PR	NICOLLET	UC	RE	TX	VR
●	●	●	Associated Abstracting Services of MN....................169	●	●	●	●
●	●	●	Olson Detective Agency....................1467	●	●	●	●

NOBLES

CV	CR	PR			UC	RE	TX	VR
●	●	●	Dirks, Lewis 635		●	●	●	●

NORMAN

CV	CR	PR			UC	RE	TX	VR
●	●	●	P.I. Services 1488		●	●	●	●
●	●	●	Port-o-Wild's Security Services 1572		●	●	●	●

OLMSTED

CV	CR	PR			UC	RE	TX	VR
●	●	●	Associated Abstracting Services of MN 169		●	●	●	●
●	●	●	Public Records Recovery Services 1628		●	●	●	●

OTTER TAIL

BK	CV	CR	PR			UC	RE	TX	VR
	●		●	N F Field Abstract Co 1403		●	●	●	
				P.I. Services 1488					
●	●	●		Walker, Marilyn 2046		●	●	●	●
●	●		●	West Central Abstracting Co 2078		●	●	●	

PENNINGTON

CV	CR	PR			UC	RE	TX	VR
●	●	●	Pennington County Abstract Co 1533			●	●	●
●	●	●	Port-o-Wild's Security Services 1572		●	●	●	●

PINE

CV	CR	PR			UC	RE	TX	VR
●	●		Reid, Ann C. 1675		●	●	●	●

PIPESTONE

CV	CR	PR			UC	RE	TX	VR
●	●	●	Dirks, Lewis 635		●	●	●	●
			Pipestone County Abstract Co 1556		●	●	●	

POLK

CV	CR	PR			UC	RE	TX	VR
●	●	●	Port-o-Wild's Security Services 1572		●	●	●	●
●			Strander Abstract Inc 1872		●	●	●	

POPE

CV	CR	PR			UC	RE	TX	VR
●		●	Douglas County Abstract Co 652		●	●	●	
●	●		Walker, Marilyn 2046		●	●	●	●

RAMSEY

DT	BK	CV	CR	PR			UC	RE	TX	VR
●	●	●	●	●	Accountable Process Servers 61		●	●	●	●
●	●	●	●	●	Acorn 3 Inc. 70		●	●	●	●
●	●	●	●	●	Associated Abstracting Services of MN 169		●	●	●	●
●	●	●	●	●	Dovolos & Associates 657		●	●	●	●
●	●	●	●	●	Heartland Information Services Inc 944		●	●	●	●
●	●	●		●	Land Title Inc 1165			●	●	●
●	●	●		●	Legal Courier Service 1195		●		●	●
●	●	●	●	●	Metro Legal Services 1334		●	●	●	●
●	●	●	●	●	Professional Research Services Inc 1617		●	●	●	●
●	●	●		●	Twin City Abstract Corp 1993		●	●	●	●
●	●	●	●	●	Verified Credentials 2028		●	●	●	●

RED LAKE

CV	CR	PR			UC	RE	TX	VR
●		●	Independent Abstracting Service Inc 1023		●	●	●	●
●	●	●	Port-o-Wild's Security Services 1572		●	●	●	●

REDWOOD

CV	CR	PR			UC	RE	TX	VR
●	●	●	Olson Detective Agency 1467		●	●	●	●
		●	Renville County Abstract Co 1681			●	●	●

RENVILLE

CV	CR	PR			UC	RE	TX	VR
		●	Renville County Abstract Co 1681			●	●	●

RICE

CV	CR	PR			UC	RE	TX	VR
●	●	●	Associated Abstracting Services of MN 169		●	●	●	●
●	●	●	Rice County Abstract & Title Co 1693		●	●	●	●

		CV	CR	PR	ROCK	UC	RE	TX	VR
		●	●	●	Dirks, Lewis 635	●	●	●	●

		CV	CR	PR	ROSEAU	UC	RE	TX	VR
		●	●	●	Port-o-Wild's Security Services..1572	●	●	●	●
		●	●	●	Roseau County Title & Abstract Co...............................1715	●	●	●	●

DT	BK	CV	CR	PR	ST. LOUIS	UC	RE	TX	VR
●	●	●			Reid, Ann C..1675	●	●	●	●
●	●	●			Seehus, Penny 1781		●	●	

		CV	CR	PR	SCOTT	UC	RE	TX	VR
		●	●	●	Acorn 3 Inc...70	●	●	●	●
		●	●	●	Associated Abstracting Services of MN............................169	●	●	●	●
		●		●	Heartland Information Services Inc..................................944	●	●	●	●
		●		●	Independent Abstracting Service Inc...............................1023	●	●	●	●
		●	●	●	Legal Courier Service...1195	●	●	●	●
		●	●	●	Metro Legal Services..1334	●	●	●	●
		●	●	●	Professional Research Services Inc 1617	●	●	●	●
		●	●	●	Public Records Recovery Services...................................1628	●	●	●	●
		●		●	Twin City Abstract Corp...1993	●	●	●	
		●	●	●	Verified Credentials 2028	●	●	●	●

		CV	CR	PR	SHERBURNE	UC	RE	TX	VR
		●	●	●	Accountable Process Servers..61	●	●	●	●
		●	●	●	Acorn 3 Inc...70	●	●	●	●
		●	●	●	Associated Abstracting Services of MN............................169	●	●	●	●
		●		●	Heartland Title and Abstract Co......................................945	●	●	●	●
		●		●	Independent Abstracting Service Inc...............................1023	●	●	●	●
		●	●	●	Legal Courier Service...1195	●	●	●	●
		●	●	●	Metro Legal Services..1334	●	●	●	●
		●	●		Reid, Ann C..1675	●	●	●	●
		●		●	Tri-County Abstract and Title Guaranty..........................1979	●	●	●	

		CV	CR	PR	SIBLEY	UC	RE	TX	VR
		●	●	●	Associated Abstracting Services of MN............................169	●	●	●	●
		●	●	●	Olson Detective Agency..1467	●	●	●	●
		●	●	●	Public Records Recovery Services...................................1628	●	●	●	●

		CV	CR	PR	STEARNS	UC	RE	TX	VR
		●	●	●	Associated Abstracting Services of MN............................169	●	●	●	●
		●		●	Heartland Title and Abstract Co......................................945	●	●	●	●
		●	●		Reid, Ann C..1675	●	●	●	●
		●		●	Tri-County Abstract and Title Guaranty..........................1979	●	●	●	
		●	●		Walker, Marilyn 2046	●	●	●	●

		CV	CR	PR	STEELE	UC	RE	TX	VR
		●	●	●	Associated Abstracting Services of MN............................169	●	●	●	●
		●	●	●	Steele County Abstract Co 1858	●	●	●	

		CV	CR	PR	STEVENS	UC	RE	TX	VR
		●	●		Walker, Marilyn 2046	●	●	●	●

		CV	CR	PR	SWIFT	UC	RE	TX	VR
		●	●		Walker, Marilyn 2046	●	●	●	●

		CV	CR	PR	TODD	UC	RE	TX	VR
		●	●		Reid, Ann C..1675	●	●	●	●
		●	●		Walker, Marilyn 2046	●	●	●	●

		CV	CR	PR	TRAVERSE	UC	RE	TX	VR
		●	●		Walker, Marilyn 2046	●	●	●	●

WABASHA

CV	CR	PR		UC	RE	TX	VR
●	●	●	Born, Shirley 327	●	●	●	●
●		●	Wabasha County Abstract Co 2041	●	●	●	●

WADENA

CV	CR	PR		UC	RE	TX	VR
●	●		Reid, Ann C 1675	●	●	●	●
●	●		Walker, Marilyn 2046	●	●	●	●

WASECA

CV	CR	PR		UC	RE	TX	VR
●	●	●	Associated Abstracting Services of MN 169	●	●	●	●

WASHINGTON

CV	CR	PR		UC	RE	TX	VR
●	●	●	Acorn 3 Inc 70	●	●	●	●
●	●	●	Associated Abstracting Services of MN 169	●	●	●	●
●	●	●	Heartland Information Services Inc 944	●	●	●	●
●		●	Independent Abstracting Service Inc 1023		●	●	●
●		●	Land Title Inc 1165		●	●	●
●	●	●	Legal Courier Service 1195	●	●	●	●
●	●	●	Metro Legal Services 1334	●	●	●	●
●	●	●	Professional Research Services Inc 1617	●	●	●	●
●		●	Twin City Abstract Corp 1993	●	●	●	●
●	●	●	Verified Credentials 2028	●	●	●	●

WATONWAN

CV	CR	PR		UC	RE	TX	VR
●	●	●	Olson Detective Agency 1467	●	●	●	●

WILKIN

CV	CR	PR		UC	RE	TX	VR
●	●	●	P.I. Services 1488	●	●	●	●
●		●	Richland County Abstract Co 1697	●	●	●	
			Wilkin County Abstract 2091		●	●	

WINONA

CV	CR	PR		UC	RE	TX	VR
●		●	Search Associates 1753	●	●	●	●

WRIGHT

CV	CR	PR		UC	RE	TX	VR
●	●	●	Acorn 3 Inc 70	●	●	●	●
●	●	●	Associated Abstracting Services of MN 169	●	●	●	●
●		●	Campbell Abstract Co 387		●	●	
●	●	●	Heartland Information Services Inc 944	●	●	●	●
●		●	Heartland Title and Abstract Co 945	●	●	●	●
●		●	Independent Abstracting Service Inc 1023	●	●	●	●
●	●	●	Legal Courier Service 1195	●	●	●	●
●	●	●	Metro Legal Services 1334	●	●	●	●
●		●	Tri-County Abstract and Title Guaranty 1979	●	●	●	

YELLOW MEDICINE

CV	CR	PR		UC	RE	TX	VR
●	●	●	Libby Law Office 1223		●	●	●

Mississippi

DT	BK	CV	CR	PR	**ALL COUNTIES**		UC	RE	TX	VR
	•	•	•	•	Hollingsworth Court Reporting Inc.................................983		•	•	•	•
•	•	•	•	•	J L & A.................................1063		•	•	•	•

		CV	CR	PR	**ADAMS**		UC	RE	TX	VR
		•	•	•	Kingsafer, John R.................................1126		•	•	•	
		•	•	•	McNeal Investigations.................................1318		•	•	•	•

		CV	CR	PR	**ALCORN**		UC	RE	TX	VR
		•	•	•	Mitchell McNutt Threadgill et al.................................1362		•	•	•	

		CV	CR	PR	**AMITE**		UC	RE	TX	VR
		•	•	•	Kingsafer, John R.................................1126		•	•	•	
		•	•	•	McNeal Investigations.................................1318		•	•	•	•
		•	•	•	Mord, John.................................1385		•	•	•	•
		•		•	Universal Research.................................2011			•		•

		CV	CR	PR	**ATTALA**		UC	RE	TX	VR
		•	•	•	Shaw, John.................................1792		•	•	•	

		CV	CR	PR	**BENTON**		UC	RE	TX	VR
		•	•	•	Taylor, Diane.................................1905		•	•	•	•

		CV	CR	PR	**BOLIVAR**		UC	RE	TX	VR
		•	•	•	Haynes, Brenette.................................943		•	•	•	
		•	•	•	Tweedle, Barbara.................................1992		•	•	•	

		CV	CR	PR	**CALHOUN**		UC	RE	TX	VR
		•	•	•	Crocker, Otis.................................565		•	•	•	•
		•		•	Teasley, Debbie.................................1907		•	•	•	

		CV	CR	PR	**CARROLL**		UC	RE	TX	VR
		•	•	•	Downs, Kenneth E.................................658		•	•	•	•
		•	•	•	Greenlee, J Lane.................................875		•	•	•	•

		CV	CR	PR	**CHICKASAW**		UC	RE	TX	VR
		•	•	•	Crocker, Otis.................................565		•	•	•	•

		CV	CR	PR	**CHOCTAW**		UC	RE	TX	VR
		•	•	•	Griffin, Joe C.................................882		•	•	•	•

		CV	CR	PR	**CLAIBORNE**		UC	RE	TX	VR
		•	•	•	Dulaney, Sim C.................................665		•	•	•	•
		•	•	•	McNeal Investigations.................................1318		•	•	•	•

		CV	CR	PR	**CLARKE**		UC	RE	TX	VR
		•	•	•	Brame Jr, Thomas Q.................................337		•	•	•	•
		•	•	•	McNeal Investigations.................................1318		•	•	•	•
		•	•	•	Williams, George.................................2094		•	•	•	•

		CV	CR	PR	**CLAY**		UC	RE	TX	VR
		•	•	•	Magnolia Title Co.................................1266		•	•	•	•

		CV	CR	PR	**COAHOMA**		UC	RE	TX	VR
		•	•	•	Haney, C Kent.................................916		•	•	•	•

		CV	CR	PR	**COPIAH**		UC	RE	TX	VR
		•	•	•	McNeal Investigations.................................1318		•	•	•	•
		•	•	•	Varas, Jeffrey A.................................2027		•	•	•	•

		CV	CR	PR	**COVINGTON**		UC	RE	TX	VR
		•	•	•	McDaniel, Ney T.................................1308		•	•	•	•
		•	•	•	McNeal Investigations.................................1318		•	•	•	•

DT	BK	CV	CR	PR	Name	Page	UC	RE	TX	VR
		•	•	•	Title Services Inc	1956	•	•	•	
		CV	**CR**	**PR**	**DE SOTO**		**UC**	**RE**	**TX**	**VR**
		•	•	•	Carl Watson & Associates	406	•	•	•	•
		•	•	•	Investigative Services for Attorneys	1049	•	•	•	•
		•	•	•	Record-Check Services Inc	1663	•	•	•	•
		•	•	•	RecordServe/John Kelley Enterprises	1664	•	•	•	
		•	•	•	Schaeffer Papers	1743	•			
DT		**CV**	**CR**	**PR**	**FORREST**		**UC**	**RE**	**TX**	**VR**
•		•	•	•	McNeal Investigations	1318	•	•	•	•
		•	•	•	Title Services Inc	1956	•	•	•	
		CV	**CR**	**PR**	**FRANKLIN**		**UC**	**RE**	**TX**	**VR**
		•	•	•	Graves Jr, K Maxwell	866	•	•	•	
		•	•	•	Kingsafer, John R	1126	•	•	•	
		•	•	•	McNeal Investigations	1318	•	•	•	•
		CV	**CR**	**PR**	**GEORGE**		**UC**	**RE**	**TX**	**VR**
		•	•	•	McNeal Investigations	1318	•	•	•	•
		CV	**CR**	**PR**	**GREENE**		**UC**	**RE**	**TX**	**VR**
		•	•	•	Dobbins, E Fred	638	•	•	•	
		•	•	•	McNeal Investigations	1318	•	•	•	•
		CV	**CR**	**PR**	**GRENADA**		**UC**	**RE**	**TX**	**VR**
		•	•	•	Crocker, Otis	565	•	•	•	•
		CV	**CR**	**PR**	**HANCOCK**		**UC**	**RE**	**TX**	**VR**
		•		•	Home Abstract & Title Co	985	•	•	•	
		•	•	•	McNeal Investigations	1318	•	•	•	•
DT		**CV**	**CR**	**PR**	**HARRISON**		**UC**	**RE**	**TX**	**VR**
		•		•	Home Abstract & Title Co	985	•	•	•	
•		•	•	•	McNeal Investigations	1318	•	•	•	•
DT	**BK**	**CV**	**CR**	**PR**	**HINDS**		**UC**	**RE**	**TX**	**VR**
•		•	•	•	C & R Associates	372	•	•	•	•
•	•	•	•	•	McAllister & Associates Inc	1298	•	•	•	•
		•	•	•	McDaniel, Ney T	1308	•	•	•	•
•	•	•	•	•	McNeal Investigations	1318	•	•	•	•
		•	•	•	Varas, Jeffrey A	2027	•	•	•	•
		CV	**CR**	**PR**	**HOLMES**		**UC**	**RE**	**TX**	**VR**
		•	•	•	Gilmore, Billy J	845	•	•	•	
		CV	**CR**	**PR**	**HUMPHREYS**		**UC**	**RE**	**TX**	**VR**
		•	•	•	Garrard & Trotter	831	•	•	•	•
		CV	**CR**	**PR**	**ISSAQUENA**		**UC**	**RE**	**TX**	**VR**
		•	•	•	Hunter, Joel A	1004	•	•	•	•
		CV	**CR**	**PR**	**ITAWAMBA**		**UC**	**RE**	**TX**	**VR**
		•	•	•	Richardson, Sharian	1695	•	•	•	•
		CV	**CR**	**PR**	**JACKSON**		**UC**	**RE**	**TX**	**VR**
		•		•	Home Abstract & Title Co	985	•	•	•	
		•	•	•	McNeal Investigations	1318	•	•	•	•
		CV	**CR**	**PR**	**JASPER**		**UC**	**RE**	**TX**	**VR**
		•	•	•	Brame Jr, Thomas Q	337	•	•	•	•
		•	•	•	McDaniel, Ney T	1308	•	•	•	•
		•	•	•	McNeal Investigations	1318	•	•	•	•

		CV	CR	PR	JEFFERSON		UC	RE	TX	VR
		•	•	•	Kingsafer, John R..1126		•	•	•	
		•	•	•	McNeal Investigations.....................................1318		•	•	•	•

		CV	CR	PR	JEFFERSON DAVIS		UC	RE	TX	VR
		•	•	•	McDaniel, Ney T...1308		•	•	•	•
		•	•	•	Title Services Inc..1956		•	•	•	

		CV	CR	PR	JONES		UC	RE	TX	VR
		•	•	•	Brame Jr, Thomas Q...337		•	•	•	•
		•	•	•	McNeal Investigations.....................................1318		•	•	•	•
		•	•	•	Title Services Inc..1956		•	•	•	

		CV	CR	PR	KEMPER		UC	RE	TX	VR
		•	•	•	Briggs, Eddie J...345		•	•	•	•

		CV	CR	PR	LAFAYETTE		UC	RE	TX	VR
DT		•	•	•	Crocker, Otis...565		•	•	•	•
		•		•	Teasley, Debbie..1907		•	•	•	

		CV	CR	PR	LAMAR		UC	RE	TX	VR
		•	•	•	McNeal Investigations.....................................1318		•	•	•	•
		•	•	•	Title Services Inc..1956		•	•	•	

		CV	CR	PR	LAUDERDALE		UC	RE	TX	VR
		•	•	•	McAllister & Associates Inc 1298			•	•	•

		CV	CR	PR	LAWRENCE		UC	RE	TX	VR
		•	•	•	McNeal Investigations.....................................1318		•	•	•	•
		•	•	•	Mord, John..1385		•	•	•	•

		CV	CR	PR	LEAKE		UC	RE	TX	VR
					See ALL COUNTIES..					

		CV	CR	PR	LEE		UC	RE	TX	VR
		•	•	•	Rainer, Vickie 1646		•	•	•	•
		•		•	Teasley, Debbie..1907		•	•	•	

		CV	CR	PR	LEFLORE		UC	RE	TX	VR
		•	•	•	Garrard & Trotter 831		•	•	•	•

		CV	CR	PR	LINCOLN		UC	RE	TX	VR
		•	•	•	Mord, John..1385		•	•	•	•
		•	•	•	Varas, Jeffrey A..2027		•	•	•	•

		CV	CR	PR	LOWNDES		UC	RE	TX	VR
		•	•	•	Magnolia Title Co 1266		•	•	•	•

		CV	CR	PR	MADISON		UC	RE	TX	VR
		•	•	•	C & R Associates 372		•	•	•	•
		•	•	•	McAllister & Associates Inc 1298		•	•	•	•

		CV	CR	PR	MARION		UC	RE	TX	VR
		•	•	•	Mord, John..1385		•	•	•	•
		•	•	•	Title Services Inc..1956		•	•	•	

		CV	CR	PR	MARSHALL		UC	RE	TX	VR
		•	•	•	Investigative Services for Attorneys...................1049		•	•	•	•
		•	•	•	Record-Check Services Inc 1663		•	•	•	•
		•	•	•	RecordServe/John Kelley Enterprises 1664		•	•	•	•
		•	•	•	Taylor, Diane...1905		•	•	•	•

			CV	CR	PR	MONROE		UC	RE	TX	VR
DT	BK		•	•	•	Magnolia Title Co 1266		•	•	•	•

CV	CR	PR	MONTGOMERY	UC	RE	TX	VR
●	●	●	Greenlee, J Lane................................875	●	●	●	●

CV	CR	PR	NESHOBA	UC	RE	TX	VR
			See ALL COUNTIES..............................				

CV	CR	PR	NEWTON	UC	RE	TX	VR
●	●	●	Brame Jr, Thomas Q................................337	●	●	●	●
●	●	●	Clearman, Danny................................474	●	●	●	●

CV	CR	PR	NOXUBEE	UC	RE	TX	VR
●	●	●	Magnolia Title Co................................1266	●	●	●	●

CV	CR	PR	OKTIBBEHA	UC	RE	TX	VR
●	●	●	Magnolia Title Co................................1266	●	●	●	●

CV	CR	PR	PANOLA	UC	RE	TX	VR
●	●	●	Baker, Gaines................................237	●	●	●	●

CV	CR	PR	PEARL RIVER	UC	RE	TX	VR
●	●	●	McNeal Investigations................................1318	●	●	●	●

CV	CR	PR	PERRY	UC	RE	TX	VR
●	●	●	McNeal Investigations................................1318	●	●	●	●
●	●	●	Title Services Inc................................1956	●	●	●	

CV	CR	PR	PIKE	UC	RE	TX	VR
●	●	●	McNeal Investigations................................1318	●	●	●	●
●	●	●	Mord, John................................1385	●	●	●	●
●	●	●	Regan, William Ben................................1671	●	●	●	●

CV	CR	PR	PONTOTOC	UC	RE	TX	VR
●	●	●	Crocker, Otis................................565	●	●	●	●
●	●	●	Rainer, Vickie................................1646	●	●	●	●
●		●	Teasley, Debbie................................1907	●	●	●	

CV	CR	PR	PRENTISS	UC	RE	TX	VR
●	●	●	Hatcher, John A................................938	●	●	●	●

CV	CR	PR	QUITMAN	UC	RE	TX	VR
●	●	●	Baker, Gaines................................237	●	●	●	●

CV	CR	PR	RANKIN	UC	RE	TX	VR
●	●	●	C & R Associates................................372	●	●	●	●
●	●	●	McAllister & Associates Inc................................1298	●	●	●	●
●	●	●	McDaniel, Ney T................................1308	●	●	●	●
●	●	●	McNeal Investigations................................1318	●	●	●	●

CV	CR	PR	SCOTT	UC	RE	TX	VR
●	●	●	Brame Jr, Thomas Q................................337	●	●	●	●
●	●	●	McDaniel, Ney T................................1308	●	●	●	●
●	●	●	Thompson & Hollingsworth PA................................1945	●	●	●	●

CV	CR	PR	SHARKEY	UC	RE	TX	VR
●	●	●	Garrard & Trotter................................831	●	●	●	●
●	●	●	Hunter, Joel A................................1004	●	●	●	●

CV	CR	PR	SIMPSON	UC	RE	TX	VR
●	●	●	Brame Jr, Thomas Q................................337	●	●	●	●
●	●	●	Buffington, B Scott................................363	●	●	●	
●	●	●	McDaniel, Ney T................................1308	●	●	●	●
●	●	●	McNeal Investigations................................1318	●	●	●	●

DT	CV	CR	PR	County / Agency	Page	UC	RE	TX	VR
				SMITH					
	•	•	•	Brame Jr, Thomas Q	337	•	•	•	•
	•	•	•	McDaniel, Ney T	1308	•	•	•	•
	•	•	•	McNeal Investigations	1318	•	•	•	•
				STONE					
	•	•	•	McNeal Investigations	1318	•	•	•	•
				SUNFLOWER					
	•	•	•	Garrard & Trotter	831	•	•	•	•
				TALLAHATCHIE					
	•	•	•	Baker, Gaines	237	•	•	•	•
	•	•	•	Cassar Jr, George P	415	•	•	•	•
				TATE					
	•	•	•	Baker, Gaines	237	•	•	•	•
	•	•	•	Carl Watson & Associates	406	•	•	•	•
	•	•	•	Record-Check Services Inc	1663	•	•	•	•
				TIPPAH					
	•	•	•	Rainer, Vickie	1646	•	•	•	•
	•	•	•	Taylor, Diane	1905	•	•	•	•
				TISHOMINGO					
	•	•	•	Segars, Mark T	1782	•	•	•	•
				TUNICA					
	•	•	•	Investigative Services for Attorneys	1049	•	•	•	•
	•	•	•	Record-Check Services Inc	1663	•	•	•	•
				UNION					
	•	•	•	Rainer, Vickie	1646	•	•	•	•
	•		•	Teasley, Debbie	1907	•	•	•	
				WALTHALL					
	•	•	•	McNeal Investigations	1318	•	•	•	•
	•	•	•	Mord, John	1385	•	•	•	•
				WARREN					
	•	•	•	C & R Associates	372	•	•	•	•
	•	•	•	Dulaney, Sim C	665	•	•	•	•
	•	•	•	McAllister & Associates Inc	1298	•	•	•	•
DT				**WASHINGTON**					
	•		•	Evans, Robert D	720	•	•	•	
				WAYNE					
	•	•	•	McNeal Investigations	1318	•	•	•	•
				WEBSTER					
	•	•	•	Crocker, Otis	565	•	•	•	•
				WILKINSON					
	•	•	•	Kingsafer, John R	1126	•	•	•	
	•	•	•	McNeal Investigations	1318	•	•		•
	•		•	Universal Research	2011		•		•
				WINSTON					
	•		•	Tucker, Taylor	1988	•	•	•	•
				YALOBUSHA					
	•	•	•	Crocker, Otis	565	•	•	•	•

Court
Records

MISSISSIPPI
119

County
Records

	CV	CR	PR	YAZOO		UC	RE	TX	VR
	●	●	●	Garrard & Trotter 831		●	●	●	●
	●	●	●	McAllister & Associates Inc 1298		●	●	●	●

SUMMARY OF CODES

COURT RECORDS

CODE*	GOVERNMENT AGENCY	TYPE OF INFORMATION
DT	US District Court	Federal civil and criminal cases
BK	Bankruptcy Court	United States bankruptcy cases
CV	Civil Court	Municipal, county and state level civil cases
CR	Criminal Court	Municipal, county and state level criminal cases
PR	Probate Court	Wills and estate cases

COUNTY RECORDS

CODE*	GOVERNMENT AGENCY	TYPE OF INFORMATION
UC	UCC Filing Office	Uniform Commercial Code and other personal property liens
RE	Recorder of Deeds	Real property transactions and liens
TX	Tax Assessor	Real property tax information
VR	Vital Records Office	Birth, death, marriage, divorce, etc.

* The "CODE designates the agency and type of information obtainable in each county."

Missouri

DT	BK	CV	CR	PR	ALL COUNTIES	UC	RE	TX	VR
		●	●	●	Real Estate Loan Services of Missouri............1658	●	●	●	

		CV	CR	PR	ADAIR	UC	RE	TX	VR
		●	●	●	Kunkel, Joan.................................1138	●	●	●	●
		●	●	●	Pickell Abstract Co 1551	●	●	●	

		CV	CR	PR	ANDREW	UC	RE	TX	VR
		●	●	●	Fred McDaniel and Associates................807	●	●	●	●
		●	●	●	Wilson Associates 2102	●	●	●	●

		CV	CR	PR	ATCHISON	UC	RE	TX	VR
		●	●	●	Wilson Associates 2102	●	●	●	●

		CV	CR	PR	AUDRAIN	UC	RE	TX	VR
		●		●	Audrain County Abstract Co...................217	●	●	●	

		CV	CR	PR	BARRY	UC	RE	TX	VR
		●	●	●	Barry County Abstract & Title................252	●	●	●	●
		●	●	●	National Investigative Services Inc..........1408	●	●	●	●

		CV	CR	PR	BARTON	UC	RE	TX	VR
		●	●	●	Barton County Title Co.......................256	●	●	●	●
		●	●	●	National Investigative Services Inc..........1408	●	●	●	●

		CV	CR	PR	BATES	UC	RE	TX	VR
		●	●	●	Akin, Nyla....................................93	●	●	●	●

		CV	CR	PR	BENTON	UC	RE	TX	VR
		●	●	●	Drake Land Title Co..........................660	●	●	●	

		CV	CR	PR	BOLLINGER	UC	RE	TX	VR
		●	●	●	Bollinger County Abstract Co.................318	●	●	●	

		CV	CR	PR	BOONE	UC	RE	TX	VR
		●		●	Guaranty Land Title..........................891	●	●	●	●
		●	●	●	Harmon Legal Process Service.................927	●	●	●	●

DT		CV	CR	PR	BUCHANAN	UC	RE	TX	VR
		●	●	●	Central-MO Investigations....................430		●	●	●
●		●	●	●	Fred McDaniel and Associates................807	●	●	●	●
●		●	●	●	Wilson Associates 2102	●	●	●	●

		CV	CR	PR	BUTLER	UC	RE	TX	VR
		●		●	Butler County Abstract and Title Inc 371	●	●	●	
		●		●	Poplar Bluff Abstract and Title Company......1571	●	●	●	

		CV	CR	PR	CALDWELL	UC	RE	TX	VR
		●		●	Daviess County Abstracts.....................601	●	●	●	
		●	●	●	Wilson Associates 2102	●	●	●	●

		CV	CR	PR	CALLAWAY	UC	RE	TX	VR
		●	●	●	Central-MO Investigations....................430		●	●	●
		●		●	Guaranty Land Title..........................891	●	●	●	●
		●	●	●	Harmon Legal Process Service.................927	●	●	●	●

		CV	CR	PR	CAMDEN	UC	RE	TX	VR
		●	●	●	Galena Abstract Co Inc.......................828	●	●	●	
		●		●	Guaranty Land Title..........................891	●	●	●	●

DT		CV	CR	PR	CAPE GIRARDEAU	UC	RE	TX	VR
		●		●	Cape Girardeau County Abstract and Title 391		●	●	●
					St Francois County Abstract Co...............1845	●	●	●	

	CV	CR	PR	CARROLL	UC	RE	TX	VR
				See ALL COUNTIES..				

	CV	CR	PR	CARTER	UC	RE	TX	VR
				See ALL COUNTIES..				

	CV	CR	PR	CASS	UC	RE	TX	VR
	●	●	●	Fred McDaniel and Associates.............................807	●	●	●	●

	CV	CR	PR	CEDAR	UC	RE	TX	VR
	●	●	●	Akin, Nyla..93	●	●	●	●
	●	●	●	Cedar County Abstract & Title Co........................419	●	●	●	●
	●	●	●	National Investigative Services Inc.....................1408	●	●	●	●

	CV	CR	PR	CHARITON	UC	RE	TX	VR
	●	●	●	Chariton Abstract 436	●	●	●	●

	CV	CR	PR	CHRISTIAN	UC	RE	TX	VR
	●	●	●	Advanced Land and Title......................................89	●	●	●	
	●		●	Hogan Land Title Co..979		●	●	
	●	●	●	National Investigative Services Inc.....................1408	●	●	●	●
	●	●	●	Ozark Abstract & Loan Co..................................1486	●	●	●	

	CV	CR	PR	CLARK	UC	RE	TX	VR
	●	●	●	Johnson, Edith F...1095	●	●	●	●

	CV	CR	PR	CLAY	UC	RE	TX	VR
	●	●	●	RSI...1643				
	●	●	●	Silk Attorney Service...1804	●	●	●	●

	CV	CR	PR	CLINTON	UC	RE	TX	VR
	●		●	Cameron Title Co Inc...384	●	●	●	
	●		●	Daviess County Abstracts....................................601	●	●	●	
	●	●	●	Fred McDaniel and Associates.............................807	●	●	●	●
	●	●	●	Wilson Associates...2102	●	●	●	●

DT	CV	CR	PR	COLE	UC	RE	TX	VR
	●	●	●	Central-MO Investigations...................................430		●	●	●
	●		●	Cole County Abstract and Title.............................485	●	●	●	
	●		●	Guaranty Land Title...891	●	●	●	●
●	●	●	●	Harmon Legal Process Service..............................927	●	●	●	●
	●	●	●	Jeff City Filing 1083	●	●	●	●

	CV	CR	PR	COOPER	UC	RE	TX	VR
	●	●	●	Forbes, Sylvia...792		●	●	●
	●		●	Guaranty Land Title...891	●	●	●	●

	CV	CR	PR	CRAWFORD	UC	RE	TX	VR
	●		●	Crawford County Title Co....................................555	●	●	●	●

	CV	CR	PR	DADE	UC	RE	TX	VR
	●	●	●	Akin, Nyla..93	●	●	●	●
	●	●	●	Ball Agency..239	●	●	●	
	●	●	●	National Investigative Services Inc.....................1408	●	●	●	

	CV	CR	PR	DALLAS	UC	RE	TX	VR
	●	●	●	Akin, Nyla..93	●	●	●	
	●		●	Hogan Land Title Co..979		●	●	
	●	●	●	National Investigative Services Inc.....................1408	●	●	●	●

	CV	CR	PR	DAVIESS	UC	RE	TX	VR
	●		●	Daviess County Abstracts....................................601	●	●	●	
	●	●	●	Wilson Associates...2102	●	●	●	●

	CV	CR	PR	DE KALB		UC	RE	TX	VR
	•		•	Cameron Title Co Inc 384		•	•	•	
	•		•	Daviess County Abstracts 601		•	•	•	
	•	•	•	Wilson Associates 2102		•	•	•	•

	CV	CR	PR	DENT		UC	RE	TX	VR
	•	•	•	Steelman Abstracting Co 1860		•	•	•	

	CV	CR	PR	DOUGLAS		UC	RE	TX	VR
	•	•	•	Douglas County Abstract & Title Co 651		•	•	•	
				Hiett Title Company 968		•	•	•	
	•	•	•	National Investigative Services Inc 1408		•	•	•	•

	CV	CR	PR	DUNKLIN		UC	RE	TX	VR
				See ALL COUNTIES					

	CV	CR	PR	FRANKLIN		UC	RE	TX	VR
	•			Hansen Franklin County Land Title 919		•	•	•	•
	•	•	•	Hayes & Associates 942		•	•	•	•
	•	•	•	Kimme and Lamke 1122		•	•	•	•
	•	•	•	St Vrain Resources 1848		•	•	•	

	CV	CR	PR	GASCONADE		UC	RE	TX	VR
	•	•	•	Mundwiller, Donna 1397		•	•	•	
	•	•	•	St Vrain Resources 1848		•	•	•	

	CV	CR	PR	GENTRY		UC	RE	TX	VR
	•		•	Holden Abstract Co 980		•	•	•	
	•	•	•	Wilson Associates 2102		•	•	•	•

DT	CV	CR	PR	GREENE		UC	RE	TX	VR
	•	•	•	Akin, Nyla 93		•	•	•	•
	•		•	Hogan Land Title Co 979			•	•	
•	•	•	•	Kunkel, Joan 1138		•	•	•	•
•	•	•	•	National Investigative Services Inc 1408		•	•	•	•

	CV	CR	PR	GRUNDY		UC	RE	TX	VR
	•	•	•	Best Abstract Title Co 291		•	•	•	•
	•	•	•	Wilson Associates 2102		•	•	•	•

	CV	CR	PR	HARRISON		UC	RE	TX	VR
	•		•	Harrison County Abstract Co Inc 930		•	•	•	
	•	•	•	Wilson Associates 2102		•	•	•	•

	CV	CR	PR	HENRY		UC	RE	TX	VR
	•		•	Henry County Abstract Co 955		•	•	•	

	CV	CR	PR	HICKORY		UC	RE	TX	VR
	•	•	•	Akin, Nyla 93		•	•	•	•
	•	•	•	Bentley Title Co 280		•	•	•	•
	•	•	•	National Investigative Services Inc 1408		•	•	•	•

	CV	CR	PR	HOLT		UC	RE	TX	VR
	•	•	•	Wilson Associates 2102		•	•	•	•

	CV	CR	PR	HOWARD		UC	RE	TX	VR
	•	•	•	Boggs, Karen V 315			•		•
	•	•	•	Central-MO Investigations 430			•	•	•
	•	•	•	Forbes, Sylvia 792			•	•	•
	•	•	•	Geo G Smith & Son Inc 840		•	•	•	•
	•		•	Guaranty Land Title 891		•	•	•	•

	CV	CR	PR	HOWELL		UC	RE	TX	VR
	•	•	•	Carroll, D Garvin 411		•	•	•	•

					UC	RE	TX	VR
•		•	Ketlett-Landis-Brill Abstr & Land Title............................1120		•	•	•	
•	•	•	Reavis, Dorotha..1661		•	•	•	•

		CV	CR	PR	**IRON**	UC	RE	TX	VR
		•		•	American Heritage Abstract...132	•	•	•	

DT	BK	CV	CR	PR	**JACKSON**	UC	RE	TX	VR
•	•	•	•	•	Executive Investigative Services...723		•		
•	•	•	•	•	Fred McDaniel and Associates...807	•	•	•	•
•	•	•	•	•	RSI 1643				
•	•	•	•	•	Silk Attorney Service...1804	•	•	•	•

		CV	CR	PR	**JASPER**	UC	RE	TX	VR
		•	•	•	Kunkel, Joan..1138	•	•	•	•
		•	•	•	National Investigative Services Inc....................................1408	•	•	•	•

		CV	CR	PR	**JEFFERSON**	UC	RE	TX	VR
		•	•	•	Hayes & Associates..942	•	•	•	
		•	•	•	Legal System Services...1213	•	•	•	
		•	•	•	St Vrain Resources..1848	•	•	•	

		CV	CR	PR	**JOHNSON**	UC	RE	TX	VR
		•	•	•	Fred McDaniel and Associates...807	•	•	•	•

		CV	CR	PR	**KNOX**	UC	RE	TX	VR
					See ALL COUNTIES..				

		CV	CR	PR	**LACLEDE**	UC	RE	TX	VR
		•	•	•	Akin, Nyla..93	•	•	•	•
		•	•	•	National Investigative Services Inc....................................1408	•	•	•	•
		•		•	Ousley, Veda..1484	•	•	•	•

		CV	CR	PR	**LAFAYETTE**	UC	RE	TX	VR
		•	•	•	Fred McDaniel and Associates...807	•	•	•	•
		•	•	•	Lafayette Land Title Company...1154	•	•	•	•

		CV	CR	PR	**LAWRENCE**	UC	RE	TX	VR
		•	•	•	Kunkel, Joan..1138	•	•	•	•
		•	•	•	National Investigative Services Inc....................................1408	•	•	•	•

		CV	CR	PR	**LEWIS**	UC	RE	TX	VR
		•	•	•	Johnson, Edith F..1095	•	•	•	•
		•	•	•	Lewis County Abstract..1222	•	•	•	
		•		•	Marion County Abstract Co..1280	•	•	•	
		•		•	Northeast Missorui Abstract Agency Inc 1442	•	•	•	

		CV	CR	PR	**LINCOLN**	UC	RE	TX	VR
		•	•	•	Assured Title Company...177	•	•	•	
		•	•	•	St Vrain Resources..1848	•	•	•	
		•	•	•	Troy Title Co..1985	•	•	•	

		CV	CR	PR	**LINN**	UC	RE	TX	VR
				•	Griffith, Charlotte..883		•	•	

		CV	CR	PR	**LIVINGSTON**	UC	RE	TX	VR
		•	•	•	Staton Abstract & Title Co...1857	•	•	•	•
		•	•	•	Wilson Associates 2102	•	•	•	•

		CV	CR	PR	**McDONALD**	UC	RE	TX	VR
		•	•	•	Kunkel, Joan..1138	•	•	•	•
		•	•	•	National Investigative Services Inc....................................1408	•	•	•	•

		CV	CR	PR	**MACON**	UC	RE	TX	VR
		•	•	•	A Verne Baker Abstract Co..10	•	•	•	•

CV	CR	PR		Page	UC	RE	TX	VR
•	•	•	White Abstract Co	2086	•	•	•	•
CV	**CR**	**PR**	**MADISON**		**UC**	**RE**	**TX**	**VR**
•		•	American Heritage Abstract	132	•	•	•	
			St Francois County Abstract Co	1845	•	•	•	
CV	**CR**	**PR**	**MARIES**		**UC**	**RE**	**TX**	**VR**
•	•	•	Hollenbeck Title Co	981	•	•	•	
	•	•	Ousley, Veda	1484	•	•	•	•
CV	**CR**	**PR**	**MARION**		**UC**	**RE**	**TX**	**VR**
•		•	Marion County Abstract Co	1280	•	•	•	•
			Wells Abstract Company	2074	•	•	•	
CV	**CR**	**PR**	**MERCER**		**UC**	**RE**	**TX**	**VR**
			Putnam County Abstract	1632	•	•	•	
•	•	•	Wilson Associates	2102	•	•	•	•
CV	**CR**	**PR**	**MILLER**		**UC**	**RE**	**TX**	**VR**
•	•	•	Central-MO Investigations	430		•	•	•
•	•	•	Harmon Legal Process Service	927	•	•	•	•
•	•	•	National Investigative Services Inc	1408	•	•	•	•
	•	•	Ousley, Veda	1484	•	•	•	•
CV	**CR**	**PR**	**MISSISSIPPI**		**UC**	**RE**	**TX**	**VR**
•	•	•	Delta Credit Bureau Inc	621	•	•	•	
•		•	Mississippi County Abstract & Loan Co	1360	•	•	•	
CV	**CR**	**PR**	**MONITEAU**		**UC**	**RE**	**TX**	**VR**
•	•	•	Central-MO Investigations	430		•	•	•
•		•	Guaranty Land Title	891	•	•	•	•
CV	**CR**	**PR**	**MONROE**		**UC**	**RE**	**TX**	**VR**
•		•	Marion County Abstract Co	1280	•	•	•	•
•	•	•	Monroe County Abstract and Title Co	1364	•	•	•	
CV	**CR**	**PR**	**MONTGOMERY**		**UC**	**RE**	**TX**	**VR**
•	•	•	Assured Title Company	177	•	•	•	
•	•	•	Montgomery County Abstract and Title Co	1374	•	•	•	
•	•	•	St Vrain Resources	1848	•	•	•	
CV	**CR**	**PR**	**MORGAN**		**UC**	**RE**	**TX**	**VR**
•	•	•	Harmon Legal Process Service	927	•	•	•	•
•		•	Hubbard-Kavanaugh Abstract and Title Co	1000	•	•	•	•
CV	**CR**	**PR**	**NEW MADRID**		**UC**	**RE**	**TX**	**VR**
•		•	Security Abstract Co	1763		•	•	
CV	**CR**	**PR**	**NEWTON**		**UC**	**RE**	**TX**	**VR**
•	•	•	Kunkel, Joan	1138	•	•	•	•
•	•	•	National Investigative Services Inc	1408	•	•	•	•
CV	**CR**	**PR**	**NODAWAY**		**UC**	**RE**	**TX**	**VR**
•		•	Nodaway County Abstract Co	1429	•	•	•	•
•	•	•	Wilson Associates	2102	•	•	•	•
CV	**CR**	**PR**	**OREGON**		**UC**	**RE**	**TX**	**VR**
•	•	•	Reavis, Dorotha	1661	•	•	•	•
CV	**CR**	**PR**	**OSAGE**		**UC**	**RE**	**TX**	**VR**
•		•	Guaranty Land Title	891	•	•	•	•
•	•	•	Harmon Legal Process Service	927	•	•	•	•
CV	**CR**	**PR**	**OZARK**		**UC**	**RE**	**TX**	**VR**
•	•	•	Carroll, D Garvin	411	•	•	•	•

CV	CR	PR	County / Company	Page	UC	RE	TX	VR
●	●	●	National Investigative Services Inc	1408	●	●	●	●
●	●	●	Reavis, Dorotha	1661	●	●	●	●
CV	**CR**	**PR**	**PEMISCOT**		**UC**	**RE**	**TX**	**VR**
●	●	●	Pemiscot County Abstract & Investment Co	1531	●	●	●	
CV	**CR**	**PR**	**PERRY**		**UC**	**RE**	**TX**	**VR**
●	●	●	Kiefer Title Co	1121	●	●	●	●
●	●	●	St Vrain Resources	1848	●	●	●	
CV	**CR**	**PR**	**PETTIS**		**UC**	**RE**	**TX**	**VR**
●	●	●	Landmann Abstract & Title Co	1166	●	●	●	●
CV	**CR**	**PR**	**PHELPS**		**UC**	**RE**	**TX**	**VR**
●			National Investigative Services Inc	1408	●	●	●	●
	●	●	Ousley, Veda	1484	●	●	●	●
CV	**CR**	**PR**	**PIKE**		**UC**	**RE**	**TX**	**VR**
		●	Griffith, Charlotte	883		●	●	
		●	Henson, Anna Marie	957		●	●	●
●	●	●	St Vrain Resources	1848	●	●	●	
●		●	Sterne, Sarah	1866	●			
CV	**CR**	**PR**	**PLATTE**		**UC**	**RE**	**TX**	**VR**
●	●	●	Fred McDaniel and Associates	807	●		●	●
●	●	●	RSI	1643				
●	●	●	Silk Attorney Service	1804	●	●	●	●
●	●	●	Wilson Associates	2102	●	●	●	●
CV	**CR**	**PR**	**POLK**		**UC**	**RE**	**TX**	**VR**
●	●	●	Akin, Nyla	93	●	●	●	●
●	●	●	National Investigative Services Inc	1408	●	●	●	●
CV	**CR**	**PR**	**PULASKI**		**UC**	**RE**	**TX**	**VR**
	●	●	Ousley, Veda	1484	●	●	●	●
CV	**CR**	**PR**	**PUTNAM**		**UC**	**RE**	**TX**	**VR**
●	●	●	Putnam County Abstract	1632	●	●	●	
CV	**CR**	**PR**	**RALLS**		**UC**	**RE**	**TX**	**VR**
●		●	Columbian National Title Ins of Wichita	498		●	●	●
●		●	Marion County Abstract Co	1280	●	●	●	
CV	**CR**	**PR**	**RANDOLPH**		**UC**	**RE**	**TX**	**VR**
●	●	●	A Verne Baker Abstract Co	10	●	●	●	
●	●	●	Central-MO Investigations	430		●	●	●
●	●	●	Town and Country Abstract Co	1970	●	●	●	
CV	**CR**	**PR**	**RAY**		**UC**	**RE**	**TX**	**VR**
●	●	●	Fred McDaniel and Associates	807	●	●	●	●
CV	**CR**	**PR**	**REYNOLDS**		**UC**	**RE**	**TX**	**VR**
			See ALL COUNTIES					
CV	**CR**	**PR**	**RIPLEY**		**UC**	**RE**	**TX**	**VR**
●	●	●	Allen, Nancy	114			●	●
CV	**CR**	**PR**	**ST. CHARLES**		**UC**	**RE**	**TX**	**VR**
●	●	●	Assured Title Company	177	●	●	●	●
●	●	●	Kyle, Michelle	1140	●	●	●	●
●	●	●	Legal System Services	1213	●	●	●	●
●	●	●	St Vrain Resources	1848	●	●	●	
CV	**CR**	**PR**	**ST. CLAIR**		**UC**	**RE**	**TX**	**VR**
●		●	Osceola Abstract & Title	1479	●	●	●	●

STE. GENEVIEVE

CV	CR	PR	Company	UC	RE	TX	VR
•		•	American Heritage Abstract 132	•	•	•	
•		•	Landmark Title and Abstr of St Genevieve 1170	•	•	•	•
			St Francois County Abstract Co 1845	•	•	•	
•	•	•	St Vrain Resources 1848	•	•	•	

ST. FRANCOIS

CV	CR	PR	Company	UC	RE	TX	VR
•		•	American Heritage Abstract 132	•	•	•	
			St Francois County Abstract Co 1845	•	•	•	
•	•	•	St Vrain Resources 1848	•	•	•	

ST. LOUIS

DT	BK	CV	CR	PR	Company	UC	RE	TX	VR
		•	•	•	D & L Invesgiations 577	•	•	•	•
•	•	•	•	•	Heil Investigations Agency Inc 948	•	•	•	•
•	•	•	•	•	Kyle, Michelle 1140	•	•	•	
•	•	•	•	•	Legal System Services 1213	•	•	•	•
•	•	•	•	•	Lueken, Patricia O 1245	•	•	•	
•	•	•	•	•	St Vrain Resources 1848	•	•	•	

CITY OF ST. LOUIS

CV	CR	PR	Company	UC	RE	TX	VR
•	•	•	D & L Invesgiations 577	•	•	•	•
•	•	•	Heil Investigations Agency Inc 948	•	•	•	•
•			Lueken, Patricia O 1245	•	•	•	
•	•	•	St Vrain Resources 1848	•	•	•	

SALINE

CV	CR	PR	Company	UC	RE	TX	VR
•	•	•	Van Dyke & Co 2023	•	•	•	

SCHUYLER

CV	CR	PR	Company	UC	RE	TX	VR
			Putnam County Abstract 1632	•	•	•	

SCOTLAND

CV	CR	PR	Company	UC	RE	TX	VR
•	•	•	Johnson, Edith F 1095	•	•	•	•
		•	Scotland County Abstract Inc 1749	•	•	•	

SCOTT

CV	CR	PR	Company	UC	RE	TX	VR
		•	Glastetter, Romana 850		•	•	•

SHANNON

CV	CR	PR	Company	UC	RE	TX	VR
•		•	Shannon County Abstract Co 1787	•	•	•	

SHELBY

CV	CR	PR	Company	UC	RE	TX	VR
•		•	Marion County Abstract Co 1280	•	•	•	•

STODDARD

CV	CR	PR	Company	UC	RE	TX	VR
•		•	County Wide Abstract and Title Co Inc 540	•	•	•	

STONE

CV	CR	PR	Company	UC	RE	TX	VR
•	•	•	Galena Abstract Co Inc 828	•	•	•	
•	•	•	National Investigative Services Inc 1408	•	•	•	•

SULLIVAN

CV	CR	PR	Company	UC	RE	TX	VR
•	•	•	Sullivan County Abstract Co 1879	•	•	•	•

TANEY

CV	CR	PR	Company	UC	RE	TX	VR
•		•	Hogan Land Title Co 979		•	•	
•	•	•	National Investigative Services Inc 1408	•	•	•	•

TEXAS

CV	CR	PR	Company	UC	RE	TX	VR
		•	Fourt, Mildred 799		•	•	•
•	•	•	Hiett Title Co 967	•	•	•	
			Hiett Title Company 968	•	•	•	
	•	•	Ousley, Veda 1484	•	•	•	•
•	•	•	Reavis, Dorotha 1661	•	•	•	•

CV	CR	PR	VERNON	UC	RE	TX	VR
●		●	Bowman's Vernon County Title Co 333		●	●	
●	●	●	National Investigative Services Inc 1408	●	●	●	●

CV	CR	PR	WARREN	UC	RE	TX	VR
●	●	●	Assured Title Company.............................177	●	●	●	
●	●	●	Hayes & Associates................................942	●	●	●	●
●	●	●	St Vrain Resources...............................1848	●	●	●	

CV	CR	PR	WASHINGTON	UC	RE	TX	VR
●		●	American Heritage Abstract...............................132	●	●	●	
			St Francois County Abstract Co...................1845	●	●	●	
●	●	●	St Vrain Resources...............................1848	●	●	●	
●	●	●	Washington County Abstract Co....................2056	●	●	●	●

CV	CR	PR	WAYNE	UC	RE	TX	VR
●	●	●	Wayne County Abstract & Title Co 2065	●	●	●	●

CV	CR	PR	WEBSTER	UC	RE	TX	VR
●	●	●	Akin, Nyla...93	●	●	●	●
●		●	D D Hamilton Abstract Co.........................578	●	●	●	
●	●	●	National Investigative Services Inc 1408	●	●	●	●

CV	CR	PR	WORTH	UC	RE	TX	VR
●		●	Nodaway County Abstract Co.......................1429	●	●	●	●
●	●	●	Wilson Associates 2102	●	●	●	●

CV	CR	PR	WRIGHT	UC	RE	TX	VR
●	●	●	Hiett Title Co 967	●	●	●	
			Hiett Title Company..............................968	●	●	●	
●	●	●	National Investigative Services Inc 1408	●	●	●	●

Montana

	CV	CR	PR	BEAVERHEAD	UC	RE	TX	VR
	•	•	•	Southern Mountain Abstract & Title Co 1830	•	•	•	•

	CV	CR	PR	BIG HORN	UC	RE	TX	VR
	•	•	•	Dunbar & Associates...666	•	•	•	•

	CV	CR	PR	BLAINE	UC	RE	TX	VR
	•	•	•	Blaine County Title Co 307	•	•	•	•

	CV	CR	PR	BROADWATER	UC	RE	TX	VR
	•	•	•	Meadowlark Search...1322	•	•	•	•

	CV	CR	PR	CARBON	UC	RE	TX	VR
	•	•	•	Dunbar & Associates...666	•	•	•	•

	CV	CR	PR	CARTER	UC	RE	TX	VR
	•	•	•	Mainstreet Business Services.....................................1272	•	•	•	•
	•	•	•	Security Abstract & Title Co....................................1761	•	•	•	

DT	CV	CR	PR	CASCADE	UC	RE	TX	VR
	•	•	•	First Montana Title Co of Great Falls 775	•	•	•	
	•	•	•	Reagan, McClure...1653	•	•	•	•

	CV	CR	PR	CHOUTEAU	UC	RE	TX	VR
	•	•	•	Chouteau County Abstract Co..457	•	•	•	

	CV	CR	PR	CUSTER	UC	RE	TX	VR
	•	•	•	Dunbar & Associates...666	•	•	•	•
	•	•	•	Mainstreet Business Services.....................................1272	•	•	•	•
	•	•	•	Security Abstract & Title Co....................................1761	•	•	•	

	CV	CR	PR	DANIELS	UC	RE	TX	VR
	•	•	•	Mainstreet Business Services.....................................1272	•	•	•	•
	•		•	Montana Abstract Co Inc 1368		•	•	•
	•		•	Nichols, Jake 1425	•	•	•	•

	CV	CR	PR	DAWSON	UC	RE	TX	VR
	•	•	•	Mainstreet Business Services.....................................1272	•	•	•	•
	•		•	Montana Title Company of Glendive Inc......................1370		•	•	

	CV	CR	PR	DEER LODGE	UC	RE	TX	VR
	•	•	•	Montana Abstract & Title Co....................................1367	•	•	•	•

	CV	CR	PR	FALLON	UC	RE	TX	VR
	•	•	•	Gill, Diana...843	•	•	•	•
	•	•	•	Mainstreet Business Services.....................................1272	•	•	•	•

	CV	CR	PR	FERGUS	UC	RE	TX	VR
	•	•	•	Realty Title Co Inc..1660	•	•	•	•

	CV	CR	PR	FLATHEAD	UC	RE	TX	VR
	•	•	•	Flathead County Title Co 782	•	•	•	•

	CV	CR	PR	GALLATIN	UC	RE	TX	VR
	•	•	•	Dunbar & Associates...666	•	•	•	•
	•		•	Security Title Co...1777	•	•	•	•

	CV	CR	PR	GARFIELD	UC	RE	TX	VR
	•	•	•	Mainstreet Business Services.....................................1272	•	•	•	•
	•	•		Security Abstract & Title Co....................................1761	•	•	•	•

	CV	CR	PR	GLACIER	UC	RE	TX	VR
	•	•	•	Reagan, McClure...1653	•	•	•	•

Court
Records

MONTANA
129

County
Records

	CV	CR	PR	GOLDEN VALLEY		UC	RE	TX	VR
	●	●	●	Dunbar & Associates................................666		●	●	●	●
				Mid Montana Title Co.............................1340			●		

	CV	CR	PR	GRANITE		UC	RE	TX	VR
	●	●	●	Montana Abstract & Title Co.........................1367		●	●	●	●

	CV	CR	PR	HILL		UC	RE	TX	VR
	●		●	Hill County Title Co.............................970		●	●	●	●

	CV	CR	PR	JEFFERSON		UC	RE	TX	VR
	●	●	●	Meadowlark Search...............................1322		●	●	●	●

	CV	CR	PR	JUDITH BASIN		UC	RE	TX	VR
	●	●	●	Realty Title Co Inc.............................1660		●	●	●	●

	CV	CR	PR	LAKE		UC	RE	TX	VR
	●	●	●	First American Title & Escrow - Polson............768		●	●	●	●
	●	●	●	Lake County Abstract & Title Co...................1155		●	●	●	●

		CV	CR	PR	LEWIS AND CLARK		UC	RE	TX	VR
DT		●	●	●	Helena Abstract & Title Co.......................950		●	●	●	●
●		●	●	●	Meadowlark Search...............................1322		●	●	●	●
		●	●	●	Montana Public Records Service 1369		●	●	●	●

	CV	CR	PR	LIBERTY		UC	RE	TX	VR
	●	●	●	Liberty County Title Co..........................1225			●	●	●

	CV	CR	PR	LINCOLN		UC	RE	TX	VR
	●	●	●	Action Agency....................................71		●	●	●	●
	●	●	●	First American Title & Escroe - Libby.............767		●	●	●	●

	CV	CR	PR	MCCONE		UC	RE	TX	VR
	●	●	●	Mainstreet Business Services.....................1272		●			
	●		●	Montana Title Company of Glendive Inc............1370			●	●	

	CV	CR	PR	MADISON		UC	RE	TX	VR
	●	●	●	Madison County Title Co..........................1264		●	●	●	●

	CV	CR	PR	MEAGHER		UC	RE	TX	VR
	●	●	●	Potter & Co 1575		●	●	●	●

	CV	CR	PR	MINERAL		UC	RE	TX	VR
	●	●	●	First American Title Co of Mineral Cnty...........770		●	●	●	●

		CV	CR	PR	MISSOULA		UC	RE	TX	VR
DT		●	●	●	Insured Titles Inc...............................1033		●	●	●	●

	CV	CR	PR	MUSSELSHELL		UC	RE	TX	VR
	●	●	●	Dunbar & Associates..............................666		●	●	●	●
	●	●	●	Musselshell County Title Inc 1402		●	●	●	●

	CV	CR	PR	PARK		UC	RE	TX	VR
	●	●	●	Security Title of Park County Inc................1780		●	●	●	●

	CV	CR	PR	PETROLEUM		UC	RE	TX	VR
	●	●	●	Realty Title Co Inc..............................1660		●	●	●	●

	CV	CR	PR	PHILLIPS		UC	RE	TX	VR
	●	●	●	Phillips County Abstract Co......................1547		●	●	●	●

	CV	CR	PR	PONDERA		UC	RE	TX	VR
	●	●	●	Pondera County Title Co..........................1570		●	●	●	●
	●	●	●	Reagan, McClure.................................1653		●	●	●	●

CV	CR	PR	**POWDER RIVER**	UC	RE	TX	VR
●	●	●	Mainstreet Business Services 1272	●	●	●	●
●	●	●	Powder River Abstract and Title Co 1577	●	●	●	●

CV	CR	PR	**POWELL**	UC	RE	TX	VR
●	●	●	Montana Abstract & Title Co.............................1367	●	●	●	●

CV	CR	PR	**PRAIRIE**	UC	RE	TX	VR
●	●	●	Mainstreet Business Services 1272	●	●	●	●
●	●	●	Prairie Abstract & Title 1580	●	●	●	●

CV	CR	PR	**RAVALLI**	UC	RE	TX	VR
●		●	Bitterrood Research..304	●	●	●	●
●	●	●	Elite Resources Inc..698				●

CV	CR	PR	**RICHLAND**	UC	RE	TX	VR
●	●	●	Mainstreet Business Services 1272	●	●	●	●
●	●	●	Security Abstract Co 1764	●	●	●	●

CV	CR	PR	**ROOSEVELT**	UC	RE	TX	VR
●	●	●	Mainstreet Business Services 1272	●	●	●	●
●		●	Nichols, Jake 1425	●	●	●	●
●	●	●	Roosevelt County Abstract Co Inc...................1714	●	●	●	

CV	CR	PR	**ROSEBUD**	UC	RE	TX	VR
●	●	●	Dunbar & Associates..666	●	●	●	●
●	●	●	First Montana Title Co of Great Falls 775	●	●	●	
●	●	●	Mainstreet Business Services 1272	●	●	●	●

CV	CR	PR	**SANDERS**	UC	RE	TX	VR
●	●	●	Action Agency..71	●	●	●	●
●	●	●	First American Title Co..769	●	●	●	●

CV	CR	PR	**SHERIDAN**	UC	RE	TX	VR
●	●	●	Mainstreet Business Services 1272	●	●	●	●
●		●	Nichols, Jake 1425	●	●	●	●

DT	BK	CV	CR	PR	**SILVER BOW**	UC	RE	TX	VR
●	●	●	●	●	Montana Abstract & Title Co.............................1367	●	●	●	●

CV	CR	PR	**STILLWATER**	UC	RE	TX	VR
●	●	●	Dunbar & Associates..666	●	●	●	●

CV	CR	PR	**SWEET GRASS**	UC	RE	TX	VR
			Mid Montana Title Co..1340		●		

CV	CR	PR	**TETON**	UC	RE	TX	VR
●	●	●	Teton County Abstract Co...................................1912	●	●	●	

CV	CR	PR	**TOOLE**	UC	RE	TX	VR
●	●	●	Reagan, McClure...1653	●	●	●	●
●	●	●	Toole County Title Co...1968	●	●	●	●

CV	CR	PR	**TREASURE**	UC	RE	TX	VR
●	●	●	Dunbar & Associates..666	●	●	●	●
●	●	●	First Montana Title Co of Great Falls 775	●	●	●	

CV	CR	PR	**VALLEY**	UC	RE	TX	VR
●	●	●	Mainstreet Business Services 1272	●	●	●	●

CV	CR	PR	**WHEATLAND**	UC	RE	TX	VR
			Mid Montana Title Co..1340		●		

CV	CR	PR	**WIBAUX**	UC	RE	TX	VR
●	●	●	Mainstreet Business Services 1272	●	●	●	●

	●	●	●	Wibaux County Abstract Company.................................2088	●	●	●	●

DT	CV	CR	PR	YELLOWSTONE	UC	RE	TX	VR
	●		●	Deister Ward & Witcher..613	●	●	●	●
●	●	●	●	Dunbar & Associates..666	●	●	●	●
	●	●	●	First Montana Title Co of Great Falls 775	●	●	●	

SUMMARY OF CODES

COURT RECORDS

CODE*	GOVERNMENT AGENCY	TYPE OF INFORMATION
DT	US District Court	Federal civil and criminal cases
BK	Bankruptcy Court	United States bankruptcy cases
CV	Civil Court	Municipal, county and state level civil cases
CR	Criminal Court	Municipal, county and state level criminal cases
PR	Probate Court	Wills and estate cases

COUNTY RECORDS

CODE*	GOVERNMENT AGENCY	TYPE OF INFORMATION
UC	UCC Filing Office	Uniform Commercial Code and other personal property liens
RE	Recorder of Deeds	Real property transactions and liens
TX	Tax Assessor	Real property tax information
VR	Vital Records Office	Birth, death, marriage, divorce, etc.

*The "CODE" designates the agency and type of information obtainable in each county.

Nebraska

CV	CR	PR	ADAMS		UC	RE	TX	VR
●	●	●	Adams Land Title..79		●	●	●	●
●	●	●	Heritage Title Inc 960		●	●	●	●

CV	CR	PR	ANTELOPE		UC	RE	TX	VR
●	●	●	Chilvers Abstract & Title Co...............................453		●	●	●	●
●	●	●	North Central Abstract Co.................................1432		●	●	●	
●	●	●	Northeast Nebraska Title & Escrow....................1443		●	●		●

CV	CR	PR	ARTHUR		UC	RE	TX	VR
●	●	●	Thalken Abstract & Title Co...............................1919		●	●	●	●

CV	CR	PR	BANNER		UC	RE	TX	VR
●	●	●	Thalken Abstract & Title Co...............................1919		●	●	●	●

CV	CR	PR	BLAINE		UC	RE	TX	VR
●	●	●	Russell Abstracting & Title................................1719		●	●	●	●

CV	CR	PR	BOONE		UC	RE	TX	VR
●	●	●	Medlin Jr, Ray P..1323		●	●	●	●

CV	CR	PR	BOX BUTTE		UC	RE	TX	VR
●		●	Buchfinck Inc...362		●	●	●	●
●	●	●	Credit Bureau of Western Nebraska.....................562		●	●	●	●

CV	CR	PR	BOYD		UC	RE	TX	VR
●	●	●	McCarthy Abstract Co.......................................1302		●	●	●	
●	●	●	North Central Abstract Co.................................1432		●	●	●	

CV	CR	PR	BROWN		UC	RE	TX	VR
		●	Brown County Abstract Co.................................350		●	●	●	

CV	CR	PR	BUFFALO		UC	RE	TX	VR
●		●	Adams Land Title..80		●	●	●	
●		●	Barney Abstract & Title Co..................................246		●	●	●	●

CV	CR	PR	BURT		UC	RE	TX	VR
●	●	●	Anderson Abstract Co 145		●	●	●	

CV	CR	PR	BUTLER		UC	RE	TX	VR
●	●	●	Beckner Abstracting & Title Co...........................272		●	●	●	●
●		●	Colfax County Title and Abstract Co....................488		●	●	●	
●		●	Mihulka, Elden...1348		●	●	●	
●	●	●	Thomas, Donna 1944				●	●

CV	CR	PR	CASS		UC	RE	TX	VR
●	●	●	Otoe County Abstract Co...................................1481		●	●	●	
●	●	●	Thomas, Donna 1944				●	●

CV	CR	PR	CEDAR		UC	RE	TX	VR
●	●	●	Chilvers Abstract & Title Co...............................453		●	●	●	●
●	●	●	Intra-Lex Investigations Inc 1043		●	●	●	●
●	●	●	Merkle Abstract & Title.....................................1330		●	●	●	
●	●	●	Stanton Co Abstract 1850		●	●	●	

CV	CR	PR	CHASE		UC	RE	TX	VR
●	●	●	Hines & Hines Lawyers.......................................976		●	●	●	●
●	●	●	Thalken Abstract & Title Co...............................1919		●	●	●	●

CV	CR	PR	CHERRY		UC	RE	TX	VR
●	●	●	Sandhills Abstracting 1738		●	●	●	●

		CV	CR	PR	CHEYENNE	UC	RE	TX	VR
				•	Cheyenne County Abstract..............450	•	•	•	
		•	•	•	Credit Bureau of Western Nebraska.............562	•	•	•	•
		•		•	Deuel County Abstract Co 627	•	•	•	

		CV	CR	PR	CLAY	UC	RE	TX	VR
		•		•	Adams Land Title..............79	•	•	•	
		•	•	•	Clay County Abstract & Title.............468	•	•	•	•

		CV	CR	PR	COLFAX	UC	RE	TX	VR
		•		•	Colfax County Title and Abstract Co................488	•	•	•	
		•		•	Mihulka, Elden..............1348	•	•	•	
		•	•	•	Stanton Co Abstract 1850	•	•	•	•

		CV	CR	PR	CUMING	UC	RE	TX	VR
		•	•	•	Intra-Lex Investigations Inc 1043	•	•	•	•
		•	•	•	Stanton Co Abstract 1850	•	•	•	•

		CV	CR	PR	CUSTER	UC	RE	TX	VR
		•	•	•	Russell Abstracting & Title.............1719	•	•	•	•

		CV	CR	PR	DAKOTA	UC	RE	TX	VR
		•		•	Harder, Mary K 922		•		•
		•	•	•	Professional Title & Escrow Inc................1620	•	•	•	•

		CV	CR	PR	DAWES	UC	RE	TX	VR
		•	•	•	Credit Bureau of Western Nebraska.............562	•	•	•	•
		•	•	•	Dawes County Abstract Co 606	•	•	•	

		CV	CR	PR	DAWSON	UC	RE	TX	VR
				•	The H O Smith Company.............1933	•	•	•	

		CV	CR	PR	DEUEL	UC	RE	TX	VR
		•		•	Deuel County Abstract Co 627	•	•	•	
		•	•	•	Thalken Abstract & Title Co.............1919	•	•	•	•

		CV	CR	PR	DIXON	UC	RE	TX	VR
		•	•	•	Intra-Lex Investigations Inc 1043	•	•	•	•

		CV	CR	PR	DODGE	UC	RE	TX	VR
		•	•	•	Intra-Lex Investigations Inc 1043	•	•	•	•
		•	•	•	Thomas, Donna.............1944		•	•	

DT	BK	CV	CR	PR	DOUGLAS	UC	RE	TX	VR
		•	•	•	Intra-Lex Investigations Inc 1043	•	•	•	•
		•	•	•	Thomas, Donna.............1944		•	•	

		CV	CR	PR	DUNDY	UC	RE	TX	VR
		•	•	•	Hines & Hines Lawyers.............976	•	•	•	•

		CV	CR	PR	FILLMORE	UC	RE	TX	VR
		•		•	Adams Land Title..............79	•	•	•	
		•	•	•	Fillmore County Abstract Co 761	•	•	•	•
		•	•		York County Title Co.............2121	•	•	•	•

		CV	CR	PR	FRANKLIN	UC	RE	TX	VR
		•		•	Adams Land Title..............80	•	•	•	
		•	•	•	Franklin Abstracts & Land Title Inc.............803	•	•	•	•

		CV	CR	PR	FRONTIER	UC	RE	TX	VR
		•	•	•	McCook Abstract Company.............1305	•	•	•	
		•	•	•	Scott Abstract.............1750	•	•	•	•

CV	CR	PR	FURNAS		UC	RE	TX	VR
•	•	•	Furnas County Title Co Inc......................821		•	•	•	•

CV	CR	PR	GAGE		UC	RE	TX	VR
•		•	Nebraska Title Company......................1414		•	•	•	

CV	CR	PR	GARDEN		UC	RE	TX	VR
•	•	•	Morrissey Morrissey & Dalluge......................1389		•	•	•	•
•	•	•	Romig, Marvin T......................1712		•	•	•	
•	•	•	Thalken Abstract & Title Co......................1919		•	•	•	•

CV	CR	PR	GARFIELD		UC	RE	TX	VR
•	•	•	Crandall, Dale C......................549		•	•	•	•

CV	CR	PR	GOSPER		UC	RE	TX	VR
•	•	•	Furnas County Title Co Inc......................821		•	•	•	•

CV	CR	PR	GRANT		UC	RE	TX	VR
•	•	•	Thalken Abstract & Title Co......................1919		•	•	•	•

CV	CR	PR	GREELEY		UC	RE	TX	VR
•	•	•	Janke Abstract Co......................1078		•	•	•	•

CV	CR	PR	HALL		UC	RE	TX	VR
•		•	Adams Land Title......................79		•	•	•	
•	•	•	Janke Abstract Co......................1078		•	•	•	•

CV	CR	PR	HAMILTON		UC	RE	TX	VR
•		•	Adams Land Title......................79		•	•	•	
•	•	•	First Securities Corp in Aurora......................776		•	•	•	•

CV	CR	PR	HARLAN		UC	RE	TX	VR
•		•	Adams Land Title......................80		•	•	•	
•	•	•	Furnas County Title Co Inc......................821		•	•	•	•

CV	CR	PR	HAYES		UC	RE	TX	VR
•	•	•	McCook Abstract Company......................1305		•	•	•	
•	•	•	Scott Abstract......................1750		•	•	•	•

CV	CR	PR	HITCHCOCK		UC	RE	TX	VR
•	•	•	Hines & Hines Lawyers......................976		•	•	•	•
•	•	•	McCook Abstract Company......................1305		•	•	•	

CV	CR	PR	HOLT		UC	RE	TX	VR
•	•	•	McCarthy Abstract Co......................1302		•	•	•	
•	•	•	North Central Abstract Co......................1432		•	•	•	

CV	CR	PR	HOOKER		UC	RE	TX	VR
•	•	•	Scott Abstract......................1750		•	•	•	•

CV	CR	PR	HOWARD		UC	RE	TX	VR
•	•	•	Janke Abstract Co......................1078		•	•	•	•

CV	CR	PR	JEFFERSON		UC	RE	TX	VR
•		•	Abstract and Title Guaranty Company Inc......................51		•	•	•	

CV	CR	PR	JOHNSON		UC	RE	TX	VR
•	•	•	Morrissey Morrissey & Dalluge......................1389		•	•	•	•

CV	CR	PR	KEARNEY		UC	RE	TX	VR
•		•	Adams Land Title......................80		•	•	•	
		•	Miller Abstract and Title Co......................1351		•	•	•	

CV	CR	PR	KEITH		UC	RE	TX	VR
•		•	Deuel County Abstract Co......................627		•	•	•	

KEYA PAHA

Company		CV	CR	PR	UC	RE	TX	VR
Brown County Abstract Co	350			•	•	•	•	
Sandhills Abstracting	1738	•	•	•	•	•	•	•

KIMBALL

Company		CV	CR	PR	UC	RE	TX	VR
Credit Bureau of Western Nebraska	562	•	•	•	•	•	•	•
Executive Title Insurance Agency Inc	726			•	•	•	•	
Steele, Betty Jo	1859			•	•	•	•	

KNOX

Company		CV	CR	PR	UC	RE	TX	VR
Chilvers Abstract & Title Co	453	•	•	•	•	•	•	•
Intra-Lex Investigations Inc	1043	•	•	•	•	•	•	•

LANCASTER

Company		DT	BK	CV	CR	PR	UC	RE	TX	VR
Morrissey Morrissey & Dalluge	1389		•	•	•	•	•	•	•	•
Records Research Inc	1666	•	•	•	•	•	•	•	•	•
Thomas, Donna	1944			•	•	•			•	•

LINCOLN

Company		CV	CR	PR	UC	RE	TX	VR
Scott Abstract	1750	•	•	•	•	•	•	•

LOGAN

Company		CV	CR	PR	UC	RE	TX	VR
Scott Abstract	1750	•	•	•	•	•	•	•

LOUP

Company		CV	CR	PR	UC	RE	TX	VR
Russell Abstracting & Title	1719	•	•	•	•	•	•	•

McPHERSON

Company		CV	CR	PR	UC	RE	TX	VR
Scott Abstract	1750	•	•	•	•	•	•	•

MADISON

Company		CV	CR	PR	UC	RE	TX	VR
Northeast Nebraska Title & Escrow	1443	•	•	•	•	•	•	•

MERRICK

Company		CV	CR	PR	UC	RE	TX	VR
Beckner Abstracting & Title Co	272	•	•	•	•	•	•	•
Janke Abstract Co	1078	•	•	•	•	•	•	•

MORRILL

Company		CV	CR	PR	UC	RE	TX	VR
Credit Bureau of Western Nebraska	562	•	•	•	•	•	•	•
Executive Title Insurance Agency Inc	726			•	•	•	•	

NANCE

Company		CV	CR	PR	UC	RE	TX	VR
Janke Abstract Co	1078	•	•	•	•	•	•	•

NEMAHA

Company		CV	CR	PR	UC	RE	TX	VR
Auburn Abstract and Title Company	216		•	•	•	•	•	
Morrissey Morrissey & Dalluge	1389	•	•	•	•	•	•	•
Otoe County Abstract Co	1481	•	•	•	•	•	•	

NUCKOLLS

Company		CV	CR	PR	UC	RE	TX	VR
Abstracts Inc	55	•	•	•	•	•	•	•
Adams Land Title	79			•	•	•	•	

OTOE

Company		CV	CR	PR	UC	RE	TX	VR
Morrissey Morrissey & Dalluge	1389	•	•	•	•	•	•	•
Otoe County Abstract Co	1481	•	•	•	•	•	•	
Thomas, Donna	1944	•	•	•			•	•

PAWNEE

Company		CV	CR	PR	UC	RE	TX	VR
Morrissey Morrissey & Dalluge	1389	•	•	•	•	•	•	•
Pawnee County Abstract Co	1526	•	•	•	•	•	•	
Stehlik Law Office	1861	•	•	•	•	•	•	

CV	CR	PR	PERKINS		UC	RE	TX	VR
●	●	●	Thalken Abstract & Title Co 1919		●	●	●	●

CV	CR	PR	PHELPS		UC	RE	TX	VR
●	●	●	Adams Land Title..80		●	●	●	●
●		●	Dealey Abstract and Title Company....................611		●	●	●	

CV	CR	PR	PIERCE		UC	RE	TX	VR
●	●	●	Chilvers Abstract & Title Co.............................453		●	●	●	●
●	●	●	Intra-Lex Investigations Inc 1043		●	●	●	●

CV	CR	PR	PLATTE		UC	RE	TX	VR
●	●	●	Platte County Title Co.....................................1560		●	●	●	●
●	●	●	Stanton Co Abstract 1850		●	●	●	●

CV	CR	PR	POLK		UC	RE	TX	VR
●	●	●	Beckner Abstracting & Title Co.........................272		●	●	●	●

CV	CR	PR	RED WILLOW		UC	RE	TX	VR
●	●	●	Hines & Hines Lawyers.....................................976		●	●	●	●
●	●	●	McCook Abstract Company...............................1305		●	●	●	

CV	CR	PR	RICHARDSON		UC	RE	TX	VR
●	●	●	Morrissey Morrissey & Dalluge..........................1389		●	●	●	●
●	●	●	Southeast Nebraska Abstract.............................1825		●	●	●	

CV	CR	PR	ROCK		UC	RE	TX	VR
		●	Brown County Abstract Co 350		●	●	●	

CV	CR	PR	SALINE		UC	RE	TX	VR
●	●	●	Slaine County Abstract.....................................1810		●	●	●	●

CV	CR	PR	SARPY		UC	RE	TX	VR
●	●	●	Intra-Lex Investigations Inc 1043		●	●	●	●
●	●	●	Thomas, Donna...1944				●	●

CV	CR	PR	SAUNDERS		UC	RE	TX	VR
●	●	●	Hamilton & Johnson Inc 911		●	●	●	
●	●	●	Thomas, Donna...1944				●	●

CV	CR	PR	SCOTTS BLUFF		UC	RE	TX	VR
●	●	●	Credit Bureau of Western Nebraska....................562		●	●	●	●

CV	CR	PR	SEWARD		UC	RE	TX	VR
●		●	Executive Title Insurance Agency Inc..................726		●	●	●	
●	●	●	Thomas, Donna...1944				●	●

CV	CR	PR	SHERIDAN		UC	RE	TX	VR
●	●	●	Credit Bureau of Western Nebraska....................562		●	●	●	●
●		●	Dawes County Abstract Co 606		●	●	●	
●		●	Janke Abstract Co..1078		●	●	●	●
●		●	Sandhills Abstracting 1737		●	●	●	●

CV	CR	PR	SHERMAN		UC	RE	TX	VR
●	●	●	Smith, Bess...1814		●	●	●	●

CV	CR	PR	SIOUX		UC	RE	TX	VR
●	●	●	Dawes County Abstract Co 606		●	●	●	
●		●	Executive Title Insurance Agency Inc..................726		●	●	●	

CV	CR	PR	STANTON		UC	RE	TX	VR
●	●	●	Intra-Lex Investigations Inc 1043		●	●	●	●
●	●	●	Stanton Co Abstract 1850		●	●	●	●

Court
Records

NEBRASKA
137

County
Records

CV	CR	PR	THAYER	UC	RE	TX	VR
●		●	Abstract and Title Guaranty Company Inc........51	●	●	●	
●		●	Thayer County Abstract Office Inc........1920	●	●	●	

CV	CR	PR	THOMAS	UC	RE	TX	VR
●	●	●	Russell Abstracting & Title........1719	●	●	●	●
●	●	●	Sandhills Abstracting........1738	●	●	●	●
●	●	●	Scott Abstract........1750	●	●	●	●

CV	CR	PR	THURSTON	UC	RE	TX	VR
●	●	●	Intra-Lex Investigations Inc........1043	●	●	●	●

CV	CR	PR	VALLEY	UC	RE	TX	VR
			See adjoining counties........				

CV	CR	PR	WASHINGTON	UC	RE	TX	VR
●	●	●	Intra-Lex Investigations Inc........1043	●	●	●	●
●	●	●	Thomas, Donna........1944			●	●

CV	CR	PR	WAYNE	UC	RE	TX	VR
●	●	●	Chilvers Abstract & Title Co........453	●	●	●	●
●	●	●	Intra-Lex Investigations Inc........1043	●	●	●	●

CV	CR	PR	WEBSTER	UC	RE	TX	VR
●		●	Adams Land Title........80	●	●	●	
●	●	●	Franklin Abstracts & Land Title Inc........803	●	●	●	●
●	●	●	Stanton Co Abstract........1850	●	●	●	●

CV	CR	PR	WHEELER	UC	RE	TX	VR
●	●	●	McCarthy Abstract Co........1302	●	●	●	
●	●	●	North Central Abstract Co........1432	●	●	●	

CV	CR	PR	YORK	UC	RE	TX	VR
●	●		York County Title Co........2121	●	●	●	●

Court
Records

NEVADA
138

County
Records

Nevada

		CV	CR	PR	CARSON CITY		UC	RE	TX	VR
		●	●	●	Nevada Records Search................................1421		●	●	●	●
		●		●	People Property Research..............................1535		●	●	●	●

		CV	CR	PR	CHURCHILL		UC	RE	TX	VR
					Nevada Land Services..................................1420		●	●	●	

DT	BK	CV	CR	PR	CLARK		UC	RE	TX	VR
●	●	●	●	●	ADP Services..24		●	●	●	●
●	●	●	●	●	Attorney's Investigative Consultants..............204		●	●	●	●
●	●	●	●	●	The Copy Store & More - Las Vegas.............1924		●	●	●	●

		CV	CR	PR	DOUGLAS		UC	RE	TX	VR
		●	●	●	Nevada Records Search................................1421		●	●	●	●
		●		●	People Property Research..............................1535		●	●	●	●

		CV	CR	PR	ELKO		UC	RE	TX	VR
					See adjoining counties....................................					

		CV	CR	PR	ESMERALDA		UC	RE	TX	VR
					Nevada Land Services..................................1420		●	●	●	
					See adjoining counties....................................					

		CV	CR	PR	EUREKA		UC	RE	TX	VR
					Nevada Land Services..................................1420		●	●	●	

		CV	CR	PR	HUMBOLDT		UC	RE	TX	VR
					Nevada Land Services..................................1420		●	●	●	

		CV	CR	PR	LANDER		UC	RE	TX	VR
					Nevada Land Services..................................1420		●	●	●	

		CV	CR	PR	LINCOLN		UC	RE	TX	VR
		●	●	●	Attorney's Document Production 202		●	●	●	●
					Nevada Land Services..................................1420		●	●	●	

		CV	CR	PR	LYON		UC	RE	TX	VR
					See adjoining counties....................................					

		CV	CR	PR	MINERAL		UC	RE	TX	VR
					Nevada Land Services..................................1420		●	●	●	

		CV	CR	PR	NYE		UC	RE	TX	VR
		●	●	●	ADP Services...24		●	●	●	●
					Nevada Land Services..................................1420		●	●	●	

		CV	CR	PR	PERSHING		UC	RE	TX	VR
					Nevada Land Services..................................1420		●	●	●	

		CV	CR	PR	STOREY		UC	RE	TX	VR
		●	●	●	Nevada Records Search................................1421		●	●	●	●
		●		●	People Property Research..............................1535		●	●	●	●

DT	BK	CV	CR	PR	WASHOE		UC	RE	TX	VR
●	●	●	●	●	Nevada Records Search................................1421		●	●	●	●
●	●	●	●		People Property Research..............................1535		●	●	●	●
●	●	●	●	●	The Copy Store & More - Reno 1925		●	●	●	●

		CV	CR	PR	WHITE PINE		UC	RE	TX	VR
					Nevada Land Services..................................1420		●	●	●	

New Hampshire

DT	BK	CV	CR	PR	ALL COUNTIES	UC	RE	TX	VR
●	●	●	●	●	Coast to Coast Research Network 480	●	●	●	●
●	●	●	●	●	New England Recovery Inc...1422	●	●	●	●

		CV	CR	PR	BELKNAP	UC	RE	TX	VR
				●	Doc*U*Search...639	●	●	●	●

		CV	CR	PR	CARROLL	UC	RE	TX	VR
					See ALL COUNTIES..				

		CV	CR	PR	CHESHIRE	UC	RE	TX	VR
		●	●		Harmon Personnel Services Inc 928				
		●	●	●	Simmons Agency 1807	●	●	●	●

		CV	CR	PR	COOS	UC	RE	TX	VR
		●	●	●	Davis, Don 604	●	●	●	●

		CV	CR	PR	GRAFTON	UC	RE	TX	VR
		●	●	●	Davis, Don 604	●	●	●	●

	BK	CV	CR	PR	HILLSBOROUGH	UC	RE	TX	VR
	●	●		●	Doc*U*Search...639	●	●	●	●
	●	●	●	●	Simmons Agency 1807	●	●	●	●

DT		CV	CR	PR	MERRIMACK	UC	RE	TX	VR
●		●		●	Doc*U*Search...639	●	●	●	●
●		●	●	●	Simmons Agency 1807	●	●	●	●

		CV	CR	PR	ROCKINGHAM	UC	RE	TX	VR
		●	●	●	Simmons Agency 1807	●	●	●	●

		CV	CR	PR	STRAFFORD	UC	RE	TX	VR
					See ALL COUNTIES..				

		CV	CR	PR	SULLIVAN	UC	RE	TX	VR
					See ALL COUNTIES..				

New Jersey

DT	BK	CV	CR	PR	ALL COUNTIES		UC	RE	TX	VR
●	●	●	●	●	Interstate Abstract Inc 1040		●	●	●	●
●	●	●	●	●	Interstate Document Filings Inc 1041		●	●	●	●
●	●	●	●	●	North East Court Services Inc 1434		●	●	●	
●	●	●	●	●	Regional Investigative Services Inc 1673		●	●		●
●	●	●	●	●	Sikoral & Associates Investigations..............1803		●	●		●
●	●	●	●	●	Teamco Inc..1906		●	●		●
				●	Worthmann, Cheri.....................................2116					●

		CV	CR	PR	ATLANTIC		UC	RE	TX	VR
		●	●	●	Anbar Corp...143		●	●	●	●
		●	●	●	Court House Legal Service............................542		●	●	●	●
		●	●		Flink Findzum...786		●	●	●	●
			●		Fuoti, Peg...820			●		
		●	●		Kerins, Karen 1119			●	●	

		CV	CR	PR	BERGEN		UC	RE	TX	VR
		●	●	●	Biamonte, Joe...297		●	●	●	●
		●		●	Callahan Lawyers Service.............................383					
		●	●		Court Data Search 541					
		●	●	●	Gamma Investigative Research Inc 829		●	●	●	
		●	●	●	Genesis Investigations..................................839		●	●		●
		●			Legal Courier 1194			●		
		●	●	●	Legal Express 1203		●	●	●	●
		●	●	●	LegalEase Inc 1215		●	●	●	●
		●	●	●	Mandelbaum-Edgerton Grooup......................1274		●	●	●	●
		●	●	●	PMD Abstract Co Inc 1492		●	●	●	●

		CV	CR	PR	BURLINGTON		UC	RE	TX	VR
		●	●		Best Legal Services Inc................................293		●	●	●	●
		●	●	●	Burlington County Abstract Co.......................368		●	●	●	
		●	●	●	Court House Legal Service............................542		●	●	●	
		●	●	●	Craig, Nancy 547		●	●	●	●
		●	●	●	Credit Lenders Service Agency Inc.................563		●	●	●	
		●	●		Flink Findzum...786		●	●	●	●
		●		●	Legal Wings Inc 1214		●	●		●
		●	●	●	O'Brien, Jack 1450		●	●	●	●
		●	●	●	Prentice Hall Legal & Financial Services.........1589		●	●	●	●
		●	●	●	Public Record Information.............................1627		●	●	●	●
		●	●		Talme and Associates...................................1900					
		●	●	●	The Coynes..1927		●	●	●	●

DT	BK	CV	CR	PR	CAMDEN		UC	RE	TX	VR
		●	●	●	Augatis, Eileen 218		●	●	●	●
●	●	●	●	●	Best Legal Services Inc................................293		●	●	●	
		●		●	Cooper Abstract Co......................................517		●	●	●	
●	●	●	●	●	Court House Legal Service............................542		●	●		●
		●	●	●	Credit Lenders Service Agency Inc.................563		●	●	●	
		●	●	●	Crystal Systems Legal Services Division..........572		●	●	●	●
●	●	●	●	●	Dennis Richman Services..............................622		●	●	●	●
●	●	●	●		Flink Findzum...786		●	●	●	●
		●		●	Hetrick, Anne 962		●	●	●	●
●	●	●	●	●	Legal Wings Inc 1214		●	●		●
●	●	●	●	●	Messmer, Craig 1333		●	●	●	
●	●	●	●		Talme and Associates...................................1900					
●	●	●	●	●	The Coynes..1927		●	●	●	●

		CV	CR	PR	CAPE MAY		UC	RE	TX	VR
		●	●		Flink Findzum...786		●	●	●	●

CV	CR	PR		UC	RE	TX	VR
●	●	●	Sterling Abstract Inc......1865	●	●	●	●

CUMBERLAND

CV	CR	PR		UC	RE	TX	VR
●	●	●	Chalow, Trish......433	●	●	●	●
●	●		Flink Findzum......786	●	●	●	●

ESSEX

DT	BK	CV	CR	PR		UC	RE	TX	VR
		●	●		Court Data Search......541				
		●	●	●	Crystal Systems Legal Services Division......572	●	●	●	●
●	●	●	●	●	Genesis Investigations......839	●	●	●	●
●	●	●			Legal Courier......1194		●		
●	●	●	●	●	Legal Express......1203	●	●	●	●
		●	●	●	PMD Abstract Co Inc......1492	●	●	●	●
		●			Quest Abstract Inc......1634	●	●		
		●	●	●	Vanderhoof, Linda......2026	●	●	●	●

GLOUCESTER

CV	CR	PR		UC	RE	TX	VR
●	●	●	Augatis, Eileen......218	●	●	●	●
●	●		Best Legal Services Inc......293	●	●	●	●
●	●	●	Court House Legal Service......542	●	●	●	●
●	●	●	Derher, Linda......624	●	●	●	●
●	●		Flink Findzum......786	●	●	●	●
●			Lester, Bruce......1220		●		
●	●		Talme and Associates......1900				

HUDSON

CV	CR	PR		UC	RE	TX	VR
●	●	●	Cook, Joseph E......516	●	●	●	●
●	●		Court Data Search......541				
			Erichsen, Carrie......714		●		
●	●	●	Gamma Investigative Research Inc......829	●	●	●	
●			Legal Courier......1194		●		
●	●	●	Legal Express......1203	●	●	●	●
●	●	●	Mandelbaum-Edgerton Grooup......1274	●	●	●	●
●	●	●	Metzler, Arthur......1337	●	●	●	●
●	●	●	PMD Abstract Co Inc......1492	●	●	●	●

HUNTERDON

CV	CR	PR		UC	RE	TX	VR
●	●	●	Blair, Joe......309	●	●	●	●
●	●	●	Crystal Systems Legal Services Division......572	●	●	●	●
●	●	●	Legal Wings Inc......1214	●	●		●

MERCER

DT	BK	CV	CR	PR		UC	RE	TX	VR
●	●	●	●	●	Court House Legal Service......542	●	●	●	●
		●	●	●	Credit Lenders Service Agency Inc......563	●	●	●	
		●	●	●	Crystal Systems Legal Services Division......572	●	●	●	●
●	●	●	●		Flink Findzum......786	●	●	●	
●	●	●	●	●	Kaufman & Harlow Inc of Dayton......1115	●	●	●	
●	●	●	●	●	Legal Wings Inc......1214	●	●		●
		●	●		Matejik, Stephen......1295	●			
●	●	●	●	●	Prentice Hall Legal & Financial Services......1589	●	●	●	●
		●	●	●	Public Record Information......1627	●	●	●	
●	●	●	●	●	The Coynes......1927	●	●	●	●

MIDDLESEX

CV	CR	PR		UC	RE	TX	VR
●	●	●	Axt, Erin......222	●	●	●	●
●	●	●	Belden, Bob......277	●	●	●	●
●	●	●	Commercial Investigation......504		●	●	
●	●		Court Data Search......541				
●	●	●	Crystal Systems Legal Services Division......572	●	●	●	
●	●	●	Kaufman & Harlow Inc of Dayton......1115	●	●	●	
●	●	●	Legal Wings Inc......1214	●	●		●

CV	CR	PR		Page	UC	RE	TX	VR
•	•	•	Trident Abstract Co	1983	•	•	•	

MONMOUTH

CV	CR	PR		Page	UC	RE	TX	VR
•	•	•	Commercial Investigation	504		•	•	•
•	•	•	Crystal Systems Legal Services Division	572	•	•	•	•
			Forlenza, Janet C	795		•		
•	•	•	G & O Abstracts Inc	823	•	•	•	
•	•	•	Hetrich, Gilbert S	961	•	•	•	
•	•	•	Kaufman & Harlow Inc of Dayton	1115	•	•	•	
•	•	•	Legal Wings Inc	1214	•	•		•
•	•	•	Trident Abstract Co	1983	•	•	•	

MORRIS

CV	CR	PR		Page	UC	RE	TX	VR
•	•		Court Data Search	541				
•	•	•	Crystal Systems Legal Services Division	572	•	•	•	•
•	•	•	Genesis Investigations	839	•	•	•	
•	•	•	Legal Express	1203	•	•	•	
•	•	•	Mandelbaum-Edgerton Grooup	1274	•	•	•	
		•	Morris Hills Abstract Co	1388	•	•	•	
•	•	•	Ronald J Axelrod and Associates	1713	•	•	•	
•	•	•	Vogel, Fred & Margaret	2033	•	•	•	•

OCEAN

CV	CR	PR		Page	UC	RE	TX	VR
•	•	•	Commercial Investigation	504		•	•	•
•	•	•	Crystal Systems Legal Services Division	572	•	•	•	
•	•		Flink Findzum	786	•	•	•	
•	•	•	Hanna, Nancy	917	•	•	•	
•	•	•	Hetrich, Gilbert S	961	•	•	•	
•	•	•	Kaufman & Harlow Inc of Dayton	1115	•	•	•	
•	•	•	Laratta & Tucker	1172	•	•	•	
•	•	•	Legal Wings Inc	1214	•	•		•
•	•	•	Trident Abstract Co	1983	•	•	•	

PASSAIC

CV	CR	PR		Page	UC	RE	TX	VR
•		•	Callahan Lawyers Service	383				
•	•		Court Data Search	541				
•	•	•	Gamma Investigative Research Inc	829	•	•	•	•
•	•	•	Genesis Investigations	839	•	•	•	•
•	•	•	Legal Express	1203	•	•	•	•
•	•	•	PMD Abstract Co Inc	1492	•	•	•	•

SALEM

CV	CR	PR		Page	UC	RE	TX	VR
			Ayars, Pamela G	223	•	•	•	
•	•	•	Chalow, Trish	433	•	•	•	•
•	•		Flink Findzum	786	•	•	•	•

SOMERSET

CV	CR	PR		Page	UC	RE	TX	VR
•	•	•	Axt, Erin	222	•	•	•	•
•	•	•	CMT Abstract	376	•	•	•	•
•	•	•	Crystal Systems Legal Services Division	572	•	•	•	•
•	•	•	Genesis Investigations	839	•	•	•	•
		•	KJK Abstract Co	1109	•	•	•	
•	•	•	Kaufman & Harlow Inc of Dayton	1115	•	•		•
•	•	•	Legal Wings Inc	1214	•	•		•

SUSSEX

CV	CR	PR		Page	UC	RE	TX	VR
•	•	•	Anthony J Fierro Abstract Co Inc	155	•	•	•	
•	•	•	Gamma Investigative Research Inc	829	•	•	•	
•	•	•	Genesis Investigations	839	•	•	•	•
•	•	•	Lora J Musilli & Associates	1240	•	•	•	•

CV	CR	PR	UNION		UC	RE	TX	VR
●	●	●	Crystal Systems Legal Services Division	572	●	●	●	●
●		●	Faithful Abstract	737	●	●	●	
●	●	●	Gamma Investigative Research Inc	829	●	●	●	
●	●	●	Genesis Investigations	839	●	●	●	●
●	●	●	Kaufman & Harlow Inc of Dayton	1115	●	●	●	●
●	●	●	PMD Abstract Co Inc	1492	●	●	●	●
●			Quest Abstract Inc	1634	●	●		
			Santillo, Marlene	1739		●		
●	●	●	Superior Subpoena Service	1887	●	●	●	●

CV	CR	PR	WARREN		UC	RE	TX	VR
●	●		Dailey Title Searching Inc	584		●		
●	●	●	Gamma Investigative Research Inc	829	●	●	●	
●	●	●	KCD Title	1108	●	●	●	●

Court
Records

NEW MEXICO
144

County
Records

New Mexico

DT	BK	CV	CR	PR	ALL COUNTIES	UC	RE	TX	VR
•	•	•	•	•	Hollingsworth Court Reporting Inc....................983	•	•	•	•

DT	BK	CV	CR	PR	BERNALILLO	UC	RE	TX	VR
•	•	•	•	•	Capitol Document Services Inc.........................394	•	•	•	•
•	•	•	•	•	Data Quest Inc..592	•	•	•	•
•	•	•	•	•	UCC Search Inc.......................................1998	•	•	•	•

		CV	CR	PR	CATRON	UC	RE	TX	VR
		•	•	•	County Abstract & Title Co.............................537	•	•	•	•

		CV	CR	PR	CHAVES	UC	RE	TX	VR
		•		•	Chaves County Abstract & Title Co...................444	•	•	•	
		•	•	•	J.P. Investigations 1070	•	•	•	•

		CV	CR	PR	CIBOLA	UC	RE	TX	VR
		•	•	•	Lopez, Alfred 1239	•	•	•	•

		CV	CR	PR	COLFAX	UC	RE	TX	VR
		•			Credit Bureau of Raton 559	•		•	•

		CV	CR	PR	CURRY	UC	RE	TX	VR
		•	•	•	Clovis Title and Abstract Company 477	•	•	•	•
		•	•	•	J.P. Investigations 1070	•	•	•	•
		•		•	Plains Title and Abstract Inc 1559	•	•	•	

		CV	CR	PR	DE BACA	UC	RE	TX	VR
		•	•	•	J.P. Investigations 1070	•	•	•	•

		CV	CR	PR	DONA ANA	UC	RE	TX	VR
		•	•	•	AGO Investigations and Polygraph Ltd 25	•	•	•	•
		•	•	•	Legal Net Process Service............................1205	•			•
		•	•	•	Legal Remedy...1207		•	•	•
		•	•	•	UCC Search Inc.......................................1998	•	•	•	•

		CV	CR	PR	EDDY	UC	RE	TX	VR
		•		•	Caprock Title Co.......................................404	•	•	•	
		•	•	•	Currier Abstract Company 574	•	•	•	
		•		•	Eddy County Abstract Co...............................691	•	•	•	•
		•	•	•	Guaranty Title Co......................................893	•	•		•
		•	•	•	J.P. Investigations 1070	•	•	•	•

		CV	CR	PR	GRANT	UC	RE	TX	VR
		•	•	•	AGO Investigations and Polygraph Ltd 25	•	•	•	•

		CV	CR	PR	GUADALUPE	UC	RE	TX	VR
		•	•	•	Territorial Title.....................................1909	•	•	•	•
		•	•	•	UCC Search Inc.......................................1998	•	•	•	•

		CV	CR	PR	HARDING	UC	RE	TX	VR
		•	•	•	Pritchett, Debbi 1604	•	•	•	•

		CV	CR	PR	HIDALGO	UC	RE	TX	VR
		•		•	Hidalgo County Abstract...............................966	•	•	•	•

		CV	CR	PR	LEA	UC	RE	TX	VR
		•		•	Caprock Title Co.......................................404	•	•	•	
		•		•	Elliott and Waldron Title and Abstract 707	•	•	•	
		•	•	•	J.P. Investigations 1070	•	•	•	•

		CV	CR	PR	LINCOLN	UC	RE	TX	VR
		•	•	•	Alamogordo Abstract & Title............................95	•	•	•	•

CV	CR	PR	Company	Page	UC	RE	TX	VR
●	●	●	J.P. Investigations	1070	●	●	●	●
●		●	Lincoln County Abstract & Title Co	1227	●	●	●	
CV	**CR**	**PR**	**LOS ALAMOS**		**UC**	**RE**	**TX**	**VR**
●	●	●	UCC Search Inc	1998	●	●	●	●
CV	**CR**	**PR**	**LUNA**		**UC**	**RE**	**TX**	**VR**
●	●	●	AGO Investigations and Polygraph Ltd	25	●	●	●	●
●	●	●	Mimbres Valley Abstract & Title Co	1358	●	●	●	●
CV	**CR**	**PR**	**MCKINLEY**		**UC**	**RE**	**TX**	**VR**
●	●	●	Lopez, Alfred	1239	●	●	●	●
CV	**CR**	**PR**	**MORA**		**UC**	**RE**	**TX**	**VR**
●	●	●	Territorial Title	1909	●	●	●	●
CV	**CR**	**PR**	**OTERO**		**UC**	**RE**	**TX**	**VR**
●	●	●	Alamogordo Abstract & Title	95	●	●	●	●
CV	**CR**	**PR**	**QUAY**		**UC**	**RE**	**TX**	**VR**
●	●	●	UCC Search Inc	1998	●	●	●	●
CV	**CR**	**PR**	**RIO ARRIBA**		**UC**	**RE**	**TX**	**VR**
●		●	Espanola Abstract Co	715	●	●	●	●
CV	**CR**	**PR**	**ROOSEVELT**		**UC**	**RE**	**TX**	**VR**
●		●	Graham Abstract Co Inc	858	●	●	●	
●	●	●	J.P. Investigations	1070	●	●		●
●	●	●	Portales Abstract	1573	●	●	●	
CV	**CR**	**PR**	**SANDOVAL**		**UC**	**RE**	**TX**	**VR**
●	●	●	Data Quest Inc	592	●	●	●	●
CV	**CR**	**PR**	**SAN JUAN**		**UC**	**RE**	**TX**	**VR**
●	●	●	San Juan County Abstract & Title	1733	●	●	●	●
CV	**CR**	**PR**	**SAN MIGUEL**		**UC**	**RE**	**TX**	**VR**
●	●	●	Territorial Title	1909	●	●	●	●
●	●	●	UCC Search Inc	1998	●	●	●	●
CV	**CR**	**PR**	**SANTA FE**		**UC**	**RE**	**TX**	**VR**
●	●	●	Capitol Document Services Inc	394	●	●	●	●
●	●	●	UCC Search Inc	1998	●		●	●
CV	**CR**	**PR**	**SIERRA**		**UC**	**RE**	**TX**	**VR**
●	●	●	AGO Investigations and Polygraph Ltd	25	●	●	●	
CV	**CR**	**PR**	**SOCORRO**		**UC**	**RE**	**TX**	**VR**
●	●	●	County Abstract & Title Co	537	●	●	●	
CV	**CR**	**PR**	**TAOS**		**UC**	**RE**	**TX**	**VR**
●	●	●	Capitol Document Services Inc	394	●	●	●	●
●	●	●	UCC Search Inc	1998	●	●	●	●
CV	**CR**	**PR**	**TORRANCE**		**UC**	**RE**	**TX**	**VR**
●	●	●	UCC Search Inc	1998	●	●	●	●
CV	**CR**	**PR**	**UNION**		**UC**	**RE**	**TX**	**VR**
●	●	●	Clayton Title Service Inc	471	●	●	●	
CV	**CR**	**PR**	**VALENCIA**		**UC**	**RE**	**TX**	**VR**
●	●	●	UCC Search Inc	1998	●	●	●	●

New York

DT	BK	CV	CR	PR	ALL COUNTIES	UC	RE	TX	VR
●	●	●	●	●	New York Institute of Legal Research 1423	●	●	●	●
●	●	●	●	●	Omni Corporate and Research Service Inc......................1468	●		●	●

DT	BK	CV	CR	PR	ALBANY	UC	RE	TX	VR
●	●	●	●	●	Attorney's Process and Research Service..........................206	●	●	●	●
●	●	●	●		Corporate Service Bureau 525	●		●	●
●	●	●	●	●	Corporation Service Company of Albany.........................530	●	●	●	●
					Four Corners Abstract...798	●	●	●	
●	●	●			Intercounty Clearance Corporation 1037	●	●	●	
●					Monroe Title Insurance Corporation...............................1366	●	●	●	
●	●	●	●	●	Prentice Hall Legal & Financial Services.......................1590	●	●	●	●
●	●	●	●	●	Relyea-Lee Services Inc..1678	●	●	●	●
●	●	●	●	●	Tracers International 1974	●	●	●	●
●	●	●	●	●	Zap! Courier Service...2123	●		●	●

CV	CR	PR	ALLEGANY	UC	RE	TX	VR
			Four Corners Abstract...798	●	●	●	
			Monroe Title Insurance Corporation...............................1366	●	●	●	

CV	CR	PR	BRONX	UC	RE	TX	VR
●	●	●	APB Information Research Center Inc................................31	●	●	●	●
●	●	●	All County Service Corp...106	●	●	●	
●	●	●	Alstate Process Service Inc 123	●	●	●	●
●	●	●	Atlantic Process Service Inc..179	●	●	●	●
●		●	B.E.S. Abstract Corp..231	●	●	●	
●		●	Barristers Abstract Corp..249	●	●	●	
●	●	●	Beck & Call Legal Support Services.................................270	●	●	●	●
●	●	●	Corporation Service Company of Albany.........................530	●	●	●	●
●		●	Eastco Abstract Corporation 682	●	●	●	
●		●	Federal Information Service..750	●	●	●	●
●	●	●	Genesis Investigations..839	●	●	●	
●		●	Gotham Process Service Inc...856				
●			Intercounty Clearance Corporation 1037	●	●	●	
●	●	●	Investigative Resources...1048	●	●		●
●	●	●	LegalEase Inc...1215	●	●	●	
●	●	●	North East Court Services Inc...1434	●	●	●	
●	●	●	Pallorium Inc..1503	●	●	●	●
●	●	●	Search NY 1757	●	●	●	●

DT	CV	CR	PR	BROOME	UC	RE	TX	VR
				Four Corners Abstract...798	●	●	●	
●				Monroe Title Insurance Corporation...............................1366	●	●	●	

CV	CR	PR	CATTARAUGUS	UC	RE	TX	VR
●	●	●	Action Process Service..73	●	●	●	●
●		●	Cattaraugus Abstract Corp 418	●		●	
			Monroe Title Insurance Corporation...............................1366	●	●	●	

CV	CR	PR	CAYUGA	UC	RE	TX	VR
●		●	Central New York Abstract Corporation............................427	●	●	●	
			Four Corners Abstract...798	●	●	●	
			Monroe Title Insurance Corporation...............................1366	●	●	●	

CV	CR	PR	CHAUTAUQUA	UC	RE	TX	VR
●	●	●	Action Process Service..73	●	●	●	●
●		●	Eastco Abstract Corporation 682	●	●	●	●
			Monroe Title Insurance Corporation...............................1366	●	●	●	

		CV	CR	PR	CHEMUNG		UC	RE	TX	VR
					Four Corners Abstract 798		•	•	•	
					Monroe Title Insurance Corporation 1366		•	•	•	

		CV	CR	PR	CHENANGO		UC	RE	TX	VR
					Four Corners Abstract 798		•	•	•	
		•		•	Iroquois Country Abstract Corp 1057		•	•	•	
					Monroe Title Insurance Corporation 1366		•	•	•	

		CV	CR	PR	CLINTON		UC	RE	TX	VR
					Monroe Title Insurance Corporation 1366		•	•	•	

		CV	CR	PR	COLUMBIA		UC	RE	TX	VR
		•	•	•	Attorney's Process and Research Service 206		•	•	•	•
					Four Corners Abstract 798		•	•	•	
					Monroe Title Insurance Corporation 1366		•	•	•	
		•	•	•	Onistagrawa Abstracting Corp 1472		•	•	•	•

		CV	CR	PR	CORTLAND		UC	RE	TX	VR
					Monroe Title Insurance Corporation 1366		•	•	•	

		CV	CR	PR	DELAWARE		UC	RE	TX	VR
					Four Corners Abstract 798		•	•	•	
		•		•	Harry W Hawley Inc 933		•	•	•	
		•		•	Iroquois Country Abstract Corp 1057		•	•	•	
					Monroe Title Insurance Corporation 1366		•	•	•	
		•	•	•	Onistagrawa Abstracting Corp 1472		•	•	•	•

	BK	CV	CR	PR	DUTCHESS		UC	RE	TX	VR
	•	•	•	•	American Legal Support Service Inc 136		•	•	•	•
	•	•	•	•	Atlantic Process Service Inc 179		•	•	•	•
	•		•	•	Eastco Abstract Corporation 682		•	•	•	•
					Four Corners Abstract 798		•	•	•	
	•	•	•	•	Fox Advertising 802		•	•	•	
	•	•	•	•	Genesis Investigations 839		•	•	•	•
	•			•	Hill-N-Dale Abstractors Inc 973		•	•	•	
	•	•	•	•	La Prade Services Inc 1146		•	•	•	•
	•	•	•	•	Orange Abstractor Services Co 1474		•		•	
	•	•	•	•	Orange Paper Placers 1476		•	•	•	•
	•	•	•	•	Walsh Process & Legal Services 2050		•	•	•	•
	•	•	•	•	Westchester Court Service 2080		•		•	•

DT	BK	CV	CR	PR	ERIE		UC	RE	TX	VR
•	•	•	•	•	Action Process Service 73		•	•	•	•
•	•	•	•	•	Ferrari 753		•	•	•	•
					Four Corners Abstract 798		•	•	•	
•	•	•	•	•	Halliwell Process Service 910			•	•	
•	•				Monroe Title Insurance Corporation 1366		•	•	•	

		CV	CR	PR	ESSEX		UC	RE	TX	VR
		•		•	Eastco Abstract Corporation 682		•	•	•	•
					Monroe Title Insurance Corporation 1366		•	•	•	

		CV	CR	PR	FRANKLIN		UC	RE	TX	VR
		•		•	Etna Abstract Corp 717		•	•	•	
				•	Marvin Abstracting 1290		•	•	•	
					Monroe Title Insurance Corporation 1366		•	•	•	

		CV	CR	PR	FULTON		UC	RE	TX	VR
		•	•	•	County Seat Abstract 539		•	•	•	
					Four Corners Abstract 798		•	•	•	
					Monroe Title Insurance Corporation 1366		•	•	•	

Court Records							County Records			
		●	●		●	Onistagrawa Abstracting Corp 1472	●	●	●	●
					●	Sacandaga Abstract Corp 1728	●	●		
		CV	**CR**	**PR**		**GENESEE**	**UC**	**RE**	**TX**	**VR**
		●	●	●		Action Process Service..73	●	●	●	●
						Four Corners Abstract...798	●	●	●	
						Monroe Title Insurance Corporation.................................1366	●	●	●	
		CV	**CR**	**PR**		**GREENE**	**UC**	**RE**	**TX**	**VR**
		●	●	●		Attorney's Process and Research Service...........................206	●	●	●	●
						Four Corners Abstract...798	●	●	●	
						Monroe Title Insurance Corporation.................................1366	●	●	●	
		●	●	●		Onistagrawa Abstracting Corp 1472	●	●	●	●
		●	●	●		Zap! Courier Service...2123	●		●	●
		CV	**CR**	**PR**		**HAMILTON**	**UC**	**RE**	**TX**	**VR**
		●	●	●		County Seat Abstract...539	●	●	●	
						Monroe Title Insurance Corporation......................1366	●	●	●	
		CV	**CR**	**PR**		**HERKIMER**	**UC**	**RE**	**TX**	**VR**
		●		●		Central New York Abstract Corporation.............................427	●	●	●	
		●		●		Eastco Abstract Corporation 682	●	●	●	●
						Four Corners Abstract...798	●	●	●	
						Monroe Title Insurance Corporation.................................1366	●	●	●	
		CV	**CR**	**PR**		**JEFFERSON**	**UC**	**RE**	**TX**	**VR**
						Monroe Title Insurance Corporation.................................1366	●	●	●	
DT	**BK**	**CV**	**CR**	**PR**		**KINGS**	**UC**	**RE**	**TX**	**VR**
●	●	●	●	●		APB Information Research Center Inc..................................31	●	●	●	●
●	●	●	●	●		All County Service Corp..106	●	●	●	
●	●	●	●	●		Alstate Process Service Inc 123	●	●	●	●
		●	●		●	Barristers Abstract Corp..249	●	●	●	
●	●	●	●	●		Beck & Call Legal Support Services...................................270	●	●	●	●
●	●	●	●	●		Corporation Service Company of Albany 530	●	●	●	●
●	●	●	●	●		Docutronics Information Services.......................................643	●			
●	●	●	●	●		Federal Information Service..750	●	●		●
●	●	●	●	●		Genesis Investigations...839	●	●	●	●
●	●	●		●		Gotham Process Service Inc..856				
●	●	●				Intercounty Clearance Corporation 1037	●	●	●	
●	●	●	●	●		Investigative Resources...1048	●			●
●	●	●	●	●		LegalEase Inc 1215	●	●	●	●
●	●	●	●	●		North East Court Services Inc 1434	●	●	●	
●	●	●	●	●		Pallorium Inc...1503	●	●	●	●
		●	●		●	Prentice Hall Legal & Financial Services.........................1591	●			
●	●	●	●	●		Search NY 1757	●	●	●	●
		CV	**CR**	**PR**		**LEWIS**	**UC**	**RE**	**TX**	**VR**
						Monroe Title Insurance Corporation.................................1366	●	●	●	
		●	●	●		National Abstract Corporation 1406	●	●	●	
		CV	**CR**	**PR**		**LIVINGSTON**	**UC**	**RE**	**TX**	**VR**
						Four Corners Abstract...798	●	●	●	
						Monroe Title Insurance Corporation.................................1366	●	●	●	
		CV	**CR**	**PR**		**MADISON**	**UC**	**RE**	**TX**	**VR**
		●		●		Central New York Abstract Corporation.............................427	●	●	●	
						Four Corners Abstract...798	●	●	●	
						Monroe Title Insurance Corporation.................................1366	●	●	●	
		●	●	●		Oneida Valley Abstract..1471	●	●	●	

MONROE

DT	BK	CV	CR	PR			UC	RE	TX	VR
		•		•	Eastco Abstract Corporation ...682		•	•	•	•
					Four Corners Abstract ...798		•	•	•	
•	•	•	•	•	Legal Recording of Rochester Inc ...1206		•	•	•	
•	•				Monroe Title Insurance Corporation ...1366		•	•	•	

MONTGOMERY

CV	CR	PR			UC	RE	TX	VR
•	•	•	County Seat Abstract ...539		•	•	•	
			Four Corners Abstract ...798		•	•	•	
			Monroe Title Insurance Corporation ...1366		•	•	•	
•	•	•	Onistagrawa Abstracting Corp ...1472		•	•		•
		•	Sacandaga Abstract Corp ...1728		•	•		

NASSAU

DT	BK	CV	CR	PR			UC	RE	TX	VR
•	•	•	•	•	APB Information Research Center Inc ...31		•	•	•	
•	•	•	•	•	All County Service Corp ...106		•	•	•	
•	•	•	•	•	Alstate Process Service Inc ...123		•	•	•	•
			•	•	B.E.S. Abstract Corp ...231		•	•	•	
•	•	•	•	•	Beck & Call Legal Support Services ...270		•	•	•	
			•	•	Eastco Abstract Corporation ...682		•	•	•	
•	•	•	•	•	Genesis Investigations ...839		•	•	•	•
•	•	•			Intercounty Clearance Corporation ...1037		•	•	•	
•	•	•	•	•	LegalEase Inc ...1215		•	•	•	
•	•	•	•	•	Pallorium Inc ...1503		•	•	•	
•	•	•	•	•	Reda's Attorney Service ...1668		•	•	•	
•	•	•	•	•	Search NY ...1757		•	•	•	•
•	•	•	•	•	Security Enforcement Inc ...1772		•	•	•	•

NEW YORK

DT	BK	CV	CR	PR			UC	RE	TX	VR
•	•	•	•	•	APB Information Research Center Inc ...31		•	•	•	•
•	•	•	•	•	All County Service Corp ...106		•	•	•	
•	•	•	•	•	Alstate Process Service Inc ...123		•	•	•	•
•	•	•	•	•	Atlantic Process Service Inc ...179		•	•	•	•
		•	•		Barristers Abstract Corp ...249		•	•		
•	•	•	•	•	Beck & Call Legal Support Services ...270		•	•	•	
•	•	•	•	•	Corporation Service Company of Albany ...530		•	•	•	•
•	•	•	•		Docutronics Information Services ...643		•			
			•	•	Eastco Abstract Corporation ...682		•	•		•
			•	•	Federal Information Service ...750		•			
•	•	•	•	•	Genesis Investigations ...839		•	•		•
•	•	•	•		Gotham Process Service Inc ...856		•			
•	•	•			Intercounty Clearance Corporation ...1037		•	•	•	
•	•	•	•	•	Investigative Resources ...1048		•	•	•	•
•	•	•			Legal Courier ...1194			•		
•	•	•	•	•	Legal Recording of Rochester Inc ...1206		•	•	•	
•	•	•	•	•	LegalEase Inc ...1215		•	•	•	•
•	•	•	•	•	North East Court Services Inc ...1434		•	•	•	
•	•	•			Pallorium Inc ...1503		•	•		•
				•	Prentice Hall Legal & Financial Services ...1591		•			
•	•	•	•	•	Search NY ...1757		•	•	•	•
•	•	•		•	Tompkins and Watkins Abstract Corp ...1965		•	•	•	

NIAGARA

CV	CR	PR			UC	RE	TX	VR
•	•	•	Action Process Service ...73		•	•	•	•
	•	•	Ferrari ...753		•	•	•	•
			Four Corners Abstract ...798		•	•	•	
•	•	•	Halliwell Process Service ...910		•	•		
			Monroe Title Insurance Corporation ...1366		•	•		

ONEIDA

DT	BK	CV	CR	PR			UC	RE	TX	VR
		•	•		Central New York Abstract Corporation ...427		•	•	•	

DT	CV	CR	PR	Provider	Pg	UC	RE	TX	VR
				Four Corners Abstract	798	●	●	●	
●	●			Monroe Title Insurance Corporation	1366	●	●	●	
●	●	●	●	Utica-Rome Legal	2016	●	●	●	●

ONONDAGA

DT	CV	CR	PR	Provider	Pg	UC	RE	TX	VR
				Four Corners Abstract	798	●	●	●	
●				Monroe Title Insurance Corporation	1366	●	●	●	

ONTARIO

CV	CR	PR	Provider	Pg	UC	RE	TX	VR
			Four Corners Abstract	798	●	●	●	
			Monroe Title Insurance Corporation	1366	●	●	●	

ORANGE

CV	CR	PR	Provider	Pg	UC	RE	TX	VR
●		●	Allied Abstract Co	116	●	●	●	
●	●	●	Atlantic Process Service Inc	179	●	●	●	●
●	●	●	Attorney Service Bureau	183	●	●	●	●
			Four Corners Abstract	798	●	●	●	
●	●	●	Fox Advertising	802	●	●	●	
●	●	●	Genesis Investigations	839	●	●	●	●
●		●	Hill-N-Dale Abstractors Inc	973	●	●	●	
●	●	●	La Prade Services Inc	1146	●	●	●	●
●	●	●	LegalEase Inc	1215	●	●	●	
			Monroe Title Insurance Corporation	1366	●	●		
●	●	●	Orange Abstractor Services Co	1474	●			
●	●	●	Orange Paper Placers	1476	●	●	●	●
●	●	●	Robert Daly Investigations	1703	●	●	●	
●	●	●	Walsh Process & Legal Services	2050	●	●	●	●
●	●	●	Westchester Court Service	2080	●	●	●	

ORLEANS

CV	CR	PR	Provider	Pg	UC	RE	TX	VR
●	●	●	Action Process Service	73	●	●	●	●
			Four Corners Abstract	798	●	●	●	

OSWEGO

CV	CR	PR	Provider	Pg	UC	RE	TX	VR
●		●	Central New York Abstract Corporation	427	●	●	●	
			Four Corners Abstract	798	●	●	●	
			Monroe Title Insurance Corporation	1366	●	●	●	

OTSEGO

CV	CR	PR	Provider	Pg	UC	RE	TX	VR
●		●	Central New York Abstract Corporation	427	●	●	●	
●		●	Eastco Abstract Corporation	682	●	●	●	●
●		●	Iroquois Country Abstract Corp	1057	●	●	●	
			Monroe Title Insurance Corporation	1366	●	●	●	
●	●	●	Onistagrawa Abstracting Corp	1472	●	●	●	●

PUTNAM

CV	CR	PR	Provider	Pg	UC	RE	TX	VR
●		●	Allied Abstract Co	116	●	●	●	
●	●	●	Atlantic Process Service Inc	179	●	●	●	●
●	●	●	Attorney Service Bureau	183	●	●	●	●
●	●	●	Fox Advertising	802	●	●	●	
●	●	●	Genesis Investigations	839	●	●	●	●
●	●	●	La Prade Services Inc	1146	●	●	●	●
●	●	●	LegalEase Inc	1215	●	●	●	
●	●	●	Orange Abstractor Services Co	1474	●			
●	●	●	Orange Paper Placers	1476	●	●	●	●
●	●	●	Walsh Process & Legal Services	2050	●	●	●	●
●	●	●	Westchester Court Service	2080	●	●	●	●

QUEENS

CV	CR	PR	Provider	Pg	UC	RE	TX	VR
●	●	●	APB Information Research Center Inc	31	●	●	●	●
●	●	●	All County Service Corp	106	●	●	●	
●	●	●	Alstate Process Service Inc	123	●	●	●	●

CV	CR	PR		UC	RE	TX	VR
●		●	B.E.S. Abstract Corp 231	●	●	●	
●		●	Barristers Abstract Corp 249	●	●	●	
●	●	●	Beck & Call Legal Support Services 270	●	●	●	●
●	●	●	Corporation Service Company of Albany 530	●	●	●	●
●	●	●	Docutronics Information Services 643	●			
●		●	Eastco Abstract Corporation 682	●	●	●	●
●	●	●	Federal Information Service 750	●	●	●	●
●	●	●	Genesis Investigations 839	●	●	●	●
●		●	Gotham Process Service Inc 856				
●			Intercounty Clearance Corporation 1037	●	●	●	
●	●	●	Investigative Resources 1048	●	●		●
●	●	●	LegalEase Inc 1215	●	●	●	●
●	●	●	North East Court Services Inc 1434	●	●	●	
●	●	●	Pallorium Inc 1503	●	●	●	●
●			Prentice Hall Legal & Financial Services 1591	●			
●	●	●	Search NY 1757	●	●	●	●

CV	CR	PR	RENSSELAER	UC	RE	TX	VR
●	●	●	Attorney's Process and Research Service 206	●	●	●	●
●	●		Corporate Service Bureau 525	●		●	●
			Four Corners Abstract 798	●	●	●	
●			Intercounty Clearance Corporation 1037	●	●	●	
			Monroe Title Insurance Corporation 1366	●	●	●	
●	●	●	Prentice Hall Legal & Financial Services 1590	●	●	●	●
●	●	●	Relyea-Lee Services Inc 1678	●	●	●	●
●	●	●	Tracers International 1974	●	●	●	●
●	●	●	Zap! Courier Service 2123	●		●	●

CV	CR	PR	RICHMOND	UC	RE	TX	VR
●	●	●	APB Information Research Center Inc 31	●	●	●	●
●	●	●	All County Service Corp 106	●	●	●	
●	●	●	Alstate Process Service Inc 123	●	●	●	●
●		●	Barristers Abstract Corp 249	●	●	●	
●	●	●	Beck & Call Legal Support Services 270	●	●	●	●
●	●	●	Federal Information Service 750	●	●	●	●
●	●	●	Genesis Investigations 839	●	●	●	●
●		●	Gotham Process Service Inc 856				
●	●	●	Investigative Resources 1048	●	●		●
●	●	●	LegalEase Inc 1215	●	●	●	●
●	●	●	North East Court Services Inc 1434	●	●	●	
●	●	●	Pallorium Inc 1503	●	●	●	●
●	●	●	Search NY 1757	●	●	●	●
●			US Title Research Inc 2002	●	●	●	

CV	CR	PR	ROCKLAND	UC	RE	TX	VR
●		●	Allied Abstract Co 116	●	●	●	
●	●	●	Atlantic Process Service Inc 179	●	●	●	●
●	●	●	Attorney Service Bureau 183	●	●	●	●
●		●	Eastco Abstract Corporation 682	●	●	●	●
●	●	●	Fox Advertising 802	●	●	●	
●	●	●	Genesis Investigations 839	●	●		●
●		●	Gotham Process Service Inc 856				
●		●	Hill-N-Dale Abstractors Inc 973	●	●	●	
●	●	●	LegalEase Inc 1215	●	●	●	●
●	●	●	Orange Abstractor Services Co 1474	●		●	
●	●	●	Orange Paper Placers 1476	●	●	●	●
●	●	●	Walsh Process & Legal Services 2050	●	●	●	●
●	●	●	Westchester Court Service 2080	●	●	●	●

ST. LAWRENCE

CV	CR	PR		UC	RE	TX	VR
●	●		J Tacchino Agency Private Investigators 1068		●	●	
			Monroe Title Insurance Corporation 1366	●	●	●	

SARATOGA

CV	CR	PR		UC	RE	TX	VR
●	●	●	Attorney's Process and Research Service 206	●	●	●	●
			Four Corners Abstract 798	●	●	●	
●			Intercounty Clearance Corporation 1037	●	●	●	
			Monroe Title Insurance Corporation 1366	●	●	●	
●	●	●	Relyea-Lee Services Inc 1678	●	●	●	●
●	●	●	Tracers International 1974	●	●	●	●
●	●	●	Zap! Courier Service 2123	●		●	●

SCHENECTADY

CV	CR	PR		UC	RE	TX	VR
●	●	●	Attorney's Process and Research Service 206	●	●	●	●
●	●		Corporate Service Bureau 525	●			●
			Four Corners Abstract 798	●	●	●	
			Monroe Title Insurance Corporation 1366	●	●	●	
●	●	●	Onistagrawa Abstracting Corp 1472	●	●	●	●
●	●	●	Prentice Hall Legal & Financial Services 1590	●	●	●	●
●	●	●	Relyea-Lee Services Inc 1678	●	●	●	●
●	●	●	Tracers International 1974	●	●	●	●
●	●	●	Zap! Courier Service 2123	●		●	●

SCHOHARIE

CV	CR	PR		UC	RE	TX	VR
●		●	Iroquois Country Abstract Corp 1057	●	●	●	
			Monroe Title Insurance Corporation 1366	●	●	●	
●	●	●	Onistagrawa Abstracting Corp 1472	●	●	●	●
●	●	●	Tracers International 1974	●	●	●	●

SCHUYLER

CV	CR	PR		UC	RE	TX	VR
			Monroe Title Insurance Corporation 1366	●	●	●	

SENECA

CV	CR	PR		UC	RE	TX	VR
			Four Corners Abstract 798	●	●	●	
			Monroe Title Insurance Corporation 1366	●	●	●	

STEUBEN

CV	CR	PR		UC	RE	TX	VR
			Four Corners Abstract 798	●	●	●	
●			Intercounty Clearance Corporation 1037	●	●	●	
			Monroe Title Insurance Corporation 1366	●	●	●	

SUFFOLK

DT	BK	CV	CR	PR		UC	RE	TX	VR
●	●	●	●	●	APB Information Research Center Inc 31	●	●	●	●
●	●	●	●	●	Alstate Process Service Inc 123	●	●	●	●
●		●		●	B.E.S. Abstract Corp 231	●	●	●	●
●	●	●	●	●	Beck & Call Legal Support Services 270	●	●	●	●
●	●	●	●	●	Corwin Attorney Service 533	●	●	●	●
●	●	●	●	●	Genesis Investigations 839	●	●	●	●
●	●	●	●	●	LegalEase Inc 1215	●	●	●	●
●	●	●	●	●	Pallorium Inc 1503	●	●	●	●
●	●	●	●	●	Reda's Attorney Service 1668	●	●	●	●
●	●	●	●	●	Security Enforcement Inc 1772	●	●	●	●
					Stovall, Donna 1871	●			●

SULLIVAN

CV	CR	PR		UC	RE	TX	VR
●	●	●	Attorney Service Bureau 183	●	●	●	●
●	●	●	Fox Advertising 802	●	●	●	
●	●	●	Genesis Investigations 839	●	●	●	●
●			Hill-N-Dale Abstractors Inc 973	●	●	●	
●	●	●	Orange Abstractor Services Co 1474	●	●	●	
●	●	●	Orange Paper Placers 1476	●	●	●	

CV	CR	PR		UC	RE	TX	VR
•	•	•	Walsh Process & Legal Services ... 2050	•	•	•	•
•	•	•	Westchester Court Service ... 2080	•	•	•	•

CV	CR	PR	TIOGA	UC	RE	TX	VR
			Four Corners Abstract ... 798	•	•	•	
			Monroe Title Insurance Corporation ... 1366	•	•	•	

CV	CR	PR	TOMPKINS	UC	RE	TX	VR
			Monroe Title Insurance Corporation ... 1366	•	•	•	

CV	CR	PR	ULSTER	UC	RE	TX	VR
•	•	•	American Legal Support Service Inc ... 136	•	•	•	•
•	•	•	Attorney Service Bureau ... 183	•	•	•	•
•		•	Eastco Abstract Corporation ... 682	•	•	•	
•	•	•	Fox Advertising ... 802	•	•	•	•
•	•	•	Genesis Investigations ... 839	•	•	•	•
•		•	Hill-N-Dale Abstractors Inc ... 973	•	•	•	
•	•	•	La Prade Services Inc ... 1146	•	•	•	
•	•	•	Orange Paper Placers ... 1476	•	•	•	
•	•	•	Ranger Recovery ... 1649	•	•	•	
•	•	•	Walsh Process & Legal Services ... 2050	•	•	•	
•	•	•	Westchester Court Service ... 2080	•	•	•	

CV	CR	PR	WARREN	UC	RE	TX	VR
			Four Corners Abstract ... 798	•	•	•	
			Monroe Title Insurance Corporation ... 1366	•	•	•	

CV	CR	PR	WASHINGTON	UC	RE	TX	VR
			Four Corners Abstract ... 798	•	•	•	
			Monroe Title Insurance Corporation ... 1366	•	•	•	

CV	CR	PR	WAYNE	UC	RE	TX	VR
			Four Corners Abstract ... 798	•	•	•	
			Monroe Title Insurance Corporation ... 1366	•	•	•	

BK	CV	CR	PR	WESTCHESTER	UC	RE	TX	VR
•	•	•	•	All County Service Corp ... 106	•	•	•	
•			•	Allied Abstract Co ... 116	•	•	•	
•	•	•	•	Atlantic Process Service Inc ... 179	•	•	•	•
•	•	•	•	Attorney Service Bureau ... 183	•	•	•	•
•	•	•	•	Beck & Call Legal Support Services ... 270	•	•	•	•
	•		•	Eastco Abstract Corporation ... 682	•	•	•	
•	•	•	•	Fox Advertising ... 802	•	•	•	•
•	•	•	•	Genesis Investigations ... 839	•	•	•	•
•	•		•	Gotham Process Service Inc ... 856				
•				Intercounty Clearance Corporation ... 1037	•	•	•	
•	•	•	•	LegalEase Inc ... 1215	•	•	•	
•	•	•	•	Pallorium Inc ... 1503	•	•	•	•
•	•	•		Search NY ... 1757	•	•	•	•
•	•	•	•	Walsh Process & Legal Services ... 2050	•	•	•	•
•	•	•	•	Westchester Court Service ... 2080	•	•	•	•

CV	CR	PR	WYOMING	UC	RE	TX	VR
•	•	•	Action Process Service ... 73	•	•	•	•
			Monroe Title Insurance Corporation ... 1366	•	•	•	

CV	CR	PR	YATES	UC	RE	TX	VR
			Four Corners Abstract ... 798	•	•	•	
			Monroe Title Insurance Corporation ... 1366	•	•	•	

Court
Records

NORTH CAROLINA
154

County
Records

North Carolina

DT	BK	CV	CR	PR	ALL COUNTIES	UC	RE	TX	VR
•	•	•	•	•	NC Search Inc 1405	•	•	•	
•	•	•	•	•	Professional Service of Process Inc.................................1618		•	•	•

		CV	CR	PR	ALAMANCE	UC	RE	TX	VR
		•	•	•	Paralegal Services of North Carolina Inc 1517	•	•	•	•
		•	•	•	Turning Wheels Inc..1990	•	•	•	•
		•	•	•	Williams, Nancy..2095	•	•	•	•

		CV	CR	PR	ALEXANDER	UC	RE	TX	VR
		•	•	•	Donna's Unlimited Searches...647	•	•	•	•

		CV	CR	PR	ALLEGHANY	UC	RE	TX	VR
		•	•	•	Murray, Dan R 1400	•	•	•	•

		CV	CR	PR	ANSON	UC	RE	TX	VR
		•	•	•	Alpha & Omega 120	•	•	•	•

		CV	CR	PR	ASHE	UC	RE	TX	VR
		•	•	•	Clue Detective Service 479	•	•	•	•
		•	•	•	Miller & Mosley..1350	•	•	•	•

		CV	CR	PR	AVERY	UC	RE	TX	VR
		•	•	•	Clue Detective Service 479	•	•	•	•
		•	•	•	Donna's Unlimited Searches...647	•	•	•	•
		•	•	•	Miller & Mosley..1350	•	•	•	•
		•	•	•	Paralegal Works 1518	•	•	•	•

		CV	CR	PR	BEAUFORT	UC	RE	TX	VR
		•	•	•	Coastal Investigative Son Inc...481	•	•	•	•
		•	•		Eastern North Carolina Invest & Process........................683			•	•
		•		•	Hamm, Sue P..912	•	•	•	•
		•	•	•	Paralegal Enterprises Inc..1511	•	•	•	•
		•	•	•	Paralegal Services of North Carolina Inc 1517	•	•	•	•

		CV	CR	PR	BERTIE	UC	RE	TX	VR
		•			Hamm, Sue P..912	•	•	•	
		•	•	•	Paralegal Enterprises Inc..1511	•	•	•	•

		CV	CR	PR	BLADEN	UC	RE	TX	VR
		•	•		Eastern North Carolina Invest & Process........................683			•	•
		•	•	•	Paralegal Services of North Carolina Inc 1517	•	•	•	•

		CV	CR	PR	BRUNSWICK	UC	RE	TX	VR
		•	•	•	Paralegal Services of North Carolina Inc 1517	•	•	•	•

DT		CV	CR	PR	BUNCOMBE	UC	RE	TX	VR
		•	•	•	Paralegal Works 1518	•	•	•	•
		•	•	•	Watson, Kathi...2063	•	•	•	•

		CV	CR	PR	BURKE	UC	RE	TX	VR
		•	•	•	Clue Detective Service 479	•	•	•	•
		•	•	•	Donna's Unlimited Searches...647	•	•	•	•

		CV	CR	PR	CABARRUS	UC	RE	TX	VR
		•	•	•	Alpha & Omega 120	•	•	•	•
		•	•	•	Sherrill, Victoria..1797	•	•	•	

		CV	CR	PR	CALDWELL	UC	RE	TX	VR
		•	•	•	Clue Detective Service 479	•	•	•	•
		•	•	•	Donna's Unlimited Searches...647	•	•	•	•

DT	CV	CR	PR		UC	RE	TX	VR
				CAMDEN				
	•	•	•	Hornthal Riley Ellis & Maland ...993	•	•	•	•
				CARTERET				
	•	•	•	Coastal Paralegal Services ...482	•	•	•	•
	•			Hamm, Sue P ...912	•	•	•	
	•	•	•	Paralegal Services of North Carolina Inc ...1517	•	•	•	•
				CASWELL				
	•	•	•	Williams, Nancy ...2095	•	•	•	•
				CATAWBA				
	•	•	•	Donna's Unlimited Searches ...647	•	•	•	•
	•	•	•	Investigative & Paralegal Services ...1045	•	•	•	•
				CHATHAM				
	•	•		Eastern North Carolina Invest & Process ...683			•	•
	•	•	•	Paralegal Services of North Carolina Inc ...1517	•	•	•	
	•	•	•	Turning Wheels Inc ...1990	•	•	•	
				CHEROKEE				
	•	•	•	Clue Detective Service ...479	•	•	•	•
	•	•	•	Lamancha Search Inc ...1161	•	•	•	•
				CHOWAN				
	•	•	•	Hornthal Riley Ellis & Maland ...993	•	•	•	•
				CLAY				
				See ALL COUNTIES ...				
				CLEVELAND				
	•	•	•	Alpha & Omega ...120	•	•	•	•
				COLUMBUS				
	•	•		Eastern North Carolina Invest & Process ...683			•	•
				CRAVEN				
•	•	•	•	Coastal Paralegal Services ...482	•	•	•	•
•	•			Eastern North Carolina Invest & Process ...683			•	•
	•			Hamm, Sue P ...912	•	•		
•	•	•	•	Paralegal Services of North Carolina Inc ...1517	•	•	•	
	•			Smith, Cheryl ...1815	•	•		
				CUMBERLAND				
•	•	•		Eastern North Carolina Invest & Process ...683			•	•
•	•	•	•	Paralegal Services of North Carolina Inc ...1517	•	•	•	•
				CURRITUCK				
	•	•	•	Coastal Investigative Son Inc ...481	•	•	•	•
				DARE				
	•	•	•	Hornthal Riley Ellis & Maland ...993	•	•	•	•
				DAVIDSON				
	•	•	•	Agency-One Investigations ...91	•	•	•	
	•	•	•	Sherrill, Victoria ...1797	•	•	•	
	•	•	•	Turning Wheels Inc ...1990	•	•	•	
				DAVIE				
	•	•	•	Paralegal Services of North Carolina Inc ...1517	•	•	•	•
				DUPLIN				
	•	•	•	Coastal Paralegal Services ...482	•	•	•	•
	•	•		Eastern North Carolina Invest & Process ...683			•	•

DT	BK	CV	CR	PR	Name	UC	RE	TX	VR
		•	•	•	Paralegal Services of North Carolina Inc ...1517	•	•	•	•

DURHAM

CV	CR	PR	Name	UC	RE	TX	VR
•	•		Eastern North Carolina Invest & Process ...683			•	•
•	•	•	Paralegal Services of North Carolina Inc ...1517	•	•	•	•

EDGECOMBE

CV	CR	PR	Name	UC	RE	TX	VR
•	•	•	Coastal Investigative Son Inc ...481	•	•	•	•
•	•		Eastern North Carolina Invest & Process ...683			•	•
•	•	•	Paralegal Enterprises Inc ...1511	•	•	•	•
•	•	•	Paralegal Services of North Carolina Inc ...1517	•	•	•	•

FORSYTH

CV	CR	PR	Name	UC	RE	TX	VR
•	•	•	Agency-One Investigations ...91	•	•	•	
•	•	•	Paralegal Services of North Carolina Inc ...1517	•	•	•	
•	•	•	Turning Wheels Inc ...1990	•	•	•	•

FRANKLIN

CV	CR	PR	Name	UC	RE	TX	VR
•	•		Eastern North Carolina Invest & Process ...683			•	•
•	•	•	Paralegal Services of North Carolina Inc ...1517	•	•	•	•

GASTON

CV	CR	PR	Name	UC	RE	TX	VR
•	•	•	Alpha & Omega ...120	•	•	•	•
•	•	•	Investigative & Paralegal Services ...1045	•	•	•	•

GATES

CV	CR	PR	Name	UC	RE	TX	VR
•	•	•	Hornthal Riley Ellis & Maland ...993	•	•	•	•

GRAHAM

CV	CR	PR	Name	UC	RE	TX	VR
•	•	•	Clue Detective Service ...479	•	•	•	•
•	•	•	Paralegal Services of North Carolina Inc ...1517	•	•	•	•

GRANVILLE

CV	CR	PR	Name	UC	RE	TX	VR
•	•		Eastern North Carolina Invest & Process ...683			•	•
•	•	•	Paralegal Services of North Carolina Inc ...1517	•	•	•	•

GREENE

CV	CR	PR	Name	UC	RE	TX	VR
•			Hamm, Sue P ...912	•	•	•	
•	•	•	Paralegal Enterprises Inc ...1511	•	•	•	•
•	•	•	Paralegal Services of North Carolina Inc ...1517	•	•	•	•

GUILFORD

DT	BK	CV	CR	PR	Name	UC	RE	TX	VR
•	•	•	•	•	Agency-One Investigations ...91	•	•	•	
•	•	•	•	•	Paralegal Services of North Carolina Inc ...1517	•	•	•	•
•	•	•	•	•	Turning Wheels Inc ...1990	•	•	•	•
		•	•	•	Williams, Nancy ...2095	•	•	•	•

HALIFAX

CV	CR	PR	Name	UC	RE	TX	VR
•	•		Eastern North Carolina Invest & Process ...683			•	•
•	•	•	Paralegal Services of North Carolina Inc ...1517	•	•	•	•

HARNETT

CV	CR	PR	Name	UC	RE	TX	VR
•	•		Eastern North Carolina Invest & Process ...683			•	•
•	•	•	Paralegal Services of North Carolina Inc ...1517	•	•	•	•

HAYWOOD

CV	CR	PR	Name	UC	RE	TX	VR
•	•	•	Watson, Kathi ...2063	•	•	•	•

HENDERSON

CV	CR	PR	Name	UC	RE	TX	VR
•	•	•	Paralegal Works ...1518	•	•	•	•
•	•	•	Watson, Kathi ...2063	•	•	•	•

HERTFORD

CV	CR	PR	Name	UC	RE	TX	VR
•	•	•	Hornthal Riley Ellis & Maland ...993	•	•	•	•

HOKE

DT	BK	CV	CR	PR		UC	RE	TX	VR
		●	●		Eastern North Carolina Invest & Process ...683			●	●

HYDE

DT	BK	CV	CR	PR		UC	RE	TX	VR
		●			Hamm, Sue P. ...912	●	●	●	

IREDELL

DT	BK	CV	CR	PR		UC	RE	TX	VR
●		●	●	●	Alpha & Omega ...120	●	●	●	●
●		●	●	●	Investigative & Paralegal Services ...1045	●	●	●	●
		●	●	●	Sherrill, Victoria ...1797	●	●	●	

JACKSON

DT	BK	CV	CR	PR		UC	RE	TX	VR
		●	●	●	Watson, Kathi ...2063	●	●	●	●

JOHNSTON

DT	BK	CV	CR	PR		UC	RE	TX	VR
		●	●		Eastern North Carolina Invest & Process ...683			●	●
		●	●	●	Paralegal Services of North Carolina Inc ...1517	●	●	●	

JONES

DT	BK	CV	CR	PR		UC	RE	TX	VR
		●	●	●	Coastal Paralegal Services ...482	●	●	●	●
		●	●		Eastern North Carolina Invest & Process ...683			●	●
		●			Hamm, Sue P. ...912	●	●	●	
		●			Smith, Cheryl ...1815	●	●	●	

LEE

DT	BK	CV	CR	PR		UC	RE	TX	VR
		●	●		Eastern North Carolina Invest & Process ...683			●	●
		●	●	●	Paralegal Services of North Carolina Inc ...1517	●	●	●	●

LENOIR

DT	BK	CV	CR	PR		UC	RE	TX	VR
		●	●	●	Coastal Investigative Son Inc ...481	●	●	●	●
		●	●	●	Coastal Paralegal Services ...482	●	●	●	●
		●			Eastern North Carolina Invest & Process ...683			●	●
		●			Hamm, Sue P. ...912	●	●	●	
		●	●	●	Paralegal Enterprises Inc ...1511	●	●	●	●
		●	●	●	Paralegal Services of North Carolina Inc ...1517	●	●	●	●

LINCOLN

DT	BK	CV	CR	PR		UC	RE	TX	VR
		●	●	●	Alpha & Omega ...120	●	●	●	●
		●	●	●	Investigative & Paralegal Services ...1045	●	●	●	●
		●	●	●	Paralegal Services of North Carolina Inc ...1517	●	●	●	●

MCDOWELL

DT	BK	CV	CR	PR		UC	RE	TX	VR
		●	●	●	Paralegal Works ...1518	●	●	●	●

MACON

DT	BK	CV	CR	PR		UC	RE	TX	VR
		●	●	●	Watson, Kathi ...2063	●	●	●	●

MADISON

DT	BK	CV	CR	PR		UC	RE	TX	VR
		●	●	●	Paralegal Works ...1518	●	●	●	●
		●	●	●	Watson, Kathi ...2063	●	●	●	●

MARTIN

DT	BK	CV	CR	PR		UC	RE	TX	VR
		●	●	●	Clue Detective Service ...479	●	●		
		●	●		Eastern North Carolina Invest & Process ...683			●	●
		●			Hamm, Sue P. ...912	●	●	●	
		●	●	●	Paralegal Enterprises Inc ...1511	●	●	●	
		●	●	●	Paralegal Services of North Carolina Inc ...1517	●	●	●	

MECKLENBURG

DT	BK	CV	CR	PR		UC	RE	TX	VR
●		●	●	●	Alpha & Omega ...120	●	●	●	●
●	●	●	●	●	Investigative & Paralegal Services ...1045	●	●	●	●

MITCHELL

DT	BK	CV	CR	PR		UC	RE	TX	VR
		●	●	●	Clue Detective Service ...479	●	●	●	●

DT	CV	CR	PR		UC	RE	TX	VR
	●	●	●	Paralegal Works 1518	●	●	●	●

MONTGOMERY

DT	CV	CR	PR		UC	RE	TX	VR
	●	●	●	Paralegal Services of North Carolina Inc 1517	●	●	●	●
	●	●	●	Turning Wheels Inc...............1990	●	●	●	●

MOORE

DT	CV	CR	PR		UC	RE	TX	VR
	●	●		Eastern North Carolina Invest & Process...............683			●	●

NASH

DT	CV	CR	PR		UC	RE	TX	VR
	●	●		Eastern North Carolina Invest & Process...............683			●	●
	●	●	●	Paralegal Services of North Carolina Inc 1517	●	●	●	●

NEW HANOVER

DT	CV	CR	PR		UC	RE	TX	VR
	●	●	●	Coastal Paralegal Services...............482	●	●	●	●
●	●	●		Eastern North Carolina Invest & Process...............683			●	●
●	●	●	●	Paralegal Services of North Carolina Inc 1517	●	●	●	●

NORTHAMPTON

DT	CV	CR	PR		UC	RE	TX	VR
	●	●		Eastern North Carolina Invest & Process...............683			●	●

ONSLOW

DT	CV	CR	PR		UC	RE	TX	VR
	●	●	●	Coastal Investigative Son Inc...............481	●	●	●	●
	●	●	●	Coastal Paralegal Services...............482	●	●	●	●
	●	●		Eastern North Carolina Invest & Process...............683			●	●
	●			Hamm, Sue P...............912	●	●	●	

ORANGE

DT	CV	CR	PR		UC	RE	TX	VR
	●	●		Eastern North Carolina Invest & Process...............683			●	●
	●	●	●	Paralegal Services of North Carolina Inc 1517	●	●	●	●

PAMLICO

DT	CV	CR	PR		UC	RE	TX	VR
	●			Hamm, Sue P...............912	●	●	●	
	●	●	●	Paralegal Services of North Carolina Inc 1517	●	●	●	●
	●			Smith, Cheryl...............1815	●	●	●	

PASQUOTANK

DT	CV	CR	PR		UC	RE	TX	VR
●	●	●	●	Hornthal Riley Ellis & Maland 993	●	●	●	●

PENDER

DT	CV	CR	PR		UC	RE	TX	VR
	●	●	●	Coastal Paralegal Services...............482	●	●	●	●
	●	●		Eastern North Carolina Invest & Process...............683			●	●
	●	●	●	Paralegal Services of North Carolina Inc 1517	●	●	●	●

PERQUIMANS

DT	CV	CR	PR		UC	RE	TX	VR
	●	●	●	Hornthal Riley Ellis & Maland 993	●	●	●	●

PERSON

DT	CV	CR	PR		UC	RE	TX	VR
	●	●	●	Paralegal Services of North Carolina Inc 1517	●	●	●	●

PITT

DT	CV	CR	PR		UC	RE	TX	VR
	●	●	●	Coastal Investigative Son Inc...............481	●	●	●	●
	●	●		Eastern North Carolina Invest & Process...............683			●	●
	●			Hamm, Sue P...............912	●	●	●	
	●	●	●	Paralegal Enterprises Inc...............1511	●	●	●	●
	●	●	●	Paralegal Services of North Carolina Inc 1517	●	●	●	●

POLK

DT	CV	CR	PR		UC	RE	TX	VR
	●	●	●	Paralegal Works 1518	●	●	●	●

RANDOLPH

DT	CV	CR	PR		UC	RE	TX	VR
	●	●		Eastern North Carolina Invest & Process...............683			●	●
	●	●	●	Turning Wheels Inc...............1990	●	●	●	●

	CV	CR	PR	RICHMOND	UC	RE	TX	VR
	●	●	●	Alpha & Omega 120	●	●	●	●
	●	●	●	Paralegal Services of North Carolina Inc 1517	●	●	●	●

	CV	CR	PR	ROBESON	UC	RE	TX	VR
	●	●		Eastern North Carolina Invest & Process.........................683			●	●

	CV	CR	PR	ROCKINGHAM	UC	RE	TX	VR
	●	●	●	Turning Wheels Inc...............................1990	●	●	●	●
	●	●	●	Williams, Nancy..................................2095	●	●	●	●

	CV	CR	PR	ROWAN	UC	RE	TX	VR
	●	●	●	Alpha & Omega 120	●	●	●	●
	●	●	●	Investigative & Paralegal Services................1045	●	●	●	●
	●	●	●	Sherrill, Victoria...............................1797	●	●	●	

	CV	CR	PR	RUTHERFORD	UC	RE	TX	VR
	●	●	●	Alpha & Omega 120	●	●	●	●
	●	●	●	Paralegal Works 1518	●	●	●	●

	CV	CR	PR	SAMPSON	UC	RE	TX	VR
	●	●		Eastern North Carolina Invest & Process.........................683			●	●
	●	●	●	Paralegal Services of North Carolina Inc 1517	●		●	

	CV	CR	PR	SCOTLAND	UC	RE	TX	VR
	●	●	●	Paralegal Services of North Carolina Inc 1517	●	●	●	●

	CV	CR	PR	STANLY	UC	RE	TX	VR
	●	●	●	Alpha & Omega 120	●	●	●	●
	●	●	●	Investigative & Paralegal Services................1045	●	●	●	●
	●	●	●	Sherrill, Victoria...............................1797	●	●	●	

	CV	CR	PR	STOKES	UC	RE	TX	VR
	●	●	●	Turning Wheels Inc...............................1990	●	●	●	●

	CV	CR	PR	SURRY	UC	RE	TX	VR
				See ALL COUNTIES.....................................				

	CV	CR	PR	SWAIN	UC	RE	TX	VR
				Warren, Maggie..................................2055	●	●		●
	●	●	●	Watson, Kathi....................................2063	●	●	●	●

	CV	CR	PR	TRANSYLVANIA	UC	RE	TX	VR
	●	●	●	Paralegal Works 1518	●	●	●	●
	●	●	●	Watson, Kathi....................................2063	●	●	●	●

	CV	CR	PR	TYRRELL	UC	RE	TX	VR
	●	●	●	Hornthal Riley Ellis & Maland 993	●	●	●	●

	CV	CR	PR	UNION	UC	RE	TX	VR
	●	●	●	Alpha & Omega 120	●	●	●	●
	●	●	●	Investigative & Paralegal Services................1045	●	●	●	●

	CV	CR	PR	VANCE	UC	RE	TX	VR
	●	●		Eastern North Carolina Invest & Process.........................683			●	●
	●	●	●	Paralegal Services of North Carolina Inc 1517	●	●	●	●

DT	BK	CV	CR	PR	WAKE	UC	RE	TX	VR
●	●	●	●		Eastern North Carolina Invest & Process.........................683			●	●
●	●	●	●	●	Paralegal Services of North Carolina Inc 1517	●	●	●	●

	CV	CR	PR	WARREN	UC	RE	TX	VR
	●	●		Eastern North Carolina Invest & Process.........................683			●	●
	●	●	●	Paralegal Services of North Carolina Inc 1517	●	●	●	●

	CV	CR	PR	WASHINGTON		UC	RE	TX	VR
	●			Hamm, Sue P...912		●	●	●	
	●	●	●	Hornthal Riley Ellis & Maland 993		●	●	●	●
	●	●	●	Paralegal Services of North Carolina Inc 1517		●	●	●	●

	CV	CR	PR	WATAUGA		UC	RE	TX	VR
	●	●	●	Clue Detective Service................................479		●	●	●	●
	●	●	●	Miller & Mosley.......................................1350		●	●	●	●

	CV	CR	PR	WAYNE		UC	RE	TX	VR
	●	●		Eastern North Carolina Invest & Process..........683				●	●
	●	●	●	Paralegal Services of North Carolina Inc 1517		●	●	●	●

	CV	CR	PR	WILKES		UC	RE	TX	VR
	●	●	●	Clue Detective Service................................479		●	●	●	●
	●	●	●	Walker, Judy L.......................................2045		●	●	●	●

BK	CV	CR	PR	WILSON		UC	RE	TX	VR
●	●	●		Eastern North Carolina Invest & Process..........683				●	●
●	●	●	●	Paralegal Enterprises Inc............................1511		●	●	●	●
●	●	●	●	Paralegal Services of North Carolina Inc 1517		●	●	●	●

	CV	CR	PR	YADKIN		UC	RE	TX	VR
				See ALL COUNTIES.................................					

	CV	CR	PR	YANCEY		UC	RE	TX	VR
	●	●	●	Paralegal Works......................................1518		●	●	●	●

North Dakota

		CV	CR	PR	ADAMS	UC	RE	TX	VR
		●			Adams County Abstract Co.....................77	●	●	●	
		●	●	●	Gion Law Office.....................846	●	●	●	●

		CV	CR	PR	BARNES	UC	RE	TX	VR
		●	●	●	Credit Bureau of Valley City.....................561	●	●	●	●
		●	●	●	P.I. Services.....................1488	●	●	●	●

		CV	CR	PR	BENSON	UC	RE	TX	VR
		●		●	Suriety Title Co.....................1893	●	●	●	

		CV	CR	PR	BILLINGS	UC	RE	TX	VR
		●			Dickinson Abstract Co.....................632	●	●	●	

		CV	CR	PR	BOTTINEAU	UC	RE	TX	VR
		●	●	●	Bottineau County Abtract Co.....................330	●	●	●	●

		CV	CR	PR	BOWMAN	UC	RE	TX	VR
		●	●	●	Bowman & Slope County Abstract Co.....................332	●	●	●	●
		●	●	●	Gion Law Office.....................846	●	●	●	●

		CV	CR	PR	BURKE	UC	RE	TX	VR
		●	●	●	Mountrail County Abstract and Title Co.....................1393	●	●	●	
		●	●	●	Wilkes Law Office.....................2090		●	●	●

DT		CV	CR	PR	BURLEIGH	UC	RE	TX	VR
		●		●	Bismark Title Co.....................303	●	●	●	
		●	●	●	Evans & Johnson Investigations Inc.....................719	●	●	●	●
●		●		●	The North Dakota Guaranty & Title Co.....................1939	●	●	●	
●		●	●	●	W T Butcher & Associates.....................2037	●	●	●	●

DT	BK	CV	CR	PR	CASS	UC	RE	TX	VR
	●	●	●	●	Cass County Abstract Co.....................414	●	●	●	●
●	●	●	●	●	P.I. Services.....................1488	●	●	●	●

		CV	CR	PR	CAVALIER	UC	RE	TX	VR
		●			McHugh Abstract Co.....................1310	●	●	●	●
		●	●	●	Welch & Ekman PC.....................2073	●	●	●	●

		CV	CR	PR	DICKEY	UC	RE	TX	VR
		●	●	●	Dickey County Abstract & Title.....................631	●	●	●	●

		CV	CR	PR	DIVIDE	UC	RE	TX	VR
		●		●	Divide Abstract Co Inc.....................637		●	●	●

		CV	CR	PR	DUNN	UC	RE	TX	VR
		●	●	●	Northwest Abstract and Title Inc.....................1446	●	●	●	●

		CV	CR	PR	EDDY	UC	RE	TX	VR
		●		●	Suriety Title Co.....................1893	●	●	●	

		CV	CR	PR	EMMONS	UC	RE	TX	VR
		●	●	●	Emmons County Abstract & Title.....................711	●	●	●	●

		CV	CR	PR	FOSTER	UC	RE	TX	VR
		●	●	●	Foster County Abstarct & Title.....................797	●	●	●	●

		CV	CR	PR	GOLDEN VALLEY	UC	RE	TX	VR
		●	●	●	The Abstract & Title Co.....................1921	●	●	●	●

		CV	CR	PR	GRAND FORKS	UC	RE	TX	VR
		●			Grand Forks Abstract Co.....................859	●	●	●	

CV	CR	PR	GRANT		UC	RE	TX	VR
•	•	•	Corant County Abstract Co.....................521		•	•	•	•
•	•	•	Gion Law Office.....................846		•	•	•	•

CV	CR	PR	GRIGGS		UC	RE	TX	VR
•	•	•	Credit Bureau of Valley City.....................561		•	•	•	•
•		•	Suriety Title Co.....................1893		•	•	•	

CV	CR	PR	HETTINGER		UC	RE	TX	VR
•	•	•	Gion Law Office.....................846		•	•	•	•

CV	CR	PR	KIDDER		UC	RE	TX	VR
•	•	•	Evans & Johnson Investigations Inc.....................719		•	•	•	•

CV	CR	PR	LA MOURE		UC	RE	TX	VR
•	•	•	Credit Bureau of Valley City.....................561		•	•	•	•
•	•	•	LaMoure County Abstract Co.....................1148		•	•	•	•

CV	CR	PR	LOGAN		UC	RE	TX	VR
			Logan County Abstract Co.....................1235		•	•	•	

CV	CR	PR	MCHENRY		UC	RE	TX	VR
•	•	•	McHenry County Abstract & Title.....................1309		•	•	•	•

CV	CR	PR	MCINTOSH		UC	RE	TX	VR
•	•	•	Ashley Abstract Co.....................167		•	•	•	•

CV	CR	PR	MCKENZIE		UC	RE	TX	VR
•		•	Abstract and Title Co.....................50		•	•	•	
•	•	•	Mountrail County Abstract and Title Co.....................1393		•	•	•	

CV	CR	PR	MCLEAN		UC	RE	TX	VR
•	•	•	Evans & Johnson Investigations Inc.....................719		•	•	•	•
•	•	•	McLean County Abstract Inc.....................1316		•	•	•	•
•	•	•	W T Butcher & Associates.....................2037		•	•	•	•

CV	CR	PR	MERCER		UC	RE	TX	VR
•			Mercer County Abstract Co Inc.....................1328			•	•	

CV	CR	PR	MORTON		UC	RE	TX	VR
•		•	Bismark Title Co.....................303		•	•	•	
•	•	•	Evans & Johnson Investigations Inc.....................719		•	•	•	•
•	•	•	W T Butcher & Associates.....................2037		•	•	•	•

CV	CR	PR	MOUNTRAIL		UC	RE	TX	VR
•	•	•	Mountrail County Abstract and Title Co.....................1393		•	•	•	

CV	CR	PR	NELSON		UC	RE	TX	VR
•	•	•	Nelson County Abstract.....................1416		•	•	•	•

CV	CR	PR	OLIVER		UC	RE	TX	VR
•	•	•	Oliver County Abstract Co.....................1465		•	•	•	

CV	CR	PR	PEMBINA		UC	RE	TX	VR
•	•	•	A Short Abstract Co.....................9		•	•	•	

CV	CR	PR	PIERCE		UC	RE	TX	VR
•		•	Pierce County Abstract.....................1552		•	•	•	

CV	CR	PR	RAMSEY		UC	RE	TX	VR
•	•	•	Credit Bureau of Devils Lake.....................558		•	•	•	•

CV	CR	PR	RANSOM		UC	RE	TX	VR
•	•	•	Ransom County Title Co.....................1650		•	•	•	•

CV	CR	PR	RENVILLE	UC	RE	TX	VR
●		●	Reniville Abstract Company Inc 1679	●	●	●	●

CV	CR	PR	RICHLAND	UC	RE	TX	VR
●	●	●	P.I. Services.................................1488	●	●	●	●
●		●	Richland County Abstract Co.....................1697	●	●	●	

CV	CR	PR	ROLETTE	UC	RE	TX	VR
●	●	●	Rolette County Abstract Inc......................1709	●	●	●	●

CV	CR	PR	SARGENT	UC	RE	TX	VR
●	●	●	Credit Bureau of Valley City....................561	●	●	●	●
●		●	Richland County Abstract Co.....................1697	●	●	●	

CV	CR	PR	SHERIDAN	UC	RE	TX	VR
●		●	Sheridan County Abstract Co.....................1796	●	●	●	●

CV	CR	PR	SIOUX	UC	RE	TX	VR
●	●	●	Evans & Johnson Investigations Inc 719	●	●	●	●

CV	CR	PR	SLOPE	UC	RE	TX	VR
●	●	●	Bowman & Slope County Abstract Co...............332	●	●	●	●
●	●	●	Gion Law Office.................................846	●	●	●	●

CV	CR	PR	STARK	UC	RE	TX	VR
●			Dickinson Abstract Co 632	●	●	●	
●	●	●	Gion Law Office.................................846	●	●	●	●

CV	CR	PR	STEELE	UC	RE	TX	VR
●			Cassell, M B..................................416		●	●	
●	●	●	Credit Bureau of Valley City....................561	●	●	●	●

CV	CR	PR	STUTSMAN	UC	RE	TX	VR
●	●	●	P.I. Services.................................1488	●	●	●	●
●	●	●	Stutsman County Abstract.......................1876	●	●	●	●

CV	CR	PR	TOWNER	UC	RE	TX	VR
●		●	Towner County Abstract Co.......................1971	●	●	●	

CV	CR	PR	TRAILL	UC	RE	TX	VR
●	●	●	P.I. Services.................................1488	●	●	●	●
●		●	Traill County Abstract Co 1976	●	●	●	

CV	CR	PR	WALSH	UC	RE	TX	VR
●	●	●	Welch & Ekman PC...............................2073	●	●	●	●

CV	CR	PR	WARD	UC	RE	TX	VR
		●	J M Devine & Co Inc 1064	●	●	●	
●	●	●	Mountrail County Abstract and Title Co..........1393	●	●	●	
●	●	●	W T Butcher & Associates.......................2037	●	●	●	

CV	CR	PR	WELLS	UC	RE	TX	VR
●	●	●	Wells County Abstract Co........................2075	●	●	●	●

CV	CR	PR	WILLIAMS	UC	RE	TX	VR
●	●	●	Mountrail County Abstract and Title Co..........1393	●	●	●	
●	●	●	Northwest Abstract and Title Inc 1446	●	●	●	●

Ohio

DT	BK	CV	CR	PR	ALL COUNTIES		UC	RE	TX	VR
	●	●	●	●	National Service Information Inc 1410		●		●	●

		CV	CR	PR	ADAMS		UC	RE	TX	VR
		●	●	●	Barber, Kevin 243		●	●	●	●

		CV	CR	PR	ALLEN		UC	RE	TX	VR
			●		CBT Services 375					
		●	●	●	Ohio Independent Title & Pub Rec Search 1460		●	●	●	
		●	●	●	Wingate Investigations 2105			●	●	●

		CV	CR	PR	ASHLAND		UC	RE	TX	VR
		●	●	●	Merritt, Brenda K 1332		●	●	●	
		●	●	●	Wayne County Title Co. 2066		●	●	●	●

		CV	CR	PR	ASHTABULA		UC	RE	TX	VR
		●	●	●	Akron/Canton/Cleveland Court Reporters 94		●	●	●	●
		●	●	●	Moore, D M 1384		●	●	●	●
		●		●	Trumbull County Abstract Co. 1986		●	●	●	

		CV	CR	PR	ATHENS		UC	RE	TX	VR
		●	●	●	Clue Detective Agency 478		●	●	●	●
		●	●	●	Gable, Norma 825		●	●	●	●
		●	●	●	West, Thomas 2079		●	●	●	●

		CV	CR	PR	AUGLAIZE		UC	RE	TX	VR
		●	●	●	Wingate Investigations 2105			●	●	●

		CV	CR	PR	BELMONT		UC	RE	TX	VR
		●	●	●	Claugus, Claudine 467		●	●	●	●
		●	●	●	Clue Detective Agency 478		●	●	●	●
		●	●	●	Doty, Dora 649		●	●	●	●
		●	●	●	Tomich, Vicki 1964		●	●	●	●

		CV	CR	PR	BROWN		UC	RE	TX	VR
		●		●	Independent Abstract Inc 1022		●	●	●	

		CV	CR	PR	BUTLER		UC	RE	TX	VR
		●		●	Independent Abstract Inc 1022		●	●	●	

		CV	CR	PR	CARROLL		UC	RE	TX	VR
		●	●	●	Akron/Canton/Cleveland Court Reporters 94		●	●	●	●
		●	●	●	Woodard and Bohse Law Office 2111		●	●	●	●

		CV	CR	PR	CHAMPAIGN		UC	RE	TX	VR
		●	●	●	Blazinski, Al 311		●	●	●	●

		CV	CR	PR	CLARK		UC	RE	TX	VR
		●	●	●	Blazinski, Al 311		●	●	●	●

		CV	CR	PR	CLERMONT		UC	RE	TX	VR
		●		●	Independent Abstract Inc 1022		●	●	●	

		CV	CR	PR	CLINTON		UC	RE	TX	VR
		●	●	●	Barber, Kevin 243		●	●	●	●
		●		●	Independent Abstract Inc 1022		●	●	●	

		CV	CR	PR	COLUMBIANA		UC	RE	TX	VR
		●	●	●	Akron/Canton/Cleveland Court Reporters 94		●	●	●	●
		●	●	●	Coats, Janet 483		●		●	●
		●		●	Trumbull County Abstract Co. 1986		●	●	●	

COSHOCTON

CV	CR	PR		UC	RE	TX	VR
●	●	●	Clue Detective Agency 478	●	●	●	●
●	●	●	Woodard and Bohse Law Office 2111	●	●	●	●

CRAWFORD

CV	CR	PR		UC	RE	TX	VR
	●		CBT Services 375				
●	●	●	Hill, Rebecca 972	●	●	●	●
●	●	●	Ohio Independent Title & Pub Rec Search 1460	●	●	●	

CUYAHOGA

DT	BK	CV	CR	PR		UC	RE	TX	VR
●	●	●	●	●	Akron/Canton/Cleveland Court Reporters 94	●	●	●	●
●	●	●	●	●	Attorney Services Inc 187		●	●	
		●		●	Bryant, Ronna K 359				●
			●		CBT Services 375				
●		●		●	Lorain County Title Co 1241	●	●	●	●
●		●	●	●	Olde Reserve Title Inc 1464	●	●	●	●
●	●	●	●	●	Records Deposition Service 1665	●	●	●	●

DARKE

CV	CR	PR		UC	RE	TX	VR
●	●	●	Blazinski, Al 311	●	●	●	●

DEFIANCE

CV	CR	PR		UC	RE	TX	VR
	●		CBT Services 375				
●	●	●	Central Investigation 425	●	●	●	●

DELAWARE

CV	CR	PR		UC	RE	TX	VR
●	●	●	ACS Tri County Title 21	●	●	●	●
●	●	●	Allstate Investigations Inc 118	●	●	●	●
●	●	●	Clue Detective Agency 478	●	●	●	●
●			Corporate Services of Ohio Inc 526	●	●	●	●
●	●	●	LDS Real Estate Services 1142	●	●	●	
●	●	●	LSW Legal Filing and Research Inc 1144	●	●	●	●
●	●	●	Miller, G Scott 1354	●	●	●	●
●	●	●	Nimrod Legal Support Services 1428	●	●	●	●
●	●	●	Records Deposition Service 1665	●	●	●	●

ERIE

CV	CR	PR		UC	RE	TX	VR
	●		CBT Services 375				
●		●	Lorain County Title Co 1241	●	●	●	●
●	●	●	Ohio Independent Title & Pub Rec Search 1460	●	●	●	

FAIRFIELD

CV	CR	PR		UC	RE	TX	VR
●	●	●	Allstate Investigations Inc 118	●	●	●	●
●	●	●	Cahill, Shani 379	●	●	●	●
●	●	●	Clue Detective Agency 478	●	●	●	●
●			Corporate Services of Ohio Inc 526	●	●	●	●
●	●	●	Gable, Norma 825	●	●	●	●
●	●		LDS Real Estate Services 1142	●	●	●	
●	●	●	LSW Legal Filing and Research Inc 1144	●	●	●	●
●	●	●	Nimrod Legal Support Services 1428	●	●	●	●

FAYETTE

CV	CR	PR		UC	RE	TX	VR
●	●	●	Barber, Kevin 243	●	●	●	●
●	●	●	Clue Detective Agency 478	●	●	●	●
●			Corporate Services of Ohio Inc 526	●	●	●	●
●	●	●	Powell, Lori 1578	●	●	●	

FRANKLIN

DT		CV	CR	PR		UC	RE	TX	VR
		●	●	●	ACS Tri County Title 21	●	●	●	●
●		●	●	●	Allstate Investigations Inc 118	●	●	●	●
		●	●	●	Cahill, Shani 379	●	●	●	●
●		●	●	●	Clue Detective Agency 478	●	●	●	●

	CV	CR	PR		Page	UC	RE	TX	VR
	●	●	●	West, Thomas	2079	●	●	●	●

HOLMES

CV	CR	PR		Page	UC	RE	TX	VR
●	●	●	Akron/Canton/Cleveland Court Reporters	94	●	●	●	●
●	●	●	Wayne County Title Co	2066	●	●	●	●
●	●	●	Woodard and Bohse Law Office	2111	●	●	●	●

HURON

CV	CR	PR		Page	UC	RE	TX	VR
	●		CBT Services	375				
●	●	●	Hill, Rebecca	972	●	●	●	●
●	●	●	Ohio Independent Title & Pub Rec Search	1460	●	●	●	

JACKSON

CV	CR	PR		Page	UC	RE	TX	VR
●	●	●	Barber, Kevin	243	●	●	●	●
●	●	●	Clue Detective Agency	478	●	●	●	●
●	●	●	Simmons & Grillo	1806	●	●	●	●

JEFFERSON

CV	CR	PR		Page	UC	RE	TX	VR
●	●	●	Akron/Canton/Cleveland Court Reporters	94	●	●	●	●
●	●	●	Claugus, Claudine	467	●	●	●	
●	●	●	Coats, Janet	483	●		●	
●	●	●	Doty, Dora	649	●	●	●	
●	●	●	Tomich, Vicki	1964	●	●	●	

KNOX

CV	CR	PR		Page	UC	RE	TX	VR
●	●	●	ACS Tri County Title	21	●	●	●	●
●	●	●	Clue Detective Agency	478	●	●	●	●
●	●	●	LDS Real Estate Services	1142	●	●	●	

LAKE

CV	CR	PR		Page	UC	RE	TX	VR
●	●	●	Akron/Canton/Cleveland Court Reporters	94	●	●	●	●
●	●	●	Moore, D M	1384	●	●	●	●

LAWRENCE

CV	CR	PR		Page	UC	RE	TX	VR
●	●	●	Daniel Agency	588	●	●	●	●
●	●	●	Davis Investigatons Inc	603	●	●	●	●

LICKING

CV	CR	PR		Page	UC	RE	TX	VR
●	●	●	ACS Tri County Title	21	●	●	●	●
●	●	●	Allstate Investigations Inc	118	●	●	●	●
●	●	●	Cahill, Shani	379	●	●	●	●
●	●	●	Clue Detective Agency	478	●	●	●	●
●			Corporate Services of Ohio Inc	526	●	●	●	●
●	●	●	LDS Real Estate Services	1142	●	●	●	
●	●	●	LSW Legal Filing and Research Inc	1144	●	●	●	
●	●	●	Nimrod Legal Support Services	1428	●	●	●	

LOGAN

CV	CR	PR		Page	UC	RE	TX	VR
●	●	●	Blazinski, Al	311	●			

LORAIN

CV	CR	PR		Page	UC	RE	TX	VR
●	●	●	Akron/Canton/Cleveland Court Reporters	94	●	●	●	●
		●	Lorain County Title Co	1241	●	●	●	●

LUCAS

DT	BK	CV	CR	PR		Page	UC	RE	TX	VR
			●		CBT Services	375				
●	●	●	●	●	Central Investigation	425	●	●	●	●

MADISON

CV	CR	PR		Page	UC	RE	TX	VR
●	●	●	Clue Detective Agency	478	●	●	●	●
●			Corporate Services of Ohio Inc	526	●	●	●	●
●	●	●	LSW Legal Filing and Research Inc	1144	●	●	●	
●	●	●	Nimrod Legal Support Services	1428	●	●	●	

	●	●	●	Powell, Lori..1578	● ● ●

BK	CV	CR	PR	**MAHONING**	UC RE TX VR
●	●	●	●	Akron/Canton/Cleveland Court Reporters..........................94	● ● ● ●
	●		●	Trumbull County Abstract Co................................1986	● ● ●

	CV	CR	PR	**MARION**	UC RE TX VR
	●			Corporate Services of Ohio Inc.............................526	● ● ● ●
	●	●	●	Miller, G Scott..1354	● ● ● ●

	CV	CR	PR	**MEDINA**	UC RE TX VR
	●	●	●	Akron/Canton/Cleveland Court Reporters..........................94	● ● ● ●
	●	●	●	Olde Reserve Title Inc.....................................1464	● ● ● ●

	CV	CR	PR	**MEIGS**	UC RE TX VR
	●	●	●	Clue Detective Agency......................................478	● ● ● ●
	●	●	●	West, Thomas..2079	● ● ● ●

	CV	CR	PR	**MERCER**	UC RE TX VR
	●	●	●	Bernard & Hirschfeld.......................................287	● ● ●

	CV	CR	PR	**MIAMI**	UC RE TX VR
	●	●	●	Blazinski, Al...311	● ● ● ●

	CV	CR	PR	**MONROE**	UC RE TX VR
	●	●	●	Claugus, Claudine..467	● ● ● ●
	●	●	●	Clue Detective Agency......................................478	● ● ● ●
	●	●	●	Doty, Dora..649	● ● ● ●
	●	●	●	Tomich, Vicki...1964	● ● ● ●

	CV	CR	PR	**MONTGOMERY**	UC RE TX VR
	●	●	●	Attorney's Dispatch Service Inc............................191	● ● ● ●
	●	●	●	Blazinski, Al...311	● ● ● ●
	●		●	Midwest Abstract Co...1345	● ●

	CV	CR	PR	**MORGAN**	UC RE TX VR
	●	●	●	Clue Detective Agency......................................478	● ● ● ●
	●	●	●	West, Thomas..2079	● ● ● ●
	●	●	●	Wilhelm, Shirley..2089	● ● ● ●

	CV	CR	PR	**MORROW**	UC RE TX VR
	●	●	●	ACS Tri County Title...21	● ● ● ●
	●	●	●	LDS Real Estate Services...................................1142	● ● ●
	●	●	●	Linder, Tina..1229	● ● ● ●

	CV	CR	PR	**MUSKINGUM**	UC RE TX VR
	●	●	●	Cahill, Shani...379	● ● ● ●
	●	●	●	Claugus, Claudine..467	● ● ● ●
	●	●	●	Clue Detective Agency......................................478	● ● ● ●
	●	●	●	LDS Real Estate Services...................................1142	● ● ●
	●	●	●	West, Thomas..2079	● ● ● ●

	CV	CR	PR	**NOBLE**	UC RE TX VR
	●	●	●	Clue Detective Agency......................................478	● ● ● ●
	●	●	●	Tomich, Vicki...1964	● ● ● ●
	●	●	●	West, Thomas..2079	● ● ● ●
	●	●	●	Wilhelm, Shirley..2089	● ● ● ●

	CV	CR	PR	**OTTAWA**	UC RE TX VR
		●		CBT Services..375	
	●	●	●	Ohio Independent Title & Pub Rec Search....................1460	● ● ●

	CV	CR	PR	**PAULDING**	UC RE TX VR
	●	●	●	Wingate Investigations.....................................2105	● ● ●

PERRY

CV	CR	PR	Provider	Page	UC	RE	TX	VR
•	•	•	Cahill, Shani	379	•	•	•	•
•	•	•	Clue Detective Agency	478	•	•	•	•
•	•	•	Gable, Norma	825	•	•	•	•
•	•	•	LDS Real Estate Services	1142	•	•	•	

PICKAWAY

CV	CR	PR	Provider	Page	UC	RE	TX	VR
•	•	•	Barber, Kevin	243	•	•	•	•
•	•	•	Clue Detective Agency	478	•	•	•	•
•			Corporate Services of Ohio Inc	526	•	•	•	•
•	•	•	LSW Legal Filing and Research Inc	1144	•	•	•	•
•	•	•	Powell, Lori	1578	•	•	•	

PIKE

CV	CR	PR	Provider	Page	UC	RE	TX	VR
•	•	•	Barber, Kevin	243	•	•	•	•
•	•	•	Clue Detective Agency	478	•	•	•	•

PORTAGE

CV	CR	PR	Provider	Page	UC	RE	TX	VR
•	•	•	Akron/Canton/Cleveland Court Reporters	94	•	•	•	•
•	•	•	Moore, D M	1384	•	•	•	•
•	•	•	Ohio Bar Title	1459	•	•	•	•
•			Trumbull County Abstract Co	1986	•	•	•	

PREBLE

CV	CR	PR	Provider	Page	UC	RE	TX	VR
•	•	•	Blazinski, Al	311	•	•	•	•

PUTNAM

CV	CR	PR	Provider	Page	UC	RE	TX	VR
•	•	•	Wingate Investigations	2105		•	•	•

RICHLAND

CV	CR	PR	Provider	Page	UC	RE	TX	VR
•	•	•	Merritt, Brenda K	1332	•	•	•	

ROSS

CV	CR	PR	Provider	Page	UC	RE	TX	VR
•	•	•	Barber, Kevin	243	•	•	•	•
•	•	•	Clue Detective Agency	478	•	•	•	•
•	•	•	Powell, Lori	1578	•	•	•	

SANDUSKY

CV	CR	PR	Provider	Page	UC	RE	TX	VR
	•		CBT Services	375				
•	•	•	National Service Information Inc	1410	•	•	•	•
•	•	•	Ohio Independent Title & Pub Rec Search	1460	•	•	•	

SCIOTO

CV	CR	PR	Provider	Page	UC	RE	TX	VR
•	•	•	Barber, Kevin	243	•	•	•	•

SENECA

CV	CR	PR	Provider	Page	UC	RE	TX	VR
	•		CBT Services	375				
•	•	•	Hill, Rebecca	972	•	•	•	•
•	•	•	Ohio Independent Title & Pub Rec Search	1460	•	•	•	

SHELBY

CV	CR	PR	Provider	Page	UC	RE	TX	VR
•	•	•	Blazinski, Al	311	•	•	•	•

STARK

BK	CV	CR	PR	Provider	Page	UC	RE	TX	VR
	•	•	•	Akron/Canton/Cleveland Court Reporters	94	•	•	•	•
•				Arrendale, Kate	162	•	•	•	
•	•	•	•	Moore, D M	1384	•	•	•	•

SUMMIT

DT	BK	CV	CR	PR	Provider	Page	UC	RE	TX	VR
•		•	•	•	Akron/Canton/Cleveland Court Reporters	94	•	•	•	•
•		•	•	•	Moore, D M	1384	•	•	•	•
•		•	•	•	Olde Reserve Title Inc	1464	•	•	•	•

CV	CR	PR	TRUMBULL		UC	RE	TX	VR
•	•	•	Akron/Canton/Cleveland Court Reporters 94		•	•	•	•
•		•	Trumbull County Abstract Co..1986		•	•	•	

CV	CR	PR	TUSCARAWAS		UC	RE	TX	VR
•	•	•	Akron/Canton/Cleveland Court Reporters 94		•	•	•	•
•	•	•	Claugus, Claudine 467		•	•	•	•
•	•	•	Woodard and Bohse Law Office 2111		•	•	•	•

CV	CR	PR	UNION		UC	RE	TX	VR
•			Corporate Services of Ohio Inc 526		•	•	•	•
•	•	•	LSW Legal Filing and Research Inc..................................1144		•	•	•	•
•	•	•	Miller, G Scott...1354		•	•	•	•
•	•	•	Nimrod Legal Support Services 1428		•	•	•	•

CV	CR	PR	VAN WERT		UC	RE	TX	VR
	•		CBT Services 375					
•	•	•	Wingate Investigations...2105			•	•	•

CV	CR	PR	VINTON		UC	RE	TX	VR
•	•	•	Barber, Kevin..243		•	•	•	•
•	•	•	Gable, Norma 825		•	•	•	•
•	•	•	Simmons & Grillo...1806		•	•	•	•

CV	CR	PR	WARREN		UC	RE	TX	VR
•		•	Independent Abstract Inc 1022		•	•	•	

CV	CR	PR	WASHINGTON		UC	RE	TX	VR
•	•	•	Clue Detective Agency..478		•	•	•	•
•	•	•	West, Thomas..2079		•	•	•	•
•	•	•	Wilhelm, Shirley 2089		•	•	•	•

CV	CR	PR	WAYNE		UC	RE	TX	VR
•	•	•	Akron/Canton/Cleveland Court Reporters 94		•	•	•	•
•	•	•	Wayne County Title Co...2066		•	•	•	•

CV	CR	PR	WILLIAMS		UC	RE	TX	VR
	•		CBT Services 375					
•	•	•	Central Investigation 425		•	•	•	•

CV	CR	PR	WOOD		UC	RE	TX	VR
	•		CBT Services 375					
•	•	•	Central Investigation 425		•	•	•	•
•	•	•	Ohio Independent Title & Pub Rec Search 1460		•	•	•	

CV	CR	PR	WYANDOT		UC	RE	TX	VR
	•		CBT Services 375					
•	•	•	Ohio Independent Title & Pub Rec Search 1460		•	•	•	

Oklahoma

DT	BK	CV	CR	PR	ALL COUNTIES		UC	RE	TX	VR
•	•				Bankruptcy Services Inc.	241				

		CV	CR	PR	ADAIR		UC	RE	TX	VR
		•	•	•	AAA Abstract Co Inc	11	•	•	•	•

		CV	CR	PR	ALFALFA		UC	RE	TX	VR
		•	•	•	Alfalfa Guaranty Abstract Co	104	•	•	•	•
		•	•	•	Territorial Title	1909	•	•	•	•

		CV	CR	PR	ATOKA		UC	RE	TX	VR
		•	•	•	Atoka Abstract Co Inc	181	•	•	•	•
		•	•	•	Moore Mowdy & Youngblood	1383	•	•	•	•

		CV	CR	PR	BEAVER		UC	RE	TX	VR
		•		•	Beaver County Abstract Co	269	•	•	•	•

		CV	CR	PR	BECKHAM		UC	RE	TX	VR
		•	•	•	Beckham County Abstract	271	•	•	•	•
		•	•	•	I S. Investigative Agency	1015	•	•	•	•

		CV	CR	PR	BLAINE		UC	RE	TX	VR
		•		•	Watonga Abstract Co	2062	•	•	•	

		CV	CR	PR	BRYAN		UC	RE	TX	VR
		•	•	•	Marshall County Abstract Co	1284	•	•	•	•
		•	•	•	Moore Mowdy & Youngblood	1383	•	•	•	•

		CV	CR	PR	CADDO		UC	RE	TX	VR
		•	•	•	Lacey Pioneer Abstract Company Inc	1152	•	•	•	•
		•	•	•	Oklahoma Legal Process Service (OLPS)	1463	•	•	•	•

		CV	CR	PR	CANADIAN		UC	RE	TX	VR
		•			Document Retrieval Service	641	•	•	•	
		•	•	•	Jayphil Investigations	1082	•	•	•	•
		•	•	•	Oklahoma Legal Process Service (OLPS)	1463	•	•	•	•
		•	•	•	United Legal Services	2009	•	•	•	

		CV	CR	PR	CARTER		UC	RE	TX	VR
		•	•	•	Legal Support Services of Oklahoma	1212	•	•	•	•
		•	•	•	Marshall County Abstract Co	1284	•	•	•	
		•	•	•	Oklahoma Legal Process Service (OLPS)	1463	•	•	•	•
		•	•	•	Superior Process Service	1886	•	•	•	

		CV	CR	PR	CHEROKEE		UC	RE	TX	VR
		•	•	•	Cherokee Capitol Abstract and Title	446	•	•	•	•

		CV	CR	PR	CHOCTAW		UC	RE	TX	VR
		•		•	Choctaw County Abstract and Title	456	•	•	•	

		CV	CR	PR	CIMARRON		UC	RE	TX	VR
				•	Rainbow Real Estate	1645	•	•	•	

		CV	CR	PR	CLEVELAND		UC	RE	TX	VR
		•		•	American First Abstract Co	131	•	•	•	
		•			Document Retrieval Service	641	•	•	•	
		•	•	•	Jayphil Investigations	1082	•	•	•	•
		•	•	•	Legal Support Services of Oklahoma	1212	•	•	•	•
		•	•	•	Oklahoma Legal Process Service (OLPS)	1463	•	•	•	•
		•	•	•	United Legal Services	2009	•	•	•	

CV	CR	PR	COAL		UC	RE	TX	VR
●	●	●	Marshall County Abstract Co	1284	●	●	●	●
●	●	●	Moore Mowdy & Youngblood	1383	●	●	●	●

CV	CR	PR	COMANCHE		UC	RE	TX	VR
●	●	●	Anderson, H Ray	150		●	●	
●	●	●	Legal Support Services of Oklahoma	1212	●	●	●	●
●	●	●	Oklahoma Legal Process Service (OLPS)	1463	●	●	●	●
●		●	Southwest Abstract Co	1834	●	●	●	●
●	●	●	Superior Process Service	1886	●	●	●	

CV	CR	PR	COTTON		UC	RE	TX	VR
●	●	●	Anderson, H Ray	150		●	●	
●	●	●	Oklahoma Legal Process Service (OLPS)	1463	●	●	●	●
●	●	●	Superior Process Service	1886	●	●	●	

CV	CR	PR	CRAIG		UC	RE	TX	VR
●		●	Vinita Title Co	2030	●	●	●	●

CV	CR	PR	CREEK		UC	RE	TX	VR
●			Document Retrieval Service	641	●	●	●	
●	●	●	Jones & Associates Inc	1098	●	●	●	●
●	●	●	Legal Support Services of Oklahoma	1212	●	●	●	●
●		●	Union-Speer Abstract Co	2006	●	●	●	

CV	CR	PR	CUSTER		UC	RE	TX	VR
●		●	Clinton Abstract Co Inc	476	●	●	●	
●	●	●	I S. Investigative Agency	1015	●	●	●	●

CV	CR	PR	DELAWARE		UC	RE	TX	VR
●		●	Delaware County Abstract Co	619	●	●	●	

CV	CR	PR	DEWEY		UC	RE	TX	VR
●	●	●	Dewey County Abstract Co	629	●	●	●	
●	●	●	I S. Investigative Agency	1015	●	●	●	●

CV	CR	PR	ELLIS		UC	RE	TX	VR
●		●	Woodward County Abstract Co	2113	●	●	●	

CV	CR	PR	GARFIELD		UC	RE	TX	VR
●	●	●	Bagenstos, Leslie	233	●	●	●	●
●		●	J C Humphrey Abstract Co	1062	●	●	●	

CV	CR	PR	GARVIN		UC	RE	TX	VR
●		●	MG Cox Abstract	1257		●	●	●

CV	CR	PR	GRADY		UC	RE	TX	VR
●			Document Retrieval Service	641	●	●	●	
●	●	●	Oklahoma Legal Process Service (OLPS)	1463	●	●	●	●
●	●	●	United Legal Services	2009	●	●	●	
●		●	Washita Valley Abstract Co	2060	●	●	●	

CV	CR	PR	GRANT		UC	RE	TX	VR
●	●	●	Bagenstos, Leslie	233	●	●	●	●
●		●	Grant County Abstract Co	862	●	●	●	

CV	CR	PR	GREER		UC	RE	TX	VR
●		●	Greer Guaranty Abstract Co	877	●	●	●	●
●	●	●	I S. Investigative Agency	1015	●	●	●	●

CV	CR	PR	HARMON		UC	RE	TX	VR
●	●	●	Harmon County Abstract	926	●	●	●	●

CV	CR	PR	HARPER	UC	RE	TX	VR
•		•	Woodward County Abstract Co ...2113	•	•	•	

CV	CR	PR	HASKELL	UC	RE	TX	VR
•		•	Guaranty Abstract Co of Stigler Inc ...890	•	•	•	
•		•	Hebert Land Services ...947	•	•	•	•

CV	CR	PR	HUGHES	UC	RE	TX	VR
•		•	Atlas Abstract Co ...180	•	•	•	

CV	CR	PR	JACKSON	UC	RE	TX	VR
•		•	Jackson County Abstract Co ...1074	•	•	•	
•	•	•	Oklahoma Legal Process Service (OLPS) ...1463	•	•	•	•
•	•	•	Superior Process Service ...1886	•	•	•	

CV	CR	PR	JEFFERSON	UC	RE	TX	VR
•	•	•	Oklahoma Legal Process Service (OLPS) ...1463	•	•	•	•
•	•	•	Superior Process Service ...1886	•	•	•	

CV	CR	PR	JOHNSTON	UC	RE	TX	VR
•		•	Johnston County Abstract Co ...1097	•	•	•	
•	•	•	Marshall County Abstract Co ...1284	•	•	•	•
•	•	•	Moore Mowdy & Youngblood ...1383	•	•	•	•

CV	CR	PR	KAY	UC	RE	TX	VR
•		•	Albright Abstract & Title Guaranty ...101	•	•	•	•

CV	CR	PR	KINGFISHER	UC	RE	TX	VR
•			Document Retrieval Service ...641	•	•	•	
•	•	•	Jayphil Investigations ...1082	•	•	•	•
•		•	Solomon Abstract Co Inc ...1817	•	•	•	

CV	CR	PR	KIOWA	UC	RE	TX	VR
•		•	Kiowa County Abstract Company ...1128	•	•	•	
•	•	•	Oklahoma Legal Process Service (OLPS) ...1463	•	•	•	•

CV	CR	PR	LATIMER	UC	RE	TX	VR
•		•	Hebert Land Services ...947	•	•	•	•
•		•	Latimer County Abstract Co ...1177	•	•	•	•
•		•	Royce, Pat ...1717	•	•	•	•

CV	CR	PR	LE FLORE	UC	RE	TX	VR
•		•	Hebert Land Services ...947	•	•	•	•
•		•	Sooner Abstract & Title Co ...1819	•	•	•	•

CV	CR	PR	LINCOLN	UC	RE	TX	VR
•		•	Abstarct & Guarantee Co ...43	•	•	•	
•	•	•	Jayphil Investigations ...1082	•	•	•	•
•	•	•	Oklahoma Legal Process Service (OLPS) ...1463	•	•	•	•
•	•	•	United Legal Services ...2009	•	•	•	

CV	CR	PR	LOGAN	UC	RE	TX	VR
•			Document Retrieval Service ...641	•	•	•	
•	•	•	Jayphil Investigations ...1082	•	•	•	•
•	•	•	Oklahoma Legal Process Service (OLPS) ...1463	•	•	•	•
•	•	•	United Legal Services ...2009	•	•	•	

CV	CR	PR	LOVE	UC	RE	TX	VR
•	•	•	Oklahoma Legal Process Service (OLPS) ...1463	•	•	•	•
•	•	•	Superior Process Service ...1886	•	•	•	

CV	CR	PR	MCCLAIN	UC	RE	TX	VR
•		•	American Abstract Company ...126	•	•	•	

DT	BK	CV	CR	PR	Company	Page	UC	RE	TX	VR
		•	•	•	Jayphil Investigations	1082	•	•	•	•
		•	•	•	Oklahoma Legal Process Service (OLPS)	1463	•	•	•	•
		•	•	•	United Legal Services	2009	•	•	•	•
					MCCURTAIN					
		•		•	Southern Abstract & Title Co	1827	•	•	•	•
					MCINTOSH					
		•		•	Eufaula Abstract & Title Co Inc	718	•	•	•	
		•		•	McIntosh County Abstract Co	1311	•	•	•	•
					MAJOR					
		•	•	•	Bagenstos, Leslie	233	•	•	•	•
		•	•	•	Fairview Abstract Co	736	•	•	•	•
					MARSHALL					
		•	•	•	Marshall County Abstract Co	1284	•	•	•	•
					MAYES					
		•		•	Mayes County Abstract	1297	•	•	•	•
		•	•	•	Oklahoma Legal Process Service (OLPS)	1463	•	•	•	•
					MURRAY					
		•	•	•	Marshall County Abstract Co	1284	•	•	•	•
		•		•	Murray County Abstract Inc	1399	•	•	•	
		•	•	•	Superior Process Service	1886	•	•	•	
					MUSKOGEE					
•		•			Document Retrieval Service	641	•	•	•	
		•	•	•	SRT Investigations	1726	•	•	•	•
					NOBLE					
		•	•	•	Powers Abstract Co Inc	1579	•	•	•	
					NOWATA					
		•		•	Title Abstract Co	1952	•	•	•	•
					OKFUSKEE					
		•		•	Okfusee County Abstract Co	1462	•	•	•	•
					OKLAHOMA					
•	•	•			Document Retrieval Service	641	•	•	•	
•	•	•	•	•	Jayphil Investigations	1082	•	•	•	•
•	•	•	•	•	Legal Support Services of Oklahoma	1212	•	•	•	•
•	•	•	•	•	Oklahoma Legal Process Service (OLPS)	1463	•	•	•	•
•	•	•	•	•	United Legal Services	2009	•	•	•	
					OKMULGEE					
	•	•	•	•	ACB Credit Services	18	•	•	•	
					OSAGE					
		•	•	•	Jones & Associates Inc	1098	•	•	•	•
					OTTAWA					
		•	•	•	Photo Abstract Co	1550	•	•	•	•
					PAWNEE					
		•	•	•	Henry, Matthew D	956	•	•	•	•
					PAYNE					
		•			Document Retrieval Service	641	•	•	•	
		•	•	•	Legal Support Services of Oklahoma	1212	•	•	•	•

PITTSBURG

CV	CR	PR			UC	RE	TX	VR
●		●	Hebert Land Services 947		●	●	●	●
●	●	●	Legal Support Services of Oklahoma 1212		●	●	●	●
●	●	●	Pioneer Abstract Co of McAlester Inc 1554		●	●	●	●

PONTOTOC

CV	CR	PR			UC	RE	TX	VR
●	●	●	Marshall County Abstract Co 1284		●	●	●	●

POTTAWATOMIE

CV	CR	PR			UC	RE	TX	VR
●			Document Retrieval Service 641		●	●	●	
●	●	●	Jayphil Investigations 1082		●	●	●	●
●	●	●	Legal Support Services of Oklahoma 1212		●	●	●	●
●	●	●	Oklahoma Legal Process Service (OLPS) 1463		●	●	●	●
●	●	●	United Legal Services 2009		●	●	●	

PUSHMATAHA

CV	CR	PR			UC	RE	TX	VR
●	●	●	Moore Mowdy & Youngblood 1383		●	●	●	●
●		●	Pushmataha County Abstract Co 1631		●	●	●	

ROGER MILLS

CV	CR	PR			UC	RE	TX	VR
●		●	Cheyenne Abstract Co Inc 449		●	●	●	
●	●	●	I S. Investigative Agency 1015		●	●	●	●

ROGERS

CV	CR	PR			UC	RE	TX	VR
●	●	●	Jones & Associates Inc 1098		●	●	●	●
●	●	●	Rogers County Abstract Co 1708		●	●	●	●

SEMINOLE

CV	CR	PR			UC	RE	TX	VR
●	●	●	Legal Support Services of Oklahoma 1212		●	●	●	●
●	●	●	Pioneer Abstract Co 1553		●	●	●	●

SEQUOYAH

CV	CR	PR			UC	RE	TX	VR
●		●	Hebert Land Services 947		●	●	●	●
●	●	●	Valley Land Title Co 2020		●	●	●	●

STEPHENS

CV	CR	PR			UC	RE	TX	VR
●	●	●	Legal Support Services of Oklahoma 1212		●	●	●	●
●	●	●	Oklahoma Legal Process Service (OLPS) 1463		●	●	●	●
●		●	Stephens County Abstract Co 1864		●	●	●	

TEXAS

CV	CR	PR			UC	RE	TX	VR
●		●	Guaranty Abstract & Title Co 886		●	●	●	

TILLMAN

CV	CR	PR			UC	RE	TX	VR
●	●	●	Oklahoma Legal Process Service (OLPS) 1463		●	●	●	●
●	●	●	Superior Process Service 1886		●	●	●	

TULSA

DT	BK	CV	CR	PR			UC	RE	TX	VR
●	●	●			Document Retrieval Service 641		●	●	●	
●	●	●	●	●	Jones & Associates Inc 1098		●	●	●	●
●	●	●	●	●	Legal Support Services of Oklahoma 1212		●	●	●	●
●	●	●	●	●	Oklahoma Legal Process Service (OLPS) 1463		●	●	●	●
		●	●	●	SRT Investigations 1726		●	●	●	●

WAGONER

CV	CR	PR			UC	RE	TX	VR
●	●	●	Jones & Associates Inc 1098		●	●	●	●
●	●	●	SRT Investigations 1726		●	●	●	
●		●	Wagoner County Abstract Co 2042		●	●	●	

WASHINGTON

CV	CR	PR			UC	RE	TX	VR
●		●	Musselman Abstract Co 1401		●	●	●	

CV	CR	PR	WASHITA		UC	RE	TX	VR
●	●	●	I S. Investigative Agency 1015		●	●	●	●

CV	CR	PR	WOODS		UC	RE	TX	VR
●	●	●	Bagenstos, Leslie...233		●	●	●	●
●	●	●	Woods County Abstract Corp 2112		●	●	●	

CV	CR	PR	WOODWARD		UC	RE	TX	VR
●		●	Woodward County Abstract Co 2113		●	●	●	

SUMMARY OF CODES

COURT RECORDS

CODE*	GOVERNMENT AGENCY	TYPE OF INFORMATION
DT	US District Court	Federal civil and criminal cases
BK	Bankruptcy Court	United States bankruptcy cases
CV	Civil Court	Municipal, county and state level civil cases
CR	Criminal Court	Municipal, county and state level criminal cases
PR	Probate Court	Wills and estate cases

COUNTY RECORDS

CODE*	GOVERNMENT AGENCY	TYPE OF INFORMATION
UC	UCC Filing Office	Uniform Commercial Code and other personal property liens
RE	Recorder of Deeds	Real property transactions and liens
TX	Tax Assessor	Real property tax information
VR	Vital Records Office	Birth, death, marriage, divorce, etc.

*The "CODE" designates the agency and type of information obtainable in each county.

Oregon

DT	BK	CV	CR	PR	ALL COUNTIES	UC	RE	TX	VR
●	●	●	●	●	Perfectly Legal Documents 1538	●	●	●	●

		CV	CR	PR	BAKER	UC	RE	TX	VR
		●	●	●	M & M Legal Services 1253		●	●	●

		CV	CR	PR	BENTON	UC	RE	TX	VR
		●	●	●	Cleveland Investigations 475	●	●	●	●
		●	●	●	Data Research Inc. 594	●		●	
		●	●	●	Joden & Associates Inc 1088	●	●	●	●
		●	●	●	McCord Company 1307	●	●	●	●
					Prentice Hall Legal & Financial Services 1593	●			

		CV	CR	PR	CLACKAMAS	UC	RE	TX	VR
		●		●	Ace Messenger Service 69	●	●	●	●
		●	●	●	Alan H Crowe & Associates Inc 97	●	●	●	●
		●	●	●	Barrister Support Service 248	●	●	●	●
		●	●	●	Cleveland Investigations 475	●	●	●	●
		●	●	●	Data Research Inc. 594	●		●	
		●	●	●	Executive Messenger 724	●			●
		●	●	●	Joden & Associates Inc 1088	●	●		●
		●	●	●	Lawyer's Legal Service 1183		●	●	
		●	●		Marosi & Associates Inc 1281		●		●
		●	●	●	McCord Company 1307	●	●	●	●

		CV	CR	PR	CLATSOP	UC	RE	TX	VR
		●	●	●	Data Research Inc. 594	●		●	
		●	●	●	Joden & Associates Inc 1088	●	●	●	●
		●	●	●	Lawyer's Legal Service 1183		●	●	

		CV	CR	PR	COLUMBIA	UC	RE	TX	VR
		●		●	Ace Messenger Service 69	●	●	●	●
		●	●	●	Cleveland Investigations 475	●	●	●	●
		●	●	●	Data Research Inc. 594	●		●	
		●	●	●	Joden & Associates Inc 1088	●	●	●	●
		●	●	●	Lawyer's Legal Service 1183		●	●	

		CV	CR	PR	COOS	UC	RE	TX	VR
		●	●	●	Joden & Associates Inc 1088	●	●	●	●
		●	●	●	North Pacific Legal 1437		●	●	●
		●	●	●	Williamette Valley Title Co 2093	●	●	●	●

		CV	CR	PR	CROOK	UC	RE	TX	VR
		●	●	●	Central Legal Service 426	●			

		CV	CR	PR	CURRY	UC	RE	TX	VR
		●		●	Ocean Title & Escrow 1454		●	●	●

		CV	CR	PR	DESCHUTES	UC	RE	TX	VR
		●	●	●	Central Legal Service 426	●	●	●	●
		●	●	●	McCord Company 1307	●	●	●	●

		CV	CR	PR	DOUGLAS	UC	RE	TX	VR
		●	●	●	Joden & Associates Inc 1088	●	●	●	●

		CV	CR	PR	GILLIAM	UC	RE	TX	VR
					See ALL COUNTIES				

		CV	CR	PR	GRANT	UC	RE	TX	VR
					See ALL COUNTIES				

		CV	CR	PR	HARNEY	UC	RE	TX	VR
					See ALL COUNTIES..				

		CV	CR	PR	HOOD RIVER	UC	RE	TX	VR
		●	●	●	Columbia Gorge Investigations.....................497	●	●	●	●
		●	●	●	Joden & Associates Inc.....................1088	●	●	●	●
		●	●	●	Lawyer's Legal Service.....................1183		●	●	

		CV	CR	PR	JACKSON	UC	RE	TX	VR
		●	●	●	Cleveland Investigations.....................475	●	●	●	●
		●	●	●	McCord Company.....................1307	●	●	●	●
		●	●	●	More Than Mail.....................1386		●	●	●

		CV	CR	PR	JEFFERSON	UC	RE	TX	VR
		●	●	●	Central Legal Service.....................426	●	●	●	●

		CV	CR	PR	JOSEPHINE	UC	RE	TX	VR
		●	●	●	Cleveland Investigations.....................475	●	●	●	●
		●	●	●	More Than Mail.....................1386		●	●	●

		CV	CR	PR	KLAMATH	UC	RE	TX	VR
		●	●	●	Cleveland Investigations.....................475	●	●	●	●

		CV	CR	PR	LAKE	UC	RE	TX	VR
					See ALL COUNTIES..				

DT	BK	CV	CR	PR	LANE	UC	RE	TX	VR
●	●	●	●	●	B & J/Barristers' Aide.....................229				
●	●	●	●	●	Cleveland Investigations.....................475	●	●	●	●
●	●	●	●	●	Data Research Inc.....................594	●		●	
●	●	●	●	●	Joden & Associates Inc.....................1088	●	●	●	●
●	●	●	●	●	McCord Company.....................1307	●	●	●	●
●	●	●	●	●	Oregon Process Service Inc.....................1477		●	●	●
					Prentice Hall Legal & Financial Services.....................1593	●			

		CV	CR	PR	LINCOLN	UC	RE	TX	VR
		●	●	●	Joden & Associates Inc.....................1088	●	●	●	●
		●	●	●	McCord Company.....................1307	●	●	●	●

		CV	CR	PR	LINN	UC	RE	TX	VR
		●	●	●	Cleveland Investigations.....................475	●	●	●	●
		●	●	●	Data Research Inc.....................594	●		●	
		●	●	●	Joden & Associates Inc.....................1088	●	●	●	●

		CV	CR	PR	MALHEUR	UC	RE	TX	VR
					See ALL COUNTIES..				

		CV	CR	PR	MARION	UC	RE	TX	VR
		●		●	Ace Messenger Service.....................69	●	●	●	●
		●	●	●	Alan H Crowe & Associates Inc.....................97	●	●	●	●
		●	●	●	Cleveland Investigations.....................475	●	●		●
		●	●	●	Data Research Inc.....................594	●		●	
		●	●	●	Executive Messenger.....................724	●			●
		●	●	●	Joden & Associates Inc.....................1088	●	●	●	●
		●	●	●	Lawyer's Legal Service.....................1183		●	●	
		●	●	●	McCord Company.....................1307	●	●	●	●

		CV	CR	PR	MORROW	UC	RE	TX	VR
		●	●	●	Data Research Inc.....................594	●		●	
		●	●	●	McCord Company.....................1307	●	●	●	●

MULTNOMAH

DT	BK	CV	CR	PR		Page	UC	RE	TX	VR
●	●	●		●	Ace Messenger Service	69	●	●	●	●
●	●	●	●	●	Alan H Crowe & Associates Inc	97	●	●	●	●
●	●	●	●	●	Barrister Support Service	248	●	●	●	●
●	●	●	●	●	Cleveland Investigations	475	●	●	●	●
●	●	●	●	●	Data Research Inc	594	●		●	
●	●	●	●	●	Executive Messenger	724	●			●
●	●	●	●	●	Joden & Associates Inc	1088	●	●		●
●	●	●	●	●	Lawyer's Legal Service	1183		●	●	
●	●	●	●	●	Marosi & Associates Inc	1281		●		●
●	●	●	●	●	McCord Company	1307	●	●	●	●
●	●	●	●		Personal Background Investigations	1542				

POLK

CV	CR	PR		Page	UC	RE	TX	VR
●	●	●	Cleveland Investigations	475	●	●	●	●
●	●	●	Data Research Inc	594	●		●	
●			Dodge, Valerie	644	●	●	●	●
●	●	●	Joden & Associates Inc	1088	●	●	●	●
●	●	●	McCord Company	1307	●	●	●	●

SHERMAN

CV	CR	PR		Page	UC	RE	TX	VR
●	●	●	Columbia Gorge Investigations	497	●	●	●	●

TILLAMOOK

CV	CR	PR		Page	UC	RE	TX	VR
●	●	●	Data Research Inc	594	●		●	
●	●	●	Joden & Associates Inc	1088	●	●	●	●

UMATILLA

CV	CR	PR		Page	UC	RE	TX	VR
●	●	●	M & M Legal Services	1253		●	●	●

UNION

CV	CR	PR		Page	UC	RE	TX	VR
●	●	●	Eastern Oregon Title	684	●	●	●	
●	●	●	M & M Legal Services	1253		●	●	●

WALLOWA

CV	CR	PR		Page	UC	RE	TX	VR
●	●	●	M & M Legal Services	1253		●	●	●

WASCO

CV	CR	PR		Page	UC	RE	TX	VR
●	●	●	Columbia Gorge Investigations	497	●	●	●	●

WASHINGTON

CV	CR	PR		Page	UC	RE	TX	VR
●		●	Ace Messenger Service	69	●	●	●	●
●	●	●	Alan H Crowe & Associates Inc	97	●	●	●	
●	●	●	Barrister Support Service	248	●	●	●	
●	●	●	Cleveland Investigations	475	●	●	●	
●	●	●	Executive Messenger	724	●			
●	●	●	Joden & Associates Inc	1088	●	●	●	●
●	●	●	Lawyer's Legal Service	1183		●	●	
●	●		Marosi & Associates Inc	1281		●	●	
●	●	●	McCord Company	1307	●	●	●	

WHEELER

CV	CR	PR		Page	UC	RE	TX	VR
●	●	●	Data Research Inc	594	●		●	

YAMHILL

CV	CR	PR		Page	UC	RE	TX	VR
●		●	Ace Messenger Service	69	●	●	●	●
●	●	●	Cleveland Investigations	475	●	●	●	●
●	●	●	Data Research Inc	594	●		●	
●	●	●	Executive Messenger	724	●			●
●	●	●	Joden & Associates Inc	1088	●	●	●	●
●	●	●	Lawyer's Legal Service	1183		●	●	

Pennsylvania

DT	BK	CV	CR	PR	ALL COUNTIES		UC	RE	TX	VR
●	●	●	●	●	Interstate Abstract Inc 1040		●	●	●	●
●	●	●	●	●	Pittsburgh Information and Research Co 1558		●	●	●	

		CV	CR	PR	ADAMS		UC	RE	TX	VR
		●	●	●	Abstract Land Associates Inc 48		●	●	●	●
		●	●	●	Abstract One Inc 49		●	●	●	●
		●	●	●	Colonial Valley Abstract Co 491		●	●	●	●
		●	●	●	D'Aiello Jr, Russell F 580		●	●	●	
		●	●	●	Patterson Abstracting 1524		●	●	●	
		●	●	●	Priority One Attorney Service.........................1603		●	●	●	●

	BK	CV	CR	PR	ALLEGHENY		UC	RE	TX	VR
	●	●	●	●	Barrett Detective Bureau.................................247		●	●	●	●
	●	●		●	Bucci, Jerry J...360		●	●	●	
	●	●	●	●	Coats, Janet 483		●		●	●
	●	●	●	●	Quest and Assoc Inc.......................................1636		●	●	●	●
	●	●	●	●	Robert Smith Abstract.....................................1704		●	●	●	●

		CV	CR	PR	ARMSTRONG		UC	RE	TX	VR
		●	●	●	Coats, Janet 483		●		●	●
		●	●	●	Lawyers' Abstract Co 1187		●	●	●	
		●	●	●	Robert Smith Abstract.....................................1704		●	●	●	●

		CV	CR	PR	BEAVER		UC	RE	TX	VR
		●	●	●	Coats, Janet 483		●		●	●

		CV	CR	PR	BEDFORD		UC	RE	TX	VR
		●	●	●	Blair Abstracting Co..308		●	●	●	

	BK	CV	CR	PR	BERKS		UC	RE	TX	VR
	●	●	●	●	Abstract Associates Ltd...................................46		●	●	●	●
	●	●	●	●	Commonwealth Investigation Agency.................506		●	●	●	●
	●	●	●	●	Docutrans Inc 642		●	●	●	●
		●	●	●	Pellish and Pellish Attorneys at Law................1530		●	●	●	●
		●	●	●	Willian C Brown and Co..................................2097		●	●	●	

		CV	CR	PR	BLAIR		UC	RE	TX	VR
		●	●	●	Blair Abstracting Co..308		●	●	●	

		CV	CR	PR	BRADFORD		UC	RE	TX	VR
					See ALL COUNTIES..					

		CV	CR	PR	BUCKS		UC	RE	TX	VR
		●	●	●	B & R Services for Professionals 230		●	●	●	●
		●	●		Best Legal Services Inc 293		●	●	●	
		●	●	●	Commonwealth Investigation Agency.................506		●	●	●	●
		●	●	●	Court House Legal Service................................542		●	●	●	●
		●	●	●	Dennis Richman Services..................................622		●	●	●	●
		●	●	●	Docutrans Inc 642		●	●	●	●
		●	●	●	Legal Wings Inc..1214		●	●	●	
		●	●	●	Pellish and Pellish Attorneys at Law................1530		●	●	●	
		●	●	●	Prentice Hall Legal & Financial Services............1589		●	●	●	
		●		●	Searchtec 1760					●
		●	●		Talme and Associates......................................1900					
		●	●	●	The Coynes...1927		●	●	●	

		CV	CR	PR	BUTLER		UC	RE	TX	VR
		●	●	●	Coats, Janet 483		●		●	●
		●	●	●	Lawyers' Abstract Co 1187		●	●	●	

DT	CV	CR	PR	CAMBRIA		UC	RE	TX	VR
	●	●	●	B & G Ltd of Hollidaysburg......227		●	●	●	
	●	●	●	Blair Abstracting Co......308		●	●	●	
	●	●	●	Mainline Researchers......1271		●	●	●	●
	●	●	●	Robert Smith Abstract......1704		●	●	●	●

	CV	CR	PR	CAMERON		UC	RE	TX	VR
	●	●	●	Reed, David......1669		●	●	●	●

	CV	CR	PR	CARBON		UC	RE	TX	VR
	●	●	●	Commonwealth Investigation Agency......506		●	●	●	●
			●	Fidelity Home Abstract......758		●	●	●	
			●	ILS Abstract......1017		●	●	●	
	●	●	●	Pellish and Pellish Attorneys at Law......1530		●	●	●	●
			●	Toma Abstract Inc......1963		●	●	●	

	CV	CR	PR	CENTRE		UC	RE	TX	VR
	●	●	●	B & G Ltd of Hollidaysburg......227		●	●	●	●

	CV	CR	PR	CHESTER		UC	RE	TX	VR
	●		●	ATACO Inc......36		●	●	●	●
	●	●		Abstract Associates Ltd......46		●	●	●	●
	●	●		Best Legal Services Inc......293		●	●	●	●
	●	●	●	Court House Legal Service......542		●	●	●	●
	●	●		Delaware Attorney Services......617		●	●	●	●
	●	●	●	Dennis Richman Services......622		●	●	●	●
	●	●	●	Docutrans Inc......642		●	●	●	●
	●	●		Golt Adjustment Service......853		●	●	●	
	●	●		National Legal Process......1409		●	●	●	●
	●		●	Searchtec......1760					●
				Signorelli, Debbie......1802		●	●	●	
	●	●		Talme and Associates......1900					
	●	●	●	The Coynes......1927		●	●	●	●

	CV	CR	PR	CLARION		UC	RE	TX	VR
	●	●	●	Falcon Abstract Co......738		●	●	●	●

	CV	CR	PR	CLEARFIELD		UC	RE	TX	VR
	●	●	●	B & G Ltd of Hollidaysburg......227		●	●	●	●
	●	●	●	Falcon Abstract Co......738		●	●	●	●

	CV	CR	PR	CLINTON		UC	RE	TX	VR
	●	●	●	Miller, Patricia......1357		●	●	●	●
	●	●	●	Pettingill, Sandra L......1545		●	●	●	●

	CV	CR	PR	COLUMBIA		UC	RE	TX	VR
	●	●	●	American Abstract & Land Co......125		●	●	●	●
			●	ILS Abstract......1017		●	●	●	●
			●	Norce, Trudi......1431		●	●	●	
	●	●	●	S.A.F.E......1723		●	●	●	●
	●		●	Toma Abstract Inc......1963		●	●	●	

	CV	CR	PR	CRAWFORD		UC	RE	TX	VR
	●			Realty Settlement Inc......1659		●	●	●	

	CV	CR	PR	CUMBERLAND		UC	RE	TX	VR
	●	●	●	Abstract Land Associates Inc......48		●	●	●	●
	●	●		Associated Services......173		●			
	●	●	●	Nationwide Information Services Inc......1412		●	●	●	●
	●	●	●	Penncorp Service Group Inc......1532		●	●	●	●
				Prentice Hall Legal & Financial Services......1594		●			

DT	BK	CV	CR	PR		UC	RE	TX	VR
		●	●	●	Priority One Attorney Service.................1603	●	●	●	●

DAUPHIN

CV	CR	PR		UC	RE	TX	VR
●	●	●	Abstract Associates Ltd..............46	●	●	●	●
●	●	●	Abstract Land Associates Inc..............48	●	●	●	●
●	●		Associated Services..............173	●			
●	●	●	Capitol Paralegal Services..............398	●			
●	●	●	Commonwealth Investigation Agency..............506		●	●	●
●	●	●	Docutrans Inc..............642	●	●	●	●
●	●	●	Nationwide Information Services Inc..............1412	●	●	●	●
●	●	●	Penncorp Service Group Inc..............1532	●	●	●	●
			Prentice Hall Legal & Financial Services..............1594	●			
●	●	●	Priority One Attorney Service..............1603	●	●	●	●

DELAWARE

CV	CR	PR		UC	RE	TX	VR
●		●	ATACO Inc..............36	●	●	●	●
●	●	●	B & R Services for Professionals..............230	●	●	●	●
●	●		Best Legal Services Inc..............293	●	●	●	●
●	●	●	Corporation Service Co - Delaware..............529	●	●	●	●
●	●	●	Court House Legal Service..............542	●	●	●	●
●	●		Delaware Attorney Services..............617	●	●	●	●
●	●	●	Dennis Richman Services..............622	●	●	●	●
●	●	●	Docutrans Inc..............642	●	●	●	●
●	●		National Legal Process..............1409	●	●	●	●
●	●	●	Prentice Hall Legal & Financial Services..............1589	●	●		●
●		●	Searchtec..............1760				●
●	●		Talme and Associates..............1900				
●	●	●	The Coynes..............1927	●	●	●	●

ELK

CV	CR	PR		UC	RE	TX	VR
●	●	●	Falcon Abstract Co..............738	●	●	●	●
●	●	●	Reed, David..............1669	●	●	●	●

ERIE

DT	BK	CV	CR	PR		UC	RE	TX	VR
		●	●	●	Chiota, Darlene..............454	●	●	●	●

FAYETTE

CV	CR	PR		UC	RE	TX	VR
●	●	●	Fayette Professional Services..............746	●	●	●	●

FOREST

CV	CR	PR		UC	RE	TX	VR
●	●	●	Falcon Abstract Co..............738	●	●	●	●

FRANKLIN

CV	CR	PR		UC	RE	TX	VR
●	●	●	Abstract Land Associates Inc..............48	●	●	●	●
●	●	●	Colonial Valley Abstract Co..............491	●	●	●	●
●	●	●	Patterson Abstracting..............1524	●	●	●	
●	●	●	Priority One Attorney Service..............1603	●	●	●	●

FULTON

CV	CR	PR		UC	RE	TX	VR
			See ALL COUNTIES..............				

GREENE

CV	CR	PR		UC	RE	TX	VR
●	●	●	Coats, Janet..............483	●		●	●
●	●	●	Fayette Professional Services..............746	●	●	●	●
●	●	●	Patterson Abstracting..............1524	●	●	●	

HUNTINGDON

CV	CR	PR		UC	RE	TX	VR
●	●	●	B & G Ltd of Hollidaysburg..............227	●	●	●	●
●	●	●	Blair Abstracting Co..............308	●	●	●	

INDIANA

CV	CR	PR		UC	RE	TX	VR
●	●	●	Robert Smith Abstract..............1704	●	●	●	●

	CV	CR	PR	JEFFERSON		UC	RE	TX	VR
	●	●	●	Brewer, Dorothy...............344		●	●	●	
	●	●	●	Falcon Abstract Co...............738		●	●	●	●
	●	●	●	Robert Smith Abstract...............1704		●	●	●	●

	CV	CR	PR	JUNIATA		UC	RE	TX	VR
	●	●	●	Rupert, Joyce...............1718		●	●	●	

DT	CV	CR	PR	LACKAWANNA		UC	RE	TX	VR
			●	Abstract Enterprises Inc...............47		●	●	●	●
	●	●	●	All Pocono Abstract Inc...............109			●	●	●
●	●	●	●	Commonwealth Investigation Agency...............506		●	●	●	●
	●	●	●	JS Industries...............1072		●	●	●	●
●	●	●	●	Maximum Protection Inc...............1296		●	●	●	●

	CV	CR	PR	LANCASTER		UC	RE	TX	VR
	●	●	●	Abstract Associates Ltd...............46		●	●	●	●
	●	●	●	Abstract Land Associates Inc...............48		●	●	●	●
	●	●	●	Colonial Valley Abstract Co...............491		●	●	●	●
	●	●	●	Commonwealth Investigation Agency...............506		●	●	●	●
	●	●	●	Docutrans Inc...............642		●	●	●	●
	●	●	●	Nationwide Information Services Inc...............1412		●	●	●	●
	●	●	●	Priority One Attorney Service...............1603		●	●	●	●

	CV	CR	PR	LAWRENCE		UC	RE	TX	VR
	●	●	●	Coats, Janet...............483		●			
	●	●	●	Turner, Helen...............1989		●	●	●	●

	CV	CR	PR	LEBANON		UC	RE	TX	VR
	●	●	●	Abstract Associates Ltd...............46		●	●	●	●
	●	●	●	Abstract Land Associates Inc...............48		●	●	●	●
	●	●	●	Commonwealth Investigation Agency...............506		●	●	●	●
	●	●	●	Nationwide Information Services Inc...............1412		●	●	●	●
	●	●	●	Priority One Attorney Service...............1603		●	●	●	●

	CV	CR	PR	LEHIGH		UC	RE	TX	VR
	●	●	●	Commonwealth Investigation Agency...............506		●	●	●	●
	●	●	●	Docutrans Inc...............642		●	●	●	●
	●		●	Zapf II, John A...............2124		●	●	●	

	CV	CR	PR	LUZERNE		UC	RE	TX	VR
			●	All Penn Abstract Co...............108		●	●	●	
	●		●	ILS Abstract...............1017		●	●	●	●
	●	●	●	Maximum Protection Inc...............1296		●	●	●	●
	●		●	Toma Abstract Inc...............1963		●	●	●	

DT	CV	CR	PR	LYCOMING		UC	RE	TX	VR
	●	●	●	Lycoming Abstract Co Inc...............1247		●	●	●	
	●	●	●	Miller, Patricia...............1357		●	●	●	●
	●	●	●	Pettingill, Sandra L...............1545		●	●	●	●

	CV	CR	PR	MCKEAN		UC	RE	TX	VR
	●		●	McKean Abstracting Co...............1313		●	●	●	●
	●	●	●	Reed, David...............1669		●	●	●	●

	CV	CR	PR	MERCER		UC	RE	TX	VR
	●			Realty Settlement Inc...............1659		●	●	●	

	CV	CR	PR	MIFFLIN		UC	RE	TX	VR
	●	●	●	Kirk, Helen...............1129		●	●	●	
	●	●	●	Rupert, Joyce...............1718		●	●	●	

CV	CR	PR	MONROE		UC	RE	TX	VR
•	•	•	All Pocono Abstract Inc 109			•	•	•
•	•	•	Commonwealth Investigation Agency 506		•	•	•	•
•		•	Toma Abstract Inc 1963		•	•	•	

CV	CR	PR	MONTGOMERY		UC	RE	TX	VR
•	•	•	B & R Services for Professionals 230		•	•	•	•
•	•		Best Legal Services Inc 293		•	•	•	•
•	•	•	Court House Legal Service 542		•	•	•	•
•	•	•	Dennis Richman Services 622		•	•	•	•
•	•	•	Docutrans Inc 642		•	•	•	•
•	•	•	Legal Wings Inc 1214		•	•		•
•	•	•	Prentice Hall Legal & Financial Services 1589		•	•	•	•
•		•	Searchtec 1760					•
•	•		Talme and Associates 1900					
•	•	•	The Coynes 1927		•	•	•	•

CV	CR	PR	MONTOUR		UC	RE	TX	VR
•	•	•	American Abstract & Land Co 125		•	•	•	•
•	•	•	S.A.F.E. 1723		•	•	•	•
•		•	Toma Abstract Inc 1963		•	•	•	

CV	CR	PR	NORTHAMPTON		UC	RE	TX	VR
•	•	•	Commonwealth Investigation Agency 506		•	•	•	•
•		•	Zapf II, John A 2124		•	•	•	

CV	CR	PR	NORTHUMBERLAND		UC	RE	TX	VR
•	•	•	S.A.F.E. 1723		•	•	•	•
•		•	Toma Abstract Inc 1963		•	•	•	

CV	CR	PR	PERRY		UC	RE	TX	VR
•	•	•	Abstract Land Associates Inc 48		•	•	•	•
•	•	•	Lyons, Helen F 1252		•	•	•	
•	•	•	Penncorp Service Group Inc 1532		•	•	•	
•	•	•	Priority One Attorney Service 1603		•	•	•	•

DT	BK	CV	CR	PR	PHILADELPHIA		UC	RE	TX	VR
•	•	•	•	•	B & R Services for Professionals 230		•	•	•	•
•	•	•	•		Best Legal Services Inc 293		•	•	•	•
•	•	•	•	•	Corporation Service Co - Delaware 529		•	•	•	•
•	•	•	•	•	Court House Legal Service 542		•	•	•	•
•	•	•	•	•	Dennis Richman Services 622		•	•	•	•
•	•	•	•	•	Docutrans Inc 642		•	•	•	•
•	•	•	•	•	Legal Wings Inc 1214		•	•		•
•	•	•	•	•	Prentice Hall Legal & Financial Services 1589		•	•	•	•
	•			•	Searchtec 1760					•
•	•	•	•		Talme and Associates 1900					
•	•	•	•	•	The Coynes 1927		•	•	•	•

CV	CR	PR	PIKE		UC	RE	TX	VR
•		•	Able Abstract Co Inc 41		•	•	•	
•	•	•	All Pocono Abstract Inc 109			•	•	•
•	•	•	Arbor Abstracting Co 157		•	•	•	•
•			Inter-County Abstract 1036			•		
•	•	•	Robert Daly Investigations 1703		•	•	•	•
•	•	•	Schroeder, Sharon 1748		•	•	•	

CV	CR	PR	POTTER		UC	RE	TX	VR
•	•	•	Reed, David 1669		•	•	•	•

CV	CR	PR	SCHUYLKILL		UC	RE	TX	VR
●		●	Assured Realty 176		●	●	●	
●		●	ILS Abstract 1017		●	●	●	●
●		●	O'Connor, Michael J 1452			●	●	
●		●	Toma Abstract Inc...................1963		●	●	●	

CV	CR	PR	SNYDER		UC	RE	TX	VR
●	●	●	S.A.F.E. 1723		●	●	●	●

CV	CR	PR	SOMERSET		UC	RE	TX	VR
●			Somerset Abstract Co Ltd 1818		●	●	●	

CV	CR	PR	SULLIVAN		UC	RE	TX	VR
●	●	●	Priority One Attorney Service...................1603		●	●	●	●

CV	CR	PR	SUSQUEHANNA		UC	RE	TX	VR
●	●	●	Bartkis, Cindy 254		●	●	●	●

CV	CR	PR	TIOGA		UC	RE	TX	VR
			See ALL COUNTIES...................					

CV	CR	PR	UNION		UC	RE	TX	VR
●	●	●	S.A.F.E. 1723		●	●	●	●

CV	CR	PR	VENANGO		UC	RE	TX	VR
●	●	●	Falcon Abstract Co...................738		●	●	●	●
●	●	●	Latchaw, Christy 1176		●	●	●	●
●			Realty Settlement Inc 1659		●	●	●	

CV	CR	PR	WARREN		UC	RE	TX	VR
			See ALL COUNTIES...................					

CV	CR	PR	WASHINGTON		UC	RE	TX	VR
●	●	●	Coats, Janet 483		●		●	●
●	●	●	Fayette Professional Services...................746		●	●	●	●

CV	CR	PR	WAYNE		UC	RE	TX	VR
●		●	Able Abstract Co Inc...................41		●	●	●	
●	●	●	All Pocono Abstract Inc...................109			●	●	●
●	●	●	Arbor Abstracting Co...................157		●	●	●	●
●		●	Fidelity Home Abstract 758		●	●	●	
●			Inter-County Abstract...................1036			●		
●	●	●	JS Industries 1072		●	●	●	●
●	●	●	Schloesser, Kathleen 1745		●	●	●	

CV	CR	PR	WESTMORELAND		UC	RE	TX	VR
●	●	●	Fayette Professional Services...................746		●	●	●	●
●	●	●	Lawyers' Abstract Co 1187		●	●	●	
●	●	●	Robert Smith Abstract...................1704		●	●	●	●

CV	CR	PR	WYOMING		UC	RE	TX	VR
●	●	●	Garbus, Catherine J...................830		●	●	●	●

Court
Records

PENNSYLVANIA

186

County
Records

CV	CR	PR	YORK		UC	RE	TX	VR
●	●	●	Abstract Associates Ltd............46		●	●	●	●
●	●	●	Abstract One Inc 49		●	●	●	●
●	●		Associated Services............173		●			
●	●	●	Campbell, Eugene R............390		●	●	●	
●	●	●	Colonial Valley Abstract Co 491		●	●	●	●
●	●	●	D'Aiello Jr, Russell F 580		●	●	●	
●	●	●	Nationwide Information Services Inc............1412		●	●	●	●

Rhode Island

DT	BK	CV	CR	PR	ALL COUNTIES	UC	RE	TX	VR
●	●	●	●	●	Barry Shuster Co...253	●	●	●	●

		CV	CR	PR	BRISTOL	UC	RE	TX	VR
					See ALL COUNTIES...				

		CV	CR	PR	KENT	UC	RE	TX	VR
					See ALL COUNTIES...				

		CV	CR	PR	NEWPORT	UC	RE	TX	VR
					See ALL COUNTIES...				

DT	BK	CV	CR	PR	PROVIDENCE	UC	RE	TX	VR
					See ALL COUNTIES...				

		CV	CR	PR	WASHINGTON	UC	RE	TX	VR
					See ALL COUNTIES...				

South Carolina

DT	BK	CV	CR	PR	ALL COUNTIES		UC	RE	TX	VR
●	●	●	●	●	Freeflight Inc.................................812		●	●	●	●
●	●	●	●	●	Professional Service of Process Inc...............1618			●	●	●

		CV	CR	PR	ABBEVILLE		UC	RE	TX	VR
		●	●	●	Upper State Title Corp 2014		●	●	●	●

		CV	CR	PR	AIKEN		UC	RE	TX	VR
		●		●	Garvin, Douglas G.....................834		●	●	●	●
		●	●	●	Hall, Franklin I.............................908		●	●	●	●

		CV	CR	PR	ALLENDALE		UC	RE	TX	VR
		●	●	●	Brunsom, Eva H..........................358		●	●	●	●

		CV	CR	PR	ANDERSON		UC	RE	TX	VR
		●	●	●	Nolan & Associates.....................1430		●	●	●	●
		●	●	●	Upper State Title Corp 2014		●	●	●	●

		CV	CR	PR	BAMBERG		UC	RE	TX	VR
		●	●	●	B & G Ltd of Hollidaysburg..................227		●	●	●	
		●	●	●	Brunsom, Eva H..........................358		●	●	●	●
		●	●	●	Horger Barnewll & Reid 991		●	●	●	●

		CV	CR	PR	BARNWELL		UC	RE	TX	VR
		●	●	●	Brunsom, Eva H..........................358		●	●	●	●

		CV	CR	PR	BEAUFORT		UC	RE	TX	VR
		●	●	●	B & G Ltd of Hollidaysburg..................227		●	●	●	
		●	●	●	NC Search Inc 1405		●	●	●	
		●	●	●	The Bister Agency.......................1922		●	●	●	●

		CV	CR	PR	BERKELEY		UC	RE	TX	VR
		●	●	●	Aubin Abstracting.......................215		●	●	●	●
		●	●	●	Process Serving Unlimited...........1611					

		CV	CR	PR	CALHOUN		UC	RE	TX	VR
		●	●	●	Hall, Franklin I............................908		●	●	●	●
		●	●	●	Horger Barnewll & Reid 991		●	●	●	●
		●	●	●	NC Search Inc 1405		●	●	●	

DT		CV	CR	PR	CHARLESTON		UC	RE	TX	VR
		●	●	●	Aubin Abstracting.......................215		●	●	●	●
●		●	●	●	NC Search Inc 1405		●	●	●	
●		●	●	●	Process Serving Unlimited...........1611					

		CV	CR	PR	CHEROKEE		UC	RE	TX	VR
		●	●	●	Alpha & Omega 120		●	●	●	●
		●	●	●	Nolan & Associates.....................1430		●	●	●	●
		●	●	●	State Line Title...........................1855		●	●	●	●

		CV	CR	PR	CHESTER		UC	RE	TX	VR
		●	●	●	Alpha & Omega 120		●	●	●	●
		●	●	●	Polk Legal Service 1566		●	●	●	●
		●	●	●	State Line Title...........................1855		●	●	●	●

		CV	CR	PR	CHESTERFIELD		UC	RE	TX	VR
		●	●	●	Alpha & Omega 120		●	●	●	●
		●	●	●	Polson, Sherrie C 1569		●	●	●	

		CV	CR	PR	CLARENDON		UC	RE	TX	VR
		●	●	●	Aubin Abstracting.......................215		●	●	●	●
		●	●	●	Cothran & Cothran......................534		●	●	●	●

	CV	CR	PR	COLLETON	UC	RE	TX	VR
				See ALL COUNTIES....................................				

	CV	CR	PR	DARLINGTON	UC	RE	TX	VR
	●	●	●	Polson, Sherrie C 1569	●	●	●	

	CV	CR	PR	DILLON	UC	RE	TX	VR
	●	●	●	Aubin Abstracting...215	●	●	●	●
	●	●	●	Polson, Sherrie C 1569	●	●	●	

	CV	CR	PR	DORCHESTER	UC	RE	TX	VR
	●	●	●	Horger Barnewll & Reid 991	●	●	●	●
	●	●	●	Process Serving Unlimited...................................1611				

	CV	CR	PR	EDGEFIELD	UC	RE	TX	VR
	●	●	●	Hall, Franklin I...908	●	●	●	
	●		●	Hastings, Renee...937	●	●	●	

	CV	CR	PR	FAIRFIELD	UC	RE	TX	VR
	●	●	●	Alpha & Omega 120	●	●	●	
	●	●	●	Carolina Information Services Inc.........................409	●	●	●	●
	●	●	●	NC Search Inc 1405	●	●	●	

DT	CV	CR	PR	FLORENCE	UC	RE	TX	VR
	●	●	●	Aubin Abstracting...215	●	●	●	●
	●	●	●	Polson, Sherrie C 1569	●	●	●	

	CV	CR	PR	GEORGETOWN	UC	RE	TX	VR
	●	●	●	Aubin Abstracting...215	●	●	●	●
	●		●	Title Services Unlimited......................................1957	●	●	●	●

DT	CV	CR	PR	GREENVILLE	UC	RE	TX	VR
●	●	●	●	Nolan & Associates...1430	●	●	●	●
	●	●	●	Upper State Title Corp 2014	●	●	●	●

	CV	CR	PR	GREENWOOD	UC	RE	TX	VR
	●	●	●	Upper State Title Corp 2014	●	●	●	●

	CV	CR	PR	HAMPTON	UC	RE	TX	VR
	●	●	●	Brunsom, Eva H..358	●	●	●	●
	●	●	●	Palmetto Title Services.......................................1508	●	●	●	●

	CV	CR	PR	HORRY	UC	RE	TX	VR
	●	●	●	Aubin Abstracting...215	●	●	●	●

	CV	CR	PR	JASPER	UC	RE	TX	VR
	●	●	●	Palmetto Title Services.......................................1508	●	●	●	●

	CV	CR	PR	KERSHAW	UC	RE	TX	VR
	●	●	●	Alpha & Omega 120	●	●	●	●
	●	●	●	NC Search Inc 1405	●	●	●	
	●	●	●	Polson, Sherrie C 1569	●	●	●	

	CV	CR	PR	LANCASTER	UC	RE	TX	VR
	●	●	●	Alpha & Omega 120	●	●	●	●
	●	●	●	Polk Legal Service 1566	●	●	●	●
	●	●	●	State Line Title 1855	●	●	●	●

	CV	CR	PR	LAURENS	UC	RE	TX	VR
	●	●	●	Nolan & Associates...1430	●	●	●	●
	●	●	●	Upper State Title Corp 2014	●	●	●	●

	CV	CR	PR	LEE	UC	RE	TX	VR
	●	●	●	Aubin Abstracting...215	●	●	●	●

DT	BK	CV	CR	PR	Company	Page	UC	RE	TX	VR
		•	•	•	Cothran & Cothran	534	•	•	•	•
		•	•	•	Polson, Sherrie C	1569	•	•	•	
		CV	CR	PR	**LEXINGTON**		UC	RE	TX	VR
		•	•	•	Carolina Information Services Inc	409	•	•	•	•
		•	•	•	Hall, Franklin I	908	•	•	•	•
		•	•	•	NC Search Inc	1405	•	•	•	
		CV	CR	PR	**MCCORMICK**		UC	RE	TX	VR
		•	•	•	Upper State Title Corp	2014	•	•	•	•
		CV	CR	PR	**MARION**		UC	RE	TX	VR
		•	•	•	Aubin Abstracting	215	•	•	•	•
		•	•	•	K.R.	1107	•	•	•	
		•	•	•	Polson, Sherrie C	1569	•	•	•	
		CV	CR	PR	**MARLBORO**		UC	RE	TX	VR
		•	•	•	Polson, Sherrie C	1569	•	•	•	
		CV	CR	PR	**NEWBERRY**		UC	RE	TX	VR
		•	•	•	Hall, Franklin I	908	•	•	•	•
		CV	CR	PR	**OCONEE**		UC	RE	TX	VR
		•	•	•	Bonham, Judy	321	•	•	•	•
				•	Lusk, Denise	1246	•	•	•	
		•	•	•	Upper State Title Corp	2014	•	•		•
		CV	CR	PR	**ORANGEBURG**		UC	RE	TX	VR
		•	•	•	Cothran & Cothran	534	•	•	•	•
		•	•	•	Horger Barnewll & Reid	991	•	•	•	•
		CV	CR	PR	**PICKENS**		UC	RE	TX	VR
		•	•	•	Nolan & Associates	1430	•	•	•	•
		•	•	•	Upper State Title Corp	2014	•	•	•	•
DT	BK	CV	CR	PR	**RICHLAND**		UC	RE	TX	VR
•	•	•	•	•	Carolina Information Services Inc	409	•	•	•	•
•	•	•	•	•	Hall, Franklin I	908	•	•	•	•
•	•	•	•	•	NC Search Inc	1405	•	•	•	
		•	•	•	Polson, Sherrie C	1569	•	•	•	
		CV	CR	PR	**SALUDA**		UC	RE	TX	VR
		•	•	•	Hall, Franklin I	908	•	•	•	•
		CV	CR	PR	**SPARTANBURG**		UC	RE	TX	VR
		•	•	•	NC Search Inc	1405	•	•	•	
		•	•	•	Nolan & Associates	1430	•	•		•
		•	•	•	Upper State Title Corp	2014	•	•	•	•
		CV	CR	PR	**SUMTER**		UC	RE	TX	VR
		•	•	•	Cothran & Cothran	534	•	•	•	•
		CV	CR	PR	**UNION**		UC	RE	TX	VR
		•	•	•	Alpha & Omega	120	•	•	•	•
		•	•	•	State Line Title	1855	•	•	•	•
		CV	CR	PR	**WILLIAMSBURG**		UC	RE	TX	VR
		•	•	•	Aubin Abstracting	215	•	•	•	•
		•	•	•	Cothran & Cothran	534	•	•	•	•

CV	CR	PR	YORK		UC	RE	TX	VR
●	●	●	Alpha & Omega 120		●	●	●	●
●	●	●	Investigative & Paralegal Services....................1045		●	●	●	●
●	●	●	NC Search Inc 1405		●	●	●	
●	●	●	Nolan & Associates..1430		●	●	●	●
●	●	●	Polk Legal Service 1566		●	●	●	●
●	●	●	State Line Title...1855		●	●	●	●

SUMMARY OF CODES

COURT RECORDS

CODE*	GOVERNMENT AGENCY	TYPE OF INFORMATION
DT	US District Court	Federal civil and criminal cases
BK	Bankruptcy Court	United States bankruptcy cases
CV	Civil Court	Municipal, county and state level civil cases
CR	Criminal Court	Municipal, county and state level criminal cases
PR	Probate Court	Wills and estate cases

COUNTY RECORDS

CODE*	GOVERNMENT AGENCY	TYPE OF INFORMATION
UC	UCC Filing Office	Uniform Commercial Code and other personal property liens
RE	Recorder of Deeds	Real property transactions and liens
TX	Tax Assessor	Real property tax information
VR	Vital Records Office	Birth, death, marriage, divorce, etc.

*The "CODE" designates the agency and type of information obtainable in each county.

Court
Records

SOUTH DAKOTA
192

County
Records

South Dakota

CV	CR	PR	AURORA	UC	RE	TX	VR
•	•	•	Aurora County Abstract 219	•	•	•	•

CV	CR	PR	BEADLE	UC	RE	TX	VR
•		•	Huron Title Co 1007	•	•	•	•

CV	CR	PR	BENNETT	UC	RE	TX	VR
•	•	•	Frontier Cultural Service..............................818	•	•	•	•
•	•	•	Home Abstract Co..............................986	•	•		•

CV	CR	PR	BON HOMME	UC	RE	TX	VR
•	•	•	Frontier Cultural Service..............................818	•	•	•	•

CV	CR	PR	BROOKINGS	UC	RE	TX	VR
•	•	•	Dirks, Lewis..............................635	•	•	•	•

CV	CR	PR	BROWN	UC	RE	TX	VR
•	•	•	Krueger, Maurice & Florence 1137	•	•	•	•

CV	CR	PR	BRULE	UC	RE	TX	VR
•	•	•	Brule County Abstract Co..............................356		•	•	
•	•	•	Brule County Title and Insurance Co..............................357	•	•	•	•
•	•	•	Frontier Cultural Service..............................818	•	•	•	•

CV	CR	PR	BUFFALO	UC	RE	TX	VR
•	•	•	Brule County Title and Insurance Co..............................357	•	•	•	•

CV	CR	PR	BUTTE	UC	RE	TX	VR
•	•	•	Frontier Cultural Service..............................818	•	•	•	•
•	•	•	Polley, Steve..............................1568	•	•		•

CV	CR	PR	CAMPBELL	UC	RE	TX	VR
•	•	•	Campbell County Abstract & Title Co..............................389	•	•	•	
•	•	•	Krueger, Maurice & Florence 1137	•	•	•	•

CV	CR	PR	CHARLES MIX	UC	RE	TX	VR
•	•	•	Frontier Cultural Service..............................818	•	•	•	•

CV	CR	PR	CLARK	UC	RE	TX	VR
•	•	•	Clark Abstract & Title Co..............................464	•	•	•	•

CV	CR	PR	CLAY	UC	RE	TX	VR
•	•	•	Dirks, Lewis..............................635	•	•	•	•
•	•	•	Intra-Lex Investigations Inc 1043	•	•	•	•

CV	CR	PR	CODINGTON	UC	RE	TX	VR
•	•	•	Watertown Title & Escrow Co..............................2061	•	•	•	•

CV	CR	PR	CORSON	UC	RE	TX	VR
•	•	•	Frontier Cultural Service..............................818	•	•	•	•

CV	CR	PR	CUSTER	UC	RE	TX	VR
•	•	•	Frontier Cultural Service..............................818	•	•	•	•

CV	CR	PR	DAVISON	UC	RE	TX	VR
•	•	•	Davison County Abstract & Title Co..............................605	•	•	•	•

CV	CR	PR	DAY	UC	RE	TX	VR
•		•	Grue Abstract Co..............................885	•	•	•	•

CV	CR	PR	DEUEL	UC	RE	TX	VR
•	•	•	Deuel County Abstract Co 628	•	•	•	•

		CV	CR	PR	**DEWEY**	UC	RE	TX	VR
		●	●	●	Frontier Cultural Service......818	●	●	●	●
		●	●	●	Titles of Dakota Inc......1960	●	●	●	●

		CV	CR	PR	**DOUGLAS**	UC	RE	TX	VR
		●	●	●	Douglas County Title Co......654		●	●	●

		CV	CR	PR	**EDMUNDS**	UC	RE	TX	VR
		●	●	●	Krueger, Maurice & Florence......1137	●	●	●	●

		CV	CR	PR	**FALL RIVER**	UC	RE	TX	VR
		●	●	●	Frontier Cultural Service......818	●	●	●	●

		CV	CR	PR	**FAULK**	UC	RE	TX	VR
		●	●	●	Krueger, Maurice & Florence......1137	●	●	●	●

		CV	CR	PR	**GRANT**	UC	RE	TX	VR
		●		●	Grant County Abstract & Title Co......861	●	●	●	

		CV	CR	PR	**GREGORY**	UC	RE	TX	VR
		●	●	●	Frontier Cultural Service......818	●	●	●	●
		●	●	●	Gregory County Abstract Co......881	●	●	●	

		CV	CR	PR	**HAAKON**	UC	RE	TX	VR
		●	●	●	Frontier Cultural Service......818	●	●	●	●
		●	●	●	Haakon County Abstract Co......905	●	●	●	

		CV	CR	PR	**HAMLIN**	UC	RE	TX	VR
		●	●	●	Dirks, Lewis......635	●	●	●	●

		CV	CR	PR	**HAND**	UC	RE	TX	VR
		●	●	●	Hand County Abstract & Title Co......915	●		●	●

		CV	CR	PR	**HANSON**	UC	RE	TX	VR
		●	●	●	Hanson County Land & Abstract......920	●	●	●	●

		CV	CR	PR	**HARDING**	UC	RE	TX	VR
		●	●	●	Frontier Cultural Service......818	●	●	●	●
		●	●	●	Harding County Abstract Co......924	●	●	●	●

DT	BK	CV	CR	PR	**HUGHES**	UC	RE	TX	VR
		●	●	●	Frontier Cultural Service......818	●	●	●	●

		CV	CR	PR	**HUTCHINSON**	UC	RE	TX	VR
		●	●	●	Dirks, Lewis......635	●	●	●	●
		●	●	●	Oplinger Abstract & Title Inc......1473	●	●	●	●

		CV	CR	PR	**HYDE**	UC	RE	TX	VR
		●	●	●	Frontier Cultural Service......818	●	●	●	●

		CV	CR	PR	**JACKSON**	UC	RE	TX	VR
		●	●	●	Frontier Cultural Service......818	●	●	●	●
		●	●	●	Jackson County Title Co......1075		●	●	●

		CV	CR	PR	**JERAULD**	UC	RE	TX	VR
		●		●	Jerauld County Abstract Co Inc......1087	●	●	●	●

		CV	CR	PR	**JONES**	UC	RE	TX	VR
		●	●	●	Frontier Cultural Service......818	●	●	●	●
		●	●	●	Jones County Abstract Co......1101	●	●	●	●

		CV	CR	PR	**KINGSBURY**	UC	RE	TX	VR
		●	●	●	Dirks, Lewis......635	●	●	●	●

		CV	CR	PR	LAKE	UC	RE	TX	VR
		●	●	●	Dirks, Lewis..635	●	●	●	●
		●		●	Weber Abstract Co...................................2069	●	●	●	●

		CV	CR	PR	LAWRENCE	UC	RE	TX	VR
		●	●	●	Frontier Cultural Service........................818	●	●	●	●
		●	●	●	Polley, Steve..1568	●	●		●

		CV	CR	PR	LINCOLN	UC	RE	TX	VR
		●	●	●	Dirks, Lewis..635	●	●	●	●
		●	●	●	Intra-Lex Investigations Inc...................1043	●	●	●	●

		CV	CR	PR	LYMAN	UC	RE	TX	VR
		●	●	●	Frontier Cultural Service........................818	●	●	●	●
		●	●	●	Lyman Title Co...1248		●	●	

		CV	CR	PR	MCCOOK	UC	RE	TX	VR
		●	●	●	Dirks, Lewis..635	●	●	●	●
		●	●	●	McCook County Abstract & Title Ins............1306	●	●	●	●

		CV	CR	PR	MCPHERSON	UC	RE	TX	VR
		●	●	●	Krueger, Maurice & Florence.................1137	●	●	●	●
				●	McPherson County Abstract Co.............1320	●	●	●	

		CV	CR	PR	MARSHALL	UC	RE	TX	VR
		●	●	●	Marshall Land & Title Co.......................1286	●	●	●	●

		CV	CR	PR	MEADE	UC	RE	TX	VR
		●	●	●	Frontier Cultural Service........................818	●	●	●	●
		●	●	●	Polley, Steve..1568	●	●		●
		●	●	●	Security Land & Abstract Co.................1775	●	●	●	●

		CV	CR	PR	MELLETTE	UC	RE	TX	VR
		●	●	●	Frontier Cultural Service........................818	●	●	●	●
		●	●	●	Mellette County Abstract Co.................1324	●	●	●	●

		CV	CR	PR	MINER	UC	RE	TX	VR
		●	●	●	Dirks, Lewis..635	●	●	●	●
		●	●	●	Fidelity Abstract & Title Co...................757	●	●	●	●

DT	BK	CV	CR	PR	MINNEHAHA	UC	RE	TX	VR
●	●	●	●	●	Dirks, Lewis..635	●	●	●	●
		●	●	●	Intra-Lex Investigations Inc...................1043	●	●	●	●

		CV	CR	PR	MOODY	UC	RE	TX	VR
		●	●	●	Dirks, Lewis..635	●	●	●	●
		●		●	Moody County Abstract Co.....................1379	●	●	●	

		CV	CR	PR	PENNINGTON	UC	RE	TX	VR
		●	●	●	Frontier Cultural Service........................818	●	●	●	●
		●	●	●	Polley, Steve..1568	●	●		●

		CV	CR	PR	PERKINS	UC	RE	TX	VR
		●	●	●	Frontier Cultural Service........................818	●	●	●	●
		●		●	Perkins County Abstract Co...................1539	●	●	●	●

		CV	CR	PR	POTTER	UC	RE	TX	VR
		●	●	●	Krueger, Maurice & Florence.................1137	●	●	●	●
		●	●	●	Potter County Land & Abstract Inc............1576		●	●	●

		CV	CR	PR	ROBERTS	UC	RE	TX	VR
		●	●	●	Dalberg, Mae...586	●	●	●	●

CV	CR	PR	SANBORN	UC	RE	TX	VR
●		●	Sanborn County Realty and Title Company....................1736	●	●		

CV	CR	PR	SHANNON	UC	RE	TX	VR
●	●	●	Frontier Cultural Service.............................818	●	●	●	●

CV	CR	PR	SPINK	UC	RE	TX	VR
●	●	●	Gillette Battey & McAreavey..............................844	●	●	●	●

CV	CR	PR	STANLEY	UC	RE	TX	VR
●	●	●	Frontier Cultural Service.............................818	●	●	●	●
●	●	●	Titles of Dakota Inc.............................1959	●	●	●	●

CV	CR	PR	SULLY	UC	RE	TX	VR
●	●	●	Frontier Cultural Service.............................818	●	●	●	●
●	●	●	Titles of Dakota Inc.............................1958	●	●	●	●

CV	CR	PR	TODD	UC	RE	TX	VR
●	●	●	Farmers State Company Abstracting...................743	●	●	●	●
●	●	●	Frontier Cultural Service.............................818	●	●	●	●

CV	CR	PR	TRIPP	UC	RE	TX	VR
●	●	●	Farmers State Company Abstracting...................743	●	●	●	●
●	●	●	Frontier Cultural Service.............................818	●	●	●	●

CV	CR	PR	TURNER	UC	RE	TX	VR
●	●	●	Dirks, Lewis.............................635	●	●	●	●
●	●	●	Intra-Lex Investigations Inc 1043	●	●	●	●

CV	CR	PR	UNION	UC	RE	TX	VR
●	●	●	Dirks, Lewis.............................635	●	●	●	●
●	●	●	Intra-Lex Investigations Inc 1043	●	●	●	●
●	●	●	Union County Abstract and Title Company...................2005	●	●	●	

CV	CR	PR	WALWORTH	UC	RE	TX	VR
●	●	●	Krueger, Maurice & Florence 1137	●	●	●	●
●	●	●	Walworth County Abstract & Title Co Inc.....................2052	●	●	●	●

CV	CR	PR	YANKTON	UC	RE	TX	VR
●	●	●	Dirks, Lewis.............................635	●	●	●	●
●	●	●	Intra-Lex Investigations Inc 1043	●	●	●	●

CV	CR	PR	ZIEBACH	UC	RE	TX	VR
●	●	●	Frontier Cultural Service.............................818	●	●	●	●
●	●	●	Titles of Dakota Inc.............................1961	●	●	●	●

Tennessee

CV	CR	PR	ANDERSON		UC	RE	TX	VR
●	●	●	Greater Tennessee Title Co 871		●	●	●	●

CV	CR	PR	BEDFORD		UC	RE	TX	VR
●	●	●	Charles F Edgar & Associates................438		●	●	●	●
●	●	●	Hollingsworth Court Reporting Inc................983		●	●	●	●

CV	CR	PR	BENTON		UC	RE	TX	VR
●	●	●	D.K. Abstract 581		●	●	●	
●	●		Lattus, Helen 1178		●	●	●	

CV	CR	PR	BLEDSOE		UC	RE	TX	VR
●		●	Real Estate Loan Services 1657		●	●	●	
●		●	Title Guaranty and Trust of Chattanooga................1953		●	●	●	

CV	CR	PR	BLOUNT		UC	RE	TX	VR
●	●	●	Clue Detective Service................479		●	●	●	●
●	●	●	Greater Tennessee Title Co 871		●	●	●	●

CV	CR	PR	BRADLEY		UC	RE	TX	VR
●		●	Hurst, Pam................1009		●	●	●	●
●		●	Real Estate Loan Services................1657		●	●	●	
●		●	Title Guaranty and Trust of Chattanooga................1953		●	●	●	

CV	CR	PR	CAMPBELL		UC	RE	TX	VR
●	●	●	Clue Detective Service................479		●	●	●	●

CV	CR	PR	CANNON		UC	RE	TX	VR
●	●	●	Hollingsworth Court Reporting Inc................983		●	●	●	●

CV	CR	PR	CARROLL		UC	RE	TX	VR
●	●	●	D.K. Abstract 581		●	●	●	
●	●		Lattus, Helen 1178		●	●	●	

CV	CR	PR	CARTER		UC	RE	TX	VR
●	●	●	Clue Detective Service................479		●	●	●	●
●	●	●	Simerly, Teresa................1805		●	●	●	●

CV	CR	PR	CHEATHAM		UC	RE	TX	VR
●	●	●	Capitol Filing Service Inc 395		●	●	●	
●	●	●	Hollingsworth Court Reporting Inc................983		●	●	●	●
●	●	●	The Search Is On................1942		●	●	●	●
●	●	●	Wells Fargo Investigative Services 2076		●	●	●	●

CV	CR	PR	CHESTER		UC	RE	TX	VR
●	●	●	D.K. Abstract 581		●	●	●	
●		●	Douglas, Howard F 656		●	●	●	●
●	●	●	Hollingsworth Court Reporting Inc................983		●	●	●	●

CV	CR	PR	CLAIBORNE		UC	RE	TX	VR
●	●	●	Clue Detective Service................479		●	●	●	●

CV	CR	PR	CLAY		UC	RE	TX	VR
●	●	●	Hollingsworth Court Reporting Inc................983		●	●	●	●

CV	CR	PR	COCKE		UC	RE	TX	VR
●	●	●	Clue Detective Service................479		●	●	●	●
●	●	●	Greater Tennessee Title Co 871		●	●	●	●
●	●	●	Harris, Eileen 929		●	●	●	

CV	CR	PR	COFFEE		UC	RE	TX	VR
●	●	●	Charles F Edgar & Associates................438		●	●	●	●

DT	BK	CV	CR	PR		UC	RE	TX	VR
		●	●	●	Hollingsworth Court Reporting Inc...................................983	●	●	●	●
		●		●	Title Guaranty and Trust of Chattanooga.......................1953	●	●	●	

		CV	CR	PR	**CROCKETT**	UC	RE	TX	VR
		●	●	●	D.K. Abstract 581	●	●	●	
		●	●	●	Hollingsworth Court Reporting Inc...................................983	●	●	●	●

		CV	CR	PR	**CUMBERLAND**	UC	RE	TX	VR
		●	●	●	Arms, Joan..160	●	●	●	●
		●	●	●	Source 1820	●	●	●	
		●	●	●	Warner, Larry M 2053	●	●	●	

DT	BK	CV	CR	PR	**DAVIDSON**	UC	RE	TX	VR
●	●	●	●	●	Capitol Filing Service Inc 395	●	●	●	
●	●	●	●		Court Record Research...545				
		●	●	●	Hollingsworth Court Reporting Inc...................................983	●	●	●	●
●	●	●	●	●	Information Retrieval Service 1029	●	●	●	●
●	●	●	●	●	Legal Eagles Attorney Services.....................................1200	●			
●	●	●	●	●	The Search Is On 1942	●	●	●	●
●	●	●	●	●	Thompson and Assoc 1946	●	●	●	●
●	●	●	●	●	Wells Fargo Investigative Services 2076	●	●	●	●

		CV	CR	PR	**DECATUR**	UC	RE	TX	VR
		●	●	●	D.K. Abstract 581	●	●	●	
		●		●	Douglas, Howard F 656	●	●	●	
		●		●	Ford Abstract Corp...793	●	●	●	

		CV	CR	PR	**DE KALB**	UC	RE	TX	VR
		●	●	●	Hollingsworth Court Reporting Inc...................................983	●	●	●	●
		●	●	●	Source 1820	●	●	●	

		CV	CR	PR	**DICKSON**	UC	RE	TX	VR
		●	●	●	Capitol Filing Service Inc 395	●	●	●	
		●	●	●	Hollingsworth Court Reporting Inc...................................983	●	●	●	●

		CV	CR	PR	**DYER**	UC	RE	TX	VR
					Crowder, Judy 568	●		●	
		●	●	●	D.K. Abstract 581	●	●	●	
		●	●	●	Hollingsworth Court Reporting Inc...................................983	●	●	●	●
		●	●		Lattus, Helen 1178	●	●	●	

		CV	CR	PR	**FAYETTE**	UC	RE	TX	VR
		●	●	●	D.K. Abstract 581	●	●	●	
		●	●	●	Hollingsworth Court Reporting Inc...................................983	●	●	●	●
		●	●	●	Investigative Services for Attorneys..............................1049	●	●	●	
		●	●	●	Record-Check Services Inc 1663	●	●	●	
		●	●	●	RecordServe/John Kelley Enterprises 1664	●	●	●	
		●	●	●	Schaeffer Papers..1743		●		

		CV	CR	PR	**FENTRESS**	UC	RE	TX	VR
		●	●	●	Arms, Joan..160	●	●	●	●

		CV	CR	PR	**FRANKLIN**	UC	RE	TX	VR
		●	●	●	Broadway, J Stephen...347	●	●	●	●
		●	●	●	Charles F Edgar & Associates...438	●	●	●	●
				●	H & M Research Co 903	●	●	●	
		●		●	Title Guaranty and Trust of Chattanooga.......................1953	●	●	●	

		CV	CR	PR	**GIBSON**	UC	RE	TX	VR
		●	●	●	D.K. Abstract 581	●	●	●	
		●	●		Lattus, Helen 1178	●	●	●	

	CV	CR	PR	GILES		UC	RE	TX	VR
	●	●	●	Broadway, J Stephen................................347		●	●	●	●
	●	●	●	Charles F Edgar & Associates....................438		●	●	●	●
			●	H & M Research Co.................................903		●	●	●	
	●	●	●	Hollingsworth Court Reporting Inc..............983		●	●	●	●

	CV	CR	PR	GRAINGER		UC	RE	TX	VR
	●	●	●	Clue Detective Service.............................479		●	●	●	●
	●	●	●	Harris, Eileen 929		●	●	●	
	●	●	●	Hollingsworth Court Reporting Inc..............983		●	●	●	●

DT	CV	CR	PR	GREENE		UC	RE	TX	VR
●	●	●	●	Clue Detective Service.............................479		●	●	●	●
	●	●	●	Harris, Eileen 929		●	●	●	

	CV	CR	PR	GRUNDY		UC	RE	TX	VR
	●	●	●	Earlene Y Speer Law Offices.....................676		●	●	●	●
	●		●	Title Guaranty and Trust of Chattanooga........1953		●	●	●	

	CV	CR	PR	HAMBLEN		UC	RE	TX	VR
	●	●	●	Clue Detective Service.............................479		●	●	●	●
	●	●	●	Harris, Eileen 929		●	●	●	

DT	BK	CV	CR	PR	HAMILTON		UC	RE	TX	VR
	●	●		●	Hurst, Pam...1009		●	●	●	●
	●	●		●	Real Estate Loan Services.........................1657		●	●	●	
●	●	●		●	Title Guaranty and Trust of Chattanooga........1953		●	●	●	

	CV	CR	PR	HANCOCK		UC	RE	TX	VR
	●	●	●	Clue Detective Service.............................479		●	●	●	●

	CV	CR	PR	HARDEMAN		UC	RE	TX	VR
	●	●	●	Carl Watson & Associates.........................406		●	●	●	
	●	●	●	D.K. Abstract 581		●	●	●	
	●	●	●	Hollingsworth Court Reporting Inc..............983		●	●	●	

	CV	CR	PR	HARDIN		UC	RE	TX	VR
	●	●	●	D.K. Abstract 581		●	●	●	
	●		●	Douglas, Howard F.................................656		●	●	●	
	●	●	●	Hollingsworth Court Reporting Inc..............983		●	●	●	●

	CV	CR	PR	HAWKINS		UC	RE	TX	VR
	●	●	●	Harris, Eileen 929		●	●	●	

	CV	CR	PR	HAYWOOD		UC	RE	TX	VR
	●	●	●	D.K. Abstract 581		●	●	●	
	●	●	●	Hollingsworth Court Reporting Inc..............983		●	●	●	●
	●	●	●	Schaeffer Papers....................................1743			●		

	CV	CR	PR	HENDERSON		UC	RE	TX	VR
	●	●	●	D.K. Abstract 581		●	●	●	
	●		●	Douglas, Howard F.................................656		●	●	●	

	CV	CR	PR	HENRY		UC	RE	TX	VR
	●	●	●	D.K. Abstract 581		●	●	●	
	●	●		Lattus, Helen 1178		●	●	●	

	CV	CR	PR	HICKMAN		UC	RE	TX	VR
	●	●	●	Capitol Filing Service Inc 395		●	●	●	
	●	●	●	D.K. Abstract 581		●	●	●	
	●	●	●	Hollingsworth Court Reporting Inc..............983		●	●	●	●
	●	●	●	Larry R Dorning PC...............................1174		●	●	●	●
	●	●		Lattus, Helen 1178		●	●	●	

		CV	CR	PR	HOUSTON			UC	RE	TX	VR
		●	●	●	D.K. Abstract 581			●	●	●	
		●	●	●	Hollingsworth Court Reporting Inc....................983			●	●	●	●

		CV	CR	PR	HUMPHREYS			UC	RE	TX	VR
		●	●	●	D.K. Abstract 581			●	●	●	
		●	●	●	Hollingsworth Court Reporting Inc....................983			●	●	●	●

		CV	CR	PR	JACKSON			UC	RE	TX	VR
		●	●	●	Hollingsworth Court Reporting Inc....................983			●	●	●	●
		●	●	●	Source 1820			●	●	●	

		CV	CR	PR	JEFFERSON			UC	RE	TX	VR
		●	●	●	Clue Detective Service 479			●	●	●	●
		●	●	●	Harris, Eileen 929			●	●	●	

		CV	CR	PR	JOHNSON			UC	RE	TX	VR
		●	●	●	Clue Detective Service 479			●	●	●	●
		●	●	●	Simerly, Teresa.....................................1805			●	●	●	●

DT	BK	CV	CR	PR	KNOX			UC	RE	TX	VR
●	●	●	●	●	Clue Detective Service 479			●	●	●	●
	●	●	●	●	Greater Tennessee Title Co 871			●	●	●	●
		●	●	●	Harris, Eileen 929			●	●	●	

		CV	CR	PR	LAKE			UC	RE	TX	VR
		●	●	●	D.K. Abstract 581			●	●	●	
		●	●	●	Hollingsworth Court Reporting Inc....................983			●	●	●	●
		●	●		Lattus, Helen 1178			●	●		

		CV	CR	PR	LAUDERDALE			UC	RE	TX	VR
		●	●	●	D.K. Abstract 581			●	●	●	
		●	●	●	Hollingsworth Court Reporting Inc....................983			●	●	●	●

		CV	CR	PR	LAWRENCE			UC	RE	TX	VR
		●	●	●	Broadway, J Stephen................................347			●	●	●	●
		●	●	●	Charles F Edgar & Associates.........................438			●	●	●	●
		●	●	●	Hollingsworth Court Reporting Inc....................983			●	●	●	●
		●	●	●	Larry R Dorning PC.................................1174			●	●	●	●

		CV	CR	PR	LEWIS			UC	RE	TX	VR
		●	●	●	Hollingsworth Court Reporting Inc....................983			●	●	●	●
		●	●	●	Larry R Dorning PC.................................1174			●	●	●	●

		CV	CR	PR	LINCOLN			UC	RE	TX	VR
		●	●	●	Broadway, J Stephen................................347			●	●	●	●
		●	●	●	Charles F Edgar & Associates.........................438			●	●	●	●
				●	H & M Research Co 903			●	●	●	
		●	●	●	Hollingsworth Court Reporting Inc....................983			●	●	●	●

		CV	CR	PR	LOUDON			UC	RE	TX	VR
		●	●	●	Clue Detective Service 479			●	●	●	●
		●	●	●	Greater Tennessee Title Co 871			●	●	●	●
		●		●	Title Guaranty and Trust of Chattanooga.....................1953			●	●	●	

		CV	CR	PR	MCMINN			UC	RE	TX	VR
		●		●	Real Estate Loan Services.............................1657			●	●	●	
		●		●	Title Guaranty and Trust of Chattanooga.....................1953			●	●	●	

		CV	CR	PR	MCNAIRY			UC	RE	TX	VR
		●	●	●	D.K. Abstract 581			●	●	●	
		●	●	●	Hollingsworth Court Reporting Inc....................983			●	●	●	●

		CV	CR	PR	MACON		UC	RE	TX	VR
		•	•	•	Hollingsworth Court Reporting Inc.................................983		•	•	•	•
		•	•	•	Source 1820		•	•	•	

DT	BK	CV	CR	PR	MADISON		UC	RE	TX	VR
•	•	•	•	•	D.K. Abstract 581		•	•	•	
				•	Douglas, Howard F 656		•	•	•	
•		•	•	•	Hollingsworth Court Reporting Inc.................................983		•	•	•	•
		•	•		Lattus, Helen 1178		•	•	•	
•	•	•	•	•	Record-Check Services Inc 1663		•	•	•	•

		CV	CR	PR	MARION		UC	RE	TX	VR
		•		•	Hurst, Pam..1009		•	•	•	•
		•		•	Real Estate Loan Services 1657		•	•	•	
		•		•	Title Guaranty and Trust of Chattanooga.......................1953		•	•	•	

		CV	CR	PR	MARSHALL		UC	RE	TX	VR
		•	•	•	Broadway, J Stephen 347		•	•	•	•
		•	•	•	Hollingsworth Court Reporting Inc.................................983		•	•	•	•

		CV	CR	PR	MAURY		UC	RE	TX	VR
		•	•	•	Capitol Filing Service Inc 395		•	•	•	
		•	•	•	Charles F Edgar & Associates................................438		•	•	•	•
		•	•	•	Hollingsworth Court Reporting Inc.................................983		•	•	•	•
		•	•	•	Larry R Dorning PC 1174		•	•	•	•

		CV	CR	PR	MEIGS		UC	RE	TX	VR
		•		•	Hurst, Pam..1009		•	•	•	•
		•		•	Real Estate Loan Services 1657		•	•	•	
		•		•	Title Guaranty and Trust of Chattanooga.......................1953		•	•	•	

		CV	CR	PR	MONROE		UC	RE	TX	VR
		•	•	•	Clue Detective Service 479		•	•	•	•
		•		•	Title Guaranty and Trust of Chattanooga.......................1953		•	•	•	

		CV	CR	PR	MONTGOMERY		UC	RE	TX	VR
		•	•	•	Capitol Filing Service Inc 395		•	•	•	
		•	•	•	Hollingsworth Court Reporting Inc.................................983		•	•	•	•

		CV	CR	PR	MOORE		UC	RE	TX	VR
		•	•	•	Charles F Edgar & Associates................................438		•	•	•	•
		•	•	•	Hollingsworth Court Reporting Inc.................................983		•	•	•	•

		CV	CR	PR	MORGAN		UC	RE	TX	VR
		•	•	•	Arms, Joan..160		•	•	•	•
		•	•	•	Clue Detective Service 479		•	•	•	•
		•	•	•	Greater Tennessee Title Co 871		•	•	•	•

		CV	CR	PR	OBION		UC	RE	TX	VR
		•	•	•	D.K. Abstract 581		•	•	•	
		•	•	•	Hollingsworth Court Reporting Inc.................................983		•	•	•	•
		•	•		Lattus, Helen 1178		•	•	•	

		CV	CR	PR	OVERTON		UC	RE	TX	VR
		•	•	•	Hollingsworth Court Reporting Inc.................................983		•	•	•	•
		•	•	•	Source 1820		•	•	•	

		CV	CR	PR	PERRY		UC	RE	TX	VR
		•	•	•	D.K. Abstract 581		•	•	•	
		•	•	•	Hollingsworth Court Reporting Inc.................................983		•	•	•	•
		•	•	•	Larry R Dorning PC 1174		•	•	•	•

PICKETT

CV	CR	PR			UC	RE	TX	VR
•	•	•	Arms, Joan ... 160		•	•	•	•

POLK

CV	CR	PR			UC	RE	TX	VR
•	•	•	Clue Detective Service ... 479		•	•	•	•
•		•	Real Estate Loan Services ... 1657		•	•	•	
•		•	Title Guaranty and Trust of Chattanooga ... 1953		•	•	•	

PUTNAM

DT		CV	CR	PR			UC	RE	TX	VR
		•	•	•	Hollingsworth Court Reporting Inc ... 983		•	•	•	•
•		•	•	•	Source ... 1820		•	•	•	

RHEA

CV	CR	PR			UC	RE	TX	VR
•		•	Real Estate Loan Services ... 1657		•	•	•	
•		•	Title Guaranty and Trust of Chattanooga ... 1953		•	•	•	

ROANE

CV	CR	PR			UC	RE	TX	VR
•	•	•	Clue Detective Service ... 479		•	•	•	•
•	•	•	Greater Tennessee Title Co ... 871		•	•	•	•
•	•	•	Source ... 1820		•	•	•	

ROBERTSON

CV	CR	PR			UC	RE	TX	VR
•	•	•	Capitol Filing Service Inc ... 395		•	•	•	
•	•	•	Hollingsworth Court Reporting Inc ... 983		•	•	•	•
•	•	•	The Search Is On ... 1942		•	•	•	•
•	•	•	Wells Fargo Investigative Services ... 2076		•	•	•	

RUTHERFORD

CV	CR	PR			UC	RE	TX	VR
•	•	•	Annie Perry Enterprises ... 154		•	•	•	
•	•	•	Capitol Filing Service Inc ... 395		•	•	•	
•	•	•	Hollingsworth Court Reporting Inc ... 983		•	•	•	•
•	•	•	The Search Is On ... 1942		•	•	•	•
•	•	•	Wells Fargo Investigative Services ... 2076		•	•	•	•

SCOTT

CV	CR	PR			UC	RE	TX	VR
•	•	•	Arms, Joan ... 160		•	•	•	•

SEQUATCHIE

CV	CR	PR			UC	RE	TX	VR
•		•	Real Estate Loan Services ... 1657		•	•	•	
•		•	Title Guaranty and Trust of Chattanooga ... 1953		•	•	•	•

SEVIER

CV	CR	PR			UC	RE	TX	VR
•	•	•	Clue Detective Service ... 479		•	•	•	•
•	•	•	Harris, Eileen ... 929		•	•	•	

SHELBY

DT	BK	CV	CR	PR			UC	RE	TX	VR
•	•	•	•	•	Guardsmark ... 897		•	•	•	•
	•	•	•	•	Hollingsworth Court Reporting Inc ... 983		•	•	•	•
•	•	•	•	•	Investigative Services for Attorneys ... 1049		•	•	•	•
•	•	•	•	•	Record-Check Services Inc ... 1663		•	•	•	•
•	•	•	•	•	RecordServe/John Kelley Enterprises ... 1664		•	•	•	•
•		•	•	•	Schaeffer Papers ... 1743			•		

SMITH

CV	CR	PR			UC	RE	TX	VR
•	•	•	Hollingsworth Court Reporting Inc ... 983		•	•	•	•
•	•	•	Source ... 1820		•	•	•	

STEWART

CV	CR	PR			UC	RE	TX	VR
•	•	•	D.K. Abstract ... 581		•	•	•	
•	•	•	Hollingsworth Court Reporting Inc ... 983		•	•	•	•

SULLIVAN

CV	CR	PR			UC	RE	TX	VR
•	•	•	Clue Detective Service ... 479		•	•	•	•

CV	CR	PR		UC	RE	TX	VR
•	•	•	Simerly, Teresa 1805	•	•	•	•

CV	CR	PR	SUMNER	UC	RE	TX	VR
•	•	•	Capitol Filing Service Inc 395	•	•	•	
•	•	•	Hollingsworth Court Reporting Inc 983	•	•	•	•
•	•	•	The Search Is On 1942	•	•	•	•
•	•	•	Wells Fargo Investigative Services 2076	•	•	•	•

CV	CR	PR	TIPTON	UC	RE	TX	VR
•	•	•	D.K. Abstract 581	•	•	•	
•	•	•	Hollingsworth Court Reporting Inc 983	•	•	•	•
•	•	•	Investigative Services for Attorneys 1049	•	•	•	•
•	•	•	Record-Check Services Inc 1663	•	•	•	•
•	•	•	RecordServe/John Kelley Enterprises 1664	•	•	•	
•	•	•	Schaeffer Papers 1743	•			

CV	CR	PR	TROUSDALE	UC	RE	TX	VR
•	•	•	Capitol Filing Service Inc 395	•	•	•	
•	•	•	Hollingsworth Court Reporting Inc 983	•	•	•	•

CV	CR	PR	UNICOI	UC	RE	TX	VR
•	•	•	Simerly, Teresa 1805	•	•	•	•

CV	CR	PR	UNION	UC	RE	TX	VR
•	•	•	Clue Detective Service 479	•	•	•	•

CV	CR	PR	VAN BUREN	UC	RE	TX	VR
•	•	•	Hollingsworth Court Reporting Inc 983	•	•	•	•
•		•	Title Guaranty and Trust of Chattanooga 1953	•	•	•	

CV	CR	PR	WARREN	UC	RE	TX	VR
•	•	•	Hollingsworth Court Reporting Inc 983	•	•	•	•

CV	CR	PR	WASHINGTON	UC	RE	TX	VR
•	•	•	Clue Detective Service 479	•	•	•	•
•	•	•	Simerly, Teresa 1805	•	•	•	•

CV	CR	PR	WAYNE	UC	RE	TX	VR
•	•	•	D.K. Abstract 581	•	•	•	
•	•	•	Hollingsworth Court Reporting Inc 983	•	•	•	•
•	•	•	Larry R Dorning PC 1174	•	•	•	•

CV	CR	PR	WEAKLEY	UC	RE	TX	VR
•	•	•	D.K. Abstract 581	•	•	•	
•	•		Lattus, Helen 1178	•	•	•	

CV	CR	PR	WHITE	UC	RE	TX	VR
•	•	•	Hollingsworth Court Reporting Inc 983	•	•	•	•
•	•	•	Source 1820	•	•	•	

CV	CR	PR	WILLIAMSON	UC	RE	TX	VR
•	•	•	Capitol Filing Service Inc 395	•	•	•	
•	•	•	Hollingsworth Court Reporting Inc 983	•	•	•	•
•	•	•	The Search Is On 1942	•	•	•	•

CV	CR	PR	WILSON	UC	RE	TX	VR
•	•	•	Capitol Filing Service Inc 395	•	•	•	
•	•	•	Clue Detective Service 479	•	•	•	•
•	•	•	Hollingsworth Court Reporting Inc 983	•	•	•	•
•	•	•	The Search Is On 1942	•	•	•	•
•	•	•	Wells Fargo Investigative Services 2076	•	•	•	•

Court
Records

TEXAS
203

County
Records

Texas

DT	BK	CV	CR	PR	ALL COUNTIES		UC	RE	TX	VR
	●				Bankruptcy Bulletin Weekly Inc..............240					
●	●				Bankruptcy Services Inc..............241					

		CV	CR	PR	ANDERSON		UC	RE	TX	VR
		●	●	●	Anderson County Abstract Co 147		●	●	●	●
		●	●	●	Brubaker & Associates 355		●	●	●	●
		●	●	●	Search Enterprises 1755		●	●	●	●

		CV	CR	PR	ANDREWS		UC	RE	TX	VR
		●	●	●	APROTEX 32		●	●	●	●
		●		●	Andrews Abstract Co 151		●	●	●	

		CV	CR	PR	ANGELINA		UC	RE	TX	VR
		●	●	●	US Legal Support-Houston 2001		●	●	●	●

		CV	CR	PR	ARANSAS		UC	RE	TX	VR
		●	●	●	Brack Warren & Associates 336		●	●	●	●
		●	●	●	John Bullock & Co 1089		●	●	●	●
		●	●	●	Professional Civil Process 1612		●	●	●	●
		●	●	●	Shawver and Associates 1793		●	●	●	●
		●	●	●	Texas Civil Process 1914		●	●	●	●
		●	●	●	Texas Legal Support Service 1917		●	●	●	●

		CV	CR	PR	ARCHER		UC	RE	TX	VR
		●	●	●	Civil Process Service 463					
		●	●	●	Superior Process Service 1886		●	●	●	

		CV	CR	PR	ARMSTRONG		UC	RE	TX	VR
		●	●	●	Rollins, Jan 1711		●	●	●	●
		●	●	●	Security Abstract Co of Claude 1766		●	●	●	●

		CV	CR	PR	ATASCOSA		UC	RE	TX	VR
		●	●	●	AKA Investigations & Process San Antonio 26		●	●	●	●
		●	●	●	Fred Meyers Company 808		●	●	●	●
		●	●	●	Professional Civil Process 1614		●	●	●	●
		●	●	●	Property Research and Documentation 1625		●	●	●	●

		CV	CR	PR	AUSTIN		UC	RE	TX	VR
		●	●	●	US Legal Support-Houston 2001		●	●	●	●

		CV	CR	PR	BAILEY		UC	RE	TX	VR
		●	●	●	Farwell Abstract Co Inc 744		●	●	●	
		●		●	Texas Abstract Services 1913		●	●		●

		CV	CR	PR	BANDERA		UC	RE	TX	VR
		●	●	●	AKA Investigations & Process San Antonio 26		●	●	●	●
		●	●	●	Fred Meyers Company 808		●	●	●	●

		CV	CR	PR	BASTROP		UC	RE	TX	VR
		●	●	●	AKA Investigations & Process of Austin 27		●	●	●	●
		●	●	●	Assured Civil Process Agency Inc 175			●		
		●	●		CPS (Capital Process Service) 378				●	
		●	●	●	Tyler-McLennon Inc 1995		●	●	●	

		CV	CR	PR	BAYLOR		UC	RE	TX	VR
		●	●	●	Civil Process Service 463					
		●	●	●	Superior Process Service 1886		●	●	●	

		CV	CR	PR	BEE		UC	RE	TX	VR
		●	●	●	Jan L Jackson Investigation 1077		●	●	●	●
		●	●	●	Professional Civil Process 1612		●	●	●	●

DT	BK	CV	CR	PR	Name	Page	UC	RE	TX	VR
		•	•	•	Shawver and Associates	1793	•	•	•	•

BELL

CV	CR	PR	Name	Page	UC	RE	TX	VR
•	•		CPS (Capital Process Service)	378			•	
•	•	•	Search Enterprises	1755	•	•	•	•
•	•	•	Shaw Title & Public Record Search	1791	•	•	•	
•	•	•	Texas Information Services	1916	•	•		•
•	•	•	Tyler-McLennon Inc	1995	•	•	•	

BEXAR

DT	BK	CV	CR	PR	Name	Page	UC	RE	TX	VR
		•	•	•	AKA Investigations & Process San Antonio	26	•	•	•	•
			•	•	Bexar Professional	296	•	•	•	•
•	•	•	•	•	Fred Meyers Company	808	•	•	•	
•		•	•	•	Inform	1026	•	•	•	
•		•	•	•	Intranet Inc	1044	•	•	•	•
•		•	•	•	Professional Civil Process	1614	•	•	•	•
•		•	•	•	Professional Civil Process	1615	•	•	•	•
•		•	•	•	Property Research and Documentation	1625	•	•	•	•
•		•	•	•	Texas Industrial Security Inc	1915	•	•	•	
		•	•	•	The Cole Group	1923	•	•	•	•
•	•	•	•	•	Tyler-McLennon Inc	1995	•	•	•	

BLANCO

CV	CR	PR	Name	Page	UC	RE	TX	VR
•	•	•	AKA Investigations & Process of Austin	27	•	•	•	•
•	•	•	Property Research and Documentation	1625	•	•	•	•

BORDEN

CV	CR	PR	Name	Page	UC	RE	TX	VR
•	•	•	APROTEX	32	•	•	•	•

BOSQUE

CV	CR	PR	Name	Page	UC	RE	TX	VR
•	•	•	Bosque Cen-Tex Title Inc	329	•	•	•	•
•	•	•	Search Enterprises	1755	•	•	•	•

BOWIE

DT	CV	CR	PR	Name	Page	UC	RE	TX	VR
•	•	•	•	Brubaker & Associates	355	•	•	•	•
			•	Twin City Title Co Inc	1994	•	•	•	

BRAZORIA

CV	CR	PR	Name	Page	UC	RE	TX	VR
•	•	•	LawServ Inc	1179	•	•	•	•
•	•	•	Legal Ease Court Service	1201	•	•	•	•
•	•		Research Staff	1687	•	•	•	
		•	Texas Abstract Services	1913	•	•	•	
	•	•	Texas Records Search	1918	•	•	•	•
	•	•	The Information Bank of Texas	1935	•	•	•	•
•	•	•	US Legal Support-Houston	2001	•	•	•	•
•	•	•	W T Smith and Associates	2038	•	•	•	
•	•	•	Walters & Associates	2051	•	•	•	•

BRAZOS

CV	CR	PR	Name	Page	UC	RE	TX	VR
•	•	•	Research Staff	1687	•	•	•	•
•	•	•	Search Enterprises	1755	•	•	•	•
•	•	•	The Court System	1926	•	•	•	•

BREWSTER

CV	CR	PR	Name	Page	UC	RE	TX	VR
•	•	•	Ellyson Abstract & Title Co of Brewster	709	•	•	•	•

BRISCOE

CV	CR	PR	Name	Page	UC	RE	TX	VR
•	•	•	Guaranty Abstract Co	888	•	•	•	

BROOKS

CV	CR	PR	Name	Page	UC	RE	TX	VR
			Border Abstract	326	•	•	•	
•	•	•	PI Unlimited	1491	•	•	•	•
•	•	•	Professional Civil Process	1612	•	•	•	•

DT	CV	CR	PR		#	UC	RE	TX	VR
	•	•	•	Shawver and Associates	1793	•	•	•	•
	•	•	•	Texas Civil Process	1914	•	•	•	•

BROWN

	CV	CR	PR		#	UC	RE	TX	VR
	•	•	•	Adams, Tommy M.	81	•	•	•	•
	•		•	Brown County Abstract Co	351	•	•	•	
	•	•	•	Burl Brown Land Title Company	366	•	•	•	

BURLESON

	CV	CR	PR		#	UC	RE	TX	VR
	•	•	•	Attorneys Title & Abstract Co	210	•	•	•	•

BURNET

	CV	CR	PR		#	UC	RE	TX	VR
	•	•	•	AKA Investigations & Process of Austin	27	•	•	•	•
	•	•	•	Assured Civil Process Agency Inc	175		•		
	•	•	•	Tyler-McLennon Inc	1995	•	•	•	

CALDWELL

	CV	CR	PR		#	UC	RE	TX	VR
	•	•	•	AKA Investigations & Process of Austin	27	•	•	•	•
	•	•	•	Assured Civil Process Agency Inc	175		•		
	•	•	•	Property Research and Documentation	1625	•	•	•	•
	•	•	•	Tyler-McLennon Inc	1995	•	•	•	

CALHOUN

	CV	CR	PR		#	UC	RE	TX	VR
	•		•	Bedgood Abstract & Title Co	275	•	•	•	•
	•	•	•	Jan L Jackson Investigation	1077	•	•	•	•
	•	•	•	Professional Civil Process	1612	•	•	•	•

CALLAHAN

	CV	CR	PR		#	UC	RE	TX	VR
	•		•	Russell-Surles Title Inc	1720	•	•	•	

CAMERON

DT	CV	CR	PR		#	UC	RE	TX	VR
•	•	•	•	Professional Civil Process	1613	•	•	•	•
•	•	•	•	Professional Civil Process	1615	•	•	•	•
•	•	•	•	Shawver and Associates	1793	•	•	•	•
•	•	•	•	Tyler-McLennon Inc	1995	•	•	•	

CAMP

	CV	CR	PR		#	UC	RE	TX	VR
	•	•	•	Brubaker & Associates	355	•	•	•	
	•		•	Camp County Land Abstract Co	385	•	•		•

CARSON

	CV	CR	PR		#	UC	RE	TX	VR
	•	•	•	Credit Bureau Services of the Panhandle	557	•	•	•	•
	•	•	•	Rollins, Jan	1711	•	•	•	•

CASS

	CV	CR	PR		#	UC	RE	TX	VR
	•	•	•	Brubaker & Associates	355	•	•	•	•
	•		•	DeSoto Abstract	609	•	•	•	

CASTRO

	CV	CR	PR		#	UC	RE	TX	VR
	•	•	•	Rollins, Jan	1711	•	•	•	•

CHAMBERS

	CV	CR	PR		#	UC	RE	TX	VR
	•	•	•	Research Staff	1687	•	•	•	•
	•	•	•	Texas Records Search	1918	•	•	•	•
	•	•	•	US Legal Support-Houston	2001	•	•	•	•

CHEROKEE

	CV	CR	PR		#	UC	RE	TX	VR
	•	•	•	Brubaker & Associates	355	•	•	•	•
	•	•	•	Cherokee County Title Co	447	•	•	•	•

CHILDRESS

	CV	CR	PR		#	UC	RE	TX	VR
	•		•	H S Black	904	•	•	•	•

	CV	CR	PR	CLAY	UC	RE	TX	VR
	●	●	●	Superior Process Service..1886	●	●	●	

	CV	CR	PR	COCHRAN	UC	RE	TX	VR
				See adjoining counties..				

	CV	CR	PR	COKE	UC	RE	TX	VR
	●	●	●	Coke County Abstract Co....................................484	●	●	●	●

	CV	CR	PR	COLEMAN	UC	RE	TX	VR
	●		●	Coleman Abstract Co 486	●	●	●	●
	●	●	●	Coleman County Title Co...................................487	●	●	●	●

BK	CV	CR	PR	COLLIN	UC	RE	TX	VR
●	●	●	●	AKA Investigations & Process of Dallas 28	●	●	●	●
				Brubaker & Associates...355				
●	●	●	●	Charles L Lager Private Investigations.....................439	●	●	●	●
●	●	●	●	Disheroon Title Consultant 636	●	●	●	●
●	●	●	●	Ed Waynick and Associates 690		●	●	●
●	●	●	●	FYI Services..730	●	●	●	●
●	●	●	●	Investigative Associates Inc 1046	●	●	●	●
●				Ricochet 1698		●		
●		●	●	Security Information Service................................1773	●	●	●	●
●		●	●	Texas Information Services..................................1916	●	●	●	●
●		●	●	The Court System..1926	●	●	●	●
●		●	●	Tyler-McLennon Inc 1995	●	●	●	

	CV	CR	PR	COLLINGSWORTH	UC	RE	TX	VR
				See adjoining counties..				

	CV	CR	PR	COLORADO	UC	RE	TX	VR
	●	●	●	Colorado County Abstract Co................................493	●	●	●	●

	CV	CR	PR	COMAL	UC	RE	TX	VR
	●	●	●	AKA Investigations & Process San Antonio.................26	●	●	●	●
		●	●	Bexar Professional 296	●	●	●	●
	●		●	Fred Meyers Company 808	●	●	●	●
	●		●	Professional Civil Process...................................1614	●	●	●	●
	●		●	Tyler-McLennon Inc 1995	●	●	●	

	CV	CR	PR	COMANCHE	UC	RE	TX	VR
	●	●	●	Adams, Tommy M...81	●	●	●	●
	●	●	●	Comanche County Abstract Co...............................502	●	●	●	●

	CV	CR	PR	CONCHO	UC	RE	TX	VR
	●	●	●	Surety Title Co of Eden.....................................1891	●	●	●	●

	CV	CR	PR	COOKE	UC	RE	TX	VR
	●	●	●	Disheroon Title Consultant 636	●	●	●	●

	CV	CR	PR	CORYELL	UC	RE	TX	VR
	●		●	American Abstract and Title Co Inc........................127	●	●	●	●
	●	●	●	Search Enterprises..1755	●	●	●	●
	●	●	●	Shaw Title & Public Record Search........................1791	●	●	●	●
	●	●	●	Tyler-McLennon Inc 1995	●	●	●	

	CV	CR	PR	COTTLE	UC	RE	TX	VR
	●	●	●	Jones & Renfrow Abstract Co...............................1099	●	●	●	●

	CV	CR	PR	CRANE	UC	RE	TX	VR
	●	●	●	APROTEX 32	●	●	●	●
	●	●	●	Crane County Abstract..550	●	●	●	●

CROCKETT

CV	CR	PR		UC	RE	TX	VR
●	●	●	Crockett County Abstract Co 566	●	●	●	●

CROSBY

CV	CR	PR		UC	RE	TX	VR
●	●	●	Robinson Agency 1706	●	●	●	●

CULBERSON

CV	CR	PR		UC	RE	TX	VR
●		●	Advance Title Co 86		●		

DALLAM

CV	CR	PR		UC	RE	TX	VR
●	●	●	Hunter & Oelke 1003	●	●	●	●

DALLAS

DT	BK	CV	CR	PR		UC	RE	TX	VR
●	●	●	●	●	AKA Investigations & Process of Dallas 28	●	●	●	●
●	●	●	●	●	Brubaker & Associates 355	●	●	●	●
●	●	●			Capitol Services Inc 402	●			
●	●	●	●	●	Charles L Lager Private Investigations 439	●	●	●	●
●	●	●	●	●	Civil Process Service 462	●	●	●	●
●	●	●	●	●	Disheroon Title Consultant 636	●	●	●	●
●	●	●	●	●	Ed Waynick and Associates 690		●	●	●
●	●	●	●	●	FYI Services 730	●	●	●	●
●	●	●	●	●	Intelnet Inc 1035	●	●	●	●
●	●	●	●	●	Investigative Associates Inc 1046	●	●	●	●
●	●	●	●	●	Litigant Services Inc of Dallas 1232	●	●	●	●
					Police Report Acquisition Service 1565				
					Prentice Hall Legal & Financial Services 1595	●			
●	●	●	●	●	Professional Civil Process 1615	●	●	●	●
●	●	●	●	●	Reliable Courier 1676		●	●	●
●	●				Ricochet 1698		●		
		●	●	●	Security Information Service 1773	●	●	●	●
●	●	●	●	●	Texas Industrial Security Inc 1915	●	●	●	●
●	●	●	●	●	Texas Information Services 1916	●	●	●	●
		●	●	●	The Cole Group 1923	●	●	●	●
●	●	●	●	●	The Court System 1926	●	●	●	●
●	●	●	●	●	The Information Bank of Texas 1935	●	●		●
●	●	●	●	●	Tyler-McLennon Inc 1995	●	●	●	

DAWSON

CV	CR	PR		UC	RE	TX	VR
●	●	●	APROTEX 32	●	●	●	●
			South Plain Abstract Co 1822	●	●	●	

DEAF SMITH

CV	CR	PR		UC	RE	TX	VR
●	●	●	Rollins, Jan 1711	●	●	●	●

DELTA

CV	CR	PR		UC	RE	TX	VR
●	●	●	Brubaker & Associates 355	●	●	●	●
●	●	●	Delta County Title Co 620	●	●	●	●
●	●	●	The Court System 1926	●	●	●	●

DENTON

CV	CR	PR		UC	RE	TX	VR
●	●	●	AKA Investigations & Process of Dallas 28	●	●	●	●
●	●	●	Brubaker & Associates 355	●	●	●	●
●	●	●	Charles L Lager Private Investigations 439	●	●	●	●
●	●	●	Disheroon Title Consultant 636	●	●	●	●
●	●	●	Ed Waynick and Associates 690		●	●	●
●	●	●	FYI Services 730	●	●	●	
●	●	●	Investigative Associates Inc 1046	●	●	●	●
●	●	●	Professional Civil Process 1615	●	●	●	●
●	●	●	Proffer, Janie 1624	●	●	●	●
			Ricochet 1698		●		
●	●	●	Security Information Service 1773	●	●	●	●
●	●	●	Texas Information Services 1916	●	●	●	●

•	•	•	The Court System..1926	•	•	•	•
•	•	•	Tyler-McLennon Inc..1995	•	•	•	

CV	CR	PR	DE WITT	UC	RE	TX	VR
•	•	•	Jan L Jackson Investigation.............................1077	•	•	•	•

CV	CR	PR	DICKENS	UC	RE	TX	VR
•		•	Caprock Title Co...404	•	•	•	

CV	CR	PR	DIMMIT	UC	RE	TX	VR
•	•	•	Elliott & Waldron Abstract Co of Dimmitt.........705	•	•	•	•

CV	CR	PR	DONLEY	UC	RE	TX	VR
•	•	•	Security Abstract Co of Clarendon....................1765	•	•	•	•

CV	CR	PR	DUVAL	UC	RE	TX	VR
•	•	•	PI Unlimited..1491	•	•	•	•
•	•	•	Professional Civil Process.................................1612	•	•	•	•
•	•	•	Shawver and Associates....................................1793	•	•	•	•
•	•	•	Texas Civil Process..1914	•	•	•	•

CV	CR	PR	EASTLAND	UC	RE	TX	VR
•	•	•	Lone Star Title & Abstract Co..........................1237	•	•	•	

CV	CR	PR	ECTOR	UC	RE	TX	VR
•	•	•	APROTEX..32	•	•	•	•
•	•		Basin Attorney Services....................................257				
•	•		Permian Court Reporters Inc............................1540				
•	•	•	Tyler-McLennon Inc..1995	•	•	•	

CV	CR	PR	EDWARDS	UC	RE	TX	VR
•		•	White Abstract & Title Co 2085	•	•	•	•

CV	CR	PR	ELLIS	UC	RE	TX	VR
•	•	•	Brubaker & Associates......................................355	•	•	•	•
•	•	•	Charles L Lager Private Investigations..............439	•	•	•	•
•	•	•	FYI Services..730	•	•	•	
•	•	•	Investigative Associates Inc.............................1046	•	•	•	•
•	•	•	Reliable Courier...1676			•	•
			Ricochet...1698		•		
•	•	•	Search Enterprises..1755	•	•		•
•	•	•	Security Information Service..............................1773	•	•		•
•	•	•	The Court System..1926	•	•	•	•
•	•	•	Tyler-McLennon Inc..1995	•	•	•	

DT	BK	CV	CR	PR	EL PASO	UC	RE	TX	VR
•	•	•	•	•	Legal Net Process Service................................1205	•	•	•	•
•	•	•	•	•	Litigant Services Inc of El Paso 1233	•	•	•	•
•	•	•	•	•	Tyler-McLennon Inc..1995	•	•	•	

CV	CR	PR	ERATH	UC	RE	TX	VR
•	•	•	Tyler-McLennon Inc..1995	•	•	•	

CV	CR	PR	FALLS	UC	RE	TX	VR
•	•	•	Falls County Abstract Co 740	•	•	•	•
•		•	Guaranty Abstract Co.......................................889	•	•	•	•
•	•	•	Search Enterprises..1755	•	•	•	•

CV	CR	PR	FANNIN	UC	RE	TX	VR
•	•	•	Tyler-McLennon Inc..1995	•	•	•	

CV	CR	PR	FAYETTE	UC	RE	TX	VR
•	•	•	Clear Title Co..473	•	•	•	•

FISHER

CV	CR	PR			UC	RE	TX	VR
•	•	•	Fisher County Abstract Co	779	•	•	•	•

FLOYD

CV	CR	PR			UC	RE	TX	VR
•	•	•	Robinson Agency	1706	•	•	•	•

FOARD

CV	CR	PR			UC	RE	TX	VR
•	•	•	Civil Process Service	463				
•	•	•	Superior Process Service	1886	•	•	•	

FORT BEND

CV	CR	PR			UC	RE	TX	VR
•	•	•	Court Record Research	546	•	•	•	
•	•	•	LawServ Inc	1179	•	•	•	
•	•		M.R.S. Datascope Inc	1256				
•		•	Professional Civil Process	1615	•	•	•	
•	•	•	Research Staff	1687	•	•	•	
•	•	•	Southwest Patrol & Investigations	1836	•	•	•	
•		•	Texas Abstract Services	1913	•	•	•	
•	•	•	Texas Records Search	1918	•	•	•	
•	•	•	The Information Bank of Texas	1935	•	•	•	
•	•	•	Tyler-McLennon Inc	1995	•	•	•	
•	•	•	US Legal Support-Houston	2001	•	•	•	•
•	•	•	W T Smith and Associates	2038	•	•	•	
•	•	•	Walters & Associates	2051	•	•	•	•

FRANKLIN

CV	CR	PR			UC	RE	TX	VR
•	•	•	Brubaker & Associates	355	•	•	•	•
•	•	•	Franklin County Abstract Co	805	•	•	•	•

FREESTONE

CV	CR	PR			UC	RE	TX	VR
•	•	•	Search Enterprises	1755	•	•	•	•

FRIO

CV	CR	PR			UC	RE	TX	VR
•	•	•	Professional Civil Process	1614	•	•	•	•

GAINES

CV	CR	PR			UC	RE	TX	VR
•		•	Gaines County Abstract Co	827		•	•	•

GALVESTON

DT	CV	CR	PR			UC	RE	TX	VR
•	•	•	•	Court Record Research	546	•	•	•	•
•	•	•	•	LawServ Inc	1179	•	•	•	•
•	•	•	•	Legal Ease Court Service	1201	•	•	•	•
	•	•		M.R.S. Datascope Inc	1256				•
•	•	•	•	Research Staff	1687	•	•	•	
•	•		•	Texas Abstract Services	1913	•	•		
•	•	•	•	Texas Records Search	1918	•	•	•	
•	•	•	•	The Information Bank of Texas	1935	•	•	•	
•	•	•	•	Tyler-McLennon Inc	1995	•	•	•	
•	•	•	•	Walters & Associates	2051	•	•	•	•

GARZA

CV	CR	PR			UC	RE	TX	VR
•	•	•	Pollard & Lott Inc	1567	•	•	•	•

GILLESPIE

CV	CR	PR			UC	RE	TX	VR
•	•	•	Fredericksburg Title Inc	811	•	•	•	

GLASSCOCK

CV	CR	PR			UC	RE	TX	VR
•	•	•	APROTEX	32	•	•	•	•
•		•	Elliott & Waldron Abstr Co of Glasscock	702	•	•	•	•

GOLIAD

CV	CR	PR			UC	RE	TX	VR
•		•	Bedgood Abstract & Title Co	273	•	•	•	
•	•	•	Jan L Jackson Investigation	1077	•	•	•	•

DT	BK	CV	CR	PR		UC	RE	TX	VR
		CV	CR	PR	**GONZALES**	UC	RE	TX	VR
		•	•	•	Property Research and Documentation 1625	•	•	•	•
		CV	CR	PR	**GRAY**	UC	RE	TX	VR
		•		•	Caprock Land Title Company 403	•	•	•	
		•	•	•	Credit Bureau Services of the Panhandle 557	•	•	•	•
		•	•	•	Rollins, Jan...1711	•	•	•	•
DT		CV	CR	PR	**GRAYSON**	UC	RE	TX	VR
•		•	•	•	The Court System...1926	•	•	•	•
		CV	CR	PR	**GREGG**	UC	RE	TX	VR
		•	•	•	Brubaker & Associates...355	•	•	•	•
		•	•	•	Intelnet Inc 1035	•	•	•	•
		CV	CR	PR	**GRIMES**	UC	RE	TX	VR
		•		•	Guaranty Title Co of Grimes County 895	•	•	•	
		•	•	•	US Legal Support-Houston..2001	•	•	•	•
		CV	CR	PR	**GUADALUPE**	UC	RE	TX	VR
		•	•	•	AKA Investigations & Process San Antonio........................26	•	•	•	•
		•	•	•	Fred Meyers Company 808	•	•	•	•
		•	•	•	Tyler-McLennon Inc 1995	•	•	•	
		CV	CR	PR	**HALE**	UC	RE	TX	VR
		•	•	•	Robinson Agency...1706	•	•	•	•
		•	•	•	Rollins, Jan...1711	•	•	•	•
		CV	CR	PR	**HALL**	UC	RE	TX	VR
		•	•	•	Security Abstract Co of Memphis.................................1767	•	•	•	•
		CV	CR	PR	**HAMILTON**	UC	RE	TX	VR
		•	•	•	Adams, Tommy M...81	•	•	•	•
		CV	CR	PR	**HANSFORD**	UC	RE	TX	VR
					See adjoining counties..				
		CV	CR	PR	**HARDEMAN**	UC	RE	TX	VR
		•	•	•	Civil Process Service..463				
		•	•	•	Superior Process Service 1886	•	•	•	
		CV	CR	PR	**HARDIN**	UC	RE	TX	VR
		•	•	•	US Legal Support-Houston..2001	•	•	•	•
DT	BK	CV	CR	PR	**HARRIS**	UC	RE	TX	VR
•	•	•			Capitol Services Inc 402	•			
•	•	•	•	•	Court Record Research...546	•	•	•	•
•	•	•	•	•	Houston Court Services...997	•	•	•	•
•	•	•	•	•	Intelnet Inc 1035	•	•	•	•
•	•	•	•	•	Intranet Inc 1044	•	•	•	•
•	•	•	•	•	LawServ Inc 1179	•	•	•	•
•	•	•	•	•	Legal Ease Court Service 1201	•	•	•	•
		•	•		M.R.S. Datascope Inc...1256				•
					Police Report Acquisition Service 1565				
•	•	•	•	•	Professional Civil Process...1615	•	•	•	•
•	•	•	•	•	Research Staff 1687	•	•	•	•
•	•	•	•	•	Southwest Patrol & Investigations 1836	•	•	•	
		•	•	•	Texas Abstract Services 1913	•	•		•
•	•	•	•	•	Texas Records Search 1918	•	•	•	•
		•	•	•	The Cole Group..1923	•	•	•	•
•	•	•	•	•	The Information Bank of Texas.....................................1935	•	•	•	•
•	•	•	•	•	Tyler-McLennon Inc 1995	•	•	•	
•	•	•	•	•	US Legal Support-Houston..2001	•	•	•	•

DT		CV	CR	PR			UC	RE	TX	VR
•	•	•	•	•	W T Smith and Associates	2038	•	•	•	
•	•	•	•	•	Walters & Associates	2051	•	•	•	•

DT		CV	CR	PR	HARRISON		UC	RE	TX	VR
		•		•	DeSoto Abstract	609	•	•		
		•	•	•	Jones, Patsy	1103	•	•	•	•
•		•	•	•	The Court System	1926	•	•	•	•

		CV	CR	PR	HARTLEY		UC	RE	TX	VR
		•	•	•	Hunter & Oelke	1003	•			•

		CV	CR	PR	HASKELL		UC	RE	TX	VR
		•	•	•	Civil Process Service	463				
		•	•	•	Haskell Abstract & TItle Co	935	•	•	•	•
		•	•	•	Superior Process Service	1886	•	•	•	

		CV	CR	PR	HAYS		UC	RE	TX	VR
		•	•	•	AKA Investigations & Process of Austin	27	•	•	•	•
		•	•	•	Assured Civil Process Agency Inc	175		•		
		•	•		CPS (Capital Process Service)	378			•	
		•	•	•	John C Dunaway and Associates	1090	•	•	•	•
		•	•	•	Professional Civil Process	1614	•	•	•	•
		•	•	•	Property Research and Documentation	1625	•	•	•	•
		•	•	•	Texas Information Services	1916	•	•	•	•
		•	•	•	Tyler-McLennon Inc	1995	•	•	•	

		CV	CR	PR	HEMPHILL		UC	RE	TX	VR
		•	•	•	Credit Bureau Services of the Panhandle	557	•	•	•	•

		CV	CR	PR	HENDERSON		UC	RE	TX	VR
		•	•	•	Brubaker & Associates	355	•	•	•	•
		•		•	DeSoto Abstract	609	•	•	•	
		•	•		Search Enterprises	1755	•	•	•	
		•	•	•	The Court System	1926	•	•	•	•

DT		CV	CR	PR	HIDALGO		UC	RE	TX	VR
•		•	•	•	Professional Civil Process	1613	•	•	•	•
•		•	•	•	Professional Civil Process	1615	•	•	•	•
•		•	•	•	Property Research and Documentation	1625	•	•	•	•
•		•	•	•	Shawver and Associates	1793	•	•	•	•

		CV	CR	PR	HILL		UC	RE	TX	VR
		•	•	•	Eastland Title Co	686	•	•	•	•
		•	•	•	Search Enterprises	1755	•	•	•	•

		CV	CR	PR	HOCKLEY		UC	RE	TX	VR
		•	•	•	Robinson Agency	1706	•	•	•	•

		CV	CR	PR	HOOD		UC	RE	TX	VR
		•	•	•	Tyler-McLennon Inc	1995	•	•	•	

		CV	CR	PR	HOPKINS		UC	RE	TX	VR
		•	•	•	Brubaker & Associates	355	•	•	•	•
		•	•	•	The Court System	1926	•	•	•	•

		CV	CR	PR	HOUSTON		UC	RE	TX	VR
		•		•	Aldrich Abstract Company	103	•	•		

		CV	CR	PR	HOWARD		UC	RE	TX	VR
		•	•	•	APROTEX	32	•	•	•	•
		•	•	•	Big Spring Abstract & Title Co Inc	299	•	•	•	•

		CV	CR	PR	HUDSPETH		UC	RE	TX	VR
		•	•	•	Legal Net Process Service	1205	•	•	•	•

	CV	CR	PR	HUNT		UC	RE	TX	VR
	●	●	●	Brubaker & Associates.................................355		●	●	●	●
	●	●	●	Charles L Lager Private Investigations..............439		●	●	●	●
	●	●	●	Security Information Service........................1773		●	●	●	●
	●	●	●	Tyler-McLennon Inc..................................1995		●	●	●	

	CV	CR	PR	HUTCHINSON		UC	RE	TX	VR
	●	●	●	Rollins, Jan...1711		●	●	●	●

	CV	CR	PR	IRION		UC	RE	TX	VR
	●		●	Irion County Abstract Co Inc........................1055		●	●	●	●

	CV	CR	PR	JACK		UC	RE	TX	VR
	●	●	●	Superior Process Service.............................1886		●	●	●	

	CV	CR	PR	JACKSON		UC	RE	TX	VR
	●	●	●	Civil Process Service................................463					
	●	●	●	Jan L Jackson Investigation.........................1077		●	●	●	●

	CV	CR	PR	JASPER		UC	RE	TX	VR
	●	●	●	US Legal Support-Houston.............................2001		●	●	●	●

	CV	CR	PR	JEFF DAVIS		UC	RE	TX	VR
	●		●	Jeff Davis County Abstract Co.......................1084		●	●	●	

DT	CV	CR	PR	JEFFERSON		UC	RE	TX	VR
●	●	●	●	Intranet Inc..1044		●	●	●	●
●	●	●	●	LawServ Inc...1179		●	●	●	●
	●	●		M.R.S. Datascope Inc................................1256					●
●	●	●	●	Texas Records Search................................1918		●	●	●	●
	●	●	●	The Cole Group......................................1923		●	●	●	●
●	●	●	●	US Legal Support-Houston............................2001		●	●	●	●
●	●	●	●	W T Smith and Associates............................2038		●	●	●	

	CV	CR	PR	JIM HOGG		UC	RE	TX	VR
			●	Border Abstract.....................................326		●	●	●	

	CV	CR	PR	JIM WELLS		UC	RE	TX	VR
	●	●	●	PI Unlimited..1491		●	●	●	●
	●	●	●	Professional Civil Process..........................1612			●	●	●
	●	●	●	Shawver and Associates..............................1793		●	●	●	●
	●	●	●	Texas Civil Process.................................1914		●	●	●	●
	●	●	●	Texas Legal Support Service.........................1917		●	●	●	●

	CV	CR	PR	JOHNSON		UC	RE	TX	VR
	●	●	●	Disheroon Title Consultant..........................636		●	●	●	●
	●	●	●	Search Enterprises..................................1755		●	●	●	●
	●	●	●	Security Information Service........................1773		●	●	●	●
	●	●	●	Tyler-McLennon Inc..................................1995		●	●	●	

	CV	CR	PR	JONES		UC	RE	TX	VR
	●	●	●	Jones County Abstract Co............................1102		●	●	●	●

	CV	CR	PR	KARNES		UC	RE	TX	VR
	●		●	Karnes Land Title Co Inc............................1113		●	●	●	●

	CV	CR	PR	KAUFMAN		UC	RE	TX	VR
	●	●	●	Brubaker & Associates...............................355		●	●	●	●
	●	●	●	Charles L Lager Private Investigations..............439		●	●	●	●
	●	●	●	Ed Waynick and Associates...........................690			●	●	●
	●	●	●	FYI Services..730		●	●	●	
	●	●	●	Investigative Associates Inc........................1046		●	●	●	●
	●	●	●	Security Information Service........................1773		●	●	●	●

Court
Records

TEXAS
213

County
Records

●	●	●	The Court System...1926	●	●	●	●
●	●	●	Tyler-McLennon Inc 1995	●	●	●	

CV	CR	PR	KENDALL	UC	RE	TX	VR
●	●	●	AKA Investigations & Process San Antonio.......26	●	●	●	●
	●	●	Bexar Professional 296	●	●	●	●
●	●	●	Fred Meyers Company 808	●	●	●	●
●	●	●	Professional Civil Process...................................1614	●	●	●	●

CV	CR	PR	KENEDY	UC	RE	TX	VR
●	●	●	Brack Warren & Associates 336	●	●	●	●
●	●	●	John Bullock & Co...1089	●	●	●	●

CV	CR	PR	KENT	UC	RE	TX	VR
●		●	Caprock Title Co...404	●	●	●	

CV	CR	PR	KERR	UC	RE	TX	VR
●	●	●	Professional Civil Process...................................1614	●	●	●	●
●	●	●	Property Research and Documentation 1625	●	●	●	●

CV	CR	PR	KIMBLE	UC	RE	TX	VR
●	●	●	Harrison, Lawrence 932	●	●	●	●

CV	CR	PR	KING	UC	RE	TX	VR
●		●	Caprock Title Co...404	●	●	●	
●	●	●	Jones & Renfrow Abstract Co.............................1099	●	●	●	●

CV	CR	PR	KINNEY	UC	RE	TX	VR
			See adjoining counties..				

CV	CR	PR	KLEBERG	UC	RE	TX	VR
●	●	●	Brack Warren & Associates 336	●	●	●	●
●	●	●	John Bullock & Co...1089	●	●	●	●
●	●	●	PI Unlimited...1491	●	●	●	●
●	●	●	Professional Civil Process...................................1612	●	●	●	●
●	●	●	Shawver and Associates 1793	●	●	●	●
●	●	●	Texas Civil Process 1914	●	●	●	●
●	●	●	Texas Legal Support Service..............................1917	●	●	●	●

CV	CR	PR	KNOX	UC	RE	TX	VR
●	●	●	Civil Process Service..463				
●	●	●	Superior Process Service...................................1886	●			

CV	CR	PR	LAMAR	UC	RE	TX	VR
●	●	●	The Court System...1926	●	●	●	●
●	●	●	Tyler-McLennon Inc 1995	●	●	●	

CV	CR	PR	LAMB	UC	RE	TX	VR
●	●	●	Robinson Agency..1706	●	●	●	●

CV	CR	PR	LAMPASAS	UC	RE	TX	VR
●	●	●	Adams, Tommy M...81	●	●	●	●
	●	●	CPS (Capital Process Service) 378			●	
●	●	●	Shaw Title & Public Record Search....................1791	●	●	●	

CV	CR	PR	LA SALLE	UC	RE	TX	VR
			Border Abstract 326	●	●	●	
●	●	●	LaSalle County Abstract Inc 1150	●	●	●	●

CV	CR	PR	LAVACA	UC	RE	TX	VR
●	●	●	Halletsville Abstract & Title Co..........................909	●	●	●	●

CV	CR	PR	LEE	UC	RE	TX	VR
●		●	Lee County Land & Abstract 1190	●	●	●	●

DT	BK	CV	CR	PR		UC	RE	TX	VR
					LEON				
		•		•	Guaranty Title Co of Leon County ... 896	•	•	•	•
					LIBERTY				
		•	•	•	Research Staff ... 1687	•	•	•	•
		•	•	•	Texas Records Search ... 1918	•	•	•	•
		•	•	•	US Legal Support-Houston ... 2001	•	•	•	•
					LIMESTONE				
		•	•	•	Groesbeck Abstract & Title Co ... 884	•	•	•	•
		•	•	•	Search Enterprises ... 1755	•	•	•	•
					LIPSCOMB				
		•	•	•	Credit Bureau Services of the Panhandle ... 557	•	•	•	
		•		•	Lipscomb County Abstract Co ... 1231	•	•	•	•
					LIVE OAK				
		•	•	•	Texas Civil Process ... 1914	•	•	•	•
					LLANO				
		•	•	•	AKA Investigations & Process of Austin ... 27	•	•	•	•
		•	•	•	AKA Investigations & Process of Dallas ... 28	•	•	•	•
		•	•		CPS (Capital Process Service) ... 378			•	
					LOVING				
		•		•	Advance Title Co ... 86	•			
					LUBBOCK				
•	•	•	•	•	Robinson Agency ... 1706	•	•	•	
•	•	•	•	•	Rollins, Jan ... 1711	•	•		•
•	•	•	•	•	Tyler-McLennon Inc ... 1995	•	•	•	
		•	•	•	US Legal Support of Lubbock ... 2000	•	•	•	•
					LYNN				
		•	•	•	Lynn County Abstract Co ... 1249	•	•	•	
					McCULLOCH				
		•	•	•	Jordan & McCulloch Abstracters Inc ... 1104		•	•	•
					McLENNAN				
•	•	•	•	•	Attorney Civil Process Service ... 182	•	•	•	•
•	•	•	•	•	Intelnet Inc ... 1035	•	•	•	•
•	•	•	•	•	Search Enterprises ... 1755	•	•	•	•
•	•	•	•	•	Tyler-McLennon Inc ... 1995	•	•	•	
					McMULLEN				
		•	•	•	McMullen County Title Co ... 1317	•	•	•	•
					MADISON				
		•		•	Landmark Title Co ... 1167	•	•	•	
					MARION				
		•	•	•	Brubaker & Associates ... 355	•	•	•	•
		•		•	DeSoto Abstract ... 609	•	•	•	
		•		•	Jones, Patsy ... 1103	•	•	•	
					MARTIN				
		•	•	•	APROTEX ... 32	•	•	•	•
		•		•	Advance Title Co ... 86		•		
					MASON				
		•	•	•	First Mason Title Co ... 774	•	•	•	•

MATAGORDA

CV	CR	PR	Company	Page	UC	RE	TX	VR
•	•	•	W T Smith and Associates	2038	•	•	•	

MAVERICK

CV	CR	PR	Company	Page	UC	RE	TX	VR
•		•	Eagle Pass Title Co Inc	674		•	•	•

MEDINA

CV	CR	PR	Company	Page	UC	RE	TX	VR
•	•	•	AKA Investigations & Process San Antonio	26	•	•	•	•
•	•	•	Fred Meyers Company	808	•	•	•	•
•	•	•	Property Research and Documentation	1625	•	•	•	•

MENARD

CV	CR	PR	Company	Page	UC	RE	TX	VR
•	•	•	Neel, Ben	1415	•	•	•	•

MIDLAND

DT	BK	CV	CR	PR	Company	Page	UC	RE	TX	VR
•	•	•	•	•	APROTEX	32	•	•	•	•
•		•		•	Advance Title Co	86		•		
•		•	•		Basin Attorney Services	257				
•	•	•	•		Permian Court Reporters Inc	1540				
•	•	•	•	•	Tyler-McLennon Inc	1995	•	•	•	

MILAM

CV	CR	PR	Company	Page	UC	RE	TX	VR
•	•	•	Tyler-McLennon Inc	1995	•	•	•	

MILLS

CV	CR	PR	Company	Page	UC	RE	TX	VR
•	•	•	Adams, Tommy M.	81	•	•	•	•

MITCHELL

CV	CR	PR	Company	Page	UC	RE	TX	VR
•	•	•	APROTEX	32	•	•	•	•
•	•	•	Colorado City Abstract Co	492	•	•	•	

MONTAGUE

CV	CR	PR	Company	Page	UC	RE	TX	VR
•	•	•	Civil Process Service	463				
•	•	•	Superior Process Service	1886	•	•	•	

MONTGOMERY

CV	CR	PR	Company	Page	UC	RE	TX	VR
•	•	•	Court Record Research	546	•	•	•	•
•	•	•	LawServ Inc	1179	•	•	•	•
•	•		M.R.S. Datascope Inc	1256				•
•	•	•	Research Staff	1687	•	•	•	
•	•	•	Southwest Patrol & Investigations	1836	•	•	•	
•		•	Texas Abstract Services	1913	•	•		•
•	•	•	Texas Records Search	1918	•	•	•	•
•	•	•	The Cole Group	1923	•	•	•	•
•	•	•	The Information Bank of Texas	1935	•	•	•	•
•	•	•	Tyler-McLennon Inc	1995	•	•	•	
•	•	•	US Legal Support-Houston	2001	•	•	•	•

MOORE

CV	CR	PR	Company	Page	UC	RE	TX	VR
•	•	•	Rollins, Jan	1711	•	•	•	•

MORRIS

CV	CR	PR	Company	Page	UC	RE	TX	VR
•	•	•	Brubaker & Associates	355	•	•	•	•

MOTLEY

CV	CR	PR	Company	Page	UC	RE	TX	VR
			See adjoining counties					

NACOGDOCHES

CV	CR	PR	Company	Page	UC	RE	TX	VR
•	•	•	Brubaker & Associates	355	•	•	•	•
•		•	East Texas Title & Abstract Co	680	•	•	•	•

NAVARRO

CV	CR	PR	Company	Page	UC	RE	TX	VR
		•	Navarro County Abstract Co	1413		•		
•	•	•	Search Enterprises	1755	•	•	•	•

DT	BK	CV	CR	PR	Company	#	UC	RE	TX	VR
		•	•	•	Tyler-McLennon Inc	1995	•	•	•	

NEWTON

CV	CR	PR	Company	#	UC	RE	TX	VR
•	•	•	US Legal Support-Houston	2001	•	•	•	•

NOLAN

CV	CR	PR	Company	#	UC	RE	TX	VR
•		•	Beall Abstract and Title Co Inc	268	•	•	•	

NUECES

DT	BK	CV	CR	PR	Company	#	UC	RE	TX	VR
•	•	•	•	•	Brack Warren & Associates	336	•	•	•	•
•	•	•	•	•	Corpus Christi Court Services	532	•	•	•	•
•	•	•	•	•	Intelnet Inc	1035	•	•	•	•
•	•	•	•	•	John Bullock & Co	1089	•	•	•	•
•	•	•	•	•	PI Unlimited	1491	•	•	•	•
•	•	•	•	•	Professional Civil Process	1612	•	•	•	•
•	•	•	•	•	Professional Civil Process	1615	•	•	•	•
•	•	•	•	•	Property Research and Documentation	1625	•	•		
•	•				Ricochet	1698				
•	•	•	•	•	Shawver and Associates	1793	•	•	•	•
•	•	•	•	•	Texas Civil Process	1914	•	•	•	•
•	•	•	•	•	Texas Legal Support Service	1917	•	•	•	•
•	•	•	•	•	Tyler-McLennon Inc	1995	•	•	•	•

OCHILTREE

CV	CR	PR	Company	#	UC	RE	TX	VR
•	•	•	Credit Bureau Services of the Panhandle	557	•	•	•	•
•		•	Ochiltree County Abstract Company	1456	•	•	•	

OLDHAM

CV	CR	PR	Company	#	UC	RE	TX	VR
			See adjoining counties					

ORANGE

CV	CR	PR	Company	#	UC	RE	TX	VR
•	•	•	US Legal Support-Houston	2001	•	•	•	•

PALO PINTO

CV	CR	PR	Company	#	UC	RE	TX	VR
•		•	Elliott & Waldron Abstr Co of Palo Pinto	703	•	•	•	•

PANOLA

CV	CR	PR	Company	#	UC	RE	TX	VR
•	•	•	Brubaker & Associates	355	•	•	•	•
•		•	DeSoto Abstract	609	•	•		
•		•	Panola County Abstract and Title	1510	•	•		

PARKER

CV	CR	PR	Company	#	UC	RE	TX	VR
•		•	Weatherford-Parker County Abstract Co	2067	•	•	•	

PARMER

CV	CR	PR	Company	#	UC	RE	TX	VR
•	•	•	Farwell Abstract Co Inc	744		•	•	

PECOS

CV	CR	PR	Company	#	UC	RE	TX	VR
•		•	Elliott & Waldron Abstract Co of Pecos	706	•	•	•	•

POLK

CV	CR	PR	Company	#	UC	RE	TX	VR
•	•	•	US Legal Support-Houston	2001	•	•	•	•

POTTER

DT	BK	CV	CR	PR	Company	#	UC	RE	TX	VR
		•	•	•	Garrison Legal Services	832	•	•	•	•
		•	•	•	Garrison Legal Services	833	•	•	•	
•	•	•	•	•	Rollins, Jan	1711	•	•	•	•
•	•	•	•	•	US Legal Support	1999				

PRESIDIO

CV	CR	PR	Company	#	UC	RE	TX	VR
•	•	•	Presidio County Abstract Co	1598	•	•	•	

RAINS

CV	CR	PR	Company	#	UC	RE	TX	VR
•	•	•	AAA Abstract Co Inc	12	•	•	•	•

DT	BK	CV	CR	PR			UC	RE	TX	VR
		●	●	●	Brubaker & Associates 355		●	●	●	●
		CV	CR	PR	**RANDALL**		UC	RE	TX	VR
		●	●	●	Garrison Legal Services 832		●	●	●	●
		●	●	●	Garrison Legal Services 833		●	●	●	●
		●	●	●	Rollins, Jan..................................1711		●	●	●	●
		●	●	●	US Legal Support..........................1999					
		CV	CR	PR	**REAGAN**		UC	RE	TX	VR
		●	●	●	APROTEX 32		●	●	●	●
		●		●	Advance Title Co 86			●		
		CV	CR	PR	**REAL**		UC	RE	TX	VR
		●	●	●	Real County Abstract & Title Co 1654		●	●	●	
		CV	CR	PR	**RED RIVER**		UC	RE	TX	VR
		●	●	●	Brubaker & Associates.......................355		●	●	●	●
		●		●	Gooding Title Co................................854		●	●	●	
DT	BK	CV	CR	PR	**REEVES**		UC	RE	TX	VR
●		●		●	Advance Title Co 86			●		
		CV	CR	PR	**REFUGIO**		UC	RE	TX	VR
		●	●	●	Jan L Jackson Investigation..............1077		●	●	●	●
		●	●	●	Professional Civil Process................1612		●	●	●	●
		●	●	●	Shawver and Associates....................1793		●	●	●	●
		●	●	●	Texas Civil Process...........................1914		●	●	●	●
		CV	CR	PR	**ROBERTS**		UC	RE	TX	VR
		●	●	●	Credit Bureau Services of the Panhandle 557		●	●	●	●
		CV	CR	PR	**ROBERTSON**		UC	RE	TX	VR
		●		●	Guaranty Title Co...............................894		●	●	●	●
		●	●	●	Search Enterprises............................1755		●	●	●	●
		CV	CR	PR	**ROCKWALL**		UC	RE	TX	VR
		●	●	●	Brubaker & Associates.......................355		●	●	●	●
		●	●	●	Charles L Lager Private Investigations.............439		●		●	●
		●	●	●	Ed Waynick and Associates...............690			●	●	●
		●	●	●	Investigative Associates Inc.............1046		●	●	●	●
		●	●	●	Security Information Service.............1773		●	●	●	●
		●	●	●	The Court System.............................1926		●	●	●	●
		●	●	●	Tyler-McLennon Inc..........................1995		●	●	●	
		CV	CR	PR	**RUNNELS**		UC	RE	TX	VR
		●	●	●	Surety Title Co of Ballenger..............1890		●	●	●	●
		CV	CR	PR	**RUSK**		UC	RE	TX	VR
		●	●	●	Brubaker & Associates.......................355		●	●	●	●
		●		●	DeSoto Abstract 609		●	●	●	
		CV	CR	PR	**SABINE**		UC	RE	TX	VR
		●	●	●	East Texas Title & Abstract Co............679		●	●	●	●
		CV	CR	PR	**SAN AUGUSTINE**		UC	RE	TX	VR
		●	●	●	Brubaker & Associates.......................355		●	●	●	●
		●	●	●	East Texas Title & Abstract Co Inc.......681		●	●	●	●
		CV	CR	PR	**SAN JACINTO**		UC	RE	TX	VR
		●	●	●	Bonds Process Service of East Texas..............320		●	●	●	●
		CV	CR	PR	**SAN PATRICIO**		UC	RE	TX	VR
		●	●	●	Brack Warren & Associates 336		●	●	●	●
		●	●	●	Corpus Christi Court Services............532		●	●	●	●

DT	BK	CV	CR	PR			UC	RE	TX	VR
		●	●	●	John Bullock & Co. 1089		●	●	●	●
		●	●	●	PI Unlimited 1491		●	●	●	●
		●	●	●	Professional Civil Process 1612		●	●	●	●
		●	●	●	Property Research and Documentation 1625		●	●	●	●
		●	●	●	Shawver and Associates 1793		●	●	●	●
		●	●	●	Texas Civil Process 1914		●	●	●	●
		●	●	●	Texas Legal Support Service 1917		●	●	●	●

		CV	CR	PR	**SAN SABA**		UC	RE	TX	VR
		●	●	●	Adams, Tommy M. 81		●	●	●	●

		CV	CR	PR	**SCHLEICHER**		UC	RE	TX	VR
		●	●	●	Benton Abstract & Title Co. 281		●	●	●	

		CV	CR	PR	**SCURRY**		UC	RE	TX	VR
		●	●	●	Scurry County Abstract Co 1752		●	●	●	

		CV	CR	PR	**SHACKELFORD**		UC	RE	TX	VR
		●		●	Albany Abstract Co. 99		●	●	●	●

		CV	CR	PR	**SHELBY**		UC	RE	TX	VR
		●		●	DeSoto Abstract 609		●	●	●	

		CV	CR	PR	**SHERMAN**		UC	RE	TX	VR
					See adjoining counties.					

DT	BK	CV	CR	PR	**SMITH**		UC	RE	TX	VR
●	●	●	●	●	Brubaker & Associates 355		●	●	●	●
		●		●	DeSoto Abstract 609		●	●	●	
●	●	●	●	●	Intranet Inc 1044		●	●	●	●
	●	●		●	Smith County Abstract 1813		●	●	●	
●		●	●	●	The Court System 1926		●	●	●	●

		CV	CR	PR	**SOMERVELL**		UC	RE	TX	VR
		●	●	●	Tyler-McLennon Inc 1995		●	●	●	

		CV	CR	PR	**STARR**		UC	RE	TX	VR
		●	●	●	Professional Civil Process 1613		●	●	●	●
		●	●	●	Shawver and Associates 1793		●	●	●	●

		CV	CR	PR	**STEPHENS**		UC	RE	TX	VR
					Stephens County Abstract 1863		●	●	●	

		CV	CR	PR	**STERLING**		UC	RE	TX	VR
		●	●	●	APROTEX 32		●	●	●	●

		CV	CR	PR	**STONEWALL**		UC	RE	TX	VR
		●		●	Caprock Title Co 404		●	●	●	
		●	●	●	Consolidated Abstract Co 514		●	●	●	●

		CV	CR	PR	**SUTTON**		UC	RE	TX	VR
		●	●	●	Neel, Ben 1415		●	●	●	●

		CV	CR	PR	**SWISHER**		UC	RE	TX	VR
		●	●	●	Rollins, Jan 1711		●	●	●	●

DT	BK	CV	CR	PR	**TARRANT**		UC	RE	TX	VR
●	●	●	●	●	AKA Investigations & Process of Dallas 28		●	●	●	●
●	●	●	●	●	Brubaker & Associates 355		●	●	●	●
●	●	●	●	●	Charles L Lager Private Investigations 439		●	●	●	●
●	●	●	●	●	Civil Process Service 462		●	●	●	●
●	●	●	●	●	Disheroon Title Consultant 636		●	●	●	●
●	●	●	●	●	Ed Waynick and Associates 690			●	●	●
●	●	●	●	●	FYI Services 730		●	●	●	

DT	BK	CV	CR	PR		UC	RE	TX	VR
•	•	•	•	•	For Your Information Inc 791	•	•	•	•
•	•	•	•	•	Intelnet Inc 1035	•	•	•	•
•	•	•	•	•	Intranet Inc 1044	•	•	•	•
•	•	•	•	•	Investigative Associates Inc 1046	•	•	•	•
					Police Report Acquisition Service 1565				
•	•	•	•	•	Professional Civil Process 1615	•			
•	•	•	•	•	Reliable Courier 1676			•	•
•	•				Ricochet 1698		•		
•	•	•	•	•	Security Information Service 1773	•		•	•
•	•	•	•	•	Texas Industrial Security Inc 1915	•		•	•
•	•	•	•	•	Texas Information Services 1916	•	•	•	•
		•	•	•	The Cole Group 1923	•	•	•	•
•	•	•	•	•	The Court System 1926	•	•	•	•
•	•	•	•	•	The Information Bank of Texas 1935	•	•	•	•
•	•	•	•	•	Tyler-McLennon Inc 1995	•	•	•	•

DT	CV	CR	PR	TAYLOR	UC	RE	TX	VR
	•	•	•	Alliance Title & Abstract Company 115	•	•	•	•

CV	CR	PR	TERRELL	UC	RE	TX	VR
			See adjoining counties				

CV	CR	PR	TERRY	UC	RE	TX	VR
•		•	Brownfield Abstract & Title Co 354		•	•	
•			Robinson Agency 1706				

CV	CR	PR	THROCKMORTON	UC	RE	TX	VR
•	•	•	Civil Process Service 463				
•	•	•	Superior Process Service 1886	•	•	•	

CV	CR	PR	TITUS	UC	RE	TX	VR
•	•	•	Brubaker & Associates 355	•	•	•	•
•		•	Titus County Title Company 1962	•	•	•	•

DT	CV	CR	PR	TOM GREEN	UC	RE	TX	VR
•	•	•	•	Robinson Agency 1706	•	•	•	•
	•	•	•	Surety Title Co of San Angelo 1892	•	•	•	•

DT	BK	CV	CR	PR	TRAVIS	UC	RE	TX	VR
•	•	•	•	•	AKA Investigations & Process of Austin 27	•	•	•	•
•	•	•	•	•	Assured Civil Process Agency Inc 175		•		
•	•	•	•		CPS (Capital Process Service) 378			•	
•	•	•			Capitol Services Inc 402	•			
•	•	•	•	•	Feaster & Associates 747	•	•	•	
•	•	•	•	•	Inform 1026	•	•		•
•	•	•	•	•	Intelnet Inc 1035	•	•	•	•
•	•	•	•	•	Intranet Inc 1044	•	•	•	•
•	•	•	•	•	John C Dunaway and Associates 1090	•	•		
•	•	•	•	•	Professional Civil Process 1615	•	•	•	•
•	•	•	•	•	Property Research and Documentation 1625	•	•	•	•
•	•	•	•	•	Texas Information Services 1916	•	•	•	•
•	•	•	•	•	The Information Bank of Texas 1935	•	•	•	•
•	•	•	•	•	Tyler-McLennon Inc 1995	•	•	•	
•	•	•	•	•	W T Smith and Associates 2038	•	•	•	

CV	CR	PR	TRINITY	UC	RE	TX	VR
•	•	•	Trinity County Abstract 1984	•	•	•	•
•	•	•	US Legal Support-Houston 2001	•	•	•	•

CV	CR	PR	TYLER	UC	RE	TX	VR
•	•	•	US Legal Support-Houston 2001	•	•	•	•

		CV	CR	PR	UPSHUR	UC	RE	TX	VR
		●	●	●	Brubaker & Associates 355	●	●	●	●

		CV	CR	PR	UPTON	UC	RE	TX	VR
		●	●	●	APROTEX 32	●	●	●	●
		●		●	Southwest Abstract & Title Co. 1833	●	●	●	

		CV	CR	PR	UVALDE	UC	RE	TX	VR
		●	●	●	Property Research and Documentation 1625	●	●	●	●

DT	BK	CV	CR	PR	VAL VERDE	UC	RE	TX	VR
		●		●	Southwest Abstract Co Inc 1835	●	●	●	●

		CV	CR	PR	VAN ZANDT	UC	RE	TX	VR
		●	●	●	Brubaker & Associates 355	●	●	●	●
		●	●	●	Elliott & Waldron Abstr Co of Van Zandt 704	●	●	●	●
		●	●	●	The Court System 1926	●	●	●	●

DT		CV	CR	PR	VICTORIA	UC	RE	TX	VR
		●		●	Bedgood Abstract & Title Co. 274	●	●	●	
●		●	●	●	Jan L Jackson Investigation 1077	●	●	●	●
●		●	●	●	Professional Civil Process 1612	●	●	●	●
●		●	●	●	Property Research and Documentation 1625	●	●	●	●
●		●	●	●	Shawver and Associates 1793	●	●	●	●
●		●	●	●	Texas Civil Process 1914	●	●	●	●
●		●	●	●	US Legal Support-Houston 2001	●	●	●	●

		CV	CR	PR	WALKER	UC	RE	TX	VR
		●	●	●	The Cole Group 1923	●	●	●	●
		●	●	●	US Legal Support-Houston 2001	●	●	●	●

		CV	CR	PR	WALLER	UC	RE	TX	VR
		●	●	●	Research Staff 1687	●	●	●	●
		●	●		Spadachene, Tony 1838				
		●	●	●	US Legal Support-Houston 2001	●	●	●	●
		●	●	●	W T Smith and Associates 2038	●	●	●	●
		●	●	●	Walters & Associates 2051	●	●	●	●

		CV	CR	PR	WARD	UC	RE	TX	VR
		●	●	●	APROTEX 32	●	●	●	●
		●		●	Pioneer-Ward County Abstract Co. 1555	●	●	●	

		CV	CR	PR	WASHINGTON	UC	RE	TX	VR
		●	●	●	Botts Abstract Co 331	●	●	●	

DT		CV	CR	PR	WEBB	UC	RE	TX	VR
					Border Abstract 326	●	●	●	
●		●	●	●	Professional Civil Process 1612	●	●	●	●
●		●	●	●	Property Research and Documentation 1625	●	●	●	●
●		●	●	●	Shawver and Associates 1793	●	●	●	●

		CV	CR	PR	WHARTON	UC	RE	TX	VR
		●		●	Texas Abstract Services 1913	●	●		●
		●	●	●	US Legal Support-Houston 2001	●	●	●	
		●	●	●	W T Smith and Associates 2038	●	●	●	
		●	●	●	Walters & Associates 2051	●	●	●	●

		CV	CR	PR	WHEELER	UC	RE	TX	VR
		●	●	●	Credit Bureau Services of the Panhandle 557	●	●	●	●

DT		CV	CR	PR	WICHITA	UC	RE	TX	VR
●		●	●	●	Civil Process Service 463				
●		●	●	●	Superior Process Service 1886	●	●	●	

CV	CR	PR	WILBARGER		UC	RE	TX	VR
•	•	•	Civil Process Service.............................463					
•	•	•	Superior Process Service.........................1886		•	•	•	

CV	CR	PR	WILLACY		UC	RE	TX	VR
•	•	•	Professional Civil Process.........................1613		•	•	•	•

CV	CR	PR	WILLIAMSON		UC	RE	TX	VR
•	•	•	AKA Investigations & Process of Austin............27		•	•	•	•
•		•	American Abstract and Title Co Inc.................127		•	•	•	•
•	•	•	Assured Civil Process Agency Inc 175			•		
•	•		CPS (Capital Process Service) 378				•	
•	•	•	Feaster & Associates 747		•	•	•	•
•	•	•	John C Dunaway and Associates...................1090		•	•	•	•
•	•	•	Property Research and Documentation 1625		•	•	•	•
•	•	•	Texas Information Services........................1916		•	•	•	•
•	•	•	Tyler-McLennon Inc 1995		•	•	•	
•	•	•	W T Smith and Associates 2038		•	•	•	

CV	CR	PR	WILSON		UC	RE	TX	VR
•	•	•	AKA Investigations & Process San Antonio........26		•	•	•	•
	•	•	Bexar Professional 296		•	•	•	•
•	•	•	Professional Civil Process........................1614		•	•	•	•
•	•	•	Property Research and Documentation 1625		•	•	•	•

CV	CR	PR	WINKLER		UC	RE	TX	VR
•		•	Advance Title Co 86			•		

CV	CR	PR	WISE		UC	RE	TX	VR
•	•	•	Civil Process Service.............................463					
•	•	•	Disheroon Title Consultant 636		•	•	•	•
•	•	•	Superior Process Service.........................1886		•	•	•	

CV	CR	PR	WOOD		UC	RE	TX	VR
•	•	•	Brubaker & Associates............................355		•	•	•	•
•		•	Wood County Title Co............................2110			•		

CV	CR	PR	YOAKUM		UC	RE	TX	VR
•	•	•	Yoakum County Abstract Co 2120		•	•	•	

CV	CR	PR	YOUNG		UC	RE	TX	VR
•	•	•	Civil Process Service.............................463					
•	•	•	Superior Process Service.........................1886		•	•	•	

CV	CR	PR	ZAPATA		UC	RE	TX	VR
			Border Abstract 326		•	•	•	

CV	CR	PR	ZAVALA		UC	RE	TX	VR
•	•	•	Zavala County Abstract Co Inc.....................2125		•	•	•	

Court
Records

UTAH
222

County
Records

Utah

DT	BK	CV	CR	PR	ALL COUNTIES		UC	RE	TX	VR
●	●	●		●	D W Moore and Assoc Inc 579		●	●	●	●
	●	●	●	●	Hollingsworth Court Reporting Inc.....................983		●	●	●	●

		CV	CR	PR	BEAVER		UC	RE	TX	VR
		●	●	●	Cedar Land Title Inc 420		●	●	●	●
		●		●	Security Title of Beaver County 1779		●	●	●	

		CV	CR	PR	BOX ELDER		UC	RE	TX	VR
		●	●	●	DataTrace Investigations Inc............................596		●	●	●	●
		●	●	●	Hillam Abstracting & Insurance Agency............974		●	●	●	
		●		●	The Home Abstract Co....................................1934		●	●	●	
		●		●	Tooele Title Company.....................................1967		●	●	●	

		CV	CR	PR	CACHE		UC	RE	TX	VR
		●	●	●	DataTrace Investigations Inc............................596		●	●	●	●
		●	●	●	Hickman Land Title..963		●	●	●	●
		●	●	●	Hillam Abstracting & Insurance Agency............974		●	●	●	
		●		●	The Home Abstract Co....................................1934		●	●	●	

		CV	CR	PR	CARBON		UC	RE	TX	VR
		●	●	●	Deister Ward & Witcher of WY 616		●	●	●	●
		●		●	Professional Title Services.............................1621		●	●	●	
		●	●	●	Southeastern Utah Title..................................1826		●	●	●	●
		●	●	●	Sunrise Title Co 1882		●	●	●	●

		CV	CR	PR	DAGGETT		UC	RE	TX	VR
		●	●	●	Deister Ward & Witcher of WY 616		●	●	●	●
		●	●	●	Sunrise Title Co 1882		●	●	●	●

		CV	CR	PR	DAVIS		UC	RE	TX	VR
		●	●	●	All-Search 111		●	●	●	●
		●	●	●	DataTrace Investigations Inc............................596		●	●	●	●
		●		●	The Home Abstract Co....................................1934		●	●	●	

		CV	CR	PR	DUCHESNE		UC	RE	TX	VR
		●		●	Professional Title Services.............................1621		●	●	●	
		●	●	●	Sunrise Title Co 1882		●	●	●	●

		CV	CR	PR	EMERY		UC	RE	TX	VR
		●		●	Professional Title Services.............................1621		●	●	●	
		●	●	●	Southeastern Utah Title..................................1826		●	●	●	●
		●	●	●	Sunrise Title Co 1882		●	●	●	●

		CV	CR	PR	GARFIELD		UC	RE	TX	VR
		●	●	●	Cedar Land Title Inc 420		●	●	●	●
		●	●	●	Security Title Co of Garfield County 1778		●	●	●	●

		CV	CR	PR	GRAND		UC	RE	TX	VR
		●	●	●	Southeastern Utah Title..................................1826		●	●	●	●

		CV	CR	PR	IRON		UC	RE	TX	VR
		●	●	●	Cedar Land Title Inc 420		●	●	●	●

		CV	CR	PR	JUAB		UC	RE	TX	VR
		●		●	Tooele Title Company.....................................1967		●	●	●	

		CV	CR	PR	KANE		UC	RE	TX	VR
		●	●	●	Cedar Land Title Inc 420		●	●	●	●
		●	●	●	Southern Utah Title Co 1832		●	●	●	●

		CV	CR	PR	MILLARD	UC	RE	TX	VR
		●	●	●	All-Search 111	●	●	●	●
		●	●	●	Utah Title & Abstract........................2015	●	●	●	

		CV	CR	PR	MORGAN	UC	RE	TX	VR
		●	●	●	DataTrace Investigations Inc........................596	●	●	●	●
		●		●	The Home Abstract Co........................1934	●	●	●	

		CV	CR	PR	PIUTE	UC	RE	TX	VR
		●	●	●	Security Title Co of Garfield County........................1778	●	●	●	●
		●	●	●	Utah Title & Abstract........................2015	●	●	●	

		CV	CR	PR	RICH	UC	RE	TX	VR
		●	●	●	Hickman Land Title........................963	●	●	●	

DT	BK	CV	CR	PR	SALT LAKE	UC	RE	TX	VR
●	●	●	●	●	All-Search 111	●	●	●	●
●	●	●	●	●	DataTrace Investigations Inc........................596	●	●	●	●
●	●	●	●	●	Detective Referral Service........................626	●	●	●	

		CV	CR	PR	SAN JUAN	UC	RE	TX	VR
		●	●	●	Southeastern Utah Title........................1826	●	●	●	●

		CV	CR	PR	SANPETE	UC	RE	TX	VR
		●	●	●	Central Utah Title........................428	●	●	●	

		CV	CR	PR	SEVIER	UC	RE	TX	VR
		●	●	●	Utah Title & Abstract........................2015	●	●	●	

		CV	CR	PR	SUMMIT	UC	RE	TX	VR
		●	●	●	All-Search 111	●	●	●	●
		●	●	●	DataTrace Investigations Inc........................596	●	●	●	●
		●	●	●	Deister Ward & Witcher of WY........................616	●	●	●	●
		●		●	The Home Abstract Co........................1934	●	●	●	

		CV	CR	PR	TOOELE	UC	RE	TX	VR
		●	●	●	All-Search 111	●	●	●	●
		●	●	●	DataTrace Investigations Inc........................596	●	●	●	●
		●		●	Tooele Title Company........................1967	●	●	●	

		CV	CR	PR	UINTAH	UC	RE	TX	VR
		●	●	●	Deister Ward & Witcher of WY........................616	●	●	●	●
		●	●	●	Sunrise Title Co 1882	●	●	●	●

		CV	CR	PR	UTAH	UC	RE	TX	VR
		●	●	●	DataTrace Investigations Inc........................596	●	●	●	●
		●	●	●	Detective Referral Service........................626	●	●	●	

		CV	CR	PR	WASATCH	UC	RE	TX	VR
		●	●	●	All-Search 111	●	●	●	●
		●	●	●	DataTrace Investigations Inc........................596	●	●	●	●
		●	●	●	Deister Ward & Witcher of WY........................616	●	●	●	●

		CV	CR	PR	WASHINGTON	UC	RE	TX	VR
		●	●	●	Washington County Title Co........................2057	●	●	●	●

		CV	CR	PR	WAYNE	UC	RE	TX	VR
		●	●	●	Utah Title & Abstract........................2015	●	●	●	

		CV	CR	PR	WEBER	UC	RE	TX	VR
		●	●	●	All-Search 111	●	●	●	●
		●	●	●	DataTrace Investigations Inc........................596	●	●	●	●
		●	●	●	Detective Referral Service........................626	●	●	●	
		●		●	The Home Abstract Co........................1934	●	●	●	

Vermont

DT	BK	CV	CR	PR	ALL COUNTIES	UC	RE	TX	VR
•	•	•	•	•	New England Recovery Inc...............1422	•	•	•	•

		CV	CR	PR	ADDISON	UC	RE	TX	VR
		•		•	Burak & Anderson 364	•	•		•

		CV	CR	PR	BENNINGTON	UC	RE	TX	VR
		•	•	•	Heritage Personnel Services Inc...............959	•	•	•	•

		CV	CR	PR	CALEDONIA	UC	RE	TX	VR
		•	•	•	Davis, Don 604	•	•	•	•

DT		CV	CR	PR	CHITTENDEN	UC	RE	TX	VR
•		•		•	Burak & Anderson 364	•	•		•

		CV	CR	PR	ESSEX	UC	RE	TX	VR
					See ALL COUNTIES...............				

		CV	CR	PR	FRANKLIN	UC	RE	TX	VR
					See ALL COUNTIES...............				

		CV	CR	PR	GRAND ISLE	UC	RE	TX	VR
					See ALL COUNTIES...............				

		CV	CR	PR	LAMOILLE	UC	RE	TX	VR
					See ALL COUNTIES...............				

		CV	CR	PR	ORANGE	UC	RE	TX	VR
					See ALL COUNTIES...............				

		CV	CR	PR	ORLEANS	UC	RE	TX	VR
					See ALL COUNTIES...............				

DT	BK	CV	CR	PR	RUTLAND	UC	RE	TX	VR
•	•	•		•	Burak & Anderson 364	•	•		•
•		•	•		Heritage Personnel Services Inc...............959				

		CV	CR	PR	WASHINGTON	UC	RE	TX	VR
		•		•	Burak & Anderson 364	•	•		•
		•	•	•	Davis, Don 604	•	•	•	•

		CV	CR	PR	WINDHAM	UC	RE	TX	VR
		•	•		Harmon Personnel Services Inc 928				

		CV	CR	PR	WINDSOR	UC	RE	TX	VR
		•	•	•	Davis, Don 604	•	•	•	•
		•	•		Heritage Personnel Services Inc...............959				

Virginia

Note: The 41 Independent Cities are listed after the counties in Virginia.

DT	BK	CV	CR	PR	ALL COUNTIES		UC	RE	TX	VR
●	●	●	●	●	CorpAssist.....524		●	●	●	●
●	●	●	●	●	Security Intelligence Bureau.....1774		●	●	●	●

		CV	CR	PR	ACCOMACK		UC	RE	TX	VR
		●	●	●	Ayres, Judith.....225		●	●	●	●

DT		CV	CR	PR	ALBEMARLE		UC	RE	TX	VR
●		●	●	●	Ellerson, H Watkins.....701		●	●	●	
		●		●	Lawyer Title/Blue Ridge Agency Inc.....1182		●	●	●	

		CV	CR	PR	ALLEGHANY		UC	RE	TX	VR
		●	●		Fletcher, Jean R.....785		●	●	●	

		CV	CR	PR	AMELIA		UC	RE	TX	VR
		●	●	●	Cumberland Title Agency Inc.....573		●	●	●	
		●	●	●	Southall Jr, Valentine W.....1824		●	●	●	

		CV	CR	PR	AMHERST		UC	RE	TX	VR
		●	●	●	Berry, William Thomas.....289		●	●	●	●

		CV	CR	PR	APPOMATTOX		UC	RE	TX	VR
		●	●	●	Brown-Browning, Gail.....353		●	●	●	●
		●	●	●	Central Virginia Investigative Service.....429		●	●	●	●

		CV	CR	PR	ARLINGTON		UC	RE	TX	VR
		●			Douglas Investigations Ltd.....655					
		●	●	●	Federal Research Corporation.....751		●	●	●	●
		●	●	●	Hylind Infoquest.....1013		●	●	●	●
		●	●	●	Instant Information Systems.....1032		●	●	●	●
		●	●	●	Legal Courier Systems Inc.....1196			●	●	●
		●	●	●	M & M Search Service Inc.....1254		●	●	●	●
		●		●	Pascal & Carter Process Service Inc.....1522			●		
		●		●	Real Estate Information Service.....1656		●	●	●	
		●	●	●	University Process Service.....2012					

		CV	CR	PR	AUGUSTA		UC	RE	TX	VR
		●	●	●	Data Abstract & Title Co Inc.....591		●	●	●	
		●		●	Lawyer Title/Blue Ridge Agency Inc.....1182		●	●	●	

		CV	CR	PR	BATH		UC	RE	TX	VR
		●	●	●	Singleton & Deeds.....1808		●	●	●	●

		CV	CR	PR	BEDFORD		UC	RE	TX	VR
		●	●	●	Biesenbach, Betsy.....298		●	●	●	
		●	●	●	Brown-Browning, Gail.....353		●	●	●	●
		●	●	●	Central Virginia Investigative Service.....429		●	●	●	●

		CV	CR	PR	BLAND		UC	RE	TX	VR
		●	●		Fletcher, Jean R.....785		●	●	●	

		CV	CR	PR	BOTETOURT		UC	RE	TX	VR
		●	●	●	Biesenbach, Betsy.....298		●	●	●	
		●	●	●	Brown-Browning, Gail.....353		●	●	●	●
		●	●		Fletcher, Jean R.....785		●	●	●	

		CV	CR	PR	BRUNSWICK		UC	RE	TX	VR
		●	●	●	Allen III, William D.....113		●	●	●	
		●	●	●	Hawthorne, Robert E.....941		●	●	●	

CV	CR	PR	BUCHANAN		UC	RE	TX	VR
●	●		Fletcher, Jean R 785		●	●	●	

CV	CR	PR	BUCKINGHAM		UC	RE	TX	VR
●	●	●	Cumberland Title Agency Inc 573		●	●	●	
●	●	●	Fette, Kitty 755					

CV	CR	PR	CAMPBELL		UC	RE	TX	VR
●	●	●	Brown-Browning, Gail 353		●	●	●	●
●	●	●	Central Virginia Investigative Service 429		●	●	●	●

CV	CR	PR	CAROLINE		UC	RE	TX	VR
●	●	●	T D Title Services 1898		●	●	●	

CV	CR	PR	CARROLL		UC	RE	TX	VR
●	●	●	Clue Detective Service 479		●	●	●	●
●	●		Fletcher, Jean R 785		●	●	●	
			Southwest Virginia Abstract & Title Co 1837		●	●	●	

CV	CR	PR	CHARLES CITY		UC	RE	TX	VR
●			UCC Retrievals 1997		●	●	●	●

CV	CR	PR	CHARLOTTE		UC	RE	TX	VR
●	●	●	Brown-Browning, Gail 353		●	●	●	●
●	●	●	Hawthorne, Robert E 941		●	●	●	

CV	CR	PR	CHESTERFIELD		UC	RE	TX	VR
●	●	●	Associated Investigative Services Inc 171		●	●	●	●
●	●	●	Hylind Infoquest 1013		●	●	●	●
●	●	●	The Marston Agency Inc 1937		●	●	●	●
●			UCC Retrievals 1997		●	●	●	●

CV	CR	PR	CLARKE		UC	RE	TX	VR
	●	●	Shenandoah Title Services Inc 1795		●	●	●	

CV	CR	PR	CRAIG		UC	RE	TX	VR
●	●		Fletcher, Jean R 785		●	●	●	

CV	CR	PR	CULPEPER		UC	RE	TX	VR
●	●	●	Ellerson, H Watkins 701		●	●	●	
●		●	Washington Title Agencies 2059		●	●	●	●

CV	CR	PR	CUMBERLAND		UC	RE	TX	VR
●	●	●	Cumberland Title Agency Inc 573		●	●	●	

CV	CR	PR	DICKENSON		UC	RE	TX	VR
●	●	●	Clue Detective Service 479		●	●	●	●
●	●		Fletcher, Jean R 785		●	●	●	

CV	CR	PR	DINWIDDIE		UC	RE	TX	VR
●	●	●	Allen III, William D 113		●	●	●	

CV	CR	PR	ESSEX		UC	RE	TX	VR
●	●	●	McKerns & McKerns 1314		●	●	●	
●	●	●	Michael B Fixman & Associates 1338		●	●	●	●

CV	CR	PR	FAIRFAX		UC	RE	TX	VR
●	●	●	ABIS Inc 17		●	●	●	
●	●	●	Associated Investigative Services Inc 171		●	●	●	●
●	●	●	Federal Information Service 749		●	●	●	●
●	●	●	Federal Research Corporation 751		●	●	●	●
●	●	●	Hylind Infoquest 1013		●	●	●	●
●	●	●	Instant Information Systems 1032		●	●	●	●
●	●	●	Legal Courier Systems Inc 1196			●	●	●

CV	CR	PR			UC	RE	TX	VR
●	●	●	M & M Search Service Inc 1254		●	●	●	●
●		●	Pascal & Carter Process Service Inc 1522			●		
●		●	Real Estate Information Service.................1656		●	●	●	
●	●	●	University Process Service.................2012					

CV	CR	PR	FAUQUIER	UC	RE	TX	VR
●	●	●	Legal Courier Systems Inc 1196		●	●	●
●		●	Washington Title Agencies 2059	●	●	●	●

CV	CR	PR	FLOYD	UC	RE	TX	VR
●	●	●	Biesenbach, Betsy 298	●	●	●	
●	●	●	Brown-Browning, Gail...............353	●	●	●	●
●	●	●	Clue Detective Service 479	●	●	●	●
●	●		Fletcher, Jean R...............785	●	●	●	

CV	CR	PR	FLUVANNA	UC	RE	TX	VR
●	●	●	Ellerson, H Watkins 701	●	●	●	
●		●	Lawyer Title/Blue Ridge Agency Inc...............1182	●	●	●	

CV	CR	PR	FRANKLIN	UC	RE	TX	VR
●	●	●	Brown-Browning, Gail...............353	●	●	●	●
●	●	●	Clue Detective Service 479	●	●	●	
●	●		Fletcher, Jean R...............785	●	●	●	

CV	CR	PR	FREDERICK	UC	RE	TX	VR
●	●	●	Shenandoah Title Services Inc 1795	●	●	●	

CV	CR	PR	GILES	UC	RE	TX	VR
●	●		Fletcher, Jean R...............785	●	●	●	

CV	CR	PR	GLOUCESTER	UC	RE	TX	VR
●	●	●	Adkins, Charles E...............85	●	●	●	●
●	●	●	O'Connell, Nikki A...............1451	●	●	●	●
●	●		Walker, Bobbi 2044	●	●	●	

CV	CR	PR	GOOCHLAND	UC	RE	TX	VR
●	●	●	Cumberland Title Agency Inc 573	●	●	●	
●	●	●	The Marston Agency Inc...............1937	●	●	●	●
●			UCC Retrievals 1997	●	●	●	●

CV	CR	PR	GRAYSON	UC	RE	TX	VR
●	●	●	Clue Detective Service...............479	●	●	●	●
●	●		Fletcher, Jean R...............785	●	●	●	
			Southwest Virginia Abstract & Title Co 1837	●	●	●	

CV	CR	PR	GREENE	UC	RE	TX	VR
●	●	●	Ellerson, H Watkins 701	●	●	●	
●		●	Lawyer Title/Blue Ridge Agency Inc...............1182	●	●	●	

CV	CR	PR	GREENSVILLE	UC	RE	TX	VR
●	●	●	Sharrett, W Allan 1790	●	●	●	

CV	CR	PR	HALIFAX	UC	RE	TX	VR
●	●		Grant, Gary...............864	●	●	●	
●	●	●	Payne, Nota 1527	●	●	●	●

CV	CR	PR	HANOVER	UC	RE	TX	VR
●	●	●	The Marston Agency Inc...............1937	●	●	●	●
●			UCC Retrievals 1997	●	●	●	●

DT	BK	CV	CR	PR	HENRICO	UC	RE	TX	VR
●	●	●	●	●	Associated Investigative Services Inc 171	●	●	●	●
●	●	●	●	●	Hylind Infoquest...............1013	●	●	●	●
●	●	●	●	●	The Marston Agency Inc...............1937	●	●	●	●

● ● ●		UCC Retrievals 1997	● ● ● ●

CV	CR	PR	**HENRY**	UC	RE	TX	VR
●	●	●	Brown-Browning, Gail..............353	●	●	●	●
●	●		Grant, Gary..............864	●	●	●	

CV	CR	PR	**HIGHLAND**	UC	RE	TX	VR
●	●	●	Singleton & Deeds 1808	●	●	●	●

CV	CR	PR	**ISLE OF WIGHT**	UC	RE	TX	VR
●	●	●	Associated Investigative Services Inc 171	●	●	●	●
●	●	●	O'Connell, Nikki A..............1451	●	●	●	●
●	●		Walker, Bobbi..............2044	●	●	●	

CV	CR	PR	**JAMES CITY**	UC	RE	TX	VR
●	●	●	Associated Investigative Services Inc 171	●	●	●	●
●	●	●	O'Connell, Nikki A..............1451	●	●	●	●
●	●		Walker, Bobbi..............2044	●	●	●	

CV	CR	PR	**KING AND QUEEN**	UC	RE	TX	VR
●	●	●	Adkins, Charles E..............85	●	●	●	●
●	●	●	T D Title Services 1898	●	●	●	

CV	CR	PR	**KING GEORGE**	UC	RE	TX	VR
●	●	●	T D Title Services 1898	●	●	●	

CV	CR	PR	**KING WILLIAM**	UC	RE	TX	VR
●	●	●	Adkins, Charles E..............85	●	●	●	●
●			UCC Retrievals 1997	●	●	●	

CV	CR	PR	**LANCASTER**	UC	RE	TX	VR
●	●	●	McKerns & McKerns 1314	●	●	●	

CV	CR	PR	**LEE**	UC	RE	TX	VR
●	●	●	Clue Detective Service 479	●	●	●	●
●	●		Fletcher, Jean R..............785	●	●	●	

CV	CR	PR	**LOUDOUN**	UC	RE	TX	VR
●	●	●	ABIS Inc 17	●	●	●	
●	●	●	Associated Investigative Services Inc 171	●	●	●	●
●	●	●	Federal Research Corporation 751	●	●	●	●
●	●	●	Legal Courier Systems Inc 1196		●	●	●
●		●	Real Estate Information Service..............1656	●	●	●	
●	●	●	Shenandoah Title Services Inc 1795	●	●	●	
●			UCC Retrievals 1997	●	●	●	●

CV	CR	PR	**LOUISA**	UC	RE	TX	VR
●	●	●	Ellerson, H Watkins..............701	●	●	●	
●		●	Lawyer Title/Blue Ridge Agency Inc..............1182	●	●	●	

CV	CR	PR	**LUNENBURG**	UC	RE	TX	VR
●	●	●	Hawthorne, Robert E..............941	●	●	●	

CV	CR	PR	**MADISON**	UC	RE	TX	VR
●	●	●	Ellerson, H Watkins..............701	●	●	●	

CV	CR	PR	**MATHEWS**	UC	RE	TX	VR
●	●		Walker, Bobbi..............2044	●	●	●	

CV	CR	PR	**MECKLENBURG**	UC	RE	TX	VR
●	●	●	Hawthorne, Robert E..............941	●	●	●	

CV	CR	PR	**MIDDLESEX**	UC	RE	TX	VR
●	●	●	Adkins, Charles E..............85	●	●	●	●
●	●	●	Michael B Fixman & Associates 1338	●	●	●	●

MONTGOMERY

CV	CR	PR	Name	Page	UC	RE	TX	VR
●	●	●	Biesenbach, Betsy	298	●	●	●	
●	●	●	Brown-Browning, Gail	353	●	●	●	●
●	●	●	Federal Research Corporation	751	●	●	●	●
●	●		Fletcher, Jean R	785	●	●	●	
●	●	●	M & M Search Service Inc	1254	●	●	●	●

NELSON

CV	CR	PR	Name	Page	UC	RE	TX	VR
●	●	●	Berry, William Thomas	289	●	●	●	●
●		●	Lawyer Title/Blue Ridge Agency Inc	1182	●	●	●	

NEW KENT

CV	CR	PR	Name	Page	UC	RE	TX	VR
●	●	●	Adkins, Charles E	85	●	●	●	●
●			UCC Retrievals	1997	●	●	●	●

NORTHAMPTON

CV	CR	PR	Name	Page	UC	RE	TX	VR
●	●	●	Associated Investigative Services Inc	171	●	●	●	
●	●	●	Ayres, Judith	225	●	●	●	

NORTHUMBERLAND

CV	CR	PR	Name	Page	UC	RE	TX	VR
●	●	●	McKerns & McKerns	1314	●	●	●	

NOTTOWAY

CV	CR	PR	Name	Page	UC	RE	TX	VR
●	●	●	Allen III, William D	113	●	●	●	
●	●	●	Southall Jr, Valentine W	1824	●	●	●	

ORANGE

CV	CR	PR	Name	Page	UC	RE	TX	VR
●	●	●	Ellerson, H Watkins	701	●	●	●	
●		●	Lawyer Title/Blue Ridge Agency Inc	1182	●	●	●	
●		●	Washington Title Agencies	2059	●	●	●	●

PAGE

CV	CR	PR	Name	Page	UC	RE	TX	VR
●	●	●	Shenandoah Title Services Inc	1795	●	●	●	

PATRICK

CV	CR	PR	Name	Page	UC	RE	TX	VR
●	●		Fletcher, Jean R	785	●	●	●	
●	●		Grant, Gary	864	●	●	●	

PITTSYLVANIA

CV	CR	PR	Name	Page	UC	RE	TX	VR
●	●	●	Brown-Browning, Gail	353	●	●	●	●
●	●		Grant, Gary	864	●	●	●	

POWHATAN

CV	CR	PR	Name	Page	UC	RE	TX	VR
●	●	●	Cumberland Title Agency Inc	573	●	●	●	
●	●	●	Hylind Infoquest	1013	●	●	●	●
●	●	●	Southall Jr, Valentine W	1824	●	●	●	

PRINCE EDWARD

CV	CR	PR	Name	Page	UC	RE	TX	VR
●	●	●	Cumberland Title Agency Inc	573	●	●	●	
●	●	●	Hawthorne, Robert E	941	●	●	●	

PRINCE GEORGE

CV	CR	PR	Name	Page	UC	RE	TX	VR
●	●	●	Allen III, William D	113	●	●	●	
●	●	●	Federal Research Corporation	751	●	●	●	●
●	●	●	M & M Search Service Inc	1254	●	●	●	●
●		●	Pascal & Carter Process Service Inc	1522		●		
●			UCC Retrievals	1997	●	●	●	●

PRINCE WILLIAM

CV	CR	PR	Name	Page	UC	RE	TX	VR
●	●	●	Associated Investigative Services Inc	171	●	●	●	●
●	●	●	Federal Research Corporation	751	●	●	●	●
●	●	●	Hylind Infoquest	1013	●	●	●	●
●	●	●	Legal Courier Systems Inc	1196		●	●	●

		CV	CR	PR	**PULASKI**		UC	RE	TX	VR
		●	●	●	Brown-Browning, Gail.................353		●	●	●	●
		●	●		Fletcher, Jean R.................785		●	●	●	

		CV	CR	PR	**RAPPAHANNOCK**		UC	RE	TX	VR
		●		●	Washington Title Agencies.................2059		●	●	●	●

		CV	CR	PR	**RICHMOND**		UC	RE	TX	VR
		●	●	●	Associated Investigative Services Inc.................171		●	●	●	●
		●	●	●	McKerns & McKerns.................1314		●	●	●	

BK		CV	CR	PR	**ROANOKE**		UC	RE	TX	VR
●		●	●	●	Biesenbach, Betsy.................298		●	●	●	
●		●	●	●	Brown-Browning, Gail.................353		●	●	●	●
●		●	●	●	Clue Detective Service.................479		●	●	●	●
●		●	●		Fletcher, Jean R.................785		●	●	●	

		CV	CR	PR	**ROCKBRIDGE**		UC	RE	TX	VR
		●	●	●	Brown-Browning, Gail.................353		●	●	●	●
		●	●	●	Haine & Murtagh.................906		●	●	●	

DT		CV	CR	PR	**ROCKINGHAM**		UC	RE	TX	VR
		●	●	●	Heatwole, Kelly.................946		●	●	●	●
		●		●	Lawyers Title.................1185		●	●	●	

		CV	CR	PR	**RUSSELL**		UC	RE	TX	VR
		●	●		Fletcher, Jean R.................785		●	●	●	

		CV	CR	PR	**SCOTT**		UC	RE	TX	VR
		●	●	●	Clue Detective Service.................479		●	●	●	●
		●	●		Fletcher, Jean R.................785		●	●	●	

		CV	CR	PR	**SHENANDOAH**		UC	RE	TX	VR
		●	●	●	Shenandoah Title Services Inc.................1795		●	●	●	

		CV	CR	PR	**SMYTH**		UC	RE	TX	VR
		●	●	●	Clue Detective Service.................479		●	●	●	●
		●	●		Fletcher, Jean R.................785		●	●	●	

		CV	CR	PR	**SOUTHAMPTON**		UC	RE	TX	VR
		●	●	●	Associated Investigative Services Inc.................171		●	●	●	●
		●	●	●	Biesenbach, Betsy.................298		●	●	●	
		●	●		Fletcher, Jean R.................785		●	●	●	

		CV	CR	PR	**SPOTSYLVANIA**		UC	RE	TX	VR
		●	●	●	Hylind Infoquest.................1013		●	●	●	●

		CV	CR	PR	**STAFFORD**		UC	RE	TX	VR
		●	●	●	Legal Courier Systems Inc.................1196			●	●	●

		CV	CR	PR	**SURRY**		UC	RE	TX	VR
		●	●	●	O'Connell, Nikki A.................1451		●	●	●	●

		CV	CR	PR	**SUSSEX**		UC	RE	TX	VR
		●	●	●	Allen III, William D.................113		●	●	●	

		CV	CR	PR	**TAZEWELL**		UC	RE	TX	VR
		●	●	●	Clue Detective Service.................479		●	●	●	●
		●	●		Fletcher, Jean R.................785		●	●	●	

		CV	CR	PR	**WARREN**		UC	RE	TX	VR
		●	●	●	Shenandoah Title Services Inc.................1795		●	●	●	

DT		CV	CR	PR	WASHINGTON	UC	RE	TX	VR
●		●	●		Fletcher, Jean R.................................785	●	●	●	

		CV	CR	PR	WESTMORELAND	UC	RE	TX	VR
		●	●	●	McKerns & McKerns.................................1314	●	●	●	

DT		CV	CR	PR	WISE	UC	RE	TX	VR
●		●	●	●	Clue Detective Service.................................479	●	●	●	●
●		●	●		Fletcher, Jean R.................................785	●	●	●	

		CV	CR	PR	WYTHE	UC	RE	TX	VR
		●	●	●	Clue Detective Service.................................479	●	●	●	●
		●	●		Fletcher, Jean R.................................785	●	●	●	

		CV	CR	PR	YORK	UC	RE	TX	VR
		●	●	●	Associated Investigative Services Inc.................................171	●	●	●	●
		●	●	●	O'Connell, Nikki A.................................1451	●	●	●	
		●	●		Walker, Bobbi.................................2044	●	●	●	

DT	BK	CV	CR	PR	CITY OF ALEXANDRIA	UC	RE	TX	VR
●	●	●	●	●	Associated Investigative Services Inc.................................171	●	●	●	●
●		●	●		Douglas Investigations Ltd.................................655				
●		●	●	●	Federal Information Service.................................749	●	●	●	
●		●	●	●	Federal Research Corporation.................................751	●	●	●	
●		●	●	●	Hylind Infoquest.................................1013	●	●	●	
●		●	●	●	Instant Information Systems.................................1032	●	●	●	
●		●	●	●	M & M Search Service Inc.................................1254	●	●	●	
●		●		●	Pascal & Carter Process Service Inc.................................1522		●		
		●		●	Real Estate Information Service.................................1656	●	●	●	
●	●	●	●	●	University Process Service.................................2012				

		CV	CR	PR	CITY OF BEDFORD	UC	RE	TX	VR
		●	●	●	Biesenbach, Betsy.................................298	●	●	●	

		CV	CR	PR	CITY OF BRISTOL	UC	RE	TX	VR
		●	●		Fletcher, Jean R.................................785	●	●	●	

		CV	CR	PR	CITY OF BUENA VISTA	UC	RE	TX	VR
		●	●	●	Haine & Murtagh.................................906	●	●	●	

		CV	CR	PR	CITY OF CHARLOTTESVILLE	UC	RE	TX	VR
		●	●	●	Ellerson, H Watkins.................................701	●	●	●	
		●		●	Lawyer Title/Blue Ridge Agency Inc.................................1182	●	●	●	

		CV	CR	PR	CITY OF CHESAPEAKE	UC	RE	TX	VR
		●	●	●	Associated Investigative Services Inc.................................171	●	●	●	●
		●	●	●	Title Search Services Inc.................................1954	●	●	●	

		CV	CR	PR	CITY OF CLIFTON FORGE	UC	RE	TX	VR
		●	●		Fletcher, Jean R.................................785	●	●	●	
		●	●	●	Singleton & Deeds.................................1808	●	●	●	●

		CV	CR	PR	CITY OF COLONIAL HEIGHTS	UC	RE	TX	VR
		●	●	●	Allen III, William D.................................113	●	●	●	
		●			UCC Retrievals.................................1997	●	●	●	●

		CV	CR	PR	CITY OF COVINGTON	UC	RE	TX	VR
		●	●		Fletcher, Jean R.................................785	●	●	●	
		●	●	●	Singleton & Deeds.................................1808	●	●	●	●

DT		CV	CR	PR	CITY OF DANVILLE	UC	RE	TX	VR
●		●	●		Grant, Gary.................................864	●	●	●	

			CV	CR	PR	CITY OF EMPORIA	UC	RE	TX	VR
			●	●	●	Sharrett, W Allan 1790	●	●	●	

			CV	CR	PR	CITY OF FAIRFAX	UC	RE	TX	VR
			●	●	●	Associated Investigative Services Inc 171	●	●	●	●
			●			Douglas Investigations Ltd............655				
			●	●	●	Instant Information Systems...............1032	●	●	●	●

			CV	CR	PR	CITY OF FALLS CHURCH	UC	RE	TX	VR
			●	●	●	Associated Investigative Services Inc 171	●	●	●	●
			●	●	●	Instant Information Systems...............1032	●	●	●	●

			CV	CR	PR	CITY OF FRANKLIN	UC	RE	TX	VR
			●	●	●	Biesenbach, Betsy 298	●	●	●	

			CV	CR	PR	CITY OF FREDERICKSBURG	UC	RE	TX	VR
			●	●	●	Hylind Infoquest............1013	●	●	●	●

			CV	CR	PR	CITY OF GALAX	UC	RE	TX	VR
			●	●		Fletcher, Jean R............785	●	●	●	
						Southwest Virginia Abstract & Title Co 1837	●	●	●	

			CV	CR	PR	CITY OF HAMPTON	UC	RE	TX	VR
			●	●	●	Associated Investigative Services Inc 171	●	●	●	●
			●	●	●	O'Connell, Nikki A............1451	●	●	●	●
			●	●		Walker, Bobbi 2044	●	●	●	

	BK		CV	CR	PR	CITY OF HARRISONBURG	UC	RE	TX	VR
					●	Lawyers Title............1185	●	●	●	

			CV	CR	PR	CITY OF HOPEWELL	UC	RE	TX	VR
			●			UCC Retrievals 1997	●	●	●	●

			CV	CR	PR	CITY OF LEXINGTON	UC	RE	TX	VR
			●	●	●	Haine & Murtagh 906	●	●	●	

DT	BK		CV	CR	PR	CITY OF LYNCHBURG	UC	RE	TX	VR
●	●		●	●	●	Brown-Browning, Gail............353	●	●	●	●
●	●		●	●	●	Central Virginia Investigative Service 429	●	●	●	●

			CV	CR	PR	CITY OF MANASSAS	UC	RE	TX	VR
			●	●	●	Associated Investigative Services Inc 171	●	●	●	●

			CV	CR	PR	CITY OF MANASSAS PARK	UC	RE	TX	VR
						See ALL COUNTIES............				

			CV	CR	PR	CITY OF MARTINSVILLE	UC	RE	TX	VR
			●	●		Grant, Gary............864	●	●	●	

DT	BK		CV	CR	PR	CITY OF NEWPORT NEWS	UC	RE	TX	VR
●	●		●	●	●	Associated Investigative Services Inc 171	●	●	●	●
●	●		●	●	●	O'Connell, Nikki A............1451	●	●	●	●
●	●		●	●		Walker, Bobbi 2044	●	●	●	

DT	BK		CV	CR	PR	CITY OF NORFOLK	UC	RE	TX	VR
●	●		●	●	●	Associated Investigative Services Inc 171	●	●	●	●
●	●		●	●	●	Michael B Fixman & Associates............1338	●	●	●	●
			●	●	●	Title Search Services Inc............1954	●	●	●	

			CV	CR	PR	CITY OF NORTON	UC	RE	TX	VR
						See ALL COUNTIES............				

			CV	CR	PR	CITY OF PETERSBURG	UC	RE	TX	VR
			●	●	●	Allen III, William D............113	●	●	●	
			●	●	●	The Marston Agency Inc............1937	●	●	●	●

DT	CV	CR	PR		Page	UC	RE	TX	VR
			•	UCC Retrievals	1997	•	•	•	•

CITY OF POQUOSON — CV CR PR | UC RE TX VR

See ALL COUNTIES

CITY OF PORTSMOUTH — CV CR PR | UC RE TX VR

	CV	CR	PR		Page	UC	RE	TX	VR
	•	•	•	Associated Investigative Services Inc	171	•	•	•	•

CITY OF RADFORD — CV CR PR | UC RE TX VR

	CV	CR	PR		Page	UC	RE	TX	VR
	•	•		Fletcher, Jean R	785	•	•	•	

CITY OF RICHMOND — CV CR PR | UC RE TX VR

	CV	CR	PR		Page	UC	RE	TX	VR
	•	•	•	Federal Information Service	749	•	•	•	•
	•	•	•	Federal Research Corporation	751	•	•	•	•
	•	•	•	Hylind Infoquest	1013	•	•	•	•
	•	•	•	The Marston Agency Inc	1937	•	•	•	•
	•			UCC Retrievals	1997	•	•	•	•

CITY OF ROANOKE — DT CV CR PR | UC RE TX VR

DT	CV	CR	PR		Page	UC	RE	TX	VR
•	•	•	•	Biesenbach, Betsy	298	•	•	•	
•	•	•	•	Brown-Browning, Gail	353	•	•	•	•
•	•	•		Fletcher, Jean R	785	•	•	•	

CITY OF SALEM — CV CR PR | UC RE TX VR

	CV	CR	PR		Page	UC	RE	TX	VR
	•	•	•	Brown-Browning, Gail	353	•	•	•	•

CITY OF SOUTH BOSTON — CV CR PR | UC RE TX VR

See ALL COUNTIES

CITY OF STAUNTON — CV CR PR | UC RE TX VR

	CV	CR	PR		Page	UC	RE	TX	VR
	•	•	•	Data Abstract & Title Co Inc	591	•	•	•	

CITY OF SUFFOLK — CV CR PR | UC RE TX VR

	CV	CR	PR		Page	UC	RE	TX	VR
	•	•	•	Associated Investigative Services Inc	171	•	•	•	•
	•	•	•	Michael B Fixman & Associates	1338	•	•	•	•

CITY OF VIRGINIA BEACH — CV CR PR | UC RE TX VR

	CV	CR	PR		Page	UC	RE	TX	VR
	•	•	•	Associated Investigative Services Inc	171	•	•	•	•
	•	•	•	Title Search Services Inc	1954	•	•	•	

CITY OF WAYNESBORO — CV CR PR | UC RE TX VR

	CV	CR	PR		Page	UC	RE	TX	VR
	•	•	•	Data Abstract & Title Co Inc	591	•	•	•	

CITY OF WILLIAMSBURG — CV CR PR | UC RE TX VR

	CV	CR	PR		Page	UC	RE	TX	VR
	•	•	•	Associated Investigative Services Inc	171	•	•	•	•
	•	•		Fletcher, Jean R	785	•	•	•	
	•	•	•	O'Connell, Nikki A	1451	•	•	•	•

CITY OF WINCHESTER — CV CR PR | UC RE TX VR

	CV	CR	PR		Page	UC	RE	TX	VR
	•	•	•	Shenandoah Title Services Inc	1795	•	•	•	
	•			UCC Retrievals	1997	•	•	•	•

Washington

DT	BK	CV	CR	PR	ALL COUNTIES	UC	RE	TX	VR
●	●	●	●	●	Joden & Associates Inc 1088	●	●	●	●

		CV	CR	PR	ADAMS	UC	RE	TX	VR
		●	●	●	AM-PM Services............30	●	●	●	●

		CV	CR	PR	ASOTIN	UC	RE	TX	VR
		●	●	●	Pullman Process Service 1630				

		CV	CR	PR	BENTON	UC	RE	TX	VR
		●			Hawley, Marlene..............940	●	●	●	
			●		Houchin, Florence..............995				
		●	●	●	McCord Company..............1307	●	●	●	●

		CV	CR	PR	CHELAN	UC	RE	TX	VR
		●	●	●	AM-PM Services............30	●	●	●	●
		●	●	●	Donald Jones Investigation/Process Svc 645	●	●	●	●

		CV	CR	PR	CLALLAM	UC	RE	TX	VR
		●	●	●	N W Legal Support Inc 1404	●	●	●	●

		CV	CR	PR	CLARK	UC	RE	TX	VR
		●	●	●	Alan H Crowe & Associates Inc..............97	●	●	●	●
		●	●	●	Lawyer's Legal Service..............1183	●	●	●	
		●	●		Marosi & Associates Inc 1282		●		●
		●	●	●	McCord Company..............1307	●	●	●	●
		●	●	●	N W Legal Support Inc 1404	●	●	●	●

		CV	CR	PR	COLUMBIA	UC	RE	TX	VR
		●	●	●	Columbia County Title Co 496	●	●	●	

		CV	CR	PR	COWLITZ	UC	RE	TX	VR
		●	●	●	N W Legal Support Inc 1404	●	●	●	●
		●	●	●	Perfectly Legal Documents 1538	●	●	●	●

		CV	CR	PR	DOUGLAS	UC	RE	TX	VR
		●	●	●	AM-PM Services............30	●	●	●	●
		●	●	●	Donald Jones Investigation/Process Svc 645	●	●	●	●

		CV	CR	PR	FERRY	UC	RE	TX	VR
		●	●	●	Ferry County Title & Escrow Co Inc 754	●	●	●	●

		CV	CR	PR	FRANKLIN	UC	RE	TX	VR
		●	●	●	AM-PM Services............30	●	●	●	●
			●		Houchin, Florence..............995				

		CV	CR	PR	GARFIELD	UC	RE	TX	VR
		●	●	●	Pacific Process Service..............1497	●	●	●	●

		CV	CR	PR	GRANT	UC	RE	TX	VR
		●	●	●	AM-PM Services............30	●	●	●	●
		●	●	●	Donald Jones Investigation/Process Svc 645	●	●	●	●

		CV	CR	PR	GRAYS HARBOR	UC	RE	TX	VR
		●	●	●	ABC Legal Messenger 15	●	●	●	●
		●	●	●	N W Legal Support Inc 1404	●	●	●	●
		●	●	●	Perfectly Legal Documents 1538	●	●	●	●

		CV	CR	PR	ISLAND	UC	RE	TX	VR
		●	●	●	ABC Legal Messenger 15	●	●	●	●
		●	●	●	N W Legal Support Inc 1404	●	●	●	●

JEFFERSON

Service	Page	CV	CR	PR	UC	RE	TX	VR
N W Legal Support Inc	1404	•	•	•	•	•	•	•

KING

Service	Page	DT	BK	CV	CR	PR	UC	RE	TX	VR
ABC Legal Messenger	15	•	•	•	•	•	•	•	•	•
All Pro Info Search	110	•	•	•	•	•	•	•	•	•
Attorney's Information Bureau Inc	203	•	•	•	•	•	•	•	•	•
Golden Information Group	852				•	•				
Hoover Professional Investigative	990	•	•	•	•	•	•	•	•	•
Legal Legwork	1204	•	•	•	•	•	•	•	•	•
LegalEze	1216	•	•	•	•	•	•	•	•	•
N W Legal Support Inc	1404	•	•	•	•	•	•	•	•	•
Perfectly Legal Documents	1538	•	•	•	•	•	•	•	•	•
Personal Background Investigations	1542			•	•					
Prentice Hall Legal & Financial Services	1596	•	•	•	•	•	•	•	•	•
Prentice Hall Legal & Financial Services	1597						•			
R & I Associates	1638	•	•	•	•	•	•		•	•
Spade and Archer Investigations	1839			•	•	•	•	•	•	•
Unisearch Inc	2007	•	•	•	•	•	•		•	•

KITSAP

Service	Page	CV	CR	PR	UC	RE	TX	VR
ABC Legal Messenger	15	•	•	•	•	•	•	•
Hoover Professional Investigative	990	•	•	•	•	•	•	•
Legal Legwork	1204	•	•	•	•	•	•	•
N W Legal Support Inc	1404	•	•	•	•	•	•	•
Personal Background Investigations	1542	•	•					

KITTITAS

Service	Page	CV	CR	PR	UC	RE	TX	VR
AM-PM Services	30	•	•	•	•	•	•	•
Attorney's Information Bureau Inc	203	•	•	•	•	•	•	•
McCord Company	1307	•	•	•	•	•	•	•

KLICKITAT

Service	Page	CV	CR	PR	UC	RE	TX	VR
Columbia Gorge Investigations	497	•	•	•	•	•	•	•

LEWIS

Service	Page	CV	CR	PR	UC	RE	TX	VR
ABC Legal Messenger	15	•	•	•	•	•	•	•
N W Legal Support Inc	1404	•	•	•	•	•	•	•
Perfectly Legal Documents	1538	•	•	•	•	•	•	•

LINCOLN

Service	Page	CV	CR	PR	UC	RE	TX	VR
AM-PM Services	30	•	•	•	•	•	•	•

MASON

Service	Page	CV	CR	PR	UC	RE	TX	VR
ABC Legal Messenger	15	•	•	•	•	•	•	•
Hoover Professional Investigative	990	•	•	•	•	•	•	•
N W Legal Support Inc	1404	•	•	•	•	•	•	•

OKANOGAN

Service	Page	CV	CR	PR	UC	RE	TX	VR
AM-PM Services	30	•	•	•	•	•	•	•
Baines Title Company Inc	234	•	•	•	•	•	•	•

PACIFIC

Service	Page	CV	CR	PR	UC	RE	TX	VR
Charter Title Corp	441	•		•	•	•	•	

PEND OREILLE

Service	Page	CV	CR	PR	UC	RE	TX	VR
Action Agency	71	•	•	•	•	•	•	•
Pacific Process Service	1497	•	•	•	•	•	•	•

PIERCE

Service	Page	DT	BK	CV	CR	PR	UC	RE	TX	VR
ABC Legal Messenger	15	•	•	•	•	•	•	•	•	•
All Pro Info Search	110	•	•	•	•	•	•	•	•	•
Attorney's Information Bureau Inc	203	•	•	•	•	•	•		•	•

CV	CR	PR		Company	Page	UC	RE	TX	VR
•	•	•	• •	Hoover Professional Investigative	990	•	•	•	•
•	•	•	• •	Legal Legwork	1204	•	•	•	•
•	•	•	• •	N W Legal Support Inc	1404	•	•	•	•
•	•	•	• •	Personal Background Investigations	1542				
•	•	•	• •	Prentice Hall Legal & Financial Services	1596	•	•		•
				Prentice Hall Legal & Financial Services	1597	•			
•		•	• •	R & I Associates	1638	•	•	•	•
		•	• •	Spade and Archer Investigations	1839	•	•	•	•
•	•	•	• •	Unisearch Inc	2007	•		•	•

SAN JUAN

CV	CR	PR	Company	Page	UC	RE	TX	VR
•	•	•	Brennan, Leslie	342	•	•	•	•
•		•	San Juan County Title Co.	1734	•	•	•	•

SKAGIT

CV	CR	PR	Company	Page	UC	RE	TX	VR
•	•	•	4th Corner Network Inc.	1	•	•	•	
•	•	•	ABC Legal Messenger	15	•	•	•	•
•	•	•	Fourth Corner Network Inc.	800	•	•	•	•
•	•	•	N W Legal Support Inc	1404	•	•	•	•
•	•	•	Spade and Archer Investigations	1839	•	•	•	•
•	•	•	Unisearch Inc	2007	•		•	•

SKAMANIA

CV	CR	PR	Company	Page	UC	RE	TX	VR
•	•	•	Skamania County Title Company	1809	•	•	•	

SNOHOMISH

CV	CR	PR	Company	Page	UC	RE	TX	VR
•	•	•	ABC Legal Messenger	15	•	•	•	•
•	•	•	All Pro Info Search	110	•	•	•	•
•	•	•	Attorney's Information Bureau Inc	203	•	•	•	•
•	•	•	Hoover Professional Investigative	990	•	•	•	•
•	•	•	LegalEze	1216	•	•	•	•
•	•	•	N W Legal Support Inc	1404	•	•	•	•
•	•	•	Perfectly Legal Documents	1538	•	•	•	•
•	•		Personal Background Investigations	1542				
•	•	•	Prentice Hall Legal & Financial Services	1596	•	•	•	•
			Prentice Hall Legal & Financial Services	1597	•			
•	•	•	Spade and Archer Investigations	1839	•	•	•	•
•	•	•	Unisearch Inc	2007	•		•	•

SPOKANE

DT	BK	CV	CR	PR	Company	Page	UC	RE	TX	VR
		•	•	•	Best Investigations	292	•	•	•	•
•	•	•	•	•	Detective Referral Service	626	•	•	•	
•	•	•	•	•	Lawyers Legal Liasion	1184	•	•	•	•
•	•	•	•	•	Pacific Process Service	1497	•	•	•	•

STEVENS

CV	CR	PR	Company	Page	UC	RE	TX	VR
•	•	•	Pacific Process Service	1497	•	•	•	•
•	•	•	Stevens County Title	1867	•	•	•	

THURSTON

CV	CR	PR	Company	Page	UC	RE	TX	VR
•	•	•	ABC Legal Messenger	15	•	•	•	•
•	•	•	Legal Legwork	1204	•	•	•	•
•	•	•	N W Legal Support Inc	1404	•	•	•	•
•	•	•	Prentice Hall Legal & Financial Services	1596	•	•	•	•
			Prentice Hall Legal & Financial Services	1597	•			
•	•	•	Unisearch Inc	2007	•		•	•

WAHKIAKUM

CV	CR	PR	Company	Page	UC	RE	TX	VR
			See ALL COUNTIES					

WALLA WALLA

CV	CR	PR	Company	Page	UC	RE	TX	VR
•		•	Walla Walla Title Co.	2047	•	•	•	•

	CV	CR	PR	WHATCOM	UC	RE	TX	VR
	●	●	●	4th Corner Network Inc............................1	●	●	●	
	●	●	●	Fourth Corner Network Inc.......................800	●	●	●	●
	●	●	●	N W Legal Support Inc 1404	●	●	●	●
	●	●	●	Spade and Archer Investigations.............1839	●	●	●	●

	CV	CR	PR	WHITMAN	UC	RE	TX	VR
	●	●	●	Detective Referral Service.......................626	●	●	●	
	●	●	●	Pacific Process Service...........................1497	●	●	●	●
	●	●	●	Pullman Process Service 1630				

DT	CV	CR	PR	YAKIMA	UC	RE	TX	VR
●	●	●	●	Executive Process Service.......................725	●	●	●	●
●	●	●	●	Legal Couriers Inc................................1197	●	●	●	●

West Virginia

DT	BK	CV	CR	PR	ALL COUNTIES		UC	RE	TX	VR
		●	●	●	Kunzelman, Fred and Rebecca	1139	●	●	●	●
●	●	●	●	●	The Croson Agency	1928	●	●	●	●

		CV	CR	PR	BARBOUR		UC	RE	TX	VR
		●	●	●	RLS Inc	1641	●	●	●	●

		CV	CR	PR	BERKELEY		UC	RE	TX	VR
		●		●	Schramm, Susan Bailey	1747	●	●	●	●

		CV	CR	PR	BOONE		UC	RE	TX	VR
		●	●	●	American Investigations	134	●	●	●	●
		●	●	●	RLS Inc	1641	●	●	●	●

		CV	CR	PR	BRAXTON		UC	RE	TX	VR
		●	●	●	RLS Inc	1641	●	●	●	●

		CV	CR	PR	BROOKE		UC	RE	TX	VR
		●	●	●	Coats, Janet	483	●		●	●
		●	●	●	Tomich, Vicki	1964	●	●	●	●

DT		CV	CR	PR	CABELL		UC	RE	TX	VR
●		●	●	●	Davis Investigatons Inc	603	●	●	●	●

		CV	CR	PR	CALHOUN		UC	RE	TX	VR
		●	●	●	RLS Inc	1641	●	●	●	●

		CV	CR	PR	CLAY		UC	RE	TX	VR
					See ALL COUNTIES					

		CV	CR	PR	DODDRIDGE		UC	RE	TX	VR
		●	●	●	RLS Inc	1641	●	●	●	●

		CV	CR	PR	FAYETTE		UC	RE	TX	VR
		●	●	●	RLS Inc	1641	●	●	●	●
		●	●	●	Reno, Connie	1680	●	●	●	●

		CV	CR	PR	GILMER		UC	RE	TX	VR
		●	●	●	RLS Inc	1641	●	●	●	●

		CV	CR	PR	GRANT		UC	RE	TX	VR
		●	●	●	Heatwole, Kelly	946	●	●	●	●
		●	●	●	Reel, Alicia	1670	●	●	●	●

		CV	CR	PR	GREENBRIER		UC	RE	TX	VR
		●	●	●	Reno, Connie	1680	●	●	●	●

		CV	CR	PR	HAMPSHIRE		UC	RE	TX	VR
		●	●	●	Heatwole, Kelly	946	●	●	●	●
		●		●	Schramm, Susan Bailey	1747	●	●	●	●

		CV	CR	PR	HANCOCK		UC	RE	TX	VR
		●	●	●	Coats, Janet	483	●		●	●
		●	●	●	Tomich, Vicki	1964	●	●	●	●

		CV	CR	PR	HARDY		UC	RE	TX	VR
		●	●	●	Heatwole, Kelly	946	●	●	●	●

DT		CV	CR	PR	HARRISON		UC	RE	TX	VR
		●	●	●	RLS Inc	1641	●	●	●	●

		CV	CR	PR	JACKSON		UC	RE	TX	VR
		●	●	●	RLS Inc	1641	●	●	●	●

DT	BK	CV	CR	PR	County / Name	Page	UC	RE	TX	VR
		CV	CR	PR	**JEFFERSON**		UC	RE	TX	VR
		•	•	•	Quality Abstractors Inc	1633	•	•	•	
		•		•	Schramm, Susan Bailey	1747	•	•	•	•
DT	BK	CV	CR	PR	**KANAWHA**		UC	RE	TX	VR
•	•	•	•	•	American Investigations	134	•	•	•	•
		CV	CR	PR	**LEWIS**		UC	RE	TX	VR
		•	•	•	Kunzelman, Fred and Rebecca	1139	•	•	•	•
		•	•	•	RLS Inc	1641	•	•	•	•
		CV	CR	PR	**LINCOLN**		UC	RE	TX	VR
		•	•	•	American Investigations	134	•	•	•	•
		•	•	•	Davis Investigatons Inc	603	•	•	•	•
		CV	CR	PR	**LOGAN**		UC	RE	TX	VR
		•	•	•	RLS Inc	1641	•	•	•	•
		CV	CR	PR	**MCDOWELL**		UC	RE	TX	VR
		•	•	•	RLS Inc	1641	•	•	•	•
		CV	CR	PR	**MARION**		UC	RE	TX	VR
		•	•	•	RLS Inc	1641	•	•	•	•
		CV	CR	PR	**MARSHALL**		UC	RE	TX	VR
		•	•	•	Tomich, Vicki	1964	•	•	•	•
		CV	CR	PR	**MASON**		UC	RE	TX	VR
		•	•	•	Davis Investigatons Inc	603	•	•	•	•
		•		•	Paralegal Services	1515	•	•	•	
DT		CV	CR	PR	**MERCER**		UC	RE	TX	VR
		•	•	•	Carr, Barbara	410	•	•	•	•
		•	•	•	Reno, Connie	1680	•	•	•	•
		CV	CR	PR	**MINERAL**		UC	RE	TX	VR
		•	•	•	Heatwole, Kelly	946	•	•	•	•
		•	•	•	RLS Inc	1641	•	•	•	•
		CV	CR	PR	**MINGO**		UC	RE	TX	VR
		•	•	•	RLS Inc	1641	•	•	•	•
		CV	CR	PR	**MONONGALIA**		UC	RE	TX	VR
		•	•	•	RLS Inc	1641	•	•	•	•
		CV	CR	PR	**MONROE**		UC	RE	TX	VR
		•	•	•	Carr, Barbara	410	•	•	•	•
		CV	CR	PR	**MORGAN**		UC	RE	TX	VR
		•			Paralegal Services	1516	•	•	•	•
		•		•	Schramm, Susan Bailey	1747	•	•	•	•
		CV	CR	PR	**NICHOLAS**		UC	RE	TX	VR
		•	•	•	RLS Inc	1641	•	•	•	•
		•	•	•	Reno, Connie	1680	•	•	•	•
DT	BK	CV	CR	PR	**OHIO**		UC	RE	TX	VR
	•	•	•	•	Coats, Janet	483	•		•	•
•		•	•	•	Tomich, Vicki	1964	•	•	•	•
		CV	CR	PR	**PENDLETON**		UC	RE	TX	VR
		•	•	•	Gum, Max L	900	•	•	•	•
		•	•	•	Heatwole, Kelly	946	•	•	•	•

	CV	CR	PR	PLEASANTS		UC	RE	TX	VR
	●	●	●	RLS Inc..1641		●	●	●	●

	CV	CR	PR	POCAHONTAS		UC	RE	TX	VR
	●	●	●	Friel, Sandra...815		●	●	●	●
	●	●	●	Gum, Max L...900		●	●	●	●

	CV	CR	PR	PRESTON		UC	RE	TX	VR
	●	●	●	RLS Inc..1641		●	●	●	●

	CV	CR	PR	PUTNAM		UC	RE	TX	VR
	●	●	●	American Investigations................................134		●	●	●	●

DT	CV	CR	PR	RALEIGH		UC	RE	TX	VR
	●	●	●	Carr, Barbara..410		●	●	●	●
●	●	●	●	Reno, Connie...1680		●	●	●	●

DT	CV	CR	PR	RANDOLPH		UC	RE	TX	VR
●	●	●	●	RLS Inc..1641		●	●	●	●

	CV	CR	PR	RITCHIE		UC	RE	TX	VR
	●	●	●	RLS Inc..1641		●	●	●	●
	●	●	●	West, Thomas..2079		●	●	●	●

	CV	CR	PR	ROANE		UC	RE	TX	VR
	●	●	●	RLS Inc..1641		●	●	●	●

	CV	CR	PR	SUMMERS		UC	RE	TX	VR
	●	●	●	Carr, Barbara..410		●	●	●	●
	●	●	●	Reno, Connie...1680		●	●	●	●

	CV	CR	PR	TAYLOR		UC	RE	TX	VR
			●	Abruzzino, Patricia..42		●	●	●	●
	●	●	●	RLS Inc..1641		●	●	●	●

	CV	CR	PR	TUCKER		UC	RE	TX	VR
	●	●	●	RLS Inc..1641		●	●	●	●

	CV	CR	PR	TYLER		UC	RE	TX	VR
	●	●	●	West, Thomas..2079		●	●	●	●

	CV	CR	PR	UPSHUR		UC	RE	TX	VR
	●	●	●	RLS Inc..1641		●	●	●	●

	CV	CR	PR	WAYNE		UC	RE	TX	VR
	●	●	●	Davis Investigatons Inc................................603		●	●	●	●

	CV	CR	PR	WEBSTER		UC	RE	TX	VR
	●	●	●	RLS Inc..1641		●	●	●	●

	CV	CR	PR	WETZEL		UC	RE	TX	VR
	●	●	●	Tomich, Vicki...1964		●	●	●	●
	●	●	●	West, Thomas..2079		●	●	●	●

	CV	CR	PR	WIRT		UC	RE	TX	VR
	●	●	●	RLS Inc..1641		●	●	●	●

DT	CV	CR	PR	WOOD		UC	RE	TX	VR
●	●	●	●	RLS Inc..1641		●	●	●	●
	●	●	●	West, Thomas..2079		●	●	●	●

	CV	CR	PR	WYOMING		UC	RE	TX	VR
	●	●	●	RLS Inc..1641		●	●	●	●

Wisconsin

CV	CR	PR	ADAMS		UC	RE	TX	VR
●	●	●	Adams County Land Titles....................78		●	●	●	●

CV	CR	PR	ASHLAND		UC	RE	TX	VR
●		●	North Wisconsin Abstract Co...................1441		●	●	●	
●	●		Reid, Ann C...................1675		●	●	●	●
●	●	●	Surety Abstract & Title Company...................1889		●	●	●	●

CV	CR	PR	BARRON		UC	RE	TX	VR
●		●	Barron County Abstract....................251		●	●	●	
●		●	Search Associates...................1753		●	●	●	

CV	CR	PR	BAYFIELD		UC	RE	TX	VR
●		●	North Wisconsin Abstract Co...................1441		●	●	●	●
●	●		Reid, Ann C...................1675		●	●	●	●

CV	CR	PR	BROWN		UC	RE	TX	VR
●		●	Bay Title and Abstract Inc...................265		●	●	●	
●	●	●	LITQIS Group...................1143		●	●	●	●

CV	CR	PR	BUFFALO		UC	RE	TX	VR
		●	Boles-Wallner Abstract and Title...................316		●	●	●	

CV	CR	PR	BURNETT		UC	RE	TX	VR
●	●	●	Burnett County Abstract Co...................369		●	●	●	
●		●	Northwest Land Title Inc...................1447		●	●	●	

CV	CR	PR	CALUMET		UC	RE	TX	VR
●		●	Bay Title and Abstract Inc...................265		●	●	●	

CV	CR	PR	CHIPPEWA		UC	RE	TX	VR
●		●	Professional Title Services Inc...................1622		●	●	●	
●		●	Search Associates...................1753		●	●	●	●

CV	CR	PR	CLARK		UC	RE	TX	VR
●	●	●	Bill Bonham "The Investigator"...................301		●	●	●	●
		●	Boles-Wallner Abstract and Title...................316		●	●	●	

CV	CR	PR	COLUMBIA		UC	RE	TX	VR
●	●	●	Gregg Investigations Inc of Janesville...................878		●	●	●	●
●	●	●	Gregg Investigations Inc of Madison...................879		●	●	●	●

CV	CR	PR	CRAWFORD		UC	RE	TX	VR
●	●	●	Donna Bean Abstractor...................646		●	●	●	●

DT	BK	CV	CR	PR	DANE		UC	RE	TX	VR
	●	●		●	Bay Title and Abstract Inc...................265		●			●
●	●	●	●		Dane County Legal Notice...................587		●			●
●	●	●	●	●	Gregg Investigations Inc of Janesville...................878		●	●	●	●
●	●	●	●	●	Gregg Investigations Inc of Madison...................879		●	●	●	●
		●		●	Search Associates...................1753		●	●	●	●

CV	CR	PR	DODGE		UC	RE	TX	VR
●	●	●	Gregg Investigations Inc of Janesville...................878		●	●	●	●
●	●	●	Gregg Investigations Inc of Madison...................879		●	●	●	●
●	●	●	LITQIS Group...................1143		●	●	●	●
●	●	●	Search Associates...................1753		●	●	●	●
●	●	●	Wisconsin Title of Fond Du Lac...................2108		●	●	●	●

CV	CR	PR	DOOR		UC	RE	TX	VR
●		●	Bay Title and Abstract Inc...................265		●	●	●	
●		●	Search Associates...................1753		●	●	●	●

CV	CR	PR	DOUGLAS		UC	RE	TX	VR
●	●		Reid, Ann C...1675		●	●	●	●
●	●		Seehus, Penny 1781			●	●	

CV	CR	PR	DUNN		UC	RE	TX	VR
●		●	Dunn County Abstract & Title Inc....................667			●	●	
●		●	Professional Title Services Inc........................1622		●	●	●	

CV	CR	PR	EAU CLAIRE		UC	RE	TX	VR
●		●	Professional Title Services Inc........................1622		●	●	●	

CV	CR	PR	FLORENCE		UC	RE	TX	VR
●		●	Florence County Abstract...................................787		●	●	●	●
●	●	●	Penninsula Title and Abstract Corp.................1534		●	●	●	

CV	CR	PR	FOND DU LAC		UC	RE	TX	VR
●		●	Search Associates...1753		●	●	●	●
●	●	●	Wisconsin Title of Fond Du Lac.....................2108		●	●	●	●

CV	CR	PR	FOREST		UC	RE	TX	VR
●		●	Star Title Company Inc 1851		●	●	●	

CV	CR	PR	GRANT		UC	RE	TX	VR
●	●	●	Grant County Abstract Co..................................863		●	●	●	●

CV	CR	PR	GREEN		UC	RE	TX	VR
●	●	●	Ekum Abstract and Title...................................694		●	●	●	
●	●	●	Gregg Investigations Inc of Janesville.............878		●	●	●	●
●	●	●	Gregg Investigations Inc of Madison 879		●	●	●	●
●		●	Search Associates...1753		●	●	●	●

CV	CR	PR	GREEN LAKE		UC	RE	TX	VR
●	●	●	Green Lake Title & Abstract Co.........................872		●	●	●	●

CV	CR	PR	IOWA		UC	RE	TX	VR
●	●	●	Gregg Investigations Inc of Janesville.............878		●	●	●	●
●	●	●	Gregg Investigations Inc of Madison 879		●	●	●	●

CV	CR	PR	IRON		UC	RE	TX	VR
●		●	Iron Title & Abstract Co 1056		●	●	●	●

CV	CR	PR	JACKSON		UC	RE	TX	VR
		●	Boles-Wallner Abstract and Title......................316		●	●	●	
●		●	Search Associates...1753		●	●	●	●

CV	CR	PR	JEFFERSON		UC	RE	TX	VR
●	●	●	Gregg Investigations Inc of Janesville.............878		●	●	●	●
●	●	●	Gregg Investigations Inc of Madison 879		●	●	●	●
●		●	Search Associates...1753		●	●	●	●

CV	CR	PR	JUNEAU		UC	RE	TX	VR
		●	Boles-Wallner Abstract and Title......................316		●	●	●	

CV	CR	PR	KENOSHA		UC	RE	TX	VR
●	●	●	LITQIS Group...1143		●	●	●	●
●	●	●	Pro Serve...1608		●	●	●	●
●		●	Search Associates...1753		●	●	●	●
●	●	●	Waller & Associates..2049		●	●	●	●

CV	CR	PR	KEWAUNEE		UC	RE	TX	VR
●		●	Bay Title and Abstract Inc................................265		●	●	●	
●		●	Search Associates...1753		●	●	●	●

	CV	CR	PR	LA CROSSE		UC	RE	TX	VR
	●	●	●	Donna Bean Abstractor 646		●	●	●	●
	●		●	Search Associates 1753		●	●	●	●

	CV	CR	PR	LAFAYETTE		UC	RE	TX	VR
	●		●	Lafayette County Abstract...............1153		●	●	●	

	CV	CR	PR	LANGLADE		UC	RE	TX	VR
	●	●	●	Bill Bonham "The Investigator"...............301		●	●	●	●
	●		●	Star Title Company Inc 1851		●	●	●	

	CV	CR	PR	LINCOLN		UC	RE	TX	VR
	●	●	●	Bill Bonham "The Investigator"...............301		●	●	●	
	●		●	Star Title Company Inc 1851		●	●	●	

	CV	CR	PR	MANITOWOC		UC	RE	TX	VR
	●	●	●	First Abstract Title Co...............765		●	●	●	●
	●		●	Search Associates 1753		●	●	●	●

	CV	CR	PR	MARATHON		UC	RE	TX	VR
	●	●	●	Bill Bonham "The Investigator"...............301		●	●	●	●
			●	Boles-Wallner Abstract and Title...............316		●	●	●	
	●		●	Wausau Abstract and Title Company Inc...............2064		●	●	●	

	CV	CR	PR	MARINETTE		UC	RE	TX	VR
	●	●	●	Packer Valley Title Corporation...............1498		●	●	●	●

	CV	CR	PR	MARQUETTE		UC	RE	TX	VR
	●	●	●	Marquette County Abstract...............1283		●	●	●	●

	CV	CR	PR	MENOMINEE		UC	RE	TX	VR
	●	●	●	Wisconsin Title of Shawano Inc...............2109		●	●	●	

DT	BK	CV	CR	PR	MILWAUKEE	UC	RE	TX	VR
●	●	●	●	●	LITQIS Group...............1143	●	●	●	●
●	●	●	●	●	Pro Serve...............1608	●	●	●	●
		●		●	Search Associates 1753	●	●	●	●
●	●	●	●	●	Waller & Associates...............2049	●	●	●	●

	CV	CR	PR	MONROE		UC	RE	TX	VR
	●	●	●	Donna Bean Abstractor 646		●	●	●	●
	●		●	Search Associates 1753		●	●	●	●

	CV	CR	PR	OCONTO		UC	RE	TX	VR
	●		●	Bay Title and Abstract Inc...............265		●	●	●	

	CV	CR	PR	ONEIDA		UC	RE	TX	VR
	●		●	Star Title Company Inc 1851		●	●	●	

	CV	CR	PR	OUTAGAMIE		UC	RE	TX	VR
	●		●	B & H Abstract and Title 228		●	●	●	
	●		●	Bay Title and Abstract Inc...............265		●	●	●	

	CV	CR	PR	OZAUKEE		UC	RE	TX	VR
	●	●	●	LITQIS Group...............1143		●	●	●	●
	●	●	●	Pro Serve...............1608		●	●	●	●
	●		●	Search Associates 1753		●	●	●	●

	CV	CR	PR	PEPIN		UC	RE	TX	VR
	●		●	Dunn County Abstract & Title Inc...............667			●	●	

	CV	CR	PR	PIERCE		UC	RE	TX	VR
	●	●	●	St Croix Valley Title Services Inc...............1844		●	●	●	

CV	CR	PR	POLK		UC	RE	TX	VR
•	•	•	Northwest Land Title Inc 1447		•	•	•	•
•	•	•	Oakey and Oakey Abstract Co 1453		•	•	•	•

CV	CR	PR	PORTAGE		UC	RE	TX	VR
•	•	•	Bill Bonham "The Investigator"...........................301		•	•	•	•
		•	Boles-Wallner Abstract and Title..........................316		•	•	•	

CV	CR	PR	PRICE		UC	RE	TX	VR
•	•	•	Phillips Land Title Company 1548		•	•	•	•

CV	CR	PR	RACINE		UC	RE	TX	VR
•	•	•	LITQIS Group...1143		•	•	•	•
•	•	•	Pro Serve..1608		•	•	•	•
•		•	Search Associates...1753		•	•	•	•
•	•	•	Waller & Associates...2049		•	•	•	•

CV	CR	PR	RICHLAND		UC	RE	TX	VR
•	•	•	Richland County Abstract....................................1696		•	•	•	•

CV	CR	PR	ROCK		UC	RE	TX	VR
•	•	•	Gregg Investigations Inc of Janesville.....................878		•	•	•	•
•	•	•	Gregg Investigations Inc of Madison.......................879		•	•	•	•
•		•	Search Associates...1753		•	•	•	•

CV	CR	PR	RUSK		UC	RE	TX	VR
			Sawyer County Abstract......................................1742		•	•	•	

CV	CR	PR	ST. CROIX		UC	RE	TX	VR
•	•	•	St Croix Valley Title Services Inc...........................1844		•	•	•	

CV	CR	PR	SAUK		UC	RE	TX	VR
•	•	•	Gregg Investigations Inc of Janesville.....................878		•	•	•	•
•	•	•	Gregg Investigations Inc of Madison.......................879		•	•	•	•

CV	CR	PR	SAWYER		UC	RE	TX	VR
•		•	Northwest Land Title Inc 1447		•	•	•	
•	•		Reid, Ann C..1675		•	•	•	•
			Sawyer County Abstract......................................1742		•	•	•	

CV	CR	PR	SHAWANO		UC	RE	TX	VR
•		•	Bay Title and Abstract Inc...................................265		•	•	•	
•	•	•	Bill Bonham "The Investigator"...........................301		•	•	•	•
•	•	•	Wisconsin Title of Shawano Inc............................2109		•	•	•	

CV	CR	PR	SHEBOYGAN		UC	RE	TX	VR
•	•	•	LITQIS Group...1143		•	•	•	•
•		•	Search Associates...1753		•	•	•	•

CV	CR	PR	TAYLOR		UC	RE	TX	VR
•	•	•	Bill Bonham "The Investigator"...........................301		•	•	•	•

CV	CR	PR	TREMPEALEAU		UC	RE	TX	VR
•		•	Search Associates...1753		•	•	•	•

CV	CR	PR	VERNON		UC	RE	TX	VR
•	•	•	Donna Bean Abstractor 646		•	•	•	•
•		•	Search Associates...1753		•	•	•	•

CV	CR	PR	VILAS		UC	RE	TX	VR
•		•	Northern Title of Vilas County 1445		•	•	•	
•		•	Star Title Company Inc 1851		•	•	•	

CV	CR	PR	WALWORTH		UC	RE	TX	VR
●	●	●	Gregg Investigations Inc of Janesville................................878		●	●	●	●
●	●	●	Gregg Investigations Inc of Madison.............................879		●	●	●	●
●	●	●	Pro Serve..1608		●	●	●	●
●		●	Search Associates..1753		●	●	●	●

CV	CR	PR	WASHBURN		UC	RE	TX	VR
●		●	Northwest Land Title Inc 1447		●	●	●	
●	●		Reid, Ann C...1675		●	●	●	●

CV	CR	PR	WASHINGTON		UC	RE	TX	VR
●	●	●	Pro Serve..1608		●	●	●	●
●		●	Search Associates..1753		●	●	●	●
●	●	●	Waller & Associates..2049		●	●	●	●

CV	CR	PR	WAUKESHA		UC	RE	TX	VR
●	●	●	Kotner, Jeff..1134		●	●	●	●
●	●	●	Pro Serve..1608		●	●	●	●
●		●	Search Associates..1753		●	●	●	●

CV	CR	PR	WAUPACA		UC	RE	TX	VR
●	●	●	Bill Bonham "The Investigator"..........................301		●	●	●	●

CV	CR	PR	WAUSHARA		UC	RE	TX	VR
		●	Boles-Wallner Abstract and Title.......................316		●	●	●	

CV	CR	PR	WINNEBAGO		UC	RE	TX	VR
●		●	Bay Title and Abstract Inc..............................265		●	●	●	

CV	CR	PR	WOOD		UC	RE	TX	VR
●	●	●	Bill Bonham "The Investigator"..........................301		●	●	●	●
		●	Boles-Wallner Abstract and Title.......................316		●	●	●	

Wyoming

DT	BK	CV	CR	PR	ALL COUNTIES	UC	RE	TX	VR
		●		●	Petroleum Title Service Inc..............................1544	●	●	●	

		CV	CR	PR	ALBANY	UC	RE	TX	VR
		●	●	●	Bontecou Investigative Services.........................322	●	●	●	
		●	●	●	Deister Ward & Witcher of WY.........................616	●	●	●	●
		●		●	Executive Title Insurance Agency Inc................726	●	●	●	

		CV	CR	PR	BIG HORN	UC	RE	TX	VR
		●	●	●	Deister Ward & Witcher of WY.........................616	●	●	●	●

		CV	CR	PR	CAMPBELL	UC	RE	TX	VR
		●	●	●	Deister Ward & Witcher of WY.........................616	●	●	●	●
		●	●	●	Frontier Cultural Service..................................818	●	●	●	●

		CV	CR	PR	CARBON	UC	RE	TX	VR
		●	●	●	Deister Ward & Witcher of WY.........................616	●	●	●	●

		CV	CR	PR	CONVERSE	UC	RE	TX	VR
		●	●	●	Deister Ward & Witcher of WY.........................616	●	●	●	●
		●	●	●	Frontier Cultural Service..................................818	●	●	●	●

		CV	CR	PR	CROOK	UC	RE	TX	VR
		●	●	●	Deister Ward & Witcher of WY.........................616	●	●	●	●
		●		●	First American Title Guaranty...........................771	●	●		
		●	●	●	Frontier Cultural Service..................................818	●	●		●
		●	●	●	Polley, Steve..1568	●	●		

		CV	CR	PR	FREMONT	UC	RE	TX	VR
		●	●	●	Deister Ward & Witcher of WY.........................616	●	●	●	●

		CV	CR	PR	GOSHEN	UC	RE	TX	VR
		●	●	●	Deister Ward & Witcher of WY.........................616	●	●	●	●
		●		●	Executive Title Insurance Agency Inc................726	●	●	●	
		●	●	●	Frontier Cultural Service..................................818	●	●	●	●

		CV	CR	PR	HOT SPRINGS	UC	RE	TX	VR
		●	●	●	Deister Ward & Witcher of WY.........................616	●	●	●	●

		CV	CR	PR	JOHNSON	UC	RE	TX	VR
		●	●	●	Deister Ward & Witcher of WY.........................616	●	●	●	●
		●	●	●	Frontier Cultural Service..................................818	●	●	●	●

DT	BK	CV	CR	PR	LARAMIE	UC	RE	TX	VR
●	●	●	●	●	Bontecou Investigative Services.........................322	●	●	●	
●	●	●	●	●	Deister Ward & Witcher of WY.........................616	●	●	●	●
●	●	●	●	●	Executive Title Insurance Agency Inc................726	●	●	●	
		●	●	●	Frontier Cultural Service..................................818	●	●	●	●

		CV	CR	PR	LINCOLN	UC	RE	TX	VR
		●	●	●	Deister Ward & Witcher of WY.........................616	●	●	●	●
		●	●	●	Land Title Co..1163	●	●	●	●

		CV	CR	PR	NATRONA	UC	RE	TX	VR
		●	●	●	Deister Ward & Witcher of WY.........................616	●	●	●	●
		●	●	●	Frontier Cultural Service..................................818	●	●	●	●

		CV	CR	PR	NIOBRARA	UC	RE	TX	VR
		●	●	●	Deister Ward & Witcher of WY.........................616	●	●	●	●
		●	●	●	Frontier Cultural Service..................................818	●	●	●	●

CV	CR	PR	PARK		UC	RE	TX	VR
●	●	●	Deister Ward & Witcher of WY.........................616		●	●	●	●
●	●	●	Park County Title...1520		●	●	●	

CV	CR	PR	PLATTE		UC	RE	TX	VR
●	●	●	Deister Ward & Witcher of WY.........................616		●	●	●	●
●		●	Executive Title Insurance Agency Inc..............726		●	●	●	
●	●	●	Frontier Cultural Service.................................818		●	●	●	●

CV	CR	PR	SHERIDAN		UC	RE	TX	VR
●	●	●	Deister Ward & Witcher of WY.........................616		●	●	●	●
●	●	●	Frontier Cultural Service.................................818		●	●	●	●

CV	CR	PR	SUBLETTE		UC	RE	TX	VR
●	●	●	Deister Ward & Witcher of WY.........................616		●	●	●	●
●	●	●	Land Title Co..1163		●	●	●	●

CV	CR	PR	SWEETWATER		UC	RE	TX	VR
●	●	●	Deister Ward & Witcher of WY.........................616		●	●	●	●

CV	CR	PR	TETON		UC	RE	TX	VR
●	●	●	Bontecou Investigative Services.......................322		●	●	●	
●	●	●	Deister Ward & Witcher of WY.........................616		●	●	●	●
●	●	●	Land Title Co..1163		●	●	●	●

CV	CR	PR	UINTA		UC	RE	TX	VR
●	●	●	Deister Ward & Witcher of WY.........................616		●	●	●	●

CV	CR	PR	WASHAKIE		UC	RE	TX	VR
●	●	●	Deister Ward & Witcher of WY.........................616		●	●	●	●

CV	CR	PR	WESTON		UC	RE	TX	VR
●	●	●	Deister Ward & Witcher of WY.........................616		●	●	●	●
●	●	●	Frontier Cultural Service.................................818		●	●	●	●

Section Two

Retriever Profiles

4th Corner Network Inc(1)
215 Flora
Bellingham WA 98225

Phone: **800-321-2455**
206-671-2455
Fax: 206-734-1286

Local Retrieval Area: WA-Skagit, Whatcom.

Normal turn around time is 2-3 days for most records (rush service is also available), 2-3 weeks for medical records. Fee basis will vary by the type of project. The first project may require a prepayment.

4th Corner Network Inc also has correspondent relationships in other jurisdictions, including throughout the rest of the state. They have direct access to SCOMIS statewide.

A & A Legal Services(2)
849 Mitten
Burlingame CA 94010

Phone: **415-697-9431**
Fax: 415-697-4640

Local Retrieval Area: CA-San Francisco, San Mateo.

Normal turn around time is a week to 10 days. However, rush service of 24-48 hours is also available. They charge by mile and/or per copy. The first project may require a prepayment. They also provide process serving.

A & M Attorney Services Inc(3)
3825 Atlantic Ave
Long Beach CA 90807

Phone: **310-426-8306**
Fax: 310-426-6384

Local Retrieval Area: CA-Los Angeles, Orange.

Normal turn around time is 1-4 days. Projects are generally billed by the hour. Credit accounts are accepted.

A California Process and Atty Svc(4)
206 S "D" St
San Bernardino CA 92401

Phone: **909-381-5185**
Fax: 909-885-5199

Local Retrieval Area: CA-Los Angeles, Orange, Riverside, San Bernardino.

Normal turn around time is 1-3 days. Online computer ordering is also available. Projects are generally billed by the hour. Credit accounts are accepted.

A California Process and Attorney Svc also has correspondent relationships in other jurisdictions, including nationwide. They specialize in civil and real estate searches.

A Fast Copy Inc(5)
397 Ray St
Pleasanton CA 94566

Phone: **510-462-9191**
Fax: 510-846-6184

Local Retrieval Area: CA-Alameda, Contra Costa.

Normal turn around time is 15-30 days. Project billing methods vary. Credit accounts are accepted.

They specialize in microfilm, photocopy and reproduce medical and legal records for personal injury or workers compensation claims.

A P Legal Support Services(6)
2031 N Charles St 2nd Floor
Baltimore MD 21218

Phone: **410-366-9109**
Fax: 410-366-9403

Local Retrieval Area: MD-Anne Arundel, Baltimore, Carroll, Harford, Howard, Prince George's, City of Baltimore.

Normal turn around time is 24-48 hours. A same day rush service is also available. Projects are generally billed by the hour. Credit accounts are accepted.

A Professional Attorney Service Inc(7)
10926 Citrus Ave
Fontana CA 92334

Phone: **909-823-3900**
Fax: 909-823-5207

Local Retrieval Area: CA-Riverside, San Bernardino.

Normal turn around time is 3 days. Projects are generally billed by the number of names searched. Credit accounts are accepted.

A Scott Broadhurst and Associates(8)
319 Commonwealth Ave Suite 10
Boston MA 02115

Phone: **617-536-3486**
Fax: 617-536-3486

Local Retrieval Area: MA-Essex, Middlesex, Norfolk, Plymouth, Suffolk, Worcester.

Normal turn around time is 24-48 hours. A same day rush service is also available. Projects are generally billed by the number of names searched. Credit accounts are accepted.

They specialize in real property, asset searches, and all local, state and federal public records.

A Short Abstract Co(9)
PO Box 657
Cavalier ND 58220

Phone: **701-265-4176**
Fax:

Local Retrieval Area: ND-Pembina.

Normal turn around time is 2 weeks. Fee basis will vary by type of project. All projects require prepayment. They specialize in title searches.

A Verne Baker Abstract Co(10)
120 W Bourke St
Macon MO 63552

Phone: **816-385-6474**
Fax: 816-385-6629

Local Retrieval Area: MO-Macon, Randolph.

Normal turn around time is next day. Projects are generally billed by the number of names searched. Credit accounts are accepted. They specialize in title company.

AAA Abstract Co Inc(11)
118 W Olive St
Stilwell OK 74960

Phone: **918-696-2770**
Fax: 918-696-2070

Local Retrieval Area: OK-Adair.

Normal turn around time is 1-10 days. Projects are generally billed by the number of records located. Credit accounts are accepted. Personal checks are accepted.

AAA Abstract Co Inc(12)
PO Box 38
Emory TX 75440

Phone: **903-473-2233**
Fax: 903-473-3069

Local Retrieval Area: TX-Rains.

Normal turn around time is 3-5 days. Fee basis varies by type of transaction. The first project may require a prepayment.

AAA Process Servers Inc(13)
PO Box 9114
Denver CO 80209
Phone: 303-680-6874
Fax: 303-752-0671

Local Retrieval Area: CO-Adams, Arapahoe, Boulder, Denver, Douglas, Jefferson.

Normal turn around time is 24 hours to 1 week. Projects are generally billed by the hour. The first project may require a prepayment. Personal checks are accepted.
AAA Process Servers Inc also has correspondent relationships in other jurisdictions, including El Paso and Pueblo. They specialize in process service, location of people and court retrieval.

ABC Investigators Inc(14)
204 Winchester Suite 1A
Lafayette LA 70506
Phone: 800-738-7300
318-783-6131
Fax: 318-783-7070

Local Retrieval Area: LA-Acadia Parish, Jefferson Davis Parish, Lafayette Parish, St. Landry Parish, Vermilion Parish.

Normal turn around time is the same week. Projects are generally billed by the hour. Credit accounts are accepted.
They are a certified legal investigative firm.

ABC Legal Messenger(15)
601 3rd Ave
Seattle WA 98104
Phone: 206-682-1675
Fax: 206-625-9247

Local Retrieval Area: WA-Grays Harbor, Island, King, Kitsap, Lewis, Mason, Pierce, Skagit, Snohomish, Thurston.

Normal turn around time is 1-2 days. Projects are generally billed by the number of names searched or records located. All projects require prepayment. Credit cards are accepted for payment. They will also invoice. Personal checks are accepted.
ABC Legal Messenger also has correspondent relationships in other jurisdictions, including Whatcom. They are on line with Scomis and Pacep, which allows them instant retrieval.

ABI Attorney Service(16)
2038 W Park Ave
Redlands CA 92373
Phone: 909-793-0613
Fax: 909-792-2590

Local Retrieval Area: CA-Los Angeles, Orange, San Bernardino.

Normal turn around time is 10 days. A 24 hour rush service is also available. Projects are generally billed by the hour. Credit accounts are accepted.
ABI Attorney Service also has correspondent relationships in other jurisdictions, including undisclosed counties in California. They specialize in investigations, statements, court indexing and mobile photocopy. They serve all types of process, civil, family law and U. S. District coourts.

ABIS Inc(17)
PO Box 426
Middleburg VA 22117
Phone: 800-669-2247
703-687-3060
Fax: 703-687-3749

Local Retrieval Area: DC-All counties; MD-Baltimore, City of Baltimore; VA-Fairfax, Loudoun.

Normal turn around time is 3-5 days. Online computer ordering is also available. Projects are generally billed by the number of names searched. Credit accounts are accepted.
They specialize in pre employment screening.

ACB Credit Services(18)
PO Box 846
Okmulgee OK 74447
Phone: 918-756-7741
Fax: 918-583-1001

Local Retrieval Area: OK-Okmulgee.

Normal turn around time is 2 days. Projects are generally billed by the number of names searched. The first project may require a prepayment. Credit cards are accepted for payment.
ACB Credit Services also has correspondent relationships in other jurisdictions, including McIntosh and Okfuskie. They specialize in judgements and titles.

ACE Legal Assistance(19)
541 Hayes St
San Francisco CA 94102
Phone: 415-864-2020
Fax:

Local Retrieval Area: CA-Alameda, Contra Costa, Marin, San Francisco, Santa Clara.

Normal turn around time is 3-5 days. They charge a flat rate per job. The first project may require a prepayment.

ACME Research(20)
Rt 1 Box 91
Guthrie MN 56461-9801
Phone: 218-244-2111
Fax: 218-224-3239

Local Retrieval Area: MN-Beltrami, Cass, Hubbard.

Normal turn around time is 72 hours. Online computer ordering is also available. Projects are generally billed by the hour. The first project may require a prepayment. Credit cards are accepted for payment. Personal checks are accepted.
They specialize in personal injury investigation.

ACS Tri County Title(21)
PO Box 747
Centerburg OH 43011
Phone: 800-798-5297
614-625-7777
Fax: 614-625-6881

Local Retrieval Area: OH-Delaware, Franklin, Knox, Licking, Morrow.

Normal turn around time is 3 days. Fee basis is per search. The first project may require a prepayment.

AD Investigations(22)
3514 Tates Creek Rd
Lexington KY 40517
Phone: 606-271-4642
Fax:

Local Retrieval Area: KY-Clark, Fayette, Jessamine, Woodford.

Normal turn around time is 1-2 days. Projects are generally billed by the hour. Credit accounts are accepted.
They specialize in insurance investigation.

AD Services(23)
39175 Liberty St Suite 207
Fremont CA 94538
Phone: 510-795-1111
Fax:

Local Retrieval Area: CA-Alameda, Contra Costa, Santa Clara.

Normal turn around time is 2-5 days. Projects are generally billed by the hour. Credit accounts are accepted. All individuals must prepay, all companies are invoiced.
A FAX service will be available in early 1993.

ADP Services(24)
3975 W Quail Suite 4
Las Vegas NV 89118

Phone: 702-798-8844
Fax: 702-798-8833

Local Retrieval Area: NV-Clark, Nye.

Normal turn around time is 24-36 hours. Rush service is also available. Projects are generally billed by the hour. Credit accounts are accepted.
ADP Services also has correspondent relationships in other jurisdictions, including undisclosed areas. They specialize in private investigation.

AGO Investigations and Polygraph(25)
PO Box 16143
Las Cruces NM 88004

Phone: 505-526-4303
Fax:

Local Retrieval Area: NM-Dona Ana, Grant, Luna, Sierra.

Normal turn around time is 36-48 hours. Projects are generally billed by the hour. Credit accounts are accepted.
AGO Investigations and Polygraph Ltd also has correspondent relationships in other jurisdictions, including El Paso, Texas and Bernallilo and Chavez. They specialize in asset checks.

AKA Investigations & Process(26)
115 E Travis - The Milam Bldg Suite 1009
San Antonio TX 78205-1606

Phone: 800-653-3817
210-224-4813
Fax: 210-224-5813

Local Retrieval Area: TX-Atascosa, Bandera, Bexar, Comal, Guadalupe, Kendall, Medina, Wilson.

Normal turn around time is 24 hours. Project billing methods vary. Credit accounts are accepted.
AKA Investigations & Process San Antonio also has correspondent relationships in other jurisdictions, including the rest of Texas. They specialize in investigations, process and document retrieval

AKA Investigations & Process(27)
603 W 13th St Suite 200
Austin TX 78701

Phone: 800-933-8706
512-335-1955
Fax: 512-335-6355

Local Retrieval Area: TX-Bastrop, Blanco, Burnet, Caldwell, Hays, Llano, Travis, Williamson.

Normal turn around time is 24 hours. Project billing methods vary. Credit accounts are accepted.
AKA Investigations & Process of Austin also has correspondent relationships in other jurisdictions, including the rest of Texas. They specialize in investigations, process and document retrieval.

AKA Investigations & Process(28)
224 W Commerce
Dallas TX 75208

Phone: 800-723-7419
214-761-1174
Fax: 214-651-6808

Local Retrieval Area: TX-Collin, Dallas, Denton, Llano, Tarrant.

Normal turn around time is 24 hours. Project billing methods vary. Credit accounts are accepted.
AKA Investigations & Process of Dallas also has correspondent relationships in other jurisdictions, including the rest of Texas. They specialize in investigations, process and document retrieval.

AM Legal Service Inc(29)
79 W Monroe St Suite 621
Chicago IL 60603

Phone: 312-782-7361
Fax: 312-782-2838

Local Retrieval Area: IL-Cook.

Normal turn around time is 24-48 hours. Projects are generally billed by the number of names searched. Credit accounts are accepted.

AM-PM Services(30)
PO Box 1776
Moses Lake WA 98837

Phone: 509-765-1776
Fax:

Local Retrieval Area: WA-Adams, Chelan, Douglas, Franklin, Grant, Kittitas, Lincoln, Okanogan.

Normal turn around time is 3 days or less. Projects are generally billed by the hour. Credit accounts are accepted.
AM-PM Services also has correspondent relationships in other jurisdictions, including the Yakima area. They specialize in process serving and repos, and will go to the Canadian border.

APB Information Research Center(31)
2047 Victory Blvd
Staten Island NY 10314

Phone: 718-494-0750
Fax: 718-494-0578

Local Retrieval Area: NY-Bronx, Kings, Nassau, New York, Queens, Richmond, Suffolk.

Normal turn around time is 2 hours to 2 weeks. Projects are generally billed by the hour. The first project may require a prepayment.
APB Information Research Center Inc also has correspondent relationships in other jurisdictions, including nationwide.

APROTEX(32)
1011 W Washington
Midland TX 79701

Phone: 915-683-3518
Fax: 915-686-1934

Local Retrieval Area: TX-Andrews, Borden, Crane, Dawson, Ector, Glasscock, Howard, Martin, Midland, Mitchell, Reagan, Sterling, Upton, Ward.

Normal turn around time is 1-2 days. Projects are generally billed by the hour. Expenses are also billed. Credit accounts are accepted. They are a private investigation agency.

APS Attorney Service(33)
1776 Peachtree Rd NW Suite 330 South
Atlanta GA 30309

Phone: 404-872-1200
Fax: 404-872-4578

Local Retrieval Area: GA-Coffee, De Kalb, Fulton, Gwinnett.

Normal turn around time is usually overnight if ordered by 2 pm. Rush service is also available. Projects are generally billed by the hour. The first project may require a prepayment.

ASAP Inc(34)
PO Box 414
Riverdale GA 30274-0414
Phone: 404-766-9700
Fax:

Local Retrieval Area: GA-Clayton, Cobb, De Kalb, Douglas, Fayette, Fulton, Gwinnett.

Normal turn around time is varied depending on project. Projects are generally billed by the hour. They also will charge a flat rate per project. All projects require prepayment.
ASAP Inc also has correspondent relationships in other jurisdictions, including Georgia. They specialize in process service.

ASAP Legal Documents(35)
3829 Natalie Wy
Ellenwood GA 30049
Phone: 404-241-8130
Fax:

Local Retrieval Area: GA-Cobb, De Kalb, Gwinnett.

Normal turn around time is within hours. Fee basis will vary by type of project. All projects require prepayment.

ATACO Inc(36)
21 W Washington St
West Chester PA 19380
Phone: 215-436-6510
Fax: 215-436-8112

Local Retrieval Area: PA-Chester, Delaware.

Normal turn around time is 2-3 days for title insurance, up to 1 week for all other searches. Rush service is available. Fee basis will vary by the type of project. Credit accounts are accepted.
ATACO Inc also has correspondent relationships in other jurisdictions, including the rest of Pennsylvania. They specialize in real estate and abstracting.

AWS Investigations Inc(37)
PO Box 4574
Yuma AZ 85366-4574
Phone: 602-329-1099
Fax: 602-329-0058

Local Retrieval Area: AZ-Yuma.

Normal turn around time is 3 working days. Projects are generally billed by the hour. The first project may require a prepayment.

Aalpha Omega Investigations Inc(38)
1213 E Cervantes St
Pensacola FL 32501
Phone: 904-433-7016
Fax: 904-433-9689

Local Retrieval Area: FL-Escambia, Okaloosa, Santa Rosa.

Normal turn around time is 24 hours for Escambia, 1 to 2 days for Santa Rosa, and 3 days for Okaloosa. Projects are generally billed by the number of names searched. The first project may require a prepayment. Credit cards are accepted for payment.

Abbas Attorney Service(39)
648 N Tustin Suite B
Orange CA 92667
Phone: 714-633-9238
Fax: 714-633-9267

Local Retrieval Area: CA-Los Angeles, Orange, Riverside, San Bernardino, San Diego.

Normal turn around time is 1-2 days. Project billing methods vary. Credit accounts are accepted. They will accept personal checks.
Abbas Attorney Service also has correspondent relationships in other jurisdictions, including the rest of California. They specialize in process service.

Abelin Abstract Co(40)
PO Box 92
Dubuque IA 52004
Phone: 319-582-7148
Fax: 319-582-7148

Local Retrieval Area: IA-Dubuque.

Normal turn around time is 1 week. Projects are generally billed by the number of names searched. A charge for time is also included. Credit accounts are accepted.
They specialize in real estate.

Able Abstract Co Inc(41)
300 Keystone St
Hawley PA 18428
Phone: 717-226-3358
Fax: 717-226-3473

Local Retrieval Area: PA-Pike, Wayne.

Normal turn around time is 1-3 days for Wayne County, and 1 to 7 days for Pike County. Projects are generally billed by the hour. Credit accounts are accepted.

Patricia Abruzzino(42)
Rt 4 Box 132A
Grafton WV 26354
Phone: 304-265-1401
Fax:

Local Retrieval Area: WV-Taylor.

Normal turn around time is 2-3 days. Projects are generally billed by the number of records located. Credit accounts are accepted.

Abstarct & Guarantee Co(43)
812 Manuel Ave
Chandler OK 74834
Phone: 405-258-1244
Fax: 405-258-1657

Local Retrieval Area: OK-Lincoln.

Normal turn around time is 48 hours. Fee basis will vary by the type of project. Credit accounts are accepted.

Abstract & Title Co of Mesa County(44)
PO Box 3738
Grand Junction CO 81502
Phone: 303-242-8234
Fax: 303-241-4925

Local Retrieval Area: CO-Mesa.

Normal turn around time is 48 hours. Fee basis will vary by the type of project. Credit accounts are accepted. Fees are usually included with close of escrow.
They specialize in real estate title and escrow services.

Abstract & Title Guaranty Co(45)
128 6th Ave S
Clinton IA 52732
Phone: 319-243-2027
Fax: 319-243-6108

Local Retrieval Area: IA-Clinton.

Normal turn around time is 2-3 days. Rush service is available. Fee basis varies by type of transaction. Credit accounts are accepted.

Abstract Associates Ltd(46)
1515 Oregon Pike
Lancaster PA 17601
Phone: 717-291-5841
Fax: 717-291-4449

Local Retrieval Area: PA-Berks, Chester, Dauphin, Lancaster, Lebanon, York.

Normal turn around time is 1 week. Rush service is also available. Fee basis will vary by the type of project. Credit accounts are accepted.

Abstract Enterprises Inc(47)
628 Spruce St
Scranton PA 18503
Phone: 717-963-5290
Fax:
Local Retrieval Area: PA-Lackawanna.
Normal turn around time is 3 days. Fee basis will vary by the type of project. Credit accounts are accepted.

Abstract Land Associates Inc(48)
3915 Market St
Camp Hill PA 17011
Phone: 717-763-1450
Fax: 717-763-1664
Local Retrieval Area: PA-Adams, Cumberland, Dauphin, Franklin, Lancaster, Lebanon, Perry.
Normal turn around time is 3 days. Fee basis will vary by the type of project. The first project may require a prepayment. They specialize in real estate.

Abstract One Inc(49)
721 S George St
York PA 17403
Phone: 717-854-3676
Fax: 717-845-1494
Local Retrieval Area: PA-Adams, York.
Normal turn around time is 24-48 hours. Fee basis will vary by the type of project. Credit accounts are accepted.
Abstract One Inc also has correspondent relationships in other jurisdictions, including Lancaster, Cumberland and Dauphin. They specialize in lien searches.

Abstract and Title Co(50)
229 N Main St
Watford City ND 58854
Phone: 701-842-3366
Fax: 701-842-2709
Local Retrieval Area: ND-McKenzie.
Normal turn around time is varied depending on project. Projects are generally billed by the number of names searched. All projects require prepayment. They will also invoice. Personal checks are accepted.

Abstract and Title Guaranty Co(51)
413 D St
Fairbury NE 68352
Phone: 402-729-2771
Fax: 402-729-5366
Local Retrieval Area: NE-Jefferson, Thayer.
Normal turn around time is 24 hours. Fee basis is per description of one ownership. Credit accounts are accepted.
Abstract and Title Guaranty Company Inc also has correspondent relationships in other jurisdictions, including Gage, Saline and Fillmore. They have been in business for 30 years and have a 100-year title plant.

Abstract and Title Services(52)
112 S Meridian St
Lebanon IN 46052
Phone: 317-482-3880
Fax: 317-873-3351
Local Retrieval Area: IN-Boone.
Normal turn around time is 24-48 hours. Projects are generally billed by the hour. Credit accounts are accepted.

Abstracting and Legal Research(53)
PO Box 12174
Alexandria LA 71315-1274
Phone: 318-473-9979
Fax:
Local Retrieval Area: LA-Allen Parish, Avoyelles Parish, Evangeline Parish, Grand Parish, Natchitoches Parish, Rapides Parish, Sabine Parish, St. Landry Parish, Vernon Parish.
Normal turn around time is 48 hours for direct parishes and over 48 hours for the remainder of the state. Projects are generally billed by the number of names searched. Credit accounts are accepted.
Abstracting and Legal Research Inc also has correspondent relationships in other jurisdictions, including the remainder of the state. They specialize in parish records. A FAX number is available upon request.

Abstracts Inc(54)
107 E Jackson
Jonesboro AR 72401
Phone: 501-935-7410
Fax: 501-935-6548
Local Retrieval Area: AR-Craighead.
Normal turn around time is 2 days. Fee is based on years searched. Credit accounts are accepted.
They specialize title insurance on land, and title searches on lots and blocks of subdivisions.

Abstracts Inc(55)
PO Box 465
Superior NE 68978
Phone: 402-879-4341
Fax:
Local Retrieval Area: NE-Nuckolls.
Normal turn around time is 1 week. Fee basis varies by type of transaction. Credit accounts are accepted.

Abstracts by Godail(56)
414 Louisiana
Baton Rouge LA 70802
Phone: 504-343-0351
Fax: 504-343-1341
Local Retrieval Area: LA-Ascension Parish, Assumption Parish, East Baton Rouge Parish, Livingston Parish, Pointe Coupee Parish, West Baton Rouge Parish.
Normal turn around time is 1-2 days. Projects are generally billed by the hour. The first project may require a prepayment.
They have been established for over 20 years.

Accelerated Legal Services (ALS)(57)
1122 B St Suite 207
Hayward CA 94541
Phone: 510-886-9067
Fax: 510-886-9067
Local Retrieval Area: CA-All counties, Alameda, Contra Costa, San Francisco.
Normal turn around time is 48-72 hours. Rush service is also available. Fee basis will vary by type of project. Credit accounts are accepted.
ALS has a second office: PO Box 1134; Sacramento, CA 95812.

Access Information(58)   Phone: **800-827-7607**
900 E Louisiana Ave Suite 209   303-778-7677
Denver CO 80210   Fax: 303-778-7691

Local Retrieval Area: CO-Arapahoe, Boulder, Denver, Jefferson.

Normal turn around time is same or next day. Projects are generally billed by the hour. Credit accounts are accepted.

Access Information also has correspondent relationships in other jurisdictions, including most of Colorado and nationwide. They specialize in document research and retrieval.

Access Louisiana Inc(59)   Phone: **800-489-5620**
400 Travis St Suite 1802   Fax: 318-222-3053
Shreveport LA 71101

Local Retrieval Area: LA-All counties.

Normal turn around time is 72 hours. Projects are generally billed by the number of names searched. They offer a discount for volume. Credit accounts are accepted. Personal check are accepted. Access Louisiana Inc also has correspondent relationships in other jurisdictions, including Louisiana, Texas and Florida extensively and nationwide.

Accessible Legal Service(60)   Phone: **209-264-3412**
538 N Fulton   Fax:
Fresno CA 93728

Local Retrieval Area: CA-Fresno, Kern, Kings, Madera, Tulare.

Normal turn around time is within 24 hours, some courts records which have been archived can take as long as 10 days depending on the county. Projects are generally billed by the hour. Credit accounts are accepted.

They specialize in criminal records research and workmen's compensation Appeal Board records.

Accountable Process Servers(61)   Phone: **612-427-0225**
222 E Main St Suite #110B   Fax:
Anoka MN 55303

Local Retrieval Area: MN-Anoka, Hennepin, Ramsey, Sherburne.

Normal turn around time is 2 days. Projects are generally billed by the number of records located. Credit accounts are accepted. They specialize in real estate record searches.

Accu-Tech Professional Services(62)   Phone: **619-232-9905**
319 Elm St Suite 101   Fax: 619-232-5928
San Diego CA 92101

Local Retrieval Area: CA-San Diego.

Normal turn around time is 4 days. Projects are generally billed by the number of names searched or records located. Credit accounts are accepted.

They specialize in court research and record retrieval.

AccuSearch Business Service(63)   Phone: **602-939-5854**
6335 W Delmonico Lane   Fax: 602-939-3671
Glendale AZ 85302

Local Retrieval Area: AZ-Maricopa, Pima.

Normal turn around time is 48 hours or less for Maricopa County, 72 hours for all other counties. Projects are generally billed by the number of names searched. Fee may also be based by index. Credit accounts are accepted.

AccuSearch Business Service also has correspondent relationships in other jurisdictions, including nationwide. They speicalize in UCC filing, corporate research, multiple jurisdiction case retrieval and searches.

Accurate Abstracts Inc(64)   Phone: **410-819-0334**
23651 Mt Pleasant Landing Circle   Fax: 410-745-9916
St Michaels MD 21663

Local Retrieval Area: MD-Caroline, Dorchester, Queen Anne's, Talbot.

Normal turn around time is 24 hours. Projects are generally billed by the number of names searched. Credit accounts are accepted.

Accurate Investigative Services(65)   Phone: **706-335-3914**
PO Box 33721   Fax:
Decatur GA 30033

Local Retrieval Area: GA-Franklin, Hart, Towns, Union.

Normal turn around time is 3-5 days. Projects are generally billed by the hour. Credit accounts are accepted.

They specialize in private investigations, domestic and insurance matters, and skip-tracing.

Accurate Legal Service Co(66)   Phone: **202-547-5710**
306 H St NE   Fax: 703-256-7865
Washington DC 20002

Local Retrieval Area: DC-All counties; MD-Montgomery, Prince George's.

Normal turn around time is 3-4 days. Projects are generally billed by the hour. All projects require prepayment.

Accurate Legal Services(67)   Phone: **813-365-3335**
PO Drawer 4635   Fax: 813-953-5616
Sarasota FL 34230

Local Retrieval Area: FL-Charlotte, De Soto, Hardee, Manatee, Sarasota.

Normal turn around time is 2-4 business days. Online computer ordering is also available. Projects are generally billed by the hour. Travel expenses will be added to the fee. All projects require prepayment.

They specialize in process service and database research including corporate, UCC, Department of Motor Vehicles, driver's license and social security number traces.

Accurate Research Inc(68)　　**Phone:** 800-628-0303
14810 S Cicer Ave Suite 2 East　　　　　708-535-0303
Midlothian IL 60445　　　　**Fax:**　708-535-2322

Local Retrieval Area: IL-All counties.

Normal turn around time is 48-72 hours. Projects are generally billed by the number of names searched. Credit accounts are accepted.

Accurate Research Inc also has correspondent relationships in other jurisdictions, including the states of Texas, Pennsylvania, Ohio, New Jersey, Indiana and Illinois. They specialize in criminal record searches.

Ace Messenger Service(69)　　**Phone:** 503-639-0836
12750 SW Pacific Hwy Suite 122　　**Fax:**
Tigard OR 97223

Local Retrieval Area: OR-Clackamas, Columbia, Marion, Multnomah, Washington, Yamhill.

Normal turn around time is 2 days. Project billing methods vary. The first project may require a prepayment. Personal checks are accepted.

Ace Messenger Service also has correspondent relationships in other jurisdictions, including all other counties within Oregon.

Acorn 3 Inc(70)　　**Phone:** 612-375-0144
PO Box 582029　　　　**Fax:**　612-332-3741
Minneapolis MN 55458-2029

Local Retrieval Area: MN-Anoka, Carver, Dakota, Hennepin, Ramsey, Scott, Sherburne, Washington, Wright.

Normal turn around time is 24 hours. Online computer ordering is also available. Projects are generally billed by the number of records located. Copy charges are added to the fee. Credit accounts are accepted. Credit cards are accepted for payment.

Acorn 3 Inc also has correspondent relationships in other jurisdictions, including counties in Minnesota. They are on-line to Hennepin County, Department of Motor Vehicles, Secretary of State and other counties.

Action Agency(71)　　**Phone:** 208-263-9586
PO Box 701　　　　**Fax:**　208-263-7032
Sandpoint ID 83864

Local Retrieval Area: ID-Benewah, Bonner, Boundary, Kootenai, Latah, Nez Perce, Shoshone; MT-Lincoln, Sanders; WA-Pend Oreille.

Normal turn around time is 48 hours. Projects are generally billed by the hour. Credit accounts are accepted.

Action Agency also has correspondent relationships in other jurisdictions, including nationwide. They specialize in locating missing persons.

Action Process(72)　　**Phone:** 209-432-3337
5528 N Palm Suite 123　　**Fax:**　209-432-1140
Fresno CA 93704

Local Retrieval Area: CA-Fresno.

Normal turn around time is within 1 week. Projects are generally billed by the number of names searched or records located. The first project may require a prepayment.

Action Process also has correspondent relationships in other jurisdictions, including Tulare, Kings, Merced, Madera and Kern.

Action Process Service(73)　　**Phone:** 716-692-5032
PO Box 215　　　　**Fax:**
Buffalo NY 14215

Local Retrieval Area: NY-Cattaraugus, Chautauqua, Erie, Genesee, Niagara, Orleans, Wyoming.

Normal turn around time is varied depending on project. Projects are generally billed by the hour. The first project may require a prepayment.

Action Process Service also has correspondent relationships in other jurisdictions, including the rest of New York.

Frances Acton(74)　　**Phone:** 301-387-4018
Rt 5 Box 3735　　　　**Fax:**
Oakland MD 21550

Local Retrieval Area: MD-Garrett.

Normal turn around time is 48 hours. Charges are varied depending on type of search. Credit accounts are accepted.

Frances specializes in property record searches.

Acumen Investigations(75)　　**Phone:** 904-668-0824
1704 Thomasville Rd Box 214　　**Fax:**　904-668-0824
Tallahassee FL 32303

Local Retrieval Area: FL-Franklin, Gadsden, Jefferson, Leon, Liberty, Wakulla.

Normal turn around time is 3-5 days for Leon County. Projects are generally billed by the hour. Credit accounts are accepted.

Acumen Investigations also has correspondent relationships in other jurisdictions, including the rest of Florida. They specialize in insurance defense/video surveillance, missing persons, process service, background investigations, matrimonial investigations, research and general investigations.

Adair County Abstract(76)　　**Phone:** 800-798-6129
230 Public Square　　　　515-743-6129
Greenfield IA 50849　　**Fax:**

Local Retrieval Area: IA-Adair.

Normal turn around time is 1-2 days. They charge a flat rate per project. Credit accounts are accepted.

Adams County Abstract Co(77)　　**Phone:** 701-567-2224
602 Adams Ave　　　　**Fax:**
Hettinger ND 58639

Local Retrieval Area: ND-Adams.

Normal turn around time is 7-10 days. Fee basis will vary by the amount of time to perform the search. All projects require prepayment. They will also invoice.

They specialize in title and mineral searches.

Adams County Land Titles(78)　　**Phone:** 608-339-6634
PO Box 189　　　　**Fax:**
Friendship WI 53934

Local Retrieval Area: WI-Adams.

Normal turn around time is 2-3 days. Fee basis varies by type of transaction. The first project may require a prepayment.

Adams Land Title(79)
PO Box 1347
Hastings NE 68901
Phone: 402-463-4198
Fax: 402-463-6480

Local Retrieval Area: NE-Adams, Clay, Fillmore, Hall, Hamilton, Nuckolls.

Normal turn around time is 2-3 days. Projects are generally billed by the number of records located. Credit accounts are accepted. Adams Land Title also has correspondent relationships in other jurisdictions, including the rest of Nebraska.

Adams Land Title(80)
405 11th Ave
Holdrege NE 68949
Phone: 308-995-5615
Fax:

Local Retrieval Area: NE-Buffalo, Franklin, Harlan, Kearney, Phelps, Webster.

Normal turn around time is 2-3 days. Projects are generally billed by the number of records located. Credit accounts are accepted. Adams Land Title also has correspondent relationships in other jurisdictions, including Adams, Clay, Fillmore, Hall, Hamilton, and Nuckolls counties. They have a FAX but would prefer not to publish the number.

Tommy M Adams(81)
PO Box 782
Goldthwaite TX 76844
Phone: 915-648-3024
Fax:

Local Retrieval Area: TX-Brown, Comanche, Hamilton, Lampasas, Mills, San Saba.

Normal turn around time is 1-2 days. Projects are generally billed by the hour. The first project may require a prepayment.
Mr. Adams is an attorney in general practice.

Addie's Attorneys Services(82)
PO Box 7475
San Jose CA 95150-7475
Phone: 408-723-3326
Fax:

Local Retrieval Area: CA-Santa Clara.

Normal turn around time is 36-48 hours. Projects are generally billed by the hour. All projects require prepayment. They only accept work from firms. They do not accept work from individuals. Addie's Attorneys Services also has correspondent relationships in other jurisdictions, including Alameda County.

Adila-Gray Process Servers(83)
PO Box 2888
Castro Valley CA 94546
Phone: 510-582-8812
Fax: 510-582-6296

Local Retrieval Area: CA-Alameda, Contra Costa.

Normal turn around time is 48 hours. Rush service is also available. Projects are generally billed by the hour. The first project may require a prepayment.
Adila-Gray Process Servers also has correspondent relationships in other jurisdictions, including undisclosed areas. Computer modem will be available in the future.

Adjuster's Photo Copy(84)
342 W Douglas Ave
El Cajon CA 92020
Phone: 619-588-6373
Fax: 619-588-9937

Local Retrieval Area: CA-San Diego.

Normal turn around time is 4-5 days. Rush service is also available. Fee basis will vary by type of search. The first project may require a prepayment.
Adjuster's Photo Copy also has correspondent relationships in other jurisdictions, including nondisclosed areas. Please call company for more information.

Charles E Adkins(85)
PO Box 112
West Point VA 23181
Phone: 804-843-4060
Fax: 804-843-4060

Local Retrieval Area: VA-Gloucester, King and Queen, King William, Middlesex, New Kent.

Normal turn around time is up to a week. Projects are generally billed by the hour. The first project may require a prepayment.

Advance Title Co(86)
206 N Main St
Midland TX 79701
Phone: 915-687-3355
Fax: 915-687-3358

Local Retrieval Area: TX-Culberson, Loving, Martin, Midland, Reagan, Reeves, Winkler.

Normal turn around time is varied depending on project. Projects are generally billed by the number of names searched or records located. All projects require prepayment. Credit cards are accepted for payment. They will also invoice. Personal checks are accepted. They specialize in title examinations, mineral take off and name searches.

Advanced Information Consultants(87)
PO Box 87127
Canton MI 48187-0127
Phone: 313-397-3660
Fax: 313-397-1762

Local Retrieval Area: MI-All counties.

Normal turn around time is 1-3 days. Projects are generally billed by the number of names searched. Credit accounts are accepted. Credit cards are accepted for payment.

Advanced Investigations Inc(88)
231 Lafayette Circle
Tallahassee FL 32303
Phone: 904-221-9989
Fax:

Local Retrieval Area: FL-Franklin, Gadsden, Jefferson, Leon, Leon, Liberty, Wakulla.

Normal turn around time is 2 working days. Corporate filings may be done the same day. A same day rush service is also available. Projects are generally billed by the hour. Incurred expenses will be added to the fee. Credit accounts are accepted. They require a retainer until the client becomes established.
Advanced Investigations Inc also has correspondent relationships in other jurisdictions, including Okaloosa County. They specialize in criminal and civil case work/investigations and process service.

Advanced Land and Title(89)
905 W Jackson
Ozark MO 65721
Phone: 417-485-8251
Fax: 417-485-8280

Local Retrieval Area: MO-Christian.

Normal turn around time is 48 hours. Projects are generally billed by the number of names searched or records located. Credit accounts are accepted. They will accept cashier's checks.

Advantage Title Co(90)
PO Box 83
Montgomery AL 36101-0083
Phone: 205-244-9992
Fax: 205-272-4165

Local Retrieval Area: AL-Autauga, Bullock, Butler, Chilton, Crenshaw, Elmore, Lowndes, Macon, Montgomery, Pike.

Normal turn around time is 48 hours. Fee basis is per search. The first project may require a prepayment.

Agency-One Investigations(91)
1332 Ashley Square
Winston-Salem NC 27103
Phone: 919-760-4000
Fax: 919-760-4155

Local Retrieval Area: NC-Davidson, Forsyth, Guilford.

Normal turn around time is 48 hours. Project billing methods vary. All projects require prepayment. They will also invoice.
They specialize in criminal, civil judgement, probate and property searches.

Aitkin County Abstract Co(92)
112 3rd St NW
Aitkin MN 56431
Phone: 218-927-3608
Fax: 218-927-6211

Local Retrieval Area: MN-Aitkin.

Normal turn around time is 3-4 days. Projects are generally billed by the number of names searched. All projects require prepayment.

Nyla Akin(93)
2252 W Drake St
Bolivar MO 65613
Phone:
Fax:

Local Retrieval Area: MO-Bates, Cedar, Dade, Dallas, Greene, Hickory, Laclede, Polk, Webster.

Normal turn around time is varied depending on project. Fee basis will vary by the type of project. All projects require prepayment. Ms. Akin prefers all correspondence by mail instead of telephone. She specializes in family histories.

Akron/Canton/Cleveland Court Rpts(94)
40 E Buchtel Ave
Akron OH 44308
Phone: 216-376-8100
Fax: 216-376-0110

Local Retrieval Area: OH-Ashtabula, Carroll, Columbiana, Cuyahoga, Geauga, Harrison, Holmes, Jefferson, Lake, Lorain, Mahoning, Medina, Portage, Stark, Summit, Trumbull, Tuscarawas, Wayne.

Normal turn around time is varied depending on project. Projects are generally billed by the hour. Credit accounts are accepted. They specialize in accomplishing rush, priorty, same day orders.

Alamogordo Abstract & Title(95)
PO Box 88
Alamogordo NM 88311
Phone: 505-437-2741
Fax: 505-437-3360

Local Retrieval Area: NM-Lincoln, Otero.

Normal turn around time is 1 week. Fee basis will vary by the type of project. Credit accounts are accepted.
They offer a full range of title functions.

Alamosa Abstract Co(96)
408 San Juan Ave
Alamosa CO 81101
Phone: 719-589-2372
Fax: 719-589-9214

Local Retrieval Area: CO-Alamosa, Conejos, Costilla, Mineral, Rio Grande, Saguache.

Normal turn around time is 3-4 days. Fee basis is determined on a "flat rate" (plus copy charges and court costs). Credit accounts are accepted. They request prepayment from individuals, but will invoice companies.

Alan H Crowe & Associates Inc(97)
PO Box 4547
Portland OR 97208
Phone: 503-222-3085
Fax: 503-222-3950

Local Retrieval Area: OR-Clackamas, Marion, Multnomah, Washington; WA-Clark.

Normal turn around time is 1-3 days unless records in archives. Can do same day turnaround if necessary. Projects are generally billed by the hour. Credit accounts are accepted.

Alaska Process(98)
PO Box 33044
Juneau AK 99803
Phone: 907-789-9276
Fax:

Local Retrieval Area: AK-Juneau Borough.

Normal turn around time is 2-3 days. Same day rush service is also available. May charge a flat fee. All projects require prepayment.

Albany Abstract Co(99)
PO Box 817
Albany TX 76430
Phone: 915-762-3077
Fax:

Local Retrieval Area: TX-Shackelford.

Normal turn around time is up to a week. Fee basis will vary by the type of project. The first project may require a prepayment.

Albert Lea Abstract Co(100)
205 S Washington Ave
Albert Lea MN 56007
Phone: 507-373-9001
Fax: 507-373-2528

Local Retrieval Area: MN-Freeborn.

Normal turn around time is 1 day. Projects are generally billed by the number of names searched. All projects require prepayment. They specialize in title searching.

Albright Abstract & Title Guaranty(101)
PO Box 467
Newkirk OK 74647
Phone: 800-522-1251
405-362-2525
Fax: 405-382-3724

Local Retrieval Area: OK-Kay.

Normal turn around time is 2-5 days. Fee basis is determined on a "per name plus time". Credit accounts are accepted.
They specialize in title insurance.

Gary Albright(102)   **Phone:** 606-474-4253
PO Box 1056   Fax:
Grayson KY 41143

Local Retrieval Area: KY-Carter.

Normal turn around time is 2 days. Fee basis will vary by the type of project. All projects require prepayment.
Gary specializes in real estate title matters.

Aldrich Abstract Company(103)   **Phone:** 409-544-2013
513 E Houston   Fax: 409-544-2411
Crockett TX 75835

Local Retrieval Area: TX-Houston.

Normal turn around time is 2-5 days. Projects are generally billed by the number of names searched. Credit accounts are accepted.

Alfalfa Guaranty Abstract Co(104)   **Phone:** 405-496-3394
201 S Grand PO Box 224   Fax: 405-596-3395
Cherokee OK 73728

Local Retrieval Area: OK-Alfalfa.

Normal turn around time is 1 to 2 days. Projects are generally billed by the hour. Credit accounts are accepted.

All Counties Attorney Service(105)   **Phone:** 714-558-1403
1617 E 17th St Suite 2   Fax: 714-558-0261
Santa Ana CA 92701

Local Retrieval Area: CA-Orange.

Normal turn around time is 1-2 days. Rush service is also available. Projects are generally billed by the hour. Credit accounts are accepted.
All Counties Attorney Service also has correspondent relationships in other jurisdictions, including undisclosed areas.

All County Service Corp(106)   **Phone:** 800-524-0099
The Professional Bldg 2111 White Plains Rd   212-792-0099
Bronx NY 10462   Fax: 212-792-3473

Local Retrieval Area: NY-Bronx, Kings, Nassau, New York, Queens, Richmond, Westchester.

Normal turn around time is 2 days. Fee basis varies by type of transaction. Credit accounts are accepted.
All County Service Corp also has correspondent relationships in other jurisdictions, including nationwide and international network. They specialize in private investigations and process serving.

All Investigations(107)   **Phone:** 708-780-8000
2831 S Austin Blvd   Fax: 708-652-7002
Cicero IL 60650

Local Retrieval Area: IL-Cook, Du Page.

Normal turn around time is 3-4 days. State criminal checks average 3 weeks to 1 month. Projects are generally billed by the number of records located. The first project may require a prepayment.
All Investigations also has correspondent relationships in other jurisdictions, including Isane, Will and Lake. They specialize in pre employment screening and background checks.

All Penn Abstract Co(108)   **Phone:** 717-823-5410
15 Public Square Suite 200 Bicentennial Bldg   Fax: 717-822-2774
Wilkes-Barre PA 18701

Local Retrieval Area: PA-Luzerne.

Normal turn around time is 1-2 weeks. They charge a flat rate per project. Credit accounts are accepted.
All Penn Abstract Co also has correspondent relationships in other jurisdictions, including Lackawanna, Columbia, Wyoming and Lycoming. They specialize in real estate.

All Pocono Abstract Inc(109)   **Phone:** 717-842-2753
PO Box 396   Fax: 717-842-8949
Gouldsboro PA 18424

Local Retrieval Area: PA-Lackawanna, Monroe, Pike, Wayne.

Normal turn around time is 1 week. Rush service is also available. Fee basis will vary by the type of project. The first project may require a prepayment.
They specialize in real estate.

All Pro Info Search(110)   **Phone:** 206-622-6994
2400 6th Ave S   Fax: 206-781-8409
Seattle WA 98134

Local Retrieval Area: WA-King, Pierce, Snohomish.

Normal turn around time is 48 hours. Rush service is also available. Fee basis will vary by the type of project. Credit accounts are accepted.
All Pro Info Search also has correspondent relationships in other jurisdictions, including Snohomish, Pierce and King. They have the capability of accessing the whole state (excluding Garfield and Spokane cities), via computer, for criminal, civil, probate and divorce.

All-Search(111)   **Phone:** 800-227-3152
743 E 400 S Suite 301   801-532-7024
Salt Lake City UT 84111   Fax: 801-532-7033

Local Retrieval Area: UT-Davis, Millard, Salt Lake, Summit, Tooele, Wasatch, Weber.

Normal turn around time is 1-2 days for Utah and 1 to 4 days nationwide. Projects are generally billed by the number of names searched. Credit accounts are accepted.
All-Search also has correspondent relationships in other jurisdictions, including all counties nationwide and Canada.

Allen Abstract Co(112)   **Phone:** 316-321-2410
PO Box 393   Fax: 316-321-2452
El Dorado KS 67042

Local Retrieval Area: KS-Butler.

Normal turn around time is 2-4 days. Fee basis varies by type of transaction. Credit accounts are accepted.

William D Allen III(113)
PO Box 366
Dinwiddie VA 23841

Phone: 804-469-3977
Fax:

Local Retrieval Area: VA-Brunswick, Dinwiddie, Nottoway, Prince George, Sussex, City of Colonial Heights, City of Petersburg.

Normal turn around time is 1-2 days for Dinwiddie. Other counties that they might do could take up to 1 week. Projects are generally billed by the hour. The first project may require a prepayment. They specialize in real estate and banking searches.

Nancy Allen(114)
H-C 5 Box 55
Doniphan MO 63935

Phone: 314-996-3789
Fax:

Local Retrieval Area: MO-Ripley.

Normal turn around time is 2-3 days. Projects are generally billed by the number of names searched. Credit accounts are accepted.

Alliance Title & Abstract Company(115)
3402 N 1st St Suite 102
Abilene TX 79603

Phone: 915-672-7021
Fax: 915-676-7911

Local Retrieval Area: TX-Taylor.

Normal turn around time is 2 days. Projects are generally billed by the number of names searched. The first project may require a prepayment.
They specialize in marriage/divorce and death searches.

Allied Abstract Co(116)
PO Box 963
Mahopac NY 10541-0963

Phone: 914-682-3433
Fax: 914-997-9017

Local Retrieval Area: NY-Orange, Putnam, Rockland, Westchester.

Normal turn around time is 5 business days. A 24 hour special service arrangement can be made. Projects are generally billed by the number of names searched. Fee may also be based per abstract. Credit accounts are accepted.
Allied Abstract Co also has correspondent relationships in other jurisdictions, including Dutchess and Sullivan Counties. They specialize in title examinations.

Allied/Northland Investigations(117)
186 Madcap Suite 9
Fairbanks AK 99709

Phone: 907-456-8106
Fax:

Local Retrieval Area: AK-Fairbanks District.

Normal turn around time is 24-48 hours. Rush service is available in 1 1/2 hours. Projects are generally billed by the hour. The first project may require a prepayment. All out of state inquiries require a retainer.
Allied/Northland Investigations also has correspondent relationships in other jurisdictions, including all the Alaska Boroughs. They specialize in investigations for lawyers and corporations.

Allstate Investigations Inc(118)
5077 Olentangy River Rd
Columbus OH 43214

Phone: 614-538-8282
Fax: 614-538-8284

Local Retrieval Area: OH-Delaware, Fairfield, Franklin, Licking.

Normal turn around time is 24-72 hours. Fee basis will vary by the type of project. Credit accounts are accepted.
Allstate Investigations Inc also has correspondent relationships in other jurisdictions, including Pickaway, Union, and Madison counties. They specialize in records research.

Alma Abstract and Title Co(119)
310 1/2 N State St
Alma MI 48801

Phone: 517-463-8325
Fax: 517-463-2363

Local Retrieval Area: MI-Gratiot.

Normal turn around time is 1 week. Fee basis will vary by type of project. Credit accounts are accepted.
They specialize in real estate.

Alpha & Omega(120)
8000 Corporate Center Dr Suite 103
Charlotte NC 28226-4467

Phone: 800-849-5474
704-543-4517
Fax: 704-543-0142

Local Retrieval Area: NC-Anson, Cabarrus, Cleveland, Gaston, Iredell, Lincoln, Mecklenburg, Richmond, Rowan, Rutherford, Stanly, Union; SC-Cherokee, Chester, Chesterfield, Fairfield, Kershaw, Lancaster, Union, York.

Normal turn around time is varied depending on project. Projects are generally billed by the hour. Credit accounts are accepted.

Alpha Attorney Service(121)
655 Fourth Ave Suite 21
San Diego CA 92101

Phone: 619-235-8008
Fax: 619-231-9535

Local Retrieval Area: CA-San Diego.

Normal turn around time is 2-7 days. Projects are generally billed by the hour. Credit accounts are accepted.
They specialize in process serving.

Alpine Title Co(122)
114 E Main
Gaylord MI 49735

Phone: 517-732-7562
Fax: 517-732-6392

Local Retrieval Area: MI-Crawford, Otsego.

Normal turn around time is 3-5 business days. Projects are generally billed by the hour. The first project may require a prepayment.
They specialize in title insurance services.

Alstate Process Service Inc(123)
1550 Deer Park Ave
Deer Park NY 11729

Phone: 516-667-1800
Fax: 516-667-0302

Local Retrieval Area: NY-Bronx, Kings, Nassau, New York, Queens, Richmond, Suffolk.

Normal turn around time is 48 hours. Fee basis will vary by the type of project. Credit accounts are accepted.

Amador/Calaveras County Atty Svc(124)
PO Box 773
Jackson CA 95642
Phone: **800-487-3272**
209-223-3068
Fax: 209-223-3068

Local Retrieval Area: CA-Alpine, Amador, Calaveras.

Normal turn around time is 1-3 days. Fee basis will vary by the type of project. The first project may require a prepayment. They specialize in criminal defense investigation.

American Abstract & Land Co(125)
6009 New Berwick Hwy
Bloomsburg PA 17815
Phone: **717-389-1174**
Fax: 717-387-0163

Local Retrieval Area: PA-Columbia, Montour.

Normal turn around time is 1-2 weeks. Rush service is also available. They charge a flat rate per project. Credit accounts are accepted.
American Abstract & Land Co also has correspondent relationships in other jurisdictions, including Luzerne.

American Abstract Company(126)
124 N 3rd
Purcell OK 73080
Phone: **405-527-7575**
Fax: 405-527-7574

Local Retrieval Area: OK-McClain.

Normal turn around time is 1-2 days. Projects are generally billed by the number of names searched or records located. Credit accounts are accepted.

American Abstract and Title Co Inc(127)
322 E Ave C
Killeen TX 76540
Phone: **817-526-9525**
Fax: 817-526-9518

Local Retrieval Area: TX-Coryell, Williamson.

Normal turn around time is 2 weeks. Fee basis will vary by the type of project. All projects require prepayment.
American Abstract and Title Co Inc also has correspondent relationships in other jurisdictions, including Coryell and Willliamson. They specialize in closing loans including commercial and single family (1-4 family).

American Abstract and Title(128)
7 8th St
Fort Madison IA 52627
Phone: **319-372-8110**
Fax:

Local Retrieval Area: IA-Lee.

Normal turn around time is 48 hours. Projects are generally billed by the number of names searched. Fee may be based per year. Credit accounts are accepted.
American Abstract and Title Gty Corp also has correspondent relationships in other jurisdictions, including South Lee County.

American Attorney Service(129)
1800 E Garry Suite 201
Santa Ana CA 92707
Phone: **714-261-0522**
Fax: 714-261-9269

Local Retrieval Area: CA-Los Angeles, Orange, San Bernardino, San Diego.

Normal turn around time is 3 days. Rush service is also available. They charge a flat fee per job. The first project may require a prepayment.

American Eagle Investigation(130)
PO Box 104
Sun Valley ID 83353
Phone: **208-788-9527**
Fax: 208-788-9527

Local Retrieval Area: ID-Blaine, Camas, Gooding, Jerome, Lincoln, Twin Falls.

Normal turn around time is 2 to 3 days. Projects are generally billed by the hour. The first project may require a prepayment.

American First Abstract Co(131)
111 E Comanche
Norman OK 73069
Phone: **405-321-7577**
Fax: 405-329-9795

Local Retrieval Area: OK-Cleveland.

Normal turn around time is 3-5 days. Fee basis will vary by the type of project. The first project may require a prepayment. They specialize in real estate title searches.

American Heritage Abstract(132)
104A N Lincoln
Desloge MO 63601
Phone: **314-431-1359**
Fax: 314-431-2137

Local Retrieval Area: MO-Iron, Madison, Ste. Genevieve, St. Francois, Washington.

Normal turn around time is 1 week. Projects are generally billed by the number of names searched or records located. Credit accounts are accepted. Personal checks are accepted.
American Heritage Abstract also has correspondent relationships in other jurisdictions, including Jeffreson and St. Louis. They specialize in title insurance and land title searches.

American Investigation Agency(133)
PO Box 24
West Burlington IA 52655
Phone: **319-753-2492**
Fax:

Local Retrieval Area: IA-Des Moines.

Normal turn around time is varied depending on project. Projects are generally billed by the hour. The first project may require a prepayment.
American Investigation Agency also has correspondent relationships in other jurisdictions, including all Iowa counties. They specialize in criminal and civil.

American Investigations(134)
242 Peoples Bldg
Charleston WV 25301
Phone: **304-343-3346**
Fax: 304-343-2211

Local Retrieval Area: WV-Boone, Kanawha, Lincoln, Putnam.

Normal turn around time is 2 days. Projects are generally billed by the hour. Credit accounts are accepted.

American Legal Services(135)
PO Box 1303
Cathedral City CA 92235
Phone: **619-328-9178**
Fax: 619-328-3185

Local Retrieval Area: CA-Riverside, San Bernardino.

Normal turn around time is 24-48 hours. Projects are generally billed by the number of names searched or records located. They also charge per page if they do any copies. The first project may require a prepayment.
American Legal Services also has correspondent relationships in other jurisdictions, including Los Angeles, Orange, San Diego, Imperial, San Francisco, and Sacramento counties.

American Legal Support Service(136)   Phone: **914-473-5676**
272 Mill St   Fax: 914-452-4731
Poughkeepsie NY 12601

Local Retrieval Area: NY-Dutchess, Ulster.

Normal turn around time is 24-48 hours. Projects are generally billed by the hour. Credit accounts are accepted.

American Messenger Service(137)   Phone: **619-741-5248**
527 10th Ave   Fax: 619-696-8976
San Diego CA 92101

Local Retrieval Area: CA-Imperial, Los Angeles, Orange, San Bernardino, San Diego.

Normal turn around time is up to 24 hours. Rush service is also available. Projects are generally billed by the hour. Driving time is included. The first project may require a prepayment.

American Title & Abstract(138)   Phone: **913-222-2712**
702 Elm St   Fax:
La Crosse KS 67548

Local Retrieval Area: KS-Rush.

Normal turn around time is up to 1 week. Fee basis varies by type of transaction. The first project may require a prepayment.

American Title & Abstr Specialists(139)   Phone: **316-624-9111**
303 N Kansas Suite 103   Fax: 316-624-6610
Liberal KS 67901

Local Retrieval Area: KS-Seward.

Normal turn around time is 1-3 days. Fee basis varies by type of transaction. The first project may require a prepayment.

American Title & Abstract (140)   Phone: **316-356-2100**
108 S Main   Fax: 316-356-2161
Ulysses KS 67880

Local Retrieval Area: KS-Grant.

Normal turn around time is 3-5 days. Fee basis varies by type of transaction. The first project may require a prepayment.

American Title Company Lenawee(141)   Phone: **517-263-4040**
237 N Main St   Fax: 517-265-2533
Adrian MI 49221

Local Retrieval Area: MI-Lenawee.

Normal turn around time is 3 days. Fee basis will vary by type of project. Credit accounts are accepted.
They specialize in real estate.

Ameripro Attorney Service Bureau(142)   Phone: **313-542-0070**
22750 Woodward Ave Suite 301   Fax: 313-542-5510
Ferndale MI 48220

Local Retrieval Area: MI-Macomb, Oakland, Wayne.

Normal turn around time is 1-2 days. Same day rush service is also available. Charges are varied depending on client needs. The first project may require a prepayment.
Ameripro Attorney Service Bureau Inc also has correspondent relationships in other jurisdictions, including the entire state of Michigan. They do also assist with filings, skiptracing, and credit asset investigations.

Anbar Corp(143)   Phone: **609-625-5146**
PO Box 593   Fax:
Egg Harbor NJ 08215

Local Retrieval Area: NJ-Atlantic.

Normal turn around time is 24 hours Projects are generally billed by the number of names searched. Credit accounts are accepted.

Anchorage and Matsu Process Svc(144)   Phone: **907-258-3211**
PO Box 212041   Fax: 907-333-3200
Anchorage AK 99521

Local Retrieval Area: AK-Anchorage Borough, Palmer District.

Normal turn around time is 2 days. Projects are generally billed by the hour. Credit accounts are accepted.
Anchorage and Matsu Process Service also has correspondent relationships in other jurisdictions, including most of Alaska. They specialize in process service.

Anderson Abstract Co(145)   Phone: **402-374-1476**
234 S 13th St Box 8   Fax: 402-374-1478
Tekamah NE 68061-0008

Local Retrieval Area: NE-Burt.

Normal turn around time is 2 days. Projects are generally billed by the hour. Credit accounts are accepted.
Anderson Abstract Co also has correspondent relationships in other jurisdictions, including Washington, Thurston and Cuming Counties. They have provided record search, title insurance and abstracting services for over 50 years. In the Nebraska 402 area code, you may dial (800) 246-1476.

Anderson County Abstract Co(146)   Phone: **913-448-2426**
109 E 4th Ave   Fax: 913-448-5458
Garnett KS 66032

Local Retrieval Area: KS-Anderson.

Normal turn around time is within 48 hours. Fee basis varies by type of transaction. The first project may require a prepayment.

Anderson County Abstract Co(147)   Phone: **903-729-5871**
PO Box 847   Fax: 903-729-1160
Palestine TX 75802

Local Retrieval Area: TX-Anderson.

Normal turn around time is 1-2 days. Fee basis varies by type of transaction. The first project may require a prepayment.
They specialize in marriage/divorce and death searches.

Anderson Land Title Co(148)   Phone: **317-459-3183**
212 W Walnut St   Fax: 317-459-3188
Kokomo IN 46901

Local Retrieval Area: IN-Howard.

Normal turn around time is 2-3 days. Fee basis varies by type of transaction. Credit accounts are accepted.

Edith L Anderson(149)
306 N Myrtle
Orangeville ID 83530
Phone: 208-898-3275
Fax:

Local Retrieval Area: ID-Idaho.

Normal turn around time is varied depending on job. Charges are varied depending on type of search. Credit accounts are accepted. There may be a minimum charge.
Edith specializes in real estate and mining record searches.

H Ray Anderson(150)
618 F Ave
Lawton OK 73501
Phone: 405-355-4450
Fax:

Local Retrieval Area: OK-Comanche, Cotton.

Normal turn around time is 24 hours. Projects are generally billed by the hour. Credit accounts are accepted. Credit cards are accepted for payment. Personal checks are accepted.

Andrews Abstract Co(151)
123 NW Ave A
Andrews TX 79714
Phone: 915-523-2295
Fax:

Local Retrieval Area: TX-Andrews.

Normal turn around time is 2-3 days. Fee basis varies by type of transaction. The first project may require a prepayment.

Andrews Agency Inc(152)
1011 N Wymore Rd Suite 202
Winter Park FL 32789
Phone: 407-628-8395
Fax: 407-628-9548

Local Retrieval Area: FL-Brevard, Lake, Orange, Osceola, Seminole.

Normal turn around time is 24 hours. Projects are generally billed by the hour. Credit accounts are accepted.
They specialize in process serving.

Sharron Andrews(153)
Star Rte 1 Box 50
Independence CA 93526
Phone: 619-878-2038
Fax: 619-872-2712

Local Retrieval Area: CA-Inyo.

Normal turn around time is 1-2 days. Projects are generally billed by the hour. The first project may require a prepayment. She will invoice companies.

Annie Perry Enterprises(154)
210 Lake Farm Rd
Smyrna TN 37167
Phone: 615-459-9117
Fax: 615-355-8838

Local Retrieval Area: TN-Rutherford.

Normal turn around time is 12-24 hours. Charges are varied depending on type of search. Credit accounts are accepted.
Annie Perry Enterprises also has correspondent relationships in other jurisdictions, including the rest of Tennessee. They specialize in criminal record searches.

Anthony J Fierro Abstract Co Inc(155)
39 Newton-Sparta Rd
Newton NJ 07860
Phone: 201-383-1252
Fax: 201-383-1973

Local Retrieval Area: NJ-Sussex.

Normal turn around time is 1-2 weeks. Fee basis will vary by the type of project. Credit accounts are accepted.
Anthony J Fierro Abstract Co Inc also has correspondent relationships in other jurisdictions, including Essex, Morris, Warren and Passaic Counties. Their specialties are 60 year title searches with plottings and title insurance.

Applied Investigative Group(156)
8 N Main St Suite 144
West Hartford CT 06107
Phone: 203-289-3390
Fax: 203-289-3088

Local Retrieval Area: CT-Hartford, Tolland.

Normal turn around time is 24 hours. Online computer ordering is also available. Projects are generally billed by the number of names searched. Credit accounts are accepted. Credit cards are accepted for payment.
Applied Investigative Group also has correspondent relationships in other jurisdictions, including the rest of the state. They specialize in record retrieval and asset location searches.

Arbor Abstracting Co(157)
109 9th St
Honesdale PA 18431
Phone: 717-253-0472
Fax:

Local Retrieval Area: PA-Pike, Wayne.

Normal turn around time is 24-48 hours. Rush service is also available. They charge a flat rate per project. Credit accounts are accepted.
They specialize in real estate.

Arenae Abstract & Title Co(158)
115 South Forest
Standish MI 48658
Phone: 517-846-6560
Fax: 517-846-6633

Local Retrieval Area: MI-Arenac.

Normal turn around time is up to a week. Projects are generally billed by the hour. All projects require prepayment. They request prepay for out of area transactions.
They specialize in title insurance.

Arkansas County Title Co Inc(159)
PO Box 644
Stuttgart AR 72160
Phone: 501-673-3981
Fax: 501-673-3981

Local Retrieval Area: AR-Arkansas.

Normal turn around time is up to 1 week. Projects are generally billed by the number of records located. Credit accounts are accepted. Out of town clients are charged a set up fee and must prepay.
They specialize in real estate abstracts.

Joan Arms(160)
Box 96 Rock Creek Rt
Jamestown TN 38556
Phone: **615-879-7818**
Fax:

Local Retrieval Area: TN-Cumberland, Fentress, Morgan, Pickett, Scott.

Normal turn around time is 1-2 days. Fee basis is per searches. Credit accounts are accepted.   Ms. Arms specializes in real estate at the register office.

Platt Arnold(161)
160 Upper Pattagansett Rd
East Lyme CT 06333
Phone: **203-691-1125**
Fax:

Local Retrieval Area: CT-New London.

Normal turn around time is 48 hours for a rundown and 1 week for a full search. Fee basis will vary by the type of project. Credit accounts are accepted.
They specialize in land records, title searches, encumbrances, taxes, flood, probate and foreclosure.

Kate Arrendale(162)
4527 7th Street SW
Canton OH 44710
Phone: **216-477-1857**
216-454-0636
Fax:

Local Retrieval Area: OH-Stark.

Normal turn around time is 24 hours. Charges are varied depending on type of search. Credit accounts are accepted.
Correspondent relationships in other jurisdictions include Tuskarawas county. Kate specializes in lien searches.

Arrow Attorney Assistance(163)
PO Box 763
Claremont CA 91711
Phone: **714-624-8377**
Fax: 714-624-8377

Local Retrieval Area: CA-Los Angeles, Orange, Riverside, San Diego.

Normal turn around time is 24-48 hours. The bankruptcy court records are normally 3 days. Projects are generally billed by the number of names searched. The first project may require a prepayment.
Arrow Attorney Assistance also has correspondent relationships in other jurisdictions, including the San Diego area.

Arval Legal Service(164)
517 Armstrong St
LeMoore CA
Phone: **209-924-1404**
Fax: 209-924-8378

Local Retrieval Area: CA-Kings, Tulare.

Normal turn around time is 1-3 days. Rush service is also available. Projects are generally billed by the number of names searched. Credit accounts are accepted.
Arval Legal Service also has correspondent relationships in other jurisdictions, including all California counties.

Ascension Title Services Inc(165)
PO Box 117
Gonzales LA 70707
Phone: **504-647-8473**
Fax:

Local Retrieval Area: LA-Ascension Parish, Iberville Parish, St. James Parish.

Normal turn around time is 2-3 days. Fee basis varies by type of transaction. The first project may require a prepayment.

Ashland Abstract & Title Co(166)
PO Box 888
Ashland KS 67831
Phone: **316-635-2716**
Fax:

Local Retrieval Area: KS-Clark.

Normal turn around time is 2-3 days. Fee basis varies by type of transaction. The first project may require a prepayment.

Ashley Abstract Co(167)
204 W Main
Ashley ND 58413
Phone: **701-288-3584**
Fax:

Local Retrieval Area: ND-McIntosh.

Normal turn around time is 1 week. Fee basis will vary by type of project. All projects require prepayment.

Elizabeth Askwith(168)
125 Alington St
Sault Sainte Marie MI 49783
Phone: **906-632-6885**
Fax: 906-632-6887

Local Retrieval Area: MI-Chippewa.

Normal turn around time is 2-3 days. Rush service is also available. Projects are generally billed by the number of names searched. The first project may require a prepayment. Prepay only for individuals. They will invoice to companies.
Elizaeth specializes in probate, real estate and commerical lawyers.

Associated Abstracting Services(169)
PO Box 39047
Edina MN 55439
Phone: **612-835-9975**
Fax: 612-835-9976

Local Retrieval Area: MN-Anoka, Benton, Blue Earth, Brown, Carver, Chisago, Dakota, Freeborn, Hennepin, Isanti, Le Sueur, McLeod, Mille Lacs, Mower, Nicollet, Olmsted, Ramsey, Rice, Scott, Sherburne, Sibley, Stearns, Steele, Waseca, Washington, Wright.

Normal turn around time is 3 days. Projects are generally billed by the number of names searched. Credit accounts are accepted.

Associated Attorney Services(170)
138 E Figueroa St
Santa Barbara CA 93101
Phone: **805-965-6542**
Fax: 805-965-6542

Local Retrieval Area: CA-Santa Barbara.

Normal turn around time is 24 hours. Projects are generally billed by the number of records located. The first project may require a prepayment.
Associated Attorney Services also has correspondent relationships in other jurisdictions, including the state of California. They specialize in process service.

Associated Investigative Services(171)   Phone: **804-483-2389**
1600 Airline Blvd Suite 2   Fax: 800-766-0740
Portsmouth VA 23707

Local retrieval area includes many cities and counties in Virginia and some in Maryland.

Normal turn around time is varied depending on project. Projects are generally billed by the hour. All projects require prepayment. Personal checks are accepted.

Associated Investigative Services Inc also has correspondent relationships in other jurisdictions, including the rest of Virginia. They specialize in infidelity, child custody, workmen's compensation, locatingheirs, missing persons, skips, pre-trial review, security consulting including employee screening/testing and risk analysis.

Associated Peninsula Title Co(172)   Phone: **906-863-7871**
1112 10th St   Fax: 906-863-1363
Menominee MI 49858

Local Retrieval Area: MI-Menominee.

Normal turn around time is 2-3 days. They charge a flat rate per project. Credit accounts are accepted.
They specialize in title insurance.

Associated Services(173)   Phone: **717-780-1497**
PO Box 5437   Fax:
Harrisburg PA 17110

Local Retrieval Area: PA-Cumberland, Dauphin, York.

Normal turn around time is 48 hours. Fee basis will vary by the type of project. The first project may require a prepayment.
They specialize in subponeas, civil process service and court filings.

Associated Title Co(174)   Phone: **815-872-9601**
717 S Main St   Fax: 815-872-9601
Princeton IL 61356

Local Retrieval Area: IL-Bureau, Putnam.

Normal turn around time is 1 day for status checks of real estate records, 1-2 weeks for title insurance orders. Projects are generally billed by the number of names searched or records located. Credit accounts are accepted.

Assured Civil Process Agency Inc(175)   Phone: **800-256-7160**
807 Nueces   512-477-2681
Austin TX 78701   Fax: 512-477-6526

Local Retrieval Area: TX-Bastrop, Burnet, Caldwell, Hays, Travis, Williamson.

Normal turn around time is 24-48 hours. Projects are generally billed by the hour. Credit accounts are accepted.

Assured Realty(176)   Phone: **717-622-1366**
2nd & Norwegian St   Fax: 717-622-4216
Pottsville PA 17901

Local Retrieval Area: PA-Schuylkill.

Normal turn around time is varied depending on search. Charges are varied depending on type of search. Credit accounts are accepted.

Assured Realty also has correspondent relationships in other jurisdictions, including Burkes county.

Assured Title Company(177)   Phone: **314-272-7511**
611 Westridge   Fax: 314-441-3689
O'Fallon MO 63366

Local Retrieval Area: MO-Lincoln, Montgomery, St. Charles, Warren.

Normal turn around time is 5 working days. Projects are generally billed by the number of names searched. Credit accounts are accepted. Personal checks are accepted.

Assured Title Company also has correspondent relationships in other jurisdictions, including St. Louis, Jefferson, boone and Calloway. They specialize in record searching for title insurance and real estate closings.

Atlanta Courthouse Services(178)   Phone: **404-872-0755**
PO Box 8632   Fax: 404-872-0755
Atlanta GA 30306-0632

Local Retrieval Area: GA-Clayton, Cobb, Coweta, De Kalb, Fulton, Gwinnett, Rockdale, Walton.

Normal turn around time is 24-48 hours for Fulton, Cobb, Dekalb, Gwinett and Clayton Counties. Projects are generally billed by the number of names searched or records located. They may give a discount for large orders. Credit accounts are accepted. Personal checks are accepted.

Atlanta Courthouse Services also has correspondent relationships in other jurisdictions, including most counties within 100 miles of Atlanta, Georgia.

Atlantic Process Service Inc(179)   Phone: **914-235-2110**
43 Davenport Ave   Fax: 914-235-0940
New Rochelle NY 10802

Local Retrieval Area: NY-Bronx, Dutchess, New York, Orange, Putnam, Rockland, Westchester.

Normal turn around time is 48 hours. Projects are generally billed by the number of records located. The first project may require a prepayment.
They specialize in process service.

Atlas Abstract Co(180)   Phone: **405-379-3311**
125 W Broadway   Fax:
Holdenville OK 74848

Local Retrieval Area: OK-Hughes.

Normal turn around time is up to one week. Fee basis will vary by the type of project. The first project may require a prepayment.

Atoka Abstract Co Inc(181)
308 E Court St
Atoka OK 74525
Phone: **405-889-7316**
Fax: 405-889-7317

Local Retrieval Area: OK-Atoka.

Normal turn around time is varied depending on project. Projects are generally billed by the hour. Credit accounts are accepted.

Attorney Civil Process Service(182)
PO Box 1247
Waco TX 76703
Phone: **817-755-6447**
Fax: 817-754-4050

Local Retrieval Area: TX-McLennan.

Normal turn around time is 2 days. Projects are generally billed by the number of names searched. All projects require prepayment. They specialize in bankruptcy and US District Court searches in the Western District of Texas.

Attorney Service Bureau(183)
PO Box 382
Pomona NY 10970
Phone: **914-354-3357**
Fax:

Local Retrieval Area: NY-Orange, Putnam, Rockland, Sullivan, Ulster, Westchester.

Normal turn around time is 7 working days. A 1 day rush service is also available. Projects are generally billed by the number of records located. Credit accounts are accepted.
Attorney Service Bureau also has correspondent relationships in other jurisdictions, including New York and New Jersey. They specialize in process service and public record investigations.

Attorney Service of California(184)
10096 Soquel Dr Suite 6
Aptos CA 95003
Phone: **408-728-1757**
Fax: 408-688-6146

Local Retrieval Area: CA-Monterey, San Benito, Santa Cruz.

Normal turn around time is 2-3 days. Rush service is also available. Projects are generally billed by the number of names searched. The first project may require a prepayment. They will invoice established clients.
They specialize in process service and investigations.

Attorney Service of Merced(185)
PO box 2351
Merced CA 95344
Phone: **209-383-3233**
Fax: 209-383-0311

Local Retrieval Area: CA-Fresno, Madera, Mariposa, Merced, Stanislaus.

Normal turn around time is up to 3 days. Projects are generally billed by the number of names searched. The first project may require a prepayment.
They specialize in process serving and private investigative services.

Attorney Services(186)
1004 13th Ave SW
Austin MN 55912
Phone: **507-437-1650**
Fax: 507-437-7513

Local Retrieval Area: MN-Mower.

Normal turn around time is varied depending on project. Fee basis will vary by the type of project. Credit accounts are accepted.
They specialize in locating missing heirs to estates.

Attorney Services Inc(187)
3214 Prospect Ave E
Cleveland OH 44115-2600
Phone: **216-431-7400**
Fax: 216-431-6149

Local Retrieval Area: OH-Cuyahoga.

Normal turn around time is 3-7 days. Fee basis will vary by type of project. Credit accounts are accepted. Personal checks are accepted.
They specialize in collections and process service.

Attorney Services--Antelope Valley(188)
PO Box 2712
Lancaster CA 93539
Phone: **805-944-5988**
Fax: 805-944-0342

Local Retrieval Area: CA-Los Angeles.

Normal turn around time is 2 days. Rush service is also available. Fee basis will vary per assignment, ususally research per hour. Credit accounts are accepted.
Attorney Services--Antelope Valley also has correspondent relationships in other jurisdictions in California.

Attorney's Aid Inc of Modesto(189)
PO Box 912
Modesto CA 95353
Phone: **209-522-9901**
Fax: 209-522-3044

Local Retrieval Area: CA-Stanislaus.

Normal turn around time is 2 days. Projects are generally billed by the hour. The first project may require a prepayment.

Attorney's Aid Inc of Sacramento(190)
PO Box 1203
Sacramento CA 95812
Phone: **916-443-3915**
Fax: 916-325-2555

Local Retrieval Area: CA-Sacramento.

Normal turn around time is 2 days. Projects are generally billed by the hour. The first project may require a prepayment.

Attorney's Dispatch Service Inc(191)
345 W 2nd St Suite 7
Dayton OH 45402   Fax: 513-222-4503
Phone: **800-528-9474**
513-222-6829

Local Retrieval Area: OH-Montgomery.

Normal turn around time is varied depending on project. Projects are generally billed by the number of names searched or records located. The first project may require a prepayment.
Attorney's Dispatch Service Inc also has correspondent relationships in other jurisdictions, including Greene, Darke, Preble, Miami, Clark, Warren and Butler.

Attorney's Diverisfied Services(192)
101 H St
Bakersfield CA 93304
Phone: **805-323-2377**
Fax: 805-323-3376

Local Retrieval Area: CA-Kern.

Normal turn around time is varied depending on project. Projects are generally billed by the number of names searched. All projects require prepayment.
They specialize in document management and litigation support.

Attorney's Diversified Services(193)
2nd St
San Francisco CA 94107
Phone: **415-882-1700**
Fax: 415-882-1705

Local Retrieval Area: CA-San Francisco.

Normal turn around time is varied depending on project. Projects are generally billed by the number of names searched. All projects require prepayment.

They specialize in document management and litigation support.

Attorney's Diversified Services(194)
860 Walnut St
San Luis Obispo CA 93401
Phone: **805-543-1458**
Fax: 805-541-4450

Local Retrieval Area: CA-San Luis Obispo.

Normal turn around time is varied depending on project. Projects are generally billed by the number of names searched. All projects require prepayment.

They specialize in document management and litigation support.

Attorney's Diversified Services(195)
741 N Fulton
Fresno CA 93728
Phone: **209-233-1475**
Fax: 209-486-4119

Local Retrieval Area: CA-Fresno.

Normal turn around time is varied depending on project. Projects are generally billed by the number of names searched. All projects require prepayment.

They specialize in document management and litigation support.

Attorney's Diversified Services(196)
342 Burney St
Modesto CA 95354
Phone: **209-576-0273**
Fax: 209-576-0238

Local Retrieval Area: CA-Stanislaus.

Normal turn around time is varied depending on project. Projects are generally billed by the number of names searched. All projects require prepayment.

They specialize in document management and litigation support.

Attorney's Diversified Services(197)
845 N California St
Stockton CA 95202
Phone: **209-948-6110**
Fax: 209-948-0806

Local Retrieval Area: CA-San Joaquin.

Normal turn around time is varied depending on project. Projects are generally billed by the number of names searched. All projects require prepayment.

They specialize in document management and litigation support.

Attorney's Diversified Services(198)
1957 Pine St
Redding CA 96001
Phone: **916-241-1228**
Fax: 916-241-1508

Local Retrieval Area: CA-Shasta.

Normal turn around time is varied depending on project. Projects are generally billed by the number of names searched. All projects require prepayment.

They specialize in document management and litigation support.

Attorney's Diversified Services(199)
2425 Cleveland Ave
Santa Rosa CA 95403
Phone: **707-545-5455**
Fax: 707-545-5454

Local Retrieval Area: CA-Sonoma.

Normal turn around time is varied depending on project. Projects are generally billed by the number of names searched. All projects require prepayment.

They specialize in document management and litigation support.

Attorney's Diversified Services(200)
300 27th St
Oakland CA 94612
Phone: **510-835-9176**
Fax: 510-835-0510

Local Retrieval Area: CA-Alameda.

Normal turn around time is varied depending on project. Projects are generally billed by the number of names searched. All projects require prepayment.

They specialize in document management and litigation support.

Attorney's Diversified Services(201)
1424 21st St
Sacramento CA 95814
Phone: **916-441-4396**
Fax: 916-443-1162

Local Retrieval Area: CA-Sacramento.

Normal turn around time is varied depending on project. Projects are generally billed by the number of names searched. All projects require prepayment.

They specialize in document management and litigation support.

Attorney's Document Production(202)
PO Box 1327
Rancho Cordova CA 95741-1327
Phone: **916-631-8844**
Fax: 916-631-8833

Local Retrieval Area: CA-Amador, Butte, Calaveras, El Dorado, Glenn, Placer, Sacramento, San Francisco, San Joaquin, Santa Clara, Solano, Sutter, Tehama, Yolo, Yuba; NV-Lincoln.

Normal turn around time is 24-36 hours. Rush service is also available. Projects are generally billed by the hour. Credit accounts are accepted.

Attorney's Document Production also has correspondent relationships in other jurisdictions in California.

Attorney's Information Bureau Inc(203)
C603 King County Courthouse
Seattle WA 98104
Phone: **206-622-1909**
Fax: 206-622-2911

Local Retrieval Area: WA-King, Kittitas, Pierce, Snohomish.

Normal turn around time is 24 hours, same day is available for a higher fee. Fee basis varies by type of transaction. The first project may require a prepayment.

They can access all of Washington county records through an on line system except for Spokane and Garfield counties.

Attorney's Investigative Consultnts(204)
PO Box 43029-4500
Las Vegas NV 89116
Phone: **702-453-4500**
Fax: 702-438-8986

Local Retrieval Area: NV-Clark.

Normal turn around time is 24-48 hours. Online computer ordering is also available. Projects are generally billed by the hour. Credit accounts are accepted.

Attorney's Messenger Service(205)   **Phone:** **510-937-4581**
1243 Alpine Rd Suite 106   Fax: 510-935-7792
Walnut Creek CA 94596

Local Retrieval Area: CA-Alameda, Contra Costa, San Francisco.

Normal turn around time is 2 days. Rush service is also available. Projects are generally billed by the number of names searched. Credit accounts are accepted.

Attorney's Process & Research (206)   **Phone:** **518-465-8951**
1 Columbia Pl   Fax: 518-465-0449
Albany NY 12207

Local Retrieval Area: NY-Albany, Columbia, Greene, Rensselaer, Saratoga, Schenectady.

Normal turn around time is 4-5 days. Motor Vehicle Records may be retrieved immediately. Rush service is also available. Online computer ordering is also available. Projects are generally billed by the hour. The first project may require a prepayment.

Attorney's Professional Process(207)   **Phone:** **407-624-6222**
3931 RCA Blvd Suite 3117   Fax: 407-624-8742
Palm Beach Gardens FL 33410

Local Retrieval Area: FL-Palm Beach.

Normal turn around time is 2-3 days. Projects are generally billed by the number of names searched. Credit accounts are accepted. Attorney's Professional Process Srvc also has correspondent relationships in other jurisdictions, including Broward and Martin. They specialize in background checks.

Attorney's Service Centers(208)   **Phone:** **916-444-2094**
PO Box 162639   Fax: 916-444-8907
Sacramento CA 95816

Local Retrieval Area: CA-El Dorado, Placer, Sacramento, Yolo.

Normal turn around time is 1 day. Rush service is also available. Fee basis is a flat fee. The first project may require a prepayment. Attorney's Service Centers also has correspondent relationships in other jurisdictions in California.

Attorney's Title Co(209)   **Phone:** **913-243-1357**
812 Washington St   Fax: 913-243-1359
Concordia KS 66901

Local Retrieval Area: KS-Clay, Cloud, Republic, Washington.

Normal turn around time is 2-3 days. Projects are generally billed by the hour. The first project may require a prepayment.

Attorneys Title & Abstract Co(210)   **Phone:** **409-567-4602**
PO Box 608   Fax: 409-567-9358
Caldwell TX 77836

Local Retrieval Area: TX-Burleson.

Normal turn around time is 1-2 days. Fee basis will vary by the type of project. Credit accounts are accepted.

Attorneys' Personal Services(211)   **Phone:** **800-245-0122**
1776 Peachtree Rd S Suite 330   404-872-1200
Atlanta GA 30309-2309   Fax: 404-872-4578

Local Retrieval Area: GA-Cherokee, Clarke, Clayton, Cobb, De Kalb, Douglas, Fayette, Floyd, Forsyth, Fulton, Gwinnett, Hall, Rockdale.

Normal turn around time is the same day. Projects are generally billed by the hour. A mileage fee is also added. The first project may require a prepayment.

Attorneys' Personal Services also has correspondent relationships in other jurisdictions, including all counties in Georgia. They specialize in court research and process service.

Attorneys' Service Limited(212)   **Phone:** **408-293-9111**
931 W Julian St   Fax: 408-293-9568
San Jose CA 95126

Local Retrieval Area: CA-Alameda, San Francisco, San Mateo, Santa Clara.

Normal turn around time is 2 hours. Fees are based on a flat rate plus expenses. Credit accounts are accepted.

They specialize in researching fictitious business names.

Attorneys' Title Agency Inc(213)   **Phone:** **303-325-4911**
PO Box 517   Fax: 303-325-7304
Ouray CO 81427

Local Retrieval Area: CO-Ouray, San Juan, San Miguel.

Normal turn around time is up to 1 week. Projects are generally billed by the hour. Credit accounts are accepted.

They specialize in real estate and title matters.

AuSable Valley Abstract and Title(214)   **Phone:** **517-826-3385**
442 1/2 S Morence Ave   Fax: 517-826-3385
Mio MI 48647

Local Retrieval Area: MI-Crawford, Ogemaw, Oscoda.

Normal turn around time is 5 working days. Projects are generally billed by the number of records located. All projects require prepayment.

Aubin Abstracting(215)   **Phone:** **803-236-1072**
PO Box 14261   Fax: 803-236-1072
Surfside Beach SC 29587

Local Retrieval Area: SC-Berkeley, Charleston, Clarendon, Dillon, Florence, Georgetown, Horry, Lee, Marion, Williamsburg.

Normal turn around time is 2 days. Fee basis varies by type of transaction. Credit accounts are accepted.

Auburn Abstract and Title Co(216)   **Phone:** **402-274-4321**
910 13th St   Fax: 402-274-4323
Auburn NE 68305

Local Retrieval Area: NE-Nemaha.

Normal turn around time is 1-2 days. Projects are generally billed by the number of names searched. All projects require prepayment. They prefer prepay request, but will invoice. Personal checks are accepted.

Auburn Abstract and Title Company also has correspondent relationships in other jurisdictions, including Richardson County.

Audrain County Abstract Co(217)
PO Box 599
Mexico MO 65265

Phone: **314-581-5136**
Fax: 314-581-8752

Local Retrieval Area: MO-Audrain.

Normal turn around time is 2-3 days. Fee basis will vary by type of project. Credit accounts are accepted.
They specialize in real estate searches.

Eileen Augatis(218)
731 Washington Ave
Woodbury NJ 08096

Phone: **609-853-9836**
Fax:

Local Retrieval Area: NJ-Camden, Gloucester.

Normal turn around time is 24 hours. Fee basis will vary by the type of project. Credit accounts are accepted. Personal checks are accepted.

Aurora County Abstract(219)
PO Box
Plankinton SD 57368

Phone: **605-942-7770**
Fax:

Local Retrieval Area: SD-Aurora.

Normal turn around time is up to 3 weeks. Projects are generally billed by the number of names searched. Credit accounts are accepted.

Autauga Abstract(220)
140 W Main St
Prattville AL 36067

Phone: **205-361-0606**
Fax: 205-361-8402

Local Retrieval Area: AL-Autauga, Elmore.

Normal turn around time is 24-48 hours. Projects are generally billed by the hour. Credit accounts are accepted. Personal checks are accepted.

Avritt & Avritt(221)
PO Box 671
Lebanon KY 40033

Phone: **502-692-4270**
Fax: 502-692-6898

Local Retrieval Area: KY-Marion.

Normal turn around time is 3-4 days. Projects are generally billed by the hour. The first project may require a prepayment.

Erin Axt(222)
180 North Ave
Fanwood NJ 07023

Phone: **908-685-9555**
Fax: 908-322-5631

Local Retrieval Area: NJ-Middlesex, Somerset.

Normal turn around time is 24-48 hours. Fee basis will vary by the type of project. Credit accounts are accepted.

Pamela G Ayars(223)
PO Box 110
Salem NJ 08079

Phone: **609-935-8185**
Fax: 609-935-4172

Local Retrieval Area: NJ-Salem.

Normal turn around time is 2-7 days. Fee basis will vary by the type of project. Credit accounts are accepted. Personal checks are accepted.
Panela specializes in credit check searches.

Aymond Investigations Inc(224)
PO Box 52004
Shreveport LA 71135

Phone: **318-797-4082**
Fax:

Local Retrieval Area: LA-Caddo Parish.

Normal turn around time is 24-48 hours. Projects are generally billed by the hour. Credit accounts are accepted. They will accept prepay orders, personal checks or they will invoice.

Judith Ayres(225)
3487 Accomack St
Chincoteague VA 23336

Phone: **804-336-5313**
Fax:

Local Retrieval Area: MD-Worcester; VA-Accomack, Northampton.

Normal turn around time is 24-48 hours. Rush service is also available. Fee basis will vary by type of project. Credit accounts are accepted.
Judith specializes in real estate and UCC searches. She also performs searches of vital statistics from the 1600s-1903 and on the state level.

B & B Reporting(226)
PO Box 191
Scottsboro AL 35768

Phone: **205-259-4323**
Fax:

Local Retrieval Area: AL-De Kalb, Jackson, Madison, Marshall.

Normal turn around time is 1 day. Projects are generally billed by the number of records located. All projects require prepayment. They will also invoice.
They specialize in civil and criminal searches.

B & G Ltd of Hollidaysburg(227)
516 Allegheny St Suite 1
Hollidaysburg PA 16648

Phone: **814-695-8414**
Fax: 814-695-8496

Local Retrieval Area: PA-Cambria, Centre, Clearfield, Huntingdon; SC-Bamberg, Beaufort.

Normal turn around time is 24-48 hours. Projects are generally billed by the number of names searched. Credit accounts are accepted.
They specialize in real estate and abstracting.

B & H Abstract and Title(228)
625 W Lawrence St
Appleton WI 54911

Phone: **414-731-5494**
Fax: 414-731-5493

Local Retrieval Area: WI-Outagamie.

Normal turn around time is 7-10 days. Projects are generally billed by the number of names searched or records located. Credit accounts are accepted. Personal checks are accepted.
They specialize in title insurance.

B & J/Barristers' Aide(229)
PO Box 88
Eugene OR 97440

Phone: **503-687-0747**
Fax: 503-687-0429

Local Retrieval Area: OR-Lane.

Normal turn around time is the next day. Projects are generally billed by the number of names searched. Credit accounts are accepted.

B & R Services for Professionals(230)   Phone: **215-546-7400**
235 S 13th St   Fax: 215-985-0169
Philadelphia PA 19107

Local Retrieval Area: PA-Bucks, Delaware, Montgomery, Philadelphia.

Normal turn around time is 24-48 hours. Projects are generally billed by the number of names searched or records located. The first project may require a prepayment.

B & R Services for Professionals also has correspondent relationships in other jurisdictions, including Dauphin. They specialize in court filings, record retrieval, process service, court reporting and private investigation.

B.E.S. Abstract Corp(231)   Phone: **212-716-2496**
3445 Lufberry Ave   Fax: 516-679-0543
Wantagh NY 11793

Local Retrieval Area: NY-Bronx, Nassau, Queens, Suffolk.

Normal turn around time is 3-5 days. They charge a flat rate per searche. Credit accounts are accepted.

B.E.S. Abstract Corp also has correspondent relationships in other jurisdictions, including Kings and Westchester Counties. They specialize in complete examination of land title records. Experienced in foreclosure work and probate proceedings on all levels.

BGB Enterprises/Investigations(232)   Phone: **303-781-5149**
PO Box 2244   Fax: 303-781-4680
Englewood CO 80150

Local Retrieval Area: CO-Adams, Arapahoe, Boulder, Denver, Douglas, El Paso, Jefferson.

Normal turn around time is 1-2 hours for real estate searches; 1 day for a 1-county search. Projects are generally billed by the hour. Credit accounts are accepted. Personal checks are accepted.

BGB Enterprises/Investigations also has correspondent relationships in other jurisdictions, including Larimer and Weld. They specialize in criminal records and real estate.

Leslie Bagenstos(233)   Phone: **405-596-3174**
1124 S Mass   Fax:
Cherokee OK 73728

Local Retrieval Area: OK-Garfield, Grant, Major, Woods.

Normal turn around time is varied depending on project. Fee basis will vary by the type of project. All projects require prepayment.

Baines Title Company Inc(234)   Phone: **509-422-3420**
PO Box 626   Fax: 509-422-1901
Okanogan WA 98840

Local Retrieval Area: WA-Okanogan.

Normal turn around time is 2 days. Fee basis varies by type of transaction. Credit accounts are accepted.

Bob Bair(235)   Phone: **515-752-6257**
1613 Fremont   Fax:
Marshalltown IA 50158

Local Retrieval Area: IA-Marshall.

Normal turn around time is 24-48 hours. Rush service is also available. Projects are generally billed by the number of names searched or records located. The first project may require a prepayment.

Baker Attorney Service(236)   Phone: **916-444-9991**
PO Box 2755   Fax: 916-444-0332
Sacramento CA 95812

Local Retrieval Area: CA-El Dorado, Placer, Sacramento, Yolo.

Normal turn around time is the same day to 1 week. Projects are generally billed by the number of names searched. Credit accounts are accepted.

Baker Attorney Service also has correspondent relationships in other jurisdictions, including the state of California.

Gaines Baker(237)   Phone: **601-563-9385**
PO Box 1417   Fax:
Batesville MS 38606

Local Retrieval Area: MS-Panola, Quitman, Tallahatchie, Tate.

Normal turn around time is 1-2 days for Panola county and 2 days for the other counties. Projects are generally billed by the hour. The first project may require a prepayment.

Mr. Baker is an attorney in general practice.

Ball Abstracting(238)   Phone: **515-664-3188**
207 S Washington St   Fax: 515-664-3486
Bloomfield IA 52537

Local Retrieval Area: IA-Davis.

Normal turn around time is 3-4 days. Fee basis will vary by the type of project. Credit accounts are accepted.

Ball Agency(239)   Phone: **417-637-2424**
12 S Main St   Fax:
Greenfield MO 65661

Local Retrieval Area: MO-Dade.

Normal turn around time is 2-5 days. Fee basis will vary by type of project. Credit accounts are accepted.

They specialize in title searches.

Bankruptcy Bulletin Weekly Inc(240)   Phone: **409-854-2777**
PO Box 311   Fax: 409-854-2594
Etoile TX 75944

Local Retrieval Area: CA-All counties; TX-All counties.

Normal turn around time is 7 days behind court and 7 days file research. They also have a an immediate on line access. Online computer ordering is also available. Projects are generally billed by the number of names searched or records located. Fee basis also per extraction. The first project may require a prepayment.

Bankruptcy Services Inc(241)   Phone: **800-256-2900**
2000 N Central Expressway Suite 215   214-424-6500
Plano TX 75074   Fax: 800-256-2800

Local Retrieval Area: OK-All counties; TX-All counties.

Normal turn around time is the same day for Texas, Oklahoma, Missouri and California. Other US cities varies from the same to 1 day. Projects are generally billed by the number of names searched. Credit accounts are accepted.
Bankruptcy Services Inc also has correspondent relationships in other jurisdictions, including nationwide. They serve 200 US cities in Bankruptcy and Federal District Courts.

Banta Abstract Co(242)   Phone: **515-342-2029**
108 E Washington St   Fax: 515-342-2029
Osceola IA 50213

Local Retrieval Area: IA-Clarke.

Normal turn around time is 5 days. They charge a flat rate per project. The first project may require a prepayment.
They specialize in real estate title.

Kevin Barber(243)   Phone: **614-792-8330**
4051 W Dublin-Granville Rd   Fax: 614-889-5588
Dublin OH 43217

Local Retrieval Area: OH-Adams, Clinton, Fayette, Gallia, Highland, Hocking, Jackson, Pickaway, Pike, Ross, Scioto, Vinton.

Normal turn around time is 3 days. Fee basis is determined on "per search". Credit accounts are accepted.
Kevin specializes in real estate and appraisal matters.

Barbour Title Co(244)   Phone: **316-221-0430**
216 E 9th Ave   Fax: 316-221-2839
Winfield KS 67156

Local Retrieval Area: KS-Cowley.

Normal turn around time is 24-48 hours. Projects are generally billed by the number of names searched. The first project may require a prepayment.

James M Barnes Jr(245)   Phone: **205-683-6060**
PO Box 639   Fax:
Marion AL 36756

Local Retrieval Area: AL-Perry.

Normal turn around time is 3 days. Fee basis will vary by the type of the project. The first project may require a prepayment.
Mr. Barnes is an attorney in general practice.

Barney Abstract & Title Co(246)   Phone: **308-234-5548**
PO Box 546   Fax: 308-236-9240
Kearney NE 68848

Local Retrieval Area: NE-Buffalo.

Normal turn around time is up to two weeks. Fee basis varies by type of transaction. Credit accounts are accepted.

Barrett Detective Bureau(247)   Phone: **412-521-2900**
4652 Desdemona Ave   Fax: 412-521-2900
Pittsburgh PA 15217

Local Retrieval Area: PA-Allegheny.

Normal turn around time is 24 hours for all Allegheny County records. Online computer ordering is also available. Projects are generally billed by the hour. Credit accounts are accepted. Barrett Detective Bureau also has correspondent relationships in other jurisdictions, including all counties in Pennsylvania.

Barrister Support Service(248)   Phone: **503-246-8934**
8700 SW 26th Suite P-6   Fax:
Portland OR 97219

Local Retrieval Area: OR-Clackamas, Multnomah, Washington.

Normal turn around time is 7-10 days. Rush service is also available. Projects are generally billed by the hour. The first project may require a prepayment.

Barristers Abstract Corp(249)   Phone: **718-624-0344**
158 Court St   Fax: 718-834-0869
Brooklyn NY 11201

Local Retrieval Area: NY-Bronx, Kings, New York, Queens, Richmond.

Normal turn around time is 4 business days. Fee basis will vary by type of project. All projects require prepayment.
Barristers Abstract Corp also has correspondent relationships in other jurisdictions, including the state of New York. They specialize in title examinations.

Barristers Attorney Service(250)   Phone: **213-747-7985**
850 Venice Blvd   Fax: 213-747-3303
Los Angeles CA 90015

Local Retrieval Area: CA-Los Angeles, Orange.

Normal turn around time is 1-3 days. Same day rush service is also available. Projects are generally billed by the hour. The first project may require a prepayment. Credit cards are accepted for payment.
Barristers Attorney Service also has correspondent relationships in other jurisdictions, including Ventura, Riverside and San Bernadino. They have over 20 years experience.

Barron County Abstract(251)   Phone: **715-537-5633**
PO Box 129   Fax: 715-537-5634
Barron WI 54812

Local Retrieval Area: WI-Barron.

Normal turn around time is 7-10 days. Projects are generally billed by the number of names searched or records located. Credit accounts are accepted. Personal checks are accepted.

Barry County Abstract & Title(252)   Phone: **417-847-3224**
700 West St   Fax: 417-847-3118
Cassville MO 65625

Local Retrieval Area: MO-Barry.

Normal turn around time is 5-10 days. Rush service is also available. Projects are generally billed by the number of records located. The first project may require a prepayment.

Barry Shuster Co(253)
PO Box 79578
North Dartmouth MA 02747
Phone: 800-367-8227
Fax: 508-990-2655

Local Retrieval Area: MA-All counties; RI-All counties.

Normal turn around time is the same day to 1 week. Fee basis will vary by jurisdiction. Credit accounts are accepted.

Cindy Bartkis(254)
RR 1 Box 137 H
Susquehanna PA 18847
Phone: 717-756-3093
Fax:

Local Retrieval Area: PA-Susquehanna.

Normal turn around time is 48 hours. Projects are generally billed by the number of names searched or records located. Credit accounts are accepted.
Cindy specializes in real estate record searches.

Barton County Abstract & Title(255)
2010 Forest
Great Bend KS 67530-4093
Phone: 316-793-3781
Fax: 316-793-5475

Local Retrieval Area: KS-Barton.

Normal turn around time is 24-48 hours. Projects are generally billed by the hour. Credit accounts are accepted.
They specialize in title insurance and special ownership searches.

Barton County Title Co(256)
122 W 10th St
Lamar MO 64759
Phone: 417-682-3100
Fax: 417-682-3100

Local Retrieval Area: MO-Barton.

Normal turn around time is about one week. Fee basis will vary by the type of project. Credit accounts are accepted.

Basin Attorney Services(257)
8502 FM 307
Midland TX 79701
Phone: 915-687-5346
Fax:

Local Retrieval Area: TX-Ector, Midland.

Normal turn around time is 24-48 hours. Projects are generally billed by the number of names searched. Credit accounts are accepted.
They specialize in bankruptcy.

Batman-Sayers Abstract & Title Co(258)
1013 6th St
Nevada IA 50201
Phone: 515-382-4127
Fax: 515-382-4358

Local Retrieval Area: IA-Story.

Normal turn around time is 3-5 days. Fee basis will vary by the type of project. Credit accounts are accepted.
They specialize in real estate title.

Baxter County Abstract Co(259)
15 E 6th St
Mountain Home AR 72653
Phone: 501-425-8989
Fax: 501-425-9080

Local Retrieval Area: AR-Baxter.

Normal turn around time is 5 days. Rush service is also available. Fee basis will vary by type of project. Credit accounts are accepted.
They specialize in real estate.

Baxter Investigations(260)
PO Box 7453
Denver CO 80207
Phone: 303-461-9007
Fax: 303-671-0986

Local Retrieval Area: CO-Adams, Arapahoe, Boulder, Clear Creek, Denver, Douglas, Elbert, El Paso, Gilpin, Jefferson, Park, Teller.

Normal turn around time is the same day to 1 week. Online computer ordering is also available. Projects are generally billed by the number of names searched or records located. The first project may require a prepayment. Special arrangements can also be made.
They specialize in adoption and family reunions, locating of missing persons and assets.

Bay Area Courthouse Services(261)
490 Winslow St Suite D
Redwood City CA 94063
Phone: 415-366-9469
Fax: 415-366-2703

Local Retrieval Area: CA-Alameda, Contra Costa, El Dorado, Kern, Kern, Los Angeles, Marin, Monterey, Napa, Orange, Placer, Riverside, Sacramento, San Bernardino, San Diego, San Francisco, San Joaquin, San Mateo, Santa Clara, Solano, Sonoma, Stanislaus.

Normal turn around time is 2-3 days. Projects are generally billed by the number of names searched or records located. Credit accounts are accepted.
Bay Area Courthouse Services also has correspondent relationships in other jurisdictions, including rural areas. They specialize in UCC, title and litigation searches.

Bay Area Search Inc(262)
PO Box 7715
St Petersburg FL 34622
Phone: 813-573-9539
Fax: 813-572-0274

Local Retrieval Area: FL-Hillsborough, Manatee, Pasco, Pinellas, Polk, Sarasota.

Normal turn around time is 24-48 hours for Hillsborough and Pinellas counties. All other counties is 2 to 3 days. Project billing methods vary. Credit accounts are accepted.

Bay County Abstract Co(263)
406 7th St
Bay City MI 48708
Phone: 517-895-9910
Fax: 517-895-5631

Local Retrieval Area: MI-Arenac, Bay, Saginaw, Tuscola.

Normal turn around time is 2-3 days. Fee basis will vary by type of project. Credit accounts are accepted. They require out of town clients to prepay.
They specialize in real estate searches.

Bay County Land and Abstract Co(264)
011-C W 23rd St
Panama City FL 32402
Phone: 800-824-0712
904-763-2399
Fax: 904-763-6570

Local Retrieval Area: FL-Bay, Gulf.

Normal turn around time is 3 days. Charges are varied depending on type of search. Credit accounts are accepted.
Bay County Land and Abstract Co Inc also has correspondent relationships in other jurisdictions, including 40 branch offices in Florida and will pull court records through the state upon request via this office. They specialize in title insurance on real estate transactions.

Bay Title and Abstract Inc(265)
345 S Monroe Ave
Green Bay WI 54301
Phone: **414-431-6100**
Fax: 414-431-6101

Local Retrieval Area: WI-Brown, Calumet, Dane, Door, Kewaunee, Oconto, Outagamie, Shawano, Winnebago.

Normal turn around time is 24 hours. Projects are generally billed by the number of names searched. Credit accounts are accepted. Personal checks are accepted.
Bay Title and Abstract Inc also has correspondent relationships in other jurisdictions, including Manitowoc County.

Bayou Investigations Inc(266)
PO Box 92825
Lafayette LA 70509
Phone: **800-256-9009**
        318-235-2322
Fax: 318-232-0365

Local Retrieval Area: LA-Acadia Parish, Evangeline Parish, Iberia Parish, Jefferson Davis Parish, Lafayette Parish, St. Landry Parish, St. Martin Parish, St. Mary Parish, Vermilion Parish.

Normal turn around time is 72 hours. Projects are generally billed by the hour. Credit accounts are accepted.
They specialize in research, investigations, surveillance and process service.

Beacom Attorney Services(267)
45 W Jefferson Suite 201
Phoenix AZ 85003
Phone: **602-258-8081**
Fax: 602-258-8864

Local Retrieval Area: AZ-Maricopa.

Normal turn around time is the same to the next day. Projects are generally billed by the number of names searched. The first project may require a prepayment.
The company has 15 years experience in research of all courts and governmental agencies at the city, county, state and federal levels.

Beall Abstract and Title Co Inc(268)
219 Oak St
Sweetwater TX 79556
Phone: **915-235-8646**
Fax: 915-235-5805

Local Retrieval Area: TX-Nolan.

Normal turn around time is 2-3 weeks. Project billing methods vary. Credit accounts are accepted. Personal checks are accepted.

Beaver County Abstract Co(269)
PO Box 928
Beaver OK 73932
Phone: **405-625-4423**
Fax:

Local Retrieval Area: OK-Beaver.

Normal turn around time is 3-4 days. Projects are generally billed by the hour. Credit accounts are accepted.

Beck & Call Legal Support Svcs(270)
1 Beckman St Suite 401
New York NY 10038
Phone: **800-466-2730**
Fax: 212-385-2708

Local Retrieval Area: NY-Bronx, Kings, Nassau, New York, Queens, Richmond, Suffolk, Westchester.

Normal turn around time is the same or the next day. Projects are generally billed by the hour. Credit accounts are accepted.
Beck & Call Legal Support Services also has correspondent relationships in other jurisdictions, including nationwide.

Beckham County Abstract(271)
211 E Main
Sayre OK 73662
Phone: **405-928-3143**
Fax: 405-928-5000

Local Retrieval Area: OK-Beckham.

Normal turn around time is 1 week. Projects are generally billed by the number of records located. Credit accounts are accepted. Personal checks are accepted.
They specialize in situations affecting mineral or surface matters in Beckham County.

Beckner Abstracting & Title Co(272)
258 N State St
Osceola NE 68651
Phone: **402-747-2141**
Fax: 402-747-2151

Local Retrieval Area: NE-Butler, Merrick, Polk.

Normal turn around time is 1 week. Fee basis varies by type of transaction. Credit accounts are accepted.
They specialize in title insurance searches.

Bedgood Abstract & Title Co(273)
PO Box 12
Goliad TX 77963
Phone: **512-645-3145**
Fax: 512-645-3265

Local Retrieval Area: TX-Goliad.

Normal turn around time is 1-2 days. Fee basis will vary by the type of project. The first project may require a prepayment.

Bedgood Abstract & Title Co(274)
PO Box 4807
Victoria TX 77903
Phone: **512-573-1785**
Fax: 512-575-7581

Local Retrieval Area: TX-Victoria.

Normal turn around time is 1-2 days. Fee basis will vary by the type of project. The first project may require a prepayment.

Bedgood Abstract & Title Co(275)
PO Box 143
Port Lavaca TX 77979
Phone: **512-552-6761**
Fax: 512-552-7421

Local Retrieval Area: TX-Calhoun.

Normal turn around time is 1-2 days. Fee basis will vary by the type of project. The first project may require a prepayment.

Behind the Scene Investigations(276)
PO Box 41
Traverse City MI 49685-0041
Phone: **616-946-7198**
Fax: 616-946-5735

Local Retrieval Area: MI-Benzie, Grand Traverse, Kalkaska, Leelanau, Wexford.

Normal turn around time is a maximum of 5 days. Projects are generally billed by the hour. Credit accounts are accepted.
They specialize in locating people and workers compensatons investigation.

Bob Belden(277)
PO Box 1234
New Brunswick NJ 08903
Phone: **908-828-9765**
Fax: 908-937-5844

Local Retrieval Area: NJ-Middlesex.

Normal turn around time is 24-48 hours. Projects are generally billed by the number of names searched. Credit accounts are accepted. Personal checks are accepted.

Jan Bele(278)
124 Valley Dr
Dalton GA 30720-4101
Phone: 706-278-7216
Fax:

Local Retrieval Area: GA-Catoosa, Gilmer, Murray, Whitfield.

Normal turn around time is 1-2 days. Rush service is also available. Projects are generally billed by the number of names searched. Credit accounts are accepted.

Jan specializes in credit searches. She also searchs open judgements, pending lawsuits, check trade names, universial codes and financial statements.

Bent County Abstract Co(279)
PO Box 183
Las Animas CO 81054
Phone: 719-456-0381
Fax: 719-456-0381

Local Retrieval Area: CO-Bent.

Normal turn around time is 2-3 days. Fee basis will vary by the type of project. The first project may require a prepayment. They specialize in title work.

Bentley Title Co(280)
PO Box 104
Hermitage MO 65668
Phone: 417-745-6626
Fax: 417-745-6160

Local Retrieval Area: MO-Hickory.

Normal turn around time is 1 week. Fee basis varies by type of transaction. All projects require prepayment.

Benton Abstract & Title Co(281)
106 W Murcheson Ave
Eldorado TX 76936
Phone: 915-853-2631
Fax:

Local Retrieval Area: TX-Schleicher.

Normal turn around time is 1-2 days. Fee basis varies by type of transaction. The first project may require a prepayment.

Benton County Abstract & Title(282)
PO Box 346
Fowler IN 47949
Phone: 317-884-1140
Fax: 317-884-1140

Local Retrieval Area: IN-Benton.

Normal turn around time is 3-5 days. Fee basis will vary by the type of project. Credit accounts are accepted.

Benton County Abstract Company(283)
481 Dewey St
Foley MN 56329-0128
Phone: 612-968-7278
Fax: 612-968-7278

Local Retrieval Area: MN-Benton.

Normal turn around time is the same day. Projects are generally billed by the number of names searched or records located. Credit accounts are accepted. Personal checks are accepted.

Benton County Title Co(284)
Box 839
Vinton IA 52349
Phone: 319-472-2369
Fax: 319-472-2360

Local Retrieval Area: IA-Benton.

Normal turn around time is 2 days. Projects are generally billed by the number of names searched. The first project may require a prepayment.

Benzie County Abstract & Title Co(285)
PO Box 27
Beulah MI 49617
Phone: 616-882-5535
Fax: 616-882-4363

Local Retrieval Area: MI-Benzie, Grand Traverse.

Normal turn around time is 5 days. Projects are generally billed by the number of names searched. All projects require prepayment. They require clients requesting a title search to prepay, otherwise, they will invoice. Personal checks are accepted. They also offer escrow service.

Berkeley Base Ltd(286)
PO Box 1134
Berkeley CA 94701
Phone: 510-524-1600
Fax: 510-524-6105

Local Retrieval Area: CA-Alameda, Contra Costa.

Normal turn around time is 3 days or less. Criminal searches take 1 to 2 days. Projects are generally billed by the number of names searched or records located. Credit accounts are accepted. Personal checks are accepted.

Berkeley Base Ltd also has correspondent relationships in other jurisdictions, including Denver. They specialize in criminal research and probate. They also track bank credit cards nationnwide. They search bankruptcy filings, civil records, fictitious bctitious business names, name lists, real property and vital statistics.

Bernard & Hirschfeld(287)
116 E Market St
Celina OH 45822
Phone: 419-586-2323
Fax: 419-586-2154

Local Retrieval Area: OH-Mercer.

Normal turn around time is 3 days. Fee basis will vary by type of project. The first project may require a prepayment. They specialize in real estate record searches.

Berry & Floyd(288)
409 N Main St
New Castle KY 40050
Phone: 502-845-2881
Fax: 502-845-4223

Local Retrieval Area: KY-Carroll, Henry, Oldham, Trimble.

Normal turn around time is 3-4 days. Fee basis is "per job". The first project may require a prepayment.

William Thomas Berry(289)
PO Box 354
Lovingston VA 22949
Phone: 804-263-4886
Fax: 804-263-4285

Local Retrieval Area: VA-Amherst, Nelson.

Normal turn around time is 2 days. Projects are generally billed by the hour. The first project may require a prepayment.

Berryville Abstract and Title Co(290)
406 Public Square
Berryville AR 72616
Phone: 501-423-2535
Fax: 501-423-6396

Local Retrieval Area: AR-Carroll.

Normal turn around time is varied depending on project. Projects are generally billed by the number of names searched. Credit accounts are accepted.

They specialize in title insurance in the Eastern District of Carroll County.

Best Abstract Title Co(291)
611 Main
Trenton MO 64683
Phone: **816-359-2377**
Fax: 816-369-2377

Local Retrieval Area: MO-Grundy.

Normal turn around time is 7 to 10 days. Fee basis varies by type of transaction. Credit accounts are accepted.

Best Investigations(292)
PO Box 1497
Coeur D' Alene ID 83814
Phone: **208-765-8412**
Fax: 208-765-8412

Local Retrieval Area: ID-Bonner, Kootenai, Shoshone; WA-Spokane.

Normal turn around time is 24 hours. Projects are generally billed by the hour. The first project may require a prepayment.

They specialize in private investigations, record checks, claims adjusting and liability investigation searches.

Best Legal Services Inc(293)
1617 JFK Blvd Suite 230
Philadelphia PA 19103
Phone: **215-567-7777**
Fax: 215-561-4546

Local Retrieval Area: NJ-Burlington, Camden, Gloucester; PA-Bucks, Chester, Delaware, Montgomery, Philadelphia.

Normal turn around time is 2 days. Projects are generally billed by the number of names searched. The first project may require a prepayment.

Best Legal Services Inc also has correspondent relationships in other jurisdictions, including Lehigh, Allegheny, Lancaster, Dauphin, Luzerne and York. They specialize in serving legal papers.

Bettendorf Abstract Co(294)
1987 Spruce Hills Dr
Bettendorf IA 52722
Phone: **319-359-3646**
Fax: 319-359-3647

Local Retrieval Area: IA-Scott.

Normal turn around time is up to 7 days. Projects are generally billed by the hour. The first project may require a prepayment. Real estate and abstracting are their specialties.

Betty M Rowell CLA(295)
1541 Highland Rd
Waycross GA 31503
Phone: **912-283-4662**
Fax:

Local Retrieval Area: GA-Appling, Atkinson, Bacon, Brantley, Charlton, Clinch, Coffee, Jeff Davis, Pierce, Ware, Wayne.

Normal turn around time is 24-48 hours. Projects are generally billed by the hour. Credit accounts are accepted.

Betty specializes in real estate matters.

Bexar Professional(296)
104 Heinman Suite 200
San Antonio TX 78205
Phone: **210-228-0083**
Fax: 210-228-0066

Local Retrieval Area: TX-Bexar, Comal, Kendall, Wilson.

Normal turn around time is the same day to the next day. Project billing methods vary. The first project may require a prepayment.

Bexar Professional also has correspondent relationships in other jurisdictions, including the state of Texas. They specialize in process service.

Joe Biamonte(297)
49 Rose St
East Rutherford NJ 07073
Phone: **201-933-3590**
Fax:

Local Retrieval Area: NJ-Bergen.

Normal turn around time is 24-48 hours. Projects are generally billed by the number of names searched. There is a minimum charge. All projects require prepayment.

Betsy Biesenbach(298)
2205 Shirley Ave SW
Roanoke VA 24015
Phone: **703-982-7892**
Fax:

Local Retrieval Area: VA-Bedford, Botetourt, Floyd, Montgomery, Roanoke, Southampton, City of Bedford, City of Franklin, City of Roanoke.

Normal turn around time is 24 hours for Roanoke City, Roanoke County and Salem City, and 48 hours for all others. Projects are generally billed by the number of names searched or records located. Credit accounts are accepted.

Big Spring Abstract & Title Co Inc(299)
210 W 3rd St
Big Spring TX 79720
Phone: **915-267-1604**
Fax:

Local Retrieval Area: TX-Howard.

Normal turn around time is 2-3 days. Fee basis will vary by the type of project. The first project may require a prepayment.

Bigler & Associates Inc(300)
PO Box 11271
Macon GA 31212
Phone: **912-742-4091**
Fax: 912-477-0456

Local Retrieval Area: GA-Baldwin, Bibb, Crawford, Houston, Jones, Monroe.

Normal turn around time is 1-3 days. Projects are generally billed by the hour. Credit accounts are accepted.

Bigler & Associates Inc also has correspondent relationships in other jurisdictions, including the rest of Georgia. They specialize in asset searches and backgrounds.

Bill Bonham "The Investigator"(301)
1314 Grand
Wausau WI 54401
Phone: **715-842-1113**
Fax: 715-845-3340

Local Retrieval Area: WI-Clark, Langlade, Lincoln, Marathon, Portage, Shawano, Taylor, Waupaca, Wood.

Normal turn around time is 24 hours for Marathon County, 24-72 hours for the remaining counties served. Projects are generally billed by the hour. Bill charges by the name for searches performed in Marathon County. The first project may require a prepayment.

Bill Bonham "The Investigator" also has correspondent relationships in other jurisdictions, including Milwaukee and Green Bay. Bill is a criminal specialist and performs civil torts.

Bill Greenberg Special Services(302) Phone: **305-829-2223**
20100 NW 83rd Pl Fax: 305-829-2223
Miami FL 33015

Local Retrieval Area: FL-Broward, Dade, Palm Beach.

Normal turn around time is 24 hours. Projects are generally billed by the hour. The first project may require a prepayment.

Bill Greenberg Special Services Inc also has correspondent relationships in other jurisdictions, including all counties in Florida. They specialize in process service.

Bismark Title Co(303) Phone: **701-222-4247**
PO Box 1811 Fax: 701-222-4413
Bismarck ND 58502

Local Retrieval Area: ND-Burleigh, Morton.

Normal turn around time is 24 hours for verbal, 48 hours for paper. Fee basis are per base rate plus name. Credit accounts are accepted.

Bismark Title Co also has correspondent relationships in other jurisdictions, including abstract companies through the rest of the state.

Bitterrood Research(304) Phone: **406-363-4408**
PO Box 1422 Fax:
Hamilton MT 59840

Local Retrieval Area: MT-Ravalli.

Normal turn around time is 1-5 days. Projects are generally billed by the hour. The first project may require a prepayment.

Black Hawk Abstract Co(305) Phone: **319-291-4000**
614 Sycamore St Fax: 319-291-3929
Waterloo IA 50703

Local Retrieval Area: IA-Black Hawk.

Normal turn around time is 24 hours. They charge a flat rate plus incurred costs. The first project may require a prepayment.

Bob & Karen Blackwell(306) Phone: **205-533-2439**
1004 Longwood Dr Fax: 205-533-2439
Huntsville AL 35801

Local Retrieval Area: AL-Limestone, Madison, Morgan.

Normal turn around time is 2-3 days. Projects are generally billed by the number of names searched or records located. Credit accounts are accepted.

Correspondent relationships in other jurisdictions include Marshall county. Bob & Karen specialize in real estate searches.

Blaine County Title Co(307) Phone: **406-357-3884**
PO Box 1328 Fax: 406-357-3114
Chinook MT 59523

Local Retrieval Area: MT-Blaine.

Normal turn around time is 3 days. Projects are generally billed by the hour. The first project may require a prepayment.

Blair Abstracting Co(308) Phone: **814-942-3701**
3615 Burgoon Rd Fax: 814-944-4299
Altoona PA 16602

Local Retrieval Area: PA-Bedford, Blair, Cambria, Huntingdon.

Normal turn around time is 24 hours for current owner or lien searches, and 1 to 2 weeks for title searches. Projects are generally billed by the number of names searched or records located. Credit accounts are accepted.

They specialize in complete, 60-year title searches, and property or current owner searches.

Joe Blair(309) Phone: **908-782-7733**
71 Main St Fax:
Flemington NJ 08822

Local Retrieval Area: NJ-Hunterdon.

Normal turn around time is 24-48 hours. Projects are generally billed by the number of names searched. The first project may require a prepayment.

Betty Blankney(310) Phone: **205-325-5112**
1129 B 3rd St Fax:
Pleasant Grove AL 35127

Local Retrieval Area: AL-Jefferson.

Normal turn around time is within 8 hours. Projects are generally billed by the number of names searched. Credit accounts are accepted.

Betty specializes in probate record searches.

Al Blazinski(311) Phone: **513-698-7283**
36 Teri Drive Fax: 513-698-7283
West Milton OH 45383

Local Retrieval Area: OH-Champaign, Clark, Darke, Greene, Logan, Miami, Montgomery, Preble, Shelby.

Normal turn around time is 48-72 hours for real estate records and 72 hours for all others. Fee basis will vary by the type of project. Credit accounts are accepted.

He specializes in title work.

Bloomington Abstract Co(312) Phone: **812-336-0121**
108 E 6th St Fax: 812-336-6445
Bloomington IN 47408-3302

Local Retrieval Area: IN-Monroe.

Normal turn around time is 3-5 days. Projects are generally billed by the number of names searched. Fee basis may include charge for length of search. Credit accounts are accepted.

They specialize in title searches.

Blue Moon Investigations(313) Phone: 303-758-1234
12203-T E Iliff Ave Suite 330   Fax: 303-695-4023
Denver CO 80231

Local Retrieval Area: CO-Adams, Arapahoe, Denver, Douglas, Jefferson.

Normal turn around time is 1-3 days. Online computer ordering is also available. Projects are generally billed by the hour. Credit accounts are accepted.
Blue Moon Investigations also has correspondent relationships in other jurisdictions, including El Paso. Easylink address is 62800442.

Bodkin Abstract Company Inc(314) Phone: 219-267-7021
122 W Main   Fax: 219-267-2502
Warsaw IN 46580

Local Retrieval Area: IN-Kosciusko, Noble.

Normal turn around time is 1 week. They charge a flat rate per project. Credit accounts are accepted.

Karen V Boggs(315) Phone: 816-848-2962
Rt 1 Box 84   Fax:
Franklin MO 65250

Local Retrieval Area: MO-Howard.

Normal turn around time is varied depending on project. Projects are generally billed by the hour. All projects require prepayment. Karen specializes in genealogy searches.

Boles-Wallner Abstract and Title(316) Phone: 715-423-6940
214 W Grand Ave   Fax: 715-423-6940
Wisconsin Rapids WI 54495-0575

Local Retrieval Area: WI-Buffalo, Clark, Jackson, Juneau, Marathon, Portage, Waushara, Wood.

Normal turn around time is 48 hours. Projects are generally billed by the number of records located. Credit accounts are accepted.

Bollinger Attorney Service(317) Phone: 310-390-2428
PO Box 41885   Fax: 310-391-1838
Los Angeles CA 90041

Local Retrieval Area: CA-Los Angeles, Orange, Riverside, San Bernardino, Ventura.

Normal turn around time is 24-36 hours. Rush (6-24 hours) and super rush (3-6 hours) service is also available. Projects are generally billed by the number of records located. The first project may require a prepayment.
Bollinger Attorney Service also has correspondent relationships in other jurisdictions, including nationwide and international. Specialities include court filings, process serving, record searches from all establishments, and paralegal services.

Bollinger County Abstract Co(318) Phone: 317-238-2823
PO Box 276   Fax:
Marble Hill MO 63764

Local Retrieval Area: MO-Bollinger.

Normal turn around time is 7-10 days. Projects are generally billed by the hour. Credit accounts are accepted. Payment acceptance may vary.
They specialize in land title and geographic land locations.

Bombet & Associates(319) Phone: 504-275-0796
12077 Old Hammond Hwy   Fax: 504-272-3631
Baton Rouge LA 70816

Local Retrieval Area: LA-Ascension Parish, East Baton Rouge Parish, Iberville Parish, West Baton Rouge Parish.

Normal turn around time is 24-48 hours. Projects are generally billed by the hour. Credit accounts are accepted.
They specialize in general investigations and research.

Bonds Process Service of E Texas(320) Phone: 409-377-4483
PO Box 585   Fax:
Pointblank TX 77364

Local Retrieval Area: TX-San Jacinto.

Normal turn around time is 1-2 days. Projects are generally billed by the hour. The first project may require a prepayment.

Judy Bonham(321) Phone: 803-882-3761
1509 Hiawassee Dr   Fax: 803-638-4191
Seneca SC 29678

Local Retrieval Area: SC-Oconee.

Normal turn around time is varied depending on project. Projects are generally billed by the number of records located. Credit accounts are accepted.
Judy specializes in title searches.

Bontecou Investigative Services(322) Phone: 307-733-2637
350 E Broadway   Fax: 307-733-5258
Jackson WY 83001

Local Retrieval Area: WY-Albany, Laramie, Teton.

Normal turn around time is 3-5 working days. Projects are generally billed by the number of names searched. The first project may require a prepayment.
Bontecou Investigative Services also has correspondent relationships in other jurisdictions, including Natrona, Sweetwater and Fremont. They specialize in background, civil litigation and investigations. They are in the process of expanding their services to Bonneville, Trenton, Ada and Madison Counties in Idaho.

Boone County Abstract Co(323) Phone: 515-432-3633
814 8th St   Fax:
Boone IA 50036

Local Retrieval Area: IA-Boone.

Normal turn around time is up to 1 week. Projects are generally billed by the number of names searched. Credit accounts are accepted.
They specialize in real estate.

Boone County Abstract Co(324) Phone: 800-773-7279
108 N Lebanon St   317-482-2270
Lebanon IN 46502   Fax: 317-852-3226

Local Retrieval Area: IN-Bartholomew, Boone, Hendricks, Montgomery, Morgan, Owen, Putnam.

Normal turn around time is 3-5 days. Projects are generally billed by the number of names searched. Credit accounts are accepted.
They specialize in title searching.

Leroy Bordelon(325)
1200 Cherry St
Mamou LA 70554
Phone: 318-468-5706
Fax:

Local Retrieval Area: LA-Acadia Parish, Allen Parish, Evangeline Parish, Jefferson Davis Parish, St. Landry Parish.

Normal turn around time is 1 day. Projects are generally billed by the hour. Credit accounts are accepted.

Leroy specializes in real estate record searches.

Border Abstract(326)
5810 San Bernado Ave
Laredo TX 78041
Phone: 210-791-5810
Fax: 210-791-5555

Local Retrieval Area: TX-Brooks, Jim Hogg, La Salle, Webb, Zapata.

Normal turn around time is 1-2 days. Fee basis varies according to the type of project. All projects require prepayment.

Shirley Born(327)
316 W 6th St
Red Wing MN 55066
Phone: 612-388-6487
Fax:

Local Retrieval Area: MN-Goodhue, Wabasha.

Normal turn around time is 1 day. Projects are generally billed by the number of names searched. Credit accounts are accepted.

Ms. Born specializes in criminal record searches.

Bosic and Bosic(328)
PO Box 2005
Riverside CA 92516
Phone: 714-788-1988
Fax: 714-788-0634

Local Retrieval Area: CA-Orange, Riverside, San Bernardino.

Normal turn around time is 1-2 days. Projects are generally billed by the hour. Credit accounts are accepted.

Bosic and Bosic also has correspondent relationships in other jurisdictions, including primarily Los Angeles and San Diego Counties, but can retrieve records thru most of the state.

Bosque Cen-Tex Title Inc(329)
PO Box 899
Meridian TX 76665
Phone: 817-435-2722
Fax: 817-435-2642

Local Retrieval Area: TX-Bosque.

Normal turn around time is 1-2 days. Fee basis will vary by the type of project. The first project may require a prepayment.

Bottineau County Abtract Co(330)
PO Box 24
Bottineau ND 58318
Phone: 701-228-2215
Fax:

Local Retrieval Area: ND-Bottineau.

Normal turn around time is 2 weeks or less. Fee basis vary by the type of project. Credit accounts are accepted. Credit cards are accepted for payment.

They specialize in oil and gas.

Botts Abstract Co(331)
116 S Park St
Brenham TX 77833
Phone: 409-836-2962
Fax: 409-830-1471

Local Retrieval Area: TX-Washington.

Normal turn around time is 2 days. Projects are generally billed by the hour. The first project may require a prepayment.

Bowman & Slope County Abstract(332)
PO Box 559
Bowman ND 58623
Phone: 701-523-5231
Fax:

Local Retrieval Area: ND-Bowman, Slope.

Normal turn around time is 1-3 days. Projects are generally billed by the hour. Credit accounts are accepted.

They specialize in title search.

Bowman's Vernon County Title Co(333)
112 W Walnut
Nevada MO 64772
Phone: 417-667-7565
Fax: 417-667-7995

Local Retrieval Area: MO-Vernon.

Normal turn around time is 5 days. Fee basis varies by type of transaction. Credit accounts are accepted. Out of state accounts must prepay.

Box & Box(334)
120 S Court
Ottumwa IA 52501
Phone: 515-682-4512
Fax:

Local Retrieval Area: IA-Wapello.

Normal turn around time is 48 hours. They charge a flat rate per project. The first project may require a prepayment.

They specialize in real estate and abstracting.

Brabston Legal Investigations Inc(335)
PO Box 91711
Mobile AL 36691-1711
Phone: 205-343-3310
Fax: 205-342-2917

Local Retrieval Area: AL-Baldwin, Clarke, Mobile.

Normal turn around time is 1 week. Projects are generally billed by the number of names searched. The first project may require a prepayment.

Brabston Legal Investigations Inc also has correspondent relationships in other jurisdictions, including the rest of Alabama. They are on-line with Alabama State Judicial Computer.

Brack Warren & Associates(336)
PO Box 6497
Corpus Christi TX 78466
Phone: 512-857-7000
Fax: 512-857-7007

Local Retrieval Area: TX-Aransas, Kenedy, Kleberg, Nueces, San Patricio.

Normal turn around time is 1-2 days. Rush service is also available. Projects are generally billed by the hour. All projects require prepayment.

Brack Warren & Associates also has correspondent relationships in other jurisdictions, including Mexico, Guatamala, and Chile. They specialize in investigative services.

Thomas Q Brame Jr(337)
PO Box 301
Bay Springs MS 39422
Phone: 601-764-4355
Fax: 601-764-4356

Local Retrieval Area: MS-Clarke, Jasper, Jones, Newton, Scott, Simpson, Smith.

Normal turn around time is 1-3 days. Projects are generally billed by the hour. The first project may require a prepayment.

Mr. Brame is in general practice.

Branch County Abstract & Title Inc(338) Phone: **517-278-7629**
13 S Monroe Street   Fax:
Coldwater MI 49036

Local Retrieval Area: MI-Branch.

Normal turn around time is 3-5 days. Fee basis will vary by the type of project. Credit accounts are accepted.
They specialize in real estate transactions and title insurance.

Attorney Leonard Brashear(339) Phone: **606-672-3577**
PO Box 677   Fax: 606-672-3627
Hyden KY 41749

Local Retrieval Area: KY-Leslie.

Normal turn around time is up to 1 week. Projects are generally billed by the hour. All projects require prepayment.

Jerry M Braud(340) Phone: **504-447-1227**
1312 Park Dr   Fax: 504-447-5800
Thibodaux LA 70301

Local Retrieval Area: LA-Assumption Parish, Jefferson Parish, Lafourche Parish, St. Charles Parish, Terrebonne Parish.

Normal turn around time is 1-2 days. Projects are generally billed by the hour. The first project may require a prepayment.
Mr. Braud has been established for over 40 years. He specializes in real estate, mineral and all public record searches.

Bremer County Abstract Co(341) Phone: **319-352-2710**
218 E Bremer Ave   Fax:
Waverly IA 50677

Local Retrieval Area: IA-Bremer.

Normal turn around time is 3 days. Projects are generally billed by the number of names searched. Fee may also be based per claim. All projects require prepayment.

Leslie Brennan(342) Phone: **206-378-3345**
PO Box 1162   Fax:
Friday Harbor WA 98250

Local Retrieval Area: WA-San Juan.

Normal turn around time is 1-2 days. Projects are generally billed by the hour. Fee basis varies by type of transaction. The first project may require a prepayment.

Billie Breuille(343) Phone: **504-785-6203**
PO Box 663   Fax:
Luling LA 70070

Local Retrieval Area: LA-St. Charles Parish, St. John the Baptist Parish.

Normal turn around time is 1-2 days. Projects are generally billed by the hour. Fee basis varies by type of transaction. The first project may require a prepayment.
Ms. Breuille has been established for over 40 years. She specializes in marriage/divorce, real estate, genealogy and court record searches.

Dorothy Brewer(344) Phone: **814-849-8296**
135 Roosevelt St   Fax:
Brookville PA 15825

Local Retrieval Area: PA-Jefferson.

Normal turn around time is 24 hours. Projects are generally billed by the number of names searched. Credit accounts are accepted.
Dorothy specializes in title searches.

Eddie J Briggs(345) Phone: **601-743-5823**
PO Box 447   Fax: 601-743-5824
De Kalb MS 39328

Local Retrieval Area: MS-Kemper.

Normal turn around time is 1-2 days. Projects are generally billed by the hour. The first project may require a prepayment.
Mr. Briggs is in general practice. He specializes in marriage/divorce searches.

Frank Britton(346) Phone: **800-343-4429**
505 Emerson Ave   619-357-6366
Calexico CA 92231   Fax: 619-357-2405

Local Retrieval Area: CA-Imperial.

Normal turn around time is 48 hours. Projects are generally billed by the number of names searched. The first project may require a prepayment.
Frank specializes in process service in Imperial County, California and all of Mexico. Skip trace service in Imperial. He performs stake-outs, investigations to locate elusive victims, witnesses, perpertrators in Mexicali, B.C Mexico and Imperial County.

J Stephen Broadway(347) Phone: **615-433-5979**
116 W Market St   Fax: 615-433-7297
Fayetteville TN 37334

Local Retrieval Area: TN-Franklin, Giles, Lawrence, Lincoln, Marshall.

Normal turn around time is 2-3 days. Charges are varied depending on type of search. Credit accounts are accepted.

Bronson Abstract Co(348) Phone: **501-521-4100**
2080 E Center   Fax: 501-521-6452
Fayetteville AR 72701

Local Retrieval Area: AR-Washington.

Normal turn around time is 2 days. Fee basis will vary by type of project. The first project may require a prepayment.
They specialize in real estate and public records.

Bronson Title Services(349) Phone: **501-631-6364**
1419 W Walnut   Fax: 501-631-6448
Rogers AR 72756

Local Retrieval Area: AR-Benton.

Normal turn around time is 2 days. Fee basis will vary by type of search. The first project may require a prepayment.
They specialize in real estate and public records.

Brown County Abstract Co(350)
127 W 3rd St
Ainsworth NE 69210
Phone: 402-387-2718
Fax:

Local Retrieval Area: NE-Brown, Keya Paha, Rock.

Normal turn around time is 2-7 days. Fee basis includes a charge by the hour but there is a mimumim. Credit accounts are accepted. They specialize in title certificates.

Brown County Abstract Co(351)
201 S Broadway St
Brownwood TX 76801
Phone: 915-643-3631
Fax:

Local Retrieval Area: TX-Brown.

Normal turn around time is 1-2 days. Projects are generally billed by the hour. The first project may require a prepayment. There is a possiblity of a retainer required.
They specialize in oil and gas searches.

Brown County Title Co(352)
108 S 7th St
Hiawatha KS 66434
Phone: 913-742-7103
Fax: 913-742-7103

Local Retrieval Area: KS-Brown.

Normal turn around time is 5-10 days. Projects are generally billed by the number of names searched. Credit accounts are accepted.

Gail Brown-Browning(353)
267 Preston Ave
Roanoke VA 24012
Phone: 703-563-5699
Fax: 703-362-7833

Local Retrieval Area: VA-Appomattox, Bedford, Botetourt, Campbell, Charlotte, Floyd, Franklin, Henry, Montgomery, Pittsylvania, Pulaski, Roanoke, Rockbridge, City of Lynchburg, City of Roanoke, City of Salem.

Normal turn around time is 24 hours unless otherwise stated. Projects are generally billed by the number of names searched. Credit accounts are accepted.
They specialize in title work.

Brownfield Abstract & Title Co(354)
305B W Broadway
Brownfield TX 79316
Phone: 806-637-9595
Fax: 806-637-7560

Local Retrieval Area: TX-Terry.

Normal turn around time is 2-3 days. It may average 1-2 weeks for difficult tracts. Projects are generally billed by the number of records located. Credit accounts are accepted. Personal checks are accepted.

Brubaker & Associates(355)
PO Box 7334
Tyler TX 75711
Phone: 903-595-4616
Fax:

Local Retrieval Area: TX-Anderson, Bowie, Camp, Cass, Cherokee, Collin, Dallas, Delta, Denton, Ellis, Franklin, Gregg, Henderson, Hopkins, Hunt, Kaufman, Marion, Morris, Nacogdoches, Panola, Rains, Red River, Rockwall, Rusk, San Augustine, Smith, Tarrant, Titus, Upshur, Van Zandt.

Normal turn around time is 1-2 days. Rush service is also available. Projects are generally billed by the hour. Credit accounts are accepted.

Brule County Abstract Co(356)
PO Box 378
Chamberlain SD 57325
Phone: 605-734-4275
Fax: 605-734-4275

Local Retrieval Area: SD-Brule.

Normal turn around time is up to 2 weeks. Fee basis varies by type of transaction. Credit accounts are accepted.
They specialize in land records.

Brule County Title and Insurance(357)
103 E Lawler
Chamberlain SD 57325
Phone: 605-734-5533
Fax:

Local Retrieval Area: SD-Brule, Buffalo.

Normal turn around time is varied depending on project. Projects are generally billed by the number of names searched. Credit accounts are accepted. Personal checks are accepted.

Eva H Brunsom(358)
PO Box 846
Allendale SC 29810
Phone: 803-584-2809
Fax:

Local Retrieval Area: SC-Allendale, Bamberg, Barnwell, Hampton.

Normal turn around time is 3-5 days. Projects are generally billed by the hour. Credit accounts are accepted.
Ms. Brunsom is an attorney.

Ronna K Bryant(359)
675 E 240 St
Euclid OH 44123-2367
Phone: 216-261-4502
Fax:

Local Retrieval Area: OH-Cuyahoga.

Normal turn around time is 3-4 days. Projects are generally billed by the hour. Credit accounts are accepted. A retainer may be required. Personal checks are accepted.
Correspondent relationships in other jurisdictions include undisclosed areas. They specialize in twentieth century descendancy research.

Jerry J Bucci(360)
2585 Washington Rd Suite 131
Pittsburgh PA 15241
Phone: 412-833-9664
Fax: 412-833-9770

Local Retrieval Area: PA-Allegheny.

Normal turn around time is 1-3 days depending on requirements. Projects are generally billed by the number of names searched. Credit accounts are accepted.
Mr. Bucci is an attorney that specializes in 2nd mortage lien searches.

Buchanan Abstract Co(361)
120 N Moore St
Algona IA 50511
Phone: 515-295-3745
Fax:

Local Retrieval Area: IA-Kossuth.

Normal turn around time is 2-3 days. Projects are generally billed by the number of names searched. Credit accounts are accepted.

Buchfinck Inc(362)
PO Box 340
Alliance NE 69301
Phone: **308-762-4715**
Fax: 308-762-4716

Local Retrieval Area: NE-Box Butte.

Normal turn around time is the same day. They charge a flat rate per project. Credit accounts are accepted.
They specialize in title search and abstract.

B Scott Buffington(363)
PO Box 745
Magee MS 39111
Phone: **601-849-4267**
Fax:

Local Retrieval Area: MS-Simpson.

Normal turn around time is 1-2 days. Fee basis varies by type of transaction. The first project may require a prepayment.
Mr. Buffington is in general practice.

Burak & Anderson(364)
PO Box 64700
Burlington VT 05406
Phone: **802-862-0500**
Fax: 802-862-8176

Local Retrieval Area: VT-Addison, Chittenden, Rutland, Washington.

Normal turn around time is same day availability. Projects are generally billed by the hour. Credit accounts are accepted.
Burak & Anderson also has correspondent relationships in other jurisdictions, including the rest of the state.

Russell Burdett(365)
204 N Walnut Ave
Demopolis AL 36732
Phone: **205-289-4928**
Fax: 205-289-3054

Local Retrieval Area: AL-Greene, Marengo, Sumter.

Normal turn around time is 2-3 days. Projects are generally billed by the hour. The first project may require a prepayment.
Mr. Burdett specializes in general practice searches.

Burl Brown Land Title Company(366)
404 N Fisk
Brownwood TX 76801
Phone: **915-646-0509**
Fax: 915-643-3322

Local Retrieval Area: TX-Brown.

Normal turn around time is 3 days. Projects are generally billed by the hour. Credit accounts are accepted.

Wade Burley(367)
3069 N Broadway Suite 5
Boulder CO 80304
Phone: **303-628-3973**
Fax:

Local Retrieval Area: CO-Adams, Adams, Arapahoe, Boulder, Denver, Jefferson, Weld.

Normal turn around time is 48 hours. Fee basis will vary by the type of search. Credit accounts are accepted. They will accept prepay or they will invoice.
Correspondent relationships in other jurisdictions include undisclosed areas. They specialize in criminal and civil records, and will search public records as requested.

Burlington County Abstract Co(368)
40 E Main St
Moorestown NJ 08057
Phone: **609-235-9435**
Fax: 609-273-1062

Local Retrieval Area: NJ-Burlington.

Normal turn around time is 1-3 days. Fee basis will vary by the type of project. Credit accounts are accepted.
Burlington County Abstract Co also has correspondent relationships in other jurisdictions, including the rest of New Jersey. They specialize in real estate.

Burnett County Abstract Co(369)
24996 Hwy 35 N
Siren WI 54872
Phone: **715-349-2269**
Fax: 715-349-7604

Local Retrieval Area: WI-Burnett.

Normal turn around time is 3 days. Projects are generally billed by the number of names searched or records located. Credit accounts are accepted. Will invoice with a prepaid deposit.
They specialize in real estate title searches.

Burr Investigation(370)
1311 W Jefferson St
Boise ID 83702
Phone: **800-582-5441**
208-342-3463
Fax: 208-342-8097

Local Retrieval Area: ID-Ada, Adams, Blaine, Boise, Canyon, Cassia, Elmore, Gem, Gooding, Minidoka, Owyhee, Twin Falls, Valley.

Normal turn around time is several days. Projects are generally billed by the hour. All projects require prepayment.
They have 20 years combined law enforcement and investigative experience.

Butler County Abstract and Title(371)
204 N Main St
Poplar Bluff MO 63901
Phone: **314-686-1495**
Fax: 314-686-3804

Local Retrieval Area: MO-Butler.

Normal turn around time is 1-3 days. Projects are generally billed by the number of names searched or records located. The first project may require a prepayment. Personal checks are accepted.

C & R Associates(372)
PO Box 31411
Jackson MS 39286
Phone: **601-982-2317**
Fax:

Local Retrieval Area: MS-Hinds, Madison, Rankin, Warren.

Normal turn around time is 48 hours. Projects are generally billed by the number of names searched. The first project may require a prepayment.
C & R Associates also has correspondent relationships in other jurisdictions, including other outlying areas around Jackson.

C W Lynn Abstract Co Inc(373)
121 N 7th St
Salina KS 67401
Phone: **913-823-3706**
Fax: 913-823-7922

Local Retrieval Area: KS-Saline.

Normal turn around time is 3-5 days. Projects are generally billed by the number of names searched. Credit accounts are accepted.

C.I. & S.(374)
1070 Highline Suite 100
Pocatello ID 83201

Phone: 208-232-3592
Fax:

Local Retrieval Area: ID-Bannock, Bingham, Caribou, Custer, Oneida, Power.

Normal turn around time is 2 to 3 days. Projects are generally billed by the number of names searched. The first project may require a prepayment.
C.I. & S. also has correspondent relationships in other jurisdictions, including northern Idaho. They specialize in child custody and domestic work.

CBT Services(375)
626 Madison Ave
Toledo OH 43604

Phone: 419-244-1991
Fax: 419-224-0901

Local Retrieval Area: OH-Allen, Crawford, Cuyahoga, Defiance, Erie, Fulton, Hancock, Henry, Huron, Lucas, Ottawa, Sandusky, Seneca, Van Wert, Williams, Wood, Wyandot.

Normal turn around time is 24-72 hours. Credit accounts are accepted.
CBT Services also has correspondent relationships in other jurisdictions, including nationwide. They specialize in employment screening.

CMT Abstract(376)
380 Catherine St
Somerville NJ 08876

Phone: 908-722-6565
Fax: 908-722-5011

Local Retrieval Area: NJ-Somerset.

Normal turn around time is 24 hours. Fee basis will vary by type of project. Credit accounts are accepted.
They also perform credit check searches.

CPD Inc(377)
901 Eastwood St
Decatur IL 62521

Phone: 217-429-2711
Fax: 217-429-2718

Local Retrieval Area: IL-Champaign, Coles, De Witt, Ford, Logan, McLean, Macon, Macoupin, Montgomery, Moultrie, Piatt, Sangamon.

Normal turn around time is 1-3 days. Projects are generally billed by the hour. Credit accounts are accepted.
CPD Inc also has correspondent relationships in other jurisdictions, including the rest of the state by ex-FBI agents. They specialize in forensic sciences, criminal investigations and process service.

CPS (Capital Process Service)(378)
404 W 9th Suite 101A
Georgetown TX 78626

Phone: 512-863-0216
Fax: 512-863-7574

Local Retrieval Area: TX-Bastrop, Bell, Hays, Lampasas, Llano, Travis, Williamson.

Normal turn around time is 24 hours. Fees are charged by case. Credit accounts are accepted. CPS (Capital Process Service) also has correspondent relationships in other jurisdictions, including the rest of Texas.

Shani Cahill(379)
4591 Dundee Ave
Columbus OH 43227

Phone: 614-864-6197
Fax: 614-864-6197

Local Retrieval Area: OH-Fairfield, Franklin, Hocking, Licking, Muskingum, Perry.

Normal turn around time is 24-72 hours. Projects are generally billed by the number of names searched. Credit accounts are accepted.

Cal Info(380)
6305 Yucca St Suite 501
Los Angeles CA 90028

Phone: 213-957-5035
Fax: 213-463-9889

Local Retrieval Area: CA-Los Angeles, Orange.

Normal turn around time is the same day. Projects are generally billed by the hour. Credit accounts are accepted.
Cal Info also has correspondent relationships in other jurisdictions, including San Diego, San Francisco and Sacramento. They can also run database searches through DB Infotek.

Calhoun-Liberty Abstract Co(381)
PO Box 216
Blountstown FL 32424

Phone: 904-674-8311
Fax: 904-674-3191

Local Retrieval Area: FL-Calhoun, Liberty.

Normal turn around time is 3-5 days. Fee basis is per search. All projects require prepayment. They specialize in title insurance.

Kevin H Caliva(382)
2905 Palmer Ave
New Orleans LA 70118

Phone: 504-866-3239
Fax:

Local Retrieval Area: LA-Jefferson Parish, La Salle Parish, Orleans Parish, Plaquemines Parish, St. Bernard Parish, Terrebonne Parish.

Normal turn around time is 2-3 days. Projects are generally billed by the hour. Credit accounts are accepted.
Correspondent relationships in other jurisdictions include all of South Louisiana.

Callahan Lawyers Service(383)
50 Main St
Hackensack NJ 07602

Phone: 201-489-2245
Fax: 201-489-8093

Local Retrieval Area: NJ-Bergen, Passaic.

Normal turn around time is 3-7 days. Fee basis is per job. The first project may require a prepayment.
Callahan Lawyers Service also has correspondent relationships in other jurisdictions, including Morris, Union, Hudson, Essex and Middlesex.

Cameron Title Co Inc(384)
1317 N Walnut St
Cameron MO 64429

Phone: 800-530-5933
             816-632-6679
Fax: 816-632-1114

Local Retrieval Area: MO-Clinton, De Kalb.

Normal turn around time is 2-5 days. Projects are generally billed by the number of names searched. Credit accounts are accepted.
They specialize in title insurance and abstracting.

Camp County Land Abstract Co(385)
PO Box 701
Pittsburg TX 75686
Phone: 903-856-3676
Fax: 903-856-0470

Local Retrieval Area: TX-Camp.

Normal turn around time is 1-7 days. Fee basis will vary by the type of project. The first project may require a prepayment.

Campanella Attorney Services Inc(386)
1461 Camino Del Rio S Suite C
San Diego CA 92108
Phone: 619-298-1820
Fax: 619-298-0612

Local Retrieval Area: CA-San Diego.

Normal turn around time is 1-3 days. Projects are generally billed by the number of records located. The first project may require a prepayment.
Campanella Attorney Services Inc also has correspondent relationships in other jurisdictions, including nationwide. They specialize in civil court research, (photocopy court records), filing of court documents and service of process. They also deal with workers compensation, County Recorders and Court of Appeals and family law at superior and municiple levels.

Campbell Abstract Co(387)
7 NW 2nd St
Buffalo MN 55313-0425
Phone: 612-682-1252
Fax: 612-682-5810

Local Retrieval Area: MN-Wright.

Normal turn around time is 1 week. Projects are generally billed by the number of names searched or records located. Credit accounts are accepted.

Campbell Abstract Inc(388)
419 N 8th St
Garden City KS 67846
Phone: 316-275-7441
Fax: 316-275-8658

Local Retrieval Area: KS-Finney.

Normal turn around time is 1-3 days. Projects are generally billed by the hour. The first project may require a prepayment.

Campbell County Abstract & Title(389)
RR 1 Box 22
Herreid SD 57632
Phone: 605-437-2222
Fax: 605-437-2220

Local Retrieval Area: SD-Campbell.

Normal turn around time is up to ten days. Projects are generally billed by the number of names searched. Credit accounts are accepted.

Eugene R Campbell(390)
11 E Market St
York PA 17401
Phone: 717-846-5830
Fax: 717-845-6664

Local Retrieval Area: PA-York.

Normal turn around time is 3 days. Projects are generally billed by the hour. All projects require prepayment.
Correspondent relationships in other jurisdictions include Lancaster. They specialize in real estate searches.

Cape Girardeau Cnty Abstr & Title(391)
400 Broadway Suite 101
Cape Girardeau MO 63701
Phone: 314-335-5890
Fax: 314-335-6381

Local Retrieval Area: MO-Cape Girardeau.

Normal turn around time is 3 days. Projects are generally billed by the number of names searched or records located. Credit accounts are accepted.
They specialize in land title record searches.

Capitol City Network(392)
1010 B Florin Rd Suite 276
Sacramento CA 95831
Phone: 800-727-9890
       916-395-2917
Fax:

Local Retrieval Area: CA-Marin, Placer, Sacramento, San Francisco, San Joaquin, Shasta, Sonoma, Stanislaus, Yolo.

Normal turn around time is 2-24 hours. Fee basis varies by type of transaction. The first project may require a prepayment.
They do provide a FAX number for ongoing accounts.

Capitol Document Services Inc(393)
245 W Roosevelt
Phoenix AZ 85003
Phone: 800-255-4052
       602-254-4489
Fax: 602-258-5833

Local Retrieval Area: AZ-Maricopa.

Normal turn around time is 24 hours in Maricopa, 1 to 2 days in Pima, and 2 to4 days in the other Arizona counties. Out of state turn around time is varied. Projects are generally billed by the number of names searched. They do sometimes charge by the hour depending on search. Credit accounts are accepted.
Capitol Document Services Inc also has correspondent relationships in other jurisdictions, including the rest of Arizona and nationwide. Both searching and filing services are specialties. They will search any public record at any level.

Capitol Document Services Inc(394)
PO Box 8803
Santa Fe NM 87504
Phone: 505-984-2696
Fax: 505-983-8511

Local Retrieval Area: NM-Bernalillo, Santa Fe, Santa Fe, Taos, Taos.

Normal turn around time is 24-48 hours. Projects are generally billed by the number of names searched. A mileage fee may also be involved. Credit accounts are accepted. Sometimes an up front fee is needed for massive record copying requests.
Capitol Document Services Inc also has correspondent relationships in other jurisdictions, including the rest of New Mexico.

Capitol Filing Service Inc(395)
214 Old Hickory Blvd Suite 199
Nashville TN 37221
Phone: 615-646-1404
Fax: 615-646-0810

Local Retrieval Area: TN-Cheatham, Davidson, Dickson, Hickman, Maury, Montgomery, Robertson, Rutherford, Sumner, Trousdale, Williamson, Wilson.

Normal turn around time is 1-3 days. Projects are generally billed by the number of names searched. Credit accounts are accepted.
Capitol Filing Service Inc also has correspondent relationships in other jurisdictions, including the rest of Tennessee. They specialize in corporate research and filing.

Capitol Legal Service Inc(396)
PO Box 22605
Sacramento CA 95822-0605
Phone: 916-443-7112
Fax: 916-443-3131

Local Retrieval Area: CA-Colusa, El Dorado, Nevada, Placer, Sacramento, Solano, Sutter, Yolo.

Normal turn around time is 5 days. Rush service is also available. Projects are generally billed by the hour. Credit accounts are accepted. Sometimes a set-up fee and prepayment is required. They specialize in research and photocoping.

Capitol Lien Records and Resrch(397)
Po Box 65727
St Paul MN 55165
Phone: 612-639-9130
Fax: 612-436-6722

Local Retrieval Area: MN-All counties.

Normal turn around time is 1-3 days. Projects are generally billed by the number of names searched or records located. Credit accounts are accepted. Personal checks are accepted.

They also provide a weekly publication of all Federal and State Tax Liens filed with the Secretary of State of Minnesota.

Capitol Paralegal Services(398)
PO Box 2775
Harrisburg PA 17105
Phone: 800-622-2300
717-234-9715
Fax: 717-233-3029

Local Retrieval Area: PA-Dauphin.

Normal turn around time is 1-2 days. Rush service is also available. Projects are generally billed by the number of names searched or records located. The first project may require a prepayment.

Capitol Paralegal Services also has correspondent relationships in other jurisdictions, including the rest of Pennsylvania. They specialize in searching and filing public records.

Capitol Services(399)
926 J St Suite 919
Sacramento CA 95814
Phone: 916-443-0657
Fax: 916-443-1908

Local Retrieval Area: CA-Sacramento.

Normal turn around time is 5 working days. Projects are generally billed by the number of records located. Credit accounts are accepted.

They provide document filing and retrieval at the California Secretary of State's office in Sacramento.

Capitol Services(400)
1020 E Lafayette St Suite 110A
Tallahassee FL 32301
Phone: 904-878-4734
Fax: 904-656-7543
800-226-7544

Local Retrieval Area: FL-Gadsden, Leon, Taylor, Wakulla.

Normal turn around time is 24 hours. Online computer ordering is also available. Projects are generally billed by the number of names searched. If the search is extra long, they will charge by the hour. Credit accounts are accepted. They request prepayment if the charges are over $50, but they will invoice. Personal checks are accepted.

Capitol Services also has correspondent relationships in other jurisdictions, including all counties in Florida. They specialize in state UCC's, preparing and filing corporations and motor vehicle record searches.

Capitol Services Inc(401)
PO Box 3738 McCormack Station
Boston MA 02101
Phone: 800-662-2202
800-662-2202
Fax: 617-523-8533

Local Retrieval Area: MA-Suffolk.

Normal turn around time is next day service. Projects are generally billed by the number of names searched. Credit accounts are accepted.

Capitol Services Inc also has correspondent relationships in other jurisdictions, including all counties and town clerks in Massachusetts. They specialize in providing state, county and town clerk UCC searches.

Capitol Services Inc(402)
1212 Guadalupe Suite 102
Austin TX 78701
Phone: 800-345-4647
Fax: 800-432-3622

Local Retrieval Area: TX-Dallas, Harris, Travis.

Normal turn around time is the next day. Projects are generally billed by the number of names searched. Credit accounts are accepted.

Capitol Services Inc also has correspondent relationships in other jurisdictions, including all Texas counties. They also search pending litigations, tax liens and judgements.

Caprock Land Title Company(403)
111 S Ballard St
Pampa TX 79065
Phone: 806-669-3281
Fax: 806-669-3282

Local Retrieval Area: TX-Gray.

Normal turn around time is the same day to several days depending on work load and search requested. Projects are generally billed by the number of names searched. Credit accounts are accepted. Personal checks are accepted.

Caprock Title Co(404)
511 W Ohio Ave Suite 100
Midland TX 79701
Phone: 915-687-3232
Fax:

Local Retrieval Area: NM-Eddy, Lea; TX-Dickens, Kent, King, Stonewall.

Normal turn around time is up to a week. Fee basis will vary by the type of project. The first project may require a prepayment.

Capstone Title Services(405)
817 22nd Ave
Tuscaloosa AL 35401
Phone: 205-759-1105
Fax: 205-759-1106

Local Retrieval Area: AL-Bibb, Dallas, Fayette, Greene, Hale, Pickens, Tuscaloosa, Walker.

Normal turn around time is 1-2 days. Projects are generally billed by the number of names searched. Fee basis may vary on length of search. Credit accounts are accepted. Personal checks are accepted.

Carl Watson & Associates(406)
663 S Cooper Suite 6
Memphis TN 38108-5350
Phone: **901-272-3006**
Fax: 901-272-2603

Local Retrieval Area: IN-Fayette, Shelby, Tipton; MS-De Soto, Tate; TN-Hardeman.

Normal turn around time is 48 hours. Online computer ordering is also available. Projects are generally billed by the number of names searched or records located. The first project may require a prepayment.
Carl Watson & Associates also has correspondent relationships in other jurisdictions, including the states of Arkansas and Alabama.

Carlton County Abstract and Title(407)
PO Box 60
Carlton MN 55718-0060
Phone: **218-384-4010**
Fax: 218-384-4010

Local Retrieval Area: MN-Carlton.

Normal turn around time is 1 day. Projects are generally billed by the number of names searched. Credit accounts are accepted. They specialize in real estate.

Carol Ann Bailey CLA Inc(408)
8178 S Airport Rd
Milton FL 32583
Phone: **904-626-1817**
Fax: 904-626-6948

Local Retrieval Area: FL-Escambia, Santa Rosa.

Normal turn around time is 7-10 days. Extra charge for expedited services. Projects are generally billed by the hour. Credit accounts are accepted. Credit cards are accepted for payment.   They require a retainer. Personal checks are accepted.
Carol Ann Bailey CLA Inc also has correspondent relationships in other jurisdictions, including all other counties in Florida. They hold a specialty certification in civil litigation, criminal law and procedure and Florida law.

Carolina Information Services Inc(409)
11071 Farrow Rd
Blythewood SC 29016
Phone: **803-786-8665**
Fax: 803-735-0399

Local Retrieval Area: SC-Fairfield, Lexington, Richland.

Normal turn around time is 3 days. Projects are generally billed by the number of names searched. Credit accounts are accepted.
Carolina Information Services Inc also has correspondent relationships in other jurisdictions, including the rest of South Carolina.

Barbara Carr(410)
PO Box 297
Hinton WV 25951
Phone: **304-466-5291**
Fax:

Local Retrieval Area: WV-Mercer, Monroe, Raleigh, Summers.

Normal turn around time is 1 day. Projects are generally billed by the number of names searched. Credit accounts are accepted. Barbara specializes in vital statistic records.

D Garvin Carroll(411)
905 E 4th
Mountain Home AR 72653
Phone: **501-425-2881**
Fax:

Local Retrieval Area: AR-Baxter, Boone, Fulton, Izard, Marion, Searcy; MO-Howell, Ozark.

Normal turn around time is varied depending on project. Projects are generally billed by the hour. Credit accounts are accepted. Correspondent relationships in other jurisdictions include undisclosed areas. They specialize in genealogy and will searches.

Cartwright Abstracting(412)
PO Box 215
Milan GA 31060
Phone: **912-362-4220**
Fax: 912-362-4783

Local Retrieval Area: GA-Bleckley, Dodge, Pulaski, Telfair, Wheeler, Wilcox.

Normal turn around time is 24 hours. Projects are generally billed by the number of names searched or records located. Credit accounts are accepted. Personal checks are accepted.
They specialize in real estate and UCC searches, including civil judgements and taxes in Superior Court Clerk's offices, Probate Courts and Tax Offices.

Cass County Abstract Co(413)
518 Chestnut St
Atlantic IA 50022
Phone: **712-243-2136**
Fax:

Local Retrieval Area: IA-Cass.

Normal turn around time is 1-14 days. Fee basis will vary by the type of project. Credit accounts are accepted.

Cass County Abstract Co(414)
PO Box 826
Fargo ND 58107
Phone: **701-232-3341**
Fax: 701-232-8702

Local Retrieval Area: ND-Cass.

Normal turn around time is 2 days. Fee basis will vary by type of search. Credit accounts are accepted.
They specialize in real estate.

George P Cassar Jr(415)
PO Box 50
CHarleston MS 38921
Phone: **601-647-5581**
Fax: 601-647-5434

Local Retrieval Area: MS-Tallahatchie.

Normal turn around time is 1-2 days. Projects are generally billed by the hour. The first project may require a prepayment.
Mr. Cassar is an attorney specializing in real estate and estate planning.

M B Cassell(416)
PO Box 235
Finley ND 58230-0235
Phone: **701-524-1961**
Fax:

Local Retrieval Area: ND-Steele.

Normal turn around time is 1-3 days. Projects are generally billed by the number of names searched or records located. Credit accounts are accepted.

Cassia County Abstract Co(417)   Phone: **208-678-8347**
PO Box 548   Fax: 208-678-8348
Burley ID 83318

Local Retrieval Area: ID-Cassia.

Normal turn around time is 10 days. Projects are generally billed by the hour. All projects require prepayment. They specialize in real estate closing.

Cattaraugus Abstract Corp(418)   Phone: **716-938-9109**
406 Erie St   Fax: 716-938-6259
Little Valley NY 14755

Local Retrieval Area: NY-Cattaraugus.

Normal turn around time is 48 hours. Projects are generally billed by the number of names searched. Credit accounts are accepted.

Cedar County Abstract & Title Co(419) Phone: **417-876-4812**
105 E Spring   Fax: 417-876-4820
El Dorado Springs MO 64744

Local Retrieval Area: MO-Cedar.

Normal turn around time is 7 days. Projects are generally billed by the number of names searched. All projects require prepayment.

Cedar Land Title Inc(420)   Phone: **801-586-9984**
PO Box 733   Fax: 801-586-5095
Cedar City UT 84721

Local Retrieval Area: UT-Beaver, Garfield, Iron, Kane.

Normal turn around time is 3 days. Projects are generally billed by the hour. Credit accounts are accepted. They specialize in title search and UCC.

Centennial Abstract of Pratt Inc(421) Phone: **316-672-6889**
100 S Main   Fax:
Pratt KS 67124

Local Retrieval Area: KS-Pratt.

Normal turn around time is 3-5 days. Projects are generally billed by the number of names searched. Credit accounts are accepted.

Centennial Coverages Inc(422)   Phone: **303-699-0444**
15200 E Girard Ave Suite 4500   Fax: 303-680-1808
Aurora CO 80014

Local Retrieval Area: CO-Adams, Arapahoe, Denver, Jefferson; IL-Cook.

Normal turn around time is 2-10 days. Projects are generally billed by the number of names searched or records located. The first project may require a prepayment. Centennial Coverages Inc also has correspondent relationships in other jurisdictions, including the United States. They specialize in real estate searches, UCC searches and skip tracing.

Centennial Title & Abstract Co(423)   Phone: **313-238-5100**
G4137 Fenton Road   Fax: 313-238-5270
Burton MI 48529

Local Retrieval Area: MI-Genesee, Monroe.

Normal turn around time is 3-4 days. Fee basis will vary by the project. The first project may require a prepayment. They specialize in real estate transactions.

Central Indiana Paralegal Service(424) Phone: **317-636-1311**
55 Monument Cir Suite 1424   Fax: 317-636-1426
Indianapolis IN 46204

Local Retrieval Area: IN-Boone, Hamilton, Hendricks, Johnson, Marion, Morgan, Shelby.

Normal turn around time is 2-5 days. Projects are generally billed by the number of names searched. Credit accounts are accepted. Central Indiana Paralegal Service Inc also has correspondent relationships in other jurisdictions, including all counties in Indiana. They specialize in legal research, collection assistance, filing of court documents, probate/estates and guardianship administration.

Central Investigation(425)   Phone: **419-474-5195**
4841 Monroe St Suite 202   Fax: 419-474-5102
Toledo OH 43614

Local Retrieval Area: MI-Lenawee, Monroe; OH-Defiance, Fulton, Hancock, Henry, Lucas, Williams, Wood.

Normal turn around time is 1 day. Fee basis is determined on "individual case". All projects require prepayment. Central Investigation also has correspondent relationships in other jurisdictions, including northern Ohio.

Central Legal Service(426)   Phone: **503-389-8133**
PO Box 409   Fax: 503-382-7068
Bend OR 97709

Local Retrieval Area: OR-Crook, Deschutes, Jefferson.

Normal turn around time is 48 hours. Rush service is also available. Projects are generally billed by the hour. Credit accounts are accepted.

Central New York Abstract Corp(427)   Phone: **315-724-1614**
24 Elizabeth St   Fax:
Utica NY 13350

Local Retrieval Area: NY-Cayuga, Herkimer, Madison, Oneida, Oswego, Otsego.

Normal turn around time is 1-2 days for reports and 1 to 2 weeks for abstracts. Projects are generally billed by the number of names searched or records located. Credit accounts are accepted. Central New York Abstract Corporation also has correspondent relationships in other jurisdictions, including Hamilton.

Central Utah Title(428)   Phone: **801-835-1111**
140 N Main   Fax: 801-835-8824
Manti UT 84642

Local Retrieval Area: UT-Sanpete.

Normal turn around time is 1 week. Projects are generally billed by the number of names searched. Credit accounts are accepted. They specialize in escrow closings.

Central Virginia Investigative Svc(429)
PO Box 760
Lynchburg VA 24505
Phone: 804-239-4657
Fax:

Local Retrieval Area: VA-Appomattox, Bedford, Campbell, City of Lynchburg.

Normal turn around time is 1-2 days. Fee basis will vary by the type of project. Credit accounts are accepted.
They handle all types of investigations and will travel throughout VA. and parts of PA.

Central-MO Investigations(430)
9120 N Brown Station Dr
Columbia MO 65202
Phone: 314-474-8735
Fax: 314-422-4338

Local Retrieval Area: MO-Buchanan, Callaway, Cole, Howard, Miller, Moniteau, Randolph.

Normal turn around time is varied depending on project. Projects are generally billed by the number of names searched or records located. Credit accounts are accepted.
They specialize in criminal investigations and military locating.

Cerro Gordo Abstract Co(431)
10 1st St NW
Mason City IA 50401
Phone: 515-423-1145
Fax: 515-423-0289

Local Retrieval Area: IA-Cerro Gordo.

Normal turn around time is 1-2 days. Projects are generally billed by the number of names searched. Fee basis may also be per description. Credit accounts are accepted.
They specialize in real estate.

Chaffee Title-Abstract Co(432)
225 "G" St
Salida CO 81201
Phone: 719-539-2215
Fax: 719-539-2588

Local Retrieval Area: CO-Chaffee.

Normal turn around time is 4-5 days. Fee basis will vary by the type of project. The first project may require a prepayment.
They specialize in real estate searching.

Trish Chalow(433)
908 Rogers Ave
Vineland NJ 08360
Phone: 609-696-2801
Fax: 609-696-1450

Local Retrieval Area: NJ-Cumberland, Salem.

Normal turn around time is 24-48 hours. Projects are generally billed by the number of names searched. Credit accounts are accepted.

Chambers Investigations(434)
606 49th St W
Bradenton FL 34209
Phone: 813-792-1107
Fax: 813-792-1107

Local Retrieval Area: FL-De Soto, Manatee, Sarasota.

Normal turn around time is 24 hours. Projects are generally billed by the hour. All projects require prepayment.
They specialize in private investigations.

Linda Chambless(435)
PO Box 437
Millry AL 36558
Phone: 205-846-3697
Fax: 205-846-3697

Local Retrieval Area: AL-Choctaw, Clarke, Marengo, Washington.

Normal turn around time is 24 hours. Projects are generally billed by the number of names searched. The first project may require a prepayment.
Linda specializes in real estate abstracts.

Chariton Abstract(436)
300 S Walnut
Keytesville MO 65261
Phone: 816-288-3446
Fax: 816-288-3446

Local Retrieval Area: MO-Chariton.

Normal turn around time is 3-4 days. Fee basis varies by type of transaction. Credit accounts are accepted. Credit cards are accepted for payment.

Chariton Abstract Co(437)
917 1/2 Braden
Chariton IA 50049
Phone: 515-774-2677
Fax:

Local Retrieval Area: IA-Lucas.

Normal turn around time is up to 2 weeks. Rush service may be available. Fee basis will vary by the type of project. Credit accounts are accepted.

Charles F Edgar & Associates(438)
904 Bob Wallace Ave Suite 222
Huntsville AL 35801
Phone: 205-539-7761
Fax: 205-539-7768

Local Retrieval Area: AL-Blount, Calhoun, Cherokee, Colbert, Cullman, De Kalb, Etowah, Franklin, Jackson, Lauderdale, Lawrence, Limestone, Madison, Marion, Marshall, Morgan, St. Clair, Winston; TN-Bedford, Coffee, Franklin, Giles, Lawrence, Lincoln, Maury, Moore.

Normal turn around time is 2-3 days. Projects are generally billed by the number of names searched. Credit accounts are accepted.
They specialize in corporation filings.

Charles L Lager Private Investig.(439)
PO Box 608
Rockwall TX 75087
Phone: 214-771-8685
Fax:

Local Retrieval Area: TX-Collin, Dallas, Denton, Ellis, Hunt, Kaufman, Rockwall, Tarrant.

Normal turn around time is 1 week. Projects are generally billed by the hour. Credit accounts are accepted. Payment acceptance was not specified.
They specialize in insurance fraud investigations and surveillance.

Charlson & Wilson Bonded Abstr(440)
111 N 4th St
Manhattan KS 66502
Phone: 913-537-2900
Fax: 913-537-2904

Local Retrieval Area: KS-Riley.

Normal turn around time is 3-5 days. Projects are generally billed by the hour. All projects require prepayment.
Charlson & Wilson Bonded Abstracters Inc also has correspondent relationships in other jurisdictions, including Pottawatomie. They specialize in any kind of title search.

Charter Title Corp(441)   Phone: 206-875-6522
PO Box 251   Fax: 206-875-5941
South Bend WA 98586

Local Retrieval Area: WA-Pacific.

Normal turn around time is 1 day. Fee basis varies by type of transaction. The first project may require a prepayment.

Chattel Mortgage Reporters Inc(442)   Phone: 708-234-8805
582 N Oakwood Ave Suite 202   Fax: 708-234-8804
Lake Forest IL 60045

Local Retrieval Area: IL-Brown, Champaign, Clay, Cook, De Kalb, Du Page, Grundy, Iroquois, Kane, Kankakee, Kendall, Lake, La Salle, Lee, Livingston, McHenry, Macon, Marion, Whiteside, Will, Winnebago.

Normal turn around time is 2-3 days. Projects are generally billed by the number of names searched or records located. Credit accounts are accepted. Personal checks are accepted.

Chautauqua County Abstract Co(443)   Phone: 316-725-3215
121 W Main St   Fax:
Sedan KS 67361

Local Retrieval Area: KS-Chautauqua.

Normal turn around time is 2-3 days. Fee basis varies by type of transaction. The first project may require a prepayment.

Chaves County Abstract & Title Co(444)   Phone: 505-622-5340
PO Box 1476   Fax: 505-622-5346
Roswell NM 88202

Local Retrieval Area: NM-Chaves.

Normal turn around time is varied depending on project. Fee basis vill vary by the type of project. The first project may require a prepayment.

Cheboygan Straits Area Title(445)   Phone: 616-627-7181
PO Box 328   Fax: 616-627-6200
Cheboygan MI 49721

Local Retrieval Area: MI-Cheboygan.

Normal turn around time is 2-5 days. Fee basis will vary by type of project. The first project may require a prepayment.
They specialize in land title searches.

Cherokee Capitol Abstract & Title(446)   Phone: 918-456-8851
107 E Delaware St   Fax: 918-456-8322
Tahlequah OK 74464

Local Retrieval Area: OK-Cherokee.

Normal turn around time is within the same day of request. Projects are generally billed by the number of records located. Credit accounts are accepted.

Cherokee County Title Co(447)   Phone: 903-586-6080
506 N Henderson   Fax:
Rusk TX 75785

Local Retrieval Area: TX-Cherokee.

Normal turn around time is 1-2 days. Fee basis will vary by the type of project. The first project may require a prepayment.

Chesapeake Services(448)   Phone: 410-643-3731
PO Box 164   Fax:
Chester MD 21619

Local Retrieval Area: MD-Anne Arundel, Queen Anne's.

Normal turn around time is 24-48 hours. Online computer ordering is also available. Projects are generally billed by the hour. The first project may require a prepayment.
An instate 800 number is available for established accounts. They have access to a statewide District Court computer system. They can communicate with accounts through Compu-Serve.

Cheyenne Abstract Co Inc(449)   Phone: 405-497-3363
PO Box 450   Fax:
Cheyenne OK 73628

Local Retrieval Area: OK-Roger Mills.

Normal turn around time is 2-3 days. Fee basis will vary by the type of project. Credit accounts are accepted.

Cheyenne County Abstract(450)   Phone: 308-254-5636
1024 Jackson St   Fax: 308-254-6159
Sidney NE 69162

Local Retrieval Area: NE-Cheyenne.

Normal turn around time is 3-5 days.] Projects are generally billed by the number of records located. Credit accounts are accepted. They specialize in oil record searches.

Cheyenne County Abstract Co(451)   Phone: 719-767-5585
130 S 1st E   Fax: 719-767-5029
Cheyenne Wells CO 80810

Local Retrieval Area: CO-Cheyenne.

Normal turn around time is up to 1 week. Projects are generally billed by the hour. Credit accounts are accepted.
They specialize in real estate title.

Chicot County Abstract(452)   Phone: 501-265-2525
PO Box 721   Fax: 501-265-2525
Lake Village AR 71653

Local Retrieval Area: AR-Chicot.

Normal turn around time is varied depending on project. Projects are generally billed by the number of names searched. The first project may require a prepayment. Personal checks are accepted.

Chilvers Abstract & Title Co(453)   Phone: 402-329-4525
101 E Main   Fax: 402-439-2145
Pierce NE 68767

Local Retrieval Area: NE-Antelope, Cedar, Knox, Pierce, Wayne.

Normal turn around time is 1-3 days. Fee bases is a flat rate and per record. Credit accounts are accepted.
They specialize in title insurance.

Darlene Chiota(454)
140 W 6th St
Erie PA 16501
Phone: 814-453-1824
Fax:

Local Retrieval Area: PA-Erie.

Normal turn around time is 24-48 hours. Turn aroune time is up to 1 week for title searches. Projects are generally billed by the number of names searched or records located. Credit accounts are accepted. Darlene request prepayment for copies, but will invoice for services.
Darlene specializes in current owner searches.

Chippewa Abstract and Title Co(455)
125 Arlington Suite 2
Sault Sainte Marie MI 49783
Phone: 906-632-7331
Fax:

Local Retrieval Area: MI-Chippewa.

Normal turn around time is 2-3 weeks in October through April and 5 to 6 weeks in May through September. Projects are generally billed by the hour. All projects require prepayment. Personal checks are accepted.
Chippewa Abstract and Title Co also has correspondent relationships in other jurisdictions, including the state of Michigan. They have been servicing Chippewa County for over 140 years.

Choctaw County Abstract and Title(456)
PO Box 636
Hugo OK 74743
Phone: 405-326-9616
Fax:

Local Retrieval Area: OK-Choctaw.

Normal turn around time is 1 week. Fee basis will vary by the type of projoct. Credit accounts are accepted. Clients may make payments upon receipt.

Chouteau County Abstract Co(457)
Box 578
Fort Benton MT 59442
Phone: 406-622-3221
Fax: 406-622-5249

Local Retrieval Area: MT-Chouteau.

Normal turn around time is 2-4 days. Projects are generally billed by the hour. Credit accounts are accepted.

Church & Grau(458)
109 W Florida Ave
Greensburg KS 67054
Phone: 316-723-2552
Fax:

Local Retrieval Area: KS-Kiowa.

Normal turn around time is 2-3 days. Fee basis varies by type of transaction. Credit accounts are accepted.

Citizen's Abstract Co(459)
104 E Race Ave
Searcy AR 72143
Phone: 501-268-5571
Fax: 501-268-7378

Local Retrieval Area: AR-White.

Normal turn around time is up to 1 week. Fee basis will vary by type of project. The first project may require a prepayment.
They specialize in land title and title insurance.

Citzen Abstract Co(460)
11 W Harrison
Sullivan IL 61951
Phone: 217-728-4389
Fax:

Local Retrieval Area: IL-Moultrie.

Normal turn around time is 2 days. Fee basis varies by type of transaction. Credit accounts are accepted.

Civil Process Plus Inc(461)
444 Brickell Ave Plaza 51 - Suite 467
Miami FL 33131
Phone: 800-497-3783
Fax: 305-883-0720

Local Retrieval Area: FL-Broward, Dade, Monroe, Palm Beach.

Normal turn around time is 48 hours. Rush service is same day. Projects are generally billed by the number of records located. The first project may require a prepayment.

Civil Process Service(462)
512 Main St Suite 615
Fort Worth TX 76102
Phone: 800-866-2214
817-335-2446
Fax: 817-335-2445

Local Retrieval Area: TX-Dallas, Tarrant.

Normal turn around time is 24-48 hours. Projects are generally billed by the hour. Credit accounts are accepted.
Civil Process Service also has correspondent relationships in other jurisdictions, including Northern Texas. They specialize in records research.

Civil Process Service(463)
2560 Wellington Lane
Wichita Falls TX 76305
Phone: 817-851-9800
Fax:

Local Retrieval Area: TX-Archer, Baylor, Foard, Hardeman, Haskell, Jackson, Knox, Montague, Throckmorton, Wichita, Wilbarger, Wise, Young.

Normal turn around time is 24-48 hours. Projects are generally billed by the number of records located. The first project may require a prepayment.
Civil Process Service also has correspondent relationships in other jurisdictions, including nationwide.

Clark Abstract & Title Co(464)
PO Box 253
Clark SD 57225
Phone: 605-532-3812
Fax:

Local Retrieval Area: SD-Clark.

Normal turn around time is 2-3 days. Fee basis varies by type of transaction. All projects require prepayment.

Clark County Abstract Co(465)
402 Clay St
Arkadelphia AR 71923
Phone: 501-246-2821
Fax: 501-246-2467

Local Retrieval Area: AR-Clark.

Normal turn around time is 3 days. A rush service is also available. Fee basis will vary by type of project. The first project may require a prepayment.

Attorney J Kirk Clarke(466)
119 Sutton
Maysville KY 41056
Phone: 606-564-5527
Fax: 606-564-4536

Local Retrieval Area: KY-Bracken, Fleming, Mason.

Normal turn around time is up to 5 days. Fee basis varies by type of transaction. Credit accounts are accepted.

Claudine Claugus(467)
34852 Hartshorne Ridge Rd
Graysville OH 45734
Phone: 614-425-1831
Fax:

Local Retrieval Area: OH-Belmont, Harrison, Jefferson, Monroe, Muskingum, Tuscarawas.

Normal turn around time is 24-72 hours. Fee basis is per piece. Credit accounts are accepted. Claudine specializes in UCC and title searches.

Clay County Abstract & Title(468)
PO Box 38
Clay Center NE 68933
Phone: 402-762-3645
Fax: 402-762-3645

Local Retrieval Area: NE-Clay.

Normal turn around time is 1-2 days. Fee basis varies by type of transaction. Credit accounts are accepted.

Clay County Abstract Co(469)
113 S 12th St
Moorhead MN 56560
Phone: 218-233-1358
Fax: 218-233-1359

Local Retrieval Area: MN-Clay.

Normal turn around time is 5-10 days. Online computer ordering is also available. Projects are generally billed by the number of names searched. Credit accounts are accepted. Personal checks are accepted.
Clay County Abstract Co also has correspondent relationships in other jurisdictions, including Becker, Otter Tail, Norman, Polk, Red Lake, Wilkin, Mahnomen, Marshall, Kittson and Roseau Counties.

Clayton County Abstract Co(470)
126 S Main
Elkader IA 52043
Phone: 319-245-1430
Fax:

Local Retrieval Area: IA-Clayton.

Normal turn around time is 1 week. Fee basis will vary by the type of project. Credit accounts are accepted.

Clayton Title Service Inc(471)
PO Box 327
Clayton NM 88415
Phone: 505-374-9789
Fax:

Local Retrieval Area: NM-Union.

Normal turn around time is 5-10 days. Fee basis will vary by the type of project. Credit accounts are accepted.

Clear Creek-Gelpin Abstract & Title(472)
PO Box 545
Georgetown CO 80444
Phone: 303-569-2391
Fax: 303-569-2670

Local Retrieval Area: CO-Clear Creek, Gilpin.

Normal turn around time is 3-5 days. Fee basis will vary by the type of project. The first project may require a prepayment.
They specialize in real estate and title matters.

Clear Title Co(473)
339 W Colorado St
La Grange TX 78945
Phone: 409-968-5885
Fax:

Local Retrieval Area: TX-Fayette.

Normal turn around time is up to a week because the court is not computerized. Fee basis will vary by the type of project. The first project may require a prepayment.

Danny Clearman(474)
PO Box 85
Decatur MS 39327
Phone: 601-635-3432
Fax: 601-635-3432

Local Retrieval Area: MS-Newton.

Normal turn around time is 1-2 days. Projects are generally billed by the hour. The first project may require a prepayment.
Mr. Clearman is in general practice. He specializes in marriage/divorce searches.

Cleveland Investigations(475)
6085 Waldlen
Talent OR 97540
Phone: 503-535-6005
Fax: 503-535-3411

Local Retrieval Area: OR-Benton, Clackamas, Columbia, Jackson, Josephine, Klamath, Lane, Linn, Marion, Multnomah, Polk, Washington, Yamhill.

Normal turn around time is up to 3 days. Rush service is also available. Projects are generally billed by the hour. The first project may require a prepayment.

Clinton Abstract Co Inc(476)
519 Gary Blvd
Clinton OK 73601
Phone: 405-323-3025
Fax:

Local Retrieval Area: OK-Custer.

Normal turn around time is 2 days. Projects are generally billed by the number of names searched. Copy charges will be added to the fee. Credit accounts are accepted. Personal checks are accepted.

Clovis Title and Abstract Company(477)
420 Mitchell St
Clovis NM 88101
Phone: 505-762-4403
Fax: 505-769-2394

Local Retrieval Area: NM-Curry.

Normal turn around time is 2 days. Projects are generally billed by the number of records located. Credit accounts are accepted. Personal checks are accepted.
They specialize in title searches, abstracts of title, title insurance and lien searches. They can retrieve all county records of Curry County.

Clue Detective Agency(478)
PO Box 2577
Lancaster OH 43130-5577

Phone: **614-536-9600**
Fax: 614-526-9601

Local Retrieval Area: OH-Athens, Belmont, Coshocton, Delaware, Fairfield, Fayette, Franklin, Gallia, Guernsey, Hocking, Jackson, Knox, Licking, Madison, Meigs, Monroe, Morgan, Muskingum, Noble, Perry, Pickaway, Pike, Ross, Washington.

Normal turn around time is 2-3 days. Fee basis will vary by the type of project. The first project may require a prepayment.

They specialize in criminal, civil, domestic matters and asset & liability searches. Nationwide record retrieval is available through their online search methods.

Clue Detective Service(479)
1209 N Eastman Rd Suite 257
Kingsport TN 37664

Phone: **800-352-2583**
    615-239-9588
Fax: 615-247-8151

Local retrieval area includes many counties in Virginia and some counties in Tennessee.

Normal turn around time is 24 hours. Project billing methods vary. Credit accounts are accepted. Established clients are invoiced. New clients must prepay.

With their network and contacts, they can provide service in NC, KY, CA, FL, NV, and TX. They carry a comprehensive library of information regarding record searches of any kind.

Coast to Coast Research Network(480)
248 S Main
Concord NH 03301

Phone: **800-933-5068**
    603-225-9222
Fax: 603-225-7268
    800-933-7268

Local Retrieval Area: NH-All counties.

Normal turn around time is 24-48 hours. Projects are generally billed by the number of names searched. They may also charge by place. Credit accounts are accepted.

Coast to Coast Research Network also has correspondent relationships in other jurisdictions, including nationwide. They specialize in UCC and corporate searches.

Coastal Investigative Son Inc(481)
3219 Landmark St Bldg 5
Greenville NC 27834

Phone: **919-355-0122**
Fax: 919-355-1842

Local Retrieval Area: NC-Beaufort, Currituck, Edgecombe, Lenoir, Onslow, Pitt.

Normal turn around time is 24-72 hours. Online computer ordering is also available. Project billing methods vary. Copy costs will be added to the total. All projects require prepayment. Credit cards are accepted for payment. They will invoice. They accept personal checks.

Coastal Paralegal Services(482)
PO Box 872
Jacksonville NC 28542

Phone: **919-577-4103**
Fax: 919-577-4095

Local Retrieval Area: NC-Carteret, Craven, Duplin, Jones, Lenoir, New Hanover, Onslow, Pender.

Normal turn around time is 24-36 hours. Projects are generally billed by the number of records located. Credit accounts are accepted.

They specialize in real estate and investigative work.

Janet Coats(483)
620 Broadhead Rd Suite 301
Pittsburgh PA 15205

Phone: **412-928-0706**
Fax:

Local Retrieval Area: OH-Columbiana, Jefferson; PA-Allegheny, Armstrong, Beaver, Butler, Greene, Lawrence, Washington; WV-Brooke, Hancock, Ohio.

Normal turn around time is 2-3 days. Fee basis varies by type of transaction. The first project may require a prepayment.

Coke County Abstract Co(484)
3 E 6th
Robert Lee TX 76945

Phone: **915-453-2049**
Fax:

Local Retrieval Area: TX-Coke.

Normal turn around time is 1-2 days. Fee basis will vary by the type of project. The first project may require a prepayment.

Cole County Abstract and Title(485)
240 E High St
Jefferson City MO 65101

Phone: **314-636-3214**
Fax: 314-636-7228

Local Retrieval Area: MO-Cole.

Normal turn around time is 3-4 days. Projects are generally billed by the number of names searched. All projects require prepayment. They will also invoice.

They specialize in land title searches.

Coleman Abstract Co(486)
PO Box 793
Coleman TX 76834

Phone: **915-625-2932**
Fax:

Local Retrieval Area: TX-Coleman.

Normal turn around time is 2 days. Fee basis will vary by the type of project. The first project may require a prepayment.

Coleman County Title Co(487)
100 Commercial Ave Suite 201
Coleman TX 76834

Phone: **915-625-4628**
Fax: 915-625-4417

Local Retrieval Area: TX-Coleman.

Normal turn around time is up to five days. Projects are generally billed by the hour. The first project may require a prepayment.

Colfax County Title and Abstract(488)
1109 C St
Schuyler NE 68661

Phone: **402-352-2027**
Fax: 402-352-2027

Local Retrieval Area: NE-Butler, Colfax.

Normal turn around time is 1 week. Projects are generally billed by the hour. Credit accounts are accepted. Personal checks are accepted.

Colfax County Title and Abstract Co also has correspondent relationships in other jurisdictions, including the rest of Nebraska.

Collier Abstracts Inc(489)
107 N Main St
Smith Center KS 66967

Phone: **913-282-3351**
Fax:

Local Retrieval Area: KS-Smith.

Normal turn around time is up to 1 week. Fee basis varies by type of transaction. Credit accounts are accepted. They request prepayment from out of state clients, but will invoice established customers.

Collins Title & Abstract Co Inc(490)　Phone: 904-829-6600
139 King St　　Fax: 904-824-2870
St Augustine FL 32084

Local Retrieval Area: FL-Duval, Flagler, Putnam, St. Johns.

Normal turn around time is varied depending on project. Fee basis will vary by the type of project. Credit accounts are accepted. They specialize in real estate title work.

Colonial Valley Abstract Co(491)　Phone: 717-848-2717
216 E Market St　　Fax: 717-845-6161
York PA 17403

Local Retrieval Area: PA-Adams, Franklin, Lancaster, York.

Normal turn around time is 3 days. Fee basis will vary by the type of project. The first project may require a prepayment. They specialize in real estate.

Colorado City Abstract Co(492)　Phone: 915-728-3475
114 W 2nd St　　Fax: 915-728-8851
Colorado City TX 79512

Local Retrieval Area: TX-Mitchell.

Normal turn around time is 2-3 days. Fee basis will vary by the type of project. The first project may require a prepayment.

Colorado County Abstract Co(493)　Phone: 409-732-6096
PO Box 428　　Fax:
Columbus TX 78934

Local Retrieval Area: TX-Colorado.

Normal turn around time is 2-3 days. Fee basis will vary by the type of project. The first project may require a prepayment.

Colorado Land Title(494)　Phone: 303-264-4178
PO Box 334　　Fax: 303-264-4775
Pagosa Springs CO 81147

Local Retrieval Area: CO-Archuleta.

Normal turn around time is up to 1 week. Fee basis is determined on a "flat rate" (plus costs). All projects require prepayment. They specialize in real estate matters.

Colorado Records Search Inc(495)　Phone: 303-972-3424
8073 W Chenango Pl　　Fax: 303-972-1068
Littleton CO 80123

Local Retrieval Area: CO-Adams, Arapahoe, Boulder, Denver, Douglas, El Paso, Gilpin, Jefferson, Larimer, Pueblo, Weld.

Normal turn around time is 24-48 hours. Projects are generally billed by the number of names searched or records located. Credit accounts are accepted.
Colorado Records Search Inc also has correspondent relationships in other jurisdictions, including the rest of the state. They specialize in public record retrieval.

Columbia County Title Co(496)　Phone: 509-382-4711
305 E Main St　　Fax: 509-382-3032
Dayton WA 99328

Local Retrieval Area: WA-Columbia.

Normal turn around time is 1-2 days. Fee basis varies by type of transaction. The first project may require a prepayment.

Columbia Gorge Investigations(497)　Phone: 503-387-2325
PO Box 371　　Fax:
The Dalles OR 97058

Local Retrieval Area: OR-Hood River, Sherman, Wasco; WA-Klickitat.

Normal turn around time is 3-5 working days. Rush service is also available. Projects are generally billed by the hour. All projects require prepayment.
Columbia Gorge Investigations also has correspondent relationships in other jurisdictions, including undisclosed names.

Columbian National Title Insurance(498)　Phone: 316-262-0387
333 S Broadway　　Fax: 316-267-8427
Wichita KS 67202

Local Retrieval Area: KS-Harvey; MO-Ralls.

Normal turn around time is 1-3 days. Fee basis varies by type of transaction. Credit accounts are accepted.

Columbus Land Title Co(499)　Phone: 706-327-4065
1811 Preston Dr　　Fax: 706-327-4065
Columbus GA 31906

Local Retrieval Area: AL-Russell; GA-Chattahoochee, Harris, Marion, Meriwether, Muscogee, Quitman, Randolph, Schley, Stewart, Talbot, Terrell, Troup, Webster.

Normal turn around time is 24 hours for Muskogee and Russell counties, 2-3 days for all others. Fee basis will vary by the type of project. The first project may require a prepayment. They specialize in real estate matters.

Melanie Colvin(500)　Phone: 318-396-6415
116 LaSalle Circle　　Fax:
West Monroe LA 71291

Local Retrieval Area: LA-Caldwell Parish, Franklin Parish, Jackson Parish, Lincoln Parish, Morehouse Parish, Ouachita Parish, Richland Parish, Tensas Parish, Union Parish, Winn Parish.

Normal turn around time is 24 hours within a 30 mile radius and 48 hours outside that radius. Projects are generally billed by the number of names searched. Credit accounts are accepted. Correspondent relationships in other jurisdictions include West Carroll and East Carroll.

Comanche Abstract and Title Co(501)　Phone: 316-582-2125
120 E Main　　Fax:
Coldwater KS 67029

Local Retrieval Area: KS-Comanche.

Normal turn around time is 7-10 days. Projects are generally billed by the number of names searched or records located. Credit accounts are accepted. Personal checks are accepted.
They specialize in title searches, ownership, mineral interest, leasehold, oil and gas searches.

Comanche County Abstract Co(502)
PO Box 762
Comanche TX 76442
Phone: **915-356-2564**
Fax: 915-356-5015

Local Retrieval Area: TX-Comanche.

Normal turn around time is 2-5 days. Fee basis will vary by type of project. The first project may require a prepayment.

Combs and Combs PSC(503)
411 Main St
Pikeville KY 41502-0031
Phone: **606-437-6226**
Fax: 606-432-4414

Local Retrieval Area: KY-Floyd, Pike.

Normal turn around time is 1 week. Projects are generally billed by the hour. All projects require prepayment.
Combs and Combs PSC also has correspondent relationships in other jurisdictions, including Knott, Johnson and Martin.

Commercial Investigation(504)
30 South St
Freehold NJ 07728
Phone: **908-431-3004**
Fax: 908-431-3680

Local Retrieval Area: NJ-Middlesex, Monmouth, Ocean.

Normal turn around time is varied depending on project. Online computer ordering is also available. Projects are generally billed by the hour. The first project may require a prepayment.
They specialize in on line civil suit, judgements, liens, bankruptcy, landlord/tenant cases, and pending litigation on individual or company names.

Commercial Process Service(505)
2051 S Victoria Ave
Oxnard CA 93063
Phone: **805-382-1036**
Fax: 805-382-1037

Local Retrieval Area: CA-Santa Barbara, Ventura.

Normal turn around time is varied depending on project. Projects are generally billed by the hour. Credit accounts are accepted. Personal checks are accepted.
Commercial Process Service also has correspondent relationships in other jurisdictions, including Los Angeles and Orange Counties. They specialize in court filings, process serving and deposition interpreting (English/Spanish).

Commonwealth Investigation Agcy(506)
461 Linden St
Allentown PA 18102
Phone: **215-433-2325**
Fax:

Local Retrieval Area: PA-Berks, Bucks, Carbon, Dauphin, Lackawanna, Lancaster, Lebanon, Lehigh, Monroe, Northampton.

Normal turn around time is 1-3 days. Projects are generally billed by the hour. All projects require prepayment.
Commonwealth Investigation Agency also has correspondent relationships in other jurisdictions, including Luzerne, Lycoming, Montgomery, Philadelphia and Schuylkill. They are a full service private investations firm.

Community Title Co(507)
PO Box 188
Grundy Center IA 50638
Phone: **319-824-3123**
Fax:

Local Retrieval Area: IA-Grundy.

Normal turn around time is 2-3 days. Fee basis varies by type of transaction. Credit accounts are accepted.

Compass Investigations(508)
1801 S Ocean Dr
Hallandale FL 33009
Phone: **305-457-0189**
Fax: 305-456-1015

Local Retrieval Area: FL-Broward, Dade, Palm Beach.

Normal turn around time is the same day. Projects are generally billed by the hour. The first project may require a prepayment. Credit cards are accepted for payment. They only accept American Express.

Complete Corporate Services(509)
PO Box 33735
Juneau AK 99803
Phone: **907-780-4956**
Fax: 907-780-4954

Local Retrieval Area: AK-Juneau Borough.

Normal turn around time is the same day. Fee basis will vary by the type of project. All projects require prepayment. They will invoice. They also will accept personal checks.
They specialize in searches at the State.

Complete Title Service of Walker(510)
PO Box 966
Walker MN 56484
Phone: **218-547-2565**
Fax: 218-547-2564

Local Retrieval Area: MN-Cass, Hubbard.

Normal turn around time is 1-3 days. New abstracts average 10 to 14 days. Projects are generally billed by the number of names searched. Credit accounts are accepted. Personal checks are accepted.
They also provide closing and title insurance services.

Comstock Search Reporting(511)
2400 W 29th Terrace
Topeka KS 66611
Phone: **913-266-7117**
Fax: 913-266-7117

Local Retrieval Area: KS-Shawnee.

Normal turn around time is 1 day. Projects are generally billed by the number of names searched or records located. Credit accounts are accepted.
They specialize in UCC record searches.

Confidential Services(512)
2700 E Main St
Columbus OH 43209
Phone: **800-752-4581**
Fax: 614-338-1515

Local Retrieval Area: OH-Franklin.

Normal turn around time is 24-72 hours. Projects are generally billed by the number of names searched or records located. The first project may require a prepayment.
Confidential Services also has correspondent relationships in other jurisdictions, including nationwide. They specialize in skip tracing.

Conover Detective Agency(513)
410 Court St
Pekin IL 61554
Phone: 309-346-5800
Fax: 309-346-5400

Local Retrieval Area: IL-De Witt, Fulton, Logan, McLean, Marshall, Mason, Menard, Peoria, Tazewell, Woodford.

Normal turn around time is varied depending on project. Projects are generally billed by the hour. The first project may require a prepayment.

Conover Detective Agency also has correspondent relationships in other jurisdictions, including Knox, Cook, and most of Illinois. They specialize in civil process and investigations.

Consolidated Abstract Co(514)
510 S Broadway St
Aspermont TX 79502
Phone: 817-989-3566
Fax: 817-989-3566

Local Retrieval Area: TX-Stonewall.

Normal turn around time is 1-2 days. Fee basis will vary by the type of project. The first project may require a prepayment.

Consolidated Abstract of Becker(515)
PO Box 376
Detroit Lakes MN 56502
Phone: 218-847-2144
Fax: 218-847-2406

Local Retrieval Area: MN-Becker.

Normal turn around time is 3-5 days. Projects are generally billed by the number of names searched. All projects require prepayment. They will also invoice.

Joseph E Cook(516)
595 Neward Ave Suite 104
Jersey City NJ 07306
Phone: 201-420-9763
Fax:

Local Retrieval Area: NJ-Hudson.

Normal turn around time is 2-3 days. Fee basis will vary by type of project. Credit accounts are accepted.

Cooper Abstract Co(517)
401 Cooper Landing Rd Suite 6
Cherry Hill NJ 08002
Phone: 609-667-4800
Fax: 609-667-1642

Local Retrieval Area: NJ-Camden.

Normal turn around time is 1 week. A rush service is also available. Fee basis will vary by the type of project. The first project may require a prepayment.

They specialize in title searches.

Copper Range Abstract & Title Co(518)
707 Shelden Ave
Houghton MI 49931
Phone: 906-482-7903
Fax: 906-482-7977

Local Retrieval Area: MI-Baraga, Houghton, Keweenaw, Ontonagon.

Normal turn around time is 3 days. Fee basis will vary by type of project. All projects require prepayment. They will invoice to established clients.

They specialize in real estate.

Copy Central(519)
255 S Grand Ave Suite 101
Los Angeles CA 90012
Phone: 213-687-3900
Fax: 213-687-7277

Local Retrieval Area: CA-Los Angeles.

Normal turn around time is 12-24 hours. Rush service is also available. Fee basis will vary with type of project. Credit accounts are accepted.

Corant County Abstract Co(520)
PO Box 897
Marion IN 46952
Phone: 317-664-7371
Fax: 317-664-0766

Local Retrieval Area: IN-Grant.

Normal turn around time is varied depending on project. Projects are generally billed by the number of names searched. All projects require prepayment. They will also invoice.

They specialize in title insurance.

Corant County Abstract Co(521)
PO Box 228
Carson ND 58529
Phone: 701-622-3556
Fax:

Local Retrieval Area: ND-Grant.

Normal turn around time is 1-5 days. Fee basis will vary by typo of project. All projects require prepayment. They will also invoice. They specialize in title histories.

Cornell Abstract Co(522)
1811 Hill Ave
Spirit Lake IA 51360
Phone: 712-336-3845
Fax:

Local Retrieval Area: IA-Dickinson.

Normal turn around time is 2 days. Fee basis will vary by the type of project. Credit accounts are accepted.
They specialize in real estate.

CorpAmerica Inc(523)
1050 S State St
Dover DE 19901
Phone: 800-622-6414
302-736-5510
Fax: 302-736-5620

Local Retrieval Area: DE-All counties.

Normal turn around time is 1-2 days pending state systems time frame. Projects are generally billed by the number of names searched or records located. The first project may require a prepayment. Credit cards are accepted for payment. Credit Cards are subject to 5% rush fee.

They specialize in form corporations and retrieve secrertary state records.

CorpAssist(524) Phone: **800-438-2996**
1090 Vermont Ave NW Suite 910   202-371-8090
Washington DC 20005   Fax: 202-371-1945

Local Retrieval Area: DC-All counties; MD-All counties; VA-All counties.

Normal turn around time is 48 hours. Projects are generally billed by the number of names searched or records located. Tax liens and civil judgements are considered 1 record. The first project may require a prepayment.
CorpAssist also has correspondent relationships in other jurisdictions, including national and international network. They specialize in fictitious business names, pending litigation, Department of Motor Vehicles and other government agency searches.

Corporate Service Bureau(525) Phone: **518-463-8550**
283 Washington Ave   Fax: 518-463-3752
Albany NY 12206

Local Retrieval Area: NY-Albany, Rensselaer, Schenectady.

Normal turn around time is 1-5 business days. Projects are generally billed by the number of names searched. The first project may require a prepayment. Credit cards are accepted for payment. They require corporation filings to prepay.
Corporate Service Bureau also has correspondent relationships in other jurisdictions, including all of New York.

Corporate Services of Ohio Inc(526) Phone: **614-464-2400**
50 W Broad St   Fax: 614-464-1505
Columbus OH 43215

Local Retrieval Area: OH-Delaware, Fairfield, Fayette, Franklin, Licking, Madison, Marion, Pickaway, Union.

Normal turn around time is 1-7 days. Projects are generally billed by the number of names searched. Credit accounts are accepted.
Corporate Services of Ohio Inc also has correspondent relationships in other jurisdictions, including Cuyahoga, Lucas, Hamilton, Summit, Butler, Clermont and Miami. They specialize in corporate filings and retrieval of certified documents from the Secretary of State.

Corporation Associates of Illinois(527) Phone: **800-877-2556**
700 S 2nd St   Fax: 217-544-4657
Springfield IL 62704

Local Retrieval Area: IL-Sangamon.

Normal turn around time is 24-48 hours. Projects are generally billed by the number of names searched. They charge by index also. The first project may require a prepayment.

Corporation Information Services(528) Phone: **800-342-8086**
1201 Hays St   Fax: 904-222-9171
Tallahassee FL 32301

Local Retrieval Area: FL-Calhoun, Franklin, Gadsden, Jackson, Jefferson, Leon, Liberty, Madison, Taylor, Wakulla, Washington.

Normal turn around time is 24-48 hours. Projects are generally billed by the number of names searched. They also charge by index. The first project may require a prepayment. Corporation Information Services also has correspondent relationships in other jurisdictions, including national network including all of Florida.

Corporation Service Co - Delaware(529) Phone: **800-927-9800**
1013 Centre Rd   Fax: 302-998-7078
Wilmington DE 19805

Local Retrieval Area: DE-Kent, New Castle, Sussex; PA-Delaware, Philadelphia.

Normal turn around time is 24-48 hours. Projects are generally billed by the number of names searched. They also charge by index. The first project may require a prepayment. Corporation Service Co - Delaware also has correspondent relationships in other jurisdictions, including national network including rest of counties in Delaware and Pennsylvania. This company has been established since 1899.

Corporation Service Company(530) Phone: **800-272-6978**
4 Central Ave   Fax: 518-432-1316
Albany NY 12210

Local Retrieval Area: NY-Albany, Bronx, Kings, New York, Queens.

Normal turn around time is 24-48 hours. Projects are generally billed by the number of names searched. They also charge by index. The first project may require a prepayment.

Corporation Service Company(531) Phone: **614-224-8882**
347-2334 85 E Gay St Suite 706   Fax: 614-337-8530
Columbus OH 43215

Local Retrieval Area: OH-Franklin.

Normal turn around time is 24-48 hours. Projects are generally billed by the number of names searched. They charge by index also. The first project may require a prepayment.

Corpus Christi Court Services(532) Phone: **512-887-8122**
545 N Upper Broadway Suite 509   Fax: 512-887-0335
Corpus Christi TX 78476

Local Retrieval Area: TX-Nueces, San Patricio.

Normal turn around time is the same day if order is received before 2:00 p.m. A 2 hour rush service is also available. Projects are generally billed by the number of records located. They charge pre hour on research only. Credit accounts are accepted.
Corpus Christi Court Services also has correspondent relationships in other jurisdictions, including all counties in Texas and most counties in the United States. They specialize in bankruptcy.

Corwin Attorney Service(533) Phone: **516-727-4718**
PO Box 1718   Fax: 516-727-4721
Riverhead NY 11901

Local Retrieval Area: NY-Suffolk.

Normal turn around time is 4 hours to 2 days. Projects are generally billed by the number of records located. The first project may require a prepayment.

Cothran & Cothran(534)
PO Drawer 700
Manning SC 29102
Phone: **803-435-8495**
Fax: 803-435-2653

Local Retrieval Area: SC-Clarendon, Lee, Orangeburg, Sumter, Williamsburg.

Normal turn around time is 24-48 hours. Projects are generally billed by the number of records located. The first project may require a prepayment.

Cothran & Cothran also has correspondent relationships in other jurisdictions, including the rest of the state.

Cottonwood County Abstract Co(535)
900 3rd Ave
Windom MN 56101
Phone: **507-831-1504**
Fax:

Local Retrieval Area: MN-Cottonwood.

Normal turn around time is varied depending on project. Projects are generally billed by the number of names searched or records located. Credit accounts are accepted. Personal checks are accepted.

They specialize in name searches, judgement searches, tax and bankruptcy searches.

Couch Abstract and Title Co(536)
119 N Jennings
Anthony KS 67003
Phone: **316-842-5512**
Fax:

Local Retrieval Area: KS-Harper.

Normal turn around time is 1-2 days. Projects are generally billed by the hour. Credit accounts are accepted. Personal checks are accepted.

County Abstract & Title Co(537)
PO Box 614
Socorro NM 87801
Phone: **505-835-0573**
Fax: 505-835-3530

Local Retrieval Area: NM-Catron, Socorro.

Normal turn around time is 1-2 weeks. Projects are generally billed by the hour. Credit accounts are accepted.

They specialize in real estate and foreclosure searches.

County Process Inc(538)
209 S 5th 2nd Floor
Louisville KY 40202
Phone: **502-587-0051**
Fax: 502-585-3480

Local Retrieval Area: KY-Bullitt, Fayette, Jefferson, Oldham, Shelby.

Normal turn around time is 2 days. Projects are generally billed by the hour. All projects require prepayment.

They specialize in Kentucky motor vehicle information, Kentucky driver license information and legal process service.

County Seat Abstract(539)
17 W Main St
Johnstown NY 12095
Phone: **518-762-3011**
Fax:

Local Retrieval Area: NY-Fulton, Hamilton, Montgomery.

Normal turn around time is 3-5 days. Projects are generally billed by the hour. Credit accounts are accepted.

County Seat Abstract also has correspondent relationships in other jurisdictions, including all counties in New York. They specialize in title insurance searches.

County Wide Abstract and Title Co(540)
4 S Elm St
Dexter MO 63841
Phone: **314-624-2436**
Fax: 314-624-5376

Local Retrieval Area: MO-Stoddard.

Normal turn around time is 2 days. Projects are generally billed by the number of names searched. Credit accounts are accepted.

Court Data Search(541)
292 Lakeview Ave Suite #A16
Paterson NJ 07503
Phone: **201-278-7529**
Fax:

Local Retrieval Area: NJ-Bergen, Essex, Hudson, Middlesex, Morris, Passaic.

Normal turn around time is 48 hours. Projects are generally billed by the number of names searched. Credit accounts are accepted. They specialize in criminal and civil judgement checks.

Court House Legal Service(542)
1020 Kings Hwy N
Cherry Hill NJ 08034
Phone: **800-242-9779**
Fax: 609-667-3438

Local Retrieval Area: NJ-Atlantic, Burlington, Camden, Gloucester, Mercer; PA-Bucks, Chester, Delaware, Montgomery, Philadelphia.

Normal turn around time is same day except for dockets which are 24 hours per court requirements. Projects are generally billed by the hour. Credit accounts are accepted. Credit cards are accepted for payment. Bulk search requests may require some prepayment.

Court House Legal Service also has correspondent relationships in other jurisdictions, including all other PA and NJ counties. They plan to have a computer/modem ordering system in place in the near future.

Court House Retrieval Inc(543)
PO Box 32825
Pikesville MD 21208
Phone: **410-823-4444**
Fax: 410-321-4538

Local Retrieval Area: DC-All counties; MD-All counties.

Normal turn around time is 2-3 days. Projects are generally billed by the number of names searched or records located. The first project may require a prepayment.

They specialize in serving summonses, subpoenas, and court house retrievals.

Court Record Consultants(544)
17029 Devonshire Suite 166
Northridge CA 91325
Phone: **818-366-1906**
Fax: 818-366-1985

Local Retrieval Area: CA-Alameda, Contra Costa, Fresno, Kern, Los Angeles, Orange, Riverside, Sacramento, San Bernardino, San Diego, San Francisco, Santa Barbara, Santa Clara, Ventura.

Normal turn around time is 1-2 days. Projects are generally billed by the number of names searched or records located. The first project may require a prepayment.

Court Record Consultants also has correspondent relationships in other jurisdictions, including the rest of the state. They also specialize in pre employment screening.

Court Record Research(545)
3601 Green Garden Ct
Antioch TN 37013
Phone: **615-367-2233**
Fax: 615-367-9748

Local Retrieval Area: TN-Davidson.

Normal turn around time is 48 hours. Projects are generally billed by the number of names searched. Credit accounts are accepted. They specialize in criminial public record retrieval.

Court Record Research(546)
PO Box 3796
Houston TX 77253-3796
Phone: **713-869-7687**
Fax: 713-869-7687

Local Retrieval Area: TX-Fort Bend, Galveston, Harris, Montgomery.

Normal turn around time is 24-48 hours. Rush service is also available. Projects are generally billed by the number of names searched or records located. Credit accounts are accepted.

Nancy Craig(547)
906 Russo Dr
Westampton NJ 08060
Phone: **609-261-5783**
Fax: 609-261-2531

Local Retrieval Area: NJ-Burlington.

Normal turn around time is 24-48 hours. Projects are generally billed by the number of names searched. Credit accounts are accepted.

Craighead County Abstract(548)
415 Union St
Jonesboro AR 72401
Phone: **501-935-9900**
Fax:

Local Retrieval Area: AR-Craighead.

Normal turn around time is up to 10 days. Rush service is also available. Fee basis will vary by type of project. Credit accounts are accepted.
They specialize in real estate.

Dale C Crandall(549)
PO Box 310
Burwell NE 68823
Phone: **308-346-4284**
Fax: 308-346-5402

Local Retrieval Area: NE-Garfield.

Normal turn around time is 1 week. Projects are generally billed by the number of records located. Credit accounts are accepted.
Mr. Crandall is an attorney. He specializes in income tax, probabe and the legal field.

Crane County Abstract(550)
PO Box 686
Crane TX 79731
Phone: **915-558-3112**
Fax: 915-558-3131

Local Retrieval Area: TX-Crane.

Normal turn around time is 3 days. Fee basis will vary by the type of project. The first project may require a prepayment.

Crawford Abstract & Real Estate(551)
113 S 5th St
Lincoln KS 67455
Phone: **913-524-4228**
Fax: 913-524-3042

Local Retrieval Area: KS-Lincoln, Lincoln.

Normal turn around time is 2-3 days. Fee basis varies by type of transaction. The first project may require a prepayment.

Crawford County Abstract & Title(552)
108 Burton Court
Grayline MI 49738
Phone: **517-348-9832**
Fax: 517-348-7511

Local Retrieval Area: MI-Crawford.

Normal turn around time is up to a week. Fee basis will vary by the type of project. All projects require prepayment. They require a prepayment for all out of area transactions.
They specialize in title insurance.

Crawford County Abstract Co(553)
424 Main Street
Van Buren AR 72956
Phone: **501-474-2711**
Fax: 501-474-2954

Local Retrieval Area: AR-Crawford.

Normal turn around time is 2 days. Projects are generally billed by the number of names searched. Credit accounts are accepted. They specialize in real estate.

Crawford County Abstract Co(554)
1223 Center St
Denison IA 51442
Phone: **712-263-5626**
Fax: 712-263-5627

Local Retrieval Area: IA-Crawford.

Normal turn around time is 3 days. Projects are generally billed by the number of records located. Credit accounts are accepted.

Crawford County Title Co(555)
PO Box G
Cuba MO 65453
Phone: **314-885-6470**
Fax: 314-885-6472

Local Retrieval Area: MO-Crawford.

Normal turn around time is 1 week. Fee basis varies by type of transaction. Credit accounts are accepted.

Credit Bureau Services Inc(556)
1135 College Dr Suite # L1
Garden City KS 67846
Phone: **316-275-6500**
Fax: 316-276-3744

Local Retrieval Area: KS-Clark, Finney, Ford, Gray, Lane, Ness, Scott, Wichita.

Normal turn around time is up to one week. Fee basis varies by type of transaction. Credit accounts are accepted.
They are affiliated with TRW and will provide credit searches. They also publish a "Public Record Bulletin".

Credit Bureau Svcs of Panhandle(557)
PO Box 2101
Pampa TX 79066-2101
Phone: **806-669-3246**
Fax: 806-669-6109

Local Retrieval Area: TX-Carson, Gray, Hemphill, Lipscomb, Ochiltree, Roberts, Wheeler.

Normal turn around time is 1-2 days. Rush service is also available. Fee basis will vary by the type of project. All projects require prepayment.

Credit Bureau of Devils Lake(558)
PO Box 792
Devils Lake ND 58301
Phone: **701-662-6690**
Fax: 701-662-6696

Local Retrieval Area: ND-Ramsey.

Normal turn around time is 3 days. Fee basis varies by type of transaction. Credit accounts are accepted.
They specialize in credit reporting and collections.

Credit Bureau of Raton(559) Phone: 505-445-2751
PO Box 98 Fax:
Raton NM 87740

Local Retrieval Area: NM-Colfax.

Normal turn around time is 2-4 days. Projects are generally billed by the number of names searched. Credit accounts are accepted. They are a credit bureau who will pull paper records for customers.

Credit Bureau of Sevier County(560) Phone: 501-642-2200
PO Box 1127 Fax:
De Queen AR 71832

Local Retrieval Area: AR-Howard, Sevier.

Normal turn around time is 48 hours. Projects are generally billed by the hour. All projects require prepayment. They publish a monthly bulletin listing small claims and civil liens.

Credit Bureau of Valley City(561) Phone: 701-845-3912
PO Box 912 Fax: 701-845-0220
Valley City ND 58072

Local Retrieval Area: ND-Barnes, Griggs, La Moure, Sargent, Steele.

Normal turn around time is 2-3 days. Fee basis will vary by the type of project. Credit accounts are accepted. They request that all out of county clients prepay.

Credit Bureau of Western Nebraska(562) Phone: 308-632-2117
PO Box 70 Fax: 308-635-0578
Scottsbluff NE 69363

Local Retrieval Area: NE-Box Butte, Cheyenne, Dawes, Kimball, Morrill, Scotts Bluff, Sheridan.

Normal turn around time is 2-3 days. Projects are generally billed by the number of records located. All projects require prepayment. They specialize in collection divisions.

Credit Lenders Service Agency Inc(563) Phone: 609-751-7400
PO Box 508 Fax: 800-648-0401
Cherry Hill NJ 08003

Local Retrieval Area: NJ-Burlington, Camden, Mercer.

Normal turn around time is 24 hours. Projects are generally billed by the number of names searched or records located. Credit accounts are accepted.
They do the Superior Courts along with the Civil division.

Crescent Legal Service(564) Phone: 707-464-2474
PO Box 1092 Fax: 707-464-2474
Crescent City CA 95531

Local Retrieval Area: CA-Del Norte.

Normal turn around time is 24 hours. Projects are generally billed by the number of names searched or records located. They also charge per page. Credit accounts are accepted.
They also provide process services and record copying.

Otis Crocker(565) Phone: 601-983-2700
PO Box 666 Fax: 601-983-4332
Bruce MS 38915

Local Retrieval Area: MS-Calhoun, Chickasaw, Grenada, Lafayette, Pontotoc, Webster, Yalobusha.

Normal turn around time is 1-2 days in Calhoun county, 2-3 days in all others. Projects are generally billed by the hour. The first project may require a prepayment.
Otis specializes in title work and public record research.

Crockett County Abstract Co(566) Phone: 915-392-2232
PO Drawer E Fax:
Ozona TX 76943

Local Retrieval Area: TX-Crockett.

Normal turn around time is 2-3 days. Fee basis will vary by the type of project. The first project may require a prepayment.

Crow Wing County Abstract Co(567) Phone: 218-829-7368
PO Box 378 Fax: 218-829-8586
Brainerd MN 56401

Local Retrieval Area: MN-Crow Wing.

Normal turn around time is 2-7 days. Projects are generally billed by the number of names searched. Credit accounts are accepted. They specialize in land title.

Judy Crowder(568) Phone: 901-627-9529
PO Box 1053 Fax:
Dyersburg TN 38025

Local Retrieval Area: TN-Dyer.

Normal turn around time is 1 day. Projects are generally billed by the number of names searched. Credit accounts are accepted. Judy specializes in UCC record searches.

Crowley County Insurance & Title(569) Phone: 719-267-4778
PO Box 398 Fax:
Ordway CO 81063

Local Retrieval Area: CO-Crowley.

Normal turn around time is up to 1 week. Fee basis will vary by the type of project. Credit accounts are accepted. Out of area clients must prepay.
They specialize in real estate title and abstract.

Crummy Investigations Inc(570) Phone: 407-724-0518
PO Box 510405 Fax: 407-728-0274
Melbourne Beach FL 32951-0405

Local Retrieval Area: FL-Bradford, Indian River.

Normal turn around time is 24 hours. Online computer ordering is also available. Projects are generally billed by the hour. The first project may require a prepayment. Personal checks are accetped. They specialize in missing persons.

Crystal Clear Copy Service(571)
8479 9th Ave
Hesperia CA 92345
Phone: 619-947-5699
Fax: 619-949-1389

Local Retrieval Area: CA-Riverside, San Bernardino.

Normal turn around time is 10 days. A 5 day rush service is also available. Fee basis will vary by the type of project. Credit accounts are accepted.
Crystal Clear Copy Service also has correspondent relationships in other jurisdictions, including undisclosed areas.

Crystal Systems Legal Svcs Div(572)
PO Box 656
Plainsboro NJ 08536-0656
Phone: 800-292-2767
Fax: 609-936-0044

Local Retrieval Area: MD-Baltimore; NJ-Camden, Essex, Hunterdon, Mercer, Middlesex, Monmouth, Morris, Ocean, Somerset, Union.

Normal turn around time is varied depending on project. Project billing methods vary. The first project may require a prepayment. Credit cards are accepted for payment. They will also invoice.
Crystal Systems Legal Services Division also has correspondent relationships in other jurisdictions, including Sussex, Warren, Passaic, Bergen, Salem, Gloucester, Atlantic, Cumberland, Hudson and Cape May.

Cumberland Title Agency Inc(573)
PO Box 295
Cumberland VA 23040
Phone: 804-492-4824
Fax: 804-492-9657

Local Retrieval Area: VA-Amelia, Buckingham, Cumberland, Goochland, Powhatan, Prince Edward, Prince Edward.

Normal turn around time is 2-3 days. Fee basis varies by type of transaction. The first project may require a prepayment.

Currier Abstract Company(574)
506 W Texas Ave
Artesia NM 88211-0680
Phone: 505-746-9823
Fax: 505-746-9661

Local Retrieval Area: NM-Eddy.

Normal turn around time is 1 week. Fee basis will vary by the type of project. Credit accounts are accepted.
The same family has been in business in Eddy County for over 50 years.

Sue Cutler(575)
Box 41
Blencoe IA 51523-0041
Phone: 712-452-2021
Fax:

Local Retrieval Area: IA-Monona.

Normal turn around time is 3-5 days. Projects are generally billed by the number of names searched. The first project may require a prepayment. A per search minimum fee will be charged. They will accept personal checks.

Cygneture Title Inc(576)
601 W Washington
Brainerd MN 56401
Phone: 800-450-0122
   218-828-0122
Fax: 218-828-0873

Local Retrieval Area: MN-Cass, Crow Wing.

Normal turn around time is 10 days. Fee basis will vary by type of project. All projects require prepayment. They will also invoice. They specialize in real estate.

D & L Invesgiations(577)
5610 W Main St
Belleville IL 62223
Phone: 618-236-2232
Fax: 618-236-7967

Local Retrieval Area: IL-Clinton, Madison, Monroe, St. Clair; MO-St. Louis, City of St. Louis.

Normal turn around time is 48 hours. Projects are generally billed by the hour. The first project may require a prepayment. They specialize in process serving.

D D Hamilton Abstract Co(578)
PO Box 11
Marshfield MO 65706
Phone: 417-468-2078
Fax: 417-468-2020

Local Retrieval Area: MO-Webster.

Normal turn around time is 48 hours. Projects are generally billed by the number of names searched or records located. Credit accounts are accepted.
They specialize in land title and civil judgements.

D W Moore and Assoc Inc(579)
1750 E Southmoon Dr
Salt Lake City UT 84117
Phone: 801-278-3528
Fax:

Local Retrieval Area: UT-All counties.

Normal turn around time is 3-5 days. Projects are generally billed by the hour. Credit accounts are accepted.
They specialize in research and historical investigation, enviornmental review, and education services.

Russell F D'Aiello Jr(580)
867 E Market St
York PA 17403
Phone: 717-845-4277
Fax: 717-852-7069

Local Retrieval Area: PA-Adams, York.

Normal turn around time is 1 week. Projects are generally billed by the hour. All projects require prepayment.
They specialize in real estate searches.

D.K. Abstract(581)
Rt 1 Box 63
Atwood IN 38220
Phone: 901-662-7394
Fax: 901-686-9373

Local Retrieval Area: TN-Benton, Carroll, Chester, Crockett, Decatur, Dyer, Fayette, Gibson, Hardeman, Hardin, Haywood, Henderson, Henry, Hickman, Houston, Humphreys, Lake, Lauderdale, McNairy, Madison, Obion, Perry, Stewart, Tipton, Wayne, Weakley.

Normal turn around time is 48 hours. Projects are generally billed by the number of names searched. Credit accounts are accepted. Personal checks are accepted.

DJM Enterprises(582)   Phone: 303-360-5854
12396 E Dakota Ave   Fax: 303-360-5854
Aurora CO 80012

Local Retrieval Area: CO-Adams, Arapahoe, Denver, Douglas, Jefferson.

Normal turn around time is 24 hours, unless requesting more than 10 separate doc files, then turnaround time would be 2 days. Fee basis is per search. The first project may require a prepayment.
DJM Enterprises also has correspondent relationships in other jurisdictions, including areas outside their immediate coverage area. They specialize in Bankruptcy Court and Federal Record Center research.

Daggett Abstract Co(583)   Phone: 501-295-3434
12 S Poplar Street   Fax: 501-295-3445
Marianna AR 72360

Local Retrieval Area: AR-Lee.

Normal turn around time is from 1 day to 1 week. Fee basis will vary by type of project. All projects require prepayment.
They specialize in title search and land ownership.

Dailey Title Searching Inc(584)   Phone: 908-475-5007
PO Box 416   Fax:
Belvidere NJ 07823

Local Retrieval Area: NJ-Warren.

Normal turn around time is 3-10 days. A 24 hour verbal response can be given for credit checks. Fee basis will vary by type of project. Credit accounts are accepted.

Dakota County Abstract Co(585)   Phone: 612-437-5600
1250 Hwy 55   Fax: 612-437-8876
Hastings MN 55033

Local Retrieval Area: MN-Dakota.

Normal turn around time is 5-10 days. Projects are generally billed by the number of names searched or records located. All projects require prepayment. They will also invoice.

Mae Dalberg(586)   Phone: 605-698-7357
516 Oak St W Suite #2   Fax:
Sisseton SD 57262-1255

Local Retrieval Area: SD-Roberts.

Normal turn around time is 1-3 days. Fee basis varies by type of transaction. Credit accounts are accepted.

Dane County Legal Notice(587)   Phone: 608-251-1181
139 W Wilson St Suite 106   Fax: 608-251-8999
Madison WI 53703

Local Retrieval Area: WI-Dane.

Normal turn around time is 24-48 hours. Projects are generally billed by the number of names searched. Credit accounts are accepted.

Daniel Agency(588)   Phone: 606-324-6029
PO Box 342   Fax:
Ashland KY 41105

Local Retrieval Area: KY-Bell, Boyd, Breathitt, Carter, Clay, Elliott, Estill, Fleming, Floyd, Greenup, Harlan, Jackson, Johnson, Knott, Knox, Laurel, Lawrence, Leslie, Letcher, Lewis, Madison, Martin, Menifee, Montgomery, Morgan, Owsley, Perry, Pike, Powell, Rowan, Whitley.

Normal turn around time is 2-3 days. Projects are generally billed by the hour. The first project may require a prepayment.
They specialize in mineral and title abstract searches.

Mabel Daniels(589)   Phone: 515-673-6507
301 Sherman St   Fax:
Beacon IA 52534-9711

Local Retrieval Area: IA-Keokuk, Mahaska.

Normal turn around time is up to one week. Projects are generally billed by the hour. Credit accounts are accepted.
Mabel specializes in genealogy searches.

Dante's Attorney Service(590)   Phone: 213-613-1417
240 S Broadway Suite 200   Fax: 213-613-1501
Los Angeles CA 90012

Local Retrieval Area: CA-Los Angeles, Orange, Riverside, San Bernardino, Ventura.

Normal turn around time is 1-3 days. Rush service is also available. Fee basis will vary with type of search. Credit accounts are accepted.
Dante's Attorney Service also has correspondent relationships in other jurisdictions, including the San Diego and surrounding cities.

Data Abstract & Title Co Inc(591)   Phone: 703-949-6676
437 Walnut Ave   Fax:
Waynesboro VA 22980

Local Retrieval Area: VA-Augusta, City of Staunton, City of Waynesboro.

Normal turn around time is 1-3 days. Fee basis is "per job". Credit accounts are accepted.

Data Quest Inc(592)   Phone: 505-891-9326
PO Box 15455   Fax: 505-891-9335
Rio Rancho NM 87174

Local Retrieval Area: NM-Bernalillo, Sandoval.

Normal turn around time is 24-48 hours. Projects are generally billed by the number of names searched. Credit accounts are accepted.
They specialize in UCC records at all New Mexico county courts and Secretary of States office.

Data Reporting Corp(593)   Phone: 203-287-1294
Sturbridge Commons 250 State St Suite D-2   Fax: 203-281-1683
North Haven CT 06473

Local Retrieval Area: CT-All counties.

Normal turn around time is 3-5 working days. Projects are generally billed by the hour. Credit accounts are accepted.

Data Research Inc(594)
Phone: **503-626-0594**
4325 SW 94th Ave No 7
Fax: 503-526-9762
Portland OR 97225

Local Retrieval Area: OR-Benton, Clackamas, Clatsop, Columbia, Lane, Linn, Marion, Morrow, Multnomah, Polk, Tillamook, Wheeler, Yamhill.

Normal turn around time is 24-72 hours. Projects are generally billed by the number of names searched or records located. Credit accounts are accepted.

Data Research Inc also has correspondent relationships in other jurisdictions, including the rest of the counties in Oregon. They specialize in all public records retrieved in State of Oregon.

DataFile(595)
Phone: **800-843-6688**
1336 E Mission
Fax: 619-747-9013
Escondido CA 92027

Local Retrieval Area: CA-San Diego.

Normal turn around time is 48-72 hours. Projects are generally billed by the number of records located. Credit accounts are accepted.

DataTrace Investigations Inc(596)
Phone: **800-748-5335**
6526 S State St Suite 203
801-261-8886
Salt Lake City UT 84107-7261
Fax: 801-261-8858

Local Retrieval Area: UT-Box Elder, Cache, Davis, Morgan, Salt Lake, Summit, Tooele, Utah, Wasatch, Weber.

Normal turn around time is 1-5 days. Online computer ordering is also available. Projects are generally billed by the number of names searched. Credit accounts are accepted. Personal checks are accepted.

DataTrace Investigations Inc also has correspondent relationships in other jurisdictions, including all counties in Utah. They specialize in investigations including background checks, asset searches and skip tracing.

Sondra Dauzat(597)
Phone: **501-772-7110**
Rt 7 Box 479 E
Fax:
Texarkana AR 75502

Local Retrieval Area: AR-Columbia, Howard, Lafayette, Little River, Miller, Sevier.

Normal turn around time is 12-72 hours. Projects are generally billed by the number of names searched. Credit accounts are accepted.

Sondra specializes in UCC record searches.

Dave Kern Attorney Service Inc(598)
Phone: **213-250-1238**
250 Glendale Blvd
Fax: 213-481-1999
Los Angeles CA 90026

Local Retrieval Area: CA-Colusa, Los Angeles, Orange, Riverside, San Diego.

Normal turn around time is 1-3 days. Rush service also is available. Projects are generally billed by the number of names searched. All projects require prepayment. Credit cards are accepted for payment.

David F Gillison Jr PA(599)
Phone: **501-265-2235**
7 N Court St
Fax: 501-265-2125
Lake Village AR 71653

Local Retrieval Area: AR-Chicot.

Normal turn around time is 3 days. Projects are generally billed by the hour. Credit accounts are accepted. Personal checks are accepted.

David F Gillison Jr PA also has correspondent relationships in other jurisdictions, including Ashley, Drew and Desha. They specialize in all land records and title insurance.

David Granger Investigations(600)
Phone: **602-945-1035**
PO Box 1001
Fax: 602-945-4132
Scottsdale AZ 85252

Local Retrieval Area: AZ-Coconino, Maricopa, Pinal.

Normal turn around time is 2 days. Projects are generally billed by the hour. Credit accounts are accepted.

David Granger Investigations also has correspondent relationships in other jurisdictions, including Pima and Yavapai counties. They specialize in locating people.

Daviess County Abstracts(601)
Phone: **816-663-2155**
106 N Market St
Fax: 816-663-2156
Gallatin MO 64640

Local Retrieval Area: MO-Caldwell, Clinton, Daviess, De Kalb.

Normal turn around time is 3 days. Projects are generally billed by the number of records located. Credit accounts are accepted.
They specialize in real estate searches.

Davis Detective Agency Inc(602)
Phone: **301-843-7288**
PO Box 1393
Fax: 301-932-4781
Waldorf MD 20604

Local Retrieval Area: DC-All counties; MD-Anne Arundel, Calvert, Charles, Howard, Prince George's, St. Mary's.

Normal turn around time is 3-5 days. Online computer ordering is also available. Projects are generally billed by the number of records located. Credit accounts are accepted. Credit cards are accepted for payment.   Personal checks are accepted.

They specialize in skips, locates, asset searches, court hourse filings, and court house records research in the Southern Maryland area.

Davis Investigations Inc(603)
Phone: **800-788-3846**
12 Heritage Village
304-523-0051
Huntington WV 25701-1044
Fax: 304-529-4552

Local Retrieval Area: KY-Boyd; OH-Lawrence; WV-Cabell, Lincoln, Mason, Wayne.

Normal turn around time is 24 hours. Online computer ordering is also available. Projects are generally billed by the hour. Credit accounts are accepted.

Their electronic mail number is ION 62778486.

Don Davis(604)
481-B Sunset Hill Rd
Sugar Hill NH 03585
Phone: 603-823-5665
Fax:

Local Retrieval Area: NH-Coos, Grafton; VT-Caledonia, Washington, Windsor.

Normal turn around time is 1 to 5 days. Project billing methods vary. Credit accounts are accepted.

Davison County Abstract & Title(605)
110 E 2nd Ave
Mitchell SD 57301
Phone: 605-996-2098
Fax: 605-334-2101

Local Retrieval Area: SD-Davison.

Normal turn around time is varied depending on project. Fee basis will vary by the type of project. Credit accounts are accepted. They specialize in title searches.

Dawes County Abstract Co(606)
PO Box 1070
Chadron NE 69337
Phone: 308-432-4840
Fax: 308-432-2960

Local Retrieval Area: NE-Dawes, Sheridan, Sioux.

Normal turn around time is 3 days. Projects are generally billed by the number of names searched. Credit accounts are accepted. They specialize in title insurance.

Day Abstract Co(607)
112 S Ave B
Washington IA 52353
Phone: 319-653-2147
Fax:

Local Retrieval Area: IA-Washington.

Normal turn around time is 2-3 days. Fee basis will vary by the type of project. Credit accounts are accepted. They specialize in real estate.

DeQueen Abstract Co(608)
PO Box 410
De Queen AR 71832
Phone: 501-642-2533
Fax: 501-642-2536

Local Retrieval Area: AR-Sevier.

Normal turn around time is up to 10 days. Projects are generally billed by the hour. The first project may require a prepayment.

DeSoto Abstract(609)
2020 E 70th St
Shreveport LA 71105
Phone: 318-798-1198
Fax: 318-797-7856

Local Retrieval Area: AR-Columbia, Lafayette, Ouachita, Union; LA-Bienville Parish, Bossier Parish, Caddo Parish, Claiborne Parish, De Soto Parish, Lincoln Parish, Webster Parish; TX-Cass, Harrison, Henderson, Marion, Panola, Rusk, Shelby, Smith.

Normal turn around time is varied depending on project. Projects are generally billed by the hour. The first project may require a prepayment.
DeSoto Abstract also has correspondent relationships in other jurisdictions, including South Louisiana. They specialize in oil, gas and environmental asessment.

DeSoto Abstract Co(610)
PO Drawer 31
Arcadia FL 33821
Phone: 813-494-3656
Fax: 813-494-3481

Local Retrieval Area: FL-De Soto.

Normal turn around time is 3 days. Projects are generally billed by the number of records located. Credit accounts are accepted.
DeSoto Abstract Co also has correspondent relationships in other jurisdictions, including Charolette, Lee and Hardee Counties.

Dealey Abstract and Title Company(611)
311 West Ave
Holdrege NE 68949
Phone: 308-995-4622
Fax:

Local Retrieval Area: NE-Phelps.

Normal turn around time is 24-48 hours. Fee basis will vary by type of project. Credit accounts are accepted.
Dealey Abstract and Title Company also has correspondent relationships in other jurisdictions, including Buffalo, Kearney and Harlan.

Deamer & Deamer(612)
109 E 9th St
Rochester IN 46975
Phone: 219-223-3129
Fax:

Local Retrieval Area: IN-Fulton.

Normal turn around time is 1 working week. Projects are generally billed by the number of records located. Credit accounts are accepted.
They specilize in title insurance.

Deister Ward & Witcher(613)
2812 1st Ave N Suite 318
Billings MT 59101
Phone: 800-443-7874
406-248-6481
Fax: 406-248-6478

Local Retrieval Area: MT-Yellowstone.

Normal turn around time is 2 days. Out of county can be done in 1 week. Projects are generally billed by the hour. Credit accounts are accepted.

Deister Ward & Witcher Inc(614)
6536 S Dayton Suite 1700
Englewood CO 80111
Phone: 303-790-8426
Fax: 303-790-7427

Local Retrieval Area: CO-Adams, Arapahoe, Cheyenne, Crowley, Douglas, Elbert, Garfield, Gunnison, Kiowa, Kit Carson, Lincoln, Logan, Mesa, Montrose, Otero, Park, Phillips, Pitkin, Rio Blanco, Sedgwick, Summit, Weld.

Normal turn around time is up to 1 week. Projects are generally billed by the hour. Credit accounts are accepted. They request prepayment from individuals, but will invoice attorneys and companies.
Deister Ward & Witcher Inc also has correspondent relationships in other jurisdictions, including natiowide. They specialize in real estate and title research.

Deister Ward & Witcher of AR(615)
412 N 6th St Suite C
Ft Smith AR 72901
Phone: 501-782-7448
Fax:

Local Retrieval Area: AR-Crawford, Franklin, Johnson, Logan, Montgomery, Perry, Pike, Polk, Scott, Sebastian, Yell.

Normal turn around time is 2-3 days. Rush service is also available. Fee basis will vary by the type of project. Credit accounts are accepted.

Deister Ward & Witcher of WY(616)
PO Box 1846
Casper WY 82602
Phone: 800-829-8434
Fax: 307-266-1823

Local Retrieval Area: UT-Carbon, Daggett, Summit, Uintah, Wasatch; WY-Albany, Big Horn, Campbell, Carbon, Converse, Crook, Fremont, Goshen, Hot Springs, Johnson, Laramie, Lincoln, Natrona, Niobrara, Park, Platte, Sheridan, Sublette, Sweetwater, Teton, Uinta, Washakie, Weston.

Normal turn around time is varied depending on project. Fee basis will vary by the type of project. Credit accounts are accepted. They specialize in oil and gas records.

Delaware Attorney Services(617)
2000 Pennsylvaina Ave Suite 207
Wilmington DE 19806
Phone: 800-457-3560
302-429-0657
Fax: 302-429-0656

Local Retrieval Area: DE-Kent, New Castle, Sussex; PA-Chester, Delaware.

Normal turn around time is 2-5 days. A same day rush service is also available. Projects are generally billed by the number of names searched. Credit accounts are accepted.
They specialize in skip tracing and process service.

Delaware County Abstract Co(618)
304 E Main St
Manchester IA 52057
Phone: 319-927-4858
Fax:

Local Retrieval Area: IA-Delaware.

Normal turn around time is 1 day to 2 weeks. Projects are generally billed by the number of names searched. Credit accounts are accepted. They request prepayment from individuals, but will invoice businesses and established customers.

Delaware County Abstract Co(619)
PO Box 930
Jay OK 74346
Phone: 918-253-4425
Fax: 918-253-6224

Local Retrieval Area: OK-Delaware.

Normal turn around time is 2-3 days. Fee basis is determined on a "per search". Credit accounts are accepted.

Delta County Title Co(620)
PO Box 127
Cooper TX 75432
Phone: 903-395-4116
Fax: 903-395-2106

Local Retrieval Area: TX-Delta.

Normal turn around time is varied depending on project. Projects are generally billed by the hour. Credit accounts are accepted.

Delta Credit Bureau Inc(621)
713 S Main
Charleston MO 63834
Phone: 314-683-6692
Fax:

Local Retrieval Area: MO-Mississippi.

Normal turn around time is 2-3 days. Projects are generally billed by the number of names searched. Credit accounts are accepted.

Dennis Richman Services(622)
601 Market St Suite 750
Philadelphia PA 19103
Phone: 215-977-9393
Fax: 215-977-9806

Local Retrieval Area: NJ-Camden; PA-Bucks, Chester, Delaware, Montgomery, Philadelphia.

Normal turn around time is 1 day Projects are generally billed by the hour. The first project may require a prepayment. Will invoice established customers.
They specialize in filings in the courts.

Linda Derher(624)
204 Sycamore Ave
Sewell NJ 08080
Phone: 609-853-9836
Fax: 609-853-9459

Local Retrieval Area: NJ-Gloucester.

Normal turn around time is 24-48 hours. Projects are generally billed by the number of names searched. Credit accounts are accepted. Personal checks are accepted.

Desert Investigations(625)
905 E 26th Pl
Yuma AZ 85365
Phone: 602-726-4398
Fax:

Local Retrieval Area: AZ-La Paz, Yuma; CA-Imperial.

Normal turn around time is 24-48 hours. Projects are generally billed by the hour. Credit accounts are accepted.

Detective Referral Service(626)
PO Box 701
Jerome ID 83338
Phone: 800-356-5009
Fax:

Local Retrieval Area: ID-All counties; UT-Salt Lake, Utah, Weber; WA-Spokane, Whitman.

Normal turn around time is 2-4 days. Rush service is also available. Projects are generally billed by the hour. The first project may require a prepayment.
Detective Referral Service also has correspondent relationships in other jurisdictions, including a nationwide network of independent correspondents.

Deuel County Abstract Co(627)
171 Vincent Ave
Chappell NE 69129
Phone: 308-874-2212
Fax: 308-874-3491

Local Retrieval Area: NE-Cheyenne, Deuel, Keith.

Normal turn around time is 7-10 days. Projects are generally billed by the number of names searched. Credit accounts are accepted.

Deuel County Abstract Co(628)
PO Box 737
Clear Lake SD 57226
Phone: 605-874-2381
Fax:

Local Retrieval Area: SD-Deuel.

Normal turn around time is 10 days. Fee basis will vary by the type of project. All projects require prepayment.
They specialize in title insurance.

Dewey County Abstract Co(629)
PO Box 157
Taloga OK 73667
Phone: 405-328-5556
Fax: 405-328-5484

Local Retrieval Area: OK-Dewey.

Normal turn around time is less than 1 week. Projects are generally billed by the number of names searched. Fee basis will vary by the type of project. Credit accounts are accepted.

DiNatale Detective Agency(630)
45 Bowdoin St
Boston MA 02114
Phone: 617-227-4115
Fax: 617-227-2587

Local Retrieval Area: MA-Essex, Middlesex, Norfolk, Plymouth, Suffolk.

Normal turn around time is 7-10 working days. Emergency requests can be taken. Online computer ordering is also available. Projects are generally billed by the hour. The first project may require a prepayment.
DiNatale Detective Agency also has correspondent relationships in other jurisdictions, including Barnstabel and Dukes. They specialize in civil and criminal pre trial investigations.

Dickey County Abstract & Title(631)
PO Box 339
Ellendale ND 58436
Phone: 701-349-3450
Fax: 701-349-4850

Local Retrieval Area: ND-Dickey.

Normal turn around time is varied depending on project. Fee basis will vary by the type of project. Credit accounts are accepted.

Dickinson Abstract Co(632)
PO Box 1055
Dickinson ND 58602
Phone: 701-225-2271
Fax:

Local Retrieval Area: ND-Billings, Stark.

Normal turn around time is 1 week. Projects are generally billed by the number of records located. All projects require prepayment.
They specialize in draw descriptions.

Nadine Dingman(633)
1623 Sparbue Ct
Webster City IA 50595
Phone: 515-832-2490
Fax:

Local Retrieval Area: IA-Hamilton.

Normal turn around time is 48 hours. Projects are generally billed by the hour. They also charge for copy fees. The first project may require a prepayment. Personal checks are accepted.

Direct Legal Support Services(634)
939 Harrison St
San Francisco CA 94107
Phone: 415-597-6630
Fax: 415-543-9935

Local Retrieval Area: CA-Alameda, Contra Costa, Contra Costa, Marin, San Francisco, San Mateo, Santa Clara.

Normal turn around time is 1 day. Rush service is also available. Projects are generally billed by the hour. Credit accounts are accepted.

Lewis Dirks(635)
PO Box 254
Sioux Falls SD 57101
Phone: 605-331-6022
Fax: 605-338-4837

Local Retrieval Area: IA-Lyon, Osceola, Sioux; MN-Lincoln, Murray, Nobles, Pipestone, Rock; SD-Brookings, Clay, Hamlin, Hutchinson, Kingsbury, Lake, Lincoln, McCook, Miner, Minnehaha, Moody, Turner, Union, Yankton.

Normal turn around time is 2-3 days. Fee basis varies by type of transaction. The first project may require a prepayment.
Mr. Dirks specializes in accident reconstruction and court investigations.

Disheroon Title Consultant(636)
6717 Calmont Ave
Ft Worth TX 76116
Phone: 800-645-0665
Fax: 817-732-2014

Local Retrieval Area: TX-Collin, Cooke, Dallas, Denton, Johnson, Tarrant, Wise.

Normal turn around time is the next day. Projects are generally billed by the number of names searched. Credit accounts are accepted.
Disheroon Title Consultant also has correspondent relationships in other jurisdictions, including undisclosed areas. They specialize in name searches.

Divide Abstract Co Inc(637)
PO Box 230
Crosby ND 58730
Phone: 701-965-6352
Fax: 701-965-4243

Local Retrieval Area: ND-Divide.

Normal turn around time is varied depending on project. Projects are generally billed by the hour. All projects require prepayment. They will also invoice.
They specialize in oil title and mineral searches.

E Fred Dobbins(638)
PO Box 1090
Leakesville MS 39451
Phone: 601-394-2377
Fax: 601-394-2778

Local Retrieval Area: MS-Greene.

Normal turn around time is 1 day. Projects are generally billed by the hour. The first project may require a prepayment.
He is an attorney specializing in property law.

Doc*U*Search(639)
PO Box 767
Concord NH 03302-0767
Phone: 800-332-3034
603-224-2871
Fax: 603-224-2794

Local Retrieval Area: NH-Belknap, Hillsborough, Merrimack.

Normal turn around time is varied depending on project. Fee basis will vary by type of search. Credit accounts are accepted.

Doc*U*Search also has correspondent relationships in other jurisdictions, including nationwide. They specialize in UCC searches.

Doc-U-Search Hawaii(640)
1188 Bishop St Suite 2609
Honolulu HI 96813
Phone: 808-523-1200
Fax: 808-533-3686

Local Retrieval Area: HI-Hawaii, Kalawao, Maui.

Normal turn around time is 2 days. Rush service is also available. Projects are generally billed by the number of names searched or records located. The first project may require a prepayment.

Document Retrieval Service(641)
PO Box 276
Oklahoma City OK 73101
Phone: 405-235-3653
Fax: 405-235-2691

Local Retrieval Area: OK-Canadian, Cleveland, Creek, Grady, Kingfisher, Logan, Muskogee, Oklahoma, Payne, Pottawatomie, Tulsa.

Normal turn around time is 24-48 hours. Projects are generally billed by the number of names searched. Credit accounts are accepted.

Document Retrieval Service also has correspondent relationships in other jurisdictions, including the rest of Oklahoma. They specialize in corporate work at the State Capitol. They also pull UCC filings in all counties in Oklahoma. Birth, death and vital statistics at the Oklahoma County only.

Docutrans Inc(642)
1520 Locust Street Suite 502
Philadelphia PA 19102
Phone: 215-735-5991
Fax: 215-790-1124

Local Retrieval Area: PA-Berks, Bucks, Chester, Dauphin, Delaware, Lancaster, Lehigh, Montgomery, Philadelphia.

Normal turn around time is 1-3 days. Rush service is also available. Fee basis will vary by the type of search. Credit accounts are accepted.

Docutronics Information Services(643)
130 W 42nd St Suite 2700
New York NY 10036
Phone: 800-227-5595
212-730-7140
Fax: 212-760-7666

Local Retrieval Area: NY-Kings, New York, Queens.

Normal turn around time is 4-24 hours. Projects are generally billed by the hour. Credit accounts are accepted. Credit cards are accepted for payment. They accept personal checks. They also accept American Express.

Docutronics Information Services also has correspondent relationships in other jurisdictions, including nationwide.

Valerie Dodge(644)
850 Main St
Dallas OR 97338
Phone: 503-623-9217
Fax: 503-623-6009

Local Retrieval Area: OR-Polk.

Normal turn around time is 1 week. Projects are generally billed by the number of names searched. Credit accounts are accepted.

Donald Jones Investigation/Proc(645)
PO Box 3243
Wenatchee WA 98807-3243
Phone: 509-662-7158
Fax:

Local Retrieval Area: WA-Chelan, Douglas, Grant.

Normal turn around time is 2-3 days. Projects are generally billed by the hour. Credit accounts are accepted.

A FAX is available for established customers. They specialize in investigation and information retrieval.

Donna Bean Abstractor(646)
95 Cetral Ave
Coon Valley WI 54623
Phone: 608-452-3169
Fax: 608-452-3167

Local Retrieval Area: WI-Crawford, La Crosse, Monroe, Vernon.

Normal turn around time is 3 days. Fee basis will vary by the type of project. The first project may require a prepayment.

They have 20 years paralegal experience and specialize in real estate, probate and UCC searches.

Donna's Unlimited Searches(647)
PO Box 63
Elk Park NC 28622
Phone: 704-765-3314
Fax:

Local Retrieval Area: NC-Alexander, Avery, Burke, Caldwell, Catawba.

Normal turn around time is 24-48 hours. Fee basis varies by type of transaction. Credit accounts are accepted.

Dotter Abstract & Associates(648)
506 Main St
Walsenburg CO 81089
Phone: 719-738-1730
Fax: 719-738-1012

Local Retrieval Area: CO-Huerfano.

Normal turn around time is 2-3 days. Fee basis will vary by the type of project. The first project may require a prepayment.

They specialize in real estate title and insurance.

Dora Doty(649)
140 S Sugar St
St Clairsville OH 43950
Phone: 614-695-4917
Fax:

Local Retrieval Area: OH-Belmont, Guernsey, Harrison, Jefferson, Monroe.

Normal turn around time is 24 hours. Projects are generally billed by the number of names searched. Credit accounts are accepted.

Dora specializes in title and lien work.

Dougherty Abstract & Title Service(650)
PO Box 841
Albany GA 31702
Phone: 912-888-9035
Fax:

Local Retrieval Area: GA-Baker, Calhoun, Clay, Dougherty, Lee, Marion, Miller, Mitchell, Quitman, Randolph, Schley, Seminole, Stewart, Sumter, Terrell, Thomas, Tift, Turner, Webster, Worth.

Normal turn around time is 48 hours. Fee basis will vary by the type of project. Credit accounts are accepted.
They specialize in real estate matters.

Douglas County Abstract & Title(651)
PO Box 97
Ava MO 65608
Phone: 417-683-4701
Fax: 417-683-5980

Local Retrieval Area: MO-Douglas.

Normal turn around time is 5 working days. Fee basis will vary by type of project. Credit accounts are accepted.

Douglas County Abstract Co(652)
616 Hawthrone St
Alexandria MN 56308
Phone: 612-763-3426
Fax: 612-762-2455

Local Retrieval Area: MN-Douglas, Pope.

Normal turn around time is 1 week. Projects are generally billed by the number of names searched. All projects require prepayment. They also invoice.

Douglas County Abstract Co Inc(653)
PO Box 167
Tuscola IL 61953
Phone: 217-253-3214
Fax: 217-253-3022

Local Retrieval Area: IL-Douglas.

Normal turn around time is the same day. Projects are generally billed by the hour. Credit accounts are accepted.

Douglas County Title Co(654)
PO Box 366
Armour SD 57313
Phone: 605-724-2235
Fax:

Local Retrieval Area: SD-Douglas.

Normal turn around time is 4 days. Fee basis varies by type of transaction. Credit accounts are accepted.

Douglas Investigations Ltd(655)
1341 G St NW Suite 510
Washington DC 20005
Phone: 800-747-0820
202-347-8840
Fax: 202-393-5657

Local Retrieval Area: DC-All counties; MD-Anne Arundel, Montgomery, Prince George's; VA-Arlington, City of Alexandria, City of Fairfax.

Normal turn around time is 1 week. Rush service is also available. Projects are generally billed by the hour. Credit accounts are accepted. Personal checks are accepted.
Douglas Investigations Ltd also has correspondent relationships in other jurisdictions, including Maryland and Virginia. They are a licensed private investigative firm.

Howard F Douglas(656)
Po Box 399
Lexington TN 38351
Phone: 901-968-9381
Fax: 901-968-0261

Local Retrieval Area: TN-Chester, Decatur, Hardin, Henderson, Madison.

Normal turn around time is 24 hours. They charge a flat rate per search. Credit accounts are accepted.
Mr. Douglas is an attorney and specializes in real estate record searches.

Dovolos & Associates(657)
401 N 3rd St Suite 430
Minneapolis MN 55401
Phone: 612-822-0271
Fax: 612-333-2261

Local Retrieval Area: MN-Anoka, Dakota, Hennepin, Ramsey.

Normal turn around time is same day if presented to them by 11 a.m., otherwise next day. Projects are generally billed by the number of names searched or records located. Credit accounts are accepted.

Kenneth E Downs(658)
PO Box 182
Carrolton MS 38917
Phone: 601-237-9391
Fax:

Local Retrieval Area: MS-Carroll.

Normal turn around time is usually the same day, but no more than 2 days. Projects are generally billed by the hour. Credit accounts are accepted.

Drake Detective Agency(659)
PO Box 44205
Boise ID 83711
Phone: 208-377-3463
Fax: 208-377-2249

Local Retrieval Area: ID-Ada, Boise, Canyon, Valley.

Normal turn around time is 24 to 48 hours. Projects are generally billed by the number of records located. All projects require prepayment.
They specialize in asset locations and fraud investigations.

Drake Land Title Co(660)
167 W Main
Warsaw MO 65355-0998
Phone: 816-438-5188
Fax: 816-438-6644

Local Retrieval Area: MO-Benton.

Normal turn around time is varied depending on project. Projects are generally billed by the number of names searched. Credit accounts are accepted.
They specialize in title insurance.

Wilson and Jay Drake(661)
PO Box 367
Centerville IA 52544
Phone: 515-437-1890
Fax: 515-437-1893

Local Retrieval Area: IA-Appanoose.

Normal turn around time is a couple of days. Fee basis will vary by the type of project, however, there is a minimum charge. Credit accounts are accepted. They will accept personal checks. Wilson and Jay Drake do 10-year searches.

Drew County Abstract & Title Co(662)
PO Box 533
Monticello AR 71655
Phone: **501-367-6607**
Fax: 501-367-8306

Local Retrieval Area: AR-Drew.

Normal turn around time is 2-3 days. Fee basis will vary by type of project. All projects require prepayment.
They specialize in title insurance.

Ray M Druley(663)
PO Box 146
Ft Branch IN 47648
Phone: **812-753-4975**
Fax: 812-753-4612

Local Retrieval Area: IN-Gibson.

Normal turn around time is 5 days. Projects are generally billed by the number of names searched. Credit accounts are accepted.
Mr. Druley is also an attorney and specializes in real estate record searches.

Dora Drum(664)
4782 E Fountain Way
Fresno CA 93726
Phone: **209-251-5193**
Fax: 209-456-3833

Local Retrieval Area: CA-Fresno.

Normal turn around time is 1-2 days. Fee basis is per search. The first project may require a prepayment.
Ms. Drum specializes in abstracting and public record searching.

Sim C Dulaney(665)
PO Box 176
Port Gibson MS 39150
Phone: **601-437-4335**
Fax: 601-437-5117

Local Retrieval Area: MS-Claiborne, Warren.

Normal turn around time is 1-2 days. Projects are generally billed by the hour. The first project may require a prepayment.
Mr. Dulaney is in general practice. He also is a public defender.

Dunbar & Associates(666)
1629 Ave D Suite #5A
Billings MT 59102
Phone: **406-252-2353**
Fax: 406-259-4211

Local Retrieval Area: MT-Big Horn, Carbon, Custer, Gallatin, Golden Valley, Musselshell, Rosebud, Stillwater, Treasure, Yellowstone.

Normal turn around time is 24-48 hours. Projects are generally billed by the hour. The first project may require a prepayment.
Dunbar & Associates also has correspondent relationships in other jurisdictions, including network in Montana, Idaho, Wyoming, North and South Dakota, Canada Providence of Sask and Alberta. They specialize in employment screening and field investigation.
Mr. Dunbar is a former FBI agent.

Dunn County Abstract & Title Inc(667)
815 7th St E
Menomonie WI 54751
Phone: **715-235-0875**
Fax: 715-235-9690

Local Retrieval Area: WI-Dunn, Pepin.

Normal turn around time is 1-2 days for Dunn county. For Pepin county up to 1 week. Fee basis varies by type of transaction. The first project may require a prepayment.

James C Duran(668)
PO Box 43
Whitehall MI 49461-0043
Phone: **616-894-8325**
Fax:

Local Retrieval Area: MI-Muskegon, Oceana.

Normal turn around time is 24 hours. Projects are generally billed by the hour. All projects require prepayment.
They specialize in serving of civil process and private investigating.

E-Z Messenger Attorney Service(669)
65 E Pennington
Tucson AZ 85701
Phone: **602-623-8436**
Fax: 602-624-1819

Local Retrieval Area: AZ-Pima.

Normal turn around time is 24 hours. Projects are generally billed by the number of names searched. All projects require prepayment.
E-Z Messenger Attorney Service Inc also has correspondent relationships in other jurisdictions, including the Phoenix region.

EJB Service Corp(670)
15111 N Longbow Bend
Davie FL 33331
Phone: **800-741-5452**
Fax: 800-741-5452

Local Retrieval Area: FL-Broward.

Normal turn around time is 24-48 hours. Projects are generally billed by the hour. Credit accounts are accepted.
EJB Service Corp also has correspondent relationships in other jurisdictions, including Dade and Palm Beach. They specialize in civil process service.

EL-Ru Inc(671)
2141 Brooks Rd
Dacula GA 30211
Phone: **404-963-8156**
Fax: 404-963-8023

Local Retrieval Area: GA-Banks, Barrow, Clarke, Clayton, Cobb, Dawson, De Kalb, Forsyth, Fulton, Gwinnett, Hall, Henry, Jackson, Lumpkin, Newton, Oconee, Oglethorpe, Rockdale, Walton, White.

Normal turn around time is 12-24 hours. Projects are generally billed by the number of names searched. Credit accounts are accepted.
They specialize in UCC searches, tax liens, suits, judgements, and retrieval of court records and mortgage searches.

EX-CEL Investigations(672)
PO Box 22124
St Petersburg FL 33742
Phone: **813-527-5440**
Fax: 813-526-9022

Local Retrieval Area: FL-Hillsborough, Pinellas.

Normal turn around time is 48 hours. Projects are generally billed by the number of names searched. Copy expenses will be added to the fee. Credit accounts are accepted.
EX-CEL Investigations also has correspondent relationships in other jurisdictions, including Manattee and Sarasota. They specialize in process service, background checks, locates and video surveillance.

Eagle Investigations Inc(673)
209 S 5th St
Louisville KY 40202
Phone: 800-344-2454
Fax: 502-585-3480

Local Retrieval Area: IN-Clark, Floyd; KY-Breckinridge, Bullitt, Hardin, Henry, Jefferson, Meade, Nelson, Oldham, Shelby, Spencer.

Normal turn around time is 24-48 hours. Projects are generally billed by the number of names searched or records located. All projects require prepayment. They will also invoice.

Eagle Pass Title Co Inc(674)
PO Box 1316
Eagle Pass TX 78853
Phone: 210-773-0555
Fax: 210-773-6886

Local Retrieval Area: TX-Maverick.

Normal turn around time is 1-2 days. All projects require prepayment.

Eagle Rock Investigations(675)
4030 Spartina
Idaho Falls ID 83406
Phone: 208-523-4317
Fax:

Local Retrieval Area: ID-Bannock, Bingham, Bonneville, Jefferson, Madison.

Normal turn around time is 48 hours. Projects are generally billed by the hour. The first project may require a prepayment.
They specialize in surveillance.

Earlene Y Speer Law Offices(676)
PO Box 310
Altamont TN 37301
Phone: 615-692-2368
Fax:

Local Retrieval Area: TN-Grundy.

Normal turn around time is 2 days. Projects are generally billed by the number of names searched. The first project may require a prepayment.
They specialize in title and UCC searches.

East Arkansas Abstract Co(677)
204 E Merriman Ave
Wynne AR 72396
Phone: 501-367-6607
Fax: 501-238-4507

Local Retrieval Area: AR-Cross.

Normal turn around time is 3-5 days. Fee basis will vary by type of project. All projects require prepayment.
They specialize in land research.

East Florida Title Services Inc(678)
1326 S Ridgewood Ave Suite 7
Daytona Beach FL 32114
Phone: 904-255-6373
Fax: 904-255-6725

Local Retrieval Area: FL-Flagler, Volusia.

Normal turn around time is 3-5 business days. Projects are generally billed by the number of names searched. Credit accounts are accepted.
They specialize in all land title research.

East Texas Title & Abstract Co(679)
PO Box 1579
Hemphill TX 75948
Phone: 409-787-2114
Fax:

Local Retrieval Area: TX-Sabine.

Normal turn around time is up to a week. Projects are generally billed by the hour. The first project may require a prepayment.

East Texas Title & Abstract Co(680)
112 S Pecan St
Nacogdoches TX 75961
Phone: 409-560-1471
Fax: 409-560-4771

Local Retrieval Area: TX-Nacogdoches.

Normal turn around time is up to a week. Projects are generally billed by the hour. Credit accounts are accepted.

East Texas Title & Abstract Co Inc(681)
PO Box 721
San Augustine TX 75972
Phone: 409-275-9786
Fax: 409-275-5069

Local Retrieval Area: TX-San Augustine.

Normal turn around time is up to a week. Projects are generally billed by the hour. The first project may require a prepayment.

Eastco Abstract Corporation(682)
148 S Swan St
Albany NY 12210
Phone: 518-463-0013
Fax: 518-463-0214

Local Retrieval Area: NY-Bronx, Chautauqua, Dutchess, Essex, Herkimer, Monroe, Nassau, New York, Otsego, Queens, Rockland, Ulster, Westchester.

Normal turn around time is 48 hours for last owner searches, 2 weeks for a full search. Fees are regulated by the state of New York. Credit accounts are accepted.
Eastco Abstract Corporation also has correspondent relationships in other jurisdictions, including Essex, Herkimer, Monroe, Otsego, Bronx, Dutchess, Nassau, New York, Queens, Suffolk, Rockland, Ulster and Westchester.

Eastern North Carolina Investig.(683)
802 Vandora Ave
Garner NC 27529
Phone: 919-772-3346
Fax: 919-772-3346

Local Retrieval Area: NC-Beaufort, Bladen, Chatham, Columbus, Craven, Cumberland, Duplin, Durham, Edgecombe, Franklin, Granville, Halifax, Harnett, Hoke, Johnston, Jones, Lee, Lenoir, Martin, Moore, Nash, New Hanover, Northampton, Onslow, Orange, Pender, Pitt, Randolph, Robes.

Normal turn around time is 1-3 days. Projects are generally billed by the hour. Credit accounts are accepted.
They also pull records from the Department of Corrections.

Eastern Oregon Title(684)
1110 Spring Ave
La Grande OR 97850
Phone: 503-963-0514
Fax: 503-963-2391

Local Retrieval Area: OR-Union.

Normal turn around time is 24-48 hours Project billing methods vary. Credit accounts are accepted.

Eastern Upper Pennensula Title Co(685)
223 W Portage Ave Suite 2
Sault Sainte Marie MI 49783
Phone: 906-632-0606
Fax: 906-632-6153

Local Retrieval Area: MI-Chippewa, Mackinac.

Normal turn around time is up to 2 weeks. Fee basis will vary by type of project. Credit accounts are accepted.
They specialize in real estate and title work.

Eastland Title Co(686)
PO Box 680
Hillsboro TX 76645
Phone: 817-582-2762
Fax: 817-582-2760

Local Retrieval Area: TX-Hill.

Normal turn around time is up to a week. Fee basis will vary by the type of project. Credit accounts are accepted.

Easy Way(687)
500 N 6 1/2 Street
Paragould AR 72450
Phone: 501-239-2760
Fax: 501-236-8982

Local Retrieval Area: AR-Craighead, Greene.

Normal turn around time is 2 days. Rush service is also available. Projects are generally billed by the hour. The first project may require a prepayment. Credit cards are accepted for payment.

Eaton Abstract Company(688)
122 S Van Buren St
Newton IL 62448
Phone: 618-783-8474
Fax: 618-783-3199

Local Retrieval Area: IL-Jasper.

Normal turn around time is 24-48 hours. Projects are generally billed by the number of names searched or records located. Credit accounts are accepted.
They specialize in complete title service searches.

Ed Knight Information Service(689)
6651 Cameron Rd
Morrow GA 30260
Phone: 800-282-6418
Fax: 800-282-6416

Local Retrieval Area: GA-All counties.

Normal turn around time is 1-2 days. Projects are generally billed by the number of names searched. Credit accounts are accepted.
Ed Knight Information Service also has correspondent relationships in other jurisdictions, including South Georgia. They have been in business since 1972. They specialize in lien searches in metropolitan Atlanta.

Ed Waynick and Associates(690)
4304 Woodbluff Dr
Mesquite TX 75150
Phone: 214-226-0403
Fax: 214-203-1314

Local Retrieval Area: TX-Collin, Dallas, Denton, Kaufman, Rockwall, Tarrant.

Normal turn around time is 7 days. Projects are generally billed by the hour. The first project may require a prepayment.
They also perform drivers license searches, moving violation record and address, and social security number searches.

Eddy County Abstract Co(691)
116 N Canyon St
Carlsbad NM 88220
Phone: 505-887-2828
Fax: 505-887-0824

Local Retrieval Area: NM-Eddy.

Normal turn around time is 12-24 hours. Projects are generally billed by the hour. The first project may require a prepayment.
They specialize in loan closing and mineral searches, and are fully computerized.

Edgar County Title Co(692)
206 W Washington St
Paris IL 61944
Phone: 217-465-5821
Fax: 217-463-7265

Local Retrieval Area: IL-Edgar.

Normal turn around time is 1-2 days. Projects are generally billed by the number of names searched. Credit accounts are accepted.

Educated Legals Inc(693)
7807 E Greenway Suite 4
Scottsdale AZ 85260
Phone: 602-994-9766
Fax: 602-483-8222

Local Retrieval Area: AZ-Maricopa, Pima, Pinal.

Normal turn around time is 1-2 days. Rush service of same day is also available. Fee basis will vary by the type of project. Credit accounts are accepted.
They also serve as a private investigation agency.

Ekum Abstract and Title(694)
912 17th Ave
Monroe WI 53566-0263
Phone: 608-328-8221
Fax: 608-328-8223

Local Retrieval Area: WI-Green.

Normal turn around time is 1-2 days. Projects are generally billed by the number of names searched or records located. Credit accounts are accepted.

El Dorado Co Attorney Service(695)
4065 Mother Lode Dr
Shingle Springs CA 95682
Phone: 916-672-0433
Fax: 916-676-2949

Local Retrieval Area: CA-El Dorado, Placer, Sacramento.

Normal turn around time is 3-5 days. Rush service is also available. Projects are generally billed by the hour. All projects require prepayment.
They specialize in process service and skip tracing.

Elder Abstracts(696)
51 Monroe St Suite 1504
Rockville MD 20850
Phone: 301-762-3533
Fax: 301-762-8479

Local Retrieval Area: MD-Montgomery, Prince George's.

Normal turn around time is 2-3 days. Fee basis will vary by type of project. All projects require prepayment.

John D Eldridge III(697)
PO Box 479
Augusta AR 72006
Phone: 501-347-2521
Fax: 501-347-5084

Local Retrieval Area: AR-Woodruff.

Normal turn around time is 1-2 days. Projects are generally billed by the hour. The first project may require a prepayment.
Mr. Eldridge specializes in general practice and marriage/divorcee searches.

Elite Resources Inc(698)
PO Box 1448
Hamilton MT 59840

Phone: 406-363-5730
Fax:

Local Retrieval Area: MT-Ravalli.

Normal turn around time is 48 hours. Projects are generally billed by the number of names searched. The first project may require a prepayment.

Elk County Abstract & Title Co(699)
PO Box 458
Howard KS 67349

Phone: 316-374-2500
Fax:

Local Retrieval Area: KS-Elk.

Normal turn around time is 1-2 days. Fee basis varies by type of transaction. All projects require prepayment.

Elkhart County Abstract Co(700)
PO Box 2540
Elkhart IN 46515

Phone: 219-295-1620
Fax: 219-295-8302

Local Retrieval Area: IN-Elkhart, Lake.

Normal turn around time is 1 week. Projects are generally billed by the number of names searched. All projects require prepayment. They will also invoice.
They specialize in title insurance and land record searches.

H Watkins Ellerson(701)
PO Box 1080
Orange VA 22960

Phone: 703-672-2109
Fax: 703-672-2117

Local Retrieval Area: VA-Albemarle, Culpeper, Fluvanna, Greene, Louisa, Madison, Orange, City of Charlottesville.

Normal turn around time is 1 day for Orange, all others up to a week. Projects are generally billed by the hour. The first project may require a prepayment.
They specialize in tax, business and real estate searches.

Elliott & Waldron Abstr Glasscock(702)
PO Box 156
Garden City TX 79739

Phone: 915-354-2231
Fax:

Local Retrieval Area: TX-Glasscock.

Normal turn around time is up to a week. Fee basis will vary by the type of project. The first project may require a prepayment.

Elliott & Waldron Abstr-Palo Pinto(703)
403 S Oak Ave
Mineral Wells TX 76067

Phone: 817-325-6564
Fax: 817-325-1036

Local Retrieval Area: TX-Palo Pinto.

Normal turn around time is 2 days. Fee basis will vary by the type of project. The first project may require a prepayment.

Elliott & Waldron Abstr-Van Zandt(704)
305 E Tyler St
Canton TX 75103

Phone: 903-567-4127
Fax: 903-567-1757

Local Retrieval Area: TX-Van Zandt.

Normal turn around time is 1-2 days. Fee basis will vary by the type of project. The first project may require a prepayment.

Elliott & Waldron Abstr of Dimmitt(705)
PO Box 248
Carrizo Springs TX 78834

Phone: 210-876-2926
Fax: 210-876-5077

Local Retrieval Area: TX-Dimmit.

Normal turn around time is 1-2 days. Fee basis will vary by the type of project. The first project may require a prepayment.

Elliott & Waldron Abstr of Pecos(706)
PO Box 1169
Fort Stockton TX 79735

Phone: 915-336-5214
Fax:

Local Retrieval Area: TX-Pecos.

Normal turn around time is up to a week. Fee basis will vary by the type of project. The first project may require a prepayment.

Elliott and Waldron Title & Abstract(707)
211 E Washington
Lovington NM 88260

Phone: 505-396-5846
Fax: 505-396-2490

Local Retrieval Area: NM-Lea.

Normal turn around time is varied depending on project. Fee basis will vary by type of project. Credit accounts are accepted.

Ellis County Abstract & Title Co(708)
110 E 12th St
Hays KS 67601

Phone: 800-794-2690
913-625-2316
Fax: 913-625-6349

Local Retrieval Area: KS-Ellis, Rooks.

Normal turn around time is 2-3 days. Projects are generally billed by the number of names searched. Credit accounts are accepted.

Ellyson Abstract & Title-Brewster(709)
PO Box 418
Alpine TX 79830

Phone: 915-837-5801
Fax: 915-837-3509

Local Retrieval Area: TX-Brewster.

Normal turn around time is 2 days. Fee basis will vary by the type of project. The first project may require a prepayment.

Elson & Fulton Abstractors(710)
203 NE Idaho
Leon IA 50144

Phone: 515-446-4621
Fax: 515-446-4888

Local Retrieval Area: IA-Decatur.

Normal turn around time is 1-2 days. Fee basis varies by type of transaction. Credit accounts are accepted.

Emmons County Abstract & Title(711)
PO Box 428
Linton ND 58552

Phone: 701-254-4261
Fax:

Local Retrieval Area: ND-Emmons.

Normal turn around time is 1-5 days. Fee basis will vary by the type of project. Credit accounts are accepted.

Equisearch Company(712)
PO Box 21838
Lexington KY 40522-1838

Phone: 606-268-1206
Fax:

Local Retrieval Area: KY-All counties.

Normal turn around time is 12-24 hours. Fee basis will vary by type of project. Credit accounts are accepted.

Eric H Swenson Co Abstracters(713)   Phone: **913-632-2535**
707 5th St   Fax: 913-632-2243
Clay Center KS 67432

Local Retrieval Area: KS-Clay.

Normal turn around time is 1-2 days. Projects are generally billed by the hour. Credit accounts are accepted. Personal checks are accepted.

Carrie Erichsen(714)   Phone: **201-420-9763**
130 Cedar Lane Suite 6   Fax: 201-928-1202
Teaneck NJ 07666

Local Retrieval Area: NJ-Hudson.

Normal turn around time is 1-2 days. Fee basis will vary by type of project. Credit accounts are accepted. Personal checks are accepted.

Espanola Abstract Co(715)   Phone: **505-753-2248**
PO Box 1282   Fax: 505-753-4392
Espanola NM 87532

Local Retrieval Area: NM-Rio Arriba.

Normal turn around time is 10-14 days. Projects are generally billed by the hour. Credit accounts are accepted.
They are the only title company with records dating back to county's inception.

Estherville Abstract Co(716)   Phone: **712-362-3148**
121 N 6th St   Fax:
Estherville IA 51334

Local Retrieval Area: IA-Emmet.

Normal turn around time is 2 days. They charge a flat rate per search. Credit accounts are accepted.

Etna Abstract Corp(717)   Phone: **518-483-7204**
11 Edward St   Fax: 518-483-7204
Malone NY 12953

Local Retrieval Area: NY-Franklin.

Normal turn around time is 1-2 weeks. Fee basis will vary per abstract. Credit accounts are accepted. Personal checks are accepted.

Eufaula Abstract & Title Co Inc(718)   Phone: **918-689-2241**
Rt 3 Box 328   Fax:
Eufaula OK 74432

Local Retrieval Area: OK-McIntosh.

Normal turn around time is 10 working days after receipt of order. Projects are generally billed by the hour. Credit accounts are accepted.

Evans & Johnson Investigations(719)   Phone: **701-224-9743**
2501 Lee Ave   Fax: 701-258-0049
Bismark ND 58504

Local Retrieval Area: ND-Burleigh, Kidder, McLean, Morton, Sioux.

Normal turn around time is 24 hours. Fee basis will vary by the type of project. Credit accounts are accepted.
They specialize in accident reconstruction, personal injury fraud, and workmen's compensation investigations.

Robert D Evans(720)   Phone: **601-378-2171**
PO Box 1498   Fax: 601-335-9049
Greenville MS 38702

Local Retrieval Area: MS-Washington.

Normal turn around time is 1-2 days. Projects are generally billed by the hour. All projects require prepayment.
Mr. Evans is an attorney in general practice.

Everhart and Everhart Abstractors(721)   Phone: **217-849-2671**
730 Courthouse Square   Fax:
Toledo IL 62468

Local Retrieval Area: IL-Clark, Cumberland.

Normal turn around time is 3-4 days. Projects are generally billed by the number of names searched or records located. Credit accounts are accepted. Personal checks are accepted.

Executive Attorney Service Inc(722)   Phone: **213-482-6680**
221 N Figueroa St Suite 980   Fax: 213-482-6688
Los Angeles CA 90012

Local Retrieval Area: CA-Los Angeles, Orange, Riverside, San Bernardino, Ventura.

Normal turn around time is varied depending on project. Projects are generally billed by the number of names searched. The first project may require a prepayment.
They specialize in service of writs.

Executive Investigative Services(723)   Phone: **913-764-9484**
PO Box 13308   Fax: 913-780-3224
Overland Park KS 66282-3308

Local Retrieval Area: KS-Johnson, Wyandotte; MO-Jackson.

Normal turn around time is the same day. Projects are generally billed by the hour. All projects require prepayment.

Executive Messenger(724)   Phone: **503-852-7222**
203 W Main   Fax:
Carlton OR 97111

Local Retrieval Area: OR-Clackamas, Marion, Multnomah, Washington, Yamhill.

Normal turn around time is 36 hours, Projects are generally billed by the hour. The first project may require a prepayment.
Executive Messenger also has correspondent relationships in other jurisdictions, including 15 counties in the surrounding area. They specialize in process serving.

Executive Process Service(725)   Phone: **509-453-8307**
PO Box 2886   Fax:
Yakima WA 98907

Local Retrieval Area: WA-Yakima.

Normal turn around time is same day with AM request. Projects are generally billed by the hour. Fee basis varies by type of transaction. The first project may require a prepayment.

Executive Title Insurance Agency(726)
110 E 16th St Suite A
Cheyenne WY 82001
Phone: 307-638-4853
Fax: 307-634-0502

Local Retrieval Area: NE-Kimball, Morrill, Seward, Sioux; WY-Albany, Goshen, Laramie, Platte.

Normal turn around time is 48 hours. Projects are generally billed by the number of names searched or records located. Credit accounts are accepted. Personal checks are accepted.

Express Network(727)
601 W 5th St Suite 350
Los Angeles CA 90071
Phone: 213-892-9090
Fax: 213-892-9095

Local Retrieval Area: CA-Los Angeles, Orange, Santa Barbara, Ventura.

Normal turn around time is varied depending on project. Projects are generally billed by the hour. The first project may require a prepayment.
Express Network also has correspondent relationships in other jurisdictions, including San Diego, Riverside and San Bernadino. They provide full service legal support.

FACFIND Network Inc(728)
PO Box 360262
Decatur GA 30036-0262
Phone: 800-343-6641
Fax: 404-289-8317

Local Retrieval Area: GA-Clayton, Cobb, De Kalb, Douglas, Fulton, Gwinnett, Haralson, Jackson, Pickens, Rockdale, Spalding.

Normal turn around time is 24-48 hours. Projects are generally billed by the number of names searched. Credit accounts are accepted.
FACFIND Network Inc also has correspondent relationships in other jurisdictions, including the rest of Georgia and all other states. They specialize in criminal research.

FLA Search Company(729)
PO Box 5346
Lake Worth FL 33466
Phone: 407-969-6594
Fax: 407-641-7516

Local Retrieval Area: FL-Broward, Dade, Martin, Palm Beach, St. Lucie.

Normal turn around time is 24 hours. Projects are generally billed by the number of records located. Credit accounts are accepted.
FLA Search Company also has correspondent relationships in other jurisdictions, including other counties in Florida. Please contact company for more information.

FYI Services(730)
3542 Wycliff Ave
Dallas TX
Phone: 214-522-1129
Fax: 214-522-5575

Local Retrieval Area: TX-Collin, Dallas, Denton, Ellis, Kaufman, Tarrant.

Normal turn around time is 2 to 3 days. Projects are generally billed by the hour. Credit accounts are accepted. They require prepay from individuals only. Companies will be invoiced.
They specialize in accounting, financial analysis, research and real estate. They also do finding and understanding financial data, and asset/lien searches.

Facts Investigative Services(731)
234 College Ave
Waterville ME 04901
Phone: 207-872-7505
Fax:

Local Retrieval Area: ME-Kennebec, Somerset.

Normal turn around time is 8 to 40 hours. Projects are generally billed by the hour. All projects require prepayment.
They specialize in workmen's compensation and criminal searches.

Facts Title Service(732)
PO Box 636
Boaz AL 35957
Phone: 205-593-8303
Fax: 205-593-5140

Local Retrieval Area: AL-Blount, Calhoun, Cherokee, Colbert, Cullman, De Kalb, Etowah, Fayette, Franklin, Jackson, Lamar, Lauderdale, Limestone, Madison, Marshall, St. Clair, Talladega.

Normal turn around time is 24-48 hours. Fee basis is per search. The first project may require a prepayment.

Fairbanks Courier Service(733)
745 8th Ave
Fairbanks AK 99707
Phone: 907-452-4292
Fax: 907-456-5049

Local Retrieval Area: AK-Bethel, Fairbanks North Star Borough, Fairbanks District.

Normal turn around time is an oral report within 24 hours. Record copies will be sent following the oral report. Projects are generally billed by the hour. Credit accounts are accepted. Fairbanks Courier Service also has correspondent relationships in other jurisdictions, including the First, Second, and Third Judicial Districts in Alaska(primarily Juneau and Anchorage). They specialize in locating persons most current whereabouts, locating and inspecting property occupancy and conditions.

Fairbanks Process Service(734)
PO Box 73087
Fairbanks AK 99707
Phone: 907-456-3023
Fax: 907-456-2084

Local Retrieval Area: AK-Fairbanks North Star Borough.

Normal turn around time is 72 hours. Fee basis will vary by the type of search. The first project may require a prepayment. They require prepay individuals only.
They specialize in process serving and are on line with state records.

Fairbanks Title Agency(735)
714 3rd Ave
Fairbanks AK 99701
Phone: 907-456-6626
Fax: 907-452-5406

Local Retrieval Area: AK-Barrow District, Cape Nome District, Fairbanks District, Fort Gibbon District, Kotzebue District, Manley Hot Springs District, Mount McKinley District, Nenana District, Nulato District, Rampart District.

Normal turn around time is 24 hours. Projects are generally billed by the hour. All projects require prepayment.
They specialize in title insurance searches.

Fairview Abstract Co(736)
PO Box 60
Fairview OK 73737
Phone: 405-227-4524
Fax:

Local Retrieval Area: OK-Major.

Normal turn around time is 1 week. Projects are generally billed by the hour. Credit accounts are accepted.

Faithful Abstract(737)
2 Broad St
Elizabeth NJ 07201
Phone: 908-351-9398
Fax: 908-654-1847

Local Retrieval Area: NJ-Union.

Normal turn around time is 1-5 days. Fee basis will vary by the type of project. The first project may require a prepayment. They have 18 years of abstract and title experience.

Falcon Abstract Co(738)
PO Box 1
Mayport PA 16240
Phone: 800-828-4081
Fax: 814-365-5019

Local Retrieval Area: PA-Clarion, Clearfield, Elk, Forest, Jefferson, Venango.

Normal turn around time is up to 1 week. Fee basis will vary by the type of project. Credit accounts are accepted.
Falcon Abstract Co also has correspondent relationships in other jurisdictions, including Erie, Cameron, and Warren counties. They specialize in land research.

Falcon Investigations(739)
30 Market St
Winchester IL 62694
Phone: 217-742-5796
Fax: 217-742-5796

Local Retrieval Area: IL-Adams, Greene, Macon, Morgan, Pike, Schuyler, Scott.

Normal turn around time is 1-2 days. Projects are generally billed by the hour. The first project may require a prepayment.
They specialize in criminal investigations.

Falls County Abstract Co(740)
122 Bridge St
Marlin TX 76661
Phone: 817-883-2051
Fax: 817-883-6260

Local Retrieval Area: TX-Falls.

Normal turn around time is up to 5 days. Fee basis will vary by the type of project. The first project may require a prepayment.

Farmers & Lawyers Title Co(741)
701 Vilymaca St
Elkhart KS 67950
Phone: 316-697-2163
Fax: 316-697-2165

Local Retrieval Area: KS-Morton, Stanton, Stevens.

Normal turn around time is 3-5 days. Fee basis varies by type of transaction. The first project may require a prepayment.

Farmers Loan and Abstract Co(742)
106 S Penn
Oberlin KS 67749
Phone: 913-475-2381
Fax: 913-475-2381

Local Retrieval Area: KS-Decatur.

Normal turn around time is 1-3 days. Projects are generally billed by the hour. Credit accounts are accepted.
Farmers Loan and Abstract Co also has correspondent relationships in other jurisdictions, including Rawlins.

Farmers State Co Abstracting(743)
PO Box 430
Winner SD 57580
Phone: 605-842-3260
Fax: 605-842-1989

Local Retrieval Area: SD-Todd, Tripp.

Normal turn around time is 5 working days. Fee basis will vary by the type of project. Credit accounts are accepted.

Farwell Abstract Co Inc(744)
402 3rd
Farwell TX 79325
Phone: 806-481-3361
Fax: 806-481-9060

Local Retrieval Area: TX-Bailey, Parmer.

Normal turn around time is 24 hours. Projects are generally billed by the hour. Credit accounts are accepted.
They specialize in title insurance.

Fax & File Legal Services Inc(745)
4000 Civic Center Dr Suite 301
San Rafael CA 94903
Phone: 415-491-0606
Fax: 415-491-0434

They also have offices in Alameda, Contra Costa, Marin, Placer, Sacramento, San Francisco, San Mateo and Santa Clara counties.

Normal turn around time is 3-5 days. Projects are generally billed by the hour. Credit accounts are accepted. Credit cards are accepted for payment.
They specialize in filing court documents and have offices also in Alameda, Contra Costa, Marin, Placer, Sacramento, San Francisco, San Mateo and Santa Clara counties.

Fayette Professional Services(746)
56 E Main St
Uniontown PA 15401
Phone: 412-439-1450
Fax: 412-439-3460

Local Retrieval Area: PA-Fayette, Greene, Washington, Westmoreland.

Normal turn around time is the same day. Fee basis will vary by type of project. Credit accounts are accepted.
They specialize in court house research.

Feaster & Associates(747)
PO Box 140543
Austin TX 78714
Phone: 512-459-1310
Fax: 512-467-0334

Local Retrieval Area: TX-Travis, Williamson, Williamson.

Normal turn around time is 24 hours. Projects are generally billed by the number of names searched. The first project may require a prepayment. They often require a deposit in place of a set-up fee.
Feaster & Associates also has correspondent relationships in other jurisdictions, including all other counties in Texas. They specialize in insurance, domestic, skip tracing and asset investigations.

Federal Information Service(749)   **Phone: 800-728-5201**
400 7th St NW 3rd Floor   202-628-5200
Washington DC 20001   Fax: 202-626-7628

Local Retrieval Area: DC-All counties; MD-Anne Arundel, Baltimore, Montgomery, City of Baltimore; VA-Fairfax, City of Alexandria, City of Richmond.

Normal turn around time is same day. Projects are generally billed by the hour. The first project may require a prepayment.
Federal Information Service also has correspondent relationships in other jurisdictions, including nationwide. They specialize in Federal court retrieval

Federal Information Service(750)   **Phone: 212-267-2800**
5 Beekman St Suite 512   Fax: 212-626-7628
New York NY 10038

Local Retrieval Area: NY-Bronx, Kings, New York, Queens, Richmond.

Normal turn around time is usually same day. Projects are generally billed by the hour. The first project may require a prepayment.
Federal Information Service also has correspondent relationships in other jurisdictions, including nationwide. They will go to the Federal Archives in Bayonne, NJ.

Federal Research Corporation(751)   **Phone: 202-783-2700**
601 Pennsylvanie Ave NW Suite 612 North Bldg Fax: 202-783-0145
Washington DC 20004

Local Retrieval Area: MD-Anne Arundel, Baltimore, Harford, Howard, City of Baltimore; VA-Arlington, Fairfax, Loudoun, Montgomery, Prince George, Prince William, City of Alexandria, City of Richmond.

Normal turn around time is 3-5 days. A 1 to 2 day rush service is also available. Online computer ordering is also available. Fee may be based per index. Federal searches are per hour. The first project may require a prepayment.
Federal Research Corporation also has correspondent relationships in other jurisdictions, including the United States. They specialize in federal agencies in the Washington DC area. They also perform patent, trademark and copyright research.

Angela Feltner(752)   **Phone: 606-436-5633**
PO Box 262   Fax:
Jeff KY 41751

Local Retrieval Area: KY-Clay, Knott, Leslie, Letcher, Perry.

Normal turn around time is 3-4 days. Projects are generally billed by the hour. The first project may require a prepayment.
Ms. Feltner specializes in researching surface and mineral titles.

Ferrari(753)   **Phone: 716-689-6577**
8 Tuder Ct   Fax: 716-689-6661
Getzville NY 14068

Local Retrieval Area: NY-Erie, Niagara.

Normal turn around time is 3-5 days. Projects are generally billed by the hour. All projects require prepayment. Credit cards are accepted for payment.
Ferrari also has correspondent relationships in other jurisdictions, including nationwide.

Ferry County Title & Escrow Co Inc(754)   **Phone: 509-775-3119**
PO Box 351   Fax: 509-775-2492
Republic WA 99166

Local Retrieval Area: WA-Ferry.

Normal turn around time is 1 day. Fee basis varies by type of transaction. The first project may require a prepayment.

Kitty Fette(755)   **Phone: 804-969-1236**
Rt 1 Box 203   Fax:
Wingina VA 24599

Local Retrieval Area: VA-Buckingham.

Normal turn around time is 1-2 days. Fee basis varies by type of transaction. The first project may require a prepayment.
She specializes in civil and criminal searches.

Fidelity Abstract & Title Co(756)   **Phone: 313-234-4554**
717 S Grand Traverse Street   Fax: 313-232-1476
Flint MI 48502

Local Retrieval Area: MI-Genesee.

Normal turn around time is 3-5 days. Fee basis will vary by the type of project. All projects require prepayment.
They specialize in title insurance, escrows and closings.

Fidelity Abstract & Title Co(757)   **Phone: 605-772-5632**
PO Box 247   Fax: 605-772-5720
Howard SD 57349

Local Retrieval Area: SD-Miner.

Normal turn around time is 1 week. Projects are generally billed by the hour. Credit accounts are accepted.

Fidelity Home Abstract(758)   **Phone: 717-424-5600**
717 Sarah St   Fax: 717-424-9860
Stroudsburg PA 18360

Local Retrieval Area: PA-Carbon, Wayne.

Normal turn around time is 10 days. Rush service is also available. Projects are generally billed by the number of records located. Credit accounts are accepted.
Fidelity Home Abstract also has correspondent relationships in other jurisdictions, including Wayne and Cargon counties.

Fidelity Legal Investigation Inc(759)   **Phone: 205-988-8644**
101 Hilltop Business Dr   Fax: 205-663-1489
Pelham AL 35124

Local Retrieval Area: AL-Jefferson, St. Clair, Shelby.

Normal turn around time is 24 hours. Rush service is available. Online computer ordering is also available. Projects are generally billed by the number of names searched. If extensive research, they charge per hour. The first project may require a prepayment.
Fidelity Legal Investigation Inc also has correspondent relationships in other jurisdictions, including Montgomery and Madison. They specialize in private investigation work, polygraph examinations, interviews and interrogations.

Fidelity Title and Guaranty Co(760)
2233 Lee Rd
Winter Park FL 32789
Phone: 407-740-7131
Fax: 407-740-6275

Local Retrieval Area: FL-Brevard, Duval, Flagler, Lake, Marion, Orange, Osceola, Polk, Seminole, Volusia.

Normal turn around time is 3 working days. Projects are generally billed by the hour. Credit accounts are accepted. Credit cards are accepted for payment.
They specialize in serving Central Florida and have a computer data base for Orange, Seminole and Volusia Counties.

Fillmore County Abstract Co(761)
PO Box 69
Geneva NE 68361
Phone: 402-759-3413
Fax:

Local Retrieval Area: NE-Fillmore.

Normal turn around time is 1 week. Fee basis will vary by the type of project. The first project may require a prepayment.
They specialize in title searches.

Finders Inc(762)
1372 Ann Terrace
Madison Heights MI 48071
Phone: 313-543-2405
Fax: 313-543-4248

Local Retrieval Area: MI-Macomb, Oakland, Washtenaw, Wayne.

Normal turn around time is the next day. Projects are generally billed by the hour. Credit accounts are accepted.
Finders Inc also has correspondent relationships in other jurisdictions, including all other counties in upper and lower Michigan. They specialize in field investigations.

Fink Abstract Co(763)
622 Madison St
Fredonia KS 66736
Phone: 316-378-2357
Fax:

Local Retrieval Area: KS-Wilson.

Normal turn around time is 2-3 days. Fee basis varies by type of transaction. The first project may require a prepayment.

Finley Abstract & Title Co(764)
309 Jefferson
Oskaloosa KS 66066
Phone: 913-863-2271
Fax: 913-863-2065

Local Retrieval Area: KS-Jefferson.

Normal turn around time is 2-3 days. Projects are generally billed by the hour. The first project may require a prepayment.

First Abstract Title Co(765)
PO Box 6
Manitowoc WI 54221
Phone: 414-684-1261
Fax: 414-684-6581

Local Retrieval Area: WI-Manitowoc.

Normal turn around time is 2-3 days. Projects are generally billed by the number of names searched. The first project may require a prepayment.

First Abstract and Loan Co(766)
512 W Main
Cherokee IA 51012
Phone: 712-225-3612
Fax:

Local Retrieval Area: IA-Cherokee.

Normal turn around time is 2 weeks. Fee basis will vary by type of project. Credit accounts are accepted.

First American Title & Escrow(767)
PO Box 155
Libby MT 59923
Phone: 406-293-3721
Fax: 406-293-3723

Local Retrieval Area: MT-Lincoln.

Normal turn around time is the next day. Fee basis varies by type of transaction. Credit accounts are accepted.

First American Title & Escrow(768)
PO Box 991
Polson MT 59860
Phone: 406-883-5258
Fax: 406-883-3056

Local Retrieval Area: MT-Lake.

Normal turn around time is the next day. Fee basis varies by type of transaction. Credit accounts are accepted.

First American Title Co(769)
Box 850
Thompson Falls MT 59873
Phone: 406-827-3591
Fax: 406-827-3848

Local Retrieval Area: MT-Sanders.

Normal turn around time is 2-3 days. Projects are generally billed by the hour. The first project may require a prepayment.

First American Title of Mineral Cty(770)
PO Box 548
Superior MT 59872
Phone: 406-822-3391
Fax: 406-822-3391

Local Retrieval Area: MT-Mineral.

Normal turn around time is 48 hours. Fee basis varies by type of transaction. Credit accounts are accepted.
They can only do real estate title information on a written basis. Will pull judgements, UCC, etc. from computer verbally only, will not charge for this information. Parent company will not allow hard copy for liability reasons.

First American Title Guaranty(771)
307 Main St
Sundance WY 82729
Phone: 307-283-1844
Fax:

Local Retrieval Area: WY-Crook.

Normal turn around time is 3-7 days. Rush service is also available. Projects are generally billed by the hour. Credit accounts are accepted.

First Coast Investigations Inc(772)
PO Box 10673
Jay FL 32247
Phone: 904-398-4076
Fax: 904-346-0329

Local Retrieval Area: FL-Clay, Clay, Duval, Nassau.

Normal turn around time is 24-48 for criminal records. Fees are based on a county schedule. Credit accounts are accepted.
First Coast Investigations Inc also has correspondent relationships in other jurisdictions, including Miami and Orlando. They can also do background investigations and Motor Vehicle Record checks.

First Insurance Agency of Hoxie(773) Phone: **913-675-3252**
700 Main Fax:
Hoxie KS 67740-0108

Local Retrieval Area: KS-Decatur, Gove, Graham, Sheridan, Thomas.

Normal turn around time is 1 day for Sheridan county and 2 to 3 days for surrounding counties. Projects are generally billed by the number of records located. Credit accounts are accepted. Personal checks are accepted.
They specialize in record searches.

First Mason Title Co(774) Phone: **915-347-6388**
PO Box 1219 Fax: **915-347-6251**
Mason TX 76856

Local Retrieval Area: TX-Mason.

Normal turn around time is 2-3 days. Projects are generally billed by the hour. The first project may require a prepayment.

First Montana Title Co-Great Falls(775) Phone: **406-727-2600**
PO Box 2249 Fax: **406-727-4404**
Great Falls MT 59403

Local Retrieval Area: MT-Cascade, Rosebud, Treasure, Yellowstone.

Normal turn around time is 24 hours. Projects are generally billed by the hour. Credit accounts are accepted.
They specialize in real estate.

First Securities Corp in Aurora(776) Phone: **402-694-6126**
1220 L St Fax:
Aurora NE 68818

Local Retrieval Area: NE-Hamilton.

Normal turn around time is 3-4 days. Fee basis varies by type of transaction. Credit accounts are accepted.
They specialize in title searches.

First Security Service Corp(777) Phone: **617-568-8750**
1 Harborside Dr Suite 302-S Fax: **617-568-8815**
Boston MA 02128

Local Retrieval Area: CT-Hartford; MA-Essex, Middlesex, Norfolk, Suffolk.

Normal turn around time is 24-48 hours. Online computer ordering is also available. Projects are generally billed by the hour. The first project may require a prepayment.

First State Abstract(778) Phone: **501-676-2486**
103 W Front Street Fax: **501-676-2486**
Lonoke AR 72086

Local Retrieval Area: AR-Lonoke.

Normal turn around time is 3-4 days. Fee basis will vary by type of project. All projects require prepayment.
They specialize in title insurance.

Fisher County Abstract Co(779) Phone: **915-776-2471**
PO Box 428 Fax: **915-776-2471**
Roby TX 79552

Local Retrieval Area: TX-Fisher.

Normal turn around time is 1-2 days. Fee basis will vary by the type of project. The first project may require a prepayment.

Five C's(780) Phone: **805-473-1825**
650 Truman Fax:
Oceano CA 93445

Local Retrieval Area: CA-Los Angeles, San Luis Obispo, Santa Barbara, Santa Barbara.

Normal turn around time is 5 days. Online computer ordering is also available. Projects are generally billed by the number of names searched. Credit accounts are accepted.
Five C's also has correspondent relationships in other jurisdictions, including all California counties.

Flagher County Abstract Co(781) Phone: **904-437-4151**
PO Box 398 Fax: **904-437-1913**
Bunnell FL 32110

Local Retrieval Area: FL-Flagler.

Normal turn around time is 24 hours. Projects are generally billed by the number of names searched. All projects require prepayment. They have been established since 1917 and specialize in titles.

Flathead County Title Co(782) Phone: **406-755-5028**
PO Box 188 Fax: **406-755-3299**
Mt Kalispell MT 59903

Local Retrieval Area: MT-Flathead.

Normal turn around time is 1-4 days. Projects are generally billed by the hour. Credit accounts are accepted.
They specialize in title insurance searches.

Fleming Attorney Service(783) Phone: **800-776-3301**
PO Box 3882 602-253-1155
Phoenix AZ 85030 Fax: **602-253-5841**

Local Retrieval Area: AZ-Coconino, Maricopa, Pima, Pinal, Yavapai.

Normal turn around time is next day for court searches. 2-3 days for UCC, tax, and vital statistic records. Projects are generally billed by the number of records located. The first project may require a prepayment.
Fleming Attorney Service also has correspondent relationships in other jurisdictions, including the rest of Arizona. They specialize in process servicng, asset searches, and skip tracing.

Glenn A Fleming(784) Phone: **504-333-4331**
PO Box 772 Fax:
Belle Chasse LA 70037

Local Retrieval Area: LA-Plaquemines Parish.

Normal turn around time is 1-3 days. Fee basis varies by type of transaction. The first project may require a prepayment.
Mr. Fleming specializes in marriage/divorce and real estate transfer searchcs.

Jean R Fletcher(785)   Phone: **703-763-2151**
Rt 1 Box 753   Fax: 703-763-2663
Riner VA 24149

Local Retrieval Area: VA-Many counties in this state are covered. See the county index for actual coverage..

Normal turn around time is 2 days. Rush service is also available. The fee is usually a flat rate based on name or by a per deed of real estate. Credit accounts are accepted.

Jean specializes in real estate, tax liens, judgements and UCC searches.

Flink Findzum(786)   Phone: **800-354-1215**
505 W Hamilton Ave Suite 201   609-653-9400
Linwood NJ 08221   Fax: 609-653-9577

Local Retrieval Area: NJ-Atlantic, Burlington, Camden, Cape May, Cumberland, Gloucester, Mercer, Ocean, Salem.

Normal turn around time is 2-3 days. Projects are generally billed by the number of names searched or records located. The first project may require a prepayment.

Florence County Abstract(787)   Phone: **715-528-3272**
425 Norway St   Fax: 715-528-4707/
Florence WI 54121

Local Retrieval Area: WI-Florence.

Normal turn around time is 24-48 hours. Projects are generally billed by the number of names searched. Credit accounts are accepted.

They have the a complete in house tract index and judgement index to serve Florence County.

Florida Information Associates(788)   Phone: **904-878-0188**
PO Box 1114   Fax: 904-656-2126
Tallahassee FL 32302

Local Retrieval Area: FL-Leon.

Normal turn around time is 2-3 days. A same day rush service is also available. Projects are generally billed by the number of names searched. They offer flexible charging for large requests. Credit accounts are accepted.

They research & retrieve for state executives, judicial & legislative agencies at the State Capital, including legislative intent, corporations, UCC, motor vehicle records, criminal records, regulatory/licensure agencies & administrative proceedings.

Floyd & Floyd(789)   Phone: **913-798-3518**
112 S Pennsylvania   Fax:
Ness City KS 67560

Local Retrieval Area: KS-Ness.

Normal turn around time is 1-2 days. Projects are generally billed by the number of names searched. Credit accounts are accepted.

Footprints(790)   Phone: **606-573-6958**
PO Box 1498   Fax: 606-573-5380
Harlan KY 40831

Local Retrieval Area: KY-Bell, Harlan.

Normal turn around time is 24-48 hours. Rush service is also avaliable. Fee basis will vary by the type of project. The first project may require a prepayment.

They specialize in 19th century genealogy, gas and oil, and curative title work.

For Your Information Inc(791)   Phone:. **817-589-2211**
2404 Gravel St   Fax: 817-448-9019
Fort Worth TX 76118

Local Retrieval Area: TX-Tarrant.

Normal turn around time is 24-48 hours. Rush service is also available. Online computer ordering is also available. Fee basis varies by the type of search. The first project may require a prepayment. Credit cards are accepted for payment.

For Your Information Inc also has correspondent relationships in other jurisdictions, including other counties in Texas. Please contact company for more information.

Sylvia Forbes(792)   Phone: **816-248-3403**
PO Box 522   Fax:
Fayette MO 65248

Local Retrieval Area: MO-Cooper, Howard.

Normal turn around time is 1 week. Charges are varied depending on type of project. The first project may require a prepayment.

Ford Abstract Corp(793)   Phone: **812-663-2190**
221 N Franklin St   Fax: 812-663-2190
Greensburg IN 47240

Local Retrieval Area: TN-Decatur.

Normal turn around time is 5 days. Projects are generally billed by the hour. Credit accounts are accepted.

Forest & Forest(794)   Phone: **318-237-7651**
110 Travis Suite 109   Fax: 318-233-5860
Lafayette LA 70503

Local Retrieval Area: LA-Acadia Parish, Lafayette Parish, St. Martin Parish, Vermilion Parish.

Normal turn around time is 48 hours. Projects are generally billed by the hour. Credit accounts are accepted.

Forest & Forest also has correspondent relationships in other jurisdictions, including all other parishes in Louisiana. They specialize in real estate and commercial transactions.

Janet C Forlenza(795)   Phone: **908-431-8730**
PO Box 609   Fax: 908-409-0310
Freehold NJ 07728

Local Retrieval Area: NJ-Monmouth.

Normal turn around time is 7-10 days. Projects are generally billed by the number of names searched. The first project may require a prepayment. Personal checks are accepted.

Fort Enterprises Process Srv & Inv(796) **Phone:** 907-451-0132
PO Box 56589 **Fax:** 907-451-0132
North Pole AK 99707

Local Retrieval Area: AK-Fairbanks North Star Borough.

Normal turn around time is 2 days to 2 weeks. Projects are generally billed by the number of names searched. The first project may require a prepayment. They will invoice with credit approval. Fort Enterprises Process Srv & Inv also has correspondent relationships in other jurisdictions, including the rest of the state. They specialize in field work and locating persons who are not "in the system".

Foster County Abstarct & Title(797) **Phone:** 701-652-3164
1005 N 1st St **Fax:** 701-652-3165
Carrington ND 58421

Local Retrieval Area: ND-Foster.

Normal turn around time is 1-2 weeks. Projects are generally billed by the number of records located. Credit accounts are accepted.

Four Corners Abstract(798) **Phone:** 716-454-2263
80 W Main St **Fax:** 716-454-6163
Rochester NY 14614

Local Retrieval Area: NY-Many counties in this state are covered. See the county index for actual coverage..

Normal turn around time is 3-5 working days. Fees are calculated on a per year basis. Credit accounts are accepted. After they run a credit check, they will invoice.

Four Corners Abstract also has correspondent relationships in other jurisdictions, including Bronx, Cattaraugus, Chautauqua, Clinton, Cortland, Essex, Franklin, Hamilton, Jefferson, Kings, Lewis, Nassau, New York, Putnam, Queens, Richmond, Rockland, St. Lawrence, Schoharie, Schuyler, Suffolk, Sullivan, Tompkins, Ulster, Westchester and Wyoming. They specialize in title insurance.

Mildred Fourt(799) **Phone:** 417-967-3517
HCR 4 Box 120A **Fax:**
Houston MO 65483

Local Retrieval Area: MO-Texas.

Normal turn around time is varied depending on project. Charge will vary with the type of search. Credit accounts are accepted. Mildred specializes in genealogy searches.

Fourth Corner Network Inc(800) **Phone:** 800-321-2455
215 Flora St **Fax:** 206-734-1286
Bellingham WA 98225

Local Retrieval Area: WA-Skagit, Whatcom.

Normal turn around time is 1-3 days for Whatcom County, and 2-5 days for Skagit County. Projects are generally billed by the number of names searched or records located. Credit accounts are accepted.

Fowler Abstract Co(801) **Phone:** 913-743-6422
110 N Main **Fax:** 913-743-5769
Keeney KS 67672

Local Retrieval Area: KS-Trego.

Normal turn around time is 3-5 days. Projects are generally billed by the hour. Credit accounts are accepted. Personal checks are accepted.

Fowler Abstract Co also has correspondent relationships in other jurisdictions, including Ness, Gove and Graham counties.

Fox Advertising(802) **Phone:** 914-948-5200
199 Main St **Fax:** 914-948-5501
White Plains NY 10601

Local Retrieval Area: NY-Dutchess, Orange, Orange, Putnam, Rockland, Sullivan, Ulster, Westchester.

Normal turn around time is varied depending on project. Projects are generally billed by the number of records located. Credit accounts are accepted.

Fox Advertising also has correspondent relationships in other jurisdictions, including New York City, Queens, King, Bronx and Long Island.

Franklin Abstracts & Land Title Inc(803) **Phone:** 308-425-3654
PO Box 185 **Fax:**
Franklin NE 68939

Local Retrieval Area: NE-Franklin, Webster.

Normal turn around time is 2 days. Projects are generally billed by the hour. Credit accounts are accepted.
They specialize in land titles.

Franklin County Abstract Co(804) **Phone:** 515-456-4551
121 1st Ave NW **Fax:**
Hampton IA 50441

Local Retrieval Area: IA-Franklin.

Normal turn around time is 2-3 days. Fee basis varies by type of transaction. The first project may require a prepayment.

Franklin County Abstract Co(805) **Phone:** 903-537-4223
103 Dallas St E **Fax:** 903-537-4223
Mt Vernon TX 75457

Local Retrieval Area: TX-Franklin.

Normal turn around time is 1-2 days. Fee basis will vary by the type of project. The first project may require a prepayment.

Barbara Fransen(806) **Phone:** 712-735-6258
Rt 2 Box 37 **Fax:**
Ocheyedan IA 51354

Local Retrieval Area: IA-Clay.

Normal turn around time is 24-48 hours. Projects are generally billed by the number of names searched. The first project may require a prepayment.

Fred McDaniel and Associates(807)
8702 NW 83rd Terrace
Kansas City MO 64152

Phone: 816-741-5557
Fax: 816-741-7453

Local Retrieval Area: KS-Atchison, Douglas, Johnson, Leavenworth, Miami, Shawnee, Wyandotte; MO-Andrew, Buchanan, Cass, Clinton, Jackson, Johnson, Lafayette, Platte, Ray.

Normal turn around time is 2-3 days. Online computer ordering is also available. Projects are generally billed by the hour. The first project may require a prepayment.

They specialize in financial investigations, personal injury and workmen's compensation.

Fred Meyers Company(808)
615 Patricia Dr
San Antonio TX 78216

Phone: 210-349-8119
Fax: 210-341-2679

Local Retrieval Area: TX-Atascosa, Bandera, Bexar, Comal, Guadalupe, Kendall, Medina.

Normal turn around time is 1 week. Rush service is also available. Projects are generally billed by the hour. The first project may require a prepayment.

Fred Meyers Company also has correspondent relationships in other jurisdictions, including the rest of Texas. They specialize in missing persons.

Fred Waters Inv(809)
8109 Watt Ave Suite 247
Elverta CA 95626

Phone: 916-331-5666
Fax: 916-331-4441

Local Retrieval Area: CA-Placer, Sacramento, Sutter, Yolo, Yuba.

Normal turn around time is the same day if the order is received early in the day. Otherwise, 24-48 hours. Online computer ordering is also available. Projects are generally billed by the hour. Credit accounts are accepted. Personal checks are accepted.

Fred Waters Inv also has correspondent relationships in other jurisdictions, including San Joaquin County and the "Bay" area. They specialize in skip tracing, background, asset searches, personal interviews, collection, auto recovery, civil and criminal fraud and insurance fraud.

June Frederick(810)
105 Park St
Folkston GA 31537

Phone: 912-496-2354
Fax:

Local Retrieval Area: GA-Charlton.

Normal turn around time is the next day. Rush service is also available. Projects are generally billed by the number of names searched. Credit accounts are accepted.

Fredericksburg Title Inc(811)
112 N Orange St
Fredericksburg TX 78624

Phone: 210-997-3852
Fax: 210-997-0193

Local Retrieval Area: TX-Gillespie.

Normal turn around time is 1-2 days. Fee basis will vary by the type of project. The first project may require a prepayment.

Freeflight Inc(812)
2819 Devine St Suite 216
Columbia SC 29205

Phone: 803-765-2637
Fax: 803-779-1666

Local Retrieval Area: GA-Columbia, McDuffie, Richmond; SC-All counties.

Normal turn around time is 2-5 days. Projects are generally billed by the number of names searched or records located. Credit accounts are accepted.

Freelance Legal Secretary(813)
911 W 8th Ave Suite 203
Anchorage AK 99501

Phone: 907-278-8855
Fax: 907-276-8967

Local Retrieval Area: AK-Anchorage Borough, Homer District, Kenai District, Kodiak District, Palmer District, Valdez District.

Normal turn around time is 1-2 days under normal circumstances. Fee basis will vary by the type of project. Credit accounts are accepted. Individuals are required to prepay. Regular customers and law firms will be invoiced.

Fremont/Custer County Abstract(814)
PO Box 1890
Canon City CO 81212

Phone: 719-275-4141
Fax: 719-275-5401

Local Retrieval Area: CO-Custer, Fremont.

Normal turn around time is 1-2 days. Projects are generally billed by the number of names searched. The first project may require a prepayment.

They specialize in real estate and title matters.

Sandra Friel(815)
Rt 2 Box 67
Buckeye WV 24924

Phone: 304-799-6748
Fax:

Local Retrieval Area: WV-Pocahontas.

Normal turn around time is 1-5 days. Fee basis varies by type of transaction. Credit accounts are accepted.

Irene Friend(816)
406 Old Hury Rd
Beattyville KY 41311

Phone: 606-464-2638
Fax:

Local Retrieval Area: KY-Breathitt, Estill, Lee, Owsley, Perry, Powell, Wolfe.

Normal turn around time is 1-2 days. Fee basis varies by type of transaction. All projects require prepayment.

Ms. Friend specializes in researching coal, oil, and mineral rights.

Fritcher Abstract Co(817)
533 Erie St
Storm Lake IA 50588

Phone: 712-732-2732
Fax:

Local Retrieval Area: IA-Buena Vista.

Normal turn around time is up to 4 days. Fee basis is "per search". Credit accounts are accepted.

Frontier Cultural Service(818)
131 N 6th St
Custer SD 57730
Phone: 605-673-2917
Fax: 605-673-2917

Local retrieval area includes 28 counties in South Dakota and 11 counties in Wyoming. Normal turn around time is 48-72 hours. Projects are generally billed by the hour. Credit accounts are accepted.
They specialize in history of property, mining claims and forest service contract searches.

Fulton Title Company(819)
PO Box 747
Salem AR 72576
Phone: 501-895-2545
Fax: 501-895-2546

Local Retrieval Area: AR-Fulton, Fulton.

Normal turn around time is 2-7 days. Projects are generally billed by the number of records located. Credit accounts are accepted. They specialize in title insurance.

Peg Fuoti(820)
35 English Lane
Mays Landing NJ 08330
Phone: 609-625-9401
Fax:

Local Retrieval Area: NJ-Atlantic.

Normal turn around time is 2-7 days. Fee basis will vary by the type of project. Credit accounts are accepted.
Peg specializes in credit check searches.

Furnas County Title Co Inc(821)
PO Box 353
Beaver City NE 68926
Phone: 308-268-4005
Fax:

Local Retrieval Area: NE-Furnas, Gosper, Harlan.

Normal turn around time is 3 days. Projects are generally billed by the hour. All projects require prepayment.

G & H Abstract(822)
PO Box 121
Ellsworth KS 67439
Phone: 913-472-3491
Fax:

Local Retrieval Area: KS-Ellsworth, Leavenworth, Russell.

Normal turn around time is 2-3 days. Fee basis varies by type of transaction. The first project may require a prepayment.

G & O Abstracts Inc(823)
10 E Main St
Freehold NJ 07728
Phone: 908-577-0459
Fax: 908-577-1063

Local Retrieval Area: NJ-Monmouth.

Normal turn around time is 24-48 hours. Projects are generally billed by the number of names searched or records located. Credit accounts are accepted. Personal checks are accepted.

G T Murphy Abstractor(824)
PO Box 345
New Hampton IA 50659
Phone: 515-394-4291
Fax:

Local Retrieval Area: IA-Chickasaw.

Normal turn around time is 1-2 days. Fee basis will vary by the type of project. The first project may require a prepayment.

Norma Gable(825)
12848 State Rt 664 South
Logan OH 43138
Phone: 614-385-3201
Fax:

Local Retrieval Area: OH-Athens, Fairfield, Hocking, Perry, Vinton.

Normal turn around time is 48 hours. Charges are varied depending on type of search. Credit accounts are accepted.

Gadsden Abstract Co(826)
120 S Madison St
Quincy FL 32351
Phone: 904-627-6811
Fax: 904-627-6440

Local Retrieval Area: FL-Gadsden.

Normal turn around time is 1-5 days. Projects are generally billed by the number of names searched. Credit accounts are accepted. They specialize in real estate.

Gaines County Abstract Co(827)
PO Box 237
Seminole TX
Phone: 915-758-3351
Fax: 915-758-3790

Local Retrieval Area: TX-Gaines.

Normal turn around time is up to a week. Fee basis will vary by the type of project. The first project may require a prepayment.

Galena Abstract Co Inc(828)
PO Box 46
Galena MO 65656
Phone: 417-357-6816
Fax: 417-357-6568

Local Retrieval Area: MO-Camden, Stone.

Normal turn around time is varied depending on project. Fee basis will vary by type of project. Credit accounts are accepted. They specialize in title insurance.

Gamma Investigative Research Inc(829)
287 Lackawanna Ave
West Paterson NJ 07424
Phone: 800-878-9393
201-785-9393
Fax: 201-785-9002

Local Retrieval Area: NJ-Bergen, Hudson, Passaic, Sussex, Union, Warren.

Normal turn around time is 24-48 hours. The on line is almost immediate. Online computer ordering is also available. Projects are generally billed by the hour. The first project may require a prepayment.
They can access many New Jersey courts through an on-line system. They also specialize in field investigations.

Catherine J Garbus(830)
Po Box 504
Tunkhannock PA 18657
Phone: 717-836-6749
Fax: 717-836-8894

Local Retrieval Area: PA-Wyoming.

Normal turn around time is 24 hours. Charges are varied depending on type of search. Credit accounts are accepted.

Garrard & Trotter(831)
PO Box 338
Belzoni MS 39038
Phone: 601-247-9362
Fax: 601-247-3156

Local Retrieval Area: MS-Humphreys, Leflore, Sharkey, Sunflower, Yazoo.

Normal turn around time is up to 1 week. Projects are generally billed by the hour. The first project may require a prepayment. This is a general practice law firm.

Garrison Legal Services(832)
400 W 15th
Amarillo TX 79101
Phone: 806-373-6204
Fax: 806-374-6501

Local Retrieval Area: TX-Potter, Randall.

Normal turn around time is varied depending on project. Projects are generally billed by the hour. Credit accounts are accepted. Personal checks are accepted.
Garrison Legal Services also has correspondent relationships in other jurisdictions, including panhandle counties.

Garrison Legal Services(833)
PO Box 1574
Amarillo TX 79105
Phone: 806-373-6204
Fax:

Local Retrieval Area: TX-Potter, Randall.

Normal turn around time is 1-2 days. Projects are generally billed by the number of records located. The first project may require a prepayment.

Douglas G Garvin(834)
PO Drawer 328
Aiken SC 29802
Phone: 803-649-6281
Fax:

Local Retrieval Area: SC-Aiken.

Normal turn around time is 2 days. Fee basis varies by type of transaction. Credit accounts are accepted.

Gary Pratt Investigations(835)
123 N Vine
West Union IA 52175
Phone: 319-422-5341
Fax: 319-425-4451

Local Retrieval Area: IA-Buchanan, Butler, Chickasaw, Fayette, Winneshiek.

Normal turn around time is 1-2 days. Projects are generally billed by the number of names searched. Credit accounts are accepted. They specialize in process serving and private investigation.

Gates Land Title Corp(836)
PO Box 369
Columbia City IN 46725
Phone: 219-244-5127
Fax: 219-244-5127

Local Retrieval Area: IN-Whitley.

Normal turn around time is 1 week. Fee basis varies by type of transaction. Credit accounts are accepted.

Gem State Investigations(837)
PO Box 1875
Lewiston ID 83501
Phone: 208-746-4152
Fax: 208-746-4152

Local Retrieval Area: ID-Benewah, Clearwater, Idaho, Latah, Lewis, Nez Perce.

Normal turn around time is varied depending on project. Fee basis varies by type of transaction. Credit accounts are accepted.
Gem State Investigations also has correspondent relationships in other jurisdictions, including northern Idaho and Eastern Washington. They specialize in insurance fraud.

General Services(838)
1645 S La Cienega Blvd
Los Angeles CA 90035
Phone: 310-859-1122
Fax: 310-859-1123

Local Retrieval Area: CA-Los Angeles, Orange.

Normal turn around time is 2-3 days. Projects are generally billed by the number of names searched. Credit accounts are accepted.

Genesis Investigations(839)
775 Brooklyn Ave Suite 101
Baldwin NY 11510-2948
Phone: 800-834-3722
      516-379-4880
Fax: 516-679-8575

Local Retrieval Area: NJ-Bergen, Essex, Morris, Passaic, Somerset, Sussex, Union; NY-Bronx, Dutchess, Kings, Nassau, New York, Orange, Putnam, Queens, Richmond, Rockland, Suffolk, Sullivan, Ulster, Westchester.

Normal turn around time is 1 week. A same day rush service is also available. Online computer ordering is also available. Projects are generally billed by the hour. The first project may require a prepayment. Personal checks are accepted.
Genesis Investigations also has correspondent relationships in other jurisdictions, including all of New York. They specialize in insurance fraud investigations.

Geo G Smith & Son Inc(840)
108 E Morrison
Fayette MO 65248
Phone: 816-248-2467
Fax:

Local Retrieval Area: MO-Howard.

Normal turn around time is 1-5 days. Projects are generally billed by the number of names searched. Fee may also be based per page. Credit accounts are accepted. Personal checks are accepted. Geo G Smith & Son Inc also has correspondent relationships in other jurisdictions, including Cooper, Boone and Randolph. (Only on property that lies within and partially within Howard County). They specialize in abstracting and title insurance.

Gietren & Associates Inc(841)
111 Parker St Suite 505
Tampa FL 33606
Phone: 813-254-4383
Fax: 813-254-1174

Local Retrieval Area: FL-Hillsborough, Pasco, Pinellas, Polk.

Normal turn around time is 1 day. Projects are generally billed by the hour. The first project may require a prepayment.
Gietren & Associates Inc also has correspondent relationships in other jurisdictions, including all Florida counties. They specialize in financial and general investigations, process and court reporting.

Gilchrist Title Services Inc(842)
PO Box 5
Trenton FL 32693
Phone: 904-463-6403
Fax: 904-463-6908

Local Retrieval Area: FL-Dixie, Gilchrist, Levy.

Normal turn around time is 24 hours. Projects are generally billed by the number of names searched or records located. Credit accounts are accepted. Personal checks are accepted.

Gilchrist Title Services Inc also has correspondent relationships in other jurisdictions, including Alachua County. They specialize in title insurance, real estate closings and all real property searches.

Diana Gill(843)
PO Box 516
Baker MT 59313
Phone: 406-778-2463
Fax:

Local Retrieval Area: MT-Fallon.

Normal turn around time is 1-2 days. Fee basis varies by type of transaction. All projects require prepayment.

Gillette Battey & McAreavey(844)
Box 60
Redfield SD 57469
Phone: 605-472-1210
Fax: 605-472-1280

Local Retrieval Area: SD-Spink.

Normal turn around time is 48 hours. Projects are generally billed by the hour. The first project may require a prepayment.
They specialize in probate, deeds and real property searches.

Billy J Gilmore(845)
PO Box 629
Lexington MS 39095
Phone: 601-834-2421
Fax: 601-834-2400

Local Retrieval Area: MS-Holmes.

Normal turn around time is 1-2 days. Fee basis varies by type of transaction. The first project may require a prepayment.
Mr. Gilmore is an attorney who specializes in public record research.

Gion Law Office(846)
PO Box 101
Regent ND 58650-0101
Phone: 701-563-4354
Fax:

Local Retrieval Area: ND-Adams, Bowman, Grant, Hettinger, Slope, Stark.

Normal turn around time is 5 to 7 days. Projects are generally billed by the hour. The first project may require a prepayment.
They specialize in general law practice.

Roger Gladden(847)
208 W Clarke St
Oxford GA 30267
Phone: 404-550-0749
Fax:

Local Retrieval Area: GA-Barrow, Butts, Clarke, Clayton, Cobb, De Kalb, Fulton, Gwinnett, Henry, Jackson, Jasper, Morgan, Newton, Oconee, Putnam, Rockdale, Walton.

Normal turn around time is 1-3 days. They charge a flat fee per county plus copy fees. The first project may require a prepayment.
Roger specializes in record searching at the SE Federal Archives.

Gladwin County Abstract Company(848)
320 W Cedar
Gladwin MI 48624
Phone: 517-426-7411
Fax: 517-426-2411

Local Retrieval Area: MI-Gladwin.

Normal turn around time is 1 week. Projects are generally billed by the number of names searched or records located. Credit accounts are accepted. Personal check are accepted.
They have the only existing complete tract index for Gladwin County.

Gladwin Title Co(849)
247 W Cedar Ave
Gladwin MI 48624
Phone: 517-426-0011
Fax: 517-426-7141

Local Retrieval Area: MI-Gladwin.

Normal turn around time is 2-3 days. Fee basis may vary by the type of project. The first project may require a prepayment.

Romana Glastetter(850)
PO Box 245
Kelso MO 63758
Phone: 314-264-2887
Fax:

Local Retrieval Area: MO-Scott.

Normal turn around time is 1 week. Projects are generally billed by the hour. All projects require prepayment.
Romana specializes in probate and census records.

Global Projects Ltd(851)
520 Washington Blvd Suite 500
Marina del Rey CA 90292
Phone: 800-859-8109
Fax: 310-306-7995

Local Retrieval Area: CA-All counties; FL-All counties; HI-All counties.

Normal turn around time is immediate on line service up to 2 hours. Online computer ordering is also available. Fee basis will vary by the type of project. Call for quote. Credit accounts are accepted. Credit cards are accepted for payment. Personal checks are accepted.
Global Projects Ltd also has correspondent relationships in other jurisdictions, including nationwide. The company has been in business for 20 years and is staffed by former law enforcement and intelligence agency personnel. They perform locates and asset searches, and retrieval of foreign courts and other records.

Golden Information Group(852)
753 N 35th Suite 312
Seattle WA 98103
Phone: 206-547-5662
Fax: 206-632-2024

Local Retrieval Area: WA-King.

Normal turn around time is 3 days. Same day service is available for an additional fee. Projects are generally billed by the hour. Credit accounts are accepted.
They are on-line with SCOMIS and WESTLAW.

Golt Adjustment Service(853)
PO Box 4377
Greenville DE 19807
Phone: **302-798-5500**
Fax: 302-429-0656

Local Retrieval Area: DE-All counties; PA-Chester.

Normal turn around time is 2-5 days. A same day rush service is also available. Projects are generally billed by the number of names searched. Credit accounts are accepted.
They specialize in process service and skip tracing.

Gooding Title Co(854)
228 N Walnut
Clarksville TX 75426
Phone: **903-427-3398**
Fax: 903-427-2423

Local Retrieval Area: TX-Red River.

Normal turn around time is varied depending on project. Fee basis will vary by the type of project. All projects require prepayment.

Goodman & Nichols(855)
PO Box 838
Munfordville KY 42765
Phone: **502-524-9292**
Fax: 502-524-9293

Local Retrieval Area: KY-Barren, Hart, Larue.

Normal turn around time is 3-5 days for title searches (only 1 1/2 days for Hart County) and 2 days for name checks (only 1 day for Hart County). Projects are generally billed by the number of records located. Credit accounts are accepted.

Gotham Process Service Inc(856)
299 Broadway Suite 1315
New York NY 10007
Phone: **212-962-2614**
Fax: 212-619-0826

Local Retrieval Area: NY-Bronx, Kings, New York, Queens, Richmond, Rockland, Westchester.

Normal turn around time is 5 days. Projects are generally billed by the number of names searched. They also charge a service fee plus a copy fee. All projects require prepayment.
They specialize in process service.

Graham Abstract Co(857)
121 Washington E
Albia IA 52531
Phone: **515-932-7156**
Fax:

Local Retrieval Area: IA-Monroe.

Normal turn around time is 2-3 days. Fee basis will vary by the type of project. The first project may require a prepayment.

Graham Abstract Co Inc(858)
107 W 2nd St
Portales NM 88130
Phone: **505-356-8505**
Fax: 505-356-8508

Local Retrieval Area: NM-Roosevelt.

Normal turn around time is 1-5 days. Fee basis will vary by the type of project. Credit accounts are accepted.
They specialize in escrow, title insurance, closings, and mineral searches.

Grand Forks Abstract Co(859)
209 S 3rd St
Grand Forks ND 58201
Phone: **701-772-3484**
Fax: 701-772-0701

Local Retrieval Area: ND-Grand Forks.

Normal turn around time is 48 hours. Projects are generally billed by the number of names searched. Credit accounts are accepted.
They specialize in title insurance.

Grand Traverse Title Co(860)
116 Boardman Ave
Traverse City MI 49684
Phone: **616-946-5686**
Fax: 616-946-2966

Local Retrieval Area: MI-Grand Traverse.

Normal turn around time is 2-3 days. Fee basis will vary by type of project. The first project may require a prepayment.
They specialize in real estate.

Grant County Abstract & Title Co(861)
210 E 1st Ave
Milbank SD 57252
Phone: **605-432-5461**
Fax: 605-432-5513

Local Retrieval Area: SD-Grant.

Normal turn around time is 1 week to 10 days. Projects are generally billed by the number of records located. All projects require prepayment.
They specialize in real estate titles.

Grant County Abstract Co(862)
PO Box 25
Medford OK 73759
Phone: **405-395-2854**
Fax:

Local Retrieval Area: OK-Grant.

Normal turn around time is 1-2 days. Projects are generally billed by the number of records located. The first project may require a prepayment.

Grant County Abstract Co(863)
138 S Madison St
Lancaster WI 53813
Phone: **608-723-4192**
Fax: 608-723-4228

Local Retrieval Area: WI-Grant.

Normal turn around time is 2-3 days. Fee basis varies by type of transaction. The first project may require a prepayment.

Gary Grant(864)
PO Box 376
Danville VA 24543
Phone: **804-799-3379**
Fax:

Local Retrieval Area: VA-Halifax, Henry, Patrick, Pittsylvania, City of Danville, City of Martinsville.

Normal turn around time is 2-3 days. Projects are generally billed by the number of records located. Credit accounts are accepted.
Gary specializes in UCC, real estate, tax and simple land searches.

Louise Grant(865)
Rt 2 Box 127
Hope Hull AL 36043
Phone: **205-548-2843**
205-548-2476
Fax:

Local Retrieval Area: AL-Lowndes.

Normal turn around time is varied depending on search. Fee basis will vary with the type of search. Credit accounts are accepted.

K Maxwell Graves Jr(866) Phone: **601-384-2733**
PO Box 607   Fax: 601-384-5568
Meadville MS 39653

Local Retrieval Area: MS-Franklin.

Normal turn around time is 1 working day. Projects are generally billed by the hour. Credit accounts are accepted. They accept personal checks.

Gray County Abstract Co Inc(867) Phone: **316-855-3128**
215 S Main   Fax:
Cimarron KS 67835

Local Retrieval Area: KS-Ford, Gray.

Normal turn around time is 1-7 days. Projects are generally billed by the number of names searched. Credit accounts are accepted. Personal checks are accepted.
Gray County Abstract Co Inc also has correspondent relationships in other jurisdictions, including Finney, Meade, Haskell and Hodgeman.

Great Lakes Title of Cadillac(868) Phone: **616-775-0561**
PO Box 877   Fax: 616-775-4221
Cadillac MI 49601

Local Retrieval Area: MI-Clare, Lake, Mecosta, Osceola, Wexford.

Normal turn around time is 3 days. Projects are generally billed by the number of names searched. All projects require prepayment. They request prepay only on the title searches.
Great Lakes Title of Cadillac also has correspondent relationships in other jurisdictions, including Missaukee County. They also offer Escrow services.

Great Lakes Title of Manistee(869) Phone: **616-723-9929**
PO Box 254   Fax: 616-723-9449
Manistee MI 49660

Local Retrieval Area: MI-Manistee, Mason.

Normal turn around time is 5 days. Projects are generally billed by the number of names searched. All projects require prepayment. They request prepay on the title searches only.
They offer escrow services.

Great Northern Title & Abstract Inc(870) Phone: **906-228-6100**
309 S 3rd Street Suite 201   Fax: 906-228-4015
Marquette MI 49855

Local Retrieval Area: MI-Marquette.

Normal turn around time is 1 week. Projects are generally billed by the hour. The first project may require a prepayment.

Greater Tennessee Title Co(871) Phone: **615-483-6311**
PO Box 5988   Fax: 615-483-4811
Oak Ridge TN 37831

Local Retrieval Area: TN-Anderson, Blount, Cocke, Knox, Loudon, Morgan, Roane.

Normal turn around time is 2 days. Fee basis is per search. Credit accounts are accepted.

Green Lake Title & Abstract Co(872) Phone: **414-294-6070**
535 Mill St   Fax: 414-294-6030
Green Lake WI 54941

Local Retrieval Area: WI-Green Lake.

Normal turn around time is 1-2 days. Fee basis varies by type of transaction. The first project may require a prepayment.

Richard J Green(873) Phone: **619-322-0402**
68-110 Tachevah Dr   Fax: 619-322-0402
Cathedral City CA 92234

Local Retrieval Area: CA-Los Angeles, Riverside, Ventura.

Normal turn around time is 24 hours. Projects are generally billed by the hour. The first project may require a prepayment.
Richard has 35 years experience in researching court and other public records.

Greene County Abstract Co(874) Phone: **515-386-2191**
102 S Wilson Ave   Fax: 515-386-2191
Jefferson IA 50129

Local Retrieval Area: IA-Greene, Iowa.

Normal turn around time is 1-7 days. Projects are generally billed by the number of names searched or records located. Fee may also be based on a combination of valuation and clerical. Credit accounts are accepted.

J Lane Greenlee(875) Phone: **601-283-1354**
PO Box 430   Fax: 601-283-4805
Winona MS 38967

Local Retrieval Area: MS-Carroll, Montgomery.

Normal turn around time is 2 days. Projects are generally billed by the hour. The first project may require a prepayment.

Greenwood Abstract Co(876) Phone: **316-342-2979**
413 Commercial St   Fax:
Emporia KS 66801

Local Retrieval Area: KS-Lyon.

Normal turn around time is 2-3 days. Fee basis varies by type of transaction. Credit accounts are accepted.

Greer Cuaranty Abstract Co(877) Phone: **405-782-3121**
Drawer C   Fax: 405-782-3000
Mangum OK

Local Retrieval Area: OK-Greer.

Normal turn around time is 1 to 2 days. Projects are generally billed by the hour. Credit accounts are accepted.

Gregg Investigations of Janesville(878) Phone: **800-866-1976**
210 Dodge St   Fax: 608-755-5853
Janesville WI 53547-0669

Local Retrieval Area: IL-Winnebago; WI-Columbia, Dane, Dodge, Green, Iowa, Jefferson, Rock, Sauk, Walworth.

Normal turn around time is the same day. Projects are generally billed by the number of names searched. Credit accounts are accepted. Credit cards are accepted for payment.
Their specialty is "Information Services". They also work with DOT records, boats, city directory library, bartenders and bowlers.

Gregg Investigations of Madison(879)
139 W Wilson Suite 211
Madison WI 53701-1641
Phone: **800-866-1976**
Fax: 608-755-5853

Local Retrieval Area: IL-Winnebago; WI-Columbia, Dane, Dodge, Green, Iowa, Jefferson, Rock, Sauk, Walworth.

Normal turn around time is the same day. Projects are generally billed by the number of names searched. Credit accounts are accepted.
They specialize in "Information Services". They also work with DOT records, boats, city directory library, bartenders and bowlers.

Gregory Abstract and Title Co Inc(880)
124 W Main
Osborne KS 67473
Phone: **913-346-5445**
Fax: 913-346-5446

Local Retrieval Area: KS-Osborne.

Normal turn around time is 12-24 hours. Projects are generally billed by the hour. Credit accounts are accepted.

Gregory County Abstract Co(881)
PO Box 352
Burke SD 57523
Phone: **605-775-2943**
Fax: 605-775-2943

Local Retrieval Area: SD-Gregory.

Normal turn around time is 10 days. Fee basis will vary by the type of project. All projects require prepayment.
They specialize in real estate.

Joe C Griffin(882)
PO Box 237
Ackerman MS 39735
Phone: **601-285-6080**
Fax:

Local Retrieval Area: MS-Choctaw.

Normal turn around time is 1-2 days. Projects are generally billed by the hour. The first project may require a prepayment.
Mr. Griffin specializes in marriage/divorce and property searches.

Charlotte Griffith(883)
Rt 1 Box 228
Clarksville MO 63336
Phone: **314-242-3488**
Fax:

Local Retrieval Area: MO-Linn, Pike.

Normal turn around time is varied depending on job. Projects are generally billed by the hour. The first project may require a prepayment.
Charlotte specializes in genealogy record searches.

Groesbeck Abstract & Title Co(884)
PO Box 127
Groesbeck TX 76642
Phone: **817-729-3806**
Fax: 817-729-5655

Local Retrieval Area: TX-Limestone.

Normal turn around time is 1-2 days. Fee basis will vary by the type of project. The first project may require a prepayment.

Grue Abstract Co(885)
PO Box 559
Webster SD 57274
Phone: **605-345-3891**
Fax:

Local Retrieval Area: SD-Day.

Normal turn around time is 5-10 days. Fee basis will vary by the type of project. Credit accounts are accepted.
They specialize in land title.

Guaranty Abstract & Title Co(886)
Box 319
Guymon OK 73942
Phone: **405-338-3374**
Fax: 405-338-3375

Local Retrieval Area: OK-Texas.

Normal turn around time is 1-3 weeks. Fee basis will vary by the type of project. Credit accounts are accepted.

Guaranty Abstract Co(887)
PO Box 859
Lamar CO 81052
Phone: **719-336-3261**
Fax: 719-336-8106

Local Retrieval Area: CO-Prowers.

Normal turn around time is 1-3 days. Fee basis is determined on "per name/description" or "flat rate". Credit accounts are accepted.
They specialize in real estate and title matters.

Guaranty Abstract Co(888)
PO Box 727
Silverton TX 79257
Phone: **806-823-2354**
Fax: 806-823-2354

Local Retrieval Area: TX-Briscoe.

Normal turn around time is 2-3 days. Projects are generally billed by the hour. The first project may require a prepayment.

Guaranty Abstract Co(889)
211 Live Oak St
Marlin TX 76661
Phone: **817-883-2112**
Fax: 817-883-3332

Local Retrieval Area: TX-Falls.

Normal turn around time is 2-3 days. Fee basis will vary by the type of project. All projects require prepayment.

Guaranty Abstract Co of Stigler Inc(890)
PO Box 278
Stigler OK 74462
Phone: **918-967-8876**
Fax:

Local Retrieval Area: OK-Haskell.

Normal turn around time is 1-2 weeks. Projects are generally billed by the hour. Credit accounts are accepted.
They specialize in land records.

Guaranty Land Title(891)
314 E High St Suite B
Jefferson City MO 65101
Phone: **314-636-8388**
Fax: 314-636-8835

Local Retrieval Area: MO-Boone, Callaway, Camden, Cole, Cooper, Howard, Moniteau, Osage.

Normal turn around time is 24-48 hours. There is a next day service on anything needed from the State government. Projects are generally billed by the number of names searched. Credit accounts are accepted.

Guaranty Title Co(892)
231 Hobson
Hot Springs AR 71913
Phone: **501-321-2856**
Fax: 501-321-9677

Local Retrieval Area: AR-Garland.

Normal turn around time is up to 1 week. Fee basis will vary by the type of project. Credit accounts are accepted.
They specialize in real estate titles.

Guaranty Title Co(893)
108 N Canyon
Carlsbad NM 88221-0430

Phone: **505-887-3593**
Fax: 505-885-5204

Local Retrieval Area: NM-Eddy.

Normal turn around time is 1 week. Fee basis will vary by the type of project. Credit accounts are accepted.
The same family has been in business in Eddy County for over 50 years.

Guaranty Title Co(894)
PO Box 481
Franklin TX 77856

Phone: **409-828-4688**
Fax: 409-828-3803

Local Retrieval Area: TX-Robertson.

Normal turn around time is up to a week. Fee basis will vary by the type of project. The first project may require a prepayment.

Guaranty Title of Grimes County(895)
PO Box 290
Anderson TX 77830

Phone: **409-873-2250**
Fax: 409-873-2056

Local Retrieval Area: TX-Grimes.

Normal turn around time is 2-4 days. Fee basis will vary by the type of project. The first project may require a prepayment.

Guaranty Title Co of Leon County(896)
PO Box 449
Centerville TX 75833

Phone: **903-536-2133**
Fax: 903-536-7643

Local Retrieval Area: TX-Leon.

Normal turn around time is up to a week. Fee basis will vary by the type of project. The first project may require a prepayment.

Guardsmark(897)
PO Box 1181
Memphis TN 38101

Phone: **901-522-7854**
Fax: 901-522-7858

Local Retrieval Area: TN-Shelby.

Normal turn around time is 24-48 hours. Fee basis will vary by the type of project. The first project may require a prepayment.
They specialize in background checks.

Jerry Guffy(898)
62 Public Square
Leitchfield KY 42754

Phone: **502-259-4828**
Fax: 502-259-8161

Local Retrieval Area: KY-Grayson.

Normal turn around time is 3-5 days. Projects are generally billed by the number of names searched. Credit accounts are accepted.
Jerry specializes in real estate searches.

Guier Abstract & Title Co(899)
137 S Main
Troy KS 66087

Phone: **913-985-3562**
Fax: 913-985-2322

Local Retrieval Area: KS-Doniphan.

Normal turn around time is 3 days. Fee basis varies by type of transaction. Credit accounts are accepted.

Max L Gum(900)
Rt 2 Box 144
Buckeye WV 24924-9651

Phone: **304-653-4631**
Fax:

Local Retrieval Area: WV-Pendleton, Pocahontas.

Normal turn around time is up to 3 weeks. Projects are generally billed by the hour. All projects require prepayment.
Max specializes in genealogy records.

Gundrum Realty Inc(901)
919 E 9th St
Rochester IN 46975

Phone: **219-223-8262**
Fax: 219-223-8425

Local Retrieval Area: IN-Cass, Fulton, Marshall, Miami.

Normal turn around time is 10 days. Projects are generally billed by the number of records located. Credit accounts are accepted. Credit cards are accepted for payment.
They specialize in real estate sales and service.

Guthrie County Abstract(902)
110 N 4th St
Guthrie Center IA 50115

Phone: **515-747-3705**
Fax:

Local Retrieval Area: IA-Guthrie.

Normal turn around time is 1-2 days. Fee basis varies by type of transaction. The first project may require a prepayment.

H & M Research Co(903)
107 Woodlawn Dr
Madison AL 35758

Phone: **205-461-8504**
Fax: 205-534-7919

Local Retrieval Area: AL-Calhoun, Cherokee, Colbert, Etowah, Jackson, Lauderdale, Lawrence, Limestone, Madison, Marshall, Morgan; TN-Franklin, Giles, Lincoln.

Normal turn around time is approximately 24 hours. Fee basis varies by type of transaction. Credit accounts are accepted.
They specialize in civil engineering, land research, public hearings, variances and oil, gas and mineral rights.

H S Black(904)
PO Box 717
Childress TX 79201

Phone: **817-937-3681**
Fax: 817-937-3682

Local Retrieval Area: TX-Childress.

Normal turn around time is 1-2 days. Fee basis will vary by the type of project. Credit accounts are accepted.

Haakon County Abstract Co(905)
Box 40
Philip SD 57567-0040

Phone: **605-859-2461**
Fax:

Local Retrieval Area: SD-Haakon.

Normal turn around time is 1 day except for real estate searches, which averages 7 days. Projects are generally billed by the number of names searched. Credit accounts are accepted. Personal checks are accepted.
Haakon County Abstract Co also has correspondent relationships in other jurisdictions, including Pennington, Jackson and Stanley. Their specialty is real esate title searches for abstracts or title insurance.

Haine & Murtagh(906)
PO Box 1258
Lexington VA 24450

Phone: 703-464-6306
Fax:

Local Retrieval Area: VA-Rockbridge, City of Buena Vista, City of Lexington.

Normal turn around time is 1-2 days. Projects are generally billed by the hour. The first project may require a prepayment. They specialize in criminal and family law searches.

Haley Abstract & Title Co(907)
320 S Main St
Ottawa KS 66067

Phone: 913-242-2457
Fax: 913-242-6830

Local Retrieval Area: KS-Franklin.

Normal turn around time is 1-2 days. Fee basis varies by type of transaction. Credit accounts are accepted.

Franklin I Hall(908)
308 Gibson Rd
Lexington SC 29072

Phone: 803-957-1243
Fax: 803-957-9359

Local Retrieval Area: SC-Aiken, Calhoun, Edgefield, Lexington, Newberry, Richland, Saluda.

Normal turn around time is 24-48 hours. ` Fee basis varies by type of transaction. Credit accounts are accepted.
Mr. Hall is associated with Lexington Title Co.

Halletsville Abstract & Title Co(909)
110 N Texana St
Halletsville TX 77964

Phone: 512-798-3291
Fax: 512-798-2257

Local Retrieval Area: TX-Lavaca.

Normal turn around time is 2 days. Fee basis will vary by the type of project. The first project may require a prepayment.

Halliwell Process Service(910)
4839 Tinawanda Creek Rd
North Tonawanda NY 14120

Phone: 800-231-4779
Fax:

Local Retrieval Area: NY-Erie, Niagara.

Normal turn around time is varied depending on project. Fee basis will vary by type of project. Credit accounts are accepted.
Halliwell Process Service also has correspondent relationships in other jurisdictions, including Cattaraugus and Chautauqua.

Hamilton & Johnson Inc(911)
PO Box 85
Wahoo NE 68066

Phone: 402-443-3081
Fax: 402-443-4120

Local Retrieval Area: NE-Saunders.

Normal turn around time is 24 hours. Projects are generally billed by the number of names searched. Credit accounts are accepted.

Sue P Hamm(912)
PO Box 46
Aurora NC 27806

Phone: 919-322-5015
Fax: 919-322-7205

Local Retrieval Area: NC-Beaufort, Bertie, Carteret, Craven, Greene, Hyde, Jones, Lenoir, Martin, Onslow, Pamlico, Pitt, Washington.

Normal turn around time is 24 -48 hours. Fee basis will vary by the type of project. Credit accounts are accepted.
Sue specializes in real estate, civil action, and lien searches.

Hancock County Abstract Co(913)
130 E 8th St
Garner IA 50438

Phone: 515-923-2454
Fax: 515-923-3381

Local Retrieval Area: IA-Hancock.

Normal turn around time is 2-3 days. Projects are generally billed by the number of records located. Credit accounts are accepted.

Hancock County Abstract Co Inc(914)
18 N State St
Greenfield IN 46140

Phone: 317-462-2446
Fax: 317-462-2488

Local Retrieval Area: IN-Hancock.

Normal turn around time is 1 day for judgement searches, and 2 to 5 days for title insurance searches. They charge by name for judgement searches only. Title insurance fees depend on amount of coverage required. Credit accounts are accepted. Personal checks are accepted.
They specialize in real estate and judgement searches, and title insurance.

Hand County Abstract & Title Co(915)
PO Box 368
Miller SD 57362

Phone: 605-853-2194
Fax:

Local Retrieval Area: SD-Hand.

Normal turn around time is 1 week. Projects are generally billed by the hour. Credit accounts are accepted.

C Kent Haney(916)
PO Box 206
Clarksdale MS 38614

Phone: 601-627-5501
Fax: 601-627-5502

Local Retrieval Area: MS-Coahoma.

Normal turn around time is 1-2 days. Fee basis varies by type of transaction. The first project may require a prepayment.
Mr. Haney specializes in personal injury and marriage/divorce searches.

Nancy Hanna(917)
PO Box 1463
Toms River NJ 08753

Phone: 908-349-9747
Fax: 908-286-6965

Local Retrieval Area: NJ-Ocean.

Normal turn around time is 24-48 hours. Projects are generally billed by the number of names searched. Credit accounts are accepted.

Hannaford Abstract & Title Co(918)
222 E Main St
Marion KS 66861

Phone: 316-382-2130
Fax: 316-382-3420

Local Retrieval Area: KS-Marion.

Normal turn around time is 3 days. Fee basis varies by type of transaction. The first project may require a prepayment.

Hansen Franklin County Land Title(919)
311 Main St
Union MO 63084

Phone: 314-583-2516
Fax: 314-583-4779

Local Retrieval Area: MO-Franklin.

Normal turn around time is 1 week. They charge a flat rate per project. Credit accounts are accepted.

Hanson County Land & Abstract(920)
PO Box 505
Alexandria SD 57311
Phone: **605-239-4559**
Fax: 605-239-4559

Local Retrieval Area: SD-Hanson.

Normal turn around time is 2 weeks. Fee basis will vary by the type of project. The first project may require a prepayment.

Harbor City Research Inc(921)
201 E Baltimore St Suite 630
Baltimore MD 21202
Phone: **410-539-0400**
Fax: 410-659-0517

Local Retrieval Area: MD-Anne Arundel, Baltimore, Harford, Howard, Montgomery, Prince George's, City of Baltimore.

Normal turn around time is 1-2 days. Projects are generally billed by the number of names searched or records located. The first project may require a prepayment.
Harbor City Research Inc also has correspondent relationships in other jurisdictions, including nationwide.

Mary K Harder(922)
Rt 1 Box 80
Dakota City NE 68731
Phone: **402-987-3684**
Fax:

Local Retrieval Area: IA-Monona, Woodbury; NE-Dakota.

Normal turn around time is varied depending on project. Projects are generally billed by the hour. Credit accounts are accepted.
Mary specializes in locating people, living or dead.

Hardin County Abstract Company(923)
158 Courthouse
Elizabethtown IL 62931
Phone: **618-287-7944**
Fax: 618-287-2161

Local Retrieval Area: IL-Hardin.

Normal turn around time is 1 week. Projects are generally billed by the number of records located. Credit accounts are accepted.
Hardin County Abstract Company also has correspondent relationships in other jurisdictions, including Pope County.

Harding County Abstract Co(924)
PO Box 87
Buffalo SD 57720
Phone: **605-375-3422**
Fax:

Local Retrieval Area: SD-Harding.

Normal turn around time is 2 weeks. Projects are generally billed by the hour. Credit accounts are accepted.
They specialize in title insurance.

Harding County Abstract and Title(925)
1330 Edgington Ave
Eldora IA 50627
Phone: **800-926-5555**
       515-858-5555
Fax: 515-858-5331

Local Retrieval Area: IA-Hardin.

Normal turn around time is 3 days. Projects are generally billed by the number of names searched. Credit accounts are accepted. Personal checks are accepted.

Harmon County Abstract(926)
PO Box 788
Hollis OK 73550
Phone: **405-688-9255**
Fax: 405-688-2287

Local Retrieval Area: OK-Harmon.

Normal turn around time is 72 hours. Projects are generally billed by the hour. Credit accounts are accepted.
They specialize in real estate and divorce matters.

Harmon Legal Process Service(927)
PO Box 1794
Jefferson City MO 65102
Phone: **314-635-6690**
Fax: 314-635-2339

Local Retrieval Area: MO-Boone, Callaway, Cole, Miller, Morgan, Osage.

Normal turn around time is 1 day. Projects are generally billed by the number of records located. Credit accounts are accepted.
They specialize in public record retrieval.

Harmon Personnel Services Inc(928)
50 Elliot St
Brattleboro VT 05301
Phone: **802-254-8639**
Fax:

Local Retrieval Area: MA-Franklin, Hampshire; NH-Cheshire; VT-Windham.

Normal turn around time is 1-2 days. Fee basis will vary by the type of search. Credit accounts are accepted. Will invoice to establised client.

Eileen Harris(929)
PO Box 381
Dandridge IN 37725
Phone: **615-397-7669**
Fax:

Local Retrieval Area: TN-Cocke, Grainger, Greene, Hamblen, Hawkins, Jefferson, Knox, Sevier.

Normal turn around time is 48 hours. Projects are generally billed by the number of names searched. Credit accounts are accepted. Personal checks are accepted.
Eileen specializes in title abstracting and registering of deeds.

Harrison County Abstract Co Inc(930)
1414 Main St
Bethany MO 64424
Phone: **816-425-3523**
Fax: 816-425-6698

Local Retrieval Area: MO-Harrison.

Normal turn around time is varied depending on project. Credit accounts are accepted.
They specialize in lien and real estate searches.

Harrison County Title and Guarnty(931)
114 N 2nd Ave
Logan IA 51546
Phone: **712-644-2703**
Fax: 712-644-2557

Local Retrieval Area: IA-Harrison.

Normal turn around time is 1 week. Projects are generally billed by the number of records located. Credit accounts are accepted.

Lawrence Harrison(932)
PO Box 385
Junction TX 76849
Phone: 915-446-2317
Fax:

Local Retrieval Area: TX-Kimble.

Normal turn around time is 24-48 hours. Projects are generally billed by the hour. Fee basis varies by type of transaction. Credit accounts are accepted.
Mr. Harrison does general law. He also does criminal and real estate.

Harry W Hawley Inc(933)
4 Couart St
Delhi NY 13753
Phone: 607-746-3864
Fax: 607-746-3339

Local Retrieval Area: NY-Delaware.

Normal turn around time is 3-10 days. Fee basis will vary by type of project. Credit accounts are accepted. Personal checks and or cash is accepted.
Harry W Hawley Inc also has correspondent relationships in other jurisdictions, including Otesgo, Scoharie and Chenango Counties.

Gayle Harvey(934)
245 Johnny Harvey Rd
Breeding KY 42715
Phone: 502-378-6452
Fax: 502-384-2116

Local Retrieval Area: KY-Adair, Cumberland, Green, Metcalfe, Taylor.

Normal turn around time is same day to 3 days. Fee basis will vary by the type of project. The first project may require a prepayment. Gayle has extensive experience as a deputy clerk at the Circuit and District Court levels.

Haskell Abstract & Title Co(935)
502 S 1st St
Haskell TX 79521
Phone: 817-864-2604
Fax:

Local Retrieval Area: TX-Haskell.

Normal turn around time is 1-2 days. Fee basis will vary by the type of project. The first project may require a prepayment.

Haskell County Abstract and Title(936)
109 S Inman
Sublette KS 67877
Phone: 316-675-2322
Fax: 316-675-2322

Local Retrieval Area: KS-Haskell.

Normal turn around time is 2 days. Projects are generally billed by the hour. Credit accounts are accepted.
They specialize in and title insurance.

Renee Hastings(937)
PO Box 561
Edgefield SC 29824
Phone: 803-637-5304
Fax: 803-637-6066

Local Retrieval Area: SC-Edgefield.

Normal turn around time is 1 week. Charges are varied depending on type of search. Credit accounts are accepted.

John A Hatcher(938)
101 W College St
Booneville MS 38829
Phone: 601-728-9444
Fax:

Local Retrieval Area: MS-Prentiss.

Normal turn around time is 1-2 days. Projects are generally billed by the hour. The first project may require a prepayment.
Mr. Hatcher is an attorney in general practice.

Hawkins and Campbell Inc(939)
800 N 4th St
Phoenix AZ 85004
Phone: 602-254-6147
Fax: 602-271-4517

Local Retrieval Area: AZ-Maricopa.

Normal turn around time is 24 hours. Projects are generally billed by the number of names searched. Credit accounts are accepted. Hawkins and Campbell Inc also has correspondent relationships in other jurisdictions, including all of Arizona.

Marlene Hawley(940)
41 Kau Trail
Pasco WA 99301
Phone: 509-547-6207
Fax:

Local Retrieval Area: WA-Benton.

Normal turn around time is 2 days. Fee basis will vary by the type of search Credit accounts are accepted.

Robert E Hawthorne(941)
PO Box 603
Kenbridge VA 23944
Phone: 804-676-3275
Fax: 804-676-2286

Local Retrieval Area: VA-Brunswick, Charlotte, Lunenburg, Mecklenburg, Prince Edward.

Normal turn around time is 1-5 days. Projects are generally billed by the hour. Credit accounts are accepted.
They specialize in real estate and commerical searches.

Hayes & Associates(942)
4235 Lindell Blvd
St Louis MO 63108
Phone: 314-535-3838
Fax: 314-534-1776

Local Retrieval Area: IL-Jersey, Madison, St. Clair; MO-Franklin, Jefferson, Warren.

Normal turn around time is 24-72 hours for St. Louis City, St. Louis County and St. Charles. 3-5 working days for all other areas. Projects are generally billed by the number of names searched. The first project may require a prepayment.

Brenette Haynes(943)
114 Belvedere Ct
Cleveland MS 38732
Phone: 601-843-2071
Fax:

Local Retrieval Area: MS-Bolivar.

Normal turn around time is 1-2 days. Projects are generally billed by the number of names searched. All projects require prepayment. Brenette specializes in the Cleveland courts. A FAX number is available upon request.

Heartland Information Services Inc(944)
821 Marquette Ave Suite 404
Minneapolis MN 55402
Phone: **612-371-9255**
Fax: 612-371-9262

Local Retrieval Area: MN-Anoka, Dakota, Hennepin, Ramsey, Scott, Washington, Wright.

Normal turn around time is 24-48 hours. Project billing methods vary. Credit accounts are accepted.

Heartland Information Services Inc also has correspondent relationships in other jurisdictions, including all counties in Minnesota and North Dakota. They have all Minnesota Secretary of State UCC microfilm on site.

Heartland Title and Abstract Co(945)
28 S 15th Ave
St Cloud MN 56301
Phone: **800-450-8860**
          612-253-8860
Fax: 612-253-5606

Local Retrieval Area: MN-Benton, Meeker, Sherburne, Stearns, Wright.

Normal turn around time is 10 days. Fee basis will vary by type of project. All projects require prepayment. Credit cards are accepted for payment. They will also invoice.

They specialize in title insurance and real estate closings.

Kelly Heatwole(946)
221 Sugar Maple Lane
Harrisonburg VA 22801
Phone: **703-434-6650**
Fax:

Local Retrieval Area: VA-Rockingham; WV-Grant, Hampshire, Hardy, Mineral, Pendleton.

Normal turn around time is 2-4 days. Projects are generally billed by the hour. Credit accounts are accepted.

Mr. Heatwole specializes in real estate.

Hebert Land Services(947)
PO Box 772
Poteau OK 74953
Phone: **918-647-9524**
Fax: 918-647-9524

Local Retrieval Area: AR-Crawford, Franklin, Logan, Pope, Scott, Sebastian, Yell; OK-Haskell, Latimer, Le Flore, Pittsburg, Sequoyah.

Normal turn around time is 1-2 days. Fee basis is determined on a "per hour/day". Credit accounts are accepted.

Hebert Land Services also has correspondent relationships in other jurisdictions, including nationwide. They specialize in oil and gas.

Heil Investigations Agency Inc(948)
10 President Wy
Belleville IL 62223
Phone: **618-277-6045**
Fax: 618-233-8759

Local Retrieval Area: IL-Clinton, Madison, Monroe, St. Clair, Washington; MO-St. Louis, City of St. Louis.

Normal turn around time is 24-48 hours. Projects are generally billed by the hour. Credit accounts are accepted.

They specialize in asset searches.

Held Abstract Co Inc(949)
26 N Monroe
Williamsport IN 47993-0068
Phone: **317-762-2457**
Fax: 317-762-2458

Local Retrieval Area: IN-Warren.

Normal turn around time is 2 weeks. Fee basis will vary by type of project. All projects require prepayment.

Helena Abstract & Title Co(950)
PO Box 853
Helena MT 59624
Phone: **406-442-5080**
Fax: 406-442-6179

Local Retrieval Area: MT-Lewis and Clark.

Normal turn around time is 2-5 days. Fee basis varies by type of transaction. All projects require prepayment.

They specialize in real estate searches.

Hempstead County Abstract & Title(951)
401 S Washington
Hope AR 71801
Phone: **501-777-2351**
Fax: 501-777-6033

Local Retrieval Area: AR-Hempstead.

Normal turn around time is 1 week. Projects are generally billed by the number of records located. Fee basis may also be by order. Credit accounts are accepted.

Hendrich Abstract Co Inc(952)
Room 1 County Courthouse
Terre Haute IN 47807
Phone: **812-232-2752**
Fax: 812-235-2718

Local Retrieval Area: IN-Clay, Vigo.

Normal turn around time is varied depending on project. Projects are generally billed by the number of names searched or records located. Credit accounts are accepted.

Henry County Abstract Co(953)
300 S Adams St
Mt Pleasant IA 52641
Phone: **319-385-9017**
Fax:

Local Retrieval Area: IA-Henry.

Normal turn around time is 2-3 days. Fee basis will vary by the type of project. Credit accounts are accepted.

Henry County Abstract Co(954)
1111 Broad St
New Castle IN 47362
Phone: **317-529-0302**
Fax:

Local Retrieval Area: IN-Henry.

Normal turn around time is 2-5 days. Projects are generally billed by the number of names searched or records located. Credit accounts are accepted.

Henry County Abstract Co(955)
101 N Main St
Clinton MO 64735
Phone: **800-748-7985**
          816-885-6188
Fax: 816-885-8278

Local Retrieval Area: MO-Henry.

Normal turn around time is 2-5 days. Fee basis will vary by the type of project. Credit accounts are accepted.

They specialize in title searches.

Matthew D Henry(956)
PO Box 149
Pawnee OK 74058
Phone: **918-762-3190**
Fax:

Local Retrieval Area: OK-Pawnee.

Normal turn around time is 1 week. Projects are generally billed by the hour. Credit accounts are accepted.

Mr. Henry is an attorney and specializes in real estate, probate, and adoptions.

Anna Marie Henson(957)
Rt 3 Box 363
Bowling Green MO 63334
Phone: 314-324-2531
Fax:

Local Retrieval Area: MO-Pike.

Normal turn around time is 2-3 weeks. Projects are generally billed by the hour. All projects require prepayment.

Herbert Abstract Co Inc(958)
1131 Pithon St
Lake Charles LA 70601
Phone: 318-439-5600
Fax: 318-439-1035

Local Retrieval Area: LA-Calcasieu Parish, Cameron Parish.

Normal turn around time is 2-10 days. Fee basis will vary by type of project. Credit accounts are accepted.
They specialize in mortgage and conveyance certificates.

Heritage Personnel Services Inc(959)
PO Box 1284
Manchester VT 05255
Phone: 802-362-5613
Fax:

Local Retrieval Area: VT-Bennington, Rutland, Windsor.

Normal turn around time is 1-2 days. Fee basis will vary by the type of project . Credit accounts are accepted. Will invoice to established client.

Heritage Title Inc(960)
421 N Burlington
Hastings NE 68901
Phone: 402-463-6208
Fax: 402-463-6203

Local Retrieval Area: NE-Adams.

Normal turn around time is 48 hours. Projects are generally billed by the hour. Credit accounts are accepted.
They specialize in title insurance searches.

Gilbert S Hetrich(961)
PO Box 743
Manahawkin NJ 08050
Phone: 908-286-9233
Fax: 609-660-0152

Local Retrieval Area: NJ-Monmouth, Ocean.

Normal turn around time is varied depending on project. Fee basis will vary by the type of project. The first project may require a prepayment.
They have 22 years experience in real estate record searches.

Anne Hetrick(962)
174 Bernard Dr
Manahawkin NJ 08050
Phone: 609-966-0030
Fax: 609-966-3460

Local Retrieval Area: NJ-Camden.

Normal turn around time is 2-3 days. Fee basis will vary by the type of project. The first project may require a prepayment. They will accept personal checks.

Hickman Land Title(963)
PO Box 386
Logan UT 84323-0386
Phone: 800-365-7760
801-752-0582
Fax: 801-752-0386

Local Retrieval Area: UT-Cache, Rich.

Normal turn around time is 1-2 days. Projects are generally billed by the hour. Credit accounts are accepted.

Carol Hickox(964)
PO Box 11
Nampa ID 83653
Phone: 208-466-2555
Fax:

Local Retrieval Area: ID-Ada, Adams, Boise, Canyon, Elmore, Gem, Owyhee, Payette, Valley, Washington.

Normal turn around time is 5 days. Rush service is available in 24 hours. Projects are generally billed by the number of records located. Credit accounts are accepted.
Carol specializes in UCC record searches.

Attorney John O Hicks III(965)
PO Box 64
Calhoun KY 42327
Phone: 502-273-5749
Fax:

Local Retrieval Area: KY-Daviess, McLean, Muhlenberg.

Normal turn around time is 2 days for McLean County and up to 1 week for Muhlenberg and Daviess Counties. Fee basis varies by type of transaction. The first project may require a prepayment.

Hidalgo County Abstract(966)
PO Box 188
Lordsburg NM 88045
Phone: 505-542-9181
Fax: 505-542-9190

Local Retrieval Area: NM-Hidalgo.

Normal turn around time is 2 days. Projects are generally billed by the number of names searched. Credit accounts are accepted. A deposit is required.
They specialize in land searches.

Hiett Title Co(967)
119 N Grand Ave
Houston MO 65689
Phone: 417-967-3660
Fax: 417-967-4840

Local Retrieval Area: MO-Texas, Wright.

Normal turn around time is 1 week. Projects are generally billed by the hour. Credit accounts are accepted. Type of payment may vary depending on project.
They specialize in title insurance.

Hiett Title Company(968)
403 W 3rd
Mountain Grove MO 65711
Phone: 417-926-6163
Fax: 417-926-6166

Local Retrieval Area: MO-Douglas, Texas, Wright.

Normal turn around time is 1-2 weeks. Projects are generally billed by the number of names searched. The first project may require a prepayment.
They specialize in real estate records, chains of title and encumbrances.

Highlands Abstract and Title Co(969)
126 E Center St
Sebring FL 33870
Phone: 813-385-0340
Fax: 813-385-5802

Local Retrieval Area: FL-Highlands.

Normal turn around time is 7-10 working days. Projects are generally billed by the number of names searched. Credit accounts are accepted.
They specialize in title insurance searches.

Hill County Title Co(970)
PO Box 1688
Havre MT 59501
Phone: **406-265-7624**
Fax: 406-265-7624

Local Retrieval Area: MT-Hill.

Normal turn around time is 2-3 days. Projects are generally billed by the hour. Credit accounts are accepted.

Hill's Records Research(971)
PO Box 702
Bridgeport CA 93517
Phone: **619-932-7296**
Fax: 619-932-7520

Local Retrieval Area: CA-Mono.

Normal turn around time is the same day to 1 day. Projects are generally billed by the hour. Fee will include copy cost and/or FAX costs. Credit accounts are accepted.
They specialize in land title, property tax, foreclosure posting and trustee sales.

Rebecca Hill(972)
420 S Monroe St
Tiffin OH 44883
Phone: **419-448-4607**
Fax:

Local Retrieval Area: OH-Crawford, Hancock, Huron, Seneca.

Normal turn around time is 10 days. Projects are generally billed by the hour. Credit accounts are accepted.
Rebecca specializes in genealogy and vital statistic searches.

Hill-N-Dale Abstractors Inc(973)
20 Scotchtown Ave
Goshen NY 10924
Phone: **914-294-5110**
Fax: 914-294-9581

Local Retrieval Area: NY-Dutchess, Orange, Rockland, Sullivan, Ulster.

Normal turn around time is 2-3 days. Projects are generally billed by the number of names searched. Credit accounts are accepted.

Hillam Abstracting & Insurance (974)
PO Box 875
Brigham City UT 84302
Phone: **801-723-5207**
Fax: 801-723-5208

Local Retrieval Area: UT-Box Elder, Cache.

Normal turn around time is 1 day. Fee basis will vary by the type of project. Credit accounts are accepted.
They specialize in real estate.

Hillsdale Title Company(975)
22 N Howell
Hillsdale MI 49242
Phone: **517-437-7345**
Fax: 517-439-1659

Local Retrieval Area: MI-Hillsdale.

Normal turn around time is up to 1 weeks. Fee basis will vary by type of project. Credit accounts are accepted.
They specialize in real estate and title research.

Hines & Hines Lawyers(976)
507 Chief St
Benkelman NE 69021-0607
Phone: **308-423-2611**
Fax: 308-423-2628

Local Retrieval Area: NE-Chase, Dundy, Hitchcock, Red Willow.

Normal turn around time is 2 days. Projects are generally billed by the hour. Credit accounts are accepted. They accept personal checks.
Hines & Hines Lawyers also has correspondent relationships in other jurisdictions, including Perkins, Hayes and Keith Counties. Their areas of expertise are title insurance, real estate and probate.

Hinsdale County Title Co(977)
PO Box 69
Lake City CO 81235
Phone: **303-944-2614**
Fax:

Local Retrieval Area: CO-Hinsdale.

Normal turn around time is 3-5 days. Projects are generally billed by the hour. The first project may require a prepayment.
They specialize in real estate.

Hodgeman County Abstract & Title(978)
112 E Bramley
Jetmore KS 67854
Phone: **316-357-8328**
Fax:

Local Retrieval Area: KS-Hodgeman.

Normal turn around time is 1-2 days. Fee basis varies by type of transaction. Credit accounts are accepted.

Hogan Land Title Co(979)
921 Boonville
Springfield MO 65802
Phone: **417-869-6319**
Fax:

Local Retrieval Area: MO-Christian, Dallas, Greene, Taney.

Normal turn around time is 3 days. Fee basis varies by type of transaction. Credit accounts are accepted.

Holden Abstract Co(980)
202 W Wood St
Albany MO 64402
Phone: **816-726-3417**
Fax:

Local Retrieval Area: MO-Gentry.

Normal turn around time is varied depending on project. Fee basis is per document. Credit accounts are accepted.
They specialize in title searches.

Hollenbeck Title Co(981)
PO Box 215
Vienna MO 65582
Phone: **314-422-3633**
Fax: 314-422-6190

Local Retrieval Area: MO-Maries.

Normal turn around time is 48 hours. Projects are generally billed by the number of names searched or records located. Credit accounts are accepted.

Mickey Holley(982)
2886 Greene St
Lake Station IN 46405
Phone: **219-962-2250**
Fax: 219-962-2250

Local Retrieval Area: IN-Elkhart, Fulton, Jasper, Kosciusko, Lagrange, La Porte, Marshall, Newton, Porter, Pulaski, St. Joseph, Starke, Steuben.

Normal turn around time is 3-5 days. They charge per county and project. Credit accounts are accepted.

Hollingsworth Court Reporting Inc(983)
10761 Perkins Rd Suite A
Baton Rouge LA 70810
Phone: 504-769-3386
Fax: 504-769-1814

Local retrieval ares include counties in Alabama, Arizona, Arkansas, Colorado, Florida, Kentucky, Louisiana, Michigan, MIssissippi, New Mexico, Tennessee and Utah.

Normal turn around time is 5 days for major metrolpolitan areas and 15 days for outlying locations. Online computer ordering is also available. Projects are generally billed by the number of names searched. Credit accounts are accepted.

They specialize in derrogatory information including: tax liens, judgements and bankruptcies. An on line data base service will be available in 1993.

Beverly Gail Holman(984)
3550 Hwy 1108
Parksville KY 40464
Phone: 606-332-7980
Fax:

Local Retrieval Area: KY-Anderson, Boyle, Casey, Garrard, Jessamine, Lincoln, Marion, Mercer, Washington.

Normal turn around time is 24 hours. Projects are generally billed by the hour. Credit accounts are accepted.
Ms. Holman specializes in deed research.

Home Abstract & Title Co(985)
2310 19th St
Gulfport MS 39501
Phone: 601-863-4783
Fax: 601-863-4783

Local Retrieval Area: MS-Hancock, Harrison, Jackson.

Normal turn around time is 1-2 days. Projects are generally billed by the hour. All projects require prepayment.

Home Abstract Co(986)
PO Box 520
Martin SD 57551
Phone: 605-685-6558
Fax:

Local Retrieval Area: SD-Bennett.

Normal turn around time is 2 weeks. Projects are generally billed by the hour. Credit accounts are accepted.

Homestead Title(987)
7600 E Grand River
Brighton MI 48116
Phone: 313-229-4770
Fax: 313-229-6360

Local Retrieval Area: MI-Genesee, Lapeer, Livingston, Oakland, Shiawassee, Washtenaw.

Normal turn around time is 4-5 days. Fee basis is per search. The first project may require a prepayment.
They specialize in real estate matters.

Honolulu Information Service(988)
1103 9th Ave Suite 202
Honolulu HI 96816
Phone: 808-733-2058
Fax:

Local Retrieval Area: HI-Hawaii, Honolulu, Kauai, Maui.

Normal turn around time is 72 hours. A 24 hour rush service is also available. Projects are generally billed by the number of records located. Credit accounts are accepted.
Honolulu Information Service also has correspondent relationships in other jurisdictions, including nationwide. They specialize in obtaining government documents, using Hawaii's FOIA if necessary.

Hood & Whaler(989)
41 E Pike St
Cynthiana KY 41031
Phone: 606-234-4321
Fax:

Local Retrieval Area: KY-Harrison.

Normal turn around time is 3-4 days. Projects are generally billed by the hour. The first project may require a prepayment.
They are a general practice law firm.

Hoover Professional Investigative(990)
3202 E "M"
Tacoma WA 98404-4027
Phone: 206-272-5090
Fax:

Local Retrieval Area: WA-King, Kitsap, Mason, Pierce, Snohomish.

Normal turn around time is 1-7 days. Projects are generally billed by the hour. The first project may require a prepayment.
Hoover Professional Investigative also has correspondent relationships in other jurisdictions, including Pierce, King, Kitsap and Mason. They specialize in all phases of investigations.

Horger Barnewll & Reid(991)
PO Drawer 329
Orangeburg SC 29116
Phone: 803-531-3000
Fax: 803-531-3030

Local Retrieval Area: SC-Bamberg, Calhoun, Dorchester, Orangeburg.

Normal turn around time is 2-3 days. Projects are generally billed by the hour. The first project may require a prepayment.
Horger Barnewll & Reid also has correspondent relationships in other jurisdictions, including the rest of the state.

Hornor-Morris Abstract Co(992)
711 Walnut St
Helena AR 72342
Phone: 501-338-8306
Fax:

Local Retrieval Area: AR-Phillips.

Normal turn around time is 3-5 days. Projects are generally billed by the hour. The first project may require a prepayment.

Hornthal Riley Ellis & Maland(993)
PO Box 220
Elizabeth City NC 27907-0220
Phone: 919-335-0871
Fax: 919-335-4223

Local Retrieval Area: NC-Camden, Chowan, Dare, Gates, Hertford, Pasquotank, Perquimans, Tyrrell, Washington.

Normal turn around time is 48 hours. Projects are generally billed by the hour. Fee basis varies by type of transaction. Credit accounts are accepted.
They are a full service law firm. They specialize in litigation, real estate, corporate practice and criminal practice.

Hot Spring County Title Services(994)
PO Box 622
Malvern AR 72104
Phone: 501-332-3770
Fax: 501-337-0729

Local Retrieval Area: AR-Garland, Grant, Hot Spring.

Normal turn around time is 3 days. Fee basis will vary by the type of project. Credit accounts are accepted.
They specialize in real estate records.

Florence Houchin(995)
Rt 14 Box 2350
Kennewick WA 99337
Phone: **509-582-7796**
Fax:

Local Retrieval Area: WA-Benton, Franklin.

Normal turn around time is 48 hours. However, Franklin City District Court only allows access on Thursdays. Projects are generally billed by the number of names searched. Credit accounts are accepted. Prepay is required from infrequent clients. They will invoice established customers.

Houghton Lake Title & Escrow Co(996)
3179 W Houghton Lake Dr
Prudenville MI 48651
Phone: **517-366-5551**
Fax: 517-366-5551

Local Retrieval Area: MI-Clare, Crawford, Gladwin, Missaukee, Ogemaw, Roscommon.

Normal turn around time is 1 day to 1 week. Fee basis is by rate sheet or per hour. Credit accounts are accepted.
They specialize in abstracting.

Houston Court Services(997)
PO Box 61645
Houston TX 77208-1645
Phone: **800-593-2023**
Fax: 713-464-7535

Local Retrieval Area: TX-Harris.

Normal turn around time is 48 hours. A 4 hour rush service is available. Projects are generally billed by the number of names searched. Credit accounts are accepted.
Houston Court Services also has correspondent relationships in other jurisdictions, including the southern states. They specialize in document retrieval and civil process.

Howard County Abstract & Title Co(998)
219 N Elm St
Cresco IA 52136
Phone: **319-547-4944**
Fax:

Local Retrieval Area: IA-Howard.

Normal turn around time is 1-2 days. Projects are generally billed by the number of names searched. The first project may require a prepayment.

Hubbard County Abstract Co Inc(999)
415 1/2 W 4th St
Park Rapids MN 56470
Phone: **218-732-3543**
Fax: 218-732-8864

Local Retrieval Area: MN-Hubbard.

Normal turn around time is 1-2 weeks. Rush service is also available. Projects are generally billed by the number of records located. Credit accounts are accepted. Personal checks are accepted.

Hubbard-Kavanaugh Abstr & Title(1000)
106 S Fisher St
Versailles MO 65084
Phone: **314-378-4411**
Fax: 314-378-6385

Local Retrieval Area: MO-Morgan.

Normal turn around time is 24 hours. Projects are generally billed by the number of records located. Credit accounts are accepted. They specialize in land titles.

Stephen P Huddleston(1001)
PO Box 807
Warsaw KY 41095
Phone: **606-567-2818**
Fax:

Local Retrieval Area: KY-Gallatin.

Normal turn around time is 2-3 days. Projects are generally billed by the hour. Credit accounts are accepted.
Mr. Huddleston is also the prosecuting attorney for the county.

Bill Hunt(1002)
PO Box 604
Double Springs AL 35553
Phone: **205-489-5743**
Fax:

Local Retrieval Area: AL-Winston.

Normal turn around time is 2 days. Projects are generally billed by the hour. The first project may require a prepayment.
Mr. Hunt is an attorney.

Hunter & Oelke(1003)
PO Box 792
Dalhart TX 79022
Phone: **806-249-5632**
Fax:

Local Retrieval Area: TX-Dallam, Hartley.

Normal turn around time is 3-4 days. Projects are generally billed by the hour. The first project may require a prepayment.

Joel A Hunter(1004)
PO Box 215
Rolling Fork MS 39159
Phone: **601-873-6258**
Fax: 601-873-6903

Local Retrieval Area: MS-Issaquena, Sharkey.

Normal turn around time is 2 days. Projects are generally billed by the hour. The first project may require a prepayment.

Huron Shares Abstract & Title(1005)
206 S 3rd Street
Rogers City MI 49779
Phone: **517-734-3344**
Fax: 517-734-4920

Local Retrieval Area: MI-Alpena, Presque Isle.

Normal turn around time is 4 days. Fee basis will vary by the type of project. All projects require prepayment.
They specialize in title insurance, oil, gas and mineral research.

Huron Title Co(1006)
330 Michigan St
Port Huron MI 48060
Phone: **313-987-2141**
Fax: 313-987-1317

Local Retrieval Area: MI-St. Clair.

Normal turn around time is 5 days. Fee basis will vary by type of project. The first project may require a prepayment.
They specialize in real estate and title insurance.

Huron Title Co(1007)
PO Box 563
Huron SD 57350
Phone: **605-352-6157**
Fax: 605-352-7354

Local Retrieval Area: SD-Beadle.

Normal turn around time is 5-10 days. Fee basis will vary by the type of project. Credit accounts are accepted.
They specialize in land title searches.

Hurst Security Service Inc(1008)   **Phone: 800-747-5770**
1015 N 5th Ave   815-933-5770
Kankakee IL 60901   Fax: 815-933-9938

Local Retrieval Area: IL-Champaign, Grundy, Kankakee, Macon, Piatt, Vermilion.

Normal turn around time is 7 to 10 days. Projects are generally billed by the number of names searched. Credit accounts are accepted.

They specialize in investigations and surveillance.

Pam Hurst(1009)   **Phone: 615-238-5400**
7322 Royal Harbour Circle   Fax: 615-238-5400
Ooltewah TN 37363

Local Retrieval Area: GA-Catoosa; TN-Bradley, Hamilton, Marion, Meigs.

Normal turn around time is 1-3 days. Fees are based on a per search charge. Credit accounts are accepted.

Hutchinson Title Co(1010)   **Phone: 316-669-8289**
327 N Main   Fax: 316-669-8280
Hutchinson KS 67501

Local Retrieval Area: KS-Harvey, McPherson, Reno, Sedgwick.

Normal turn around time is 5 days. Fee basis varies by type of transaction. The first project may require a prepayment.

Hyland Abstract Co(1011)   **Phone: 913-325-2166**
PO Box 255   Fax: 913-325-2046
Washington KS 66968

Local Retrieval Area: KS-Washington.

Normal turn around time is 2-3 days. Fee basis varies by type of transaction. All projects require prepayment.

Hylind Info Quest(1012)   **Phone: 800-292-9493**
230 Broadway Suite 100   Fax: 800-437-3796
Springfield IL 62701

Local Retrieval Area: IL-Cass, Christian, Logan, Macon, Menard, Morgan, Sangamon.

Normal turn around time is 1-2 days. Projects are generally billed by the number of names searched. Credit accounts are accepted.
Hylind Info Quest also has correspondent relationships in other jurisdictions, including all counties in Illinois.

Hylind Infoquest(1013)   **Phone: 800-468-4310**
1901 Anderson Hwy   Fax: 800-448-5350
Powhatan VA 23139

Local Retrieval Area: VA-Arlington, Chesterfield, Fairfax, Henrico, Powhatan, Prince William, Spotsylvania, City of Alexandria, City of Fredericksburg, City of Richmond.

Normal turn around time is 1-3 days. Projects are generally billed by the number of names searched or records located. Credit accounts are accepted.
Hylind Infoquest also has correspondent relationships in other jurisdictions, including all counties in Virginia and nationwide. They specialize in UCC searches. An on-line computer link system will be available in 1993.

I & S Consulting(1014)   **Phone: 616-846-0719**
PO Box 822   Fax: 616-846-4165
Grand Haven MI 49417

Local Retrieval Area: MI-Allegan, Kent, Muskegon, Oceana, Ottawa.

Normal turn around time is 2 working days. Projects are generally billed by the hour. Credit accounts are accepted.
I & S Consulting also has correspondent relationships in other jurisdictions, including Mason, Grand Traverse, Ingam, Ionia, Kalamazoo, Mecosta and Van Buren. They specialize in surveillance.

I.N.S. Investigative Agency(1015)   **Phone: 405-323-6362**
PO Box 771   Fax: 405-323-6109
Clinton OK 73601

Local Retrieval Area: OK-Beckham, Custer, Dewey, Greer, Roger Mills, Washita.

Normal turn around time is 3 to 4 days. Projects are generally billed by the hour. A mileage charge is also added. Credit accounts are accepted.

They specialize in criminal and vital statistic searches.

IH Publishing(1016)   **Phone: 410-668-1559**
8743 Cimarron Circle   Fax: 410-537-4744
Baltimore MD 21234

Local Retrieval Area: MD-Anne Arundel, Baltimore, Carroll, Cecil, Harford, Howard, Montgomery, City of Baltimore.

Normal turn around time is 24 hours. Online computer ordering is also available. Projects are generally billed by the number of names searched. Credit accounts are accepted.
IH Publishing also has correspondent relationships in other jurisdictions, including Frederick and Washington counties as well as Washington, DC. They specialize in reporting for title companies and other types of courthouse research.

ILS Abstract(1017)   **Phone: 717-455-9030**
1201 N Church St Bldg A Suite 208   Fax: 717-455-9036
Hazleton PA 18201

Local Retrieval Area: PA-Carbon, Columbia, Luzerne, Schuylkill.

Normal turn around time is 4-7 days. Projects are generally billed by the number of names searched or records located. The first project may require a prepayment.

They specialize in real estate searches and prepare deeds.

Ida County Abstract Co(1018)   **Phone: 712-364-2287**
217 Main St   Fax:
Ida Grove IA 51445

Local Retrieval Area: IA-Ida.

Normal turn around time is 2-3 days. Fee basis will vary by the type of project. Credit accounts are accepted.

Incorporating Services Ltd(1019)
15 E North St
Dover DE 19903

Phone: **800-346-4646**
302-678-0855
Fax: 302-678-3150

Local Retrieval Area: DE-All counties.

Normal turn around time is 1-5 working days. Projects are generally billed by the number of names searched. Credit accounts are accepted. Credit cards are accepted for payment. Personal checks, certified checks, money orders or cash are accepted.

Independence County Abstract(1020)
150 S Broad St
Batesville AR 72501

Phone: **501-793-3333**
Fax: 501-793-3343

Local Retrieval Area: AR-Independence.

Normal turn around time is 5-10 days. Rush service is also available. Projects are generally billed by the hour. A minimum charge also applies. Credit accounts are accepted.
They specialize in real estate.

Independent Abstract & Title(1021)
525 Caroline St
Key West FL 33040

Phone: **305-294-5105**
Fax: 305-294-5354

Local Retrieval Area: FL-Monroe.

Normal turn around time is 2 weeks. They charge a flat rate per project. The first project may require a prepayment.
They specialize in title insurance.

Independent Abstract Inc(1022)
45 N Market St
Batavia OH 45103

Phone: **513-732-9103**
Fax: 513-732-9154

Local Retrieval Area: KY-Boone, Campbell, Kenton; OH-Brown, Butler, Clermont, Clinton, Hamilton, Highland, Warren.

Normal turn around time is 24-72 hours. Projects are generally billed by the number of records located. Credit accounts are accepted.
They specialize in 40 year and current owner real estate title searches.

Independent Abstracting Service(1023)
4111 Central Ave NE
Columbia Heights MN 55421

Phone: **612-789-8440**
Fax: 612-789-9294

Local Retrieval Area: MN-Anoka, Carver, Chisago, Dakota, Hennepin, Isanti, Red Lake, Scott, Sherburne, Washington, Wright.

Normal turn around time is 3-5 days. Fee basis will vary by type of project. All projects require prepayment. They will also invoice.

Independent Research(1024)
746 Dunhill Dr
Orlando FL 32825

Phone: **407-277-0076**
Fax:

Local Retrieval Area: FL-Brevard, Orange, Osceola, Seminole, Volusia.

Normal turn around time is 24 hours or less. Projects are generally billed by the number of names searched. Credit accounts are accepted.
They specialize in pending litigation and asset searches.

Indiana Title Co(1025)
203-05 W Tipton St
Seymour IN 47274

Phone: **812-522-3216**
Fax: 812-523-1018

Local Retrieval Area: IN-Many counties in this state are covered. See the county index for actual coverage..

Normal turn around time is 24-96 hours. Projects are generally billed by the number of names searched or records located. Credit accounts are accepted.
They specialize in abstracts and title searches.

Inform(1026)
8200 Neely Dr Suite 159
Austin TX 78759

Phone: **512-345-4136**
Fax: 512-345-4371

Local Retrieval Area: TX-Bexar, Travis.

Normal turn around time is 24-48 hours. Project billing methods vary. Credit accounts are accepted. Personal checks are accepted.
Inform also has correspondent relationships in other jurisdictions, including the state of Texas. They specialize in bankruptcy, researching, paralegal "in-depth" searching, attending docket calls and hearings for out of town attorneys in the Austin cours. They also perform environmental research and monitor Texas Legislature.

Informa Alaska Inc(1027)
PO Box 190908
Anchorage AK 99519-0793

Phone: **907-563-4375**
Fax: 907-345-0793

Local Retrieval Area: AK-Anchorage Borough.

Normal turn around time is 48 hours. Projects are generally billed by the hour. The first project may require a prepayment.
Informa Alaska Inc also has correspondent relationships in other jurisdictions, including the rest of the state. They specialize in public record retrieval.

Information Research(1028)
251 Florida St Suite 402
Baton Rouge LA 70801

Phone: **504-387-3878**
Fax: 504-383-4507

Local Retrieval Area: LA-East Baton Rouge Parish, Livingston Parish, West Baton Rouge Parish.

Normal turn around time is 4-5 days. Rush service is also available. Projects are generally billed by the hour. The first project may require a prepayment.
They provide on-line and library research, document delivery and background support for litigation and business development, and court records.

Information Retrieval Service(1029)
404 James Robertson Pkwy
Nashville TN 37219-1505

Phone: **615-255-1708**
Fax:

Local Retrieval Area: TN-Davidson.

Normal turn around time is 2-24 hours. Online computer ordering is also available. Fee basis will vary by the type of project. The first project may require a prepayment.
They specialize in public records search, locate skips and assets. Their computer link number is 62052334.

Information Svcs of Anchorage(1030)
PO Box 220647
Anchorage AK 99522-0647
Phone: 907-272-4688
Fax: 907-274-6449

Local Retrieval Area: AK-Anchorage Borough.

Normal turn around time is 2-3 days. Online computer ordering is also available. Projects are generally billed by the hour. All projects require prepayment.

Ingham County Sheriff-Civil Div(1031)
PO Box 80165
Lansing MI 48908-0165
Phone: 517-393-1200
Fax: 517-393-9330

Local Retrieval Area: MI-Clinton, Eaton, Ingham.

Normal turn around time is 2-3 days. Projects are generally billed by the hour. Credit accounts are accepted.
They can also visit the Department of Corrections.

Instant Information Systems(1032)
9916 Oakdale Woods Court
Vienna VA 22181
Phone: 703-281-9312
Fax: 703-281-7669

Local Retrieval Area: DC-All counties; MD-Montgomery; VA-Arlington, Fairfax, City of Alexandria, City of Fairfax, City of Falls Church.

Normal turn around time is typically the same day as the order is received. Projects are generally billed by the hour. Credit accounts are accepted.
They also specialize in retrieval from federal sources in the Washington DC area.

Insured Titles Inc(1033)
PO Box 4706
Missoula MT 59806
Phone: 406-728-7900
Fax: 406-728-5892

Local Retrieval Area: MT-Missoula.

Normal turn around time is 3-5 days. Projects are generally billed by the number of names searched. Credit accounts are accepted.
They specialize in real estate record searches.

Intelligence Network Inc(1034)
PO Box 727
Clearwater FL 34617-0727
Phone: 813-449-0072
Fax: 813-448-0949

Local Retrieval Area: FL-Hillsborough, Pinellas.

Normal turn around time is 24 hours. Projects are generally billed by the number of names searched or records located. Credit accounts are accepted.
They can search Dade, Broward and Palm Beach via computer data base.

Intelnet Inc(1035)
1177 W Loop S Suite 1620
Houston TX 77027
Phone: 800-876-0018
713-964-0018
Fax: 713-964-0064

Local Retrieval Area: TX-Dallas, Gregg, Harris, McLennan, Nueces, Nueces, Tarrant, Travis.

Normal turn around time is 24 hours. Projects are generally billed by the number of names searched. Credit accounts are accepted.
Intelnet Inc also has correspondent relationships in other jurisdictions, including a network of 480 paralegals nationwide. They specialize in pulling physical records as opposed to pulling only index information.

Inter-County Abstract(1036)
925 Main St
Honesdale PA 18431
Phone: 717-253-4734
Fax: 717-253-1359

Local Retrieval Area: PA-Pike, Wayne.

Normal turn around time is 10 days. Projects are generally billed by the number of names searched. All projects require prepayment. Inter-County Abstract also has correspondent relationships in other jurisdictions, including Lackawanna. They specialize in information certificats for real estate abstract.

Intercounty Clearance Corp(1037)
105 Chambers St
New York NY 10007
Phone: 800-229-4422
Fax: 212-349-0145

Local Retrieval Area: NY-Albany, Bronx, Kings, Nassau, New York, Queens, Rensselaer, Saratoga, Steuben, Westchester.

Normal turn around time is 2-3 days. Online computer ordering is also available. Projects are generally billed by the number of names searched. Fee may be based on location searched. Credit accounts are accepted. Credit cards are accepted for payment.
Intercounty Clearance Corporation also has correspondent relationships in other jurisdictions, including all counties nationwide. They have a nationwide network of correspondants. They have been in business since 1935. They also search pending suits, tax liens and mechanics liens.

International Investigators Inc(1038)
3216 N Pennsylvania St
Indianapolis IN 46205-3414
Phone: 317-925-7496
Fax: 317-926-1177

Local Retrieval Area: IN-Boone, Hamilton, Hancock, Hendricks, Johnson, Marion, Shelby.

Normal turn around time is 1-4 days. Projects are generally billed by the hour. The first project may require a prepayment.

International Research Bureau(1039)
1331 E Lafayette St Suite D
Tallahassee FL 32301
Phone: 800-447-2112
Fax: 904-561-1377

Local Retrieval Area: FL-Leon.

Normal turn around time is varied depending on project. Projects are generally billed by the number of names searched or records located. Credit accounts are accepted. Credit cards are accepted for payment. Personal checks are accepted.
International Research Bureau Inc (IRB) also has correspondent relationships in other jurisdictions, including the western portions of Florida.

Interstate Abstract Inc(1040)
413 Rt 70 E
Cherry Hill NJ 08876
Phone: 800-222-0090
609-795-4000
Fax: 609-795-9457

Local Retrieval Area: DE-All counties; NJ-All counties; PA-All counties.

Normal turn around time is varied depending on project. Projects are generally billed by the number of records located. Credit accounts are accepted.

Interstate Document Filings Inc(1041)   Phone: **908-530-4413**
2930 S Broad St   Fax: 908-530-6335
Trenton NJ 08610

Local Retrieval Area: NJ-All counties.

Normal turn around time is 24-48 hours. Projects are generally billed by the number of names searched. The first project may require a prepayment. Personal checks are accepted.

They also file at courts for clients and have a monitoring service, which follows action on pending cases.

Interwest Investigations(1042)   Phone: **303-223-2212**
PO Box 1773   Fax:
Ft Collins CO 80522

Local Retrieval Area: CO-Adams, Arapahoe, Boulder, Denver, Jefferson, Larimer, Weld.

Normal turn around time is 2-3 days. Projects are generally billed by the hour. All projects require prepayment.

They specialize in skip tracing.

Intra-Lex Investigations Inc(1043)   Phone: **712-233-1639**
505 6th St Suite 502   Fax: 712-255-1127
Sioux City IA 51101

Local Retrieval Area: IA-Cherokee, Dickinson, Monona, Plymouth, Sioux, Woodbury; NE-Cedar, Cuming, Dixon, Dodge, Douglas, Knox, Pierce, Sarpy, Stanton, Thurston, Washington, Wayne; SD-Clay, Lincoln, Minnehaha, Turner, Union, Yankton.

Normal turn around time is 24 hours. Projects are generally billed by the hour. Mileage charges will be added to the fee. A miminum fee applies. The first project may require a prepayment. They are a full line investigation agency.

Intranet Inc(1044)   Phone: **903-593-9817**
107 E Erwin   Fax: 903-593-1830
Tyler TX 75702

Local Retrieval Area: TX-Bexar, Harris, Jefferson, Smith, Tarrant, Travis.

Normal turn around time is 24-48 hours. Projects are generally billed by the number of names searched. Credit accounts are accepted. Personal checks are accepted.

Intranet Inc also has correspondent relationships in other jurisdictions, including Nueces County. They specialize in bankruptcy document retrieval.

Investigative & Paralegal Services(1045)   Phone: **704-552-2000**
3008 Fieldpointe Lane   Fax: 704-552-0053
Charlotte NC 28210

Local Retrieval Area: NC-Catawba, Gaston, Iredell, Lincoln, Mecklenburg, Rowan, Stanly, Union; SC-York.

Normal turn around time is 24-48 hours for Mecklenburg, 48-72 hours for all other counties. Project billing methods vary. A mileage expense may be encurred outside of Mecklenburg. Credit accounts are accepted.

Investigative & Paralegal Services also has correspondent relationships in other jurisdictions, including Guilford, Avery and Forsyth. They specialize in skip tracing, process service, background/asset searches, jury profiles, interviews and document retrieval.

Investigative Associates Inc(1046)   Phone: **214-235-9884**
800 E Campbell Rd Suite 199   Fax: 214-235-9885
Richardson TX 75081

Local Retrieval Area: TX-Collin, Dallas, Denton, Ellis, Kaufman, Rockwall, Tarrant.

Normal turn around time is one week. Projects are generally billed by the hour. The first project may require a prepayment.

They can retrieve records throught most of the US as needed.

Investigative Legal Services(1047)   Phone: **407-426-7433**
111 N Orange Ave Suite 1430   Fax: 407-426-6968
Orlando FL 32801

Local Retrieval Area: FL-Orange, Osceola, Seminole.

Normal turn around time is 5 days. Projects are generally billed by the hour. The first project may require a prepayment. Personal checks are accepted.

Investigative Legal Services also has correspondent relationships in other jurisdictions, including Florida. Mr. Eisenberg was a practicing trial lawyer for 30 years.

Investigative Resources(1048)   Phone: **718-317-0043**
150 Nassau St   Fax: 718-967-0688
New York NY 10038

Local Retrieval Area: NY-Bronx, Kings, New York, Queens, Richmond.

Normal turn around time is as soon as 4 hours. An emergency rush service is available. Projects are generally billed by the number of names searched or records located. The first project may require a prepayment.

They provide 1 hour service for Department of Motor Vehicle records.

Investigative Services for Attys(1049)   Phone: **901-278-6778**
PO Box 3092   Fax: 901-274-7640
Memphis TN 38173-0092

Local Retrieval Area: AR-Crittenden; MS-De Soto, Marshall, Tunica; TN-Fayette, Shelby, Tipton.

Normal turn around time is 24 hours. Online computer ordering is also available. Projects are generally billed by the hour. Credit accounts are accepted.

They specialize in located records when limited information is available.

Investigative and Attorney Svcs(1050)   Phone: **800-428-0419**
7210 Jordan Ave Suite B-65   818-905-5628
Canoga Park CA 91303   Fax:

Local Retrieval Area: CA-Los Angeles, Orange, Ventura.

Normal turn around time is 1-5 days. Projects are generally billed by the number of names searched or records located. They will give a discount to volume orders. All projects require prepayment. They will also invoice.

Investigative and Attorney Services also has correspondent relationships in other jurisdictions, including nationwide. They are a licensed private investigatinve agency and a full attorney service.

Iosco County Abstract Office Ltd(1051)
432 W Lake St
Tawas City MI 48764-0420
Phone: **517-362-3231**
Fax: 517-362-7844

Local Retrieval Area: MI-Iosco.

Normal turn around time is 5 working days or less. Projects are generally billed by the number of names searched or records located. The first project may require a prepayment. A setup fee is required for abstracts and searches only. Personal checks are accepted.
They specialize in title insurance and closings.

Iowa County Abstract Company(1052)
1048 Court Ave
Marengo IA 52301
Phone: **319-642-7321**
Fax: 319-642-7321

Local Retrieval Area: IA-Iowa.

Normal turn around time is 2-3 days for personal lien searches, and 1 to 2 weeks for a full, written search. Fee basis is per transaction. Credit accounts are accepted. Personal checks are accepted.

Iowa Title & Guaranty Co(1053)
115 S 2nd St
Maquoketa IA 52060
Phone: **319-652-6081**
Fax:

Local Retrieval Area: IA-Jackson.

Normal turn around time is 1-3 days. Fee basis will vary by the type of project. Credit accounts are accepted.
They also provide credit bureau services.

Iowa Title & Realty Co(1054)
203 1/2 N Main St
Charles City IA 50616
Phone: **515-228-1515**
Fax:

Local Retrieval Area: IA-Floyd.

Normal turn around time is 1-7 days. Fee basis will vary by the type of project. The first project may require a prepayment.

Irion County Abstract Co Inc(1055)
PO Box 800
Mertzon TX 76941
Phone: **915-835-2811**
Fax:

Local Retrieval Area: TX-Irion.

Normal turn around time is 2-3 days. Fee basis will vary by the type of project. The first project may require a prepayment.

Iron Title & Abstract Co(1056)
402 Silver St
Hurley WI 54534
Phone: **715-561-3576**
Fax: 715-561-5050

Local Retrieval Area: MI-Gogebic; WI-Iron, Iron.

Normal turn around time is 1-2 days. Fee basis varies by type of transaction. Credit accounts are accepted.

Iroquois Country Abstract Corp(1057)
PO Box 850
Oneonta NY 13820
Phone: **800-564-2466**
607-432-3614
Fax: 607-432-9761

Local Retrieval Area: NY-Chenango, Delaware, Otsego, Schoharie.

Normal turn around time is 4-7 days. Projects are generally billed by the number of names searched or records located. Credit accounts are accepted. Personal checks are accepted.

Isabella County Abstract(1058)
209 E Broadway
Mt Pleasant MI 48858
Phone: **517-773-3241**
Fax: 517-773-6221

Local Retrieval Area: MI-Isabella.

Normal turn around time is 1 week. Projects are generally billed by the number of records located. Credit accounts are accepted. Personal checks are accepted.

Reeda Ison(1059)
C/O PO Box 225
Sandy Hook KY 41171
Phone: **606-738-5671**
Fax:

Local Retrieval Area: KY-Elliott.

Normal turn around time is 2 days. Fee basis will vary by the type or project. The first project may require a prepayment.
Reeda specializes in real estate matters.

Itasca County Abstract Co(1060)
410 2nd Ave NE
Grand Rapids MN 55744
Phone: **218-326-9601**
Fax: 218-326-4348

Local Retrieval Area: MN-Itasca.

Normal turn around time is 24 hours for name and UCC searches. 5 to 10 days for owner's and encumbrance reports and abstracts. Projects are generally billed by the number of names searched. Credit accounts are accepted. Personal checks are accepted.
They specialize in complete title service.

Izard County Abstract Co(1061)
PO Box 579
Melbourne AR 72556
Phone: **501-368-4818**
Fax: 501-368-5511

Local Retrieval Area: AR-Izard.

Normal turn around time is 3-5 days. Fee basis will vary by the type of project. Credit accounts are accepted.
They specialize in real estate.

J C Humphrey Abstract Co(1062)
217 W Broadway
Enid OK 73702
Phone: **405-237-3136**
Fax: 405-237-1948

Local Retrieval Area: OK-Garfield.

Normal turn around time is 1-2 days. Projects are generally billed by the number of records located. The first project may require a prepayment.
J C Humphrey Abstract Co also has correspondent relationships in other jurisdictions, including Grant County, Oklahoma.

J L & A(1063)
PO Box 844
Crystal Springs MS 39059
Phone: **800-927-0251**
Fax: 601-892-4404

Local Retrieval Area: LA-All counties; MS-All counties.

Normal turn around time is 2-3 days. Projects are generally billed by the number of names searched. Credit accounts are accepted.
They specialize in UCC's, tax liens, judgements, motor vehicle records and bankruptcy court searches.

J M Devine & Co Inc(1064)
Phone: **701-852-6800**
Fax: 701-852-6806
PO Box 1316
Minot ND 58702

Local Retrieval Area: ND-Ward.

Normal turn around time is 1-2 days. Projects are generally billed by the number of names searched. All projects require prepayment. They will also invoice.

They specialize real estate closings and title insurance.

J M White Investigations(1065)
Phone: **309-794-1499**
Fax: 309-794-9952
PO Box 5404
Rock Island IL 61204

Local Retrieval Area: IL-Henry, Mercer, Peoria, Rock Island, Stark, Tazewell; IA-Scott.

Normal turn around time is 3-4 days. Projects are generally billed by the hour. Credit accounts are accepted.

They specialize in criminal defense.

J Mike Kelley Investigative Svcs(1066)
Phone: **407-423-3038**
Fax:
PO Box 608082
Orlando FL 32860-8082

Local Retrieval Area: FL-Brevard, Citrus, Hernando, Lake, Marion, Orange, Osceola, Seminole, Sumter.

Normal turn around time is 1 week. Projects are generally billed by the hour. Fee basis includes copy costs. Credit accounts are accepted.

J R Investigations(1067)
Phone: **515-965-8828**
Fax: 515-964-0064
313 SW Westlawn Dr
Ankeny IA 50021

Local Retrieval Area: IA-Dallas, Jasper, Keokuk, Mahaska, Polk, Story, Warren.

Normal turn around time is 48 hours. Projects are generally billed by the number of records located. Credit accounts are accepted.

J R Investigations also has correspondent relationships in other jurisdictions, including Sac, Boone, Johnson, Madison, Henry, VanBuren, Lee and Jefferson. They specialize in all types of surveillance and accident investigation.

J Tacchino Agency Private Inv(1068)
Phone: **315-344-8828**
Fax:
HC 62 Box 22
Heuvelton NY 13654-9503

Local Retrieval Area: NY-St. Lawrence.

Normal turn around time is 7 working days. Projects are generally billed by the hour. The first project may require a prepayment.

J-C Investigations(1069)
Phone: **219-262-2832**
Fax:
PO Box 4655
Elkhart IN 46514

Local Retrieval Area: IN-Elkhart, Lagrange, La Porte, St. Joseph.

Normal turn around time is 48 hours. Projects are generally billed by the hour. The first project may require a prepayment.

J-C Investigations also has correspondent relationships in other jurisdictions, including the rest of the state. They specialize in civil, criminal, domestic, workmen's compensation, and accident investigation.

J.P. Investigations(1070)
Phone: **505-623-9542**
Fax:
1005 Malamute Rd
Roswell NM 88201

Local Retrieval Area: NM-Chaves, Curry, De Baca, Eddy, Lea, Lincoln, Roosevelt.

Normal turn around time is 24 to 48 hours. Projects are generally billed by the hour. All projects require prepayment.

They specialize in criminal and workmen's compensation searches.

JMAC Enterprises(1071)
Phone: **303-789-7176**
Fax: 303-879-7710
PO Box 771214
Steamboat Springs CO 80477

Local Retrieval Area: CO-Eagle, Grand, Jackson, Moffat, Routt.

Normal turn around time is 24-48 hours. Rush service is also available. Projects are generally billed by the hour. Credit accounts are accepted.

They specializes in water record and real estate searches.

JS Industries(1072)
Phone: **717-253-3136**
Fax:
643 R Park St
Honesdale PA 18431

Local Retrieval Area: PA-Lackawanna, Wayne.

Normal turn around time is several hours. Charges are varied depending on type of search. Credit accounts are accepted.

They specialize in working with attorneys.

Jackson Abstract Inc(1073)
Phone: **501-423-2285**
Fax:
PO Box 89
Berryville AR 72616

Local Retrieval Area: AR-Carroll.

Normal turn around time is 1 day. Projects are generally billed by the number of records located. Credit accounts are accepted. Personal checks are accepted.

Jackson Abstract Inc also has correspondent relationships in other jurisdictions, including Arkansas.

Jackson County Abstract Co(1074)
Phone: **405-482-1235**
Fax: 405-482-9180
PO Box 756
Altus OK 73521

Local Retrieval Area: OK-Jackson.

Normal turn around time is varied depending on project. Projects are generally billed by the hour. The first project may require a prepayment.

They specialize in real estate records.

Jackson County Title Co(1075)
Phone: **605-837-2286**
Fax:
PO Box 544
Kadoka SD 57543

Local Retrieval Area: SD-Jackson.

Normal turn around time is up to two weeks. Fee basis varies by type of transaction. Credit accounts are accepted.

They specialize in land records.

James F Havill Attorney PC(1076) Phone: **812-254-0050**
401 E South St   Fax: 812-254-7633
Washington IN 47501

Local Retrieval Area: IN-Daviess.

Normal turn around time is 1 week. Projects are generally billed by the number of records located. Credit accounts are accepted. Personal checks are accepted.

James F Havill Attorney at Law PC also has correspondent relationships in other jurisdictions, including Knox, Martin and Pike Counties. They specialize in title opinions, abstracts and title insurance.

Jan L Jackson Investigation(1077) Phone: **512-578-0243**
PO Box 4866   Fax: 512-576-0948
Victoria TX 77903

Local Retrieval Area: TX-Bee, Calhoun, De Witt, Goliad, Jackson, Refugio, Victoria.

Normal turn around time is 1-3 days. Projects are generally billed by the hour. All projects require prepayment.

Janke Abstract Co(1078) Phone: **308-754-4251**
PO Box 114   Fax:
St Paul NE 68873

Local Retrieval Area: NE-Greeley, Hall, Howard, Merrick, Nance, Sheridan.

Normal turn around time is 2-3 days. Projects are generally billed by the number of names searched. Credit accounts are accepted. They specialize in real estate.

Jasper County Abstract Company(1079) Phone: **219-866-7333**
PO Box 336   Fax:
Rensselaer IN 47978

Local Retrieval Area: IN-Jasper.

Normal turn around time is 2 days. Projects are generally billed by the number of names searched. Credit accounts are accepted.

Jay County Abstract Company Inc(1080) Phone: **219-726-4303**
125 W Main St   Fax:
Portland IN 47371

Local Retrieval Area: IN-Jay.

Normal turn around time is 5-6 working days. Fee basis will vary by type of project. All projects require prepayment. They will also invoice.

They specialize in real estate searches.

Jay Portland Abstract Inc Co(1081) Phone: **219-726-6466**
109 S Commerce St   Fax: 219-726-4222
Portland IN 47371

Local Retrieval Area: IN-Jay.

Normal turn around time is 5 days. Projects are generally billed by the number of names searched. All projects require prepayment. They will also invoice.

Jayphil Investigations(1082) Phone: **405-348-3410**
1005 Pine Oak Dr   Fax: 405-341-2002
Edmond OK 73034

Local Retrieval Area: OK-Canadian, Cleveland, Kingfisher, Lincoln, Logan, McClain, Oklahoma, Pottawatomie.

Normal turn around time is 2 working days for county and 4 working days for court searches. Online computer ordering is also available. Projects are generally billed by the hour. The first project may require a prepayment. Credit cards are accepted for payment. Personal checks are accepted.

Jeff City Filing(1083) Phone: **314-634-3894**
1701 Swifts Hwy   Fax: 314-634-5159
Jefferson City MO 65109

Local Retrieval Area: MO-Cole.

Normal turn around time is 1 day. Projects are generally billed by the number of names searched. Credit accounts are accepted.

They specialize in filing & recording legal instruments with local & Missouri Supreme Courts, "walking through" filings with state agencies, UCC searches, ts, tax clearances & recissions, copying documents. They are a registered agent for foreign corps.

Jeff Davis County Abstract Co(1084) Phone: **915-426-3288**
PO Box 813   Fax: 915-426-3844
Fort Davis TX 79734

Local Retrieval Area: TX-Jeff Davis.

Normal turn around time is 2 days. Projects are generally billed by the hour. The first project may require a prepayment.

Jefferson County Abstr & Title(1085) Phone: **515-472-5052**
PO Box 170   Fax: 515-472-5052
Fairfield IA 52556

Local Retrieval Area: IA-Jefferson.

Normal turn around time is 1-2 days. Fee basis varies by type of transaction. The first project may require a prepayment.

Keith A Jeffries(1086) Phone: **502-845-7603**
PO Box 478   Fax:
New Castle KY 40050

Local Retrieval Area: KY-Henry, Trimble.

Normal turn around time is varied depending on project. Projects are generally billed by the hour. Credit accounts are accepted. He will ask for a retainer.

Keith is an attorney and is very familiar with the local courts.

Jerauld County Abstract Co Inc(1087) Phone: **605-539-1541**
Box 341   Fax:
Wessington Springs SD 57382

Local Retrieval Area: SD-Jerauld.

Normal turn around time is varied depending on project. Projects are generally billed by the number of records located. Credit accounts are accepted.

Joden & Associates Inc(1088)   Phone: **206-441-5833**
1601 2nd Ave Suite 710   Fax: 206-448-1008
Seattle WA 98101

Local Retrieval Area: OR-Benton, Clackamas, Clatsop, Columbia, Coos, Douglas, Hood River, Lane, Lincoln, Linn, Marion, Multnomah, Polk, Tillamook, Washington, Yamhill; WA-All counties.

Normal turn around time is 1-3 days in the metro areas, up to 2 weeks in the outlying regions. Online computer ordering is also available. Projects are generally billed by the hour. Credit accounts are accepted.

They specialize in general records research including asset searches with emphasis on locating real property and determining one's equity in said real property. They also have access to SCOMIS.

John Bullock & Co(1089)   Phone: **512-851-8855**
PO Box 721309   Fax: 512-851-8899
Corpus Christi TX 78472

Local Retrieval Area: TX-Aransas, Kenedy, Kleberg, Nueces, San Patricio.

Normal turn around time is 1-3 days. Projects are generally billed by the hour. All projects require prepayment.

They specialize in private investigation.

John C Dunaway and Associates(1090)   Phone: **512-835-5888**
PO Box 202102   Fax: 512-835-2136
Austin TX 78720-2102

Local Retrieval Area: TX-Hays, Travis, Williamson.

Normal turn around time is 24 hours. Online computer ordering is also available. Projects are generally billed by the hour. Credit accounts are accepted.

John C Dunaway and Associates also has correspondent relationships in other jurisdictions, including the rest of Texas. They specialize in "All Lines" Civil Investigations and skip tracing.

John E Jones Jr Land Title Svcs(1091)   Phone: **912-685-3027**
231 S Broad St   Fax: 912-685-3393
Metter GA 30439

Local retrieval area includes more than 60 counties in Georgia.

Normal turn around time is 1-4 days. Rush service is also available. Fee basis will vary by type of search plus costs of copies. Credit accounts are accepted.

They specialize in appraisals and title searches.

John H Rider Abstract & Real Est(1092)   Phone: **515-872-1966**
PO Box 208   Fax:
Corydon IA 50060

Local Retrieval Area: IA-Wayne.

Normal turn around time is 2-3 days. Fee basis varies by type of transaction. The first project may require a prepayment.

John Reberson Investigations(1093)   Phone: **404-461-8958**
746 Hwy 314   Fax: 404-461-0119
Fayetteville GA 30214

Local Retrieval Area: GA-De Kalb, Fulton.

Normal turn around time is 2 days. Projects are generally billed by the hour. Credit accounts are accepted.

John Reberson Investigations also has correspondent relationships in other jurisdictions, including nationwide.

Johnson County Abstract(1094)   Phone: **618-658-3721**
405 Poplar   Fax: 618-658-3721
Vienna IL 62995

Local Retrieval Area: IL-Johnson.

Normal turn around time is 2-3 business days. Projects are generally billed by the number of records located. Credit accounts are accepted. Personal checks are accepted.

Johnson County Abstract also has correspondent relationships in other jurisdictions, including Williamson, Pope and Union Counties. They specialize in title insurance through Chicago Title Insurance Company.

Edith F Johnson(1095)   Phone: **816-948-3671**
Rt 1 Box 83   Fax:
Revere MO 63465

Local Retrieval Area: IA-Lee; MO-Clark, Lewis, Scotland.

Normal turn around time is varied depending on project. Projects are generally billed by the hour. Credit accounts are accepted. A retainer is required.

Edith specializes in genealogy searches.

Janice I Johnson(1096)   Phone: **712-423-1912**
1205 7th St   Fax:
Onawa IA 51040

Local Retrieval Area: IA-Monona.

Normal turn around time is 1-2 days. Projects are generally billed by the number of records located. The first project may require a prepayment. A setup fee is only charged for first time clients.

Johnston County Abstract Co(1097)   Phone: **405-371-9375**
103 N Kemp Ave   Fax:
Tishomingo OK 73460

Local Retrieval Area: OK-Johnston.

Normal turn around time is two to five days. Projects are generally billed by the hour. They also charge per page or per certificate. Credit accounts are accepted.

Jones & Associates Inc(1098)   Phone: **918-583-4779**
1611 S Utica Suite 117   Fax: 918-587-8571
Tulsa OK 74104

Local Retrieval Area: OK-Creek, Osage, Rogers, Tulsa, Wagoner.

Normal turn around time is 24-72 hours. Projects are generally billed by the hour. The first project may require a prepayment.

Jones & Associates Inc also has correspondent relationships in other jurisdictions, including the rest of Oklahoma. They specialize in private investigation, process service, medical research and interpretation.

Jones & Renfrow Abstract Co(1099)
PO Drawer I
Paducah TX 79248
Phone: 806-492-3823
Fax: 806-492-3574

Local Retrieval Area: TX-Cottle, King.

Normal turn around time is 1-2 days. Fee basis will vary by the type of project. The first project may require a prepayment.

Jones Abstract & Title Co Inc(1100)
313 Warren St
Huntington IN 46750
Phone: 219-356-2122
Fax: 219-356-2122

Local Retrieval Area: IN-Huntington.

Normal turn around time is 3-5 days. Fee basis will vary by the type of project. Credit accounts are accepted.
Jones Abstract & Title Co Inc also has correspondent relationships in other jurisdictions, including most of the state through an alliance of title companies. They specialize in title searching.

Jones County Abstract Co(1101)
PO Box 485
Murdo SD 57559
Phone: 605-669-2231
Fax:

Local Retrieval Area: SD-Jones.

Normal turn around time is 1 week. Projects are generally billed by the hour. Credit accounts are accepted.
They specialize in land titles.

Jones County Abstract Co(1102)
PO Box 71
Anson TX 79501
Phone: 915-823-3236
Fax: 915-823-3224

Local Retrieval Area: TX-Jones.

Normal turn around time is 1-2 days. Fee basis will vary by the type of project. The first project may require a prepayment.

Patsy Jones(1103)
304 N Canal
Jefferson TX 75657
Phone: 903-665-8262
Fax:

Local Retrieval Area: TX-Harrison, Marion.

Normal turn around time is 1-2 days. Fee basis is a flat fee schedule. The first project may require a prepayment.

Jordan & McCulloch Abstracters(1104)
101 1/2 E Main St
Brady TX 76825
Phone: 915-597-2172
Fax:

Local Retrieval Area: TX-McCulloch.

Normal turn around time is 3-4 days. Fee basis will vary by the type of project. The first project may require a prepayment.

Cheryl S Josey(1105)
PO Box 394
Pembroke GA 31321
Phone: 912-653-2707
Fax:

Local Retrieval Area: GA-Bryan, Bulloch, Chatham, Evans, Glynn, Liberty, Long, Tattnall.

Normal turn around time is 24-48 hours. Fee basis will vary by the type of search. Credit accounts are accepted.

Julien Process Service(1106)
12265 S Dixie Hwy Suite 957
Miami FL 33156
Phone: 305-256-7700
Fax: 305-256-7711

Local Retrieval Area: FL-Dade.

Normal turn around time is the same day to 24 hours. Online computer ordering is also available. Projects are generally billed by the number of records located. The first project may require a prepayment. Personal checks are accepted.
Julien Process Service also has correspondent relationships in other jurisdictions, including Dade, Broward, Palm Beach and Monroe.

K.R.(1107)
PO Box 635
Marion SC 29571
Phone: 803-423-3041
Fax:

Local Retrieval Area: SC-Marion.

Normal turn around time is varied depending on search. Projects are generally billed by the hour. Credit accounts are accepted.

KCD Title(1108)
Greystone Ave
Phillipsburg NJ 08865
Phone: 908-475-8202
Fax: 908-859-1102

Local Retrieval Area: NJ-Warren.

Normal turn around time is 24 hours. Projects are generally billed by the number of names searched. The first project may require a prepayment. Personal checks are accepted.

KJK Abstract Co(1109)
38 Alpine Wy
Raritan NJ 08869
Phone: 908-725-6336
Fax: 908-253-9228

Local Retrieval Area: NJ-Somerset.

Normal turn around time is 5-10 days. Fee basis will vary by type of project. Credit accounts are accepted.
They specialize in real estate searches.

KOBS Abstracting(1110)
PO Box 458
Meade KS 67864
Phone: 316-873-2421
Fax:

Local Retrieval Area: KS-Meade.

Normal turn around time is 2-3 days. Fee basis varies by type of transaction. The first project may require a prepayment.

Kansas Investigative Services Inc(1111)
219 N Washington
Wichita KS 67202
Phone: 316-267-1356
Fax: 316-267-5476

Local Retrieval Area: KS-Barton, Butler, Cowley, Ellis, Ellsworth, Ford, Harvey, Reno, Russell, Sedgwick, Seward, Sumner.

Normal turn around time is the same day. Projects are generally billed by the hour. All projects require prepayment. They will also invoice.
Kansas Investigative Services Inc also has correspondent relationships in other jurisdictions, including Shawnee County.

Kansas Title Service(1112)
209 N Washington
Wellington KS 67152
Phone: 316-326-8508
Fax: 316-326-8049

Local Retrieval Area: KS-Sumner.

Normal turn around time is up to 48 hours. Fee basis varies by type of transaction. The first project may require a prepayment.

Karnes Land Title Co Inc(1113)
108 N Panna Maria St
Karnes TX 78118
Phone: 210-780-2221
Fax: 210-780-2795

Local Retrieval Area: TX-Karnes.

Normal turn around time is 1 day. Fee basis will vary by the type of project. The first project may require a prepayment.

Kaufman & Harlow of Cambridge(1114)
93 6th St
Cambridge MA 02141
Phone: 617-876-3347
Fax: 617-868-6749

Local Retrieval Area: MA-Essex, Middlesex, Norfolk, Suffolk, Worcester.

Normal turn around time is 3 days. Projects are generally billed by the number of names searched. Credit accounts are accepted. Kaufman & Harlow Inc of Cambridge also has correspondent relationships in other jurisdictions, including the rest of Massachusetts. They specialize in UCC, corporate records, state and federal tax liens, and federal, state, county and local courts.

Kaufman & Harlow Inc of Dayton(1115)
N7 Quincy Cir
Dayton NJ 08810
Phone: 908-329-3186
Fax: 908-274-1370

Local Retrieval Area: NJ-Mercer, Middlesex, Monmouth, Ocean, Somerset, Union.

Normal turn around time is 3 days. Projects are generally billed by the number of names searched. Credit accounts are accepted. Kaufman & Harlow Inc of Dayton also has correspondent relationships in other jurisdictions, including the rest of New Jersey. They specialize in UCC, corporate records, state and federal tax liens, and federal, state, county and local courts.

Keesee Abstracting Co(1116)
785 3rd St
Phillipsburg KS 67661
Phone: 913-543-5115
Fax:

Local Retrieval Area: KS-Phillips.

Normal turn around time is 2-3 days. Fee basis varies by type of transaction. Credit accounts are accepted.

Kelley Law Offices(1117)
Box 668
Wickliffe KY 42087
Phone: 502-335-3504
Fax: 502-335-3025

Local Retrieval Area: KY-Ballard, Calloway, Carlisle, Fulton, Graves, Hickman, McCracken, Marshall.

Normal turn around time is 1-3 days. Fee basis will vary by the type of project. All projects require prepayment. They specialize in real estate research.

Kennedy's Private Eye(1118)
PO Box 201646
Anchorage AK
Phone: 907-278-8910
Fax: 907-276-5309

Local Retrieval Area: AK-Anchorage Borough.

Normal turn around time is 1-7 days. Projects are generally billed by the hour. Credit accounts are accepted. They require a retainer for out-of-state requests.

Karen Kerins(1119)
6109 11th St
Mays Landing NJ 08330
Phone: 609-625-3565
Fax: 609-625-3408

Local Retrieval Area: NJ-Atlantic.

Normal turn around time is 24-48 hours. Fee basis will vary by the type of project. Credit accounts are accepted.

Ketlett-Landis-Brill Abstr & Title(1120)
PO Box 527
West Plains MO 65775
Phone: 417-256-2951
Fax: 417-256-0928

Local Retrieval Area: MO-Howell.

Normal turn around time is 2-3 days. Projects are generally billed by the number of names searched. Credit accounts are accepted. They specialize in title insurance.

Kiefer Title Co(1121)
2 W St Maries Suite B
Perryville MO 63775
Phone: 314-547-7755
Fax: 314-547-1452

Local Retrieval Area: MO-Perry.

Normal turn around time is 1-2 weeks. They charge a flat rate per project. Credit accounts are accepted.

Kimme and Lamke(1122)
415 Cedar St
Washington MO 63090
Phone: 314-239-7808
Fax: 314-621-1922

Local Retrieval Area: MO-Franklin.

Normal turn around time is 7 working days. Fee basis will vary by type of project. Fee may be based per tract of land. Credit accounts are accepted. Credit cards are accepted for payment. They specialize in title insurance.

King & King(1123)
PO Box 249
Pine Knot KY 42635
Phone: 606-354-2153
Fax: 606-354-2005

Local Retrieval Area: KY-McCreary, Pulaski, Wayne, Whitley.

Normal turn around time is up to 1 week. Fee basis varies by type of transaction. Credit accounts are accepted. They are a general practice law firm.

King's Title & Abstract Co(1124)
210 S Main
New Castle IN 47362
Phone: 800-860-2990
317-521-2990
Fax: 317-529-0633

Local Retrieval Area: IN-Blackford, Decatur, Delaware, Fayette, Franklin, Henry, Jay, Madison, Randolph, Rush, Shelby, Wayne.

Normal turn around time is 2-3 days. Projects are generally billed by the hour. Credit accounts are accepted. They specialize in railroad records.

Kingman Abstract and Title Co 1125)
221 N Main
Kingman KS 67068
Phone: 316-532-2011
Fax: 316-532-5383

Local Retrieval Area: KS-Kingman.

Normal turn around time is 24-48 hours. Projects are generally billed by the hour. Credit accounts are accepted.
They specialize in title insurance, escrow and closings.

John R Kingsafer(1126)
PO Box 1472
Natchez MS 39121
Phone: 601-444-6628
Fax:

Local Retrieval Area: MS-Adams, Amite, Franklin, Jefferson, Wilkinson.

Normal turn around time is 1-2 days in Adams county, others county records may take up to one week. Projects are generally billed by the hour. The first project may require a prepayment.
Mr. Kingsafer is a general practice attorney.

Kiowa County Abstract Co(1127)
PO Box 128
Eads CO 81036
Phone: 719-438-5811
Fax:

Local Retrieval Area: CO-Kiowa.

Normal turn around time is 1-2 weeks. Fee basis will vary by the type of project. Credit accounts are accepted.
They specialize in real estate title.

Kiowa County Abstract Company(1128)
108 E 4th
Hobart OK 73651
Phone: 405-726-5283
Fax: 405-726-5283

Local Retrieval Area: OK-Kiowa.

Normal turn around time is varied depending on project. Projects are generally billed by the number of names searched or records located. Credit accounts are accepted. They will accept personal checks.

Helen Kirk(1129)
RR 1 Box 218
Lewistown PA 17044
Phone: 717-248-4560
Fax: 717-248-3904

Local Retrieval Area: PA-Mifflin.

Normal turn around time is 48 hours. Charges are varied depending on type of search. Credit accounts are accepted.
Helen specializes in "current owner" searches.

R Carrol Kirkland Jr(1130)
110 Circle Dr
Statesboro GA 30458
Phone: 912-764-5232
Fax:

Local Retrieval Area: GA-Bulloch.

Normal turn around time is 2 days. Projects are generally billed by the number of names searched. Credit accounts are accepted. They will accept personal checks.

Katherine G Kittrell(1131)
40 Seneca Dr
Noank CT 06340
Phone: 203-572-9162
Fax:

Local retrieval area includes town and superior court levels within New London.

Normal turn around time is 1 week. They charge a flat rate per search. Credit accounts are accepted.
Katherine specializes in boundary dispute records.

Thomas W Klyce(1132)
1538 Gult Shores Pkwy
Gulf Shores AL 36547
Phone: 205-568-7291
Fax: 205-568-4491

Local Retrieval Area: AL-Baldwin.

Normal turn around time is 3-5 business days. Project billing methods vary. All projects require prepayment. They will also invoice. Personal checks are accepted.

Koogler and Associates Inc(1133)
6020 Covewood Ct
Citrus Heights CA 95621
Phone: 800-676-7528
916-721-7528
Fax: 916-729-7157

Local Retrieval Area: CA-El Dorado, Placer, Sacramento, San Joaquin, Sutter, Yolo, Yuba.

Normal turn around time is 2 hours for computer searches and 24 hours for physical searches. Online computer ordering is also available. Projects are generally billed by the number of names searched. They may charge by contract if it is a large client. Credit accounts are accepted. Credit cards are accepted for payment. Personal checks are accepted.
Koogler and Associates Inc also has correspondent relationships in other jurisdictions, including all counties in California. They have a large in house computer data base with direct access to several civil courts, Department of Motor Vehicles, Department of Corporations and UCC.

Jeff Kotner(1134)
1333 B Locust St
Eldorado IL 62930
Phone: 618-273-7611
Fax:

Local Retrieval Area: IL-Franklin, Gallatin, Hamilton, Hardin, Jackson, Johnson, Pope, Saline, White, Williamson; WI-Waukesha.

Normal turn around time is 24 hours. Projects are generally billed by the number of names searched or records located. Credit accounts are accepted.
Jeff specializes in abstracts of title and title insurance. He is a policy issuing agent for First American Title and National Land Title Insurance Companies.

Kroes Detective Agency(1135)
7301 E 22nd St
Tucson AZ 85710
Phone: 602-886-8397
Fax: 602-298-6334

Local Retrieval Area: AZ-Pima.

Normal turn around time is 24-48 hours. Online computer ordering is also available. Projects are generally billed by the number of names searched. Credit accounts are accepted.
Kroes Detective Agency also has correspondent relationships in other jurisdictions, including nationwide. They have 20 years experience, knowledge and equipment in debugging services. They also perform pre employment screening.

Krotzer Legal Service(1136)
319 Elm St Suite 101M
San Diego CA 92101
Phone: 619-232-1291
Fax: 619-232-0910

Local Retrieval Area: CA-San Diego.

Normal turn around time is 3-4 days. A same day rush service is also available. Projects are generally billed by the hour. The first project may require a prepayment.
Krotzer Legal Service also has correspondent relationships in other jurisdictions, including all of California. They also work with the Assessor's office, and search ficititious business names, statements and voter's registration.

Maurice & Florence Krueger(1137)
Rt 2 Box 80
Mina SD 57462
Phone: 605-226-0707
Fax:

Local Retrieval Area: SD-Brown, Campbell, Edmunds, Faulk, McPherson, Potter, Walworth.

Normal turn around time is varied depending on project. Projects are generally billed by the hour. The first project may require a prepayment.
They specialize in genealogy searches.

Joan Kunkel(1138)
Rt 3 Box 117
Carthage MO 64836
Phone: 417-358-6494
Fax: 417-358-6840

Local Retrieval Area: KS-Cherokee, Crawford, Labette; KY-Taylor; MO-Adair, Greene, Jasper, Lawrence, McDonald, Newton.

Normal turn around time is 1-2 days. They charge a flat rate per search. Credit accounts are accepted. Personal checks are accepted. They have 20 year experience with specialties in lost heirs and genealogy.

Fred and Rebecca Kunzelman(1139)
Rt 1 Box 270 C
Jane Lew WV 26378
Phone: 304-269-1553
Fax: 304-269-1553

Local Retrieval Area: WV-All counties, Lewis.

Normal turn around time is 1-7 days. Projects are generally billed by the hour. Credit accounts are accepted.
They specialize in real estate, coal, oil, gas, leasing and acquistion record searches.

Michelle Kyle(1140)
208 Bayless Ave
St Louis MO 63125
Phone: 314-544-3493
Fax: 314-544-6804

Local Retrieval Area: MO-St. Charles, St. Louis.

Normal turn around time is 24-48 hours. Projects are generally billed by the number of records located. Credit accounts are accepted.
Correspondent relationships in other jurisdictions include St. Charles County.

L Fay Hedden Abstract Office Inc(1141)
122 N 7th St
Vincennes IN 47591
Phone: 812-882-5273
Fax: 812-882-9886

Local Retrieval Area: IN-Knox.

Normal turn around time is 5-10 days. Projects are generally billed by the number of names searched or records located. Credit accounts are accepted.
They specialize in real estate title.

LDS Real Estate Services(1142)
27 1/2 S Park Pl
Newark OH 43055
Phone: 800-926-4871
Fax: 800-926-5780

Local Retrieval Area: OH-Delaware, Fairfield, Guernsey, Knox, Licking, Morrow, Muskingum, Perry.

Normal turn around time is 48 hours or less. Fee basis will vary by the type of project. Credit accounts are accepted.
LDS Real Estate Services also has correspondent relationships in other jurisdictions, including the southern 2/3's of Ohio.

LITQIS Group(1143)
757 N Broadway
Milwaukee WI 53202
Phone: 414-271-0909
Fax:

Local Retrieval Area: WI-Brown, Dodge, Kenosha, Milwaukee, Ozaukee, Racine, Sheboygan.

Normal turn around time is 4 hours to 4 days. Online computer ordering is also available. Projects are generally billed by the hour. The first project may require a prepayment.
LITQIS Group also has correspondent relationships in other jurisdictions, including Illinois, Wisconsin, Maryland, Washington DC, Ohio, Michigan, Minnesota and Iowa.

LSW Legal Filing and Research(1144)
2783A Calumet St
Columbus OH 43202
Phone: 614-329-3832
Fax: 614-268-3485

Local Retrieval Area: OH-Delaware, Fairfield, Franklin, Licking, Madison, Pickaway, Union.

Normal turn around time is 1-2 business days. Project billing methods vary. Credit accounts are accepted.
LSW Legal Filing and Research Inc also has correspondent relationships in other jurisdictions, including nationwide and international. They specialize in public record research.

La Plata Abstract Co(1145)
PO Box 197
Durango CO 81302
Phone: 303-247-5464
Fax: 303-385-4332

Local Retrieval Area: CO-La Plata.

Normal turn around time is up to 1 week. Fee basis is determined on a "flat rate" (plus costs). All projects require prepayment.

La Prade Services Inc(1146)
PO Box 5218
Poughkeepsie NY 12602-5218
Phone: **914-473-0468**
Fax: 914-473-1667

Local Retrieval Area: NY-Dutchess, Orange, Putnam, Ulster.

Normal turn around time is 2-4 days. Rush service is also available. Fee basis will vary by the type of project. Credit accounts are accepted. They may require a retainer.
La Prade Services Inc also has correspondent relationships in other jurisdictions, including Westchester, NYC, and Long Island. They have the "county contract for social services and handle 125 court papers a week".

LaGrange Title Company(1147)
127 W Spring
LaGrange IN 46761
Phone: **219-463-3232**
Fax: 219-463-3232

Local Retrieval Area: IN-Lagrange.

Normal turn around time is 1 week. Projects are generally billed by the number of names searched. Credit accounts are accepted.

LaMoure County Abstract Co(1148)
103 S Main St
LaMoure ND 58458
Phone: **701-883-4246**
Fax: 701-883-4425

Local Retrieval Area: ND-La Moure.

Normal turn around time is 2-5 days. Fee basis will vary by type of project. All projects require prepayment. They will also invoice.

LaPeer County Abstract & Title(1149)
303 W Nepessing St
LaPeer MI 48446
Phone: **313-664-9951**
Fax: 313-664-8331

Local Retrieval Area: MI-Lapeer.

Normal turn around time is 1 week. Projects are generally billed by the number of names searched or records located. Credit accounts are accepted.
They specialize in real estate.

LaSalle County Abstract Inc(1150)
PO Box 486
Cotulla TX 78014
Phone: **210-879-3712**
Fax:

Local Retrieval Area: TX-La Salle.

Normal turn around time is 2-3 days. Fee basis will vary by the type of project. The first project may require a prepayment.

LaSalle Process Servers(1151)
29 S LaSalle St Suite 956
Chicago IL 60603
Phone: **312-263-0620**
Fax: 312-263-0622

Local Retrieval Area: IL-Cook.

Normal turn around time is the same day to 1 day. If archives need to be searched, the turnaround time averages 1-2 weeks. Projects are generally billed by the hour. Copy expenses will be added to the fee. The first project may require a prepayment.
LaSalle Process Servers also has correspondent relationships in other jurisdictions, including Will, DuPage, Kane, McHenry and Lake. They specialize in process service.

Lacey Pioneer Abstract Company(1152)
209 W Broadway
Anadarko OK 73005
Phone: **405-247-5152**
Fax: 405-247-5777

Local Retrieval Area: OK-Caddo.

Normal turn around time is 2-3 days. Projects are generally billed by the number of names searched. Credit accounts are accepted. Personal checks are accepted.
They specialize in closings, title insurance and title searches.

Lafayette County Abstract(1153)
330 Main St
Darlington WI 53530
Phone: **608-776-3338**
Fax: 608-776-4798

Local Retrieval Area: WI-Lafayette.

Normal turn around time is 1-2 days. Fee basis varies by type of transaction. Credit accounts are accepted.

Lafayette Land Title Company(1154)
1007 Franklin Ave
Lexington MO 64067
Phone: **816-259-4631**
Fax: 816-259-3142

Local Retrieval Area: MO-Lafayette.

Normal turn around time is 2-3 days. Fee basis will vary by type of project. Credit accounts are accepted.
They specialize in real estate title.

Lake County Abstract & Title Co(1155)
PO Box 331
Polson MT 59860
Phone: **406-883-6226**
Fax: 406-883-2586

Local Retrieval Area: MT-Lake.

Normal turn around time is 3 days. Projects are generally billed by the hour. Credit accounts are accepted.

Lake County Abstract Co(1156)
PO Box 931
Leadville CO 80461
Phone: **719-486-2688**
Fax: 719-486-3039

Local Retrieval Area: CO-Lake.

Normal turn around time is up to 1 week. Fee basis will vary by the type of project. The first project may require a prepayment.
They specialize in real estate title searches.

Lake County Abstract Co Inc(1157)
815 N Michigan Ave
Baldwin MI 49304
Phone: **616-745-3432**
Fax: 616-745-7660

Local Retrieval Area: MI-Lake, Osceola.

Normal turn around time is up to 1 week. Fee basis will vary by type of project. All projects require prepayment. They will also invoice.
They specialize in real estate.

Lake Michigan Title Co(1158)
501 Quaker Street
South Haven MI 49090
Phone: **616-637-8595**
Fax: 616-637-1857

Local Retrieval Area: MI-Van Buren.

Normal turn around time is up to 1 week. Fee basis will vary by they type of project. Credit accounts are accepted.
They specialize in title insurance.

Lake Research Inc(1159)
PO Box 1392
Eustis FL 32727
Phone: 904-483-3310
Fax: 904-589-6899
Local Retrieval Area: FL-Lake, Marion, Sumter.
Normal turn around time is 3 days. Fee basis will vary by the type of search. Credit accounts are accepted.
They specialize is real estate record searches.

Lake of the Woods County Title(1160)
PO Box 511
Baudette MN 56623
Phone: 218-634-2544
Fax: 218-634-1890
Local Retrieval Area: MN-Lake of the Woods.
Normal turn around time is 2-5 days. Fees are billed by the search. All projects require prepayment.

Lamancha Search Inc(1161)
102 Bayless St
Murphy NC 28906
Phone: 704-837-7580
Fax:
Local Retrieval Area: NC-Cherokee.
Normal turn around time is 1 day. They charge by half day and full day. Credit accounts are accepted.

Land Title & Abstract Inc(1162)
247 W Cedar Ave
Gladwin MI 48624
Phone: 517-426-0011
Fax: 517-426-7141
Local Retrieval Area: MI-Clare, Gladwin.
Normal turn around time is 2-3 days. Fee basis will vary by type of project. Credit accounts are accepted. They require out of town clients to prepay.
They specialize in real estate.

Land Title Co(1163)
160 E Broadway
Jackson WY 83001
Phone: 800-365-7720
307-733-4713
Fax: 307-733-6186
Local Retrieval Area: WY-Lincoln, Sublette, Teton.
Normal turn around time is 1-2 days. Projects are generally billed by the hour. Credit accounts are accepted.

Land Title Corp(1164)
501 Cedar St
Tipton IA 52772
Phone: 319-886-6915
Fax:
Local Retrieval Area: IA-Cedar.
Normal turn around time is up to 3 days. Fee basis will vary by the type of project. The first project may require a prepayment.

Land Title Inc(1165)
8 Pine Tree Dr Suite 150
Arden Hills MN 55112
Phone: 612-482-8223
Fax: 612-481-9044
Local Retrieval Area: MN-Anoka, Chisago, Dakota, Hennepin, Ramsey, Washington.
Normal turn around time is 2-3 days. Projects are generally billed by the number of names searched. Credit accounts are accepted. Personal checks are accepted.
They specialize in distressed property and foreclosure information.

Landmann Abstract & Title Co(1166)
119 E 4th
Sedalia MO 65301
Phone: 816-826-0051
Fax: 816-826-1266
Local Retrieval Area: MO-Pettis.
Normal turn around time is 24 hours. Projects are generally billed by the hour. Fee basis varies by type of transaction. Credit accounts are accepted.

Landmark Title Co(1167)
202 N Madison St
Madisonville TX 77864
Phone: 409-348-5618
Fax: 409-348-5604
Local Retrieval Area: TX-Madison.
Normal turn around time is 2-4 days. Fee basis will vary by the type of project. The first project may require a prepayment.

Landmark Title Corp(1168)
PO Box 666
Oscoda MI 48750
Phone: 517-739-1471
Fax: 517-739-0606
Local Retrieval Area: MI-Alcona, Iosco, Ogemaw.
Normal turn around time is 3-5 days. Fee basis will vary by the type of project. Credit accounts are accepted.

Landmark Title Service(1169)
10315 E Grand River Suite 201
Brighton MI 48116
Phone: 313-227-1733
Fax: 313-227-1570
Local Retrieval Area: MI-Livingston, Oakland, Washtenaw.
Normal turn around time is 3 days. Fee basis will vary by the type of project. All projects require prepayment. They will invoice to established customers.
They specialize in title insurance and escrow closings.

Landmark Title and Abstract(1170)
70 S 3rd St
Ste Genevieve MO 63670
Phone: 314-883-5609
Fax:
Local Retrieval Area: MO-Ste. Genevieve.
Normal turn around time is 10 days or less. Projects are generally billed by the hour. The amount charged may be a flat fee. Credit accounts are accepted. Personal checks are accepted.

Lane County Abstract Co Inc(1171)
125 E Long
Dighton KS 67839
Phone: 316-397-5911
Fax:
Local Retrieval Area: KS-Lane.
Normal turn around time is 72 hours. Projects are generally billed by the hour. Credit accounts are accepted. Personal checks are accepted.
They specialize in title work.

Laratta & Tucker(1172)
935 Indian Hill Rd
Toms River NJ 08753
Phone: 908-349-1301
Fax: 908-341-7224
Local Retrieval Area: NJ-Ocean.
Normal turn around time is 1-2 days. Projects are generally billed by the number of names searched or records located. Credit accounts are accepted.

Larry Nasi LTD(1173)
PO Box 1034
Longmont CO 80502-1034
Phone: 303-776-0291
Fax:

Local Retrieval Area: CO-Adams, Arapahoe, Boulder, Denver, Jefferson, Larimer, Weld.

Normal turn around time is 1-3 days. Rush service is also available. Projects are generally billed by the hour. The first project may require a prepayment.

Larry Nasi LTD also has correspondent relationships in other jurisdictions, including the rest of the state as needed.

Larry R Dorning PC(1174)
1113 S Court St
Hohenwald TN 38462
Phone: 615-796-5959
Fax: 615-796-5950

Local Retrieval Area: TN-Hickman, Lawrence, Lewis, Maury, Perry, Wayne.

Normal turn around time is 48 hours. Charges are varied depending on type of search. Credit accounts are accepted. They specialize in real estate record searches.

Larson Abstract Co(1175)
PO Box 387
Little Falls MN 56345
Phone: 612-632-5667
Fax: 612-632-4583

Local Retrieval Area: MN-Morrison.

Normal turn around time is 10 days. Fee basis will vary by type of project. All projects require prepayment. They will also invoice. They specialize in real estate.

Christy Latchaw(1176)
23 Parker Ave
Franklin PA 16323
Phone: 814-437-5828
Fax:

Local Retrieval Area: PA-Venango.

Normal turn around time is 12-24 hours. Projects are generally billed by the number of names searched. Credit accounts are accepted.

Christy specializes in real estate record searches.

Latimer County Abstract Co(1177)
PO Box 68
Wilburton OK 74578
Phone: 918-465-2131
Fax: 918-465-3545

Local Retrieval Area: OK-Latimer.

Normal turn around time is up to 2 weeks. Fee basis is per page. Credit accounts are accepted.

Helen Lattus(1178)
PO Box 96
Woodland Mills TN 38271
Phone: 901-885-0891
Fax:

Local Retrieval Area: KY-Calloway, Fulton, Graves, McCracken; TN-Benton, Carroll, Dyer, Gibson, Henry, Hickman, Lake, Madison, Obion, Weakley.

Normal turn around time is 2-3 days. Projects are generally billed by the number of names searched. Credit accounts are accepted. They speicalize in real estate title searches.

LawServ Inc(1179)
801 Congress Suite 230
Houston TX 77062
Phone: 713-228-1055
Fax: 713-228-1056

Local Retrieval Area: TX-Brazoria, Fort Bend, Galveston, Harris, Jefferson, Montgomery.

Normal turn around time is 1-3 days. Projects are generally billed by the hour. The first project may require a prepayment.

LawServ Inc also has correspondent relationships in other jurisdictions, including Travis, Bexar, Nueces, Tarrant and Dallas.

Lawrence County Title(1180)
908 Jefferson
Lawrenceville IL 62439
Phone: 618-943-4464
Fax: 618-943-4643

Local Retrieval Area: IL-Crawford, Lawrence, Richland, Wabash.

Normal turn around time is 24-48 hours for liens and judgement searches, and 1 to 2 weeks for abstracts and title insurance. Projects are generally billed by the hour. A charge per page and length of period (years) searched will be added to the fee. Credit accounts are accepted. Some clients are required to pay a retainer. Personal checks are accepted.

Lawyer Support Services(1181)
751 7th Ave
Fairbanks AK 99701
Phone: 907-456-8142
Fax: 907-452-8157

Local Retrieval Area: AK-Fairbanks North Star Borough, Fairbanks District.

Normal turn around time is the same day. Projects are generally billed by the hour. Credit accounts are accepted.

Lawyer Title/Blue Ridge Agency(1182)
218 5th St NE
Charlottesville VA 22902
Phone: 804-295-7196
Fax: 804-979-7208

Local Retrieval Area: VA-Albemarle, Augusta, Fluvanna, Greene, Louisa, Nelson, Orange, City of Charlottesville.

Normal turn around time is 1-2 days in Albemarle and 3-5 days in other counties. Fee basis varies by type of transaction. The first project may require a prepayment.

They specialize in real estate and title searches.

Lawyer's Legal Service(1183)
3301 SW Barbur Blvd Suite 200, PO Box 9007
Portland OR 97207
Phone: 503-224-7911
Fax: 503-224-9611

Local Retrieval Area: OR-Clackamas, Clatsop, Columbia, Hood River, Marion, Multnomah, Washington, Yamhill; WA-Clark.

Normal turn around time is 1-2 days. Projects are generally billed by the number of records located. The first project may require a prepayment.

Lawyer's Legal Service also has correspondent relationships in other jurisdictions, including the entire State of Oregon and the Southwest part of Washington. They specialize in process servicing and case file management.

Lawyers Legal Liasion(1184)   Phone: **509-325-0001**
2032 Northwest Blvd   Fax: 509-838-1005
Spokane WA 99205

Local Retrieval Area: WA-Spokane.

Normal turn around time is 2 days. Projects are generally billed by the hour. The first project may require a prepayment.
Lawyers Legal Liasion also has correspondent relationships in other jurisdictions, including network for the rest of Washington. They specialize in marriage/divorce and birth/death searches.

Lawyers Title(1185)   Phone: **703-433-8112**
66 W Water St   Fax: 703-433-5804
Harrisonburg VA 22801

Local Retrieval Area: VA-Rockingham, City of Harrisonburg.

Normal turn around time is 5-7 days. Projects are generally billed by the hour. All projects require prepayment.

Lawyers Title Insurance Corp(1186)   Phone: **517-372-9450**
603 S Washington Ave Suite 100   Fax: 517-372-1412
lansing MI 48933

Local Retrieval Area: MI-Clinton, Eaton, Ingham, Shiawassee.

Normal turn around time is 7 working days. Projects are generally billed by the hour. Credit accounts are accepted.

Lawyers' Abstract Co(1187)   Phone: **412-283-3510**
220 S Main St Holly Point Suite A   Fax: 412-283-2258
Butler PA 16001

Local Retrieval Area: PA-Armstrong, Butler, Westmoreland.

Normal turn around time is 2-14 days. Projects are generally billed by the hour. All projects require prepayment. They will also invoice. Personal checks are accepted.
Lawyers' Abstract Co also has correspondent relationships in other jurisdictions, including Lawrence, Mercer, Crawford and Clarion Counties. They specialize in title searching and title insurance. The company is owned by Butler County Lawyers and has been in business since 1965. They have the only title plant in Butler County.

Lawyers' Abstract Service Inc(1188)   Phone: **813-774-2627**
2670 Airport Road S   Fax: 813-774-0063
Naples FL 33962

Local Retrieval Area: FL-Collier.

Normal turn around time is 5-7 days. Fee basis will vary by the type of project. The first project may require a prepayment.
They specialize in land records.

Attorney David K Layton(1189)   Phone: **606-792-4613**
13 Public Square   Fax:
Lancaster KY 40444

Local Retrieval Area: KY-Boyle, Garrard, Jessamine, Lincoln, Madison.

Normal turn around time is 1-2 days. Projects are generally billed by the hour. Credit accounts are accepted.

Lee County Land & Abstract(1190)   Phone: **409-542-3636**
PO Drawer 1039   Fax: 409-542-5604
Giddings TX 78942

Local Retrieval Area: TX-Lee.

Normal turn around time is 2-3 days. Fee basis will vary by the type of project. The first project may require a prepayment.

Leelanau Title Co(1191)   Phone: **616-271-6191**
PO Box 10   Fax: 616-271-3516
Suttons Bay MI 49682

Local Retrieval Area: MI-Leelanau.

Normal turn around time is 2-3 days. Fee basis will vary by transactions. The first project may require a prepayment.
They specialize in real estate.

Legal Abstract Co(1192)   Phone: **319-263-3171**
301 E 2nd St   Fax: 319-263-0829
Muscatine IA 52761

Local Retrieval Area: IA-Muscatine.

Normal turn around time is up to 1 week. Fee basis will vary by the type of project. Credit accounts are accepted.

Legal Beagles Inc(1193)   Phone: **302-322-9897**
PO Box 886   Fax:
New Castle DE 19720

Local Retrieval Area: DE-New Castle.

Normal turn around time is 1 week. 1 day rush service is also available. Projects are generally billed by the number of names searched. Credit accounts are accepted.
Legal Beagles Inc also has correspondent relationships in other jurisdictions, including Sussex county.

Legal Courier(1194)   Phone: **201-798-1139**
1315 Garden   Fax: 201-216-1541
Hoboken NJ 07030

Local Retrieval Area: NJ-Bergen, Essex, Hudson; NY-New York.

Normal turn around time is 24 hours. Projects are generally billed by the number of records located. The first project may require a prepayment.
They specialize in bankruptcy searches.

Legal Courier Service(1195)   Phone: **612-332-7203**
607 Marquette Ave Suite 309   Fax: 612-334-3245
Minneapolis MN 55402

Local Retrieval Area: MN-Anoka, Carver, Dakota, Hennepin, Ramsey, Scott, Sherburne, Washington, Wright.

Normal turn around time is 12 hours. Projects are generally billed by the hour. Mileage expenses are added to the hourly fee. Credit accounts are accepted. They will invoice with a deposit. Legal Courier Service also has correspondent relationships in other jurisdictions, including Beltrami. They specialize in federal litigation document retrieval.

Legal Courier Systems Inc(1196) **Phone:** 800-869-8586
PO Box 30443 **Fax:** 301-320-9219
Bethesda MD 20824

Local Retrieval Area: VA-Arlington, Fairfax, Fauquier, Loudoun, Prince William, Stafford.

Normal turn around time is the same day. A one hour rush service is also available. Projects are generally billed by the hour. Travel expenses will be added to the fee. Credit accounts are accepted.

They specialize in court filings and research, and bankruptcy courts.

Legal Couriers Inc(1197) **Phone:** 509-453-1134
22 S 3rd Ave **Fax:** 509-575-6680
Yakima WA 98902

Local Retrieval Area: WA-Yakima.

Normal turn around time is 24 hours. They charge per hour plus costs. The first project may require a prepayment. They will invoice law firms.

Legal Couriers Inc also has correspondent relationships in other jurisdictions, including nondisclosed counties. Please call company for information.

Legal Data Resources(1198) **Phone:** 800-735-9207
2816 W Summerdale Suite 200 312-512-2468
Chicago IL 60625 **Fax:** 312-561-2488

Local Retrieval Area: IL-Cook, Du Page, Lake, Will.

Normal turn around time is 24 hours. Online computer ordering is also available. Project billing methods vary. Credit accounts are accepted. Personal checks are accepted.

Legal Data Resources also has correspondent relationships in other jurisdictions, including nationwide. They specialize in legal research including case law, federal and state legislation, property, patent, trademark and copyright searches.

Legal Data Services(1199) **Phone:** 504-892-5194
PO Box 1119 **Fax:** 504-898-0837
Covington LA 70434-1119

Local Retrieval Area: LA-St. Tammany Parish, Washington Parish.

Normal turn around time is 5 working days. Fee basis will vary by type of project. Credit accounts are accepted.

Legal Data Services also has correspondent relationships in other jurisdictions, including Orleans, Jefferson, St. Bernard, St. Charles, Tangipahoa and Livingston Parishes. They specialize in metes and bounds, and lot and block abstracting.

Legal Eagles Attorney Services(1200) **Phone:** 615-665-1211
321 Boxmore Pl **Fax:**
Nashville TN 37215-6128

Local Retrieval Area: TN-Davidson.

Normal turn around time is 1-2 days. Projects are generally billed by the hour. The first project may require a prepayment.

They specialize in the Federal Courts. A FAX number is available upon request.

Legal Ease Court Service(1201) **Phone:** 713-338-1687
PO Box 137 **Fax:**
League City TX 77574

Local Retrieval Area: TX-Brazoria, Galveston, Harris.

Normal turn around time is 24-48 hours. Turnaround time can be the same day, if the request is received before noon. Fee basis will vary by type of project. The first project may require a prepayment. They specialize in filing documents for attorneys, check certification of good standing, and state comptroller.

Legal Express(1202) **Phone:** 719-578-0407
15 S Weber **Fax:**
Colorado Springs CO 80903

Local Retrieval Area: CO-El Paso, Teller.

Normal turn around time is 2 working days. Projects are generally billed by the number of names searched. Credit accounts are accepted.

Legal Express(1203) **Phone:** 201-941-5032
250 Gorge Rd Suite 8J **Fax:**
Cliffside Park NJ 07010

Local Retrieval Area: NJ-Bergen, Essex, Hudson, Morris, Passaic.

Normal turn around time is varied depending on project. Projects are generally billed by the hour. Credit accounts are accepted.

Legal Legwork(1204) **Phone:** 206-272-9429
945 Tacoma Ave S Suite F **Fax:** 206-272-9482
Tacoma WA 98402

Local Retrieval Area: WA-King, Kitsap, Pierce, Thurston.

Normal turn around time is 24 hours for most requests. Independent contractors is normally 48 to 72 hours. Projects are generally billed by the number of names searched. Credit accounts are accepted.

Legal Legwork also has correspondent relationships in other jurisdictions, including Snohomish, Spokane and Clark. They specialize in litigation research. They have extensive experience in dealing with lawyers and litigation clients. They also provides UCC searching.

Legal Net Process Service(1205) **Phone:** 915-532-7871
1023 E Yandell **Fax:** 915-532-7874
El Paso TX 79902

Local Retrieval Area: NM-Dona Ana; TX-El Paso, Hudspeth.

Normal turn around time is 1 day in El Paso and 2-3 days in the other counties. Fee basis will vary by the type of project. The first project may require a prepayment.

Legal Recording of Rochester Inc(1206) **Phone:** 716-232-6710
807 Wilder Bldg **Fax:**
Rochester NY 14614

Local Retrieval Area: NY-Monroe, New York.

Normal turn around time is 24-48 hours. Projects are generally billed by the number of names searched or records located. Credit accounts are accepted.

They specialize in real property tax searches for lenders.

Legal Remedy(1207)   **Phone:** **915-545-1525**
444 Executive Center Suite 223   Fax: 915-533-7217
El Paso TX 79901

Local Retrieval Area: NM-Dona Ana.

Normal turn around time is 1-3 days. Projects are generally billed by the hour. All projects require prepayment.

Legal Remedy also has correspondent relationships in other jurisdictions, including Brewster, Culberson, Presidio and Hudspeth. They specialize in paralegal services.

Legal Research Services Inc(1208)   **Phone:** **205-757-4153**
Rt 13 Box 133   Fax: 205-757-5357
Florence AL 35630

Local Retrieval Area: AL-Colbert, Franklin, Lauderdale, Lawrence, Limestone, Madison.

Normal turn around time is 2 days. Projects are generally billed by the hour. The first project may require a prepayment.

They specialize in pre employment screening and document retrieval.

Legal Search(1209)   **Phone:** **907-258-4752**
205 East 4th Ave   Fax:
Anchorage AK 99501

Local Retrieval Area: AK-Anchorage Borough, Matanuska-Susitna Borough.

Normal turn around time is 3-14 days. Projects are generally billed by the hour. Credit accounts are accepted.

Legal Search also has correspondent relationships in other jurisdictions, including the Kenai and Fairbanks regions.

Legal Services(1210)   **Phone:** **313-353-0990**
PO Box 267-250   Fax: 313-356-4655
Franklin MI 48025

Local Retrieval Area: IL-All counties; MI-All counties.

Normal turn around time is 3-4 days. Projects are generally billed by the hour. Copy expenses will be added to the fee. Credit accounts are accepted.

They specialize in obtaining medical insurance, court records, obtaining information about foreign companies and corporations.

Legal Support Svcs of Oklahoma(1212)   **Phone:** **800-336-1024**
217 N Harvey   405-232-1025
Oklahoma City OK 73102   Fax: 405-232-4446

Local Retrieval Area: OK-Carter, Cleveland, Comanche, Creek, Oklahoma, Payne, Pittsburg, Pottawatomie, Seminole, Stephens, Tulsa.

Normal turn around time is 24-48 hours for most cases. Fee basis will vary by the type of project. All projects require prepayment.

Legal Support Services of Oklahoma also has correspondent relationships in other jurisdictions, including the rest of Oklahoma. They specialize in providing support services to attorneys.

Legal System Services(1213)   **Phone:** **314-725-6919**
7536 Forsyth Blvd Suite 126   Fax: 314-862-0903
Clayton MO 63105

Local Retrieval Area: IL-Madison, Monroe, St. Clair; MO-Jefferson, St. Charles, St. Louis.

Normal turn around time is 5 working days. Project billing methods vary. Copy fees will be added to the per hour charge. Credit accounts are accepted.

Legal System Services also has correspondent relationships in other jurisdictions, including outlying counties in eastern Missouri and western Illinois.

Legal Wings Inc(1214)   **Phone:** **800-339-1286**
425 Greenwood Ave Suite 300   609-393-6700
Trenton NJ 08609   Fax: 609-393-8001

Local Retrieval Area: NJ-Burlington, Camden, Hunterdon, Mercer, Middlesex, Monmouth, Ocean, Somerset; PA-Bucks, Montgomery, Philadelphia.

Normal turn around time is 48 hours for limited partnership records, bankrupcy or corporate. All other records average 24 hours. Projects are generally billed by the number of names searched. The first project may require a prepayment.

Legal Wings Inc also has correspondent relationships in other jurisdictions, including nationwide. They are connected by modem for all U.S. District and Bankruptcy docket sheets in New Jersey. They also search foreclosure, matrimonial, DMV records, corporatioins, partnership, trade names and indexes.

LegalEase Inc(1215)   **Phone:** **212-393-9070**
139 Fulton St Suite 1013   Fax: 212-393-9796
New York NY 10038

Local Retrieval Area: CT-Fairfield; NJ-Bergen; NY-Bronx, Kings, Nassau, New York, Orange, Putnam, Queens, Richmond, Rockland, Suffolk, Westchester.

Normal turn around time is 24-48 hours. Projects are generally billed by the number of names searched or records located. Volume searches will be charged by the hour. The first project may require a prepayment.

LegalEase Inc also has correspondent relationships in other jurisdictions, including all areas outside an 85 mile radius of New York City.

LegalEze(1216)   **Phone:** **206-670-6551**
7009 212th SW Suite 202   Fax: 206-778-2274
Edmonds WA 98026

Local Retrieval Area: WA-King, Snohomish.

Normal turn around time is 24-48 hours. Rush service is also available. Projects are generally billed by the hour. The first project may require a prepayment.

LegalNet Inc(1217)
2510 W 237th Street Suite 110
Torrance CA 90505
Phone: 310-530-2200
Fax: 310-530-1014

Local Retrieval Area: CA-Los Angeles, Orange.

Normal turn around time is 1-3 weeks. Projects are generally billed by the number of records located. Credit accounts are accepted. LegalNet Inc also has correspondent relationships in other jurisdictions, including Ventura, San Diego, Riverside, and San Bernardino.

Legalese(1218)
1814 27th St Suite 100
Sacramento CA 95816
Phone: 916-455-9133
Fax: 916-751-7722

Local Retrieval Area: CA-El Dorado, Placer, Sacramento, Sutter, Yolo, Yuba.

Normal turn around time is 2 days. Projects are generally billed by the number of records located. Credit accounts are accepted.

Lemhi Title Co(1219)
PO Box J
Salmon ID 83467
Phone: 208-756-2977
Fax: 208-756-6286

Local Retrieval Area: ID-Lemhi.

Normal turn around time is 3 days. Fee basis varies by type of transaction. Credit accounts are accepted.

Bruce Lester(1220)
7 Laurel Ct
Deptford NJ 08096
Phone: 609-853-9836
Fax: 609-853-5008

Local Retrieval Area: NJ-Gloucester.

Normal turn around time is 24 hours. Fee basis will vary by the type of project. Credit accounts are accepted. Personal checks are accepted.

Lewis County Abstract(1221)
PO Box 36
Nezperce ID 83543
Phone: 208-937-2621
Fax:

Local Retrieval Area: ID-Lewis.

Normal turn around time is 4-5 days. Fee basis will vary by the type of project. Credit accounts are accepted.
They specialze in providing title insurance.

Lewis County Abstract(1222)
200 A E Lafayette
Monticello MO 63457
Phone: 314-767-5204
Fax:

Local Retrieval Area: MO-Lewis.

Normal turn around time is the same day. Projects are generally billed by the number of records located. Credit accounts are accepted. Personal checks are accepted.

Libby Law Office(1223)
204 S 1st St
Montevideo MN 56265-1413
Phone: 612-269-5508
Fax:

Local Retrieval Area: MN-Chippewa, Lac qui Parle, Yellow Medicine.

Normal turn around time is 1 day. Fee basis varies by type of transaction. The first project may require a prepayment.
They specialize in real estate and family law.

Liberty Corporate Services Inc(1224)
3998 Ashford Dunwoody Rd
Atlanta GA 30319
Phone: 800-334-2735
Fax: 404-986-9326

Local Retrieval Area: GA-All counties.

Normal turn around time is 1-5 days. Online computer ordering is also available. Fee basis is by name and county. Credit accounts are accepted.
They specialize in UCC and corporate work.

Liberty County Title Co(1225)
235 Main St
Shelby MT 59474
Phone: 406-434-5156
Fax: 406-434-5157

Local Retrieval Area: MT-Liberty.

Normal turn around time is 5 days. Projects are generally billed by the hour. All projects require prepayment.

Lincoln Abstract Co(1226)
PO Box 598
Star City AR 71667
Phone: 501-628-3144
Fax:

Local Retrieval Area: AR-Lincoln.

Normal turn around time is 5 working days. Projects are generally billed by the hour. All projects require prepayment.

Lincoln County Abstract & Title(1227)
PO Drawer 1979
Ruidoso NM 88345
Phone: 800-635-4692
505-257-5665
Fax: 505-257-9010

Local Retrieval Area: NM-Lincoln.

Normal turn around time is varied depending on project. Projects are generally billed by the number of records located. Credit accounts are accepted.
They specialize in title insurance.

Lincoln Trail Title Services Inc(1228)
PO Box 111
Elizabethtown KY 42702
Phone: 502-765-5566
Fax: 502-769-3267

Local Retrieval Area: KY-Hardin.

Normal turn around time is 3-5 days. Projects are generally billed by the hour. Credit accounts are accepted.

Tina Linder(1229)
240 W Marion St
Mt Gilead OH 43338
Phone: 419-947-7240
Fax: 419-947-7240

Local Retrieval Area: OH-Morrow.

Normal turn around time is 12-24 hours. Fee basis is "per job". Credit accounts are accepted.

Linn County Abstract Co(1230)
PO Box 98
Mound City KS 66056
Phone: 913-795-2949
Fax: 913-795-2449

Local Retrieval Area: KS-Bourbon, Linn.

Normal turn around time is 1 day. They fee basis is a set fee. The first project may require a prepayment. Personal checks are accepted.

Lipscomb County Abstract Co(1231)　　**Phone:** 806-658-4525
PO Box L　　　　　　　　　　　　　　　**Fax:** 806-658-2421
Booker TX 79005

Local Retrieval Area: TX-Lipscomb.

Normal turn around time is 2-3 days. Fee basis will vary by the type of project. The first project may require a prepayment.

Litigant Services Inc of Dallas(1232)　　**Phone:** 214-880-0070
3232 McKinney Ave Suite 1270　　　　　　**Fax:** 214-880-0071
Dallas TX 75204

Local Retrieval Area: TX-Dallas.

Normal turn around time is 1-3 days. Online computer ordering is also available. Projects are generally billed by the number of names searched. Credit accounts are accepted.
Litigant Services Inc of Dallas also has correspondent relationships in other jurisdictions, including Tarrant and Collin. They specialize in accident reconstruction, computer record retrieval, financial/assets, insurance, security/loss prevention and general investigations.

Litigant Services Inc of El Paso(1233)　　**Phone:** 915-545-2309
State National Plaza, 221 N Kansas Suite 1201　**Fax:** 915-545-1436
El Paso TX 79901

Local Retrieval Area: TX-El Paso.

Normal turn around time is 1-3 days. Online computer ordering is also available. Projects are generally billed by the number of names searched. Credit accounts are accepted.
Litigant Services Inc of El Paso also has correspondent relationships in other jurisdictions, including Dona Ana, New Mexico and Jualez Chihuaha, Mexico. They specialize in accident reconstruction, comoputer records retrieval, financial/assets, insurance security/loss prevention and general investigations.

Locke-Neosho Abstracts Inc(1234)　　**Phone:** 316-244-3641
PO Box 178　　　　　　　　　　　　　　**Fax:** 316-244-3234
Erie KS 66733

Local Retrieval Area: KS-Neosho.

Normal turn around time is up to 1 week. Fee basis varies by type of transaction. Credit accounts are accepted. They request prepayment from out of area clients, but will invoice established customers.

Logan County Abstract Co(1235)　　**Phone:** 701-754-2200
Box C　　　　　　　　　　　　　　　　**Fax:**
Napoleon ND 58561

Local Retrieval Area: ND-Logan.

Normal turn around time is 1-2 days. Projects are generally billed by the number of records located. Credit accounts are accepted.

Lone Star Legal(1236)　　**Phone:** 415-389-1464
PO Box 2262　　　　　　　　**Fax:** 415-389-1464
Mill Valley CA 94942

Local Retrieval Area: CA-Alameda, Contra Costa, Marin, Napa, San Francisco, San Mateo, Santa Clara, Sonoma.

Normal turn around time is 2 days. Projects are generally billed by the hour. The first project may require a prepayment.
Lone Star Legal also has correspondent relationships in other jurisdictions, including Sacramento, Santa Cruz, and Mendicino counties. They specialize in complete court research and on site copy work.

Lone Star Title & Abstract Co(1237)　　**Phone:** 817-629-2683
PO Box 855　　　　　　　　　　　　　　**Fax:** 817-629-2684
Eastland TX 76448

Local Retrieval Area: TX-Eastland.

Normal turn around time is 2-3 days. Fee basis will vary by the type of project. The first project may require a prepayment.

Gordon B Long(1238)　　**Phone:** 606-349-1558
PO Box 531　　　　　　　　**Fax:** 606-349-2441
Salyersville KY 41465

Local Retrieval Area: KY-Breathitt, Johnson, Knott, Magoffin, Pike, Wolfe.

Normal turn around time is up to 1 week. Projects are generally billed by the hour. All projects require prepayment.

Alfred Lopez(1239)　　**Phone:** 505-863-3396
PO Box 563　　　　　　　　**Fax:**
Gallup NM 87305

Local Retrieval Area: NM-Cibola, McKinley.

Normal turn around time is 2 days. Projects are generally billed by the hour. Credit accounts are accepted.

Lora J Musilli & Associates(1240)　　**Phone:** 201-383-7763
PO Box 635　　　　　　　　　　　　　　**Fax:** 201-875-0650
Branchville NJ 07826

Local Retrieval Area: NJ-Sussex.

Normal turn around time is 24 hours. Projects are generally billed by the number of names searched. Credit accounts are accepted. Personal checks are accepted.
They also provide credit check searches.

Lorain County Title Co(1241)　　**Phone:** 800-624-5507
424 Middle Ave　　　　　　　　　　　　　　　216-777-4686
Elyria OH 44035　　　　　　　　　　　　**Fax:** 216-284-5161

Local Retrieval Area: OH-Cuyahoga, Erie, Lorain.

Normal turn around time is 3 days. Fee basis varies by type of transaction. Credit accounts are accepted.

Lord and Associates(1242)
PO Box 909
Eagle ID 83616
Phone: **208-939-8258**
Fax: 208-939-7244

Local Retrieval Area: ID-Ada, Boise, Canyon, Elmore, Gem, Owyhee, Payette, Valley, Washington.

Normal turn around time is 72 hours. Online computer ordering is also available. Projects are generally billed by the hour. Credit accounts are accepted.

They specialize in general investigations.

Los Angeles Legal Service(1243)
PO Box 41411
Los Angeles CA 90041
Phone: **213-259-9499**
Fax: 213-257-0605

Local retrieval area includes Los Angeles County for record retrieval and the entire state of California for process serving and photocopying.

Normal turn around time is 24-48 hours. Bankruptcy may take longer than 48 hours. Fees basis will vary by the type of project. Credit accounts are accepted. Prepay and invoice payment is negotiable.

Los Angeles Legal Service also has correspondent relationships in other jurisdictions, including CAPP Members in California.

Loss Protection & Investigations (1244)
122 Walker
Fresno CA 93721
Phone: **209-268-7472**
Fax: 209-268-7459

Local Retrieval Area: CA-Fresno, Madera, Tulare.

Normal turn around time is 2 days. Project billing methods vary. The first project may require a prepayment.

Patricia O Lueken(1245)
9864 Diamond Point Dr
St Louis MO 63123
Phone: **314-631-5928**
Fax:

Local Retrieval Area: MO-St. Louis, City of St. Louis.

Normal turn around time is the next day. Projects are generally billed by the number of names searched. Credit accounts are accepted.

They specialize in enviornmental lien searches.

Denise Lusk(1246)
1609 Playground Rd
Walhalla SC 29691
Phone: **803-638-2766**
Fax: 803-638-4191

Local Retrieval Area: SC-Oconee.

Normal turn around time is 1-2 days per record. Projects are generally billed by the number of records located. Credit accounts are accepted.

Lycoming Abstract Co Inc(1247)
PO Box 402
Williamsport PA 17703-0402
Phone: **717-327-2264**
Fax: 717-321-9698

Local Retrieval Area: PA-Lycoming.

Normal turn around time is 24 hours. Projects are generally billed by the number of names searched. Credit accounts are accepted.

Lyman Title Co(1248)
PO Box 187
Kennebec SD 57544
Phone: **605-869-2269**
Fax:

Local Retrieval Area: SD-Lyman.

Normal turn around time is up to 2 weeks. Fee basis varies by type of transaction. Credit accounts are accepted.
They specialize in land records.

Lynn County Abstract Co(1249)
PO Box 968
Tahoka TX 79373
Phone: **806-998-4022**
Fax:

Local Retrieval Area: TX-Lynn.

Normal turn around time is up to a week. Fee basis will vary by the type of project. The first project may require a prepayment.

Lynn County Title(1250)
109 S Marshall St
Rock Rapids IA 51246
Phone: **712-472-3753**
Fax:

Local Retrieval Area: IA-Lyon.

Normal turn around time is 1-3 days. Fee basis will vary by the type of project. The first project may require a prepayment.

Lyon Abstract Company(1251)
PO Box 216
Camden AR 71701
Phone: **501-836-8084**
Fax: 501-836-4811

Local Retrieval Area: AR-Calhoun, Columbia, Dallas, Lafayette, Ouachita, Union.

Normal turn around time is varied depending on project. Projects are generally billed by the number of names searched. The first project may require a prepayment.

Lyon Abstract Company also has correspondent relationships in other jurisdictions, including the rest of Arkansas.

Helen F Lyons(1252)
Box 86
New Bloomfield PA 17608
Phone: **717-582-2504**
Fax: 717-582-2131

Local Retrieval Area: PA-Perry.

Normal turn around time is 24 hours. Charges are varied depending on type of search. Credit accounts are accepted.
Helen specializes in lien searches.

M & M Legal Services(1253)
PO Box 364
La Grande OR 97850
Phone: **503-963-9703**
Fax: 503-963-8219

Local Retrieval Area: OR-Baker, Umatilla, Union, Wallowa.

Normal turn around time is 1 day for Union County, 1-2 days for Baker County, and 4 days for Wallowa and Umatilla Counties. Projects are generally billed by the hour. Credit accounts are accepted. They request prepayment from out of state clients, but will invoice established customers.

M & M Search Service Inc(1254)
601 Indiana Ave NW Suite 619
Washington DC 20004
Phone: 202-393-3144
Fax: 202-393-3242

Local Retrieval Area: DC-All counties; VA-Arlington, Fairfax, Montgomery, Prince George, City of Alexandria.

Normal turn around time is 8 hours for Court Records and UCC's. Full 60 year searches take 2 to 3 days. They charge by name and address. Credit accounts are accepted. They will accept personal checks.

M & M Search Service Inc also has correspondent relationships in other jurisdictions, including Howard County, Ann Arundel County and Prince William County. They specialize in real estate and UCC searches.

M R Daniel & Associates(1255)
78 N 3167 E
Idaho Falls ID 83402
Phone: 208-523-4166
Fax:

Local Retrieval Area: ID-Bannock, Bonneville, Butte, Caribou, Jefferson, Madison, Teton.

Normal turn around time is 1 day. Projects are generally billed by the hour. All projects require prepayment.

They specialize in criminal cases and workmen's compensation claims.

M.R.S. Datascope Inc(1256)
7155 Old Katy Rd Suite 160
Houston TX 77025
Phone: 800-899-3282
713-861-3900
Fax: 713-864-0439

Local Retrieval Area: TX-Fort Bend, Galveston, Harris, Jefferson, Montgomery.

Normal turn around time is 2-3 days. Projects are generally billed by the hour. All projects require prepayment.
They specialize in record retrieval for pre trial discovery.

MG Cox Abstract(1257)
PO Box 608
Pauls Valley OK 73075
Phone: 405-238-2600
Fax: 405-238-7553

Local Retrieval Area: OK-Garvin.

Normal turn around time is 1 week. Projects are generally billed by the hour. The first project may require a prepayment.

MGC Courier Inc(1258)
1564 Norman Dr
College Park GA 30349
Phone: 800-822-1084
404-991-1084
Fax: 404-991-6928

Local Retrieval Area: .

Normal turn around time is the same day. The fee basis is by mileage and time. Credit accounts are accepted.
MGC Courier Inc also has correspondent relationships in other jurisdictions, including nationwide.

MGI(1259)
22777 Harper Suite 102
St Clair Shores MI 48080
Phone: 313-445-3160
Fax: 313-445-3163

Local Retrieval Area: MI-Macomb, Oakland, Wayne.

Normal turn around time is 1 week. Online computer ordering is also available. Projects are generally billed by the hour. Credit accounts are accepted.

MGI also has correspondent relationships in other jurisdictions, including the remaining 83 counties in Michigan. They specialize in insurance defense investigations.

MHR and Associates(1260)
543 E Andy Devine
Kingman AZ 86401
Phone: 602-753-4777
Fax: 602-753-2875

Local Retrieval Area: AZ-Mohave.

Normal turn around time is 1-3 days. Projects are generally billed by the hour. Credit accounts are accepted.

MLQ Attorney Services(1261)
3200 Professional Pkwy Bldg 200 Suite 225
Atlanta GA 30339
Phone: 800-446-8794
404-984-7007
Fax: 404-984-7049

Local Retrieval Area: GA-All counties.

Normal turn around time is 24 hours within Atlanta metropolitan area, and 3 days outside the metropolitan area. Online computer ordering is also available. Projects are generally billed by the number of names searched. The first project may require a prepayment. Credit cards are accepted for payment.
MLQ Attorney Services also has correspondent relationships in other jurisdictions, including the state of Georgia.

Mac Abstract & Title Insurance Co(1262)
PO Box 2124
Fort Smith AR 72902
Phone: 501-782-3053
Fax: 501-782-5432

Local Retrieval Area: AR-Crawford, Sebastian.

Normal turn around time is 3 days. Fee basis will vary by the type of project. All projects require prepayment. They will invoice to established clients.
They specialize in real estate.

Mackinac Abstract and Title Co(1263)
291 Stockbridge
St Ignace MI 49781
Phone: 906-643-7452
Fax: 906-643-7452

Local Retrieval Area: MI-Chippewa, Luce, Mackinac.

Normal turn around time is 7-10 business days. Fee basis will vary by type of project. Credit accounts are accepted.
They specialize in real estate and tax record searches, title insurance and abstracts of title.

Madison County Title Co(1264)
PO Box 54
Virginia City MT 59755
Phone: 406-843-5337
Fax: 406-843-5431

Local Retrieval Area: MT-Madison.

Normal turn around time is 1-3 days. Projects are generally billed by the hour. Credit accounts are accepted.

Magic P I & Security Inc(1265)
201 E Ransom St
Kalamazoo MI 49007
Phone: **616-381-7772**
Fax: 616-381-2324

Local Retrieval Area: MI-Kalamazoo.

Normal turn around time is 48-72 hours. Projects are generally billed by the hour. The first project may require a prepayment. They specialize in civil process and private investigations.

Magnolia Title Co(1266)
PO Box 427
Columbus MS 39703
Phone: **601-329-9964**
Fax:

Local Retrieval Area: AL-Pickens; MS-Clay, Lowndes, Monroe, Noxubee, Oktibbeha.

Normal turn around time is 3 days. Fee basis will vary by type of project. Credit accounts are accepted. They specialize in title searches.

Mahaska Title - Johnson Abstract(1267)
209 A Ave E
Oskaloosa IA 52577
Phone: **515-673-5666**
Fax: 515-673-9224

Local Retrieval Area: IA-Mahaska.

Normal turn around time is 1-2 days. Projects are generally billed by the number of names searched. Credit accounts are accepted.

Mahnomen County Abstract Co(1268)
PO Box 325
Mahnomen MN 56557
Phone: **218-935-5227**
Fax:

Local Retrieval Area: MN-Mahnomen.

Normal turn around time is the same day. Projects are generally billed by the number of names searched or records located. Credit accounts are accepted.

They specialize in title searches, owner and encumbrance reports, and registered property abstracts.

Main Abstract & Title Co(1269)
100 Aherwood Drive
Roscommon MI 48653
Phone: **517-275-5600**
Fax: 517-275-8649

Local Retrieval Area: MI-Crawford, Roscommon.

Normal turn around time is up to 1 week. Fee basis will vary by type of project. All projects require prepayment. They specialize in real estate transactions.

Main Street Title Corp(1270)
118 N Main St
Goshen IN 46526
Phone: **219-533-3774**
Fax: 219-534-5445

Local Retrieval Area: IN-Elkhart.

Normal turn around time is 7-10 days. A 2 day rush service is available for established customers. Projects are generally billed by the number of records located. Credit accounts are accepted. They specialize in real estate records.

Mainline Researchers(1271)
PO Box 741
Ebensburg PA 15931-0741
Phone: **814-472-7936**
Fax: 814-472-7936

Local Retrieval Area: PA-Cambria.

Normal turn around time is 24 hours. 60 year title searches take longer. Charges are varied depending on type of search. Credit accounts are accepted.

Mainline Researchers also has correspondent relationships in other jurisdictions, including most counties in western Pennsylvania.

Mainstreet Business Services(1272)
Box 674
Miles City MT 59301
Phone: **406-232-6111**
Fax: 406-232-0319

Local Retrieval Area: MT-Carter, Custer, Daniels, Dawson, Fallon, Garfield, McCone, Powder River, Prairie, Richland, Roosevelt, Rosebud, Sheridan, Valley, Wibaux.

Normal turn around time is varied depending on project. Fee basis varies by type of transaction. Credit accounts are accepted.

Mainstreet Business Services also has correspondent relationships in other jurisdictions, including Garfield and Powder River counties. They specialize in private investigations and bail bonds.

Mallard Investigations(1273)
PO Box 157
Clarkston MI 48347
Phone: **313-627-6605**
Fax: 313-627-6666

Local Retrieval Area: MI-Genesee, Lapeer, Macomb, Oakland, Wayne.

Normal turn around time is 24-48 hours. Projects are generally billed by the number of records located. Credit accounts are accepted. They require partial prepayment.

Mandelbaum-Edgerton Group(1274)
7855 Blvd East Suite 40
North Bergen NJ 07047
Phone: **908-899-9439**
Fax:

Local Retrieval Area: CT-Fairfield; NJ-Bergen, Hudson, Morris.

Normal turn around time is 1-3 days days, database searching will take 1-2 hours. Projects are generally billed by the hour. The first project may require a prepayment. Mandelbaum-Edgerton Group also has correspondent relationships in other jurisdictions, including all of NJ, CT, and NY. They specialize in plaintiff and defense fact finding, asset and financial worth searching, and general investigations.

Manistee Abstract & Title Co(1275)
63 Maple St
Manistee MI 49660
Phone: **616-723-3397**
Fax: 616-723-5382

Local Retrieval Area: MI-Manistee.

Normal turn around time is 3-5 days. Fee basis will vary by type of project. All projects require prepayment. They will also invoice. They specialize in real estate.

Marco & Company(1276)
PO Box 302
Benicia CA 94516
Phone: 707-747-1802
Fax: 707-747-5602

Local Retrieval Area: CA-Alameda, Marin, San Francisco.

Normal turn around time is varied depending on project. Online computer ordering is also available. Fee basis will vary by type of project. Credit accounts are accepted.
Marco & Company also has correspondent relationships in other jurisdictions, including the United States. They specialize in general investigations.

Hannah Marcum(1277)
198 Clearview
Irvine KY 40336
Phone: 606-723-4438
Fax:

Local Retrieval Area: KY-Estill.

Normal turn around time is up t 1 week. Fee basis varies by type of transaction. Credit accounts are accepted.

Marion County Abstract Co(1278)
PO Box 388
Yellville AR 72687
Phone: 501-449-4218
Fax: 501-449-4220

Local Retrieval Area: AR-Miller.

Normal turn around time is 3 days. Fee basis will vary by type of project. All projects require prepayment.
They have 27 years experience in real estate.

Marion County Abstract Co(1279)
117 S 3rd St
Knoxville IA 50138
Phone: 515-842-3518
Fax:

Local Retrieval Area: IA-Marion.

Normal turn around time is 1-2 days. Fee basis varies by type of transaction. The first project may require a prepayment.

Marion County Abstract Co(1280)
104 E Lafayette
Palmyra MO 63461
Phone: 800-952-5314
314-769-2212
Fax: 314-769-4916

Local Retrieval Area: IL-Adams, Hancock, Pike; MO-Lewis, Marion, Monroe, Ralls, Shelby.

Normal turn around time is 4-5 days. Fee basis will vary by the type of project. Credit accounts are accepted.
They specialize in title insurance and updating.

Marosi & Associates Inc(1281)
510 SW 3rd Ave Suite 400
Portland OR 97204
Phone: 503-760-2072
Fax:

Local Retrieval Area: OR-Clackamas, Multnomah, Washington.

Normal turn around time is 3 days. Projects are generally billed by the hour. The first project may require a prepayment.
Marosi & Associates Inc also has correspondent relationships in other jurisdictions, including Seattle area, Portland area and Boise area.

Marosi & Associates Inc(1282)
39713 NE Sunset Dr
Yacolt WA 98675
Phone: 206-686-3668
Fax:

Local Retrieval Area: WA-Clark.

Normal turn around time is 3 days. Projects are generally billed by the hour. The first project may require a prepayment.
Marosi & Associates Inc also has correspondent relationships in other jurisdictions, including King County.

Marquette County Abstract(1283)
16 Main St
Montello WI 53949
Phone: 608-297-2472
Fax: 608-297-2994

Local Retrieval Area: WI-Marquette.

Normal turn around time is 3-5 days. Fee basis varies by type of transaction. The first project may require a prepayment.

Marshall County Abstract Co(1284)
PO Box 50
Madill OK 73446
Phone: 405-795-3212
Fax: 405-795-3212

Local Retrieval Area: OK-Bryan, Carter, Coal, Johnston, Marshall, Murray, Pontotoc.

Normal turn around time is 2 days. Fee basis will vary by the type of project. Credit accounts are accepted.

Marshall County Abstract Co(1285)
30 W Main Room 102
Marshalltown IA 50158
Phone: 515-752-5358
Fax:

Local Retrieval Area: IA-Marshall.

Normal turn around time is 2 days. Fee basis will vary by type of project. Credit accounts are accepted.

Marshall Land & Title Co(1286)
PO Box 898
Britton SD 57430
Phone: 605-448-5796
Fax:

Local Retrieval Area: SD-Marshall.

Normal turn around time is 3-4. Fee basis is "by evaluation". Credit accounts are accepted.

Marshall Services Inc(1287)
3887 Durango Dr
Pensacola FL 32504
Phone: 904-478-5848
Fax: 904-478-8878

Local Retrieval Area: FL-Escambia, Okaloosa, Santa Rosa, Walton.

Normal turn around time is 2 days. A 1 day rush service is also available. Projects are generally billed by the hour. Credit accounts are accepted.
Marshall Services Inc also has correspondent relationships in other jurisdictions, including Leon, Bay and Washington Counties. They specialize in process service.

Martin Abstract Co(1288)
520 DeQueen St
Mena AR 71953
Phone: 501-394-1963
Fax: 501-394-3091

Local Retrieval Area: AR-Polk.

Normal turn around time is 2-3 days. Fee basis will vary by the type of project. All projects require prepayment. They will invoice to established clients.

Martin Abstract Co(1289)
PO Box 191
Warren AR 71671
Phone: **501-226-7487**
Fax: 501-226-2685

Local Retrieval Area: AR-Bradley, Cleveland.

Normal turn around time is up to 7 days. Projects are generally billed by the number of names searched. The first project may require a prepayment.

Marvin Abstracting(1290)
63 W Main St
Malone NY 12953
Phone: **518-483-3994**
Fax: 518-483-3994

Local Retrieval Area: NY-Franklin.

Normal turn around time is 1-3 days. Projects are generally billed by the number of names searched or records located. Credit accounts are accepted.

Maryland Research and Abstract(1291)
400 W Pennsylvania Ave
Towson MD 21204
Phone: **410-823-1944**
Fax: 410-823-7254

Local Retrieval Area: MD-Baltimore, Harford.

Normal turn around time is 1 week. Projects are generally billed by the number of names searched. Fee may be charged per property. Credit accounts are accepted.

Mason County Abstract(1292)
111 South Rath Avenue
Ludington MI 49431
Phone: **616-843-2645**
Fax: 616-843-1330

Local Retrieval Area: MI-Mason.

Normal turn around time is varied depending on project. Projects are generally billed by the number of names searched or records located. Credit accounts are accepted.
They specialize in searches covering real estate in Mason County, MI.

Mason and Associates(1293)
1372 Ann Terrace
Madison Heights MI 48071
Phone: **313-543-2405**
Fax: 313-543-4248

Local Retrieval Area: MI-Macomb, Oakland, Washtenaw, Wayne.

Normal turn around time is the next day. Projects are generally billed by the hour. Credit accounts are accepted.
Mason and Associates also has correspondent relationships in other jurisdictions, including all other counties in upper and lower Michigan.

Massey Abstract and Real Estate(1294)
307 Washington St
Covington IN 47932
Phone: **317-793-4547**
Fax: 317-793-0636

Local Retrieval Area: IN-Fountain, Vermillion, Warren.

Normal turn around time is 7 working days. Projects are generally billed by the number of names searched. Credit accounts are accepted.
They specialize in title searches.

Stephen Matejik(1295)
27 Mistletoe Lane
Levittown PA 19054
Phone: **609-394-9232**
Fax: 215-949-2030

Local Retrieval Area: NJ-Mercer.

Normal turn around time is 1 day to several weeks, depending on the number of years searched. Fee basis will vary by the type of project. Credit accounts are accepted. They require all national inquiries to prepay. Personal checks are accepted.

Maximum Protection Inc(1296)
101 Elmwood Dr
Wilkes-Barre PA 18702-7246
Phone: **717-655-5335**
Fax: 717-347-7273

Local Retrieval Area: PA-Lackawanna, Luzerne.

Normal turn around time is 24 hours. Projects are generally billed by the hour. Credit accounts are accepted. Personal checks are accepted.

Mayes County Abstract(1297)
PO Box 967
Pryor OK 74362
Phone: **918-825-3074**
Fax: 918-825-3571

Local Retrieval Area: OK-Mayes.

Normal turn around time is 1-2 days. Projects are generally billed by the hour. Credit accounts are accepted.

McAllister & Associates Inc(1298)
1998 Plantation Blvd
Jackson MS 39236-2082
Phone: **601-977-0406**
Fax: 601-957-2160

Local Retrieval Area: MS-Hinds, Lauderdale, Madison, Rankin, Warren, Yazoo.

Normal turn around time is varied depending on project. Projects are generally billed by the hour. All projects require prepayment. They will also invoice.
McAllister & Associates Inc also has correspondent relationships in other jurisdictions, including the rest of Mississippi. They are a general investigative agency.

McBrayer McDennis Leslie et al(1299)
PO Box 347
Greenup KY 41144
Phone: **606-473-7303**
Fax: 606-473-9003

Local Retrieval Area: KY-Boyd, Carter, Fayette, Franklin, Greenup, Lewis.

Normal turn around time is 2 days. Projects are generally billed by the hour. Credit accounts are accepted.

McCabe and Hubly Adj Co(1300)
2917 N Main St
Rockford IL 61103
Phone: **815-877-3053**
Fax: 815-877-3361

Local Retrieval Area: IL-Boone, Stephenson, Winnebago.

Normal turn around time is 48 hours for criminal and taxes, all others average up to 5 days. Projects are generally billed by the number of names searched. Credit accounts are accepted.
McCabe and Hubly Adj Co also has correspondent relationships in other jurisdictions, including Carroll, Ogle, De Kaib, Lee and Bureau. They specialize in criminal record searches.

McCarn Abstract Co(1301)　　Phone: **319-462-4828**
2200 W Jackson St　　　　　　　Fax: 319-462-4958
Anamosa IA 52205
Local Retrieval Area: IA-Jones.
Normal turn around time is 1-5 days. Projects are generally billed by the number of names searched. Credit accounts are accepted. McCarn Abstract Co also has correspondent relationships in other jurisdictions, including Linn and Scott Counties in Iowa and Rock Island Illinois.

McCarthy Abstract Co(1302)　　Phone: **402-336-2860**
PO Box 528　　　　　　　　　　Fax: 402-336-4489
O Neill NE 68763
Local Retrieval Area: NE-Boyd, Holt, Wheeler.
Normal turn around time is 3 days. Projects are generally billed by the hour. Credit accounts are accepted.
They specialize in real estate records.

Attorney John McCarty(1303)　　Phone: **502-927-8800**
PO Box 189　　　　　　　　　　Fax: 502-927-8810
Hawesville KY 42348
Local Retrieval Area: KY-Breckinridge, Daviess, Hancock, Ohio.
Normal turn around time is up to 1 week. Projects are generally billed by the hour. Credit accounts are accepted. A "retainer" fee is required.
He specializes in all types of legal work (excluding patent or immigration issues).

McCay Marcum & Triplett(1304)　　Phone: **606-298-3449**
PO Box 1087　　　　　　　　　　Fax: 606-298-5012
Inez KY 41224
Local Retrieval Area: KY-Johnson, Lawrence, Martin.
Normal turn around time is 2-3 days. Projects are generally billed by the hour. All projects require prepayment.

McCook Abstract Company(1305)　　Phone: **308-345-5120**
316 Norris Ave　　　　　　　　　Fax: 308-345-3812
McCook NE 69001
Local Retrieval Area: NE-Frontier, Hayes, Hitchcock, Red Willow.
Normal turn around time is 3-8 days. Projects are generally billed by the hour. Credit accounts are accepted. Personal checks are accepted.

McCook County Abstract & Title(1306)　　Phone: **605-425-2612**
PO Box 506　　　　　　　　　　Fax:
Salem SD 57058
Local Retrieval Area: SD-McCook.
Normal turn around time is 1 week. Fee basis is set by state law. All projects require prepayment.
They specialize in title insurance.

McCord Company(1307)　　Phone: **800-874-8820**
49 Stevenson St Suite 300　　　Fax: 800-828-3066
San Francisco CA 94105

Local retrieval area includes parts of Alaska, California, Idaho, Oregon, and Washington.
Normal turn around time is a 2 day verbal response and copies will follow. Projects are generally billed by the number of names searched or records located. Credit accounts are accepted. McCord Company also has correspondent relationships in other jurisdictions, including 95% of the counties nationwide. They specialize in UCC and litigation searches. They also handle filings in all jurisdictions.

Ney T McDaniel(1308)　　Phone: **601-782-9080**
158 Main St PO Box 476　　　Fax:
Raleigh MS 39153
Local Retrieval Area: MS-Covington, Hinds, Jasper, Jefferson Davis, Rankin, Scott, Simpson, Smith.
Normal turn around time is 1-2 days, although Smith county may be available on the same day. Projects are generally billed by the hour. Other billing methods are possible. The first project may require a prepayment.
Mr. McDaniel is an attorney in general practice as well as County Prosecutor.

McHenry County Abstract & Title(1309)　　Phone: **701-537-5723**
PO Box 420　　　　　　　　　　Fax:
Towner ND 58788
Local Retrieval Area: ND-McHenry.
Normal turn around time is about 1 week. Projects are generally billed by the hour. Credit accounts are accepted.

McHugh Abstract Co(1310)　　Phone: **701-256-2851**
PO Box 151　　　　　　　　　　Fax:
Langdon ND 58249
Local Retrieval Area: ND-Cavalier.
Normal turn around time is 2-5 days. Projects are generally billed by the number of names searched. Credit accounts are accepted.

McIntosh County Abstract Co(1311)　　Phone: **918-689-2311**
PO Box 150　　　　　　　　　　Fax:
Eufaula OK 74432
Local Retrieval Area: OK-McIntosh.
Normal turn around time is 2 days. Projects are generally billed by the number of records located. Credit accounts are accepted.

McIver Abstract & Insurance Co(1312)　　Phone: **501-898-3502**
440 W Main St　　　　　　　　　Fax:
Ashdown AR 71822
Local Retrieval Area: AR-Little River.
Normal turn around time is 3-4 days. Fee basis will vary by type of project. The first project may require a prepayment.
They specialize in real estate and title work.

McKean Abstracting Co(1313)
437 Main St
Smethport PA 16749
Phone: 814-887-5562
Fax:

Local Retrieval Area: PA-McKean.

Normal turn around time is 1-7 days. Projects are generally billed by the hour. Credit accounts are accepted. Out of county clients are charged a setup fee.

McKerns & McKerns(1314)
PO Box 188
Heathsville VA 22473
Phone: 804-580-8225
Fax: 804-580-8626

Local Retrieval Area: VA-Essex, Lancaster, Northumberland, Richmond, Westmoreland.

Normal turn around time is 2-3 days. Projects are generally billed by the hour. Credit accounts are accepted. Fee basis is per case. There is a possible retainer fee.
They specialize in criminal law and litigation.

McKesson Title Corp(1315)
201 W Jefferson St
Plymouth IN 46563
Phone: 219-936-2555
Fax: 219-936-2555

Local Retrieval Area: IN-Marshall.

Normal turn around time is 48 hours. Projects are generally billed by the number of names searched. Credit accounts are accepted. Personal or cashier checks are accepted.
McKesson Title Corp also has correspondent relationships in other jurisdictions, including Fulton and Starke counties. They specialize in title insurance and escrow closings.

McLean County Abstract Inc(1316)
PO Box 370
Washburn ND 58577
Phone: 701-462-3244
Fax:

Local Retrieval Area: ND-McLean.

Normal turn around time is 2 weeks. Fee basis will vary by type of project. All projects require prepayment. They will also invoice.

McMullen County Title Co(1317)
PO Box 395
Tilden TX 78072
Phone: 512-274-3312
Fax: 512-274-3590

Local Retrieval Area: TX-McMullen.

Normal turn around time is 2-3 days. Fee basis will vary by the type of project. The first project may require a prepayment.

McNeal Investigations(1318)
23000 Hwy 57
Ocean Springs MS 39564
Phone: 601-826-5104
Fax:

Local retrieval area includes southern Alabama and Southern Mississippi.

Normal turn around time is varied depending on project. Projects are generally billed by the hour. The first project may require a prepayment.
They specialize in investigations, process serving, and pre employment evaluations. They cover a wide range of counties in Southern AL and MS.

McPherson County Abstract(1319)
206 S Main St
McPherson KS 67460
Phone: 316-241-1317
Fax:

Local Retrieval Area: KS-McPherson.

Normal turn around time is up to 1 week. Fee basis varies by type of transaction. Credit accounts are accepted.

McPherson County Abstract Co(1320)
PO Box 440
Leola SD 57456
Phone: 605-439-3614
Fax:

Local Retrieval Area: SD-McPherson.

Normal turn around time is 1-5 days. Projects are generally billed by the hour. Credit accounts are accepted.
They specialize in real estate.

McQueen Abstract Company(1321)
PO Box 549
Hugoton KS 67951
Phone: 316-544-2311
Fax: 316-544-8029

Local Retrieval Area: KS-Stevens.

Normal turn around time is 3-5 days. Projects are generally billed by the hour. Credit accounts are accepted.

Meadowlark Search(1322)
3045 Meadowlark Dr
East Helena MT 59635
Phone: 406-227-5613
Fax:

Local Retrieval Area: MT-Broadwater, Jefferson, Lewis and Clark.

Normal turn around time is 2 days. Projects are generally billed by the hour. Credit accounts are accepted.
They specialize in mortgages, mining, oil, gas and water right searches.

Ray P Medlin Jr(1323)
PO Box 266
Albion NE 68620
Phone: 402-395-6183
Fax:

Local Retrieval Area: NE-Boone.

Normal turn around time is 1-2 days. Projects are generally billed by the hour. Credit accounts are accepted.
Mr. Medlin specializes in real estate and probate searches.

Mellette County Abstract Co(1324)
PO Box D
White River SD 57579
Phone: 605-259-3181
Fax: 605-259-3118

Local Retrieval Area: SD-Mellette.

Normal turn around time is 1 week to 10 days. Projects are generally billed by the number of records located. Credit accounts are accepted. Credit cards are accepted for payment.

Menard Title & Abstract Co Inc(1325)
121 Court St
Clarendon AR 72029
Phone: 501-747-3712
Fax:

Local Retrieval Area: AR-Monroe.

Normal turn around time is up to 2 weeks. Fee basis will vary by the type of project. Credit accounts are accepted.
They specialize in real estate and title insurance.

Mendo-Lake Paralegals(1326)
485 N Main St
Lakeport CA 95453
Phone: 707-263-8755
Fax: 707-263-4319

Local Retrieval Area: CA-Lake.

Normal turn around time is 2-3 days. Projects are generally billed by the number of names searched. The first project may require a prepayment.
Mendo-Lake Paralegals also has correspondent relationships in other jurisdictions, including Mendocino. They specialize in process serving and court filings.

Mercantile Data Resources(1327)
PO Box 1467
Russellville AR 72801
Phone: 800-242-5675
501-968-2163
Fax: 501-968-4596

Local Retrieval Area: AR-Conway, Crawford, Faulkner, Franklin, Johnson, Madison, Newton, Pope, Searcy, Stone, Van Buren, Washington, Yell.

Normal turn around time is varied depending on type of project. Projects are generally billed by the number of names searched or records located. Credit accounts are accepted. Credit cards are accepted for payment. Personal checks are accepted.
Mercantile Data Resources also has correspondent relationships in other jurisdictions, including the State of Arkansas. They specialize in asset and liability searches.

Mercer County Abstract Co Inc(1328)
614 4th Ave NE
Hazen ND 58545
Phone: 701-748-2190
Fax:

Local Retrieval Area: ND-Mercer.

Normal turn around time is 2 days. Projects are generally billed by the number of names searched. Credit accounts are accepted.

Mercury Messengers Inc(1329)
500 S Kansas Ave
Topeka KS 66603
Phone: 913-357-0078
Fax:

Local Retrieval Area: KS-Douglas, Osage, Shawnee.

Normal turn around time is up to 48 hours. Rush service is also available. Projects are generally billed by the hour. Fee basis will vary by the type of search. Credit accounts are accepted. They specialize in filings for attorneys.

Merkle Abstract & Title(1330)
216 N Broadway
Hartington NE 68739
Phone: 402-254-3547
Fax:

Local Retrieval Area: NE-Cedar.

Normal turn around time is 2 days. Project billing methods vary. Credit accounts are accepted.

Charles W Merritt Jr(1331)
120 S Main St
Madison GA 30650
Phone: 706-342-9668
Fax: 706-342-9843

Local Retrieval Area: GA-Greene, Jasper, Morgan, Oconee, Putnam.

Normal turn around time is varied depending on project. Projects are generally billed by the hour. The first project may require a prepayment. They accept personal checks.
Mr. Merritt specializes in real estate searches.

Brenda K Merritt(1332)
324 Colonial Dr
Mansfield OH 44903
Phone: 419-589-4729
Fax: 419-774-5603

Local Retrieval Area: OH-Ashland, Richland.

Normal turn around time is 24 hours. Projects are generally billed by the number of names searched. Credit accounts are accepted. Brenda specializes in real estate record searches.

Craig Messmer(1333)
29 Summer Dr
Berlin NJ 08009
Phone: 609-964-5453
Fax: 609-964-9880

Local Retrieval Area: NJ-Camden.

Normal turn around time is 1-7 days. Projects are generally billed by the number of names searched. The first project may require a prepayment. Personal checks are accepted.

Metro Legal Services(1334)
1 Financial Plaza Suite 1115
Minneapolis MN 55402
Phone: 612-332-0202
Fax:

Local Retrieval Area: MN-Anoka, Carver, Dakota, Hennepin, Ramsey, Scott, Sherburne, Washington, Wright.

Normal turn around time is 2-3 days. Some projects may be done the same day. Projects are generally billed by the number of names searched. Credit accounts are accepted.
Metro Legal Services also has correspondent relationships in other jurisdictions, including St. Louis, Blue Earth, Winona and Olmsted. They specialize in real estate searches.

Metro Legal Services Inc(1335)
1322 Webster St Suite 207
Oakland CA 94612-3232
Phone: 510-444-4800
Fax:

Local Retrieval Area: CA-Alameda, Contra Costa, Marin, Napa, San Francisco, San Mateo, Santa Clara, Solano, Sonoma.

Normal turn around time is the same day to 1 day. Projects are generally billed by the hour. Credit accounts are accepted. Credit cards are accepted for payment. Personal checks are accepted. They specialize in long distance rush court filings and research. They are California's largest trained legal courier staff.

Metropolitan Title Co(1336)
201 E State St
Hastings MI 49058
Phone: 616-945-9447
Fax: 616-945-5350

Local Retrieval Area: MI-Barry.

Normal turn around time is 3 days. Fee basis will vary by the type of project. Credit accounts are accepted.
They specialize in real estate title work.

Arthur Metzler(1337)
595 Newark Ave
Jersey City NJ 07306
Phone: 201-653-9676
Fax: 201-288-8835

Local Retrieval Area: NJ-Hudson.

Normal turn around time is 48 hours. Projects are generally billed by the number of names searched. The first project may require a prepayment. Personal checks are accepted.

Michael B Fixman & Associates(1338)
72 Hancock St
Everett MA 02149
Phone: **617-387-1100**
Fax: 617-884-8388

Local Retrieval Area: MA-Barnstable, Bristol, Plymouth; VA-Essex, Middlesex, City of Norfolk, City of Suffolk.

Normal turn around time is 1 day. Projects are generally billed by the hour. The first project may require a prepayment. Personal checks are accepted.

Michael B Fixman & Associates also has correspondent relationships in other jurisdictions, including Suffok, Essex, Norfolk, Middlesex, Plymouth, Barnstable and Bristol. Michael is a private detective and process server.

Mid Michigan Title & Abstract Co(1339)
26 E Sanilac Rd
Sandusky MI 48471
Phone: **313-648-4060**
Fax: 313-648-9137

Local Retrieval Area: MI-Sanilac.

Normal turn around time is 2-4 days. Fee basis will vary by type of project. The first project may require a prepayment.
They specialize in real estate.

Mid Montana Title Co(1340)
PO Box 2909
Harlowton MT 59036
Phone: **406-632-4145**
Fax: 406-632-4145

Local Retrieval Area: MT-Golden Valley, Sweet Grass, Wheatland.

Normal turn around time is varied depending on project. Fee basis varies by type of transaction. Credit accounts are accepted.
They specialize in title policies governed by the state, lot book reports in company form and real estate searches. They will give verbal replies on "simple searches" but will not send hard copy.

Mid-Point Services(1341)
PO Box 1546
Frederick MD 21702
Phone: **301-293-6997**
Fax: 301-371-6897

Local Retrieval Area: MD-All counties.

Normal turn around time is 12-24 hours. Real estate and tax searches average 24 hours. Projects are generally billed by the number of records located. Credit accounts are accepted. Personal checks are accepted.

Mid-Point Services also has correspondent relationships in other jurisdictions, including the State of Maryland.

Mid-South Investigations Inc(1342)
PO Box 100428
Birmingham AL 35210
Phone: **205-951-2301**
Fax:

Local Retrieval Area: AL-Bibb, Blount, Calhoun, Chilton, Cullman, Etowah, Jefferson, Madison, Montgomery, St. Clair, Shelby, Talladega, Tuscaloosa, Walker.

Normal turn around time is 24-48 hours. Project billing methods vary. Credit accounts are accepted.
They specialize in process service, asset searches, and skip tracing. A FAX # is available to established accounts.

Mid-State Attorney Service Inc(1343)
321 Cindy Lane
Montgomery AL 36116
Phone: **205-288-5975**
Fax: 205-288-3443

Local Retrieval Area: AL-Autauga, Butler, Chilton, Dallas, Elmore, Lee, Montgomery, Pike. Normal turn around time is 2 working days. Project billing methods vary. The first project may require a prepayment.
They specialize in retrieval of records from agencies located at the state capitol.

Midland Title Co(1344)
5103 Eastman Pl Suite 223
Midland MI 48640
Phone: **517-839-1003**
Fax: 517-839-0860

Local Retrieval Area: MI-Isabella, Midland.

Normal turn around time is 2-3 days. Fee basis will vary on the type of project. Credit accounts are accepted. They require out of town clients to prepay.
They specialize in real estate.

Midwest Abstract Co(1345)
4 S Main St Suite 200
Dayton OH 45402
Phone: **513-228-2292**
Fax: 513-228-0640

Local Retrieval Area: OH-Hamilton, Montgomery.

Normal turn around time is 5-7 days. The fee basis is per exam. Credit accounts are accepted. Midwest Abstract Co also has correspondent relationships in other jurisdictions, including Miami, Parke, Clark, Preble, Warren, Butler, Clermont and Green counties. They specialize in full 42-year title exams searches.

Midwest Search Ltd(1346)
36920 Ridgedale Court
Farmington Hills MI 48331
Phone: **313-788-7140**
Fax: 313-788-8930

Local Retrieval Area: MI-Oakland, Wayne.

Normal turn around time is 1-3 days. Projects are generally billed by the hour. The first project may require a prepayment.
They are specialists at reading and understanding files and motions.

Midwest Title Guarantee Co of Fla(1347)
3936 N Tamiami Trail Suite A
Naples FL 33940
Phone: **813-262-2164**
Fax: 813-262-7904

Local Retrieval Area: FL-Collier, Lee.

Normal turn around time is 48 hours. Rush service is also available. Fee basis will vary by type of project. Credit accounts are accepted.

Midwest Title Guarantee Company of Fl also has correspondent relationships in other jurisdictions, including all of Florida. Their specialty is real estate title searches.

Elden Mihulka(1348)
1115 C St
Schuyler NE 68661
Phone: **402-352-3053**
Fax:

Local Retrieval Area: NE-Butler, Colfax.

Normal turn around time is 2 days. Projects are generally billed by the number of names searched. Credit accounts are accepted.

Mike Moore Private Investigations(1349) Phone: **209-627-6824**
PO Box 2401   Fax: 209-734-3212
Visalia CA 93279

Local Retrieval Area: CA-Kings, Tulare.

Normal turn around time is 24 hours. Projects are generally billed by the hour. Credit accounts are accepted. Personal checks are accepted.

Mike Moore Private Investigations also has correspondent relationships in other jurisdictions, including Fresno and Keizn. They specialize in process serving and investigation.

Miller & Mosley(1350)   Phone: **704-264-1125**
PO Box 49   Fax: 704-262-3544
Boone NC 28607

Local Retrieval Area: NC-Ashe, Avery, Watauga.

Normal turn around time is 2 days. Projects are generally billed by the hour. Credit accounts are accepted.

They specialize in real estate and forclosures.

Miller Abstract and Title Co(1351)   Phone: **308-832-0969**
506 N Minden   Fax: 308-832-0969
Minden NE 68959

Local Retrieval Area: NE-Kearney.

Normal turn around time is 1-4 days. Fee basis is per search. Credit accounts are accepted. Personal checks are accepted.

Miller Abstract and Title Co also has correspondent relationships in other jurisdictions, including Phelps, Franklin and Buffalo counties. They specialize in title insurance, abstracting and limited title reports.

Miller County Abstract Co(1352)   Phone: **501-774-2539**
225 E 4th St   Fax: 501-772-3302
Texarkana AR 75502

Local Retrieval Area: AR-Miller.

Normal turn around time is 3 days. Projects are generally billed by the hour. Credit accounts are accepted.

Miller Newell Abstract(1353)   Phone: **501-523-8976**
514 3rd St   Fax: 501-523-3969
Newport AR 72112

Local Retrieval Area: AR-Jackson.

Normal turn around time is up to 10 days. Projects are generally billed by the hour. Credit accounts are accepted.

They specialize in real estate abstracting and title insurance.

G Scott Miller(1354)   Phone: **614-363-1324**
30 Troy Road Shopping Center   Fax: 614-548-5443
Delaware OH 43015

Local Retrieval Area: OH-Delaware, Marion, Union.

Normal turn around time is 24 hours. Fee basis will vary by the type of project. Credit accounts are accepted.

Gail L Miller(1355)   Phone: **913-378-3128**
208 N Commercial   Fax: 913-378-3543
Mankato KS 66956

Local Retrieval Area: KS-Jewell.

Normal turn around time is 1-7 days. Projects are generally billed by the hour. Credit accounts are accepted. Personal checks are accepted.

Joan Miller(1356)   Phone: **319-332-7767**
2704 29th St   Fax:
Bettendorf IA 52722

Local Retrieval Area: IA-Cedar, Clinton, Johnson, Muscatine, Scott.

Normal turn around time is 24-48 hours. Fee basis varies by type of transaction. Credit accounts are accepted.

Patricia Miller(1357)   Phone: **717-769-6880**
HCR 80 Box 65   Fax:
Lock Haven PA 17745

Local Retrieval Area: PA-Clinton, Lycoming.

Normal turn around time is 1-2 days. 1 to 2 weeks for 60 year title searches. They charge a flat rate per search. Credit accounts are accepted.

Patricia is a paralegal and specializes is real estate record searches.

Mimbres Valley Abstract & Title(1358)   Phone: **505-546-8896**
PO Drawer 2849   Fax: 505-546-9697
Deming NM 88031

Local Retrieval Area: NM-Luna.

Normal turn around time is 2-5 days. Fee basis is determined on a per name or "per legal". Credit accounts are accepted.

They specialize in title searches.

Missaukee Realty Co(1359)   Phone: **616-839-4563**
119 Prospect St   Fax: 616-839-4563
Lake City MI 49651

Local Retrieval Area: MI-Missaukee.

Normal turn around time is within 2 days. A rush service is also available. Projects are generally billed by the number of records located. Credit accounts are accepted.

Mississippi County Abstract(1360)   Phone: **314-683-4671**
105 E Court St   Fax:
Charleston MO 63834

Local Retrieval Area: MO-Mississippi.

Normal turn around time is 3-5 days. Fee basis will vary by type of project. All projects require prepayment.

They specialize in title insurance.

Mitchell County Abstract Co(1361)   Phone: **515-732-4571**
631 Main St   Fax:
Osage IA 50461

Local Retrieval Area: IA-Mitchell.

Normal turn around time is 3-5 days. They charge a flat rate per project. All projects require prepayment.

Mitchell McNutt Threadgill et al(1362)
PO Box 1200
Corinth MS 38834
    Phone: **601-286-9931**
    Fax: 601-286-8984

Local Retrieval Area: MS-Alcorn.

Normal turn around time is 1-2 days. Projects are generally billed by the hour. Credit accounts are accepted. They specialize in insurance investigations.

Kent D Mitchener(1363)
2075 Bypass Rd
Brandenburg KY 40108-0568
    Phone: **502-422-2611**
    Fax: 502-422-2011

Local Retrieval Area: KY-Breckinridge, Meade.

Normal turn around time is 2 working days. Fee basis varies by type of transaction. The first project may require a prepayment. Kent is a lawyer and specializes in criminal, bankruptcy, divorce, and personal injury cases.

Monroe County Abstract and Title(1364)
229 N Main St
Paris MO 65275
    Phone: **816-327-4109**
    Fax:

Local Retrieval Area: MO-Monroe.

Normal turn around time is 3 days. Projects are generally billed by the number of names searched. A fee for the length of the search may also be added to the per name charge. Credit accounts are accepted.

Monroe County Title Co(1365)
111 S Main St
Waterloo IL 62298
    Phone: **618-939-8292**
    Fax: 618-939-3931

Local Retrieval Area: IL-Marion.

Normal turn around time is 5 days except for US District and Bankruptcy Courts, which takes 10 days. Projects are generally billed by the number of names searched. Credit accounts are accepted. Personal checks are accepted.
Monroe County Title Co also has correspondent relationships in other jurisdictions, including undisclosed. They are an agent of Chicago Title Insurance Company and Lawyers Title Insurance Corporation. They specialize in insured real estate title searches.

Monroe Title Insurance Corp(1366)
47 W Main St
Rochester NY 14604
    Phone: **716-232-2070**
    Fax: 716-232-4988

Local Retrieval Area: NY-Many counties in this state are covered. See the county index for actual coverage..

Normal turn around time is 48 hours. Projects are generally billed by the number of names searched or records located. All projects require prepayment. Credit cards are accepted for payment. They will also invoice.

Montana Abstract & Title Co(1367)
400 W Granite
Butte MT 59701
    Phone: **406-723-6521**
    Fax: 406-723-6523

Local Retrieval Area: MT-Deer Lodge, Granite, Powell, Silver Bow.

Normal turn around time is 2 days. Projects are generally billed by the hour. Credit accounts are accepted.

Montana Abstract Co Inc(1368)
PO Box 128
Scobey MT 59263
    Phone: **406-487-5961**
    Fax:

Local Retrieval Area: MT-Daniels.

Normal turn around time is 1 week. Project billing methods vary. The first project may require a prepayment. They specialize in title insurance and abstract updating.

Montana Public Records Service(1369)
PO Box 516
Helena MT 59624
    Phone: **406-447-8337**
    Fax:

Local Retrieval Area: MT-Lewis and Clark.

Normal turn around time is 2-5 days. Projects are generally billed by the number of names searched. All projects require prepayment. They specialize in corporate searches.

Montana Title Co of Glendive(1370)
114 W Benham St
Glendive MT 59330
    Phone: **406-365-5482**
    Fax:

Local Retrieval Area: MT-Dawson, McCone.

Normal turn around time is 1 week or less. Projects are generally billed by the hour. Credit accounts are accepted.

Monterey County Attorneys Svc(1371)
395 Del Monte Center Suite 138
Monterey CA 93940-6156
    Phone: **408-649-5870**
    Fax: 408-649-8523

Local Retrieval Area: CA-Monterey, San Benito, Santa Cruz.

Normal turn around time is 1-2 days. Projects are generally billed by the hour. All projects require prepayment. Personal checks are accepted.
Monterey County Attorneys Service also has correspondent relationships in other jurisdictions, including statewide and nationwide. They specialize in process serving.

Montezuma-Dolores Title Co(1372)
236 W North St
Cortez CO 81321
    Phone: **303-565-8491**
    Fax: 303-565-7050

Local Retrieval Area: CO-Dolores, Montezuma.

Normal turn around time is 5-7 days. Projects are generally billed by the hour. Credit accounts are accepted. Personal checks are accepted.
They specialize in real estate title searches.

Montgomery County Abstract Co(1373)
108 N Pennsylvania Ave
Independence KS 67301
    Phone: **316-331-1440**
    Fax: 316-331-4760

Local Retrieval Area: KS-Montgomery.

Normal turn around time is 1-2 days. Fee basis varies by type of transaction. The first project may require a prepayment.

Montgomery County Abstr & Title(1374)
106 N Sturgeon St
Montgomery City MO 63361
Retrieval Area: MO-Montgomery.

Phone: **314-564-2298**
Fax: 314-564-6158
                                        Local

Normal turn around time is 5-10 days. Fee basis will vary by the type ofo project. All projects require prepayment. They will also invoice.
They maintain a complete set of in house record books for Montgomery County.

Montgomery Investigative Svcs(1375)
12073 Tech Rd
Silver Spring MD 20904

Phone: **301-384-7777**
Fax: 301-680-8966

Local Retrieval Area: MD-Montgomery.

Normal turn around time is 24-48 hours. Online computer ordering is also available. Projects are generally billed by the hour. Mileage expenses are added to the fee. Credit accounts are accepted.

Montmorency County Abstract(1376)
PO Box 212
Atlanta MI 49709

Phone: **517-785-4889**
Fax: 517-785-3689

Local Retrieval Area: MI-Montmorency.

Normal turn around time is 4-5 days. Projects are generally billed by the number of records located. The first project may require a prepayment.
They specialize in real estate.

Mary Ann Montz(1377)
302 23rd Street
Tuscaloosa AL 35401

Phone: **205-345-6643**
Fax:

Local Retrieval Area: AL-Tuscaloosa.

Normal turn around time is varied depending on search. Fee basis will vary by the type of search. Credit accounts are accepted.
Mary Ann specializes in UCC and judgement record searches.

Moody Abstract Co(1378)
PO Box 325
De Valls Bluff AR 72041

Phone: **501-998-2314**
Fax:

Local Retrieval Area: AR-Prairie.

Normal turn around time is 3-5 days. Fee basis will vary by the type of project. The first project may require a prepayment.
They have been in business for over 40 years.

Moody County Abstract Co(1379)
PO Box 304
Flandreau SD 57028

Phone: **605-997-3723**
Fax: 605-997-3722

Local Retrieval Area: SD-Moody.

Normal turn around time is 1 week. Fee basis will vary by the typr or project. The first project may require a prepayment.
They specialize in title insurance and record searches.

Moomaw Abstract Corp(1380)
8 E Main St
Bloomfield IN 47424

Phone: **812-384-4702**
Fax: 812-384-8936

Local Retrieval Area: IN-Clay, Daviess, Greene, Sullivan.

Normal turn around time is 1 week. Projects are generally billed by the number of names searched or records located. Credit accounts are accepted. Personal checks are accepted.
Moomaw Abstract Corp also has correspondent relationships in other jurisdictions, including Monroe, Owen and Martin Counties.

Moon Abstract Co(1381)
421 Commercial St
Emporia KS 66801

Phone: **316-342-1917**
Fax: 316-342-6888

Local Retrieval Area: KS-Chase, Coffey, Greenwood, .Morris, Osage, Wabaunsee.

Normal turn around time is "as soon as possible" for Lyon County and up to 1 week for other counties served. Fee basis varies by type of transaction. Credit accounts are accepted.
They specialize in long term escrow holdings.

Attorney Reed Moore Jr(1382)
107 Second St
Tompkinsville KY 42167

Phone: **502-487-6262**
Fax: 502-487-8000

Local Retrieval Area: KY-Barren, Monroe.

Normal turn around time is 2-3 days. Fee basis varies by type of transaction. The first project may require a prepayment.

Moore Mowdy & Youngblood(1383)
PO Box 540
Atoka OK 74525-0540

Phone: **405-889-5656**
Fax: 405-889-7149

Local Retrieval Area: OK-Atoka, Bryan, Coal, Johnston, Pushmataha.

Normal turn around time is 48 hours. Projects are generally billed by the hour. Credit accounts are accepted.
They specialize in probate and real estate record searches.

D M Moore(1384)
PO Box 2373
Streetsboro OH 44241

Phone: **216-626-5655**
Fax:

Local Retrieval Area: OH-Ashtabula, Geauga, Lake, Portage, Stark, Summit.

Normal turn around time is 1-7 days Projects are generally billed by the hour. The first project may require a prepayment.
Correspondent relationships in other jurisdictions include nationwide. Mr. Moore specializes in polygraph.

John Mord(1385)
PO Drawer 311
Tylertown MS 39667

Phone: **601-876-2611**
Fax: 601-876-4379

Local Retrieval Area: MS-Amite, Lawrence, Lincoln, Marion, Pike, Walthall.

Normal turn around time is 1 day in Walthall and 2-3 days in the other counties. Projects are generally billed by the hour. The first project may require a prepayment.
Mr. Mord is an attorney in general practice, including real estate and family law.

More Than Mail(1386)   Phone: 503-474-6692
322 Redwood Hwy   Fax: 503-474-6692
Grants Pass OR 97527
Local Retrieval Area: OR-Jackson, Josephine.

Normal turn around time is 24-48 hours. Projects are generally billed by the number of names searched or records located. Credit accounts are accepted.

Morrilton Abstract Co(1387)   Phone: 501-354-2611
110 S Chestnut Suite C   Fax:
Morrilton AR 72110
Local Retrieval Area: AR-Conway.

Normal turn around time is 1 week. Fee basis will vary by the type of project. All projects require prepayment. They will also invoice. They specialize in title and real estate research.

Morris Hills Abstract Co(1388)   Phone: 201-267-0450
44 Washington St   Fax: 201-267-0981
Morristown NJ 07960
Local Retrieval Area: NJ-Morris.

Normal turn around time is up to 2 weeks. Projects are generally billed by the hour. Credit accounts are accepted.

Morrissey Morrissey & Dalluge(1389)   Phone: 402-335-3344
PO Box 597   Fax: 402-335-3345
Tecumseh NE 68450
Local Retrieval Area: NE-Garden, Johnson, Lancaster, Nemaha, Otoe, Pawnee, Richardson. Normal turn around time is 1 week. Projects are generally billed by the hour. The first project may require a prepayment. Credit cards are accepted for payment. They specialize in probate and real estate.

Ralph J Moses(1390)   Phone: 618-576-2632
PO Box 326   Fax:
Hardin IL 62047
Local Retrieval Area: IL-Calhoun.

Normal turn around time is 12-24 hours. Projects are generally billed by the hour. Credit accounts are accepted.
Ralph specializes in real estate record searches.

Mosley Abstract Co(1391)   Phone: 501-782-3053
PO Box 2124   Fax: 501-782-5432
Fort Smith AR 72902-2124
Local Retrieval Area: AR-Crawford, Franklin, Scott, Sebastian.

Normal turn around time is 2-3 days. Projects are generally billed by the number of names searched. Credit accounts are accepted.

Mountain View Abstract Co(1392)   Phone: 501-269-8410
PO Box 130   Fax: 501-269-8410
Mountain View AR 72560
Local Retrieval Area: AR-Stone.

Normal turn around time is 1-2 weeks. Fee basis will vary by the type of project. All projects require prepayment. They will also invoice.
They specialize in real estate and title work.

Mountrail Cty Abstr & Title(1393)   Phone: 701-628-2886
PO Box 519   Fax:
Stanley ND 58784
Local Retrieval Area: ND-Burke, McKenzie, Mountrail, Ward, Williams.

Normal turn around time is 1-5 days. Fee basis will vary by type of project. Credit accounts are accepted.

Mt Pleasant Abstract and Title Co(1394)   Phone: 517-773-3651
116 Court   Fax: 517-773-0751
Mt Pleasant MI 48858
Local Retrieval Area: MI-Clare, Isabella.

Normal turn around time is 1 week. Fee basis will vary by type of project. Credit accounts are accepted.
They specialize in real estate and title insurance.

David Mulberry(1395)   Phone: 407-640-0506
931 Village Blvd Suite 907-184   Fax:
West Palm Beach FL 33409
Local Retrieval Area: FL-Palm Beach.

Normal turn around time is varied depending on project. Projects are generally billed by the number of records located. The first project may require a prepayment.
David is a private investigator and certified process server.

Mullen Abstract Co(1396)   Phone: 501-886-2452
119 SW 2nd St   Fax:
Walnut Ridge AR 72476
Local Retrieval Area: AR-Lawrence.

Normal turn around time is 3-5 days. Fee basis will vary by the type of project. Credit accounts are accepted.
They specialize in real estate abstracting and title.

Donna Mundwiller(1397)   Phone: 314-486-2925
118 E 4th St   Fax: 314-486-2059
Hermann MO 65041
Local Retrieval Area: MO-Gasconade.

Normal turn around time is varied depending on project. Projects are generally billed by the hour. All projects require prepayment.
Donna specializes in genealogy searches.

Maxine Munsinger(1398)   Phone: 515-858-3585
402 9th Ave   Fax:
Eldora IA 50627
Local Retrieval Area: IA-Hardin.

Normal turn around time is normally 24 to 48 hours plus mail time. Rush service is available in 24 hours plus mail time. Projects are generally billed by the number of names searched or records located. Credit accounts are accepted. They will accept personal checks.

Murray County Abstract Inc(1399)   Phone: 405-622-5294
108 W Muskogee   Fax: 405-622-2866
Sulphur OK 73086
Local Retrieval Area: OK-Murray.

Normal turn around time is 24 hours. Projects are generally billed by the hour. Credit accounts are accepted.

Dan R Murray(1400)
PO Box 639
Sparta NC 28675
Phone: **919-372-5681**
Fax: 919-372-8617

Local Retrieval Area: NC-Alleghany.

Normal turn around time is 1-2 days. Fee basis varies by type of transaction. The first project may require a prepayment.
Mr. Murray is a trial lawyer.

Musselman Abstract Co(1401)
PO Box 1072
Bartlesville OK 74005
Phone: **918-336-6410**
Fax: 918-336-4880

Local Retrieval Area: OK-Washington.

Normal turn around time is 24 hours. Fee basis will vary by the type of project. Credit accounts are accepted.

Musselshell County Title Inc(1402)
PO Box 838
Roundup MT 59072
Phone: **406-323-3165**
Fax: 406-323-3165

Local Retrieval Area: MT-Musselshell.

Normal turn around time is 3-5 days. Fee basis varies by type of transaction. Credit accounts are accepted.

N F Field Abstract Co(1403)
PO Box 697
Fergus Falls MN 56538
Phone: **218-736-6844**
Fax: 218-739-5331

Local Retrieval Area: MN-Otter Tail.

Normal turn around time is 5-10 days. Projects are generally billed by the number of names searched. Fee may also be based per entry. All projects require prepayment. They will also invoice.
They specialize in title insurance and closings.

N W Legal Support Inc(1404)
703 Columbia St Suite 201
Seattle WA 98104
Phone: **206-223-9426**
Fax: 206-223-9475

Local Retrieval Area: WA-Clallam, Clark, Cowlitz, Grays Harbor, Island, Jefferson, King, Kitsap, Lewis, Mason, Pierce, Skagit, Snohomish, Thurston, Whatcom.

Normal turn around time is the same day. Projects are generally billed by the hour. Credit accounts are accepted.
N W Legal Support Inc also has correspondent relationships in other jurisdictions, including Washington.

NC Search Inc(1405)
620 S Elm St Suite 363
Greensboro NC 27406
Phone: **919-273-4999**
Fax: 919-273-5155

Local Retrieval Area: NC-All counties; SC-Beaufort, Calhoun, Charleston, Fairfield, Kershaw, Lexington, Richland, Spartanburg, York.

Normal turn around time is 2-3 days. Rush service orders are possible. Projects are generally billed by the number of names searched. Asset searches are done on a per hour basis. Credit accounts are accepted.

National Abstract Corporation(1406)
7659 N State St
Lowville NY 13367
Phone: **315-376-3911**
Fax: 315-376-8305

Local Retrieval Area: NY-Lewis.

Normal turn around time is 24 hours for court records, taxes and UCC's, and 5 working days for real estate searches. Projects are generally billed by the number of names searched or records located. Credit accounts are accepted.
National Abstract Corporation also has correspondent relationships in other jurisdictions, including Chenango, Deleware, Jefferson, Madison, Oneida, Ononoaga, Oswego, Otsego and St. Lawrence counties.

National Document Retrieval Inc(1407)
3101 N Central Ave Suite 1050
Phoenix AZ 85012
Phone: **602-258-8223**
Fax: 602-243-1589

Local Retrieval Area: AZ-Maricopa, Pima, Pinal.

Normal turn around time is 48 hours. Projects are generally billed by the number of names searched. Credit accounts are accepted.
National Document Retrieval Inc also has correspondent relationships in other jurisdictions, including all of Arizona and nationwide.

National Investigative Services 1408)
1736 E Sunshine Suite 308
Springfield MO 65804
Phone: **417-883-1213**
Fax: 417-883-4521

Local Retrieval Area: MO-Barry, Barton, Cedar, Christian, Dade, Dallas, Douglas, Greene, Hickory, Jasper, Laclede, Lawrence, McDonald, Miller, Newton, Ozark, Phelps, Polk, Stone, Taney, Vernon, Webster, Wright.

Normal turn around time is two weeks. Projects are generally billed by the hour. The first project may require a prepayment.

National Legal Process(1409)
49 Bancroft Mills Suite 3-H
Wilmington DE 19806
Phone: **302-429-0649**
Fax: 302-429-0656

Local Retrieval Area: DE-All counties; PA-Chester, Delaware.

Normal turn around time is 2-5 days. A same day rush service is also available. Projects are generally billed by the number of names searched. Credit accounts are accepted.
They specialize in process service and skip tracing.

National Service Information Inc(1410)
145 Baker St
Marion OH 43302
Phone: **614-387-6806**
Fax: 614-382-1256

Local Retrieval Area: IN-All counties; KY-All counties; OH-All counties, Sandusky.

Normal turn around time is varied depending on project. Fee basis will vary by type of project. Credit accounts are accepted.
National Service Information Inc also has correspondent relationships in other jurisdictions, including nationwide.

Nationwide Information Services(1411)
505 Willard Ave
Newington CT 06111
Phone: 203-666-3090
Fax: 203-667-2038

Local Retrieval Area: CT-All counties.

Normal turn around time is the same day for Secretary of State in Connecticut, and next day service for all other states or counties. Projects are generally billed by the number of names searched. Credit accounts are accepted.
Nationwide Information Services also has correspondent relationships in other jurisdictions, including nationwide. They specialize in UCC searches, filing and recording.

Nationwide Information Services(1412)
117 Liberty St
Harrisburg PA 17101
Phone: 800-443-0824
Fax: 717-238-6522

Local Retrieval Area: PA-Cumberland, Dauphin, Lancaster, Lebanon, York.

Normal turn around time is 24-48 hours. Projects are generally billed by the number of names searched or records located. Credit accounts are accepted.
Nationwide Information Services Inc also has correspondent relationships in other jurisdictions, including the state of Pennsylvania. They specialize in asset searches and state level searches.

Navarro County Abstract Co(1413)
PO Box 685
Corsicana TX 75151
Phone: 903-874-3768
Fax:

Local Retrieval Area: TX-Navarro.

Normal turn around time is varied depending on project. Fee basis will vary by type of project. Credit accounts are accepted.

Nebraska Title Company(1414)
110 N 5th St
Beatrice NE 68310
Phone: 402-228-2233
Fax: 402-228-4543

Local Retrieval Area: NE-Gage.

Normal turn around time is 36 hours. Projects are generally billed by the number of names searched. Credit accounts are accepted.

Ben Neel(1415)
PO Box 355
Menard TX 76859
Phone: 915-396-2351
Fax:

Local Retrieval Area: TX-Menard, Sutton.

Normal turn around time is 1-2 days. Projects are generally billed by the hour. All projects require prepayment.

Nelson County Abstract(1416)
112 Main
Lakota ND 58344
Phone: 701-247-2221
Fax:

Local Retrieval Area: ND-Nelson.

Normal turn around time is 24-48 hours. Projects are generally billed by the number of names searched or records located. Fee basis may vary according to laws. Credit accounts are accepted. A setup fee may be charged depending on type of work requested. Personal checks are accepted.

Nemaha County Abstract Co(1417)
419 Main St
Seneca KS 66538
Phone: 913-336-2137
Fax:

Local Retrieval Area: KS-Nemaha.

Normal turn around time is 1-2 days. Fee basis varies by type of transaction. The first project may require a prepayment.

Neuf & Associates(1418)
PO Box 2445
Paducah KY 42002-2445
Phone: 502-443-2867
Fax: 502-443-2867

Local Retrieval Area: IL-Hardin, Johnson, Massac; KY-Livingston, McCracken, Marshall.

Normal turn around time is 1-3 days. There is an additional charge for rush service. Projects are generally billed by the hour. The first project may require a prepayment.
Neuf & Associates also has correspondent relationships in other jurisdictions, including the state of Kentucky and Nashville, Tennessee. They specialize in legal investigation, recorded interviews, and person location.

Tim Neuroth(1419)
813 Des Moines St
Webster City IA 50595
Phone: 515-832-3156
Fax:

Local Retrieval Area: IA-Hamilton.

Normal turn around time is 1-2 days. Projects are generally billed by the hour. The first project may require a prepayment. They will accept personal checks.

Nevada Land Services(1420)
PO Box 1169
Tonopah NV 89049
Phone: 702-482-5641
Fax: 702-482-8935

Local Retrieval Area: NV-Churchill, Esmeralda, Eureka, Humboldt, Lander, Lincoln, Mineral, Nye, Pershing, White Pine.

Normal turn around time is 10 days. Projects are generally billed by the number of names searched. Credit accounts are accepted. Personal checks are accepted.
They specialize in unpatented mining claim reports.

Nevada Records Search(1421)
PO Box 8759
Incline Village NV 89450
Phone: 702-832-0490
Fax: 702-832-0944

Local Retrieval Area: NV-Douglas, Storey, Washoe, Carson City.

Normal turn around time is is 1-2 days for the listed counties and 3-5 days for the network counties. Projects are generally billed by the number of names searched. Credit accounts are accepted.
Nevada Records Search also has correspondent relationships in other jurisdictions, including the rest of the counties in Nevada. They specialize in UCC searches and filings and Motor Vehicle Record searches.

New England Recovery Inc(1422)
PO Box 1025
Barre VT 05641
Phone: 802-433-6145
Fax: 802-433-6742

Local Retrieval Area: NH-All counties; VT-All counties.

Normal turn around time is 2 to 4 days. They charge a base fee and per hour. They also charge extra for the copy charges. Credit accounts are accepted.

New York Institute of Legal Rsrch(1423)   Phone: 914-245-8400
PO Box 398   Fax: 914-245-7660
Yorktown Heights NY 10598-0398

Local Retrieval Area: NY-All counties.

Normal turn around time is 24 hours. Projects are generally billed by the number of names searched or records located. Credit accounts are accepted.

New York Institute of Legal Research also has correspondent relationships in other jurisdictions, including nationwide.

Newaygo County Abstract & Title(1424)   Phone: 800-536-5263
24 E Main St   616-924-2000
Fremont MI 49412   Fax: 616-924-2111

Local Retrieval Area: MI-Newaygo.

Normal turn around time is 1 week. They charge a flat rate per project. Credit accounts are accepted.

They specialize in real estate.

Jake Nichols(1425)   Phone: 406-765-1651
PO Box 441   Fax:
Plentywood MT 59254

Local Retrieval Area: MT-Daniels, Roosevelt, Sheridan.

Normal turn around time is varied depending on project. Projects are generally billed by the hour. The first project may require a prepayment.

Mr. Nichols specializes in mineral searches.

Leslie Niemier(1426)   Phone: 208-425-3841
59 S 3rd E Suite 2   Fax:
Soda Springs ID 83276

Local Retrieval Area: ID-Bear Lake, Caribou.

Normal turn around time is 1-2 days. Fee basis will vart by type of project. The first project may require a prepayment.

Nierman & Nierman Law Office(1427)   Phone: 812-358-4766
111 W Walnut St   Fax:
Brownstown IN 47220

Local Retrieval Area: IN-Jackson.

Normal turn around time is 10 working days. Projects are generally billed by the number of names searched. Copy charges may be added to the fee. Credit accounts are accepted.

Nimrod Legal Support Services(1428)   Phone: 614-497-1655
1099 Belford Ave   Fax: 614-497-1655
Columbus OH 43207

Local Retrieval Area: OH-Delaware, Fairfield, Franklin, Licking, Madison, Union.

Normal turn around time is 24 hours. Projects are generally billed by the number of names searched or records located. Credit accounts are accepted.

Nimrod Legal Support Services also has correspondent relationships in other jurisdictions, including the rest of Ohio. They specialize in preparing subpoenas in order to obtain medical and other records.

Nodaway County Abstract Co(1429)   Phone: 816-582-2332
118 E 3rd St   Fax:
Maryville MO 64468

Local Retrieval Area: MO-Nodaway, Worth.

Normal turn around time is 1 day. Projects are generally billed by the number of names searched. Credit accounts are accepted. They specialize in complete searches of land records.

Nolan & Associates(1430)   Phone: 803-244-9925
117 Bendingwood Cir   Fax: 803-244-2394
Taylors SC 29687

Local Retrieval Area: SC-Anderson, Cherokee, Greenville, Laurens, Pickens, Spartanburg, York.

Normal turn around time is 1-5 days. Projects are generally billed by the hour. Credit accounts are accepted.

Nolan & Associates also has correspondent relationships in other jurisdictions, including nationwide. They specialize in background checks and skip tracing/missing person.

Trudi Norce(1431)   Phone: 717-752-5710
304 Mary St   Fax:
Berwick PA 18603

Local Retrieval Area: PA-Columbia.

Normal turn around time is 24-48 hours. Projects are generally billed by the number of names searched. Credit accounts are accepted.

Trudi specializes in real estate record searches.

North Central Abstract Co(1432)   Phone: 800-456-4705
1017 E Douglas St   402-336-1588
O'Neill NE 68763   Fax: 402-336-1590

Local Retrieval Area: NE-Antelope, Boyd, Holt, Wheeler.

Normal turn around time is 14 days. Projects are generally billed by the hour. Credit accounts are accepted.

They specialize in title searches.

North Coast Attorney Service(1433)   Phone: 707-462-6877
107 W Perkins Suite 16   Fax: 707-462-6878
Ukiah CA 95482

Local Retrieval Area: CA-Lake, Mendocino.

Normal turn around time is 5 days. Rush or next day service is available for an additional charge. Projects are generally billed by the hour. Credit accounts are accepted.

North Coast Attorney Service also has correspondent relationships in other jurisdictions, including nationwide. They specialize in private investigation and legal video.

North East Court Services Inc(1434)   Phone: 800-235-0794
43 Winchester Dr   Fax: 908-755-5797
Scotch Plains NJ 07076

Local Retrieval Area: CT-Fairfield; NJ-All counties; NY-Bronx, Kings, New York, Queens, Richmond.

Normal turn around time is 24-72 hours. Projects are generally billed by the number of names searched or records located. Credit accounts are accepted.

North Florida Abstract(1435)
PO Box 838
Monticello FL 32344
Phone: **904-997-2670**
Fax:

Local Retrieval Area: FL-Jefferson.

Normal turn around time is 1 week. Fee basis will vary by the type of project Credit accounts are accepted.
They specialize in real estate searches.

North Louisiana Title Co Inc(1436)
1101 Royal Ave
Monroe LA 71201
Phone: **318-323-3800**
Fax: 318-325-8357

Local retrieval area includes 23 parishes in Louisiana.

Normal turn around time is 1-3 days. Fee will vary with the type of search. All projects require prepayment.
They specialize in title searches.

North Pacific Legal(1437)
PO Box 1217
Coos Bay OR 97420
Phone: **503-267-5118**
Fax: 503-267-0823

Local Retrieval Area: OR-Coos.

Normal turn around time is varied depending on project. Projects are generally billed by the hour. Credit accounts are accepted.
They specialize in locating people.

North State Process(1438)
2701 Eureka Wy
Redding CA 96001
Phone: **916-241-2228**
Fax: 916-241-6928

Local Retrieval Area: CA-Butte, Shasta, Siskiyou, Tehama.

Normal turn around time is varied depending on project. Projects are generally billed by the number of names searched or records located. All projects require prepayment. They will invoice. Cash is accepted.
North State Process also has correspondent relationships in other jurisdictions, including all counties in California. Their specialty is process locating and record search.

North Vernon Abstract Co Inc(1439)
16 Main St
North Vernon IN 47265
Phone: **812-346-2259**
Fax: 812-346-6056

Local Retrieval Area: IN-Jennings.

Normal turn around time is varied depending on project. Projects are generally billed by the number of names searched. Credit accounts are accepted. Personal checks are accepted.

North Winds Investigations Inc(1440)
PO Box 1654
Rogers AR 72752
Phone: **800-530-4514**
501-925-1612
Fax: 501-925-2819

Local Retrieval Area: AR-Benton, Carroll, Crawford, Pulaski, Sebastian, Washington.

Normal turn around time is 2-3 days. Projects are generally billed by the hour. Credit accounts are accepted.
North Winds Investigations Inc also has correspondent relationships in other jurisdictions, including the rest of Arkansas. They specialize in worker's compensation, liability surveillance and skip tracing.

North Wisconsin Abstract Co(1441)
212 W Main St
Ashland WI 54806
Phone: **715-682-4234**
Fax: 715-682-4234

Local Retrieval Area: WI-Ashland, Bayfield.

Normal turn around time is varied depending on project. Projects are generally billed by the number of names searched. Credit accounts are accepted. Personal checks are accepted.
They specialize in real estate title searches.

Northeast Missorui Abstr Agy(1442)
106 W Jefferson
Monticello MO 63457
Phone: **314-767-5430**
Fax: 314-767-5430

Local Retrieval Area: MO-Lewis.

Normal turn around time is 4 days. Projects are generally billed by the number of names searched or records located. Fee basis will vary by type of project. The first project may require a prepayment. Personal checks and cash are accepted.
Northeast Missorui Abstract Agency Inc also has correspondent relationships in other jurisdictions, including Knox, Scotland, Clark, Marion, Shelby and Adair Counties in Missouri. They have over 25 years experience in legal work.

Northeast Nebraska Title(1443)
1105 S 13th St Suite 208
Norfolk NE 68701
Phone: **800-870-2142**
402-371-1221
Fax: 402-439-2145

Local Retrieval Area: NE-Antelope, Madison.

Normal turn around time is 1-3 days. Fee basis is a flat rate and per record. Credit accounts are accepted.
They specialize in title insurance.

Northern Arizona Investigations(1444)
PO Box 1326
Flagstaff AZ 86002
Phone: **800-657-2747**
Fax: 602-779-2823

Local Retrieval Area: AZ-Coconino, Navajo.

Normal turn around time is 1-2 days. Projects are generally billed by the hour. Credit accounts are accepted.
They specialize in skiptracing.

Northern Title of Vilas County(1445)
Box 877
Eagle River WI 54521
Phone: **715-479-6459**
Fax: 715-479-7482

Local Retrieval Area: WI-Vilas.

Normal turn around time is 2 days. Projects are generally billed by the number of names searched. Credit accounts are accepted.

Northwest Abstract and Title Inc(1446)
PO Box 1265
Williston ND 58801
Phone: **701-774-8829**
Fax: 701-774-8400

Local Retrieval Area: ND-Dunn, Williams.

Normal turn around time is 3 days. Projects are generally billed by the hour. Credit accounts are accepted.

Northwest Land Title Inc(1447) Phone: **715-825-4411**
97 W Main Fax: 715-825-4226
Milltown WI 54858

Local Retrieval Area: WI-Burnett, Polk, Sawyer, Washburn.

Normal turn around time is 2 days for title insurance, and 3 days for abstracting. Projects are generally billed by the number of names searched. Credit accounts are accepted.

They specialize in title insurance and insured closings.

Northwestern Illinois Title(1448) Phone: **815-235-1477**
116 W Exchange St Fax:
Freeport IL 61032

Local Retrieval Area: IL-Boone, Bureau, Carroll, De Kalb, Henry, Jo Daviess, La Salle, Lee, McHenry, Marshall, Ogle, Putnam, Rock Island, Stephenson, Whiteside, Winnebago.

Normal turn around time is 48 hours. Projects are generally billed by the number of records located. Credit accounts are accepted.

They specialize in land title.

O H Vivell Title Co(1449) Phone: **217-942-3733**
506 N Court House Square PO Box 31 Fax: 217-942-3207
Carrollton IL 62016-0031

Local Retrieval Area: IL-Greene.

Normal turn around time is varied depending on project. Projects are generally billed by the number of records located. The first project may require a prepayment.

O H Vivell Title Co also has correspondent relationships in other jurisdictions, including the counties of Calhoun and Jersey.

Jack O'Brien(1450) Phone: **609-265-1303**
462 Connecticut Ave Fax: 609-587-0984
Trenton NJ 08629

Local Retrieval Area: NJ-Burlington.

Normal turn around time is 1-3 days. Projects are generally billed by the number of names searched. The first project may require a prepayment. Personal checks are accepted.

Nikki A O'Connell(1451) Phone: **804-877-8469**
155 Princess Margaret Dr Fax:
Newport News VA 23602

Local Retrieval Area: VA-Gloucester, Isle of Wight, James City, Surry, York, City of Hampton, City of Newport News, City of Williamsburg.

Normal turn around time is 24-48 hours. Projects are generally billed by the number of names searched. Credit accounts are accepted. Personal checks are accepted.

Nikki specializes in UCC, judgement and property/title searches.

Michael J O'Connor(1452) Phone: **717-874-3300**
56 N Lehigh Ave Fax: 717-874-4822
Frackville PA 17931

Local Retrieval Area: PA-Schuylkill.

Normal turn around time is 1 week. Projects are generally billed by the number of names searched. Credit accounts are accepted. They accept personal checks.

Correspondent relationships in other jurisdictions include Columbia and Northumberland.

Oakey and Oakey Abstract Co(1453) Phone: **715-294-2624**
108 Chieftain Fax: 715-755-3535
Osceola WI 54020

Local Retrieval Area: WI-Polk.

Normal turn around time is 2-7 days. Projects are generally billed by the number of names searched or records located. Credit accounts are accepted.

Oakey and Oakey Abstract Co also has correspondent relationships in other jurisdictions, including Burnett and Barron. They specialize in DOT searches for new road set ups, title searches and full abstracting.

Ocean Title & Escrow(1454) Phone: **503-247-7021**
PO Box 505 Fax: 503-247-2421
Gold Beach OR 97444

Local Retrieval Area: OR-Curry.

Normal turn around time is 2-3 days. Projects are generally billed by the hour. The first project may require a prepayment.

Oceana Land Title Co(1455) Phone: **800-466-5263**
117 N State St 616-873-2166
Hart MI 49420 Fax: 616-873-2824

Local Retrieval Area: MI-Oceana.

Normal turn around time is 1 week. They charge a flat rate per project. Credit accounts are accepted.

They specialize in real estate.

Ochiltree County Abstract Co(1456) Phone: **806-435-4572**
316 S Main St Fax:
Perryton TX 79070

Local Retrieval Area: TX-Ochiltree.

Normal turn around time is 2 days. Projects are generally billed by the hour. Credit accounts are accepted. Personal checks are accepted.

They specialize in preparing abstracts of title, issuance of title insurance, lien searches, abstracts of judgement, copies of filed documents and courtesy filings. They also can search District Court minutes and pending lawsuits.

Ogeman Title Co(1457) Phone: **517-345-7240**
PO Box 384 Fax: 517-345-4777
West Branch MI 48661

Local Retrieval Area: MI-Ogemaw.

Normal turn around time is up to a week, rush service may be available. Fee basis will vary by the type of project. Credit accounts are accepted. They request prepay on out of area transactions. They specialize in title insurance.

Ogemaw County Abstract Co(1458) Phone: **517-345-0110**
111 N 3rd St Fax: 517-345-2907
West Branch MI 48661

Local Retrieval Area: MI-Ogemaw.

Normal turn around time is 24 hours. Projects are generally billed by the number of names searched. Credit accounts are accepted.

Ohio Bar Title(1459)
250 S Prospect St
Ravenna OH 44266
Phone: 216-296-7003
Fax: 216-296-9642

Local Retrieval Area: OH-Portage.

Normal turn around time is 24 hours for most searches, and full real estate title searches average 3 working days. Fee basis will vary by type of project. Credit accounts are accepted. Personal checks are accepted.

Ohio Independent Title & Pub Rec(1460)
PO Box 593
Tiffin OH 44883
Phone: 419-447-7474
Fax: 419-447-0007

Local Retrieval Area: OH-Allen, Crawford, Erie, Hancock, Hardin, Huron, Ottawa, Sandusky, Seneca, Wood, Wyandot.

Normal turn around time is 24-48 hours. Projects are generally billed by the number of names searched or records located. Credit accounts are accepted. Personal checks are accepted. Ohio Independent Title & Pub Rec Search also has correspondent relationships in other jurisdictions, including Putnam, Lucas, Definane, Fulton, Williams, Henry, Richland, Morrow, Ashland, Marion, Deleware and Paulding. They specialize in title searches.

Okeechobee Abstract and Title(1461)
302 NW 3rd St
Okeechobee FL 34972
Phone: 813-763-3710
Fax: 813-763-3787

Local Retrieval Area: FL-Glades, Martin, Okeechobee.

Normal turn around time is the same day for name and UCC searches, and 2 to 3 days for real state commitments. Projects are generally billed by the number of names searched. Credit accounts are accepted.
Okeechobee Abstract and Title Ins Inc also has correspondent relationships in other jurisdictions, including Palm Beach, Martin, St. Lucie, Broward, Dade and Monroe Counties. They are a family owned company that has been in business for over 50 years at the same location.

Okfusee County Abstract Co(1462)
PO Box 66
Okemah OK 74859
Phone: 918-623-0565
Fax:

Local Retrieval Area: OK-Okfuskee.

Normal turn around time is 2-3 days. Projects are generally billed by the hour. Credit accounts are accepted.

Oklahoma Legal Process Service(1463)
431 SW C Ave
Lawton OK 73501
Phone: 405-353-0248
Fax: 405-353-1170
800-383-7978

Local Retrieval Area: OK-Caddo, Canadian, Carter, Cleveland, Comanche, Cotton, Grady, Jackson, Jefferson, Kiowa, Lincoln, Logan, Love, McClain, Mayes, Oklahoma, Pottawatomie, Stephens, Tillman, Tulsa.

Normal turn around time is 48 hours. Projects are generally billed by the hour. Credit accounts are accepted.
Oklahoma Legal Process Service (OLPS) also has correspondent relationships in other jurisdictions, including all counties in Oklahoma. Their specialty is process service.

Olde Reserve Title Inc(1464)
677 W Liberty Street
Medina OH 44256
Phone: 216-273-3007
Fax: 216-722-4764

Local Retrieval Area: OH-Cuyahoga, Medina, Summit.

Normal turn around time is 1-3 days. No project billing information was given. Credit accounts are accepted. Credit cards are accepted for payment.

Oliver County Abstract Co(1465)
Box 105
Center ND 58530
Phone: 701-794-3496
Fax:

Local Retrieval Area: ND-Oliver.

Normal turn around time is varied depending on project. Projects are generally billed by the hour. A base rate is charged in addition to the hourly rate. All projects require prepayment. They will also invoice.

Olson Abstract and Title Co(1466)
122 W 11th
Baxter Springs KS 66713
Phone: 316-856-2355
Fax: 316-856-2354

Local Retrieval Area: KS-Cherokee.

Normal turn around time is 48-72 hours. Projects are generally billed by the number of names searched. Credit accounts are accepted.

Olson Detective Agency(1467)
Rt 1 Box 173
Gibbon MN 55335
Phone: 507-834-6845
Fax:

Local Retrieval Area: MN-Blue Earth, Brown, Nicollet, Redwood, Sibley, Watonwan.

Normal turn around time is a few days. Fee basis is per project. All projects require prepayment.

Omni Corporate and Research(1468)
451 Sunrise Hwy
Lynbrook NY 11563
Phone: 516-887-7810
Fax: 516-887-9440

Local Retrieval Area: NY-All counties.

Normal turn around time is the next day, which is subject to state limitations. Projects are generally billed by the number of names searched or records located. All projects require prepayment. Credit cards are accepted for payment. They will also invoice.
They specialize in public record information, court cases and litigations.

On-Line Investigation & Recovery(1469)
PO Box 70188
Ocala FL 34470
Phone: 904-368-5991
Fax:

Local Retrieval Area: FL-Citrus, Marion.

Normal turn around time is 48 hours. Fee basis varies by type of transaction. The first project may require a prepayment.
On-Line Investigation & Recovery Inc also has correspondent relationships in other jurisdictions, including Volusia, Orange, Seminole, Dade and Osceola counties.

One Hour Court Services(1470)   Phone: 714-558-1403
PO Box 12194   Fax: 714-558-0261
Santa Ana CA 92712-2194

Local Retrieval Area: CA-Orange.

Normal turn around time is the same day for federal courts and 1 to 2 days for archives. Fee basis will vary by type of project. Bankruptcy is by case number, indexing is per name. All projects require prepayment.

Oneida Valley Abstract(1471)   Phone: 315-363-1444
PO Box 29   Fax: 315-363-9547
Wampsville NY 13163

Local Retrieval Area: NY-Madison.

Normal turn around time is 48 hours. Fee basis will vary by years searched. Credit accounts are accepted. Personal checks are accepted.

Onistagrawa Abstracting Corp(1472)   Phone: 518-827-8088
PO Box 777   Fax: 518-295-7459
Middleburgh NY 12122-0777

Local Retrieval Area: NY-Columbia, Delaware, Fulton, Greene, Montgomery, Otsego, Schenectady, Schoharie.

Normal turn around time is 2-4 days for UCC's, judgements (civil and criminal), probate, taxes and simple deed searches. Full abstract and title insurance will take 1 to 2 weeks. The fee basis for real estate is figured on a per parcel basis. Credit accounts are accepted.

Oplinger Abstract & Title Inc(1473)   Phone: 605-387-2335
PO Box 133   Fax:
Olivet SD 57052

Local Retrieval Area: SD-Hutchinson.

Normal turn around time is 5 days. Projects are generally billed by the hour. All projects require prepayment.

Orange Abstractor Services Co(1474)   Phone: 914-294-3331
222 Greenwich Ave   Fax: 914-294-8748
Goshen NY 10924

Local Retrieval Area: NY-Dutchess, Orange, Putnam, Rockland, Sullivan.

Normal turn around time is 1-14 days. Fee basis will vary by type of project. Credit accounts are accepted.
Orange Abstractor Services Co also has correspondent relationships in other jurisdictions, including Queens, Nassau, Westchester and Suffolk.

Orange County Abstract and Title(1475) Phone: 812-723-3044
204 E Main St   Fax:
Paoli IN 47454

Local Retrieval Area: IN-Orange.

Normal turn around time is 24-72 hours. Projects are generally billed by the number of names searched or records located. Credit accounts are accepted. Personal checks are accepted. They specialize in title searches and lien searches.

Orange Paper Placers(1476)   Phone: 914-294-7810
PO Box 22   Fax:
Goshen NY 10924

Local Retrieval Area: NY-Dutchess, Orange, Putnam, Rockland, Sullivan, Ulster.

Normal turn around time is 7 days. A rush service is also available. Projects are generally billed by the number of records located. All projects require prepayment.

Oregon Process Service Inc(1477)   Phone: 503-746-3021
PO Box 768   Fax: 503-687-1656
Springfield OR 97477

Local Retrieval Area: OR-Lane.

Normal turn around time is 3 days. Rush service is also available. Fee basis will vary by type of project. The first project may require a prepayment.
Oregon Process Service Inc also has correspondent relationships in other jurisdictions, including other counties in Oregon. They specialize in process serving.

Oressner & Company Inc(1478)   Phone: 219-936-2020
PO Box 207   Fax: 219-962-2582
Plymouth IN 46563

Local Retrieval Area: IN-Marshall.

Normal turn around time is 3 days. Projects are generally billed by the number of records located. Credit accounts are accepted. They specialize in real estate title and abstract.

Osceola Abstract & Title(1479)   Phone: 417-646-2417
PO Box E   Fax:
Osceola MO 64776

Local Retrieval Area: MO-St. Clair.

Normal turn around time is 1 week. Projects are generally billed by the number of records located. Credit accounts are accepted.

Oscoda County Abstract Inc(1480)   Phone: 517-826-5832
210 S Morenci Ave   Fax: 517-826-5832
Mio MI 48647

Local Retrieval Area: MI-Oscoda.

Normal turn around time is 24 hours. Projects are generally billed by the number of names searched. All projects require prepayment.

Otoe County Abstract Co(1481)   Phone: 402-873-5511
PO Box 488   Fax: 402-873-7746
Nebraska City NE 68410

Local Retrieval Area: NE-Cass, Nemaha, Otoe.

Normal turn around time is 1-2 days. They charge a flat fee per project. The first project may require a prepayment.
They specialize in title records.

Otsego County Abstract Co(1482)   Phone: 517-732-5765
120 E Main St   Fax: 517-732-7288
Gaylord MI 49735

Local Retrieval Area: MI-Otsego.

Normal turn around time is 7-10 days. Rush service is also available. Fee basis will vary by type of project. The first project may require a prepayment.

Ouren Title Inc(1483)
1009 7th St
Harlan IA 51537
Phone: **712-755-2174**
Fax: 712-755-3865

Local Retrieval Area: IA-Shelby.

Normal turn around time is 24 hours. Projects are generally billed by the number of names searched. Credit accounts are accepted. They specialize in preparing abstracts, and record ownership and lien reports.

Veda Ousley(1484)
Rt 1 Box 292 A
Crocker MO 65452
Phone: **314-736-5357**
Fax:

Local Retrieval Area: MO-Laclede, Maries, Miller, Phelps, Pulaski, Texas.

Normal turn around time is varied depending on project. Fee basis will vary with the type of search. The first project may require a prepayment.
Veda specializes in genealogy searches.

Owens & Associates Investig(1485)
2254 Moore St Suite 203A
San Diego CA 92110-3015
Phone: **619-297-1343**
Fax: 619-297-7622

Local Retrieval Area: CA-San Diego.

Normal turn around time is 24 hours. Online computer ordering is also available. Projects are generally billed by the hour. All projects require prepayment.
They can search nationwide with their online capabilities.

Ozark Abstract & Loan Co(1486)
PO Box 224
Ozark MO 65721
Phone: **417-485-2431**
Fax: 417-485-2431

Local Retrieval Area: MO-Christian.

Normal turn around time is 2-3 days. Fee basis will vary by the type of project. Credit accounts are accepted.
They specialize in title insurance.

Ozark Title & Guaranty Co(1487)
PO Box 6
Harrison AR 72602-0006
Phone: **501-743-3333**
Fax: 501-743-3333

Local Retrieval Area: AR-Boone, Carroll, Newton.

Normal turn around time is 7 days. Online computer ordering is also available. Fee basis will vary by the type of project. All projects require prepayment.

P.I. Services(1488)
PO Box 2383
Fargo ND 58108
Phone: **701-235-4842**
Fax: 701-232-9368

Local Retrieval Area: MN-Becker, Clay, Norman, Otter Tail, Wilkin; ND-Barnes, Cass, Richland, Stutsman, Traill.

Normal turn around time is 48 hours. Projects are generally billed by the hour. Credit accounts are accepted.
P.I. Services also has correspondent relationships in other jurisdictions, including Grand Forks.

PC Fraze Abstract Co(1489)
301 N Main
Syracuse KS 67878
Phone: **316-384-7828**
Fax: 316-384-7828

Local Retrieval Area: KS-Grant, Hamilton, Kearny, Stanton.

Normal turn around time is 1 day for Hamilton County, 2 days for Stanton and Grant Counties, and 3 days for Kearney County. Projects are generally billed by the hour. Credit accounts are accepted.

PFC Information Services(1490)
6114 LaSalle Ave Suite 149
Oakland CA 94611
Phone: **510-653-0666**
Fax: 510-653-0842

Local Retrieval Area: CA-Alameda, San Francisco.

Normal turn around time is 24 hours. Projects are generally billed by the number of records located. Credit accounts are accepted. Credit cards are accepted for payment. Personal checks are accepted.
PFC Information Services also has correspondent relationships in other jurisdictions, including Marin, Santa Clara, Contra Costa and San Mateo. They specialize in asset searches, corporate profiles, skip trace and employment screening.

PI Unlimited(1491)
3313 S Staples
Corpus Christi TX 78411
Phone: **512-851-8129**
Fax: 512-850-0879

Local Retrieval Area: TX-Brooks, Duval, Jim Wells, Kleberg, Nueces, San Patricio.

Normal turn around time is varied depending on project. Online computer ordering is also available. Projects are generally billed by the hour. The first project may require a prepayment.
PI Unlimited also has correspondent relationships in other jurisdictions, including network contacts throughout Texas.

PMD Abstract Co Inc(1492)
127 Chestnut St
Roselle Park NJ 07204
Phone: **908-241-7644**
Fax: 908-241-0775

Local Retrieval Area: NJ-Bergen, Essex, Hudson, Passaic, Union.

Normal turn around time is 12 hours or more. Projects are generally billed by the number of names searched. Credit accounts are accepted.

Pacific Photocopy & Research(1493)
200 N Andrews Ave Suite 100
Ft Lauderdale FL 33301
Phone: **305-764-5646**
Fax: 305-764-5447

Local Retrieval Area: FL-Broward, Collier, Hendry, Palm Beach.

Normal turn around time is 1-3 days. Fee basis will vary by the type of project. The first project may require a prepayment.
Pacific Photocopy & Research also has correspondent relationships in other jurisdictions, including the rest of the state with nationwide capabilities through a network. They specialize in bankruptcy court records.

Pacific Photocopy & Research(1494)   Phone: 904-355-1062
404 Julia St Suite 300   Fax: 904-355-0958
Jacksonville FL 32202

Local Retrieval Area: FL-Calhoun, Clay, Nassau, St. Johns.

Normal turn around time is 1-3 days. Fee basis will vary by the type of project. The first project may require a prepayment.

Pacific Photocopy & Research also has correspondent relationships in other jurisdictions, including the rest of the state with nationwide capabilities through a network. They specialize in bankruptcy court records.

Pacific Photocopy & Research(1495)   Phone: 305-371-7694
55 NE 2nd St   Fax: 305-371-9657
Miami FL 33132

Local Retrieval Area: FL-Dade.

Normal turn around time is 1 hour to availability of the file. Fee basis will vary by the type of project. The first project may require a prepayment.

Pacific Photocopy & Research - Miami also has correspondent relationships in other jurisdictions, including the rest of the state with nationwide capabilities through a network. They specialize in bankruptcy court records.

Pacific Photocopy & Research(1496)   Phone: 813-885-3854
6005 Jarvis St   Fax: 813-885-3942
Tampa FL 33634

Local Retrieval Area: FL-Hillsborough, Manatee, Pasco, Polk.

Normal turn around time is 1-3 days. Fee basis will vary by the type of project. The first project may require a prepayment.

Pacific Photocopy & Research Services also has correspondent relationships in other jurisdictions, including the rest of the state with nationwide capabilities thourgh a network. They specialize in bankruptcy court records.

Pacific Process Service(1497)   Phone: 509-325-1371
PO Box 9212   Fax: 509-327-1830
Spokane WA 99209

Local Retrieval Area: WA-Garfield, Pend Oreille, Spokane, Stevens, Whitman.

Normal turn around time is 1-2 days. Projects are generally billed by the hour. The first project may require a prepayment.

Packer Valley Title Corporation(1498)   Phone: 715-735-9791
1943 Hall Ave PO Box 543   Fax: 715-735-9791
Marinette WI 54143

Local Retrieval Area: WI-Marinette.

Normal turn around time is 1-2 days. Fee basis varies by type of transaction. The first project may require a prepayment.

Page County Abstract and Title(1499)   Phone: 712-542-3613
118 N 16th St   Fax: 712-542-2629
Clarinda IA 51632

Local Retrieval Area: IA-Page.

Normal turn around time is 48 hours. Fee basis will bary by the type of project. Credit accounts are accepted. Personal checks are accepted.

They specialize in searching county records and abstracting real estate titles.

Pagosa Springs Title Co(1500)   Phone: 303-264-4141
PO Box 146   Fax: 303-264-4835
Pagosa Springs CO 81147

Local Retrieval Area: CO-Archuleta.

Normal turn around time is up to 1 week. Projects are generally billed by the hour. Credit accounts are accepted. Out of town clients are charged a setup fee and must prepay.

They specialize in real estate and title matters.

Paladin Investigations Inc(1501)   Phone: 407-862-2228
PO Box 915593   Fax: 407-862-8846
Longwood FL 32791

Local Retrieval Area: FL-Brevard, Lake, Marion, Orange, Osceola, Polk, Seminole, Sumter, Volusia.

Normal turn around time is 3 days. Projects are generally billed by the hour. Credit accounts are accepted.

Please call the FAX number first before sending. They specialize in local city & occupational licenses, domestic relations records, and marriage licenses.

Paladin Legal Services(1502)   Phone: 907-272-1497
745 W 4th Ave Suite 300   Fax:
Anchorage AK 99501

Local Retrieval Area: AK-Anchorage Borough, Matanuska-Susitna Borough.

Normal turn around time is 48 hours. Rush service is also available. Projects are generally billed by the hour. Credit accounts are accepted. Set up fee varies. They require prepay for out of state customers and will invoice in state and established customers.

They specialize in private investigations.

Pallorium Inc(1503)   Phone: 212-696-0286
PO Box 155   Fax: 800-275-4329
Brooklyn NY 11230

Local Retrieval Area: NY-Bronx, Kings, Nassau, New York, Queens, Richmond, Suffolk, Westchester.

Normal turn around time is 1-3 days. Online computer ordering is also available. Project billing methods vary. The first project may require a prepayment.

Pallorium Inc also has correspondent relationships in other jurisdictions, including San Antonio and Los Angeles. They maintain an online database of voter registration for NYC. They also maintain an online network of 700+ investigative agencies.

Palm Title Inc(1504)
PO Box 2550
La Belle FL 33935
Phone: 813-675-4545
Fax:

Local Retrieval Area: FL-Hendry.

Normal turn around time is 3-5 days. Projects are generally billed by the hour. Credit accounts are accepted. They specialize in title policy work.

Palmer Abstract Inc(1505)
19 1st Ave NW
Waukon IA 52172
Phone: 319-568-3488
Fax:

Local Retrieval Area: IA-Allamakee.

Normal turn around time is 48 hours. Projects are generally billed by the number of names searched or records located. Credit accounts are accepted.

Palmer Investigative Services(1506)
PO Box 10760
Prescott AZ 86304
Phone: 602-778-2951
Fax: 602-445-7204

Local Retrieval Area: AZ-Yavapai, Yavapai.

Normal turn around time is 48 hours. Rush service is also available. Projects are generally billed by the hour. Fee will also include incurred costs if any. All projects require prepayment. Palmer Investigative Services also has correspondent relationships in other jurisdictions, including Coconino and Mohave counties.

Palmer and Murrie Abstract Co(1507)
506 N Market St
Marion IL 62959
Phone: 618-993-3861
Fax: 618-993-3015

Local Retrieval Area: IL-Franklin, Johnson, Saline, Williamson.

Normal turn around time is 5-6 working days. Projects are generally billed by the number of names searched or records located. Credit accounts are accepted. Personal checks are accepted. Palmer and Murrie Abstract Co also has correspondent relationships in other jurisdictions, including Union and Jackson Counties.

Palmetto Title Services(1508)
PO Box 1343
Estill SC 29918
Phone: 803-625-2004
Fax:

Local Retrieval Area: SC-Hampton, Jasper.

Normal turn around time is 3-4 days. Projects are generally billed by the number of names searched. Credit accounts are accepted.

Palo Alto County Abstract Co(1509)
1009-1011 Broadway St
Emmetsburg IA 50536
Phone: 712-852-4313
Fax:

Local Retrieval Area: IA-Palo Alto.

Normal turn around time is varied depending on project. Fee basis will vary by the type of project. Credit accounts are accepted.

Panola County Abstract and Title(1510)
202 W Wellington
Carthage TX 75633
Phone: 903-693-3266
Fax: 903-693-2819

Local Retrieval Area: TX-Panola.

Normal turn around time is varied depending on project. Project billing methods vary. Credit accounts are accepted. Personal checks are accepted.

Paralegal Enterprises Inc(1511)
401 W First St Suite 2-D
Greenville NC 27835
Phone: 919-758-6622
Fax: 919-758-6622

Local Retrieval Area: NC-Beaufort, Bertie, Edgecombe, Greene, Lenoir, Martin, Pitt, Wilson.

Normal turn around time is 48 hours. Projects are generally billed by the number of names searched. Fee basis will vary with portions of tracts of land. The first project may require a prepayment. They specialize in real estate searches.

Paralegal Field Research Service(1512)
PO Box 7095
West Palm Beach FL 33405
Phone: 407-588-5828
Fax: 407-588-2799

Local Retrieval Area: FL-Broward, Dade, Indian River, Martin, Okeechobee, Palm Beach, St. Lucie.

Normal turn around time is varied depending on project. Projects are generally billed by the hour. The first project may require a prepayment.
Paralegal Field Research Service also has correspondent relationships in other jurisdictions, including the rest of Florida.

Paralegal Resource Center Inc(1513)
4 Fanevil Hall Marketplace
Boston MA 02109
Phone: 617-742-1939
Fax: 617-742-1417

Local Retrieval Area: MA-Suffolk.

Normal turn around time is 7 business days. A same day rush service is also available. Projects are generally billed by the number of names searched. Credit accounts are accepted.
Paralegal Resource Center Inc also has correspondent relationships in other jurisdictions, including the rest of Massachusetts. They provide paralegal specialists, on a temporary basis to law firms, banks and insurance companies for special in house research projects.

Paralegal Services(1514)
26322 Tunis Mills Rd
Easton MD 21601
Phone: 410-820-8717
Fax: 410-820-5147

Local Retrieval Area: MD-Caroline, Dorchester, Kent, Queen Anne's, Talbot.

Normal turn around time is 48 hours. Projects are generally billed by the number of names searched. Credit accounts are accepted. They specialize in full title searches.

Paralegal Services(1515)
PO Box 247
Point Pleasant WV 25550
Phone: 304-675-4008
Fax: 304-675-1362

Local Retrieval Area: WV-Mason.

Normal turn around time is 24-48 hours. Projects are generally billed by the number of names searched. Credit accounts are accepted.

Paralegal Services(1516)
Rt 2 Box 492
Berkeley Springs WV 25411
Phone: 304-258-3771
Fax:

Local Retrieval Area: WV-Morgan.

Normal turn around time is 24-48 hours. Projects are generally billed by the number of names searched. Credit accounts are accepted.

Paralegal Services of N Carolina(1517)
120 Penmarc Dr Suite 118
Raleigh NC 27603
Phone: 919-821-7762
Fax: 919-832-6378

Local Retrieval Area: NC-Many counties in this state are covered. See the county index for actual coverage..

Normal turn around time is 3-4 days. Projects are generally billed by the number of records located. Credit accounts are accepted.
Paralegal Services of North Carolina Inc also has correspondent relationships in other jurisdictions, including the rest of North Carolina. They specialize in real property, probate and Secretary of State Information searches.

Paralegal Works(1518)
20 Brentwood Dr
Asheville NC 28806
Phone: 704-254-5044
Fax: 704-254-8960

Local Retrieval Area: NC-Avery, Buncombe, Henderson, McDowell, Madison, Mitchell, Polk, Rutherford, Transylvania, Yancey.

Normal turn around time is 48 hours. Projects are generally billed by the number of names searched. Credit accounts are accepted. They specialize in real estate title searches.

Parasec(1519)
1007 7th St 2nd Floor
Sacramento CA 95814
Phone: 916-441-1001
Fax: 916-447-6091

Local Retrieval Area: CA-Los Angeles, Sacramento, San Diego.

Normal turn around time is 24-72 hours. Projects are generally billed by the number of names searched or records located. Credit accounts are accepted. Credit cards are accepted for payment. Personal checks are accepted.
They specialize in document filing and retrieval for UCC, corporate, limited partnership, trademark and service marks.

Park County Title(1520)
1025 12th St
Cody WY 82414
Phone: 307-587-4926
Fax: 307-587-9784

Local Retrieval Area: WY-Park.

Normal turn around time is 1 day-3 weeks. Projects are generally billed by the hour. Credit accounts are accepted.

June Parks(1521)
Rt 4 Box 199
Bedford IA 50833
Phone: 712-523-3490
Fax:

Local Retrieval Area: IA-Taylor.

Normal turn around time is a week. Projects are generally billed by the number of names searched. Credit accounts are accepted. A prepay set up fee is charged for first time customers only. Personal checks are accepted.

Pascal & Carter Process Service(1522)
700 13th St NW Suite 950
Washington DC 20005
Phone: 202-434-4578
Fax: 202-434-4599

Local Retrieval Area: DC-All counties; MD-Montgomery; VA-Arlington, Fairfax, Prince George, City of Alexandria.

Normal turn around time is 48 hours. Projects are generally billed by the hour. All projects require prepayment.
Pascal & Carter Process Service Inc also has correspondent relationships in other jurisdictions, including Baltimore. They provide business development services to persons who have a desire to start legal support companies.

Patten Investigations(1523)
PO Box 311
Benicia CA 94510
Phone: 707-745-1922
Fax: 707-746-1337

Local Retrieval Area: CA-Alameda, Contra Costa, Napa, Solano.

Normal turn around time is 4 working days or less. Projects are generally billed by the hour. Credit accounts are accepted.
Patten Investigations also has correspondent relationships in other jurisdictions, including South Alameda, San Francisco, Marin, and Sonoma counties. They also specialize in process serving.

Patterson Abstracting(1524)
173 Lincoln Wy E
Chambersburg PA 17201
Phone: 717-263-5239
Fax: 717-263-3395

Local Retrieval Area: PA-Adams, Franklin, Greene.

Normal turn around time is 24 hours Projects are generally billed by the number of names searched. Credit accounts are accepted.

Patton Abstract and Title Inc(1525)
PO Box 943
Lewisville AR 71845
Phone: 501-921-5262
Fax:

Local Retrieval Area: AR-Lafayette.

Normal turn around time is 1 week. Projects are generally billed by the hour. Credit accounts are accepted.

Pawnee County Abstract Co(1526)
637 G St
Pawnee City NE 68420
Phone: 402-852-2577
Fax: 402-852-2035

Local Retrieval Area: NE-Pawnee.

Normal turn around time is varied depending on project. Projects are generally billed by the number of names searched or records located. Credit accounts are accepted.

Nota Payne(1527)
Rt 2 Box 943
Halifax VA 24558

Phone: 804-476-2595
Fax:

Local Retrieval Area: VA-Halifax.

Normal turn around time is 1-2 days. Fee basis varies by type of transaction. Credit accounts are accepted.
Ms. Payne specializes in real estate title searches.

Paul Peduska(1528)
74 Court Square
Pocahontas IA 50574

Phone: 712-335-4257
Fax:

Local Retrieval Area: IA-Pocahontas.

Normal turn around time is 1-2 days. Projects are generally billed by the hour. Credit accounts are accepted. Personal checks are accepted.

Pelican Land and Abstract Co Inc(1529)
PO Box 608
Lake Charles LA 70601

Phone: 318-436-3419
Fax: 318-436-3419

Local Retrieval Area: LA-Acadia Parish, Beauregard Parish, Calcasieu Parish, Cameron Parish, East Baton Rouge Parish, Jefferson Davis Parish.

Normal turn around time is varied depending on project. Fee basis will vary by the type of project. The first project may require a prepayment.
Pelican Land and Abstract Co Inc also has correspondent relationships in other jurisdictions, including the rest of Louisiana. They specialize in oil, gas and leasing research.

Pellish and Pellish Attorneys(1530)
809 W Market St
Pottsville PA 17901

Phone: 717-622-2338
Fax: 717-622-2339

Local Retrieval Area: PA-Berks, Bucks, Carbon.

Normal turn around time is 1-14 days. Projects are generally billed by the hour. Credit accounts are accepted. Personal checks are accepted.
Pellish and Pellish Attorneys at Law also has correspondent relationships in other jurisdictions, including Lehigh and Dauphin Counties.

Pemiscot County Abstract & Inv(1531)
404 Carleton Ave
Caruthersville MO 63830

Phone: 314-333-4666
Fax: 314-333-2641

Local Retrieval Area: MO-Pemiscot.

Normal turn around time is 1-3 days. Fee basis will vary by the type of project. Credit accounts are accepted.
They specialize in title probate and title insurance.

Penncorp Service Group Inc(1532)
600 N 2nd St Suite 500
Harrisburg PA 17101

Phone: 800-544-9050
Fax: 717-238-8232

Local Retrieval Area: PA-Cumberland, Dauphin, Perry.

Normal turn around time is 24 hours. If certification is needed, allow 3 to 7 days. Projects are generally billed by the number of records located. Credit accounts are accepted. Credit cards are accepted for payment. Personal checks are accepted.
Penncorp Service Group Inc also has correspondent relationships in other jurisdictions, including nationwide and Canada. They specialize in LCB transfers and renewals, and working with the Pennsylvania Department of Transportation.

Pennington County Abstract Co(1533)
PO Box 508
Thief River Falls MN 56701

Phone: 218-681-2527
Fax: 218-681-2528

Local Retrieval Area: MN-Pennington.

Normal turn around time is varied depending on project. Fee basis will vary by type of project. All projects require prepayment. They will also invoice.

Penninsula Title and Abstract(1534)
15 S 4th St
Crystal Falls MI 49920

Phone: 906-875-6618
Fax: 906-875-4382

Local Retrieval Area: MI-Dickinson, Iron; WI-Florence.

Normal turn around time is 1 day. Fee basis will vary by type of project. The first project may require a prepayment.
They specialize in real estate.

People Property Research(1535)
330 E Liberty St Suite 215
Reno NV 89501

Phone: 702-329-6600
Fax: 702-323-6863

Local Retrieval Area: NV-Douglas, Storey, Washoe, Carson City.

Normal turn around time is 48 hours. Projects are generally billed by the number of names searched or records located. Credit accounts are accepted. Payment depends on client and work requested. They specialize in real estate searches, and assisting lenders, attorneys and investors.

Peregrine Investigation & Resrch(1537)
PO Box 3601
Boulder CO 80307-3601

Phone: 303-441-7442
Fax:

Local Retrieval Area: CO-Adams, Arapahoe, Boulder, Denver, Douglas.

Normal turn around time is 2 days to 1 week. Projects are generally billed by the number of names searched or records located. Credit accounts are accepted.
Peregrine Investigation & Research also has correspondent relationships in other jurisdictions, including Larimer, Weld, and El Paso counties. They specialize in finding those who default on consumer and commercial loans.

Perfectly Legal Documents(1538)   Phone: 800-256-2447
1404 NE 111th Ave   503-256-2447
Portland OR 97220   Fax:

Local Retrieval Area: OR-All counties; WA-Cowlitz, Grays Harbor, King, King, Lewis, Snohomish.

Normal turn around time is 4-5 days. Rush service is also available. Projects are generally billed by the hour. The first project may require a prepayment.

They perform a wide variety of legal support services from private investigation to document preparation.

Perkins County Abstract Co(1539)   Phone: 605-244-5544
PO Box 157   Fax: 605-244-7199
Bison SD 57620

Local Retrieval Area: SD-Perkins.

Normal turn around time is 2 weeks. Projects are generally billed by the hour. All projects require prepayment.

Permian Court Reporters Inc(1540)   Phone: 915-683-3032
605 W Texas   Fax: 915-683-5324
Midland TX 79701

Local Retrieval Area: TX-Ector, Midland.

Normal turn around time is 2 days. Projects are generally billed by the hour. Credit accounts are accepted.

Perry Field Services(1541)   Phone: 800-783-7904
PO Box 506   Fax: 404-978-8672
Snellville GA 30278

Local Retrieval Area: GA-Bartow, Cherokee, Clayton, Cobb, Coweta, De Kalb, Douglas, Fayette, Forsyth, Fulton, Gwinnett, Hall, Henry, Rockdale.

Normal turn around time is 24-48 hours. Projects are generally billed by the number of names searched or records located. Credit accounts are accepted. Personal checks are accepted.

They specialize in current owner searches, 50 year title searches, UCC and tax records.

Personal Background Investig(1542)   Phone: 800-949-9982
PO Box 77308   206-233-1948
Seattle WA 98177   Fax: 206-546-3677

Local Retrieval Area: OR-Multnomah; WA-King, Kitsap, Pierce, Snohomish.

Normal turn around time is 24-48 hours for most records. Fee basis varies by type of transaction. The first project may require a prepayment.

They have on-line retrieval capabilities for all of Washington except Spokane and Garfield counties. They also specialize in education, Motor Vehicle Records, and credit checks.

Peterson Abstract Co(1543)   Phone: 612-257-4200
209 N Main Street   Fax: 612-462-7820
Center City MN 55012

Local Retrieval Area: MN-Chisago.

Normal turn around time is 1 week. Projects are generally billed by the number of names searched or records located. Credit accounts are accepted.

Petroleum Title Service Inc(1544)   Phone: 307-235-6237
3603 Hawthorne   Fax:
Casper WY 82604

Local Retrieval Area: WY-All counties.

Normal turn around time is 1 week. Projects are generally billed by the hour. Mileage expenses will be added to the fee. Credit accounts are accepted.

They prepare abstracts of title, title certificates and any research pertaining to title information on surface, minerals, research for ownership for probates, leasehold checks or any type of title research across the State of Wyoming.

Sandra L Pettingill(1545)   Phone: 717-769-6070
RD 2 Box 856   Fax:
Lock Haven PA 17745

Local Retrieval Area: PA-Clinton, Lycoming.

Normal turn around time is Charges are varied depending on type of search. Credit accounts are accepted.

Sandra is a paralegal and specializes in mineral and pipeline record searches.

Phelps & Phelps Investigations(1546)   Phone: 800-633-6125
1235 S Gilbert Rd Suite 3-73   602-545-0626
Mesa AZ 85204   Fax: 602-926-8733
                                                     800-347-9918

Local Retrieval Area: AZ-Maricopa.

Normal turn around time is 24-48 hours. Online computer ordering is also available. Projects are generally billed by the number of names searched. The first project may require a prepayment. Personal checks are accepted.

Phelps & Phelps Investigations also has correspondent relationships in other jurisdictions, including Pima, Coconino, Mohave Counties in Arizona, and Clark County in Nevada.

Phillips County Abstract Co(1547)   Phone: 406-654-1413
PO Box 250   Fax: 406-654-1413
Malta MT 59538

Local Retrieval Area: MT-Phillips.

Normal turn around time is 1 week. Projects are generally billed by the hour. Credit accounts are accepted.

Phillips Land Title Company(1548)   Phone: 715-339-2230
174 N Avon Ave   Fax:
Phillips WI 54555

Local Retrieval Area: WI-Price.

Normal turn around time is 2 days. Fee basis varies by type of transaction. The first project may require a prepayment.

Phoenix Investigations(1549)   Phone: 404-992-4700
1025 Old Roswell Rd Suite 202   Fax: 404-992-4941
Roswell GA 30076

Local Retrieval Area: GA-Cobb, De Kalb, Fulton, Gwinnett.

Normal turn around time is 2 days. Projects are generally billed by the number of names searched. All projects require prepayment. They will also invoice.

Photo Abstract Co(1550)   Phone: **918-542-1871**
22 E Central Ave   Fax: 918-542-9748
Miami OK 74354

Local Retrieval Area: OK-Ottawa.

Normal turn around time is 1-3 days. Projects are generally billed by the number of records located. Credit accounts are accepted.

Pickell Abstract Co(1551)   Phone: **816-665-8342**
113 E Washington St   Fax: 816-627-1733
Kirksville MO 63501

Local Retrieval Area: MO-Adair.

Normal turn around time is 48 hours. Projects are generaliy billed by the number of names searched. Credit accounts are accepted. They specialize in land titles.

Pierce County Abstract(1552)   Phone: **701-776-6961**
216 2nd Ave SE   Fax:
Rugby ND 58368

Local Retrieval Area: ND-Pierce.

Normal turn around time is 2 weeks. Fee basis will vary by type of project. There is a set fee for abstracting. Credit accounts are accepted.

Pioneer Abstract Co(1553)   Phone: **405-257-3351**
PO Box 1100   Fax:
Wewoka OK 74884

Local Retrieval Area: OK-Seminole.

Normal turn around time is 1-3 days. Fee basis is determined on a per hour or "per name plus service charge". Credit accounts are accepted.
They specialize in county records.

Pioneer Abstract Co of McAlester(1554) Phone: **918-423-0817**
PO Box 926   Fax: 918-423-7650
McAlester OK 74502

Local Retrieval Area: OK-Pittsburg.

Normal turn around time is three days. Projects are generally billed by the hour. The first project may require a prepayment. Credit cards are accepted for payment.

Pioneer-Ward County Abstract Co(1555)   Phone: **915-943-5561**
PO Box 1876   Fax: 915-943-3716
Monahans TX 79756

Local Retrieval Area: TX-Ward.

Normal turn around time is 2-3 days. Projects are generally billed by the hour. The first project may require a prepayment.

Pipestone County Abstract Co(1556)   Phone: **507-825-5519**
PO Box 335   Fax:
Pipestone MN 56164

Local Retrieval Area: MN-Pipestone.

Normal turn around time is 2-3 days. Projects are generally billed by the number of names searched. Credit accounts are accepted. They specialize in recorder and deeds.

Julie Pittman(1557)   Phone: **515-644-5114**
RR #1 Box 124   Fax:
Montezuma IA 50171

Local Retrieval Area: IA-Poweshiek.

Normal turn around time is weekly. Fee basis varies by type of transaction. Credit accounts are accepted. All customers outside of the county are asked to prepay.
Julie specializes in credit research and publishes a monthly bulletin.

Pittsburgh Information and Rsrch(1558) Phone: **412-766-3832**
PO Box 99181   Fax: 412-761-3591
Pittsburgh PA 15233

Local Retrieval Area: PA-All counties.

Normal turn around time is 24-48 hours for a verbal. Fee basis is per index. Credit accounts are accepted.

Plains Title and Abstract Inc(1559)   Phone: **505-762-4589**
1520 Mitchell St Suite 2   Fax: 505-769-1417
Clovis NM 88101-4617

Local Retrieval Area: NM-Curry.

Normal turn around time is 3-5 days. Projects are generally billed by the number of names searched. Credit accounts are accepted. They specialize in title insurance.

Platte County Title Co(1560)   Phone: **402-563-4519**
PO Box 946   Fax: 402-564-0588
Columbus NE 68601

Local Retrieval Area: NE-Platte.

Normal turn around time is 1 week. Fee basis varies by type of transaction. Credit accounts are accepted.
Platte County Title Co also has correspondent relationships in other jurisdictions, including the counties of Boone, Nance, Butler and Merrick. They specialize in escrow closings.

Plymouth County Abstract(1561)   Phone: **712-546-4564**
PO Box 1126   Fax: 712-546-7999
Le Mars IA 51031

Local Retrieval Area: IA-Plymouth.

Normal turn around time is 2-7 days. Fee basis will vary by type of project. Credit accounts are accepted. Personal checks are accepted.
They search information provided in the Clerk's office, not in the courts.

Pofessional Services Bureau(1562) Phone: 318-234-9931
315 S College Rd Suite 245   Fax: 318-235-5318
Lafayette LA 70503

Local Retrieval Area: LA-Acadia Parish, East Baton Rouge Parish, Evangeline Parish, Iberia Parish, Jefferson Davis Parish, Lafayette Parish, Rapides Parish, St. Landry Parish, St. Martin Parish, St. Mary Parish, Vermilion Parish, West Baton Rouge Parish.

Normal turn around time is 24 hours. A 1 hour rush is also available for extra charge. Project billing methods vary. Credit accounts are accepted. Credit cards are accepted for payment. Personal checks and bank wires are accepted.

Pofessional Services Bureau also has correspondent relationships in other jurisdictions, including the rest of Louisiana. They specialize in domestic, civil investigations, criminal investigations, surveillance and process service.

Marilyn Pohlpeter(1563) Phone: 319-754-5979
1500 Summer St   Fax:
Burlington IA 52601

Local Retrieval Area: IA-Des Moines.

Normal turn around time is 1-2 days. Projects are generally billed by the number of names searched. Credit accounts are accepted. They will accept personal checks.

They will no do written confirmation, only verbal information is given.

Poinsett County Abstract Co(1564) Phone: 501-578-5914
411 Court St   Fax: 501-578-5914
Harrisburg AR 72432

Local Retrieval Area: AR-Poinsett.

Normal turn around time is 1 week. Fee basis will vary by the type of project. Credit accounts are accepted.

They are a full service title company.

Police Report Acquisition Service(1565) Phone: 214-783-9505
613 Sheffield Dr   Fax: 214-669-9090
Richardson TX 75081

Local Retrieval Area: TX-Dallas, Harris, Tarrant.

Normal turn around time is 24 hours. Projects are generally billed by the number of records located. The first project may require a prepayment.

They specialize in police reports and only retrieve from police departments.

Polk Legal Service(1566) Phone: 803-366-9772
619 North Ave   Fax: 803-366-9382
Rock Hill SC 29732

Local Retrieval Area: SC-Chester, Lancaster, York.

Normal turn around time is 1-3 days. Project billing methods vary. All projects require prepayment.

Pollard & Lott Inc(1567) Phone: 806-495-2989
PO Box 850   Fax: 806-495-3876
Post TX 79356

Local Retrieval Area: TX-Garza.

Normal turn around time is 1-2 days. Fee basis will vary by the type of project. The first project may require a prepayment. They specialize in abstract and title searches.

Steve Polley(1568) Phone: 605-642-7146
19 Nickel Pl   Fax: 605-642-5099
Spearfish SD 57783

Local Retrieval Area: SD-Butte, Lawrence, Meade, Pennington; WY-Crook.

Normal turn around time is 1-5 days. Rush service is also available. They charge per record on real estate searches. Credit accounts are accepted. Personal and business checks are accepted. They specialize in document filing, searches and retrieval of public records from federal, state and county agencies.

Sherrie C Polson(1569) Phone: 803-383-5067
PO Box 362   Fax: 803-383-2759
Hartsville SC 29551

Local Retrieval Area: SC-Chesterfield, Darlington, Dillon, Florence, Kershaw, Lee, Marion, Marlboro, Richland.

Normal turn around time is 24 hours. Charges are varied depending on type of search. Credit accounts are accepted. Sherrie specializes in real estate title searches.

Pondera County Title Co(1570) Phone: 406-278-5823
PO Box 755   Fax: 406-278-5820
Conrad MT 59425

Local Retrieval Area: MT-Pondera.

Normal turn around time is 2 days. Projects are generally billed by the hour. All projects require prepayment.

Poplar Bluff Abstract and Title Co(1571) Phone: 314-785-7790
310 Vine   Fax: 314-785-0370
Poplar Bluff MO 63901

Local Retrieval Area: MO-Butler.

Normal turn around time is 1 day for abstracts, 1 to 5 days for title insurance. Fee is based per order and per page. Credit accounts are accepted.

Port-o-Wild's Security Services(1572) Phone: 218-751-8200
PO Box 521   Fax: 218-751-3132
Bemidji MN 56601

Local Retrieval Area: MN-Aitkin, Becker, Beltrami, Cass, Clearwater, Crow Wing, Hubbard, Itasca, Kittson, Koochiching, Lake of the Woods, Mahnomen, Marshall, Norman, Pennington, Polk, Red Lake, Roseau.

Normal turn around time is varied depending on project. Projects are generally billed by the hour. Credit accounts are accepted. Some projects may require prepayment.

Portales Abstract(1573)   **Phone: 505-356-4062**
218 S Ave A   Fax: 505-356-5811
Portales NM 88130

Local Retrieval Area: NM-Roosevelt.

Normal turn around time is 48 hours. Projects are generally billed by the number of names searched or records located. The first project may require a prepayment.

Pottawatomie County Abstract Co(1574)   **Phone: 913-457-3441**
108 N 2nd   Fax: 913-457-3441
Westmoreland KS 66549

Local Retrieval Area: KS-Pottawatomie.

Normal turn around time is 2-3 days. Fee basis varies by type of transaction. The first project may require a prepayment.

Potter & Co(1575)   **Phone: 406-547-3355**
PO Box 650   Fax:
White Sulphur Springs MT 59645

Local Retrieval Area: MT-Meagher.

Normal turn around time is 2 weeks. Projects are generally billed by the hour. Credit accounts are accepted.
They specialize in real estate.

Potter County Land & Abstract(1576)   **Phone: 605-765-2858**
PO Box 203   Fax: 605-765-2252
Gettysburg SD 57442

Local Retrieval Area: SD-Potter.

Normal turn around time is 5 days. Projects are generally billed by the hour. Credit accounts are accepted.
They specialize in real estate.

Powder River Abstract and Title(1577)   **Phone: 406-436-2209**
PO Box 413   Fax: 406-436-2604
Broadus MT 59317

Local Retrieval Area: MT-Powder River.

Normal turn around time is 3 days. Projects are generally billed by the number of records located. Credit accounts are accepted.

Lori Powell(1578)   **Phone: 614-836-1342**
438 Benson Dr   Fax:
Groveport OH 43125

Local Retrieval Area: OH-Fayette, Madison, Pickaway, Ross.

Normal turn around time is 24-48 hours. Projects are generally billed by the number of names searched or records located. Credit accounts are accepted.
Lori specializes in real estate records.

Powers Abstract Co Inc(1579)   **Phone: 405-336-4068**
PO Box 707   Fax: 405-336-4078
Perry OK 73077

Local Retrieval Area: OK-Noble.

Normal turn around time is five to seven days. Fee basis will vary by the type of project. Credit accounts are accepted.
They specialize in real estate and titles.

Prairie Abstract & Title(1580)   **Phone: 406-637-2160**
PO Box 215   Fax: 406-637-5576
Terry MT 59349

Local Retrieval Area: MT-Prairie.

Normal turn around time is 2-3 days. Projects are generally billed by the hour. The first project may require a prepayment.

Preferred Research Inc(1581)   **Phone: 912-781-9344**
3092 Pio Nono Ave   Fax: 912-781-9682
Macon GA 30728

Local Retrieval Area: GA-Baldwin, Bibb, Bleckley, Butts, Crawford, Dodge, Dooly, Hancock, Jasper, Johnson, Jones, Lamar, Laurens, Macon, Monroe, Peach, Pike, Pulaski, Putnam, Taylor, Telfair, Treutlen, Twiggs, Upson, Washington, Wheeler, Wilkinson.

Normal turn around time is 24 hours. Fee basis is per search and per county. The first project may require a prepayment.
They specialize in public record retrieval.

Prentice Hall Legal & FInancial (1582)   **Phone: 800-222-2122**
1455 Response Rd Suite 250   916-649-9916
Sacramento CA 95815   Fax: 916-649-9933

Local Retrieval Area: CA-Sacramento.

Normal turn around time is 4 days. Rush service is also available. Projects are generally billed by the number of names searched. The first project may require a prepayment.
Prentice Hall Legal & FInancial Services also has correspondent relationships in other jurisdictions, including all jurisdictions nationwide. They specialize in UCC and corporate work.

Prentice Hall Legal & Financial (1583)   **Phone: 800-458-0700**
5670 Wilshire Blvd Suite 750   213-954-3854
Los Angeles CA 90036   Fax: 213-954-0871

Local Retrieval Area: CA-Los Angeles, Orange.

Normal turn around time is 24 hours. Projects are generally billed by the number of names searched. The first project may require a prepayment.
Prentice Hall Legal & Financial Services also has correspondent relationships in other jurisdictions, including all jurisdictions nationwide. They specialize in UCC and corporate work.

Prentice Hall Legal & Financial (1584)   **Phone: 800-423-7398**
1560 Broadway Suite 620   303-860-7052
Denver CO 80202   Fax: 303-832-9050

Local Retrieval Area: CO-Adams, Arapahoe, Boulder, Jefferson.

Normal turn around time is 24 hours. Projects are generally billed by the number of names searched. The first project may require a prepayment.
Prentice Hall Legal & Financial Services also has correspondent relationships in other jurisdictions, including all jurisdictions nationwide. They specialize in both UCC and corporate work.

Prentice Hall Legal & Financial (1585) **Phone:** 800-826-7847
110 N Magnolia St   904-222-7495
Tallahassee FL 32301   **Fax:** 904-222-5513

Local Retrieval Area: FL-Leon.

Normal turn around time is 4 days. Rush service is also available. Projects are generally billed by the number of names searched. The first project may require a prepayment.

Prentice Hall Legal & Financial Services also has correspondent relationships in other jurisdictions, including all jurisdictions nationwide.

Prentice Hall Legal & Financial (1586) **Phone:** 800-772-2068
105 W Allen St   217-522-6712
Springfield IL 62704   **Fax:** 217-522-1922

Local Retrieval Area: IL-Sangamon.

Normal turn around time is 4 days. Rush service is also available. Projects are generally billed by the number of names searched. The first project may require a prepayment.

Prentice Hall Legal & Financial Services also has correspondent relationships in other jurisdictions, including all jurisdictions nationwide. They specialize in UCC and corporate work.

Prentice Hall Legal & Financial (1587) **Phone:** 617-227-9590
84 State St 5th Floor   **Fax:** 617-523-3189
Boston MA 02109

Local Retrieval Area: MA-Suffolk.

Normal turn around time is 4 days. Rush service is also available. Projects are generally billed by the number of names searched. The first project may require a prepayment.

Prentice Hall Legal & Financial Services also has correspondent relationships in other jurisdictions, including all jurisdictions nationwide.

Prentice Hall Legal & Financial (1588) **Phone:** 301-728-8441
1123 N Eutaw St Suite 521   **Fax:** 301-669-3878
Baltimore MD 21201

Local Retrieval Area: MD-Baltimore, City of Baltimore.

Normal turn around time is 4 days. Rush service is also available. Projects are generally billed by the number of names searched. The first project may require a prepayment.

Prentice Hall Legal & Financial Services also has correspondent relationships in other jurisdictions, including all jurisdictions nationwide.

Prentice Hall Legal & Financial (1589) **Phone:** 800-631-2155
830 Bear Mountain Rd Suite 305   **Fax:** 609-771-1800
West Trenton NJ 08628

Local Retrieval Area: NJ-Burlington, Mercer; PA-Bucks, Delaware, Montgomery, Philadelphia.

Normal turn around time is 4 days. Rush service is also available. Projects are generally billed by the number of names searched. The first project may require a prepayment.

Prentice Hall Legal & Financial Services also has correspondent relationships in other jurisdictions, including all jurisdictions nationwide. They specialize in UCC and corporate work.

Prentice Hall Legal & Financial (1590) **Phone:** 800-833-9848
500 Central Avenue   518-458-8111
Albany NY 12206   **Fax:** 518-482-8864

Local Retrieval Area: NY-Albany, Rensselaer, Schenectady.

Normal turn around time is 4 days. Rush service is also available. Projects are generally billed by the number of names searched. The first project may require a prepayment.

Prentice Hall Legal & Financial Services also has correspondent relationships in other jurisdictions, including all jurisdictions nationwide. They specialize in UCC and corporate work.

Prentice Hall Legal & Financial (1591) **Phone:** 212-406-2510
225 Broadway Suite 330   **Fax:** 212-791-2836
New York NY 10007

Local Retrieval Area: NY-Kings, New York, Queens.

Normal turn around time is 2 days. Projects are generally billed by the number of names searched. The first project may require a prepayment.

Prentice Hall Legal & Financial (1592) **Phone:** 800-688-9901
16 E Broad St Suite 910   614-463-9901
Columbus OH 43215   **Fax:** 614-463-9903

Local Retrieval Area: OH-Franklin.

Normal turn around time is 4 days. Rush service is also available. Projects are generally billed by the number of names searched. The first project may require a prepayment.

Prentice Hall Legal & Financial Services also has correspondent relationships in other jurisdictions, including all jurisdictions nationwide. They specialize in UCC and corporate work.

Prentice Hall Legal & Financial (1593) **Phone:** 800-452-7856
144 Chemawa Rd N   503-390-3735
Salem OR 97303   **Fax:** 503-393-9401

Local Retrieval Area: OR-Benton, Lane.

Normal turn around time is 4 days. Rush service is also available. Projects are generally billed by the number of names searched. The first project may require a prepayment.

Prentice Hall Legal & Financial Services also has correspondent relationships in other jurisdictions, including all jurisdictions nationwide. They specialize in UCC and corporate work.

Prentice Hall Legal & Financial (1594) **Phone:** 717-236-1535
100 Pine St Suite 330   **Fax:** 717-236-1592
Harrisburg PA 17101

Local Retrieval Area: PA-Cumberland, Dauphin.

Normal turn around time is 2 days. Rush service is also available. Projects are generally billed by the number of names searched. The first project may require a prepayment.

Prentice Hall Legal & Financial Services also has correspondent relationships in other jurisdictions, including all jurisdictions nationwide.

Prentice Hall Legal & Financial (1595)   Phone: 800-654-3398
400 N St Paul Suite 1025   214-220-2061
Dallas TX 75201   Fax: 214-720-3872

Local Retrieval Area: TX-Dallas.

Normal turn around time is 3 days. Rush service is also available. Projects are generally billed by the number of names searched. The first project may require a prepayment.
Prentice Hall Legal & Financial Services also has correspondent relationships in other jurisdictions, including all jurisdictions nationwide. They specialize in UCC and corporate work.

Prentice Hall Legal & Financial (1596)   Phone: 206-343-9436
600 First St   Fax: 206-343-7318
Seattle WA 98104

Local Retrieval Area: WA-King, Pierce, Snohomish, Thurston.

Normal turn around time is 24 hours. Projects are generally billed by the number of names searched. The first project may require a prepayment.
Prentice Hall Legal & Financial Services also has correspondent relationships in other jurisdictions, including all jurisdictions nationwide. They specialize in both UCC and corporate work.

Prentice Hall Legal & Financial (1597)   Phone: 206-754-9333
508 E Union St Suite 1   Fax: 206-754-5781
Olympia WA 98501

Local Retrieval Area: WA-King, Pierce, Snohomish, Thurston.

Normal turn around time is 4 days. Rush service is also available. Projects are generally billed by the number of names searched. The first project may require a prepayment.
Prentice Hall Legal & Financial Services also has correspondent relationships in other jurisdictions, including all jurisdictions nationwide. They specialize in UCC and corporate work.

Presidio County Abstract Co(1598)   Phone: 915-729-4264
PO Box 666   Fax: 915-729-3286
Marfa TX 79843

Local Retrieval Area: TX-Presidio.

Normal turn around time is 1-2 days. Fee basis will vary by the type of project. All projects require prepayment.

Presque Isle County Abstract(1599)   Phone: 517-734-2816
283 N 3rd St   Fax: 517-734-3896
Rogers City MI 49779

Local Retrieval Area: MI-Presque Isle.

Normal turn around time is 48-72 hours. Fee basis will vary by type of project. All projects require prepayment.
They specialize in real estate.

Preston Land Title Co(1600)   Phone: 800-365-7720
PO Box 148   208-852-2810
Preston ID 83263   Fax: 208-852-2811

Local Retrieval Area: ID-Franklin.

Normal turn around time is 1-2 days. Projects are generally billed by the hour. Credit accounts are accepted.

Prewitt-Rogers Abstract Co(1601)   Phone: 501-563-2137
203 E Hale Ave   Fax: 501-563-3558
Osceola AR 72370

Local Retrieval Area: AR-Mississippi.

Normal turn around time is 2-5 days. Projects are generally billed by the number of names searched or records located. Credit accounts are accepted. Personal checks are accepted. Prewitt-Rogers Abstract Co also has correspondent relationships in other jurisdictions, including Mississippi County (Chickasawba District). They specialize in abstracts of title and title insurance.

Bob Prins(1602)   Phone: 319-232-4752
401 Ardmore   Fax:
Waterloo IA 50703

Local Retrieval Area: IA-Black Hawk.

Normal turn around time is 2 days. They charge by the hour plus a minimum fee. Credit accounts are accepted. They request prepayment for copies only, and they will accept personal checks.

Priority One Attorney Service(1603)   Phone: 717-257-1365
955 S Cameron St   Fax: 717-234-0953
Harrisburg PA 17108-0454

Local Retrieval Area: PA-Adams, Cumberland, Dauphin, Franklin, Lancaster, Lebanon, Perry, Sullivan.

Normal turn around time is 3-4 days. Rush service is also available. Projects are generally billed by the number of records located. The first project may require a prepayment. Set-up fee required for volume work.
They specialize in searches, retrieval and filings for Pennsylvania Secretary of State and motor vehicle records.

Debbi Pritchett(1604)   Phone: 505-673-2301
PO Box 1002   Fax:
Mosquero NM 87733

Local Retrieval Area: NM-Harding.

Normal turn around time is 2-3 days. Projects are generally billed by the number of names searched. Fee basis may also be per year. Credit accounts are accepted.

Private Eyes Investigations(1605)   Phone: 207-947-9819
PO Box 2745   Fax:
Bangor ME 04402

Local Retrieval Area: ME-Aroostook, Hancock, Penobscot.

Normal turn around time is varied depending on project. Projects are generally billed by the hour. The first project may require a prepayment.
They specialize in surveillance and freedom of information act searches.

Pro Facto Inc(1606)   Phone: 501-376-8556
200 W Capitol Ave Suite 1118   Fax:
Little Rock AR 72201

Local Retrieval Area: AR-Faulkner, Jefferson, Pulaski, Saline.

Normal turn around time is 1-2 days. Rush service is also available. Fee basis will vary by the type of search. The first project may require a prepayment.

Pro Search Inc(1607)
91 Dora St
Stamford CT 06902
Phone: 203-348-6994
Fax: 203-325-3179

Local Retrieval Area: CT-Fairfield.

Normal turn around time is 3-5 days. Projects are generally billed by the number of names searched. Credit accounts are accepted.
Pro Search Inc also has correspondent relationships in other jurisdictions, including all counties in Connecticut. They also have a beeper phone number: (203) 977-9035.

Pro Serve(1608)
740 N Plankinton Suite 634
Milwaukee WI 53203
Phone: 414-271-9574
Fax: 414-271-4018

Local Retrieval Area: WI-Kenosha, Milwaukee, Ozaukee, Racine, Walworth, Washington, Waukesha.

Normal turn around time is usually the same day, but maximum 1 day. Projects are generally billed by the hour. Fee may include incurred costs. Credit accounts are accepted.
Pro Serve also has correspondent relationships in other jurisdictions, including the state of Wisconsin.

Process Associates(1609)
1100 Fleming Bldg
Des Moines IA 50309
Phone: 515-244-2488
Fax: 515-288-2163

Local Retrieval Area: IA-Polk.

Normal turn around time is 1-2 days. Projects are generally billed by the hour. Credit accounts are accepted. Personal checks are accepted.
They are also licensed private investigators.

Process Service Unlimited Inc(1610)
204 S Main St PO Box 258
Mount Airy MD 21771
Phone: 800-726-7068
Fax: 301-729-1935

Local Retrieval Area: MD-Baltimore, Carroll, Frederick, Howard, Montgomery.

Normal turn around time is 24-72 hours. Projects are generally billed by the hour. The first project may require a prepayment.
Process Service Unlimited Inc also has correspondent relationships in other jurisdictions, including all counties in Maryland.

Process Serving Unlimited(1611)
1832 Gippy Lane
Charleston SC 29407
Phone: 803-728-2732
Fax:

Local Retrieval Area: SC-Berkeley, Charleston, Dorchester.

Normal turn around time is 2 days. Projects are generally billed by the hour. The first project may require a prepayment.
They specialize in process serving.

Professional Civil Process(1612)
PO Box 181293
Corpus Christi TX 78480-1293
Phone: 512-884-1657
Fax: 512-884-1658

Local Retrieval Area: TX-Aransas, Bee, Brooks, Calhoun, Duval, Jim Wells, Kleberg, Nueces, Refugio, San Patricio, Victoria, Webb.

Normal turn around time is 24-48 hours. Projects are generally billed by the hour. The first project may require a prepayment.
Professional Civil Process also has correspondent relationships in other jurisdictions, including Starr, Hidalgo, Camaron, Willacy, Bexar, Travis, Harris, Dallas, Tarrant, Brazoria, Fetor and Midland. They specialize in service of civil process. They also have investigators available for background, surveillance, statements and skiptracing.

Professional Civil Process(1613)
7417 N 10th St
McAllen TX 78504
Phone: 800-880-4223
210-630-4223
Fax: 210-630-4223

Local Retrieval Area: TX-Cameron, Hidalgo, Starr, Willacy.

Normal turn around time is 5 working days. Rush service is also available. Projects are generally billed by the hour. All projects require prepayment. Credit cards are accepted for payment. They will invoice to NAPPS member only.
Professional Civil Process also has correspondent relationships in other jurisdictions, including the state of Texas They are liscensed investigators and their specialties include medical recordsand process service.

Professional Civil Process(1614)
410 S Main Suite 217
San Antonio TX 78204
Phone: 210-225-1239
Fax: 210-225-1243

Local Retrieval Area: TX-Atascosa, Bexar, Comal, Frio, Hays, Kendall, Kerr, Wilson.

Normal turn around time is 1 day. Projects are generally billed by the hour. Credit accounts are accepted.
They specialize in process service.

Professional Civil Process(1615)
603 W 13th St Suite 347
Austin TX 78701
Phone: 512-263-4141
Fax: 512-261-5811

Local Retrieval Area: TX-Bexar, Cameron, Dallas, Denton, Fort Bend, Harris, Hidalgo, Nueces, Tarrant, Travis.

Normal turn around time is 2-3 days. A same day rush service is also available. Projects are generally billed by the hour. The first project may require a prepayment.
Professional Civil Process also has correspondent relationships in other jurisdictions, including the rest of Texas. They have been in business since 1978.

Professional Courier Service(1616)
Waters Bldg 161 Ottowa Suite 200J
Grand Rapids MI 49503
Phone: 616-451-4445
Fax: 616-459-0025

Local Retrieval Area: MI-Kent, Muskegon, Ottawa.

Normal turn around time is 24-48 hours. Rush service is also available. Projects are generally billed by the hour. A flat fee is also charged in addition to the per hour fee. The first project may require a prepayment.

Professional Research Services(1617)
7151 Metro Blvd Suite 210
Minneapolis MN 55439
Phone: **612-941-9040**
Fax: 612-941-9041

Local Retrieval Area: MN-Anoka, Carver, Dakota, Hennepin, Ramsey, Scott, Washington.

Normal turn around time is 48 hours for surrounding counties, 1-4 days for the rest of Minnesota and the United States. Projects are generally billed by the number of records located. Credit accounts are accepted.
Professional Research Services Inc also has correspondent relationships in other jurisdictions, including nationwide. They specialize in background screening.

Professional Service of Process(1618)
500 N College St Suite 195
Charlotte NC 28202
Phone: **704-375-4353**
Fax: 704-333-0233

Local Retrieval Area: NC-All counties; SC-All counties.

Normal turn around time is 48 hours. Projects are generally billed by the hour. The first project may require a prepayment.
They specialize in process serving and skip tracing.

Professional Title & Abstract Co(1619)
112 S 4th St
Heber Springs AR 72543
Phone: **501-362-3136**
Fax: 501-362-2930

Local Retrieval Area: AR-Cleburne.

Normal turn around time is within 5 days. Fee basis will vary by the type of project. The first project may require a prepayment.
They specialize in real estate and closings.

Professional Title & Escrow Inc(1620)
PO Box 339
South Sioux City NE 68776-0339
Phone: **402-494-5223**
Fax: 402-494-1478

Local Retrieval Area: NE-Dakota.

Normal turn around time is 2-3 days. Projects are generally billed by the hour. Credit accounts are accepted.

Professional Title Services(1621)
248 E Main
Price UT 84501
Phone: **801-637-2320**
Fax: 801-637-2323

Local Retrieval Area: UT-Carbon, Duchesne, Emery.

Normal turn around time is 24 hours for UCC and name searches, 48 hours for title commitments, 3 days for mineral title memo's, and 1 week for abstracts. Projects are generally billed by the number of names searched. Credit accounts are accepted. .
They specialize in all services regarding real esate records, abstracts, title insurance, closing and escrow services.

Professional Title Services Inc(1622)
220 W Willow St
Chippewa Falls WI 54729
Phone: **715-723-7706**
Fax: 715-726-9507

Local Retrieval Area: WI-Chippewa, Dunn, Eau Claire.

Normal turn around time is varied depending on project. Title insurance search fees are preset by insurance. Credit accounts are accepted.
They specialize in title insurance, abstracting and judgement searches.

Professional Title of Edgewater(1623)
2102 S Ridgewood Ave Suite 25
Edgewater FL 32141
Phone: **904-427-0505**
Fax: 904-428-1031

Local Retrieval Area: FL-Volusia.

Normal turn around time is 3 days. They can complete within 24 hours with verbal callback if necessary. Projects are generally billed by the number of names searched. Credit accounts are accepted.
Professional Title of Edgewater Inc also has correspondent relationships in other jurisdictions, including nationwide. They specialize in title searches, real estate and loan closings.

Janie Proffer(1624)
313 W Sherman Dr
Aubrey TX 76227
Phone: **817-387-1214**
Fax:

Local Retrieval Area: TX-Denton.

Normal turn around time is 1-2 days. Projects are generally billed by the number of names searched. Credit accounts are accepted.

Property Research and Doc(1625)
2502 Babcock Rd Suite 1106
San Antonio TX 78229
Phone: **210-614-0456**
Fax: 210-614-0445

Local Retrieval Area: TX-Atascosa, Bexar, Blanco, Caldwell, Gonzales, Hays, Hidalgo, Kerr, Medina, Medina, Nueces, San Patricio, Travis, Uvalde, Victoria, Webb, Williamson, Wilson.

Normal turn around time is 1-3 days. Owner histories average 5 days. Projects are generally billed by the hour. Credit accounts are accepted.
They specialize in 50 year owner histories and survey packages, which include: deeds, plats, easements on subject properties and adjoiners.

Public Information Resource(1626)
239 Sunderland Dr
Auburn ME 04210
Phone: **207-795-6350**
Fax: 207-795-6313

Local Retrieval Area: ME-Androscoggin, Cumberland, Franklin, Kennebec, Oxford, Sagadahoc, York.

Normal turn around time is the same day to 48 hours. Projects are generally billed by the number of names searched. The first project may require a prepayment. Personal checks are accepted. Public Information Resource also has correspondent relationships in other jurisdictions, including the state of Maine. They perform UCC-11's on a daily basis at the State Department. They file UCC's, articles of Inc., annual reports and obtain Certificates of Good Standing. (CGS).

Public Record Information(1627)
209 Fairview Ave
Voorhees NJ 08043
Phone: **609-429-0225**
Fax:

Local Retrieval Area: NJ-Burlington, Mercer.

Normal turn around time is 24-48 hours. Fee basis will vary by the type of search. The first project may require a prepayment. Personal checks are accepted.

Public Records Recovery Srvs(1628)   Phone: 612-448-2952
2529 Woodcrest Dr   Fax: 612-448-2398
Chaska MN 55318
Local Retrieval Area: MN-McLeod, Olmsted, Scott, Sibley.
Normal turn around time is 48-72 hours. Projects are generally billed by the number of names searched or records located. All projects require prepayment. They will also invoice. Personal checks are accepted.

Pulaski County Abstract Co(1629)   Phone: 618-748-9233
232 Main St   Fax:
Mound City IL 62963
Local Retrieval Area: IL-Pulaski.
Normal turn around time is 2-14 days. Fee basis will vary by complexity and time of the job. Credit accounts are accepted. Personal checks are accepted.
They specialize in real estate transactions and court records

Pullman Process Service(1630)   Phone: 509-334-7588
PO Box 356   Fax:
Pullman WA 99163
Local Retrieval Area: ID-Latah; WA-Asotin, Whitman.
Normal turn around time is 2 days. Projects are generally billed by the hour. The first project may require a prepayment.
They search only in the criminal and civil courts.

Pushmataha County Abstract Co(1631)   Phone: 405-298-3189
Box 849   Fax: 405-298-2322
Antlers OK 74523
Local Retrieval Area: OK-Pushmataha.
Normal turn around time is 3-7 days. Projects are generally billed by the number of names searched or records located. All projects require prepayment.

Putnam County Abstract(1632)   Phone: 816-947-3105
PO Box 303   Fax:
Unionville MO 63565
Local Retrieval Area: MO-Mercer, Putnam, Schuyler.
Normal turn around time is 1 week. Fee basis varies by type of transaction. Credit accounts are accepted.

Quality Abstractors Inc(1633)   Phone: 301-695-9329
140-F W Patrick St   Fax: 301-695-5016
Frederick MD 21701
Local Retrieval Area: MD-Frederick; WV-Jefferson.
Normal turn around time is 1-14 days. Projects are generally billed by the number of names searched. Credit accounts are accepted. Personal checks are accepted.
They have been in the land title abstracting business for more than 25 years.

Quest Abstract Inc(1634)   Phone: 201-624-6558
291 Willow Ave   Fax: 201-622-6216
Lyndhurst NJ 07071
Local Retrieval Area: NJ-Essex, Union.
Normal turn around time is 2-3 days. Projects are generally billed by the number of names searched. Credit accounts are accepted. Quest Abstract Inc also has correspondent relationships in other jurisdictions, including Bergen.

Quest Research Inc(1635)   Phone: 501-374-4712
101 S Spring St Suite 220   Fax: 501-374-3029
Little Rock AR 72201
Local Retrieval Area: AR-All counties.
Normal turn around time is 1-3 days. Projects are generally billed by the number of names searched or records located. Credit accounts are accepted.
They specialize in corporate retrieval and filing service.

Quest and Assoc Inc(1636)   Phone: 412-563-1007
PO Box 23323   Fax: 412-563-6869
Pittsburgh PA 15222
Local Retrieval Area: PA-Allegheny.
Normal turn around time is 24-72 hours. Projects are generally billed by the number of names searched. Credit accounts are accepted.
Quest and Assoc Inc also has correspondent relationships in other jurisdictions, including all counties in Pennsylvania. They specialize in criminal and Department of Motor Vehicle records.

Quirk Associates(1637)   Phone: 617-326-1202
PO Box 226   Fax: 617-326-0916
Dedham MA 02027
Local Retrieval Area: MA-Middlesex, Norfolk, Suffolk.
Normal turn around time is within one week. The fee basis will vary with the type of search. Credit accounts are accepted.
Quirk Associates also has correspondent relationships in other jurisdictions, including Plymouth, Essex, and Bristol counties. They specialize in real estate record searches.

R & I Associates(1638)   Phone: 206-324-6300
2508 5th Ave Suite 162   Fax:
Seattle WA 98121
Local Retrieval Area: WA-King, Pierce.
Normal turn around time is 48-72 hours. Projects are generally billed by the hour. The first project may require a prepayment. Personal checks or money orders are accepted.
R & I Associates also has correspondent relationships in other jurisdictions, including most of the United States. They specialize in personal injury, child custody and missing or unable to locate persons.

R A Heales & Associates Ltd(1639)   Phone: **303-671-8700**
2530 S Parker Rd Suite 220   Fax: 303-671-6063
Aurora CO 80014

Local Retrieval Area: CO-Adams, Arapahoe, Denver, Douglas, Jefferson.

Normal turn around time is 2-3 days. Projects are generally billed by the hour. All projects require prepayment. Credit cards are accepted for payment. Personal checks are accepted. They will invoice to established clients and P.I. Association members only.

RASCAL(1640)   Phone: **909-677-9833**
24977 Washington Ave Suite D   Fax: 909-677-6205
Murrieta CA 92564-0840

Local Retrieval Area: CA-Riverside, San Diego.

Normal turn around time is 1-5 days. Projects are generally billed by the number of names searched. All projects require prepayment. They will also invoice. They accept personal checks.
RASCAL also has correspondent relationships in other jurisdictions, including Los Angeles, Orange, Ventura, San Bernardino, Riverside and San Diego.

RLS Inc(1641)   Phone: **304-472-4932**
1 Riley Heights   Fax: 304-457-2788
Buckhannon WV 26201

Local Retrieval Area: WV-Barbour, Boone, Braxton, Calhoun, Doddridge, Fayette, Gilmer, Harrison, Jackson, Lewis, Logan, McDowell, Marion, Mineral, Mingo, Monongalia, Nicholas, Pleasants, Preston, Randolph, Ritchie, Roane, Taylor, Tucker, Upshur, Webster, Wirt, Wood, Wyoming.

Normal turn around time is from 3 days to 3 weeks. Projects are generally billed by the hour. The first project may require a prepayment.
RLS Inc also has correspondent relationships in other jurisdictions, including the rest of West Virginia. They specialize in oil, gas and coal records and also serve as private investigators.

RND Realty Corp(1642)   Phone: **318-234-9061**
100 E Vermilion St Suite 300A-5   Fax: 318-237-8556
Lafayette LA 70501-6930

Local Retrieval Area: LA-Iberia Parish, Lafayette Parish, St. Martin Parish, Vermilion Parish.

Normal turn around time is 3-5 days. Projects are generally billed by the hour. Copy, mileage and per day cost will be added to the fee. Credit accounts are accepted. Deposit or retainer is required.
RND Realty Corp also has correspondent relationships in other jurisdictions, including undisclosed areas. They specialize in 52-year abstracts for real estate and mortgage purposes.

RSI(1643)   Phone: **800-633-6125**
1828 Walnut 6th Floor   816-471-1414
Kansas City MO 64108   Fax: 816-472-7155

Local Retrieval Area: KS-Johnson, Wyandotte; MO-Clay, Jackson, Platte.

Normal turn around time is 1-3 days. Projects are generally billed by the hour. Credit accounts are accepted.

Rafael Jorge Investigations(1644)   Phone: **818-846-5038**
2219 W Olive Suite 295   Fax: 818-846-5977
Burbank CA 91506

Local Retrieval Area: CA-Many counties in this state are covered. See the county index for actual coverage..

Normal turn around time is 1-3 days. Projects are generally billed by the number of names searched. Credit accounts are accepted. Rafael Jorge Investigations also has correspondent relationships in other jurisdictions, including the rest of California. Thay also have network affiliations with AZ, CO, DC, FL, Md, MI, NM, NV, VA, and WA. They specialize in court record retrieval and pre-employment investigations.

Rainbow Real Estate(1645)   Phone: **405-544-3274**
PO Box 233   Fax: 405-544-2451
Boise City OK 73933

Local Retrieval Area: OK-Cimarron.

Normal turn around time is 48 hours. Projects are generally billed by the hour. Credit accounts are accepted.
They specialize in real estate, oil, and gas.

Vickie Rainer(1646)   Phone: **601-534-6326**
C/O Sumners, Carter PO Drawer 730   Fax: 601-534-5205
New Albany MS 38652

Local Retrieval Area: MS-Lee, Pontotoc, Tippah, Union.

Normal turn around time is 1-2 days in Union county, up to 1 week in others. Fee basis varies by type of transaction. The first project may require a prepayment.

Ramey Investigative Services(1647)   Phone: **510-933-9730**
PO Box 4471   Fax: 510-820-8896
Walnut Creek CA 94596-0471

Local Retrieval Area: CA-Alameda, Marin, San Francisco.

Normal turn around time is 1-3 weeks. Projects are generally billed by the hour. Credit accounts are accepted.

Jean Randall(1648)   Phone: **415-897-2361**
501 Louis Dr   Fax: 415-897-2305
Novato CA 94945

Local Retrieval Area: CA-Marin.

Normal turn around time is 1 day. Projects are generally billed by the number of names searched. The first project may require a prepayment. Personal checks are accepted.
They specialize in voter registration and fictitious business filing searches.

Ranger Recovery(1649)   Phone: **914-679-2957**
PO Box 1184   Fax: 914-336-5480
Woodstock NY 12498

Local Retrieval Area: NY-Ulster.

Normal turn around time is less than 1 week. Projects are generally billed by the hour. Credit accounts are accepted.

Ransom County Title Co(1650) Phone: **701-683-5511**
PO Box 511 Fax: 701-683-5511
Lisbon ND 58054
Local Retrieval Area: ND-Ransom.
Normal turn around time is 12-36 hours. Fee basis will vary by the type of project. The first project may require a prepayment.

Rawlings County Abstract & Title(1651) Phone: **913-626-3011**
408 Main St Fax: 913-626-3104
Atwood KS 67730
Local Retrieval Area: KS-Rawlins.
Normal turn around time is 1-3 days. Project billing methods vary. Credit accounts are accepted. Personal checks are accepted.
They specialize in real estate titles and title insurance.

Ray Feller Investigatons(1652) Phone: **209-576-8531**
1320 Standiford Ave Suite 252 Fax: 209-529-3424
Modesto CA 95350
Local Retrieval Area: CA-Calaveras, Merced, San Joaquin, Stanislaus, Tuolumne.
Normal turn around time is 24 hours for Stanislaus, Merced and San Joaquin, and 48 hours for other counties. Online computer ordering is also available. Projects are generally billed by the hour. Credit accounts are accepted. Personal checks are accepted.
They specialize in asset location, real estate and investment fraud embezzlement. Their computer link number is 62956884.

McClure Reagan(1653) Phone: **406-873-4742**
138 3rd Ave SE Fax:
Cut Bank MT 59427
Local Retrieval Area: MT-Cascade, Glacier, Pondera, Toole.
Normal turn around time is 3-5 days. Projects are generally billed by the hour. The first project may require a prepayment.
Mr. Reagan specializes in real estate, oil and gas searches.

Real County Abstract & Title Co(1654) Phone: **210-232-5303**
PO Box 298 Fax: 210-232-5399
Leakey TX 78873
Local Retrieval Area: TX-Real.
Normal turn around time is 1-2 days. Fee basis will vary by the type of project. Credit accounts are accepted.

Real Estate Data Inc(1655) Phone: **618-964-1907**
Rt 5 Box 334 Fax: 618-964-1366
Marion IL 62959
Local Retrieval Area: IL-Franklin, Jackson, Johnson, Saline, Union, Williamson.
Normal turn around time is 3 days. Projects are generally billed by the number of names searched. Credit accounts are accepted.
They specialize in real estate searches.

Real Estate Information Service(1656) Phone: **703-787-0506**
PO Box 5178 Fax: 703-787-0509
Herndon VA 22070
Local Retrieval Area: VA-Arlington, Fairfax, Loudoun, City of Alexandria.
Normal turn around time is 3 days. Fee basis is per case. Credit accounts are accepted.
They specialize in real estate title examinations.

Real Estate Loan Services(1657) Phone: **615-855-0581**
Uptain Building Suite 312 Fax: 615-894-3184
Chattanooga TN 37411
Local Retrieval Area: TN-Bledsoe, Bradley, Hamilton, McMinn, Marion, Meigs, Polk, Rhea, Sequatchie.
Normal turn around time is 24 hours. Projects are generally billed by the number of records located. All projects require prepayment. They will also invoice.
Real Estate Loan Services also has correspondent relationships in other jurisdictions, including counties in Georgia and Alabama. They specialize in title openings and closing.

Real Estate Loan Services of MO(1658) Phone: **314-893-4898**
911 A E High Fax: 314-893-6282
Jefferson City MO 65101
Local Retrieval Area: MO-All counties.
Normal turn around time is 48 hours. Fee basis will vary per county. Credit accounts are accepted.
They specialize in real estate and titles. They also have access to the Secretary of State office.

Realty Settlement Inc(1659) Phone: **814-336-1802**
915 Liberty St Fax: 814-336-5881
Meadville PA 16335
Local Retrieval Area: PA-Crawford, Mercer, Venango.
Normal turn around time is up to 7 days. Fee basis will vary by the type of project. Credit accounts are accepted.
They specialize in title insurance.

Realty Title Co Inc(1660) Phone: **406-538-8176**
517 W Janeaux Fax: 406-538-5184
Lewistown MT 59457
Local Retrieval Area: MT-Fergus, Judith Basin, Petroleum.
Normal turn around time is 2-3 days. Projects are generally billed by the hour. Credit accounts are accepted.

Dorotha Reavis(1661) Phone: **417-256-4755**
708 Nichols Dr Fax:
West Plains MO 65775
Local Retrieval Area: AR-Fulton; MO-Howell, Oregon, Ozark, Texas.
Normal turn around time is 1 day. Projects are generally billed by the hour. A mileage charge is also added. The first project may require a prepayment.

Record Search and Information(1662)
2219 N Curtis
Boise ID 83706
Phone: **208-375-1906**
Fax: 208-322-5469

Local Retrieval Area: ID-All counties.

Normal turn around time is 24 hours. Projects are generally billed by the number of names searched. Credit accounts are accepted. They also have access to abstract court files for liens, judgements and bankruptcy cases.

Record-Check Services Inc(1663)
1556 W Crestwood Rd
Memphis TN 38119
Phone: **800-530-7226**
Fax: 901-761-3409

Local Retrieval Area: MS-De Soto, Marshall, Tate, Tunica; TN-Fayette, Madison, Shelby, Tipton.

Normal turn around time is 72 hours. Projects are generally billed by the number of names searched or records located. Credit accounts are accepted.
Record-Check Services Inc also has correspondent relationships in other jurisdictions, including all counties in Tennessee, Kentucky and North Mississippi.

RecordServe/John Kelley Ent(1664)
1315 Ridgeway Suite 104-200
Memphis TN 38119
Phone: **901-853-5320**
Fax: 901-853-6372

Local Retrieval Area: AR-Crittenden; MS-De Soto, Marshall; TN-Fayette, Shelby, Tipton.

Normal turn around time is 2-3 days. Projects are generally billed by the number of names searched. Credit accounts are accepted.
RecordServe/John Kelley Enterprises also has correspondent relationships in other jurisdictions, including nationwide. They specialize in hard to locate records, i.e. post office box, change of address, FAA and expert witness identifications.

Records Deposition Service(1665)
51 N High St Suite 461
Columbus OH 43215
Phone: **614-365-9092**
Fax: 614-365-9198

Local Retrieval Area: OH-Cuyahoga, Delaware, Franklin.

Normal turn around time is 2-3 weeks. A 1 week rush service is also available. Project billing methods vary. They may also charge per page. Credit accounts are accepted.
They specialize in hospital, doctor's offices, clinics and Bureau of Workers Compensation searches.

Records Research Inc(1666)
PO Box 81227
Lincoln NE 68501-1227
Phone: **402-476-3869**
Fax:

Local Retrieval Area: NE-Lancaster.

Normal turn around time is 24 hours to 2 weeks. Projects are generally billed by the number of names searched. The first project may require a prepayment.
Records Research Inc also has correspondent relationships in other jurisdictions, including all the counties in the state. They specialize in UCC searches.

Red River Title Research(1667)
PO Box 305
Coushatta LA 71019
Phone: **318-932-6264**
Fax: 318-932-3301

Local Retrieval Area: LA-Red River Parish.

Normal turn around time is 1-2 days. Fee basis varies by type of transaction. The first project may require a prepayment.

Reda's Attorney Service(1668)
PO Box 579
Shoreham NY 11786
Phone: **516-821-6060**
Fax: 516-744-5314

Local Retrieval Area: NY-Nassau, Suffolk.

Normal turn around time is 24 hours for Suffolk County and 48 hours for Nassau County. Rush service is also available. Fee basis will vary by the type of search. The first project may require a prepayment.
Reda's Attorney Service also has correspondent relationships in other jurisdictions, including nondisclosed counties.

David Reed(1669)
315 W 4th St
Emporium PA 15834
Phone: **814-486-3349**
Fax:

Local Retrieval Area: PA-Cameron, Elk, McKean, Potter.

Normal turn around time is 24 hours to 1 week. Fee basis is determined by a established fee schedule. Credit accounts are accepted. They request that individuals prepay, but will invoice attorneys and companies.

Alicia Reel(1670)
5 Highland Ave
Petersburg WV 26847
Phone: **304-257-4550**
Fax: 304-257-2593

Local Retrieval Area: WV-Grant.

Normal turn around time is 1 week. Fee basis varies by type of transaction. Credit accounts are accepted.
Alicia has several associates who work with her and specialize in searching all records in the County Clerk's office.

William Ben Regan(1671)
225 E Bay St
Magnolia MS 39652
Phone: **601-783-2491**
Fax: 601-783-2492

Local Retrieval Area: MS-Pike.

Normal turn around time is 1 day. Fee basis varies by type of transaction. The first project may require a prepayment.
Mr. Regan is in general practice. He specializes in marriage/divorce searches.

Regier Agency Inc(1672)
616 N Main St
Newton KS 67114
Phone: **316-283-2750**
Fax: 316-283-5680

Local Retrieval Area: KS-Harvey.

Normal turn around time is 2-3 days. Fee basis varies by type of transaction. The first project may require a prepayment.

Regional Investigative Services(1673)
PO Box 4322
Cherry Hill NJ 08034
Phone: **609-667-4098**
Fax: 609-667-2847

Local Retrieval Area: NJ-All counties.

Normal turn around time is 1 day-2 weeks. Projects are generally billed by the hour. All projects require prepayment.

Regional Investigative Services Inc also has correspondent relationships in other jurisdictions, including New Jersey, Pennsylvania and Deleware. Their specialty is the combined use of public records and computer databases in background, assets and locate investigations.

Registry Research(1674)
PO Box 448
South Egremont MA 01258
Phone: **413-528-3919**
Fax: 413-528-0907

Local Retrieval Area: MA-Berkshire.

Normal turn around time is 2 weeks. Projects are generally billed by the hour. Credit accounts are accepted. A downpayment is required.

They specialize in title abstracts and historical or genealogical documentation.

Ann C Reid(1675)
339 2nd St
Cloquet MN 55720
Phone: **218-878-0619**
Fax: 218-878-0619

Local Retrieval Area: MN-Aitkin, Beltrami, Benton, Carlton, Cass, Cook, Crow Wing, Hubbard, Itasca, Kanabec, Koochiching, Lake, Lake, McLeod, Meeker, Morrison, Pine, St. Louis, Sherburne, Stearns, Todd, Wadena; WI-Ashland, Bayfield, Douglas, Sawyer, Washburn.

Normal turn around time is 24-48 hours. For counties outside immediate area, turnaround time is 3 to 5 days. Projects are generally billed by the number of records located. Mileage is also charged. The first project may require a prepayment. Personal checks are accepted.

Reliable Courier(1676)
4300 N Central Suite 108A
Dallas TX 75206
Phone: **214-821-5596**
Fax: 214-821-5598

Local Retrieval Area: TX-Dallas, Ellis, Tarrant.

Normal turn around time is 2 days. Projects are generally billed by the hour. Credit accounts are accepted.

Reliance Title Services(1677)
1016 A Gilbert Ct
Iowa City IA 52244
Phone: **319-354-6505**
Fax:

Local Retrieval Area: IA-Johnson.

Normal turn around time is 48 hours for court searches, and 3 to 5 working days for real estate. Projects are generally billed by the number of records located. A flat fee charge is also included. Credit accounts are accepted.

Relyea-Lee Services Inc(1678)
14 Sleepy Hollow PO Box 172
Clifton Park NY 12065
Phone: **800-854-4111**
Fax: 800-854-4112

Local Retrieval Area: NY-Albany, Rensselaer, Saratoga, Schenectady.

Normal turn around time is same day. Projects are generally billed by the number of names searched. Credit accounts are accepted.

Relyea-Lee Services Inc also has correspondent relationships in other jurisdictions, including every court in the county/nationwide. They specialize in court record retrieval, UCC, searching and filing and corporate work.

Reniville Abstract Company Inc(1679)
PO Box 189
Mohall ND 58761
Phone: **701-756-6487**
Fax:

Local Retrieval Area: ND-Renville.

Normal turn around time is 10 days. Fee basis will vary by type of project. Credit accounts are accepted.

Connie Reno(1680)
PO Box 356
Mabscott WV 25871
Phone: **304-253-3215**
Fax:

Local Retrieval Area: WV-Fayette, Greenbrier, Mercer, Nicholas, Raleigh, Summers.

Normal turn around time is 24-48 hours. Projects are generally billed by the number of records located. Credit accounts are accepted.

Connie specializes in property searches and title work.

Renville County Abstract Co(1681)
PO Box 86
Olivia MN 56277
Phone: **612-523-5321**
Fax: 612-523-5321

Local Retrieval Area: MN-Redwood, Renville.

Normal turn around time is 2 days. Fee basis will vary by type of project. Credit accounts are accepted.

They specialize in real estate title searches.

Research & Revisions Etc(1682)
PO Box 1115
Greeley CO 80632
Phone: **303-351-6276**
Fax:

Local Retrieval Area: CO-Adams, Larimer, Logan, Morgan, Phillips, Sedgwick, Washington, Weld, Yuma.

Normal turn around time is 2-3 days. Projects are generally billed by the hour. The first project may require a prepayment.

They specialize in abstract judgements.

Research Information Services(1683)
53 W Jackson Blvd Suite 664
Chicago IL 60604
Phone: **800-388-3320**
312-922-7171
Fax: 312-922-7736

Local Retrieval Area: IL-Cook, Du Page.

Normal turn around time is the same or next day. Projects are generally billed by the hour. The first project may require a prepayment.

Research Information Services also has correspondent relationships in other jurisdictions, including nationwide.

Research North Inc of Alpena(1684)
122 N 2nd St Suite C
Alpena MI 49707-2802

Phone: **517-356-4500**
Fax: 517-354-2106

Local Retrieval Area: MI-Alcona, Alpena, Montmorency, Oscoda, Presque Isle.

Normal turn around time is varied depending on project. Online computer ordering is also available. Projects are generally billed by the hour. The first project may require a prepayment. Research North Inc of Alpena also has correspondent relationships in other jurisdictions, including Chippewa, Ingham, Wayne, Oakland, Macomb and Kent. They specialize in insurance defense investigation.

Research North Inc of Petoskey(1685)
207 Michigan
Petoskey MI 49770-2607

Phone: **616-347-7366**
Fax: 616-347-7685

Local Retrieval Area: MI-Charlevoix, Cheboygan, Emmet, Mackinac, Otsego.

Normal turn around time is varied depending in project. Online computer ordering is also available. Projects are generally billed by the hour. The first project may require a prepayment. Research North Inc of Petoskey also has correspondent relationships in other jurisdictions, including Chippewa, Ingham, Wayne, Oakland, Macomb and Kent. They specialize in insurance defense investigations.

Research North of Traverse City(1686)
160 E State St
Traverse City MI 49684-2572

Phone: **616-947-6300**
Fax: 616-947-0706

Local Retrieval Area: MI-Antrim, Benzie, Grand Traverse, Kalkaska, Lenawee, Manistee, Missaukee, Wexford.

Normal turn around time is variable. Online computer ordering is also available. Projects are generally billed by the hour. Credit accounts are accepted.
Research North Inc of Traverse City also has correspondent relationships in other jurisdictions, including Chippewa, Ingham, Wayne, Oakland, Macomb and Kent. Insurance defense investigation is their specialty.

Research Staff(1687)
5718 Hewitt St
Houston TX 77092

Phone: **713-688-3584**
Fax: 713-688-1121

Local Retrieval Area: TX-Brazoria, Brazos, Chambers, Fort Bend, Galveston, Harris, Liberty, Montgomery, Waller.

Normal turn around time is 24-48 hours. Rush service is also available. Fee basis will vary by the type of search. The first project may require a prepayment.
Research Staff also has correspondent relationships in other jurisdictions, including the entire state of Texas. They specialize in enviromental, UCC, and real estate asset searches.

Research and Investigative Assoc(1688)
PO Box 1321
Eureka CA 95502

Phone: **707-444-8767**
Fax: 707-444-2164

Local Retrieval Area: CA-Del Norte, Humboldt, Mendocino, Trinity.

Normal turn around time is 48 hours for verbal request and 5 days for a written request. Projects are generally billed by the hour. Credit accounts are accepted. A 50% retainer is required. Personal checks are accepted.
Research and Investigative Associates also has correspondent relationships in other jurisdictions, including Sanoma, Lake, Sacramento, Marin, San Francisco, Alameda and San Mateo. They specialize in investigation and trial preparation.

Research and Retrieval(1689)
2715 Orange Ave
Torrance CA 90501

Phone: **310-782-6200**
Fax: 310-782-6303

Local Retrieval Area: CA-Los Angeles, San Francisco.

Normal turn around time is the same day. Projects are generally billed by the number of names searched. Credit accounts are accepted.
Research and Retrieval also has correspondent relationships in other jurisdictions, including the rest of California and nationwide. They specialize in case files/newspaper monitors, library research, lot book & property information, fictitious business name filing & searches, UCC search & filings, tax lien judgement searches, and all courts including bankruptcy & document retrieval.

Researchers(1690)
130 Townsend St
San Francisco CA 94107

Phone: **415-543-9555**
Fax: 415-974-6119

Local Retrieval Area: CA-Alameda, Contra Costa, El Dorado, Marin, Monterey, Nevada, Placer, Sacramento, San Francisco, San Mateo, Santa Clara, Santa Cruz, Solano, Sonoma, Stanislaus, Sutter, Yolo, Yuba.

Normal turn around time is 1-3 days. Projects are generally billed by the number of names searched or records located. Credit accounts are accepted. They request new clients to pay C.O.D. Their Public Records Division provides extensive record retrieval services for state agencies, such as the California Public Utilities Commission, Departmennt of Insurance, Department of Corporations and Department of Real Estate.

Researchers Ltd(1691)
105 S Race St
Georgetown DE 19947

Phone: **302-856-7442**
Fax: 302-856-7462

Local Retrieval Area: DE-Sussex.

Normal turn around time is 1-48 hours for document retrieval, and 2 to 5 days for title searches. Projects are generally billed by the number of names searched. Credit accounts are accepted. Researchers Ltd also has correspondent relationships in other jurisdictions, including Kent and New castle counties.

Ricard Assocates Inc(1692)
PO Box 653
Manchester CT 06045

Phone: **203-646-4333**
Fax:

Local Retrieval Area: CT-Hartford, Middlesex, New London, Tolland, Windham.

Normal turn around time is 2 weeks. Projects are generally billed by the number of records located. Credit accounts are accepted.

Rice County Abstract & Title Co(1693)
PO Box 97
Faribault MN 55021

Phone: **507-332-2259**
Fax:

Local Retrieval Area: MN-Rice.

Normal turn around time is 1-3 days. Projects are generally billed by the hour. Credit accounts are accepted.
They will go only to the County Recorders office for real estate.

Richardson Abstract Co Inc(1694)
521 Marsh
Kinsley KS 67547

Phone: **316-659-2592**
Fax:

Local Retrieval Area: KS-Edwards.

Normal turn around time is the same day. Projects are generally billed by the hour. Credit accounts are accepted. Personal checks are accepted.

Sharian Richardson(1695)
PO Box 506
Fulton MS 38843

Phone: **601-862-7879**
Fax: 601-862-2655

Local Retrieval Area: MS-Itawamba.

Normal turn around time is 1-2 days. Projects are generally billed by the hour. The first project may require a prepayment.
Ms. Richardson is in general practice. She specializes in marriage/divorce searches.

Richland County Abstract(1696)
133 N Central Ave Suite 223
Richland Center WI 53581

Phone: **608-647-4596**
Fax: 608-647-8033

Local Retrieval Area: WI-Richland.

Normal turn around time is 1-2 days. Fee basis varies by type of transaction. The first project may require a prepayment.

Richland County Abstract Co(1697)
123 N 3rd St
Wahpeton ND 58074

Phone: **701-642-3781**
Fax:

Local Retrieval Area: MN-Wilkin; ND-Richland, Sargent.

Normal turn around time is 1 week. Projects are generally billed by the number of names searched or records located. Credit accounts are accepted.
Richland County Abstract Co also has correspondent relationships in other jurisdictions, including North Dakota and Minnesota. They specialize in real estate records, taxes, judgements and UCC searches.

Ricochet(1698)
3031 Allen Suite 202
Dallas TX 75204

Phone: **214-855-0303**
Fax: 214-855-7877

Local Retrieval Area: TX-Collin, Dallas, Denton, Ellis, Nueces, Tarrant.

Normal turn around time is 3 days. Archive records average 10 days. Project billing methods vary. Credit accounts are accepted.
Ricochet also has correspondent relationships in other jurisdictions, including Harris, Bexar and Travis. They specialize in process service and court record searches.

Ringgold County Abstract Co(1699)
109 S Fillmore St
Mt Ayr IA 50854

Phone: **515-464-3902**
Fax: 515-464-3185

Local Retrieval Area: IA-Ringgold.

Normal turn around time is 3-5 days. Fee basis will vary by the type of project. The first project may require a prepayment.

Frances Rittenour(1700)
HC Rt 2 Box 351
Minter AL 36761

Phone: **205-548-2843**
205-227-4517
Fax:

Local Retrieval Area: AL-Lowndes.

Normal turn around time is varied depending on search. Fee basis will vary with type of search. Credit accounts are accepted.

Riviera Research(1701)
PO Box 2259
Riviera AZ 86442

Phone: **602-763-7273**
Fax:

Local Retrieval Area: AZ-La Paz, Mohave.

Normal turn around time is 1-3 days. Rush service is also available. Projects are generally billed by the number of names searched. The first project may require a prepayment.
Riviera Research also has correspondent relationships in other jurisdictions, including other counties in Arizona.

Roadrunner Messenger Service(1702)
547 Halekauwila Suite 101
Honolulu HI 96813

Phone: **808-526-9101**
Fax: 808-528-3475

Local Retrieval Area: HI-Honolulu.

Normal turn around time is 2 days. Rush service is also available. Fee basis is per stop and waiting. All projects require prepayment. They will invoice to established customers.

Robert Daly Investigations(1703)
PO Box 2076
Monroe NY 10950

Phone: **914-858-8888**
Fax: 914-858-8889

Local Retrieval Area: NY-Orange; PA-Pike.

Normal turn around time is varied depending on project. Projects are generally billed by the hour. The first project may require a prepayment. Personal checks are accepted.
Robert Daly Investigations also has correspondent relationships in other jurisdictions, including all of New York, New Jersey and Pennsylvania. They are a licensed private investigation firm in New York, New Jersey and Pennsylvania that specializes in skip tracing, data searches, polygraph and photographs (video and 35mm).

Robert Smith Abstract(1704)
840 Philadelphia St
Indiana PA 15701
Phone: **412-349-9200**
Fax: 412-349-9200

Local Retrieval Area: PA-Allegheny, Armstrong, Cambria, Indiana, Jefferson, Westmoreland.

Normal turn around time is 24 hours. Charges are varied depending on type of search. Credit accounts are accepted.
Robert Smith Abstract also has correspondent relationships in other jurisdictions, including East Central Pennsylvania.

Roberts Abstracting Inc(1705)
Rt 1 Box 315
Alapaha GA 31622
Phone: **912-532-5105**
Fax:

Local Retrieval Area: GA-Atkinson, Berrien, Cook, Lanier, Lowndes, Tift.

Normal turn around time is 3-5 days. Rush service is also available. Fee basis is determined on "flat rate plus costs". The first project may require a prepayment.
They specialize in real estate matters.

Robinson Agency(1706)
3104 Indiana Ave Suite D
Lubbock TX 79410
Phone: **800-658-6656**
806-791-2783
Fax: 806-795-0798

Local Retrieval Area: TX-Crosby, Floyd, Hale, Hockley, Lamb, Lubbock, Terry, Tom Green.

Normal turn around time is 24-48 hours. Projects are generally billed by the number of names searched. The first project may require a prepayment. Personal checks are accepted.
They specialize in location and asset searches.

Robinson Real Estate Services(1707)
4 N Main St Suite 10
Cedartown GA 30125
Phone: **706-748-8155**
Fax:

Local Retrieval Area: GA-Bartow, Floyd, Gordon, Haralson, Paulding, Polk.

Normal turn around time is 2 days for real estate and 3 days for UCC searches. Projects are generally billed by the number of records located. Credit accounts are accepted.
They specialize in real estate sales data, mortgage inspector research, property tax information, insurance research on real estate and property inspection.

Rogers County Abstract Co(1708)
PO Box 38
Claremore OK 74018
Phone: **918-341-0525**
Fax: 918-341-0637

Local Retrieval Area: OK-Rogers.

Normal turn around time is three to four days. Fee basis will vary by the type of project. Credit accounts are accepted.
They specialize in title insurance and closings.

Rolette County Abstract Inc(1709)
PO Box 549
Rolla ND 58367
Phone: **701-477-3149**
Fax:

Local Retrieval Area: ND-Rolette.

Normal turn around time is 1-2 weeks. Fee basis will vary by the type of project. Credit accounts are accepted.

Rollins and Ives PA(1710)
143 Jackson
Camden AR 71701
Phone: **501-836-4166**
Fax: 501-836-4167

Local Retrieval Area: AR-Calhoun, Columbia, Dallas, Nevada, Ouachita, Union.

Normal turn around time is 2-5 days. Project billing methods vary. Credit accounts are accepted.

Jan Rollins(1711)
6412 Alpine Lane
Amarillo TX 79109
Phone: **806-353-7886**
Fax: 806-353-7886

Local Retrieval Area: TX-Armstrong, Carson, Castro, Deaf Smith, Gray, Hale, Hutchinson, Lubbock, Moore, Potter, Randall, Swisher.

Normal turn around time is 24 hours for Potter and Randall Counties, and 48 to 72 hours for all other counties. Projects are generally billed by the number of names searched or records located. Credit accounts are accepted.
Correspondent relationships in other jurisdictions include Childress and Hardeman. They specialize in title runs for foreclosures or second liens, UCC and asset searches.

Marvin T Romig(1712)
PO Box 467
Oshkosh NE 69154
Phone: **308-772-4420**
Fax:

Local Retrieval Area: NE-Garden.

Normal turn around time is 3-5 days. Projects are generally billed by the number of records located. Credit accounts are accepted.
They specialize in real estate.

Ronald J Axelrod and Assoc(1713)
PO Box 275
Morris Plains NJ 07950
Phone: **201-538-4606**
Fax: 201-267-4606

Local Retrieval Area: NJ-Morris.

Normal turn around time is unknown. Projects are generally billed by the number of names searched. Credit accounts are accepted.
They specialize in title searches.

Roosevelt County Abstract Co(1714)
PO Box 176
Wolf Point MT 59201
Phone: **406-653-2800**
Fax:

Local Retrieval Area: MT-Roosevelt.

Normal turn around time is 4 days. Projects are generally billed by the hour. Credit accounts are accepted.
They specialize in title insurance.

Roseau County Title & Abstract(1715)
PO Box 297
Roseau MN 56751
Phone: **218-463-3313**
Fax: 218-463-1174

Local Retrieval Area: MN-Roseau.

Normal turn around time is 2-5 days. Fee basis is per search. All projects require prepayment.

Ross Legal Services(1716)　Phone: **800-765-7833**
PO Box 9107　415-485-1290
San Rafael CA 94912　Fax:　415-457-3325

Local Retrieval Area: CA-Alameda, Contra Costa, Marin, San Francisco, San Mateo, Sonoma.

Normal turn around time is unknown. Projects are generally billed by the hour. The first project may require a prepayment.

Ross Legal Services also has correspondent relationships in other jurisdictions, including Napa, Santa Clara, and Solano counties. They are a family owned business. Larry Ross has experience as an investigative journalist and photographer.

Pat Royce(1717)　Phone: **918-465-3425**
PO Box 280　Fax:
Wilburton OK 74578

Local Retrieval Area: OK-Latimer.

Normal turn around time is varied depending on search. Pat charges on a per day basis. Credit accounts are accepted.

Pat specializes in mineral interest searches.

Joyce Rupert(1718)　Phone: **717-248-4649**
Rd 2 Box 235K　Fax:
Lewistown PA 17044

Local Retrieval Area: PA-Juniata, Mifflin.

Normal turn around time is 48 hours. Projects are generally billed by the number of names searched. Credit accounts are accepted.

Joyce specializes in real estate record searches.

Russell Abstracting & Title(1719)　Phone: **308-872-5938**
420 S 10th　Fax:　308-872-5938
Broken Bow NE 68822

Local Retrieval Area: NE-Blaine, Custer, Loup, Thomas.

Normal turn around time is 1 week. Fee basis varies by type of transaction. Credit accounts are accepted.

Russell-Surles Title Inc(1720)　Phone: **915-854-1115**
337 Market St　Fax:　915-854-1459
Baird TX 79504

They only serve the State District Court, 42nd Judicial District, Tri-County District and Callahan County.

Normal turn around time is varied depending on project. Projects are generally billed by the number of names searched. Credit accounts are accepted. Personal checks are accepted.

S & J Attorney Service(1721)　Phone: **310-558-8088**
Box 1612　Fax:
Beverly Hills CA 90213

Local Retrieval Area: CA-Los Angeles, Orange, Ventura.

Normal turn around time is 3-5 days. Projects are generally billed by the hour. Credit accounts are accepted.

S & J Attorney Service also has correspondent relationships in other jurisdictions, including the remaining counties in California. They specialize in process serving.

S D Moody Co(1722)　Phone: **404-956-9530**
901 Cedar Canyon Square　Fax:　404-956-9534
Marietta GA 30067

Local Retrieval Area: GA-Barrow, Bartow, Carroll, Cherokee, Clayton, Cobb, Dawson, De Kalb, Douglas, Fayette, Forsyth, Fulton, Gwinnett, Paulding, Walton.

Normal turn around time is 2-4 days. Fee basis is per search. Credit accounts are accepted. S D Moody Co also has correspondent relationships in other jurisdictions, including rest of Georgia. They specialize in real estate.

S.A.F.E.(1723)　Phone: **717-622-0172**
1014 N Front Street　Fax:　717-286-8774
Sunbury PA 17801

Local Retrieval Area: PA-Columbia, Montour, Northumberland, Snyder, Union.

Normal turn around time is 24-48 hours. Projects are generally billed by the number of names searched. Charges are varied depending on type of search. Credit accounts are accepted. S.A.F.E. also has correspondent relationships in other jurisdictions, including the rest of Pennsylvania.

SIC Inc(1724)　Phone: **305-751-0015**
986 NE 84th St　Fax:　305-758-3341
Miami FL 33138

Local Retrieval Area: FL-Alachua, Broward, Collier, Dade, Duval, Monroe, Orange, Palm Beach, Pinellas, Volusia.

Normal turn around time is varied depending on project. Online computer ordering is also available. Projects are generally billed by the number of names searched. The first project may require a prepayment. Credit cards are accepted for payment. They will also invoice.

SIC Inc also has correspondent relationships in other jurisdictions, including the state of Florida.

SPS Investigations & Process Srv(1725)　Phone: **303-233-1785**
8007 W Colfax Ave Suite #215　Fax:
Lakewood CO 80215

Local Retrieval Area: CO-Adams, Arapahoe, Boulder, Denver, Douglas, Jefferson.

Normal turn around time is varied depending on project. Project billing methods vary. The first project may require a prepayment.

They specialize in criminal and civil searches, skip tracing, and witness locating.

SRT Investigations(1726)　Phone: **800-800-7119**
PO Box 35403　918-481-6045
Tulsa OK 74153　Fax:　918-491-9774

Local Retrieval Area: OK-Muskogee, Tulsa, Wagoner.

Normal turn around time is 24 hours. Projects are generally billed by the hour. The first project may require a prepayment.

SRT Investigations also has correspondent relationships in other jurisdictions, including network for the rest of Oklahoma. They specialize in marriage/divorce searches.

Sac County Abstract Co(1727)
420 Main
Sac City IA 50583
Phone: **712-662-7317**
Fax: 712-662-4090

Local Retrieval Area: IA-Sac.

Normal turn around time is 2-3 days. Fee basis will vary by the type of project. The first project may require a prepayment.

Sacandaga Abstract Corp(1728)
6-8 Fremont St
Gloversville NY 12078
Phone: **518-773-2828**
Fax: 518-725-9875

Local Retrieval Area: NY-Fulton, Montgomery.

Normal turn around time is 1-7 days. Projects are generally billed by the number of names searched or records located. Credit accounts are accepted. Personal checks are accepted.

Saline County Abstract(1729)
316 N Maih St
Benton AR 72015
Phone: **501-778-2471**
Fax: 501-778-4128

Local Retrieval Area: AR-Saline.

Normal turn around time is 1 week. Projects are generally billed by the hour. Credit accounts are accepted.
They specialize in real estate and title insurance.

Sam Steele Investigations(1730)
226 S 7th St
Louisville KY 40202
Phone: **502-587-0965**
Fax: 502-584-3244

Local Retrieval Area: IN-Clark, Floyd; KY-Jefferson, Oldham, Shelby.

Normal turn around time is 24-48 hours. Vital statistics searches average 7-10 days. Projects are generally billed by the number of names searched or records located. Credit accounts are accepted.
Sam Steele Investigations also has correspondent relationships in other jurisdictions, including the state of Kentucky. They specialize in disability surveillance and covert video.

Samford Denson Horsley et al(1731)
PO Box 2345
Opelika AL 36803-2345
Phone: **205-745-3504**
Fax: 205-745-3506

Local Retrieval Area: AL-Lee.

Normal turn around time is within 1 week. Projects are generally billed by the number of records located. Credit accounts are accepted.

San Diego Attorney Service Inc(1732)
525 Hawthron St Suite 1
San Diego CA 92101
Phone: **619-236-9585**
Fax: 619-236-9136

Local Retrieval Area: CA-San Diego.

Normal turn around time is the same day, if requested. Project billing methods vary. The first project may require a prepayment.
San Diego Attorney Service Inc also has correspondent relationships in other jurisdictions, including all of California.

San Juan County Abstract & Title(1733)
111 N Orchard Ave
Farmington NM 87401
Phone: **505-325-2808**
Fax: 505-327-7485

Local Retrieval Area: NM-San Juan.

Normal turn around time is 1-3 days, Fee basis will vary by the type of project. A minimum fee is involved. Credit accounts are accepted.

San Juan County Title Co(1734)
104 Fern St
Eastsound WA 98245
Phone: **206-376-4939**
Fax: 206-376-4951

Local Retrieval Area: WA-San Juan.

Normal turn around time is 1 day. Projects are generally billed by the hour. The first project may require a prepayment.

Sanborn County Realty and Title(1736)
PO Box 127
Woonsocket SD 57385-0127
Phone: **605-796-4417**
Fax: 605-796-4417

Local Retrieval Area: SD-Sanborn.

Normal turn around time is 1-2 weeks. The fee basis is a flat fee. Credit accounts are accepted. Personal checks and cash are accepted.
Sanborn County Realty and Title Company also has correspondent relationships in other jurisdictions. They specialize in abstracts and title insurance. They also search liens and real estate taxes.

Sandhills Abstracting(1737)
218 N Main St
Gordon NE 69343
Phone: **308-282-0715**
Fax:

Local Retrieval Area: NE-Sheridan.

Normal turn around time is 1 week. Projects are generally billed by the number of names searched or records located. Credit accounts are accepted. Personal checks are accepted.
They specialize in real estate sales.

Sandhills Abstracting(1738)
PO Box 181
Valentine NE 69201
Phone: **402-376-2639**
Fax: 402-376-1989

Local Retrieval Area: NE-Cherry, Keya Paha, Thomas.

Normal turn around time is 1 week. Projects are generally billed by the hour. Credit accounts are accepted.
They specialize in record searches.

Marlene Santillo(1739)
PO Box 9642
Elizabeth NJ 07202
Phone: **908-353-6665**
Fax: 908-820-3808

Local Retrieval Area: NJ-Union.

Normal turn around time is 2-5 days. Fee basis will vary by type of project. Credit accounts are accepted.

Sargents Abstract & Title Co(1740)
625 S Grand Traverse St
Flint MI 48502
Phone: **313-767-2355**
Fax: 313-767-2430

Local Retrieval Area: MI-Genesee.

Normal turn around time is 5 days. Projects are generally billed by the hour. All projects require prepayment.
They specialize in title insurance.

Sathre Abstractors Inc(1741)   Phone: **218-751-4565**
720 Beltrami Ave NW   Fax: 218-751-7991
Bemidji MN 56601
Local Retrieval Area: MN-Beltrami.

Normal turn around time is varied depending on project. Fee basis will vary by type of project. Credit accounts are accepted. They specialize in real estate and property reports.

Sawyer County Abstract(1742)   Phone: **715-866-2312**
PO Box 128   Fax: 715-266-2312
Winter WI 54896
Local Retrieval Area: WI-Rusk, Sawyer.

Normal turn around time is 48 hours. Projects are generally billed by the number of names searched or records located. Credit accounts are accepted. Credit cards are accepted for payment. Personal checks are accepted.

Schaeffer Papers(1743)   Phone: **800-867-9919**
436 S Greer St   901-458-3421
Memphis TN 38111   Fax: 901-458-8438
Local Retrieval Area: AR-Crittenden; MS-De Soto; TN-Fayette, Haywood, Shelby, Tipton.

Normal turn around time is 24-72 hours. Projects are generally billed by the hour. Incurred expenses will be added to the fee. All projects require prepayment. Personal checks are accepted. They specialize in civil court matters and process service.

Scheibeler's(1744)   Phone: **913-392-3145**
217 N Ottawa St   Fax:
Minneapolis KS 67467
Local Retrieval Area: KS-Ottawa.

Normal turn around time is 2-3 days. Fee basis varies by type of transaction. The first project may require a prepayment.

Kathleen Schloesser(1745)   Phone: **717-253-5368**
RR 3 Box 630   Fax:
Honesdale PA 18431
Local Retrieval Area: PA-Wayne.

Normal turn around time is 24 hours. Projects are generally billed by the number of names searched. Credit accounts are accepted. Prepayment is required for individuals and they will invoice to companies. Personal checks are accepted.
Kathleen specializes in current owner searches.

Scholtes Investigation & Atty Svc(1746)   Phone: **407-683-4174**
PO Box 1262   Fax: 407-683-4174
West Palm Beach FL 33402
Local Retrieval Area: FL-Palm Beach.

Normal turn around time is varied depending on project. Projects are generally billed by the number of names searched. All projects require prepayment.
Scholtes Investigation & Attorney Svcs also has correspondent relationships in other jurisdictions, including Broward, Dade, Martin and St. Lucie. They specialize in private investigating.

Susan Bailey Schramm(1747)   Phone: **304-876-2750**
PO Box 308   Fax:
Shepherdstown WV 25443
Local Retrieval Area: WV-Berkeley, Hampshire, Jefferson, Morgan.

Normal turn around time is 48 hours. Fee basis will vary by name or index. Credit accounts are accepted.
Susan has 19 years experience and specializes in record searching and real estate.

Sharon Schroeder(1748)   Phone: **717-296-6604**
RR 4 Box 7146   Fax:
Milford PA 18337
Local Retrieval Area: PA-Pike.

Normal turn around time is 24 hours for last owner. Other search time is varied. Projects are generally billed by the number of names searched. Credit accounts are accepted.

Scotland County Abstract Inc(1749)   Phone: **816-465-7052**
205 E Monroe St   Fax: 816-465-7052
Memphis MO 63555
Local Retrieval Area: MO-Scotland.

Normal turn around time is 3 days. Projects are generally billed by the number of records located. All projects require prepayment. They specialize in title insurance.

Scott Abstract(1750)   Phone: **308-532-8535**
PO Box 929   Fax: 308-532-6559
North Platte NE 69103
Local Retrieval Area: NE-Frontier, Hayes, Hooker, Lincoln, Logan, McPherson, Thomas.

Normal turn around time is 3 days for Lincoln county. Longer for other counties. Fee basis varies by type of transaction. Credit accounts are accepted.

Scott County Abstract and Title(1751)   Phone: **316-872-3470**
310 Court St   Fax: 316-872-3873
Scott City KS 67871
Local Retrieval Area: KS-Greeley, Lane, Logan, Scott, Wichita.

Normal turn around time is 24 hours. Projects are generally billed by the number of records located. Credit accounts are accepted. Personal checks are accepted.

Scurry County Abstract Co(1752)   Phone: **915-728-3475**
1816 26th St   Fax: 915-728-8851
Snyder TX 79549
Local Retrieval Area: TX-Scurry.

Normal turn around time is 2-3 days. Fee basis will vary by the type of project. The first project may require a prepayment.

Search Associates(1753)
3716 S 86th St
Milwaukee WI 53228

Phone: 414-541-7506
Fax: 414-541-2080

Local Retrieval Area: MN-Houston, Winona; WI-Barron, Chippewa, Dane, Dodge, Door, Fond du Lac, Green, Jackson, Jefferson, Kenosha, Kewaunee, La Crosse, Manitowoc, Milwaukee, Monroe, Monroe, Ozaukee, Racine, Rock, Sheboygan, Trempealeau, Vernon, Walworth, Washington, Waukesha.

Normal turn around time is 24-48 hours. Projects are generally billed by the number of names searched. Credit accounts are accepted.

They specialize in real estate title searches.

Search Company International(1754)
1535 Grant St Suite 140
Denver CO 80203-1843

Phone: 800-727-2120
Fax:

Local Retrieval Area: CO-Adams, Arapahoe, Boulder, Denver, Douglas, Jefferson, Larimer.

Normal turn around time is 1-5 days. Projects are generally billed by the number of names searched. Credit accounts are accepted. Credit cards are accepted for payment. Personal checks are accepted.

Search Company International also has correspondent relationships in other jurisdictions, including the rest of Colorado.

Search Enterprises(1755)
PO Box 1613
Waco TX 76703

Phone: 817-752-2057
Fax: 817-752-8201

Local Retrieval Area: TX-Anderson, Bell, Bosque, Brazos, Coryell, Ellis, Falls, Freestone, Henderson, Hill, Johnson, Limestone, McLennan, Navarro, Robertson.

Normal turn around time is 48-72 hours. Projects are generally billed by the number of names searched or records located. The first project may require a prepayment.

They specialize in real estate, environmental, and other public record research.

Search In USA(1756)
Rt 4 Box 2220
Oakland MD 21550

Phone: 301-334-4205
Fax:

Local Retrieval Area: MD-Garrett.

Normal turn around time is the next day. Projects are generally billed by the number of names searched. Credit accounts are accepted.

They specialize in UCC searches.

Search NY(1757)
161 Prospect Pk SW
Brooklyn NY 11218

Phone: 718-854-1492
Fax: 718-854-1492

Local Retrieval Area: NY-Bronx, Kings, Nassau, New York, Queens, Richmond, Westchester.

Normal turn around time is 24-72 hours. Projects are generally billed by the number of names searched. Credit accounts are accepted.

Search Network(1758)
2 Corp Pl, 1501 42nd St Suite 100
West Des Moines IA 50266

Phone: 800-383-5050
Fax: 800-383-5050

Local Retrieval Area: IA-All counties; KS-All counties.

Normal turn around time is varied depending on project. Online computer ordering is also available. Projects are generally billed by the number of names searched or records located. Credit accounts are accepted.

Search Network also has correspondent relationships in other jurisdictions, including all state and county agencies in the Unites States. They have been in business since 1965, and specialize in UCC and lien searches, and national document filing.

Search Network Ltd(1759)
700 SW Jackson Suite 100
Topeka KS 66603

Phone: 913-235-5777
Fax: 913-235-5788

Local Retrieval Area: KS-Shawnee.

Normal turn around time is 1-2 days. Projects are generally billed by the number of records located. Credit accounts are accepted.

Search Network Ltd also has correspondent relationships in other jurisdictions, including nationwide. They are on-line with State UCC.

Searchtec(1760)
211 N 13th St Suite 703
Philadelphia PA 19107

Phone: 800-762-5018
Fax: 215-851-8775

Local Retrieval Area: PA-Bucks, Chester, Delaware, Montgomery, Philadelphia.

Normal turn around time is 24-48 hours. Online computer ordering is also available. Projects are generally billed by the number of names searched. Credit accounts are accepted.

Searchtec also has correspondent relationships in other jurisdictions, including all of New Jersey and Delaware. They specialize in record searches, title insurance and appraisal services.

Security Abstract & Title Co(1761)
PO Box 339
Miles City MT 59301

Phone: 406-232-3415
Fax: 406-232-7107

Local Retrieval Area: MT-Carter, Custer, Garfield.

Normal turn around time is as much as two weeks. Projects are generally billed by the hour. Credit accounts are accepted.

Security Abstract Co(1762)
112 E Calhoun St
Magnolia AR 71753

Phone: 501-234-5990
501-234-1291
Fax:

Local Retrieval Area: AR-Columbia.

Normal turn around time is 2-3 days for civil, criminal and UCC searches, 5-7 days for real estate and probate. Fee basis will vary by the type of project. Credit accounts are accepted.

They specialize in title insurance.

Security Abstract Co(1763)   Phone: 314-748-2372
305 Main   Fax: 314-748-2372
New Madrid MO 63869

Local Retrieval Area: MO-New Madrid.

Normal turn around time is 1 week or less. Projects are generally billed by the number of names searched. Credit accounts are accepted. Personal checks are accepted.

Security Abstract Co(1764)   Phone: 406-482-1010
122 2nd Ave SW   Fax:
Sidney MT 59270

Local Retrieval Area: MT-Richland.

Normal turn around time is 3-4 days. Projects are generally billed by the hour. Credit accounts are accepted. They specialize in title insurance.

Security Abstract of Clarendon(1765) Phone: 806-874-3511
PO Box 673   Fax: 806-874-3160
Clarendon TX 79226

Local Retrieval Area: TX-Donley.

Normal turn around time is 1-2 days. Projects are generally billed by the hour. The first project may require a prepayment.

Security Abstract Co of Claude(1766) Phone: 806-226-3621
PO Box 527   Fax: 806-874-3160
Claude TX 79019

Local Retrieval Area: TX-Armstrong.

Normal turn around time is 1-2 days. Projects are generally billed by the hour. The first project may require a prepayment.

Security Abstract Co of Memphis(1767) Phone: 806-259-2931
205 S 6th St   Fax: 806-874-3160
Memphis TX 79245

Local Retrieval Area: TX-Hall.

Normal turn around time is 1-2 days. Projects are generally billed by the hour. The first project may require a prepayment.

Security Abstract Company(1768)   Phone: 913-877-2141
PO Box 444   Fax:
Norton KS 67654-0444

Local Retrieval Area: KS-Norton.

Normal turn around time is 24 hours. Projects are generally billed by the hour. Credit accounts are accepted.
Security Abstract Company also has correspondent relationships in other jurisdictions, including Phillips County. They specialize in title insurance.

Security Abstract and Title Inc(1769) Phone: 515-462-1691
114 N 1st Ave   Fax: 515-462-3927
Winterset IA 50273

Local Retrieval Area: IA-Madison.

Normal turn around time is 2-5 days. Projects are generally billed by the number of names searched. Credit accounts are accepted.

Security Consulting Cassopolis(1770) Phone: 800-578-2406
PO Box 53   Fax: 219-234-7224
Cassopolis MI 49031-0053

Local Retrieval Area: MI-Berrien, Cass.

Normal turn around time is varied depending on project. Projects are generally billed by the hour. The first project may require a prepayment.

Security Consulting Svc S Bend(1771) Phone: 219-289-0500
PO Box 2731   Fax: 219-234-7224
South Bend IN 46680-2731

Local Retrieval Area: IN-Elkhart, St. Joseph.

Normal turn around time is varied depending on project. Projects are generally billed by the hour. The first project may require a prepayment.

Security Enforcement Inc(1772)   Phone: 516-678-0344
2983 Long Beach Rd   Fax: 516-678-7134
Oceanside NY 11572

Local Retrieval Area: NY-Nassau, Suffolk.

Normal turn around time is varied depending on project. Project billing methods vary. The first project may require a prepayment. Credit cards are accepted for payment.   Personal checks are accepted.
Security Enforcement Inc also has correspondent relationships in other jurisdictions, including Westchester, Kings, Queens, Richmond, New York City and Albany.

Security Information Service(1773)   Phone: 214-241-3384
11500 Stemmons Fwy Suite 151   Fax: 214-241-8668
Dallas TX 75229

Local Retrieval Area: TX-Collin, Dallas, Denton, Ellis, Hunt, Johnson, Kaufman, Rockwall, Tarrant.

Normal turn around time is 1-3 days. Online computer ordering is also available. Projects are generally billed by the hour. Credit accounts are accepted.
Security Information Service also has correspondent relationships in other jurisdictions, including all of Texas. They specialize in survelliance.

Security Intelligence Bureau(1774)   Phone: 202-515-1365
PO Box 1578   Fax:
Laurel MD 20725

Local Retrieval Area: DC-All counties; MD-All counties; VA-All counties.

Normal turn around time is 24 hours. Projects are generally billed by the number of names searched or records located. The first project may require a prepayment. Personal checks are accepted. They specialize in asset searches.

Security Land & Abstract Co(1775)   Phone: 800-310-3442
PO Box 718   605-347-3443
Sturgis SD 57785   Fax: 605-347-4817

Local Retrieval Area: SD-Meade.

Normal turn around time is 1-4 days. Projects are generally billed by the hour. Credit accounts are accepted.
They specialize in title insurance.

Security Land Title Co(1776)
607 1st Ave Box 5333
Spencer IA 51301
Phone: **712-262-1074**
Fax: 712-262-1082

Local Retrieval Area: IA-Clay.

Normal turn around time is varied depending on project. They charge a flat fee. Credit accounts are accepted.

Security Title Co(1777)
PO Box 6550
Bozeman MT 59715
Phone: **406-586-1319**
Fax: 406-586-1024

Local Retrieval Area: MT-Gallatin.

Normal turn around time is 3-5 days. Projects are generally billed by the hour. Credit accounts are accepted. They may require prepayment.

Security Title of Garfield County(1778)
15 N Main St
Panguitch UT 84759
Phone: **801-676-8808**
Fax: 801-676-2421

Local Retrieval Area: UT-Garfield, Piute.

Normal turn around time is 3-5 days. Projects are generally billed by the hour. Credit accounts are accepted. They specialize in recreational properties.

Security Title of Beaver County(1779)
PO Box 819
beaver UT 84713
Phone: **801-438-2354**
Fax: 801-438-5805

Local Retrieval Area: UT-Beaver.

Normal turn around time is 24 hours. Projects are generally billed by the number of names searched. All projects require prepayment.

Security Title of Park County Inc(1780)
PO Box 928
Livingston MT 59047
Phone: **406-222-0362**
Fax: 406-222-8764

Local Retrieval Area: MT-Park.

Normal turn around time is 24 hours. Fee basis varies by type of transaction. Credit accounts are accepted.

Penny Seehus(1781)
31 S 65th Ave W
Duluth MN 55807
Phone: **218-624-0753**
Fax:

Local Retrieval Area: MN-Carlton, Cook, Itasca, Lake, St. Louis; WI-Douglas.

Normal turn around time is 1 week. Fee basis will vary by the type of project. Credit accounts are accepted. A retainer is required.

Mark T Segars(1782)
PO Box 1106
Iuka MS 38852
Phone: **601-423-1989**
Fax:

Local Retrieval Area: MS-Tishomingo.

Normal turn around time is 1-2 days. Fee basis will vary by type of project. The first project may require a prepayment.
Mr. Segars is an attorney in general practice, including real estate.

Sentry Security(1783)
PO Box 873
Waterville ME 04901
Phone: **207-873-2674**
Fax: 207-873-2674

Local Retrieval Area: ME-Kennebec, Somerset.

Normal turn around time is 3 to 4 days. Fee basis will vary by the type of project. Credit accounts are accepted.

Service Abstract Company(1784)
208 E Everett
Pocahontas AR 72455
Phone: **501-892-4538**
Fax: 501-892-9808

Local Retrieval Area: AR-Randolph.

Normal turn around time is varied depending on project. Fee basis will vary by the type of project. Credit accounts are accepted. Personal checks are accepted.
Service Abstract Company also has correspondent relationships in other jurisdictions, including various counties within the state. The specialize in title insurance and loan closings.

Services for Attorneys(1785)
1032 Santa Barbara St
Santa Barbara CA 93101
Phone: **805-564-4107**
Fax:

Local Retrieval Area: CA-Santa Barbara.

Normal turn around time is varied depending on project. Fee basis will vary by type of project. All projects require prepayment. They will invoice. Personal checks are accepted.
Services for Attorneys also has correspondent relationships in other jurisdictions, including nationwide. They specialize in litigation/trial support, legal research, drafting, and processing.

Shanks Abstract and Title Co(1786)
62 Public Square
Salem IN 47167
Phone: **812-883-5806**
Fax:

Local Retrieval Area: IN-Clark, Crawford, Floyd, Harrison, Jackson, Lawrence, Orange, Scott, Washington.

Normal turn around time is 1 day for judgement or UCC search, and 3 to 5 days for complete title searches. Fee basis will vary by the type of project. Credit accounts are accepted. Personal checks are accepted.
They maintain a title plant in their office.

Shannon County Abstract Co(1787)
PO Box 334
Eminence MO 65466
Phone: **314-226-3331**
Fax:

Local Retrieval Area: MO-Shannon.

Normal turn around time is 1-2 weeks. Fee basis will vary by the type of project. Credit accounts are accepted.
They specialize in real estate.

Sharon K Hannaman Abstracter(1788)
PO Box 246
Blue Earth MN 56013
Phone: **507-526-5144**
Fax:

Local Retrieval Area: MN-Faribault.

Normal turn around time is 1-2 weeks. Projects are generally billed by the number of names searched. The first project may require a prepayment.

Sharp County Abstract Co Inc(1789) **Phone:** 501-994-7314
PO Box 81 **Fax:** 501-994-2880
Ash Flat AR 72513

Local Retrieval Area: AR-Sharp.

Normal turn around time is 10 days. A rush service is also available. Fee basis will vary by the type of project. Credit accounts are accepted. A down payment is required.
They specialize in title insurance, escrow and closings.

W Allan Sharrett(1790) **Phone:** 804-634-2167
314 S Main St **Fax:** 804-634-3798
Emporia VA 23847

Local Retrieval Area: VA-Greensville, City of Emporia.

Normal turn around time is 2 days. Projects are generally billed by the hour. The first project may require a prepayment.
Mr. Sharrett is a trial lawyer.

Shaw Title & Public Record Srch(1791) **Phone:** 817-539-8374
51451-6 Coushatta St **Fax:** 817-539-8374
Ft Hood TX 76544

Local Retrieval Area: TX-Bell, Coryell, Lampasas.

Normal turn around time is within 24 hours. Projects are generally billed by the number of names searched. Credit accounts are accepted.

John Shaw(1792) **Phone:** 601-289-3110
PO Box 744 **Fax:** 601-289-2048
Kosciusko MS 39090

Local Retrieval Area: MS-Attala.

Normal turn around time is 1-2 days. Fee basis varies by type of transaction. All projects require prepayment.
Mr. Shaw is a country lawyer.

Shawver and Associates(1793) **Phone:** 512-991-5055
PO Box 1592 **Fax:** 512-887-1005
Corpus Christi TX 78403

Local Retrieval Area: TX-Aransas, Bee, Brooks, Cameron, Duval, Hidalgo, Jim Wells, Kleberg, Nueces, Refugio, San Patricio, Starr, Victoria, Webb.

Normal turn around time is 2 days for areas within a 50 mile radius. Projects are generally billed by the hour. Credit accounts are accepted.
They specialize in third party liability identification.

Shelby County Land Title Corp(1794) **Phone:** 217-774-2623
PO Box 473 **Fax:** 217-774-3702
Shelbyville IL 62565

Local Retrieval Area: IL-Shelby.

Normal turn around time is 2 days. Projects are generally billed by the number of records located. Credit accounts are accepted.

Shenandoah Title Services Inc(1795) **Phone:** 703-465-5231
212 S Braddock St **Fax:** 703-667-0464
Winchester VA 22601

Local Retrieval Area: VA-Clarke, Frederick, Loudoun, Page, Shenandoah, Warren, City of Winchester.

Normal turn around time is 3-5 days. Rush service is also available. Fee basis will vary by type of project. Credit accounts are accepted.
They specialize in real estate searches.

Sheridan County Abstract Co(1796) **Phone:** 701-363-2285
Box 428 **Fax:**
McClusky ND 58463

Local Retrieval Area: ND-Sheridan.

Normal turn around time is 3-4 days. Fee basis will vary by type of project. Credit accounts are accepted.
They specialize in title and land ownership.

Victoria Sherrill(1797) **Phone:** 704-938-9529
323 E 20th St **Fax:**
Kannapolis NC 28083

Local Retrieval Area: NC-Cabarrus, Davidson, Iredell, Rowan, Stanly.

Normal turn around time is 48 hours. Projects are generally billed by the number of names searched. Credit accounts are accepted.
They have 21 years of legal experience. They specialize in real estate title searches.

Valerie Shickel(1798) **Phone:** 203-767-2269
42 Book Hill Rd **Fax:** 203-767-7621
Essex CT 06426

Local Retrieval Area: CT-Middlesex, New Haven, New London.

Normal turn around time is 2-3 days. Fees are based on a per search basis. Credit accounts are accepted.
Valerie specializes in 40 or 60 year land and probate record searches.

Michael A Shurn(1799) **Phone:** 219-946-3521
PO Box 227 **Fax:**
Winamac IN 46996

Local Retrieval Area: IN-Pulaski.

Normal turn around time is 1-5 days. Projects are generally billed by the hour. Credit accounts are accepted.
Michael specializes in probate.

Sierra Attorney Service(1800) **Phone:** 619-872-1208
PO Box 1193 **Fax:**
Bishop CA 93515

Local Retrieval Area: CA-Inyo.

Normal turn around time is 1-2 days. Rush service is also available. Projects are generally billed by the hour. The first project may require a prepayment.
They specialize in process serving and photocopying documents.

Sierra Legal Services(1801)
1449 Lincoln Wy Suite A
Auburn CA 95603
Phone: **916-888-6613**
Fax: 916-888-6613

Local Retrieval Area: CA-El Dorado, Nevada, Placer, Sacramento, Yuba.

Normal turn around time is 3-4 business days. Rush service is also available. Projects are generally billed by the hour. Fee may also be based per trip. The first project may require a prepayment. Personal checks are accepted.

Sierra Legal Services also has correspondent relationships in other jurisdictions, including Placer, Nevada, Yuba, Sacramento and Eldorado. They specialize in Judicial Court systems searches and the Secretary of State.

Debbie Signorelli(1802)
14 W Market St
West Chester PA 19382
Phone: **215-436-5148**
Fax: 215-436-5890

Local Retrieval Area: PA-Chester.

Normal turn around time is 24 hours. Projects are generally billed by the number of names searched. Credit accounts are accepted. They specialize in credit and business searches.

Sikoral & Associates Investig(1803)
12 Salem Rd
East Brunswick NJ 08816
Phone: **908-257-2550**
Fax: 908-257-9266

Local Retrieval Area: NJ-All counties.

Normal turn around time is 3-4 working days. Projects are generally billed by the hour. Credit accounts are accepted. They specialize in background investigations.

Silk Attorney Service(1804)
5301 W 50th St
Shawnee Mission KS 66205-1219
Phone: **913-432-2755**
Fax:

Local Retrieval Area: KS-Johnson, Leavenworth, Wyandotte; MO-Clay, Jackson, Platte.

Normal turn around time is 24-36 hours. Projects are generally billed by the hour. Mileage and copy expenses are added to the fee. Credit accounts are accepted. They request prepayment for process serving.

They specialize in Northeast Kansas and Northwest Missouri. They will also go to Federal Records Center in Kansas City, Missouri.

Teresa Simerly(1805)
Rt 1 Box 613
Hampton TN 37658
Phone: **615-725-3901**
Fax:

Local Retrieval Area: TN-Carter, Johnson, Sullivan, Unicoi, Washington.

Normal turn around time is 24-48 hours. Projects are generally billed by the number of records located. Credit accounts are accepted.

Ms. Simerly is a certified legal assistant. She specializes in real estate.

Simmons & Grillo(1806)
116 W Main
McArthur OH 45651
Phone: **614-596-5291**
Fax:

Local Retrieval Area: OH-Jackson, Vinton.

Normal turn around time is varied depending on search. Charges are varied depending on the type of search. Credit accounts are accepted.

They are attorneys and specialize in real estate record searches.

Simmons Agency(1807)
200 Lincoln St Suite 211
Boston MA 02111
Phone: **617-523-2288**
Fax: 617-695-1815

Local Retrieval Area: MA-Barnstable, Bristol, Essex, Franklin, Hampden, Hampshire, Middlesex, Norfolk, Plymouth, Suffolk, Worcester; NH-Cheshire, Hillsborough, Merrimack, Rockingham.

Normal turn around time is 1-2 days. Projects are generally billed by the hour. They may also charge a flat fee. The first project may require a prepayment.

Simmons Agency also has correspondent relationships in other jurisdictions, including Belknap, Carroll, Coos, Grafton, Strafford and Sullivan. They specialize in full background investigations. They are on line for real estate records in Massachusetts, Rhode Island and New Hampshire.

Singleton & Deeds(1808)
PO Box 116
Warm Springs VA 24484
Phone: **703-839-5009**
Fax: 703-839-5969

Local Retrieval Area: VA-Bath, Highland, City of Clifton Forge, City of Covington.

Normal turn around time is 24 hours. Projects are generally billed by the hour. Credit accounts are accepted.

Skamania County Title Company(1809)
Box 277
Stevenson WA 98648
Phone: **509-427-5681**
Fax: 509-427-5610

Local Retrieval Area: WA-Skamania.

Normal turn around time is 1 day. Fee basis varies by type of transaction. The first project may require a prepayment. They specialize in title searches.

Slaine County Abstract(1810)
PO Box 627
Wilber NE 68465
Phone: **402-821-3246**
Fax:

Local Retrieval Area: NE-Saline.

Normal turn around time is 1-2 days. Projects are generally billed by the number of records located. Credit accounts are accepted.

Slamal & Swayden Inc(1811)
105 E Kansas
Medicine Lodge KS 67104
Phone: **316-886-5141**
Fax:

Local Retrieval Area: KS-Barber.

Normal turn around time is 1 week. Projects are generally billed by the hour. Credit accounts are accepted. They specialize in title and abstract work.

Smith Abstract Co Inc(1812)   Phone: 501-222-5001
PO Box 261   Fax: 501-222-6159
McGehee AR 71654

Local Retrieval Area: AR-Desha.

Normal turn around time is 1-2 weeks. Projects are generally billed by the hour. All projects require prepayment. They will also invoice.
They specialize in real estate, civil judgements and probate.

Smith County Abstract(1813)   Phone: 903-597-7711
200 W Erwin   Fax: 903-595-6738
Tyler TX 75702

Local Retrieval Area: TX-Smith.

Normal turn around time is 1-3 days. Projects are generally billed by the number of names searched. Credit accounts are accepted. Personal checks are accepted.

Bess Smith(1814)   Phone: 308-745-0172
PO Box 219   Fax: 308-745-0170
Loup City NE 68853

Local Retrieval Area: NE-Sherman.

Normal turn around time is 1 day. Projects are generally billed by the number of names searched. Credit accounts are accepted.

Cheryl Smith(1815)   Phone: 919-633-3890
1405 Hwy 55 W   Fax: 919-633-3890
New Bern NC 28562

Local Retrieval Area: NC-Craven, Jones, Pamlico.

Normal turn around time is 1-3 days. Projects are generally billed by the hour. Credit accounts are accepted. Personal checks are accepted.
Cheryl specializes in title examinations.

Ed Snyder(1816)   Phone: 515-332-3675
205 5th St N   Fax:
Humboldt IA 50548

Local Retrieval Area: IA-Humboldt.

Normal turn around time is 2-3 days. Projects are generally billed by the number of names searched or records located. Credit accounts are accepted. A setup fee is required for first time clients.

Solomon Abstract Co Inc(1817)   Phone: 405-375-4151
PO Box 449   Fax: 405-375-5023
Kingfisher OK 73750-0449

Local Retrieval Area: OK-Kingfisher.

Normal turn around time is three to seven days. Fee basis will vary by the type of project. The first project may require a prepayment.

Somerset Abstract Co Ltd(1818)   Phone: 814-445-9525
124 N Center Ave   Fax:
Somerset PA 15501

Local Retrieval Area: PA-Somerset.

Normal turn around time is up to 1 week. Fee basis is determined on "per transaction". Credit accounts are accepted. Payment is invoiced at closing.
They specialize in real estate.

Sooner Abstract & Title Co(1819)   Phone: 918-647-3202
PO Drawer F   Fax: 918-647-8784
Poteau OK 74953

Local Retrieval Area: OK-Le Flore.

Normal turn around time is 1-2 days. Fee basis is determined on a "per hour/day". Credit accounts are accepted.

Source(1820)   Phone: 800-678-8774
PO Box 88   Fax: 615-537-3682
Cookeville TN 38503

Local Retrieval Area: TN-Cumberland, De Kalb, Jackson, Macon, Overton, Putnam, Roane, Smith, White.

Normal turn around time is 1-7 working days. Projects are generally billed by the number of names searched. All projects require prepayment. Credit cards are accepted for payment. Source also has correspondent relationships in other jurisdictions, including natonwide.
They specialize in extended court filings and searches for New Jersey, Pennsylvania and New York. They also search public record information on individuals and businesses.

South Georgia Title(1821)   Phone: 912-273-1977
PO Box 938   Fax:
Cordele GA 31015

Local Retrieval Area: GA-Crisp, Dodge, Dooly, Dougherty, Houston, Lee, Pulaski, Sumter, Thomas, Turner, Wilkes, Worth.

Normal turn around time is 2 days. Projects are generally billed by the hour. The first project may require a prepayment. A minimum fee is required.
They specialize in real estate and UCC's.

South Plain Abstract Co(1822)   Phone: 806-872-3023
PO Box 418   Fax:
LaMesa TX 79331

Local Retrieval Area: TX-Dawson.

Normal turn around time is 2 days. Fee basis will vary by the type of project. All projects require prepayment.

South Ridge Abstract and Title Co(1823) Phone: 813-385-2521
229 S Commerce   Fax: 813-382-6438
Sebring FL 33870

Local Retrieval Area: FL-Highlands.

Normal turn around time is 7-10 working days. Projects are generally billed by the number of names searched. Credit accounts are accepted.
They maintain an in house title plant.

Valentine W Southall Jr(1824)   Phone: 804-561-2157
PO Box 78   Fax: 804-561-2552
Amelia VA 23002

Local Retrieval Area: VA-Amelia, Nottoway, Powhatan.

Normal turn around time is 1-2 days. Projects are generally billed by the hour. The first project may require a prepayment.
Mr. Southall is from the law firm of Stark and Southall. He specializes in real estate and general practice searches.

Southeast Nebraska Abstract(1825)
1524 Stone St
Falls City NE 68355
Phone: **402-245-4222**
Fax: 402-245-3859

Local Retrieval Area: NE-Richardson.

Normal turn around time is 24-48 hours. Fee basis will vary by the type of project. Credit accounts are accepted.
They specialize in real estate transactions, probate and family practice.

Southeastern Utah Title(1826)
PO Box 855
Price UT 84501
Phone: **801-637-4455**
Fax:

Local Retrieval Area: UT-Carbon, Emery, Grand, San Juan.

Normal turn around time is 24 hours. Fee basis will vary by the type of project. Credit accounts are accepted.

Southern Abstract & Title Co(1827)
PO Box 507
Idabel OK 74745
Phone: **405-286-2288**
Fax: 405-286-7885

Local Retrieval Area: OK-McCurtain.

Normal turn around time is 2-3 weeks. Projects are generally billed by the hour. Fee basis is also determined on a "per abstract". Credit accounts are accepted. Clients pay before searches are released.

Southern Colorado Title Co(1828)
100 E Main St Suite 311
Trinidad CO 81082
Phone: **719-846-4944**
Fax: 719-846-4944

Local Retrieval Area: CO-Las Animas.

Normal turn around time is 3-5 days. Projects are generally billed by the hour. Credit accounts are accepted.
They specialize in real estate matters.

Southern Indiana Abstract & Title(1829)
411 W 1st
New Albany IN 47150
Phone: **812-944-4931**
Fax: 812-948-9329

Local Retrieval Area: IN-Clark, Floyd, Harrison.

Normal turn around time is 2-10 days. Projects are generally billed by the number of names searched. Credit accounts are accepted.
Southern Indiana Abstract & Title Co also has correspondent relationships in other jurisdictions, including Kentucky. They specialize in title searches.

Southern Mountain Abstr & Title(1830)
PO Box 390
Dillon MT 59725
Phone: **406-683-4445**
Fax: 406-683-4445

Local Retrieval Area: MT-Beaverhead.

Normal turn around time is 5 days. Fee basis varies by type of transaction. Credit accounts are accepted.

Southern Research Company(1831)
1700 Buckner Square Suite #240
Shreveport LA 71165
Phone: **318-227-9700**
Fax: 318-424-1801

Local Retrieval Area: LA-Bossier Parish, Caddo Parish.

Normal turn around time is 48 hours. Projects are generally billed by the hour. Credit accounts are accepted.
Southern Research Company also has correspondent relationships in other jurisdictions, including networking for the remainder of state. They specialize in employment screening, localized court documents and field investigation searchs.

Southern Utah Title Co(1832)
PO Box T
Kanab UT 84741
Phone: **801-644-5891**
Fax: 801-644-8136

Local Retrieval Area: UT-Kane.

Normal turn around time is 1-2 weeks. Fee basis will vary by the type of project. All projects require prepayment.

Southwest Abstract & Title Co(1833)
PO Box 13
Rankin TX 79778
Phone: **915-693-2242**
Fax: 915-693-2249

Local Retrieval Area: TX-Upton.

Normal turn around time is 2-3 days. Fee basis will vary by the type of project. Credit accounts are accepted.

Southwest Abstract Co(1834)
PO Box 1149
Lawton OK 73502
Phone: **405-355-3680**
Fax: 405-248-1849

Local Retrieval Area: OK-Comanche.

Normal turn around time is two to four days. Fee basis will vary by the type of project. Credit accounts are accepted.
They specialize in title insurance.

Southwest Abstract Co Inc(1835)
PO Box 1175
Del Rio TX 78841
Phone: **210-775-8508**
Fax: 210-775-9183

Local Retrieval Area: TX-Val Verde.

Normal turn around time is 2 days. Fee basis will vary by the type of project. All projects require prepayment.

Southwest Patrol & Investigations(1836)
607 Sunnyside
Houston TX 77076
Phone: **713-697-1577**
Fax: 713-697-1580

Local Retrieval Area: TX-Fort Bend, Harris, Montgomery.

Normal turn around time is varied depending on project. Fee basis will vary by type of project. All projects require prepayment.
They specialize in family law, asset and child recovery.

Southwest Virginia Abstr & Title(1837)
102 Windsor Drive
Galax VA 24333
Phone: **703-236-7267**
Fax: 703-236-4411

Local Retrieval Area: VA-Carroll, Grayson, City of Galax.

Normal turn around time is 24 to 48 hours. Projects are generally billed by the number of names searched. Credit accounts are accepted.
They do real estate title searches and title insurance only.

Tony Spadachene(1838)
1345 13th
Hempstead TX 77445
Phone: 409-826-8610
Fax:

Local Retrieval Area: TX-Waller.

Normal turn around time is 24-48 hours. Projects are generally billed by the number of names searched. Credit accounts are accepted.

Spade and Archer Investigations(1839)
PO Box 576
Lake Stevens WA 98258
Phone: 206-334-6945
Fax:

Local Retrieval Area: WA-King, Pierce, Skagit, Snohomish, Whatcom.

Normal turn around time is 24 hours. Online computer ordering is also available. Projects are generally billed by the hour. Credit accounts are accepted. Credit cards are accepted for payment. Personal checks are accepted.

Special Private Investigations Inc(1840)
PO Box 2174
Grand Rapids MI 49501-2174
Phone: 616-887-8574
Fax: 616-887-8775

Local Retrieval Area: MI-Allegan, Barry, Ionia, Kent, Muskegon, Ottawa.

Normal turn around time is 3-10 days for UCC, tax, real estate, and vital stats. 2 days for civil cases and probate. Projects are generally billed by the hour. The first project may require a prepayment.

Specialized Investigations(1841)
14530 Deland St 2nd Floor
Van Nuys CA 91411
Phone: 818-909-9607
Fax: 818-909-7365

Local Retrieval Area: CA-Alameda, Los Angeles, San Diego, Santa Barbara.

Normal turn around time is 1-7 working days. Online computer ordering is also available. Projects are generally billed by the hour. Credit accounts are accepted.
They specialize in insurance fraud.

Toni Speed(1842)
PO Box 992
Hammond LA 70404
Phone: 504-542-0355
Fax: 504-345-9006

Local Retrieval Area: LA-Livingston Parish, St. Helena Parish, St. Tammany Parish, Tangipahoa Parish, Washington Parish.

Normal turn around time is 1-3 days. Fee basis varies by type of transaction. The first project may require a prepayment.
Correspondent relationships in other jurisdictions include network in the other Louisanna parishes. Ms. Speed has been established for 27 years. She specializes in marriage/divorce searches.

R Scott Spidel(1843)
444 Moats Lane
Bowling Green KY 42103
Phone: 502-782-8471
Fax:

Local Retrieval Area: KY-Warren.

Normal turn around time is up to 1 week. Projects are generally billed by the hour. The first project may require a prepayment.
They specialize in mineral ownership and deed plotting.

St Croix Valley Title Services Inc(1844)
219 N Main St PO Box 138
River Falls WI 54022
Phone: 715-425-1519
Fax: 715-425-7586

Local Retrieval Area: WI-Pierce, St. Croix.

Normal turn around time is 1-2 days. Fee basis varies by type of transaction. The first project may require a prepayment.

St Francois County Abstract Co(1845)
PO Box 708
Farmington MO 63640
Phone: 314-756-6721
Fax: 314-756-0519

Local Retrieval Area: MO-Cape Girardeau, Madison, Ste. Genevieve, St. Francois, Washington.

Normal turn around time is 3-5 working days. Fee basis is per chain of title. Credit accounts are accepted. Personal checks are accepted.
They maintain complete geographical indexed title plants in each county they do business in.

St Ives(1846)
1124 2nd St
Old Sacramento CA 95814
Phone: 800-995-9443
Fax: 916-446-7459

Local Retrieval Area: CA-Many counties in this state are covered. See the county index for actual coverage..

Normal turn around time is 2 days within California and 3-5 days outside California. Projects are generally billed by the number of records located. The first project may require a prepayment. St Ives also has correspondent relationships in other jurisdictions, including nationwide, Canada and Philipines. They specialize in pre employment background searches and asset searches.

St Joseph County Abstract Office(1847)
PO Box 217
Centreville MI 49302
Phone: 616-497-6075
Fax: 616-467-4314

Local Retrieval Area: MI-Cass, St. Joseph.

Normal turn around time is 3 days. Projects are generally billed by the hour. Credit accounts are accepted.
They specialize in title and real estate.

St Vrain Resources(1848)
Jenkins Bldg 699 W Woodbine
St Louis MO 63122
Phone: 314-821-9029
Fax: 314-821-9035

Local Retrieval Area: IL-Clinton, Jersey, Madison, Monroe, Randolph, St. Clair; MO-Franklin, Gasconade, Jefferson, Lincoln, Montgomery, Perry, Pike, St. Charles, Ste. Genevieve, St. Francois, St. Louis, Warren, Washington, City of St. Louis.

Normal turn around time is 24 hours. Projects are generally billed by the hour. The first project may require a prepayment.
St Vrain Resources also has correspondent relationships in other jurisdictions, including Northwest Missouri in the Kansas City area and Northeast Illinois in the Chicago area. They specialize in trial preparation and background information.

Stafford County Abstract & Title(1849)
PO Box 265
St John KS 67576
Phone: 316-549-3579
Fax: 316-549-6594

Local Retrieval Area: KS-Stafford.

Normal turn around time is up to 1 week. Projects are generally billed by the hour. All projects require prepayment.

Stanton Co Abstract(1850)
PO Box 86
Stanton NE 68779
Phone: 402-439-2142
Fax: 402-439-2145

Local Retrieval Area: NE-Cedar, Colfax, Cuming, Platte, Stanton, Webster.

Normal turn around time is 1-3 days Fee basis is flat rate and per record. Credit accounts are accepted.
They specialize in title insurance.

Star Title Company Inc(1851)
203 E Anderson St
Rhinelander WI 54501
Phone: 715-369-0777
Fax: 715-369-9107

Local Retrieval Area: WI-Forest, Langlade, Lincoln, Oneida, Vilas.

Normal turn around time is 24 hours. Projects are generally billed by the number of names searched. Credit accounts are accepted. Personal checks are accepted.
They specialize in searching county records for title insurance purposes.

Starke County Abstract Title(1852)
14 E Washington St
Knox TN 46534
Phone: 219-772-3733
Fax: 219-772-3733

Local Retrieval Area: IN-Starke.

Normal turn around time is 3-5 days. Fee basis will vary by type of project. Credit accounts are accepted.
They specialize in record searching.

Starr Investigations & Security(1853)
1848 43rd St NE
Cedar Rapids IA 52402-3008
Phone: 800-779-0557
        319-393-1007
Fax: 319-378-1377

Local Retrieval Area: IA-Benton, Black Hawk, Cedar, Iowa, Johnson, Jones, Linn.

Normal turn around time is 24 hours. Projects are generally billed by the hour. The first project may require a prepayment.
Starr Investigations & Security also has correspondent relationships in other jurisdictions, including Buchanan county and Eastern Iowa. They specialize in process serving and divorce matters.

State Information Bureau(1854)
842 E Park Ave
Tallahassee FL 32301
Phone: 904-561-3990
Fax: 904-561-3995

Local Retrieval Area: FL-Gadsden, Jefferson, Leon, Wakulla.

Normal turn around time is 24-48 hours for Leon County. Fee basis will vary by type of project. Credit accounts are accepted.
State Information Bureau also has correspondent relationships in other jurisdictions, including major counties in Florida. They specialize in locations and asset development searches.

State Line Title(1855)
7 Smith St
York SC 29745
Phone: 803-684-3422
Fax: 803-684-3422

Local Retrieval Area: SC-Cherokee, Chester, Lancaster, Union, York.

Normal turn around time is 24-48 hours. Projects are generally billed by the number of records located. Credit accounts are accepted.

Statewide Abstract and Title(1856)
8712 Quarters Lake Rd
Baton Rouge LA 70809
Phone: 800-673-5567
        504-922-7752
Fax: 504-922-7732
        800-364-7201

Local Retrieval Area: LA-East Baton Rouge Parish, West Baton Rouge Parish.

Normal turn around time is 24-48 hours. Projects are generally billed by the number of names searched. Credit accounts are accepted.
Statewide Abstract and Title Co Inc also has correspondent relationships in other jurisdictions, including the rest of the parishes in Louisiana. They specialize in UCC searches statewide and corporate work.

Staton Abstract & Title Co(1857)
PO Box 168
Chillicothe MO 64601
Phone: 816-646-1421
Fax: 816-646-1441

Local Retrieval Area: MO-Livingston.

Normal turn around time is 2 days. Fee basis varies by type of transaction. Credit accounts are accepted.

Steele County Abstract Co(1858)
PO Box 413
Owatonna MN 55060
Phone: 507-451-6487
Fax:

Local Retrieval Area: MN-Steele.

Normal turn around time is 4 days. Projects are generally billed by the number of names searched. All projects require prepayment. They will also invoice.

Betty Jo Steele(1859)
706 S Howard
Kimball NE 69145
Phone: 308-235-3801
Fax:

Local Retrieval Area: NE-Kimball.

Normal turn around time is varied depending on project. Fee basis will vary by type of project. Credit accounts are accepted.
They specialize in oil, gas and mineral searches.

Steelman Abstracting Co(1860)
PO Box 544
Salem MO 65560
Phone: 314-729-6183
Fax: 314-729-6183

Local Retrieval Area: MO-Dent.

Normal turn around time is 2 weeks. Projects are generally billed by the number of records located. Credit accounts are accepted.
They specialize in title insurance.

Stehlik Law Office(1861)   Phone: 402-852-2973
653 G St   Fax: 402-852-2940
Pawnee City NE 68420

Local Retrieval Area: NE-Pawnee.

Normal turn around time is 24 hours. Projects are generally billed by the hour. Credit accounts are accepted. Personal checks are accepted.
They specialize in general law and abstracting.

Stephen's Research(1862)   Phone: 502-686-3222
PO Box 477   Fax:
Owensboro KY 42302

Local Retrieval Area: KY-Daviess.

Normal turn around time is the same day, if the client has a toll free number. Projects are generally billed by the number of names searched. All projects require prepayment.

Stephens County Abstract(1863) Phone: 817-559-9089
PO Box 1537   Fax: 817-559-8935
Breckenridge TX 76424

Local Retrieval Area: TX-Stephens.

Normal turn around time is 1 day. Fee basis will vary by the type of project. All projects require prepayment.

Stephens County Abstract Co(1864) Phone: 405-255-2525
PO Box 220   Fax: 405-255-3844
Duncan OK 73534

Local Retrieval Area: OK-Stephens.

Normal turn around time is 4-5 days. Fee basis is per page and time. Credit accounts are accepted.

Sterling Abstract Inc(1865)   Phone: 609-465-2220
311 Mechanic St   Fax: 609-465-1362
Cape May NJ 08210

Local Retrieval Area: NJ-Cape May.

Normal turn around time is 24-48 hours. Projects are generally billed by the number of names searched. Credit accounts are accepted.

Sarah Sterne(1866)   Phone: 314-242-3240
Rt 1 Box 67   Fax:
Clarksville MO 63336

Local Retrieval Area: MO-Pike.

Normal turn around time is varied depending on job. Projects are generally billed by the hour. Credit accounts are accepted.
Sarah specializes in genealogy record searches.

Stevens County Title(1867)   Phone: 509-684-4589
PO Box 349   Fax: 509-684-5448
Colville WA 99114

Local Retrieval Area: WA-Stevens.

Normal turn around time is 24-48 hours. Projects are generally billed by the hour. The first project may require a prepayment.
They specialize in title searches.

Steward and Associates Inc(1868) Phone: 815-235-3807
1001 State Bank Center   Fax: 815-235-4937
Freeport IL 61032

Local Retrieval Area: IL-Carroll, Jo Daviess, Lee, Ogle, Stephenson, Whiteside, Winnebago.

Normal turn around time is 24-48 hours for Winnebago and Stephenson, other counties average 1-5 business days. Projects are generally billed by the number of names searched. Credit accounts are accepted.
Steward and Associates Inc also has correspondent relationships in other jurisdictions, including Dubuque and Iowa. They are a licensed private detective agency that specializes in professional investigative services.

Frances Stimpson(1869)   Phone: 205-927-2424
PO Drawer 603   Fax: 205-927-2500
Centre AL 35960

Local Retrieval Area: AL-Cherokee.

Normal turn around time is 1 week, Rush service is also available. Projects are generally billed by the hour. Credit accounts are accepted.
Frances specializes in title and UCC record searches.

Attorney Alan Stout(1870)   Phone: 502-965-4600
PO Box 81   Fax: 502-965-4848
Marion KY 42064

Local Retrieval Area: KY-Caldwell, Crittenden, Livingston, Lyon, Union, Webster.

Normal turn around time is 3 days. Projects are generally billed by the hour. Credit accounts are accepted. Setup fee may sometimes be required.
They specialize in real estate and corporate matters.

Donna Stovall(1871)   Phone: 516-727-9809
28 Solitaire Rd   Fax: 516-744-9379
Rocky Point NY 11778

Local Retrieval Area: NY-Suffolk.

Normal turn around time is 24 hours. Projects are generally billed by the number of records located. Fee basis will vary by type of project. All projects require prepayment.

Strander Abstract Inc(1872)   Phone: 218-281-1191
PO Box 622   Fax: 218-281-1191
Crookston MN 56716

Local Retrieval Area: MN-Polk.

Normal turn around time is 1 week. Projects are generally billed by the number of names searched. All projects require prepayment.

Street Abstract Co(1873)   Phone: 316-625-2421
118 1/2 N Main St   Fax:
Yates Center KS 66783

Local Retrieval Area: KS-Coffey, Woodson.

Normal turn around time is 48 hours. Fee basis varies by type of transaction. The first project may require a prepayment.

Kieth Street(1874) Phone: 319-523-8164
325 Franklin Fax:
Wapello IA 52653-1515

Local Retrieval Area: IA-Louisa.

Normal turn around time is 1-7 days. Projects are generally billed by the number of names searched. Credit accounts are accepted. Keith specializes in genealogy searches.

Strother-Wilbourn Land Title Co(1875) Phone: 501-268-8273
308 E Market Ave Fax: 501-268-3275
Searcy AR 72143

Local Retrieval Area: AR-White.

Normal turn around time is 5-10 days. Fee basis will vary by the type of project. Credit accounts are accepted. They specialize in title insurance.

Stutsman County Abstract(1876) Phone: 701-252-4870
113 3rd St SW Fax: 701-252-4960
Jamestown ND 58401

Local Retrieval Area: ND-Stutsman.

Normal turn around time is 2-5 days. Fee basis will vary by type of project. All projects require prepayment. They will also invoice.

Suburban Record Research(1877) Phone: 617-536-3486
58 Alder Rd Fax:
Westwood MA 02090

Local Retrieval Area: MA-Middlesex, Norfolk.

Normal turn around time is 24-48 hours. A same day rush service is also available. Projects are generally billed by the number of names searched. Credit accounts are accepted. They specialize in UCC and court record searches.

Suit McCartney Price(1878) Phone: 606-849-2338
207 Court Square Fax: 606-845-8701
Flemingsburg KY 41041

Local Retrieval Area: KY-Fleming.

Normal turn around time is up to 1 week. Projects are generally billed by the hour. The first project may require a prepayment.

Sullivan County Abstract Co(1879) Phone: 816-265-3744
217 E 3rd St Fax:
Milan MO 63556

Local Retrieval Area: MO-Sullivan.

Normal turn around time is 2 days. Fee basis will vary by the type of project. Credit accounts are accepted. They specialize in title insurance.

Sullivan County Abstract Inc(1880) Phone: 812-268-4242
PO Box 430 Fax:
Sullivan IN 47882

Local Retrieval Area: IN-Sullivan.

Normal turn around time is 3 weeks. Fee basis will vary by type of project. Credit accounts are accepted.

Joan Sullivan(1881) Phone: 203-488-6251
32 Windhill Rd Fax: 203-488-6251
Branford CT 06405

Local Retrieval Area: CT-New Haven.

Normal turn around time is 1 week. Projects are generally billed by the number of names searched. Charges can also be based on a per address fee. Credit accounts are accepted.

Sunrise Title Co(1882) Phone: 800-244-1644
193 N State #73-13 801-722-2257
Roosevelt UT 84066 Fax: 801-722-2258

Local Retrieval Area: UT-Carbon, Daggett, Duchesne, Emery, Uintah.

Normal turn around time is 1 week to 10 days for mineral. 3 days for "others." Projects are generally billed by the hour. Credit accounts are accepted. They specialize in real estate.

Sunshine State Abstract & Title(1883) Phone: 813-382-9797
5606 US 27 N Fax: 813-382-8513
Sebring FL 33870

Local Retrieval Area: FL-Highlands.

Normal turn around time is 1 week. Fee basis will vary by the type of project. Credit accounts are accepted.

Sunstate Research Associates Inc(1884) Phone: 800-621-7234
143 Whetherbine Way W 904-656-5454
Tallahassee FL 32301 Fax:

Local Retrieval Area: FL-Calhoun, Gadsden, Holmes, Jackson, Jefferson, Leon, Liberty, Madison, Wakulla, Washington; GA-Brooks, Colquitt, Cook, Decatur, Grady, Lowndes, Miller, Mitchell, Seminole, Thomas.

Normal turn around time is the same or next day for Secretary of State and 1 to 3 days for the remainder of our service area. Projects are generally billed by the number of names searched. The first project may require a prepayment. Personal checks are accepted. Sunstate Research Associates Inc also has correspondent relationships in other jurisdictions, including Pinellas and Hillsborough Counties. They specialize in filing and retrieval of UCC and corporate documents from the Florida Secretary of State. They also search federal and state tax liens.

SuperBureau Inc(1885) Phone: 408-655-7700
2600 Garden Rd 224 West Fax: 408-372-7166
Monterey CA 93942

Local Retrieval Area: CA-Monterey.

Normal turn around time is varied depending on project. Online computer ordering is also available. Fee basis will vary by the type of project. Credit accounts are accepted. They specialize in online searches for corporate, UCC, licensed occupations, and skip tracing.

Superior Process Service(1886)
900 8th St Hamilton Bldg Suite 115
Wichita Falls TX 76301

Phone: 817-726-6624
Fax:

Local Retrieval Area: OK-Carter, Comanche, Cotton, Jackson, Jefferson, Love, Murray, Tillman; TX-Archer, Baylor, Clay, Foard, Hardeman, Haskell, Jack, Knox, Montague, Throckmorton, Wichita, Wilbarger, Wise, Young.

Normal turn around time is varied depending on project. Projects are generally billed by the hour. Credit accounts are accepted.

Superior Subpoena Service(1887)
214 1st Ave
Linden NJ 07036

Phone: 908-245-1661
Fax: 908-298-8157

Local Retrieval Area: NJ-Union.

Normal turn around time is varied depending on project. Projects are generally billed by the hour. Credit accounts are accepted. Superior Subpoena Service also has correspondent relationships in other jurisdictions, including the rest of New Jersey. They also go to the Federal Archives in Bayonne NJ.

Superior Title and Abstract(1888)
615 S Stephenson Ave
Iron Mountain MI 49801

Phone: 906-774-9010
Fax: 906-774-8994

Local Retrieval Area: MI-Dickinson.

Normal turn around time is 2 days. Projects are generally billed by the hour. Credit accounts are accepted. Superior Title and Abstract also has correspondent relationships in other jurisdictions, including all counties in the upper penisula of Michigan.

Surety Abstract & Title Company(1889)
174 N Avon Ave
Phillips WI 54555

Phone: 715-339-2110
Fax:

Local Retrieval Area: WI-Ashland.

Normal turn around time is 48 hours. Fee basis varies by type of transaction. The first project may require a prepayment.

Surety Title Co of Ballenger(1890)
207 Hutchings
Ballinger TX 76821

Phone: 915-365-5713
Fax:

Local Retrieval Area: TX-Runnels.

Normal turn around time is 1-2 days. Fee basis will vary by the type of project. The first project may require a prepayment.

Surety Title Co of Eden(1891)
19 Market
Eden TX 76837

Phone: 915-869-7081
Fax:

Local Retrieval Area: TX-Concho.

Normal turn around time is 1-2 days. Fee basis will vary by the type of project. The first project may require a prepayment.

Surety Title Co of San Angelo(1892)
136 W Twohig Ave
San Angelo TX 76903

Phone: 915-658-7588
Fax:

Local Retrieval Area: TX-Tom Green.

Normal turn around time is 1-2 days. Fee basis will vary by the type of project. The first project may require a prepayment.

Suriety Title Co(1893)
PO Box 551
New Rockford ND 58356

Phone: 701-947-2446
Fax: 701-947-2443

Local Retrieval Area: ND-Benson, Eddy, Griggs.

Normal turn around time is 5 days. Fee basis will vary by the type of project. Credit accounts are accepted.

Suveyors Title Co Inc(1894)
105 W Church Ave
Reed City MI 49677

Phone: 616-832-9916
Fax: 616-832-5077

Local Retrieval Area: MI-Lake, Mecosta, Osceola, Wexford.

Normal turn around time is 1 weeks for Osceola and Mecosta counties, 2 weeks for other counties. Projects are generally billed by the hour. Credit accounts are accepted.
They specialize in title searches on real estate.

Suwanne Title and Abstract Inc(1895)
PO Box 889
Chiefland FL 32626

Phone: 904-493-2564
Fax: 904-493-1673

Local Retrieval Area: FL-Dixie, Gilchrist, Levy.

Normal turn around time is 5-10 working days. Projects are generally billed by the number of names searched. Fee basis may per parcel for real estate searches. Credit accounts are accepted. They require a non refundable deposit. Payment is deducted from closing proceeds, if they handle the closing.
They specialize in title searches and real estate closings.

Swayze Abstract(1896)
PO Box 275
Newport IN 47966

Phone: 317-492-3767
Fax:

Local Retrieval Area: IN-Vermillion.

Normal turn around time is 48 hours. Projects are generally billed by the number of names searched. Credit accounts are accepted.
They specialize in title insurance.

Systems Resource(1897)
1671 The Alameda Suite 201
San Jose CA 95126

Phone: 408-292-2360
Fax: 408-279-5899

Local Retrieval Area: CA-Alameda, San Benito, San Francisco, San Mateo, Santa Clara, Santa Cruz.

Normal turn around time is 1-3 days. Rush service is also available. Project billing methods vary. The first project may require a prepayment.
Systems Resource also has correspondent relationships in other jurisdictions, including Monterey, Marin, Contra Costa, Sonoma and Solano. They specialize in skip tracing and court records research.

T D Title Services(1898)
PO Box 1072
Bowling Green VA 22427

Phone: 804-633-6900
Fax: 804-633-9436

Local Retrieval Area: VA-Caroline, King and Queen, King George.

Normal turn around time is 1-2 days. Fee basis varies by type of transaction. The first project may require a prepayment.

TWT Title(1899)
100 S Main St
Wolcottville IN 46795

Phone: **800-742-9362**
Fax: 800-824-2563

Local Retrieval Area: IN-DeKalb, Lagrange, Noble, Steuben.

Normal turn around time is 2 days for all counties directly served. Approximately 1 week for all others. Projects are generally billed by the hour. Credit accounts are accepted. Personal checks are accepted.
TWT Title also has correspondent relationships in other jurisdictions, including all counties in Indiana. They have an on staff attorney who specializes in real estate law including quiet title actions, zoning, title insurance and insured closings.

Talme and Associates(1900)
423 S 15th St
Philadelphia PA 19146

Phone: **215-546-6080**
Fax: 215-546-2412

Local Retrieval Area: NJ-Burlington, Camden, Gloucester; PA-Bucks, Chester, Delaware, Montgomery, Philadelphia.

Normal turn around time is varied depending on project. Projects are generally billed by the hour. Credit accounts are accepted.

Tama County Abstract(1901)
PO Box 2
Toledo IA 52342

Phone: **515-484-4386**
Fax:

Local Retrieval Area: IA-Tama.

Normal turn around time is 3-5 days. Fee basis varies by type of transaction. All projects require prepayment.
They will provide a FAX number to current clients.

Tappan Abstract(1902)
430 Ohio St
Helena AR 72342

Phone: **501-338-3311**
Fax:

Local Retrieval Area: AR-Phillips.

Normal turn around time is 2-3 days. Projects are generally billed by the hour. All projects require prepayment.
They specialize in title insurance.

Taylor Abstract Co(1903)
114 W 5th St
Larned KS 67550

Phone: **316-285-2026**
Fax:

Local Retrieval Area: KS-Pawnee.

Normal turn around time is 3 days. Fee basis varies by type of transaction. The first project may require a prepayment.

Taylor Title Inc(1904)
PO Box 5377
Bossier City LA 71171-5377

Phone: **318-741-1373**
Fax: 318-741-1821

Local Retrieval Area: LA-Bossier Parish, Caddo Parish.

Normal turn around time is 1 week. Projects are generally billed by the hour. Credit accounts are accepted.
Taylor Title Inc also has correspondent relationships in other jurisdictions, including Webster, Red River, DeSoto and Natchitoches. They specialize in title searches and real estate.

Diane Taylor(1905)
PO Box 98
Ashland MS 38603

Phone: **601-224-6300**
Fax: 601-224-3229

Local Retrieval Area: MS-Benton, Marshall, Tippah.

Normal turn around time is 2 days. Fee basis varies by type of transaction. The first project may require a prepayment.
Diane has been a paralegal for 25 years.

Teamco Inc(1906)
415 Rt 18 Suite 140
East Brunswick NJ 08816

Phone: **800-759-3691**
Fax: 800-392-2705
Fax: 908-254-5169

Local Retrieval Area: NJ-All counties.

Normal turn around time is 24-72 hours. Online computer ordering is also available. Projects are generally billed by the number of names searched. The first project may require a prepayment. Credit cards are accepted for payment. The rates are the same per type of search for each county. Searches have different charges but they are uniform for all counties.
Requests may be received by electronic mail through AT&T Easy Link Compuserve.They specialize in private investigations.

Debbie Teasley(1907)
106 Meadow Lane
Houston MS 38851

Phone: **601-456-5579**
Fax:

Local Retrieval Area: MS-Calhoun, Lafayette, Lee, Pontotoc, Union.

Normal turn around time is 2 days. Fee basis varies by type of transaction. The first project may require a prepayment.

Teeters Abstract and Title Co(1908)
1200 Main St
Goodland KS 67735

Phone: **913-899-7138**
Fax: 913-899-6644

Local Retrieval Area: KS-Sherman, Wallace.

Normal turn around time is 2 days. Projects are generally billed by the hour. Credit accounts are accepted.
Teeters Abstract and Title Co also has correspondent relationships in other jurisdictions, including Greeley and Cheyenne Counties. They specialize in real estate searches.

Territorial Title(1909)
PO Box 1007
Las Vegas NM 87701

Phone: **505-425-3563**
Fax: 505-425-9637

Local Retrieval Area: NM-Guadalupe, Mora, San Miguel; OK-Alfalfa.

Normal turn around time is 1 week for San Miguel, 4 weeks for Mora and 2 weeks for Guadalupe. Projects are generally billed by the hour. Credit accounts are accepted.
They specialize in title insurance and closings.

Terry Investigations Inc(1910)
18115 SR 23 Box 245
South Bend IN 46637

Phone: **219-631-4014**
Fax: 219-631-4014

Local Retrieval Area: IN-Marshall, St. Joseph.

Normal turn around time is 3 days. Projects are generally billed by the hour. A mileage expense will be added to the hourly fee. Credit accounts are accepted.
They specialize in criminal history records.

Terry Sharp Law Office(1911)　　　Phone: **618-242-0246**
PO Box 906　　　　　　　　　　　　Fax:　　618-242-1170
Mt Vernon IL 62864

Local Retrieval Area: IL-Alexander, Bond, Clay, Clinton, Crawford, Edwards, Effingham, Fayette, Franklin, Gallatin, Hamilton, Hardin, Jackson, Jasper, Jefferson, Johnson, Lawrence, Madison, Marion, Massac, Monroe, Perry, Pope, Pulaski, Randolph, Richland, St. Clair, Saline, U.

Normal turn around time is 3-5 days. Projects are generally billed by the hour. Credit accounts are accepted.
They specialize in real estate searches.

Teton County Abstract Co(1912)　　Phone: **406-466-2181**
PO Box 468　　　　　　　　　　　　Fax:
Mt Coteau MT 59422-0468

Local Retrieval Area: MT-Teton.

Normal turn around time is 1 week. Projects are generally billed by the hour. Credit accounts are accepted.

Texas Abstract Services(1913)　　　Phone: **713-862-8244**
2100 W 18th St Suite 101　　　　　　Fax:　　713-880-3224
Houston TX 77008

Local Retrieval Area: TX-Bailey, Brazoria, Fort Bend, Galveston, Harris, Montgomery, Wharton.

Normal turn around time is 1-3 days. Fee basis is per instrument. Credit accounts are accepted.
Texas Abstract Services also has correspondent relationships in other jurisdictions, including nationwide. They specialize in historical deed searches (environmental) and foreclosure reports.

Texas Civil Process(1914)　　　　Phone: **512-887-9595**
1731 S Staples　　　　　　　　　　Fax:　　512-897-9597
Corpus Christi TX 78463-3785

Local Retrieval Area: TX-Aransas, Brooks, Duval, Jim Wells, Kleberg, Live Oak, Nueces, Refugio, San Patricio, Victoria.

Normal turn around time is 1 day. Projects are generally billed by the number of names searched or records located. Credit accounts are accepted.
Texas Civil Process also has correspondent relationships in other jurisdictions, including Bexar, Travis, Harris, Tarrant, Dallas, McMillian, Cameron, Hidalgo, Williamson and Taylor. They specialize in process service, record research and skip tracing.

Texas Industrial Security Inc(1915)　Phone: **214-634-2791**
1440 W Mockingbird Lane Suite 205　Fax:
Dallas TX 75247

Local Retrieval Area: TX-Bexar, Dallas, Tarrant.

Normal turn around time is 2-5 days. Project billing methods vary. All projects require prepayment.
They specialize in asset locations.

Texas Information Services(1916)　　Phone: **800-822-8084**
PO Box 912　　　　　　　　　　　　　　　512-480-0123
Austin TX 78767　　　　　　　　　Fax:　　512-480-0147

Local Retrieval Area: TX-Bell, Collin, Dallas, Denton, Hays, Tarrant, Travis, Williamson.

Normal turn around time is 24-48 hours. Projects are generally billed by the number of records located. Credit accounts are accepted.
Texas Information Services also has correspondent relationships in other jurisdictions, including networking nationwide. They specialize in UCC filing and recording searches.

Texas Legal Support Service(1917)　Phone: **512-883-2247**
615 Leopard Suite 430　　　　　　　Fax:　　512-883-4515
Corpus Christi TX 78476

Local Retrieval Area: TX-Aransas, Jim Wells, Kleberg, Nueces, San Patricio.

Normal turn around time is the same day for Nueces County. Other counties is 24 to 48 hours. Projects are generally billed by the number of names searched. Credit accounts are accepted. They specialize in bankruptcy and lien searches.

Texas Records Search(1918)　　　Phone: **800-869-1405**
401 Studewood Suite 301　　　　　　　　　713-863-8003
Houston TX 77008　　　　　　　　Fax:　　713-863-8006

Local Retrieval Area: TX-Brazoria, Chambers, Fort Bend, Galveston, Harris, Jefferson, Liberty, Montgomery.

Normal turn around time is 24 hours. Projects are generally billed by the number of names searched or records located. Credit accounts are accepted. Personal checks are accepted.
They specialize in courthouse research.

Thalken Abstract & Title Co(1919)　Phone: **308-284-3972**
PO Box 307　　　　　　　　　　　　Fax:　　308-284-6802
Ogallala NE 69153

Local Retrieval Area: NE-Arthur, Banner, Chase, Deuel, Garden, Grant, Perkins.

Normal turn around time is 1 day. Fee basis varies by type of transaction. Credit accounts are accepted.
They specialize in title insurance searches.

Thayer County Abstract Office Inc(1920)　Phone: **402-768-6324**
PO Box 207　　　　　　　　　　　　Fax:
Hebron NE 68370

Local Retrieval Area: NE-Thayer.

Normal turn around time is 3-5 days. They charge a flat rate per project. Credit accounts are accepted.
They specialize in title insurance.

The Abstract & Title Co(1921)　　　Phone: **701-872-4531**
PO Box 369　　　　　　　　　　　　Fax:　　701-872-4112
Beach ND 58621

Local Retrieval Area: ND-Golden Valley.

Normal turn around time is 3-5 days. Projects are generally billed by the number of names searched. The first project may require a prepayment.

The Bister Agency(1922)
PO Box 1172
Beaufort SC 29901
Phone: 803-838-2307
Fax: 803-838-2307

Local Retrieval Area: SC-Beaufort.

Normal turn around time is 1-3 working days. A rush service is also available. Projects are generally billed by the hour. Mileage and expenses are added to the hourly fee. Credit accounts are accepted.

The Bister Agency also has correspondent relationships in other jurisdictions, including the state of South Carolina and Savannah, Georgia. They specialize in investigation, surveillance and process service.

The Cole Group(1923)
5225 Katy Fwy Suite 490
Houston TX 77007
Phone: 800-232-5602
713-880-9494
Fax: 713-880-9595

Local Retrieval Area: TX-Bexar, Dallas, Harris, Jefferson, Montgomery, Tarrant, Walker.

Normal turn around time is 1 day. Projects are generally billed by the number of records located. Credit accounts are accepted.

The Cole Group also has correspondent relationships in other jurisdictions, including nationwide. They specialize in applicant screening.

The Copy Store & More(1924)
823 S 3rd St
Las Vegas NV 89101
Phone: 702-385-0999
Fax:

Local Retrieval Area: NV-Clark.

Normal turn around time is same day. Fee basis varies by type of transaction. The first project may require a prepayment.

The Copy Store & More - Las Vegas also has correspondent relationships in other jurisdictions, including the rest of Nevada. They specialize in legal support services.

The Copy Store & More - Reno(1925)
333 Flint St
Reno NV 89501
Phone: 702-329-0999
Fax: 702-329-3402

Local Retrieval Area: NV-Washoe.

Normal turn around time is the same day. Fee basis varies by type of transaction. The first project may require a prepayment.

The Copy Store & More - Reno also has correspondent relationships in other jurisdictions, including the rest of Nevada. They specialize in legal support services.

The Court System(1926)
708 Creekview Ct
Mesquite TX 75181
Phone: 214-222-0041
Fax: 214-222-0042

Local Retrieval Area: TX-Brazos, Collin, Dallas, Delta, Denton, Ellis, Grayson, Harrison, Henderson, Hopkins, Kaufman, Lamar, Rockwall, Smith, Tarrant, Van Zandt.

Normal turn around time is 1-2 days in Dallas, and 3 to 5 days in most areas outside of Dallas. A rush service is also available. Projects are generally billed by the number of names searched or records located. Credit accounts are accepted.

The Court System also has correspondent relationships in other jurisdictions, including the rest of Texas. They also network through other retrievers nationwide. They specialize in UCC searches.

The Coynes(1927)
87 Jonquil Lane
Levittown PA 19055
Phone: 215-945-6227
Fax: 215-945-9470

Local Retrieval Area: NJ-Burlington, Camden, Mercer; PA-Bucks, Chester, Delaware, Montgomery, Philadelphia.

Normal turn around time is 24 hours. They charge per name and per index. Credit accounts are accepted.

The Croson Agency(1928)
211 Peoples Building 179 Summers St
Charleston WV 25301
Phone: 304-343-1564
Fax: 304-722-4240

Local Retrieval Area: WV-All counties.

Normal turn around time is often the same day. A search may take 24 to 48 hours. Projects are generally billed by the number of names searched or records located. Credit accounts are accepted.

The Croson Agency also has correspondent relationships in other jurisdictions, including Kentucky, Virginia, Ohio, Tennessee and Indiana. They are the oldest investigation agency in West Virgina.

The Daily Report(1929)
1705 K St
Bakersfield CA 93301
Phone: 805-322-3226
Fax: 805-322-9084

Local Retrieval Area: CA-Kern.

Normal turn around time is 2 days. Projects are generally billed by the hour. Credit accounts are accepted.

They specializing legal advertising. They also search at the municipal court level.

The Eaton County Sheriff Civil Div(1930)
242 S Bostwick
Charlotte MI 48813
Phone: 517-543-1610
Fax:

Local Retrieval Area: MI-Eaton.

Normal turn around time is 2-3 days. Fee basis varies by type of transaction. The first project may require a prepayment.

The Fatman Intl Private Detective(1931)   Phone: **616-964-2445**
194 N Union St   Fax: 616-949-4800
Battle Creek MI 49017

Local Retrieval Area: MI-Calhoun, Kent.

Normal turn around time is 1-2 days. Fee basis varies by type of transaction. Credit accounts are accepted. They ask for a retainer. The Fatman Intl Private Detective Svc also has correspondent relationships in other jurisdictions, including worldwide. They specialize in investigations.

The Gordon Company of Colby(1932)   Phone: **913-462-7555**
450 N Franklin   Fax: 913-462-2099
Colby KS 67701-0489

Local Retrieval Area: KS-Logan, Sheridan, Sherman, Thomas.

Normal turn around time is 24 hours. Projects are generally billed by the number of names searched or records located. Credit accounts are accepted. Credit cards are accepted for payment. Personal checks are accepted.
They specialize in title insurance searches.

The H O Smith Company(1933)   Phone: **308-324-2216**
104 E 7th   Fax: 308-324-7228
Lexington NE 68850

Local Retrieval Area: NE-Dawson.

Normal turn around time is 2-7 days. Projects are generally billed by the number of names searched or records located. Credit accounts are accepted.
The H O Smith Company also has correspondent relationships in other jurisdictions, including Frontier and Gosper Counties. They specialize in title insurance and abstracting.

The Home Abstract Co(1934)   Phone: **801-631-7861**
2404 Washington Suite 200   Fax: 801-621-7850
Ogden UT 84401

Local Retrieval Area: UT-Box Elder, Cache, Davis, Morgan, Summit, Weber.

Normal turn around time is 72 hours. Projects are generally billed by the number of names searched. Credit accounts are accepted. Personal checks are accepted.
The Home Abstract Co also has correspondent relationships in other jurisdictions, including all counties in Utah. They specialize in title insurance.

The Information Bank of Texas(1935)   Phone: **713-864-9122**
111 W 14th St   Fax: 713-862-6237
Houston TX 77008

Local Retrieval Area: TX-Brazoria, Dallas, Fort Bend, Galveston, Harris, Montgomery, Tarrant, Travis.

Normal turn around time is 5-7 working days. Projects are generally billed by the number of names searched. Credit accounts are accepted. Credit cards are accepted for payment. Personal checks are accepted.
The Information Bank of Texas also has correspondent relationships in other jurisdictions, including most Texas counties and many counties nationwide. They specialize with in depth asset investigations and public record searches.

The Legal Source(1936)   Phone: **916-845-8163**
PO Box 1542   Fax: 916-891-6616
Chico CA 95927

Local Retrieval Area: CA-Butte, Colusa, Glenn, Lassen, Nevada, Plumas, Shasta, Sierra, Sutter, Tehama, Yuba.

Normal turn around time is up to 5 days for remote counties. Rush service is also available. Projects are generally billed by the number of names searched. The first project may require a prepayment.
They also prepare subpoenas and provide photocopies.

The Marston Agency Inc(1937)   Phone: **804-784-0111**
PO Box 29940   Fax:
Richmond VA 23242

Local Retrieval Area: VA-Chesterfield, Goochland, Hanover, Henrico, Henrico, City of Petersburg, City of Richmond.

Normal turn around time is 24-72 hours. Projects are generally billed by the hour. Credit accounts are accepted.

The Niles Agency(1938)   Phone: **808-533-7707**
350 Ward Ave Suite 106   Fax: 808-533-7324
Honolulu HI 96814

Local Retrieval Area: HI-Honolulu.

Normal turn around time is 48 hours. Online computer ordering is also available. Project billing methods vary. The first project may require a prepayment. Personal checks are accepted. They specialize in fraud investigations.

The North Dakota Guaranty & Title1939)   Phone: **701-223-6835**
400 E Broadway Ave Suite 409   Fax: 701-224-1571
Bismarck ND 58501

Local Retrieval Area: ND-Burleigh.

Normal turn around time is 2-3 days. They charge a minimum charge, however, the fee basis will vary by type of project. Credit accounts are accepted.
They specialize in title and UCC searches.

The R M Jaqua Abstract Co(1940)   Phone: **913-332-3041**
Box 665   Fax:
St Francis KS 67756

Local Retrieval Area: KS-Cheyenne.

Normal turn around time is within 48 hours. Projects are generally billed by the number of names searched. Credit accounts are accepted. Personal checks are accepted.

The Records Reviewer Inc(1941)   Phone: **305-947-1186**
13899 Biscayne Blvd   Fax: 305-944-6933
North Miami Beach FL 33181

Local Retrieval Area: FL-Broward, Dade.

Normal turn around time is 48 hours. Projects are generally billed by the number of names searched. They may also charge by the quarter hour. Credit accounts are accepted. They only invoice to professionals.
The Records Reviewer Inc also has correspondent relationships in other jurisdictions, including Palm Beach county.

The Search Is On(1942)
PO Box 120598
Nashville TN 37212

Phone: **615-352-5580**
Fax: 615-356-3269

Local Retrieval Area: TN-Cheatham, Davidson, Robertson, Rutherford, Sumner, Williamson, Wilson.

Normal turn around time is 1-3 days. Projects are generally billed by the number of names searched. Credit accounts are accepted.

The Search Is On also has correspondent relationships in other jurisdictions, including all the other counties in Tennessee. They specialize in UCC and Corporate documents.

The Title Co Inc(1943)
319 9th St
Sibley IA 51249

Phone: **712-754-2284**
Fax:

Local Retrieval Area: IA-Osceola.

Normal turn around time is 1-3 days. Fee basis will vary by the type of project. The first project may require a prepayment.

Donna Thomas(1944)
1019 Tekamah Ln
Papillion NE 68128

Phone: **402-339-7291**
Fax:

Local Retrieval Area: IA-Adair, Adams, Audubon, Carroll, Cass, Crawford, Fremont, Harrison, Iowa, Mills, Monona, Montgomery, Page, Pottawattamie, Shelby, Taylor, Union; NE-Butler, Cass, Dodge, Douglas, Lancaster, Otoe, Sarpy, Saunders, Seward, Washington.

Normal turn around time is up to 2 weeks. Rush service is also available. Projects are generally billed by the hour. Credit accounts are accepted. Personal checks are accepted.

Donna specializes in genealogy. She is compiling a book on cemetary inscriptions. Performs research for maiden and married names.

Thompson & Hollingsworth PA(1945)
PO Drawer 119
Forest MS 39074

Phone: **601-469-0341**
Fax: 601-469-3411

Local Retrieval Area: MS-Scott.

Normal turn around time is 1 day. Projects are generally billed by the hour. The first project may require a prepayment.

They are in general practice. They specialize in marriage/divorce searches.

Thompson and Assoc(1946)
930 Jefferson St Bldg 100
Nashville TN 37208

Phone: **615-272-9754**
Fax: 615-242-9762

Local Retrieval Area: TN-Davidson.

Normal turn around time is up to 3 days. Rush service is available. Fee basis will vary by the type of search. The first project may require a prepayment.

Three Rivers Title Co(1947)
731 Court St
Ft Wayne IN 46802

Phone: **219-424-2929**
Fax: 219-424-0037

Local Retrieval Area: IN-Huntington, Noble, Wabash, Wells, Whitley.

Normal turn around time is 2-3 days. Fee basis varies by type of transaction. Credit accounts are accepted.

Thurman Investigative Services(1948)
PO Box 259
Albany GA 31702

Phone: **912-883-6227**
Fax: 912-888-2447

Local Retrieval Area: GA-Baker, Calhoun, Clay, Crisp, Dougherty, Early, Lee, Mitchell, Thomas.

Normal turn around time is 24-48 hours. Projects are generally billed by the hour. Credit accounts are accepted.

They specialize in criminal and civil matters as well as insurance fraud investigation.

Tinnon Beshear Abstract Co(1949)
PO Box 487
Rison AR 71665

Phone: **501-325-6832**
Fax: 501-325-6265

Local Retrieval Area: AR-Cleveland.

Normal turn around time is 3-5 days. Fee basis will vary by the type of project. The first project may require a prepayment.

They specialize in title insurance, searches, and reports.

Tippecanoe Title Services Inc(1950)
133 N 4th St Suite 42
Lafayette IN 47901

Phone: **317-423-2457**
Fax: 317-742-0194

Local Retrieval Area: IN-Benton, Carroll, Cass, Clinton, Fountain, Jasper, Montgomery, Steuben, Warren, White.

Normal turn around time is 3-7 days. Projects are generally billed by the number of records located. Credit accounts are accepted.

Title Abstract Co(1951)
120 W 5th Courthouse Square
Holton KS 66436

Phone: **913-364-2040**
Fax: 913-364-3420

Local Retrieval Area: KS-Jackson.

Normal turn around time is 2 days for name searches, 1 week for title insurance and 2 weeks for abstracting. Projects are generally billed by the number of names searched. Credit accounts are accepted. Personal checks are accepted.

Title Abstract Co(1952)
119 N Maple St
Nowata OK 74048

Phone: **918-273-0225**
Fax: 918-273-0259

Local Retrieval Area: OK-Nowata.

Normal turn around time is 24-36 hours. Projects are generally billed by the hour. All projects require prepayment.

They are the county's only source of complete records (the court house burned in 1911), and the only company in the county with computerized records.

Title Guaranty Chattanooga(1953)   Phone: **615-266-5751**
617 Walnut St   Fax: 615-265-8855
Chattanooga TN 37402

Local Retrieval Area: AL-Cherokee, De Kalb, Houston; GA-Catoosa, Chattooga, Dade, Fannin, Gilmer, Gordon, Murray, Walker, Whitfield; TN-Bledsoe, Bradley, Coffee, Coffee, Franklin, Grundy, Hamilton, Loudon, McMinn, Marion, Meigs, Monroe, Polk, Rhea, Sequatchie, Van Buren.

Normal turn around time is 2 days. Projects are generally billed by the hour. The first project may require a prepayment.
Title Guaranty and Trust of Chattanooga also has correspondent relationships in other jurisdictions, including nationwide. They specialize in title insurance.

Title Search Services Inc(1954)   Phone: **804-490-7009**
804 Newtown Rd Suite 104   Fax: 804-456-0069
Virginia Beach VA 23462

Local Retrieval Area: VA-City of Chesapeake, City of Norfolk, City of Virginia Beach.

Normal turn around time is 1-2 days. Projects are generally billed by the number of names searched or records located. Credit accounts are accepted.
Title Search Services Inc also has correspondent relationships in other jurisdictions.

Title Searchers Inc(1955)   Phone: **904-797-7822**
2730 US 1 South Suite F   Fax: 904-797-2429
St Augustine FL 32086

Local Retrieval Area: FL-Seminole.

Normal turn around time is 2-3 days. Fee basis will vary by type of project. Credit accounts are accepted.
Title Searchers Inc also has correspondent relationships in other jurisdictions, including the state of Florida. They specialize in land title searches.

Title Services Inc(1956)   Phone: **601-264-3500**
804 Westover Dr   Fax: 601-264-5377
Hattiesburg MS 39402

Local Retrieval Area: MS-Covington, Forrest, Jefferson Davis, Jones, Lamar, Marion, Perry.

Normal turn around time is 1 day in Forrest county, 2 days all others. Fee basis varies by type of transaction. The first project may require a prepayment.

Title Services Unlimited(1957)   Phone: **803-527-6326**
PO Box 611   Fax:
Georgetown SC 29442

Local Retrieval Area: SC-Georgetown.

Normal turn around time is varied depending on project. Fee basis is per project. Credit accounts are accepted.

Titles of Dakota Inc(1958)   Phone: **605-258-2291**
PO Box 167   Fax: 605-223-9237
Onida SD 57564-0167

Local Retrieval Area: SD-Sully.

Normal turn around time is 1 week. Fee basis will vary by the type of project. Credit accounts are accepted.

Titles of Dakota Inc(1959)   Phone: **800-794-2725**
PO Box 278   605-223-2727
Fort Pierre SD 57532-0278   Fax: 605-223-9237

Local Retrieval Area: SD-Stanley.

Normal turn around time is 1 week. Fee basis will vary by the type of project. Credit accounts are accepted.

Titles of Dakota Inc(1960)   Phone: **605-365-5247**
PO Box 402   Fax: 605-365-5248
Timber Lake SD 57656-0402

Local Retrieval Area: SD-Dewey.

Normal turn around time is 1 week. Fee basis will vary by the type of project. Credit accounts are accepted.

Titles of Dakota Inc(1961)   Phone: **605-365-5247**
PO Box 100   Fax: 605-365-5248
Dupree SD 57623-0100

Local Retrieval Area: SD-Ziebach.

Normal turn around time is 1 week. Fee basis will vary by the type of project. Credit accounts are accepted.

Titus County Title Company(1962)   Phone: **903-577-0333**
103 N Madison   Fax: 903-577-1666
Mt Pleasant TX 75455

Local Retrieval Area: TX-Titus.

Normal turn around time is 2-3 days. Fee basis will vary by the type of project. The first project may require a prepayment.

Toma Abstract Inc(1963)   Phone: **800-726-8134**
11 E Diamond Ave   717-454-7899
Hazleton PA 18201   Fax: 717-454-5999

Local Retrieval Area: PA-Carbon, Columbia, Luzerne, Monroe, Montour, Northumberland, Schuylkill.

Normal turn around time is 2 weeks or less. Projects are generally billed by the number of names searched. Credit accounts are accepted.
They specialize in title searching and title insurance and have a secod office at 2691 New Berwick Hwy, Suite A, Bloomburg, PA.

Vicki Tomich(1964)   Phone: **304-845-5213**
727 Echo Valley   Fax:
Glen Dale WV 26038

Local Retrieval Area: OH-Belmont, Belmont, Guernsey, Harrison, Jefferson, Monroe, Noble; WV-Brooke, Hancock, Marshall, Ohio, Wetzel.

Normal turn around time is 24-48 hours. Fee basis varies by type of transaction. Credit accounts are accepted.
Vicki specializes in non commercial property searches.

Tompkins and Watkins Abstract(1965)   Phone: **607-273-0884**
202 E Court St   Fax: 607-277-5584
Ithaca NY 14850

Local Retrieval Area: NY-New York.

Normal turn around time is 5-7 days. Projects are generally billed by the number of names searched. Credit accounts are accepted.

Tomson Abstract Co(1966)
111 N Main St
Johnson KS 67855
Phone: 316-492-6810
Fax: 316-492-6801

Local Retrieval Area: KS-Stanton.

Normal turn around time is up to 1 week. Fee basis varies by type of transaction. The first project may require a prepayment.

Tooele Title Company(1967)
526 S 525 W
Tooele UT 84074
Phone: 801-882-1120
Fax: 801-882-1111

Local Retrieval Area: UT-Box Elder, Juab, Tooele.

Normal turn around time is 2-3 days for Grantsville, 3 to 5 days for Utah, 3 to 5 days for mining searches. Fee basis will vary by the type of project. Credit accounts are accepted. A setup fee and prepayment is required by individuals, and no setup fee is required of companies. Companies will be invoiced.

They specialize in tax sales, mining, special county searches, foreclosure reports, plating problems, escrow services and any title service.

Toole County Title Co(1968)
235 Main St
Shelby MT 59474
Phone: 406-434-5156
Fax: 406-434-5157

Local Retrieval Area: MT-Toole.

Normal turn around time is 5 days. Projects are generally billed by the hour. All projects require prepayment.

Town & Country Abstract Co(1969)
Hwy 412W
Huntsville AR 72740
Phone: 501-738-2055
Fax: 501-738-2075

Local Retrieval Area: AR-Madison.

Normal turn around time is 1-2 days. Fee basis will vary by the type of project. The first project may require a prepayment. They specialize in title insurance.

Town and Country Abstract Co(1970)
101 S Main
Huntsville MO 65259
Phone: 816-277-3467
Fax:

Local Retrieval Area: MO-Randolph.

Normal turn around time is 24-48 hours. Projects are generally billed by the number of names searched or records located. Credit accounts are accepted. Personal checks are accepted.
Town and Country Abstract Co also has correspondent relationships in other jurisdictions, including nationwide.

Towner County Abstract Co(1971)
PO Box 668
Cando ND 58324
Phone: 701-963-3651
Fax:

Local Retrieval Area: ND-Towner.

Normal turn around time is 2 weeks. Fee basis are also based per entry. All projects require prepayment. They will also invoice.

Trace Investigations(1972)
PO Box 2603
Bloomington IN 47402
Phone: 812-334-8857
Fax: 812-333-4048

Local Retrieval Area: IN-Bartholomew, Brown, Greene, Johnson, Lawrence, Marion, Monroe, Morgan, Owen.

Normal turn around time is 24-48 hours for county courts and 48-72 hours for US courts. Projects are generally billed by the hour. Credit accounts are accepted.
Trace Investigations also has correspondent relationships in other jurisdictions, including all of Southern and Central Indiana. They specialize in legal investigations, i.e. investigations for plaintiff attorney in personal injury and negligence civil actions and investigations for criminal defense.

Trace Unlimited(1973)
5501 N Swan Rd Suite 225
Tucson AZ 85718-5445
Phone: 602-299-0015
Fax: 602-299-0524

Local Retrieval Area: AZ-Pima.

Normal turn around time is 2 days. Tucson municipal averages 5 days. Projects are generally billed by the hour. Credit accounts are accepted.
Trace Unlimited also has correspondent relationships in other jurisdictions, including Maricopa. They specialize in skip tracing and locating individuals.

Tracers International(1974)
PO Box 1049
Schenectady NY 12305
Phone: 800-872-2377
Fax: 518-374-1814

Local Retrieval Area: NY-Albany, Rensselaer, Saratoga, Schenectady, Schoharie.

Normal turn around time is 3-5 days. Online computer ordering is also available. Projects are generally billed by the number of records located. Credit accounts are accepted. Credit cards are accepted for payment.
Tracers International also has correspondent relationships in other jurisdictions, including Orange, Dutchess, Rockland, Bronx, New York, Queens, Nassau, Suffolk and Ulster. They specialize in asset searches and skip tracing.

Track Down Inc(1975)
115 W McDowell Rd Suite 2
Phoenix AZ 85003
Phone: 602-252-8521
Fax: 602-252-8682

Local Retrieval Area: AZ-Maricopa.

Normal turn around time is 24 hours. Projects are generally billed by the hour. All projects require prepayment. Will invoice to established clients.
Track Down Inc also has correspondent relationships in other jurisdictions, including the rest of Arizona. They specialize in service of process and special investigations/research.

Traill County Abstract Co(1976)
PO Box 69
Hillsboro ND 58045
Phone: 701-436-4880
Fax:

Local Retrieval Area: ND-Traill.

Normal turn around time is 2-3 weeks. Fees are based according to state law. All projects require prepayment. They also invoice.

Treasure Coast Abstract & Title(1977)
401-B S Indian River Dr
Fort Pierce FL 34950
Phone: 407-461-7190
Fax: 407-468-8461

Local Retrieval Area: FL-Indian River, Martin, Okeechobee, St. Lucie.

Normal turn around time is 7 days. Fee basis will vary by the type of project. Credit accounts are accepted.
They specialize in residential and commercial title searches.

Tri County Process Service(1978)
PO Box 3026
Salinas CA 93912
Phone: 408-758-2580
Fax: 408-757-0693

Local Retrieval Area: CA-Monterey, San Benito, Santa Cruz.

Normal turn around time is 1 week. Projects are generally billed by the hour. All projects require prepayment.
Tri County Process Service also has correspondent relationships in other jurisdictions, including all of California. They specialize in process service.

Tri-County Abstract and Title(1979)
400 1st St S Suite 530
St Cloud MN 56302
Phone: 612-253-2096
Fax: 612-253-4536

Local Retrieval Area: MN-Benton, Morrison, Sherburne, Stearns, Wright.

Normal turn around time is 5-10 business days. Projects are generally billed by the number of names searched or records located. Credit accounts are accepted. Personal checks are accepted.

Tri-County Land Title(1980)
PO Box 303
Berne IN 46711
Phone: 219-589-3139
Fax: 219-589-3130

Local Retrieval Area: IN-Adams, Jay, Wells.

Normal turn around time is 1-5 days. Projects are generally billed by the number of records located. Credit accounts are accepted.

Tri-County Process Serving(1981)
417 W Fort St
Boise ID 83702
Phone: 800-473-3454
208-344-4132
Fax: 208-338-1530

Local Retrieval Area: ID-Ada, Boise, Canyon, Elmore, Gem, Payette, Valley.

Normal turn around time is varied depending on project. Projects are generally billed by the number of records located. Credit accounts are accepted.
Tri-County Process Serving also has correspondent relationships in other jurisdictions, including Twin Falls, Gooding, Jerome, Bonneville, Madison, Jefferson, Power, and most counties in northern Idaho. They specialize in process service and skip tracing.

Tri-County Title Services(1982)
2091 S 1st St
Lake City FL 32055
Phone: 904-755-5566
Fax: 904-755-5799

Local Retrieval Area: FL-Baker, Columbia, Gilchrist, Hamilton, Lafayette, Suwannee, Union.

Normal turn around time is 3-5 days. Fee basis will vary by the type of project. Credit accounts are accepted.
They specialize in ownership and encumbrance searches and title insurance.

Trident Abstract Co(1983)
8 Broad St
Freehold NJ 07728
Phone: 800-464-3434
908-431-3134
Fax: 908-431-8408

Local Retrieval Area: NJ-Middlesex, Monmouth, Ocean.

Normal turn around time is 2-3 days for title searches. Judgements and probate average 1-2 hours. Projects are generally billed by the number of records located. Credit accounts are accepted. Trident Abstract Co also has correspondent relationships in other jurisdictions, including the entire state.

Trinity County Abstract(1984)
107 Main St
Groveton TX 75845
Phone: 409-642-1698
Fax:

Local Retrieval Area: TX-Trinity.

Normal turn around time is 5-10 working days. Commitments and land searches take 15 working days. Projects are generally billed by the number of names searched. Credit accounts are accepted. A payment program may be used. Personal checks are accepted.
They specialize in land title searches and title insurance.

Troy Title Co(1985)
115 N Lincoln Dr
Troy MO 63379
Phone: 314-528-2220
Fax: 314-528-2220

Local Retrieval Area: MO-Lincoln.

Normal turn around time is 2 days. Projects are generally billed by the number of names searched. Credit accounts are accepted. Personal checks are accepted.
They specialize in real estate title searches.

Trumbull County Abstract Co(1986)
174 N Park Ave
Warren OH 44482
Phone: 216-399-1891
Fax: 216-399-1892

Local Retrieval Area: OH-Ashtabula, Columbiana, Geauga, Mahoning, Portage, Trumbull.

Normal turn around time is 3 days. Projects are generally billed by the hour. Credit accounts are accepted.

Tucker Abstract Co(1987)
202 E Central
Bentonville AR 72712
Phone: 501-273-2111
Fax: 501-273-9247

Local Retrieval Area: AR-Benton.

Normal turn around time is 3 days for UCC and taxes and 7-10 days for real estate. Projects are generally billed by the hour. All projects require prepayment.

Taylor Tucker(1988)
PO Box 7
Louisville MS 39339

Phone: **601-773-9254**
Fax: 601-773-9255

Local Retrieval Area: MS-Winston.

Normal turn around time is 2 days. Projects are generally billed by the hour. The first project may require a prepayment.
Mr. Tucker is an attorney in general practice.

Helen Turner(1989)
931 Marshall Ave
New Castle PA 16101

Phone: **412-652-5402**
Fax:

Local Retrieval Area: PA-Lawrence.

Normal turn around time is 24-48 hours. Fee basis will vary by the type of project. The first project may require a prepayment. Out of state clients are charged a setup fee.

Turning Wheels Inc(1990)
PO Box 13002
Greensboro NC 27415

Phone: **919-621-9064**
Fax: 919-621-8202

Local Retrieval Area: NC-Alamance, Chatham, Davidson, Forsyth, Guilford, Montgomery, Randolph, Rockingham, Stokes.

Normal turn around time is 24-48 hours. Fee basis varies by type of transaction. Credit accounts are accepted.
They specialize in litigation support, document preparation and forclosure searches.

Turnquist & Associates(1991)
PO Box 607
Galesburg IL 61402-0607

Phone: **309-343-6614**
Fax: 309-343-6165

Local Retrieval Area: IL-Fulton, Henry, Knox, McDonough, Peoria, Warren.

Normal turn around time is 3-4 days. Fee basis varies by type of transaction. The first project may require a prepayment.
Turnquist & Associates also has correspondent relationships in other jurisdictions, including the rest of the state. They specialize in private investigations, criminal, workmen's compensation, fraud and process serving.

Barbara Tweedle(1992)
PO Box 9
Rosedale MS 38769

Phone: **601-759-3762**
Fax:

Local Retrieval Area: MS-Bolivar.

Normal turn around time is 1-2 days. Projects are generally billed by the number of names searched. All projects require prepayment. Barbara specializes in records at the Rosedale courts. A FAX machine is available upon request.

Twin City Abstract Corp(1993)
730 Meritor Tower
St Paul MN 55101

Phone: **612-224-7072**
Fax: 612-223-5819

Local Retrieval Area: MN-Anoka, Carver, Dakota, Hennepin, Ramsey, Scott, Washington.

Normal turn around time is 3 days. Projects are generally billed by the number of names searched. Fee basis can also be per entry for abstracts. Credit accounts are accepted.

Twin City Title Co Inc(1994)
PO Box 2791
Texarkana TX 75504

Phone: **903-793-7671**
Fax: 903-792-2847

Local Retrieval Area: TX-Bowie.

Normal turn around time is 1-2 days. Projects are generally billed by the hour. All projects require prepayment.

Tyler-McLennon Inc(1995)
1306 Nueces St
Austin TX 78701

Phone: **512-482-0808**
Fax: 512-482-0912

Local Retrieval Area: TX-Many counties in this state are covered. See the county index for actual coverage..

Normal turn around time is 24-72 hours. Online computer ordering is also available. Projects are generally billed by the number of names searched. Credit accounts are accepted. Tyler-McLennon Inc also has correspondent relationships in other jurisdictions, including Texas, Maryland, Virginia, California and Oklahoma. They specialize in criminal record searches.

UCC Network Inc(1996)
PO Box 255869
Sacramento CA 95865

Phone: **800-998-0433**
Fax: 916-929-0368

Local Retrieval Area: CA-El Dorado, Placer, Sacramento.

Normal turn around time is 24-48 hours. Projects are generally billed by the number of names searched. They charge by index also. The first project may require a prepayment.

UCC Retrievals(1997)
4809 Brook Rd
Richmond VA 23227

Phone: **804-266-3499**
Fax: 804-266-0348

Local Retrieval Area: VA-Charles City, Chesterfield, Goochland, Hanover, Henrico, King William, Loudoun, New Kent, Prince George, City of Colonial Heights, City of Hopewell, City of Petersburg, City of Richmond, City of Richmond, City of Winchester.

Normal turn around time is 48 hours. Rush service is also available. Fee basis will vary by type of project. Credit accounts are accepted.
UCC Retrievals also has correspondent relationships in other jurisdictions, including the state of Virginia. They also search motor vehicle records, do coporate filings and retrievals and assist with pending cases.

UCC Search Inc(1998)
PO Box 9315
Santa Fe NM 87504

Phone: **505-983-4228**
Fax: 505-983-1169

Local Retrieval Area: NM-Bernalillo, Dona Ana, Guadalupe, Los Alamos, Quay, San Miguel, Santa Fe, Taos, Torrance, Valencia.

Normal turn around time is 24-48 hours. Verbals may be available in several hours. Projects are generally billed by the number of names searched. Credit accounts are accepted.
UCC Search Inc also has correspondent relationships in other jurisdictions, including the rest of the state of New Mexico.

US Legal Support(1999) Phone: **806-374-2900**
PO Box 1053 Fax: 806-374-2954
Amarillo TX 79105

Local Retrieval Area: TX-Potter, Randall.

Normal turn around time is 24 hours. Projects are generally billed by the number of names searched or records located. The first project may require a prepayment.
They also provide process service.

US Legal Support of Lubbock(2000) Phone: **806-747-8500**
PO Box 11564 Fax: 806-741-0947
Lubbock TX 79408

Local Retrieval Area: TX-Lubbock.

Normal turn around time is 2 days. Fee basis varies by type of transaction. The first project may require a prepayment.
US Legal Support of Lubbock also has correspondent relationships in other jurisdictions, including network for the panhandle of Texas. They specialize in marriage/divorce searches.

US Legal Support-Houston(2001) Phone: **800-775-2524**
1314 Texas Ave Suite 519   713-225-2524
Houston TX 77002 Fax: 713-225-2524

Local Retrieval Area: TX-Angelina, Austin, Brazoria, Chambers, Fort Bend, Grimes, Hardin, Harris, Jasper, Jefferson, Liberty, Montgomery, Newton, Orange, Polk, Trinity, Tyler, Victoria, Walker, Waller, Wharton.

Normal turn around time is 2-3 days. A rush service is also available. Projects are generally billed by the hour. The first project may require a prepayment.
They specialize in civil process.

US Title Research Inc(2002) Phone: **718-256-2776**
146 86th St Fax: 718-206-4761
Brooklyn NY 11228

Local Retrieval Area: NY-Richmond.

Normal turn around time is 3-5 days. Projects are generally billed by the number of names searched. Credit accounts are accepted.
US Title Research Inc also has correspondent relationships in other jurisdictions, including all New York counties, Nassau and Surfolk. They specialize in title searching and examinations.

Lois Uhe(2003) Phone: **618-357-8747**
Rt 2 Box 470 Fax:
Pinckneyville IL 62274

Local Retrieval Area: IL-Perry.

Normal turn around time is 2 days. Projects are generally billed by the hour. Credit accounts are accepted.

Union Abstract Co(2004) Phone: **501-863-6053**
200 N Jeffersn Ave Suite 214 Fax:
El Dorado AR 71730

Local Retrieval Area: AR-Union.

Normal turn around time is 1 day. Projects are generally billed by the hour. All projects require prepayment.

Union County Abstract and Title(2005) Phone: **605-356-3180**
104 W Main St Fax: 605-356-3112
Elk Point SD 57025

Local Retrieval Area: SD-Union.

Normal turn around time is 24-48 hours. Projects are generally billed by the hour. Credit accounts are accepted.
They specialize in title searches, lien searches, abstracting and title insurance. They are a licensed abstractor for Union County, South Dakota.

Union-Speer Abstract Co(2006) Phone: **918-224-4540**
PO Box 710 Fax: 918-224-4549
Sapulpa OK 74067

Local Retrieval Area: OK-Creek.

Normal turn around time is varied depending on project. Fees basis is per page. Credit accounts are accepted.

Unisearch Inc(2007) Phone: **800-722-0708**
525 Columbia Ave NW Suite 205 Fax: 800-531-1717
Olympia WA 98501-1098

Local Retrieval Area: WA-King, Pierce, Skagit, Snohomish, Thurston.

Normal turn around time is 24-48 hours. Projects are generally billed by the number of names searched or records located. Copy costs and disbursements are added to the search charge. Credit accounts are accepted.
Unisearch Inc also has correspondent relationships in other jurisdictions, including Nationwide. Unisearch, Inc. also has a second office at 3789 River Rd. N, Suite C, Salem, Oregon 97303-5631 and has on-line access to 16 states' records.

United Attorneys' Services(2008) Phone: **916-457-3000**
601 University Ave Suite 125 Fax:
Sacramento CA 95825

Local Retrieval Area: CA-Placer, Sacramento, San Joaquin, Yolo.

Normal turn around time is 4 days. Projects are generally billed by the number of names searched. Credit accounts are accepted. Personal checks are accepted.
United Attorneys' Services also has correspondent relationships in other jurisdictions, including Solano, El Dorado and Nevada.

United Legal Services(2009) Phone: **405-232-8432**
217 N Harvey Suite 102 Fax: 405-232-8442
Oklahoma City OK 73102

Local Retrieval Area: OK-Canadian, Cleveland, Grady, Lincoln, Logan, McClain, Oklahoma, Pottawatomie.

Normal turn around time is 48 hours for close in counties. Contract areas average 3-4 days. Projects are generally billed by the hour. The first project may require a prepayment. Personal checks are accepted.
United Legal Services also has correspondent relationships in other jurisdictions, including all of Oklahoma

United Title Services Inc(2010)
312 1st St SE
Cedar Rapids IA 52401

Phone: 319-365-1478
Fax: 319-364-3217

Local Retrieval Area: IA-Linn.

Normal turn around time is 24-48 hours. Fee basis varies by type of transaction. Credit accounts are accepted. They request prepayment from individials, but will invoice companies.

Universal Research(2011)
18733 Samuel Rd Suite 221
Zachary LA 70791

Phone: 504-654-4920
Fax:

Local Retrieval Area: LA-East Baton Rouge Parish, East Feliciana Parish, Livingston Parish, St. Helena Parish, West Feliciana Parish; MS-Amite, Wilkinson.

Normal turn around time is 5 working days. Projects are generally billed by the hour. Credit accounts are accepted. Personal checks are accepted.

They specialize in genealogy. They also search probate, land, marriage, and all county court house records.

University Process Service(2012)
609 University Blvd W
Silver Spring MD 20901

Phone: 301-681-7206
Fax: 301-593-1583

Local Retrieval Area: DC-All counties; MD-Anne Arundel, Baltimore, Carroll, Frederick, Howard, Montgomery, Prince George's, City of Baltimore; VA-Arlington, Fairfax, City of Alexandria.

Normal turn around time is 1-2 days. Projects are generally billed by the number of records located. Credit accounts are accepted.

Upper Penninsula Title and Abstr(2013)
810 Ludington St
Escanaba MI 49829

Phone: 906-786-3821
Fax: 906-786-7910

Local Retrieval Area: MI-Alger, Delta, Marquette, Menominee, Schoolcraft.

Normal turn around time is 1-5 days. Fee basis will vary by type of project. Credit accounts are accepted.
They specialize in full title service.

Upper State Title Corp(2014)
PO Box 2205
Anderson SC 29625-2205

Phone: 803-260-4649
Fax: 803-231-8419

Local Retrieval Area: SC-Abbeville, Anderson, Greenville, Greenwood, Laurens, McCormick, Oconee, Pickens, Spartanburg.

Normal turn around time is 1 day. Projects are generally billed by the hour. Credit accounts are accepted.

Utah Title & Abstract(2015)
PO Box 337
Richfield UT 84754

Phone: 801-896-5429
Fax: 801-896-4084

Local Retrieval Area: UT-Millard, Piute, Sevier, Wayne.

Normal turn around time is as long as 2-3 weeks. Projects are generally billed by the hour. All projects require prepayment.

Utica-Rome Legal(2016)
PO Box 7
Utica NY 13503

Phone: 315-797-8609
Fax: 315-797-8609

Local Retrieval Area: NY-Oneida.

Normal turn around time is 72 hours. Projects are generally billed by the number of names searched or records located. Credit accounts are accepted.

They specialize in judgement enforcement and process service.

VISTA Inc(2017)
29524 Southfield Rd
Southfield MI 48076-2004

Phone: 313-559-3500
Fax: 313-559-4757

Local Retrieval Area: MI-Macomb, Monroe, Oakland, Washtenaw, Wayne.

Normal turn around time is 1-2 weeks depending on the county. Projects are generally billed by the number of names searched. The first project may require a prepayment.
VISTA Inc also has correspondent relationships in other jurisdictions, including the state of Michigan. They specialize in surveillance and defense sub rosa.

VTS(2018)
PO Box 971
Elgin IL 60121-0971

Phone: 708-888-4464
Fax: 708-888-8588

Local Retrieval Area: IL-Cook, De Kalb, Du Page, Kane, Kendall, Lake, McHenry, Will. Normal turn around time is 24-48 hours. Online computer ordering is also available. Projects are

generally billed by the number of names searched or records located. The first project may require a prepayment. Personal checks are accepted.

They are a licensed investigative agency that specializes in paralegal service, computerized information service and foreign language translation.

Valley Copy Service Inc(2019)
PO Box 3449
Modesto CA 95353

Phone: 209-524-0223
Fax: 209-524-1505

Local Retrieval Area: CA-Amador, Fresno, Merced, Sacramento, San Joaquin, Stanislaus, Tehama, Tulare.

Normal turn around time is 5-10 days. Projects are generally billed by the number of names searched or records located. Credit accounts are accepted.
Valley Copy Service Inc also has correspondent relationships in other jurisdictions, including all of California. They are an attorney service. They prepare subpoenas, serve and copy medical employment and other records for many hospitals in the valley.

Valley Land Title Co(2020)
100 N Oak St
Sallisaw OK 74955

Phone: 918-775-4872
Fax: 918-775-4812

Local Retrieval Area: OK-Sequoyah.

Normal turn around time is 12-24 hours. Projects are generally billed by the number of records located. All projects require prepayment.
They specialize in real estate.

Valley Legal Support Services Inc(2021)
20720 Ventura Blvd Suite 160
Woodland Hills CA 91364
Phone: **818-888-7166**
Fax: 818-704-4668

Local Retrieval Area: CA-Los Angeles.

Normal turn around time is 1 day. Projects are generally billed by the number of records located. The first project may require a prepayment.
Valley Legal Support Services Inc also has correspondent relationships in other jurisdictions, including Orange, Ventura, Riverside, San Bernardino and San Diego.

Van Buren Abstract Co(2022)
PO Box 310
Keosauqua IA 52565
Phone: **319-293-3783**
Fax:

Local Retrieval Area: IA-Van Buren.

Normal turn around time is 2-3 days. Fee basis will vary by the type of project. The first project may require a prepayment.

Van Dyke & Co(2023)
74 E Arrow PO Box 520
Marshall MO 65340
Phone: **816-886-7444**
Fax: 816-886-9511

Local Retrieval Area: MO-Saline.

Normal turn around time is 1 week. Charges are varied depending on type of search. Credit accounts are accepted.

Leona Van Dyke(2024)
12168 Still Pond Creek Rd
Worton MD 21678
Phone: **410-778-2468**
Fax:

Local Retrieval Area: MD-Kent, Queen Anne's.

Normal turn around time is 24-48 hours. Fee basis will vary with type of search. The first project may require a prepayment.
Leona specializes in real estate record searches.

VanBuren County Abstract Office(2025)
207 Paw Paw
Paw Paw MI 49079
Phone: **616-657-4250**
Fax: 616-657-3207

Local Retrieval Area: MI-Van Buren.

Normal turn around time is 2-3 days. Rush service also available. Fee basis will vary by type of project. All projects require prepayment.
They specialize in real estate matters.

Linda Vanderhoof(2026)
60 Parkway Dr E Suite 11M
East Orange NJ 07017
Phone: **201-674-0870**
Fax: 201-674-0870

Local Retrieval Area: NJ-Essex.

Normal turn around time is 24-48 hours. Projects are generally billed by the number of names searched. Credit accounts are accepted. Personal checks are accepted.

Jeffrey A Varas(2027)
PO Box 886
Hazlehurst MS 39083
Phone: **601-894-4088**
Fax:

Local Retrieval Area: MS-Copiah, Hinds, Lincoln.

Normal turn around time is 1-2 days. Projects are generally billed by the hour. The first project may require a prepayment.
He is an attorney and specializes in criminal law and domestic relations.

Verified Credentials(2028)
1020 E 146th St
Burnsville MN 55337
Phone: **612-431-1811**
Fax: 612-431-6235

Local Retrieval Area: MN-Anoka, Carver, Dakota, Hennepin, Ramsey, Scott, Washington.

Normal turn around time is 1-3 days. Online computer ordering is also available. Projects are generally billed by the number of names searched. Credit accounts are accepted.
Verified Credentials also has correspondent relationships in other jurisdictions, including all of Minnesota and other states. They specialize in background screening.

Vigil Enterprises(2029)
1804 Tribute Rd Suite 210
Sacramento CA 95815
Phone: **916-927-3282**
Fax: 916-927-3389

Local Retrieval Area: CA-Amador, El Dorado, Nevada, Placer, Sacramento, Yolo.

Normal turn around time is 24 hours unless files need to be ordered. Projects are generally billed by the hour. Credit accounts are accepted. They will accept personal checks.
They specialize in the investigation and structuring of white collar crime cases and the location of hidden assets.

Vinita Title Co(2030)
PO Box 306
Vinita OK 74301
Phone: **918-256-2617**
Fax: 918-256-3412

Local Retrieval Area: OK-Craig.

Normal turn around time is 48 hours. Projects are generally billed by the number of names searched. Credit accounts are accepted.

Vinson Detective Agency(2031)
955 Howard
New Orleans LA 70113
Phone: **800-441-7899**
Fax: 504-529-4393

Local Retrieval Area: LA-Jefferson Parish, Orleans Parish, St. Bernard Parish.

Normal turn around time is 1-2 days. Projects are generally billed by the hour. The first project may require a prepayment.

Lynda P Vinson(2032)
503 Poplar St
Cambridge MD 21613
Phone: **410-228-1188**
Fax: 410-228-1572

Local Retrieval Area: MD-Caroline, Dorchester, Talbot, Wicomico.

Normal turn around time is 48 hours. Fee basis will vary with type of search. All projects require prepayment.
Lynda specializes in title searches.

Fred & Margaret Vogel(2033)
46 Ferry St
Lambertville NJ 08530
Phone: 201-539-5093
Fax: 609-397-3562

Local Retrieval Area: NJ-Morris.

Normal turn around time is 24-48 hours. They charge by name for civil and criminal searches and by the type of search for real estate. Credit accounts are accepted. They require all out of state client to prepay. Personal checks are accepted.

Robert Vollrath(2034)
2895 Biscayne Blvd Suite 528
Miami FL 33137
Phone: 305-939-0375
Fax: 305-649-0114

Local Retrieval Area: FL-Dade.

Normal turn around time is 1 week. Projects are generally billed by the number of names searched. All projects require prepayment. Robert is a liscensed private investigator that specialize in process service. Can network through all 50 states.

Volusia Legal Services(2035)
10 Lake Ruby Dr
Deland FL 32724
Phone: 904-822-9067
Fax:

Local Retrieval Area: FL-Volusia.

Normal turn around time is 24 hours. Some same day service is available. Projects are generally billed by the number of names searched. The first project may require a prepayment.
They specialize in criminal misdemeamor records and process serving.

W A Haag & Associates Inc(2036)
PO Box 7065
Alexandria VA 22307
Phone: 703-765-2138
Fax: 703-765-1264

Local Retrieval Area: DC-All counties.

Normal turn around time is 1-3 days. Projects are generally billed by the hour. Credit accounts are accepted.
W A Haag & Associates Inc also has correspondent relationships in other jurisdictions, including the states of Virginia and Maryland.

W T Butcher & Associates(2037)
1424 W Sentry Ave Suite 106
Bismark ND 58501
Phone: 701-224-1541
Fax: 701-258-2637

Local Retrieval Area: ND-Burleigh, McLean, Morton, Ward.

Normal turn around time is 24-48 hours. Fee basis varies by type of transaction. Credit accounts are accepted. Credit cards are accepted for payment.
W T Butcher & Associates also has correspondent relationships in other jurisdictions, including all of the state and nationwide. They specialize in asset locations, skip tracing, private investigations and computer information services.

W T Smith and Associates(2038)
9525 Katy Fwy Suite 400
Houston TX 77024
Phone: 713-461-4230
Fax: 713-984-9237

Local Retrieval Area: TX-Brazoria, Fort Bend, Harris, Jefferson, Matagorda, Travis, Waller, Wharton, Williamson.

Normal turn around time is 5 working days. Projects are generally billed by the hour. Credit accounts are accepted. Payment type depends on type of case.
W T Smith and Associates also has correspondent relationships in other jurisdictions, including all of Texas and many counties outside of Texas. They specialize in background investigations, surveillance, workman's compensation cases and asset searches.

WE Investigate Inc(2039)
PO Box 720160
San Diego CA 92172
Phone: 619-672-1664
Fax: 619-672-0676

Local Retrieval Area: CA-San Diego.

Normal turn around time is 2-3 days. Projects are generally billed by the hour. Credit accounts are accepted.
They specialize in asset searches, interviews and skip tracing.

Wabash Valley Abstract Co Inc(2040)
PO Box 1350
Peru IN 46970
Phone: 317-472-4351
Fax: 317-472-4352

Local Retrieval Area: IN-Miami.

Normal turn around time is 5-7 days. Projects are generally billed by the number of records located. Credit accounts are accepted.

Wabasha County Abstract Co(2041)
100 W Main St
Wabasha MN 55981
Phone: 612-565-3391
Fax: 612-565-3391

Local Retrieval Area: MN-Wabasha.

Normal turn around time is 1 week. Projects are generally billed by the number of names searched. Credit accounts are accepted.

Wagoner County Abstract Co(2042)
PO Box 188
Wagoner OK 74467-0188
Phone: 918-485-2215
Fax: 918-485-9162

Local Retrieval Area: OK-Wagoner.

Normal turn around time is 24 hours for name, UCC and abstract continuation; 5 days for complete abstract searches. Projects are generally billed by the number of names searched or records located. Credit accounts are accepted. Personal checks and cash are accepted.
They have serviced Wagoner County since 1907.

Wakeman Microfilm Service(2043)
22283 Main Street
Hayward CA 94541
Phone: 510-886-7667
Fax: 510-886-1523

Local Retrieval Area: CA-Alameda, Contra Costa, Marin, San Francisco, San Mateo, Santa Clara, Solano.

Normal turn around time is 3-5 business days depending on size of job. Projects are generally billed by the number of names searched or records located. The first project may require a prepayment.
All records copied on microfilm copier and re-produced according to request. Also offer subpoena preparation and service.

Bobbi Walker(2044)
627 Redheart Dr
Hampton VA 23666
Phone: 804-838-6587
Fax:

Local Retrieval Area: VA-Gloucester, Isle of Wight, James City, Mathews, York, City of Hampton, City of Newport News.

Normal turn around time is 24-48 hours. Rush service is also available. Projects are generally billed by the number of names searched or records located. Fee basis will vary by type of project. Credit accounts are accepted.

Judy L Walker(2045)
Rt 4 Box 985
North Wilkesboro NC 28659
Phone: 919-838-2052
Fax:

Local Retrieval Area: NC-Wilkes.

Normal turn around time is 1 day. Projects are generally billed by the number of names searched. Credit accounts are accepted.

Marilyn Walker(2046)
Rt 1 Box 119
Villard MN 56385
Phone: 612-554-7205
Fax:

Local Retrieval Area: MN-Benton, Big Stone, Cass, Chippewa, Douglas, Grant, Kandiyohi, Otter Tail, Pope, Stearns, Stevens, Swift, Todd, Traverse, Wadena.

Normal turn around time is 1-7 days Fee basis is determined on "per name plus mileage". The first project may require a prepayment.

Walla Walla Title Co(2047)
102 W Main Suite 100
Walla Walla WA 99362
Phone: 509-525-8660
Fax: 509-529-4713

Local Retrieval Area: WA-Walla Walla.

Normal turn around time is 1-2 days. Fee basis is determined on "per job". Credit accounts are accepted. Out of area clients are asked to prepay.
They specialize in real estate matters.

Wallace Investigations(2048)
10120 Ave F
Yuma AZ 85364
Phone: 602-726-5055
Fax:

Local Retrieval Area: AZ-Yuma.

Normal turn around time is 12-24 hours. Projects are generally billed by the number of names searched. Credit accounts are accepted.
They specialize in recorders office searches and federal and state liens.

Waller & Associates(2049)
10701 W North Ave
Milwaukee WI 53226
Phone: 414-771-5252
Fax: 414-771-5202

Local Retrieval Area: WI-Kenosha, Milwaukee, Racine, Washington.

Normal turn around time is 2 working days. Projects are generally billed by the hour. The first project may require a prepayment. A retainer is requested of first time clients.
They specialize in background investigations.

Walsh Process & Legal Services(2050)
124 Old Glenham Rd
Fishkill NY 12524
Phone: 914-838-2398
Fax: 914-838-3345

Local Retrieval Area: NY-Dutchess, Orange, Putnam, Rockland, Sullivan, Ulster, Westchester.

Normal turn around time is 2-4 days. Rush is available on a same or next day basis. Projects are generally billed by the hour. Credit accounts are accepted.
Walsh Process & Legal Services also has correspondent relationships in other jurisdictions, including New York county, Long Island and Albany.

Walters & Associates(2051)
10707 Corporate Dr Suite 104
Stafford TX 77477
Phone: 713-240-0908
Fax: 713-240-0913

Local Retrieval Area: TX-Brazoria, Fort Bend, Galveston, Harris, Waller, Waller, Wharton.

Normal turn around time is 3 days. Online computer ordering is also available. Project billing methods vary. The first project may require a prepayment. Persona checks are accepted.
Walters & Associates also has correspondent relationships in other jurisdictions, including Bexar, Comal and Kendall. They specialize in background, asset and liability, and legal investigations.

Walworth County Abstract & Title(2052)
PO Box 418
Selby SD 57472-0418
Phone: 605-649-7772
Fax:

Local Retrieval Area: SD-Walworth.

Normal turn around time is 1 week. Projects are generally billed by the hour. Credit accounts are accepted.

Larry M Warner(2053)
PO Box 601
Crossville TN 38557
Phone: 615-484-1611
Fax: 615-484-4509

Local Retrieval Area: TN-Cumberland.

Normal turn around time is 1-2 days. Fee basis will vary with type of search. Credit accounts are accepted.
Larry is an attorney who specializes in real estate record searches.

Warren County Abstract Co(2054)
210 W Ashland
Indianola IA 50047
Phone: 515-961-7479
Fax: 515-961-7470

Local Retrieval Area: IA-Warren.

Normal turn around time is 24 hours for most abstract continuations and 1 week for marketabel title abstracts. Projects are generally billed by the number of names searched or records located. Credit accounts are accepted. Personal checks are accepted.

Maggie Warren(2055)
PO Box 417
Bryson City NC 28713
Phone: 704-488-9273
Fax:

Local Retrieval Area: NC-Swain.

Normal turn around time is the same day. Projects are generally billed by the number of records located. All projects require prepayment.

Washington County Abstract Co(2056)
108 N Missouri St
Potosi MO 63664
Phone: 314-438-3431
Fax:

Local Retrieval Area: MO-Washington.

Normal turn around time is 1-2 weeks. Fee basis will vary by the type of project. Credit accounts are accepted. They specialize in notary work.

Washington County Title Co(2057)
90 E 100 S Suite 201
St George UT 84770
Phone: 800-576-6770
801-628-6717
Fax: 801-628-6874

Local Retrieval Area: UT-Washington.

Normal turn around time is 24-48 hours. Fee basis are determined on a "variable per name". Credit accounts are accepted. They specialize in title examination.

Washington County Title Co(2058)
158 Main St
Akron CO 80720
Phone: 303-345-2256
Fax: 303-345-2953

Local Retrieval Area: CO-Washington.

Normal turn around time is 3 days for abstracting and title memos, and 3 to 7 days for title insurance commitment. Projects are generally billed by the hour. Credit accounts are accepted. They provide title memos for oil companies.

Washington Title Agencies(2059)
PO Box 375
Washington VA 22747
Phone: 703-675-1567
Fax: 703-675-3698

Local Retrieval Area: VA-Culpeper, Fauquier, Orange, Rappahannock.

Normal turn around time is up to 2 weeks. Fee basis varies by type of transaction. Credit accounts are accepted.

Washita Valley Abstract Co(2060)
PO Box 458
Chickasha OK 73023
Phone: 405-224-6111
Fax: 405-222-4429

Local Retrieval Area: OK-Grady.

Normal turn around time is 4-5 days. Fee basis is per page and time. Credit accounts are accepted.

Watertown Title & Escrow Co(2061)
PO Box 1444
Watertown SD 57201
Phone: 605-886-8406
Fax: 605-882-3473

Local Retrieval Area: SD-Codington.

Normal turn around time is 2-5 days. Fee basis varies by type of transaction. Credit accounts are accepted.

Watonga Abstract Co(2062)
101 N Noble
Watonga OK 73772
Phone: 405-623-7248
Fax: 405-623-7268

Local Retrieval Area: OK-Blaine.

Normal turn around time is 1 week. Projects are generally billed by the hour. Credit accounts are accepted. Personal checks are accepted.

Kathi Watson(2063)
19 Means Ave
Canton NC 28716
Phone: 704-648-5830
Fax:

Local Retrieval Area: NC-Buncombe, Haywood, Henderson, Jackson, Macon, Madison, Swain, Transylvania.

Normal turn around time is 1 day. Projects are generally billed by the hour. The first project may require a prepayment. Ms. Watson specializes in real estate and title searches.

Wausau Abstract and Title Co(2064)
500 3rd St Suite 318
Wausau WI 54401
Phone: 715-842-9300
Fax: 715-842-5877

Local Retrieval Area: WI-Marathon.

Normal turn around time is 1-4 days. Projects are generally billed by the number of names searched or records located. Credit accounts are accepted. They require prepayment only if ordered by an individual. They will invoice to a company. They specialize in examining county records and real estate closings.

Wayne County Abstract & Title Co(2065)
PO Box 554
Greenville MO 63944
Phone: 314-224-3616
Fax: 314-224-3196

Local Retrieval Area: MO-Wayne.

Normal turn around time is 1 week. Fee basis varies by type of transaction. Credit accounts are accepted.

Wayne County Title Co(2066)
141 E Liberty St
Wooster OH 44691
Phone: 216-262-2916
Fax: 216-263-1738

Local Retrieval Area: OH-Ashland, Holmes, Wayne.

Normal turn around time is 1-5 days. Projects are generally billed by the hour. All projects require prepayment.

Weatherford-Parker County Abstr(2067)
PO Box 278
Weatherford TX 76086
Phone: 817-594-4435
Fax: 817-594-0861

Local Retrieval Area: TX-Parker.

Normal turn around time is 2-3 days. Fee basis will vary by the type of project. The first project may require a prepayment.

Weatherly Law Office(2068)
309 S Broad St
London KY 40741
Phone: 606-878-9661
Fax: 606-878-6948

Local Retrieval Area: KY-Bell, Clay, Knox, Laurel, Pulaski, Rockcastle, Whitley.

Normal turn around time is 2-3 days. Projects are generally billed by the hour. Credit accounts are accepted. They will ask for out of area or first time clients to prepay.

They are a small town law office that works closely with the County Attorney's office. They will also go to Pulaski county as needed.

Weber Abstract Co(2069)   Phone: **605-256-4640**
PO Box 263   Fax:
Madison SD 57042

Local Retrieval Area: SD-Lake.

Normal turn around time is 1 day to 2 weeks. Fee basis is set by law. The first project may require a prepayment.
They specialize in real estate.

Attorney David V Weber(2070)   Phone: **706-860-8160**
PO Box 211149   Fax: 706-860-8607
Martinez GA 30917-1149

Local Retrieval Area: GA-Columbia, Richmond.

Normal turn around time is usually up to 3 days. Fee basis will vary by the type of project. Credit accounts are accepted.
David specializes in real estate, criminal, and domestic matters.

Webster County Records(2071)   Phone: **515-576-3911**
1503 4th Ave N   Fax:
Ft Dodge IA 50501

Local Retrieval Area: IA-Webster.

Normal turn around time is 2-3 days. Projects are generally billed by the number of names searched. The first project may require a prepayment.
They specialize in legal record publishing.

Webster County-Butler & Rhodes(2072)   Phone: **515-573-3341**
805 Central Ave   Fax: 515-576-7962
Fort Dodge IA 50501

Local Retrieval Area: IA-Webster.

Normal turn around time is 1-2 days. Fee basis will vary by the type of project. The first project may require a prepayment.

Welch & Ekman PC(2073)   Phone: **701-284-7833**
PO Box 198   Fax: 701-284-7832
Park River ND 58270

Local Retrieval Area: MN-Kittson, Marshall; ND-Cavalier, Walsh.

Normal turn around time is 1 day. Projects are generally billed by the hour. Credit accounts are accepted.

Wells Abstract Company(2074)   Phone: **314-221-0644**
Court House Box 732   Fax:
Hannibal MO 63401

Local Retrieval Area: MO-Marion, Marion.

Normal turn around time is 2 days. Projects are generally billed by the number of records located. Credit accounts are accepted. Personal checks are accepted.

Wells County Abstract Co(2075)   Phone: **701-547-3433**
PO Box 597   Fax:
Fessenden ND 58438

Local Retrieval Area: ND-Wells.

Normal turn around time is 2 days. Projects are generally billed by the number of records located. Credit accounts are accepted.
They specialize in real estate.

Wells Fargo Investigative Svcs(2076)   Phone: **615-254-6685**
269 Cumberland Bend Dr   Fax: 615-248-6951
Nashville TN 37228

Local Retrieval Area: TN-Cheatham, Davidson, Robertson, Rutherford, Sumner, Wilson.

Normal turn around time is 24-48 hours. Projects are generally billed by the hour. Credit accounts are accepted.
Wells Fargo Investigative Services also has correspondent relationships in other jurisdictions, including Hamilton, Knox, Shelby and Montgomery.

Weltmer Law Office(2077)   Phone: **913-378-3172**
Box 303   Fax: 913-378-3203
Mankato KS 66956

Local Retrieval Area: KS-Jewell.

Normal turn around time is 24 hours. Projects are generally billed by the number of records located. Credit accounts are accepted. They accept personal checks.
Weltmer Law Office also has correspondent relationships in other jurisdictions, including Mitchell, Republic and Smith. They also operate Woltmer Abstract and Title Company, which specializes in title searches, abstracts and title insurance. The company has been in business for 57 years.

West Central Abstracting Co(2078)   Phone: **218-736-5685**
125 N Union Ave   Fax: 218-739-4610
Fergus Falls MN 56537

Local Retrieval Area: MN-Otter Tail.

Normal turn around time is 3-5 days. Fees basis are per entry. Credit accounts are accepted.

Thomas West(2079)   Phone: **614-373-6688**
PO Box 5557   Fax: 614-373-7442
Athens OH 45701

Local Retrieval Area: OH-Athens, Hocking, Meigs, Morgan, Muskingum, Noble, Washington; WV-Ritchie, Tyler, Wetzel, Wood.

Normal turn around time is up to one week. Fee basis will vary by the type of project. Credit accounts are accepted.
He specializes in current owner searches, oil and gas.

Westchester Court Service(2080)   Phone: **914-948-5200**
199 Main St   Fax: 914-948-5501
White Plains NY 10601

Local Retrieval Area: NY-Dutchess, Orange, Putnam, Rockland, Sullivan, Ulster, Westchester.

Normal turn around time is 1-2 days. Projects are generally billed by the number of records located. The first project may require a prepayment.
They specialize in process serving.

Western Attorney Services(2081)
75 Columbia Square
San Francisco CA 94103-4099

Phone: 415-864-1113
Fax: 415-864-6238

Local Retrieval Area: CA-Alameda, Contra Costa, Marin, San Francisco, San Mateo, Santa Clara.

Normal turn around time is the same day. Fee basis is per hour and a distance charge. The first project may require a prepayment. Western Attorney Services also has correspondent relationships in other jurisdictions, including nationwide. They specialize in civil case record searches.

Western Title Insurance Agency(2082)
PO Box 528
Delta CO 81416

Phone: 303-874-8286
Fax: 303-874-4762

Local Retrieval Area: CO-Delta.

Normal turn around time is 1 week to 10 days. Fee basis will vary by the type of project. Credit accounts are accepted. They specialize in title insurance.

Western Title Insurance Agency(2083)
PO Box 579
Montrose CO 81401

Phone: 303-249-7944
Fax: 303-249-5341

Local Retrieval Area: CO-Montrose.

Normal turn around time is 1 week to 10 days. Fee basis will vary by the type of project. Credit accounts are accepted. They specialize in title insurance.

Richard Wetherill(2084)
215 Main St
Rockport IN 47635

Phone: 812-649-2221
Fax: 812-649-2222

Local Retrieval Area: IN-Spencer.

Normal turn around time is varied depending on search. Charges vary with the type of record. Credit accounts are accepted.

White Abstract & Title Co(2085)
401 Main St
Rocksprings TX 78880

Phone: 210-683-2149
Fax: 210-683-4100

Local Retrieval Area: TX-Edwards.

Normal turn around time is 1 day. Fee basis will vary by the type of project. The first project may require a prepayment.

White Abstract Co(2086)
PO Box 85
Macon MO 63552

Phone: 816-385-2515
Fax:

Local Retrieval Area: MO-Macon.

Normal turn around time is 1 week to 10 days. Projects are generally billed by the number of names searched. Credit accounts are accepted. They specialize in title insurance.

Whiteside Abstract and Title Ins(2087)
132 N State St
St Ignace MI 49781

Phone: 906-643-9292
Fax: 906-643-7157

Local Retrieval Area: MI-Mackinac.

Normal turn around time is up to 1 week. Fee basis will vary by type of project. The first project may require a prepayment. They specialize in real estate and title insurance.

Wibaux County Abstract Co(2088)
PO Box 239
Wibaux MT 59353

Phone: 406-228-2350
Fax:

Local Retrieval Area: MT-Wibaux.

Normal turn around time is varied depending on project. Projects are generally billed by the hour. Credit accounts are accepted. They specialize in mineral searches and title insurance.

Shirley Wilhelm(2089)
909 Phillips St
Marietta OH 45750

Phone: 614-374-8444
Fax:

Local Retrieval Area: OH-Morgan, Noble, Washington.

Normal turn around time is 48 hours. Projects are generally billed by the number of names searched. Credit accounts are accepted.

Wilkes Law Office(2090)
PO Box 190
Bowbells ND 58721

Phone: 701-377-4357
Fax:

Local Retrieval Area: ND-Burke.

Normal turn around time is varied depending on project. Fee basis will vary by type of project. Credit accounts are accepted.

Wilkin County Abstract(2091)
PO Box 200
Breckenridge MN 56520

Phone: 218-643-4002
Fax:

Local Retrieval Area: MN-Wilkin.

Normal turn around time is 2-4 weeks. Projects are generally billed by the number of names searched. Credit accounts are accepted.

William Olmsted Investigations(2092)
455 University Ave Suite 230
Sacramento CA 95825

Phone: 800-662-3443
916-646-3443
Fax: 916-921-0125

Local Retrieval Area: CA-El Dorado, Placer, Sacramento, San Joaquin, Sutter, Yolo, Yuba.

Normal turn around time is varied depending on project. Same day service is available. Projects are generally billed by the hour. Mileage and expenses will be added to the hourly charge. The first project may require a prepayment. William Olmsted Investigations also has correspondent relationships in other jurisdictions, including California. They specialize in investigations including civil, criminal, background, assets and fraud.

Williamette Valley Title Co(2093)
454 Commercial St
Coos Bay OR 97420

Phone: 503-269-0119
Fax: 503-269-0470

Local Retrieval Area: OR-Coos.

Normal turn around time is 1-2 days. Projects are generally billed by the hour. Their hourly rate is varied. The first project may require a prepayment. They specialize in title insurance.

George Williams(2094)
PO Box 63
Quitman MS 39355

Phone: **601-776-2111**
Fax:

Local Retrieval Area: MS-Clarke.

Normal turn around time is 2-3 days. Projects are generally billed by the hour. The first project may require a prepayment.
Mr. Williams is a lawyer.

Nancy Williams(2095)
2703 Barton Court
Elon College NC 27244

Phone: **919-584-0450**
Fax: 919-584-1679

Local Retrieval Area: NC-Alamance, Caswell, Guilford, Rockingham.

Normal turn around time is 12 hours. Projects are generally billed by the number of names searched. Credit accounts are accepted.
Ms. Williams specializes in title searches.

Williamson Abstract Co(2096)
Box 43
Greenfield IA 50849

Phone: **515-743-2175**
Fax: 515-743-6313

Local Retrieval Area: IA-Adair.

Normal turn around time is 2-5 days. Fee basis will vary by the type of search. Credit accounts are accepted. They require a retainer and will accept personal checks.
They specialize in abstract and real estate searches.

Willian C Brown and Co(2097)
629 Walnut St
Reading PA 19601

Phone: **215-373-1516**
Fax: 215-373-7360

Local Retrieval Area: PA-Berks.

Normal turn around time is 1 week. Fee basis will vary by the type of project. The first project may require a prepayment.
They specialize in title searches.

Jeanette Willingham(2098)
PO Box 670
Geneva AL 36340

Phone: **205-898-7625**
Fax:

Local Retrieval Area: AL-Coffee, Covington, Dale, Geneva, Henry, Houston.

Normal turn around time is 1-3 days. Fee basis varies by type of transaction. Credit accounts are accepted.
Ms. Willingham has 18 1/2 years experience at an attorney paralegal.

Sally Wilmot(2099)
PO Box 68
Athens GA 30603

Phone: **706-354-1831**
Fax: 706-354-4177

Local Retrieval Area: GA-Banks, Barrow, Clarke, Elbert, Gwinnett, Hall, Jackson, Madison, Oconee, Oglethorpe, Walton.

Normal turn around time is 24-48 hours. Projects are generally billed by the number of names searched. Credit accounts are accepted.

Wilson & Associates(2100)
425 W Capital Suite 1500
Little Rock AR 72201

Phone: **501-375-1820**
Fax: 501-375-8609

Wilson & Associates' employees cover every county in the state of Arkansas.

Normal turn around time is varied depending on search. Fee basis will vary with type of search. Credit accounts are accepted.
They specialize in real estate records and banking work.

Wilson Abstract Co(2101)
215 W Washington
Macomb IL 61455

Phone: **309-833-2049**
Fax:

Local Retrieval Area: IL-Fulton, Hancock, Henderson, McDonough, Schuyler, Warren. Normal turn around time is 2 days for a judgement search, 4 days for title work. Projects are generally billed by the hour. Travel expenses will be included in the fee. All projects require prepayment.
They have been in business for 45 years.

Wilson Associates(2102)
2031 N 36th St
St Joseph MO 64508

Phone: **816-233-6334**
Fax: 816-233-4855

Local Retrieval Area: KS-Atchison, Doniphan, Leavenworth; MO-Andrew, Atchison, Buchanan, Caldwell, Clinton, Daviess, De Kalb, Gentry, Grundy, Harrison, Holt, Livingston, Mercer, Nodaway, Platte, Worth.

Normal turn around time is 1-4 days depending on county. Fee basis will vary by the type and location of project. The first project may require a prepayment.

Wilson Associates also has correspondent relationships in other jurisdictions, including Carrol, Carrollton, Clay, Jackson, Johnson, Lafayette, Ray, Saline and Sullivan. They specialize in process service and surveillance.

Wilson Enterprises(2103)
4705 N Sonora #112B
Fresno CA 93722

Phone: **209-276-3821**
Fax: 209-276-3834

Local Retrieval Area: CA-Fresno.

Normal turn around time is 1-2 days. Fee basis will vary by the type of project. All projects require prepayment.
They specialize in workmen's compensation and other private investigation.

Cindy Wilson(2104)
C/O 100 Oak St
Baxley GA 31513

Phone: **912-367-8109**
Fax:

Local Retrieval Area: GA-Appling.

Normal turn around time is usually within the same day. Projects are generally billed by the number of names searched or records located. Credit accounts are accepted.
Cindy specializes in criminal matters.

Wingate Investigations(2105)
660 S Roberts Ave
Lima OH 45804
Phone: **419-225-6534**
Fax:

Local Retrieval Area: OH-Allen, Auglaize, Paulding, Putnam, Van Wert.

Normal turn around time is 3 days. Projects are generally billed by the number of names searched or records located. All projects require prepayment. Credit cards are accepted for payment. Personal checks are accepted.
They specialize in real estate, civil, crimial, probate, and domestic relations on the county level.

Wendell D Winkler(2106)
133 S Pearl
Paola KS 66071
Phone: **913-294-2339**
Fax: 913-294-5702

Local Retrieval Area: KS-Miami.

Normal turn around time is 2-5 days. Projects are generally billed by the number of names searched. Credit accounts are accepted.

Winnebago County Abstract(2107)
133 E J St
Forest City IA 50436
Phone: **515-582-3101**
Fax:

Local Retrieval Area: IA-Winnebago.

Normal turn around time is 2-3 days. Fee basis varies by type of transaction. The first project may require a prepayment.

Wisconsin Title of Fond Du Lac(2108)
113 S Main St
Fond Du Lac WI 54935
Phone: **414-922-2200**
Fax: 414-922-3867

Local Retrieval Area: WI-Dodge, Fond du Lac.

Normal turn around time is 2 days. Fee basis varies by type of transaction. The first project may require a prepayment.

Wisconsin Title of Shawano Inc(2109)
218 N Washington St PO Box 330
Shawano WI 54166
Phone: **715-524-2413**
Fax: 715-526-9110

Local Retrieval Area: WI-Menominee, Shawano.

Normal turn around time is 1-2 days. Fee basis varies by type of transaction. The first project may require a prepayment.

Wood County Title Co(2110)
PO Box 266
Mineola TX 75773
Phone: **903-569-3863**
Fax:

Local Retrieval Area: TX-Wood.

Normal turn around time is 48 hours for federal tax liens and judgements, and 2 to 4 weeks for real estate records. Projects are generally billed by the hour. Credit accounts are accepted. Personal checks are accepted.

Woodard and Bohse Law Office(2111)
121 W 3rd St
Dover OH 44622
Phone: **216-343-8848**
Fax: 216-343-3496

Local Retrieval Area: OH-Carroll, Coshocton, Harrison, Holmes, Tuscarawas.

Normal turn around time is 1 week. Projects are generally billed by the hour. Credit accounts are accepted. They will accept personal checks.
Woodard and Bohse Law Office also has correspondent relationships in other jurisdictions, including Tuscarawas, Coshocton, Carroll, Holmes and Harrison Counties.

Woods County Abstract Corp(2112)
PO Box 686
Alva OK 73717
Phone: **405-327-1746**
Fax: 405-327-1780

Local Retrieval Area: OK-Woods.

Normal turn around time is 1-5 days. Fee basis will vary by the type of project. Credit accounts are accepted.
They specialize in title work and special certificates.

Woodward County Abstract Co(2113)
1513 Main
Woodward OK 73802
Phone: **405-256-3344**
Fax: 405-256-4530

Local Retrieval Area: OK-Ellis, Harper, Woodward.

Normal turn around time is 2 days. Projects are generally billed by the hour. Credit accounts are accepted.
They specialize in abstracts of title and title insurance.

World Class Investigations(2114)
PO Box 510548
Melbourne Beach FL 32951-0548
Phone: **407-728-0641**
Fax: 407-728-0818

Local Retrieval Area: FL-Brevard, Indian River.

Normal turn around time is 2-3 days. Projects are generally billed by the number of records located. Credit accounts are accepted.
World Class Investigations also has correspondent relationships in other jurisdictions, including the rest of Florida.

Worth County Abstract Co Inc(2115)
736 Central Ave
Northwood IA 50459
Phone: **515-324-1761**
Fax:

Local Retrieval Area: IA-Worth.

Normal turn around time is 1-3 days. Projects are generally billed by the hour. All projects require prepayment. They will also invoice.

Cheri Worthmann(2116)
5093 Grace Dr
Morrisville PA 19067
Phone: **215-736-0486**
Fax:

Local Retrieval Area: NJ-All counties.

Normal turn around time is 2 weeks. Projects are generally billed by the number of records located. Credit accounts are accepted. They will invoice if the charges are under $50.00
They specialize in New Jersey vital records and probate.

Wright County Land Title Co(2117)   Phone: 515-532-2259
112 Central Ave E   Fax:
Clarion IA 50525
Local Retrieval Area: IA-Wright.
Normal turn around time is up to 1 week. Fee basis will vary by the type of project. Credit accounts are accepted.

Wyatt Wright III(2118)   Phone: 205-357-4933
PO Box 66   205-357-4978
Wedowee AL 36278   Fax:
Local Retrieval Area: AL-Chambers, Clay, Cleburne, Randolph, Tallapoosa; GA-Carroll, Heard, Troup.
Normal turn around time is 36 hours. Projects are generally billed by the hour. Credit accounts are accepted.

Wyatt Land Title Services Inc(2119)   Phone: 913-263-7722
PO Box 503   Fax:
Abilene KS 67410
Local Retrieval Area: KS-Dickinson.
Normal turn around time is 2 days. Fee basis varies by type of transaction. Credit accounts are accepted.

Yoakum County Abstract Co(2120)   Phone: 806-456-2615
PO Box 457   Fax: 806-456-2625
Plains TX 79355
Local Retrieval Area: TX-Yoakum.
Normal turn around time is 2-3 days. Fee basis will vary by the type of project. The first project may require a prepayment.

York County Title Co(2121)   Phone: 402-362-4405
611 Corant Ave   Fax:
York NE 68467
Local Retrieval Area: NE-Fillmore, York.
Normal turn around time is 24 hours. Fee basis varies by type of transaction. Credit accounts are accepted.

Youngblood Process Service(2122)   Phone: 813-743-4952
97 Robina St   Fax: 813-637-4663
Port Charlotte FL 33954
Local Retrieval Area: FL-Charlotte.
Normal turn around time is 1-3 days. Projects are generally billed by the hour. Credit accounts are accepted.
They specialize in civil process service.

Zap! Courier Service(2123)   Phone: 518-449-3361
90 S Swan St   Fax: 518-449-1332
Albany NY 12210
Local Retrieval Area: NY-Albany, Greene, Rensselaer, Saratoga, Schenectady.
Normal turn around time is 24 hours. Projects are generally billed by the number of names searched. Credit accounts are accepted.
Zap! Courier Service also has correspondent relationships in other jurisdictions, including Monroe and New York City

---

John A Zapf II(2124)   Phone: 215-868-5101
628 W Broad St   Fax: 215-691-1216
Bethlehem PA 18016
Local Retrieval Area: PA-Lehigh, Northampton.
Normal turn around time is 1 week. Projects are generally billed by the number of names searched or records located. Credit accounts are accepted.
They specialize in real estate title searches and abstracts.

Zavala County Abstract Co Inc(2125)   Phone: 210-374-3218
PO Drawer F   Fax: 210-374-3947
Crystal City TX 78839
Local Retrieval Area: TX-Zavala.
Normal turn around time is up to a week. Fee basis will vary by the type of project. The first project may require a prepayment.

Ziegler and Associates Inc(2126)   Phone: 904-788-7255
200 Forest Lake Blvd Suite 5   Fax: 904-788-7261
Daytona Beach FL 32119
Local Retrieval Area: FL-Volusia.
Normal turn around time is 1-2 days. Fee basis will vary by type of project. All projects require prepayment.
They specialize in locating and insurance investigations.

Pacific Photocopy & Research(2127)   Phone: 407-425-7234
35 W Pine St Suite 229   Fax: 407-425-7218
Orlando FL 32801
Local Retrieval Area: FL-Brevard, Lake, Orange, Osceola, Volusia.
Normal turn around time is 1-3 days. Fee basis will vary by the type of project. The first project may require a prepayment.
Pacific Photocopy & Research - Orlando also has correspondent relationships in other jurisdictions, including the rest of the state with nationwide capabilities through a network. They specialize in bankruptcy court records.

THE PUBLIC RECORD RESEARCH LIBRARY

The PUBLIC RECORD RESEARCH LIBRARY is a growing collection of reference books (we call them *Sourcebooks*) designed to guide you through the maze of public records. The PRRL Sourcebooks:

- tell you what each type of public record means and how to use it.
- help you locate the information you need to know about companies or individuals, so you can obtain the documents behind the information.
- include directory editions that contain comprehensive listings of companies that specialize in obtaining different types of public record information.

PRRL *Sourcebooks* are THE SOURCE for public record research.

P-095

LOCAL COURT & COUNTY RECORD RETRIEVERS

A county-by-county directory, listing and profiling firms and individuals who "hands-on" retrieve criminal, civil, and probate case files at the county, state, US District, and Bankruptcy courts, and lien, tax, real estate, and vital statistics at local county offices. 432+ pages, $45.00.

P-052

COUNTY COURT RECORDS

A directory of over 5,300 local courts detailing where and how you can obtain information on civil and criminal cases, probate, liens, UCC, real estate, tax, and vital statistic records. Each state chapter also includes a city-county cross reference index. 544 pages, $33.00.

P-060

PUBLIC RECORD PROVIDERS

A compendium profiling and indexing 400 companies that specialize in online public record access and retrieval, proprietary databases, UCC and state record retrieval, public record related CD-ROM products, screening search firms, and more. 224 pages, $18.00.

P-071

ASSET/LIEN SEARCHING

A national directory of names, addresses, and phone numbers for all 4,283 US jurisdictions where real property, lien, and corporate records are located. 240 pages, $19.00.

P-079

THE 1993 MVR BOOK

A national reference detailing, and summarizing in practical terms, the descriptions, access, automation, regulations, and privacy restrictions of all the state driver and vehicle records. 256 page, $17.00.

P-087

THE 1993 DECODER DIGEST

A companion to The MVR Book, translating the codes and abbreviations of violations, classes, restrictions, endorsements, etc. that appear on motor vehicle related records. 256 pages, $17.00.

P-117

LOCUS — THE ULTIMATE LOCATOR!

The ONLY directory with over 90,000+ place names that accurately matches ZIP codes to places to county — 2 cross reference indexes — over 10,000 ZIPS that cross county borders. 600+ pages, $25.00.

P-109

FEDERAL COURTS — US DISTRICT AND BANKRUPTCY

The only complete guide to searching the more than 500 US Court locations and 12 Federal Records Centers for information about criminal, civil, and bankruptcy cases. 500+ pages, $33.00.

P-044

INSURANCE SERVICES VENDORS

A unique directory for Property and Casualty Insurers, profiling those firms who provide premium audits, property inspections, motor vehicle record reporting, and more. 224+ pages, $15.00.
